Christoph Mohr, Bastian Barenbrock, Oliver Fülling

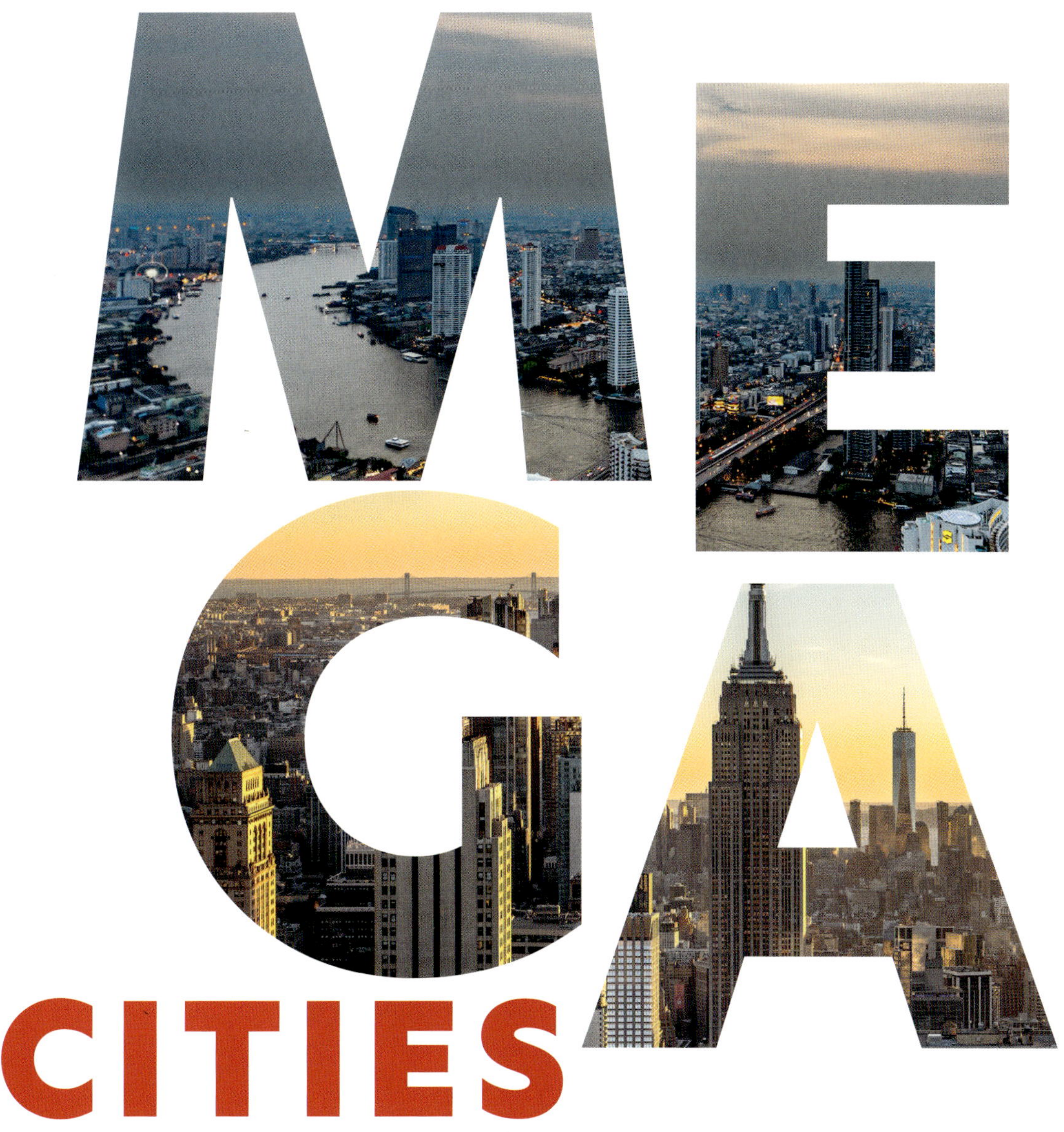

MEGA CITIES

Living in the World's Largest Cities
Vom Leben in den größten Städten der Welt

teNeues

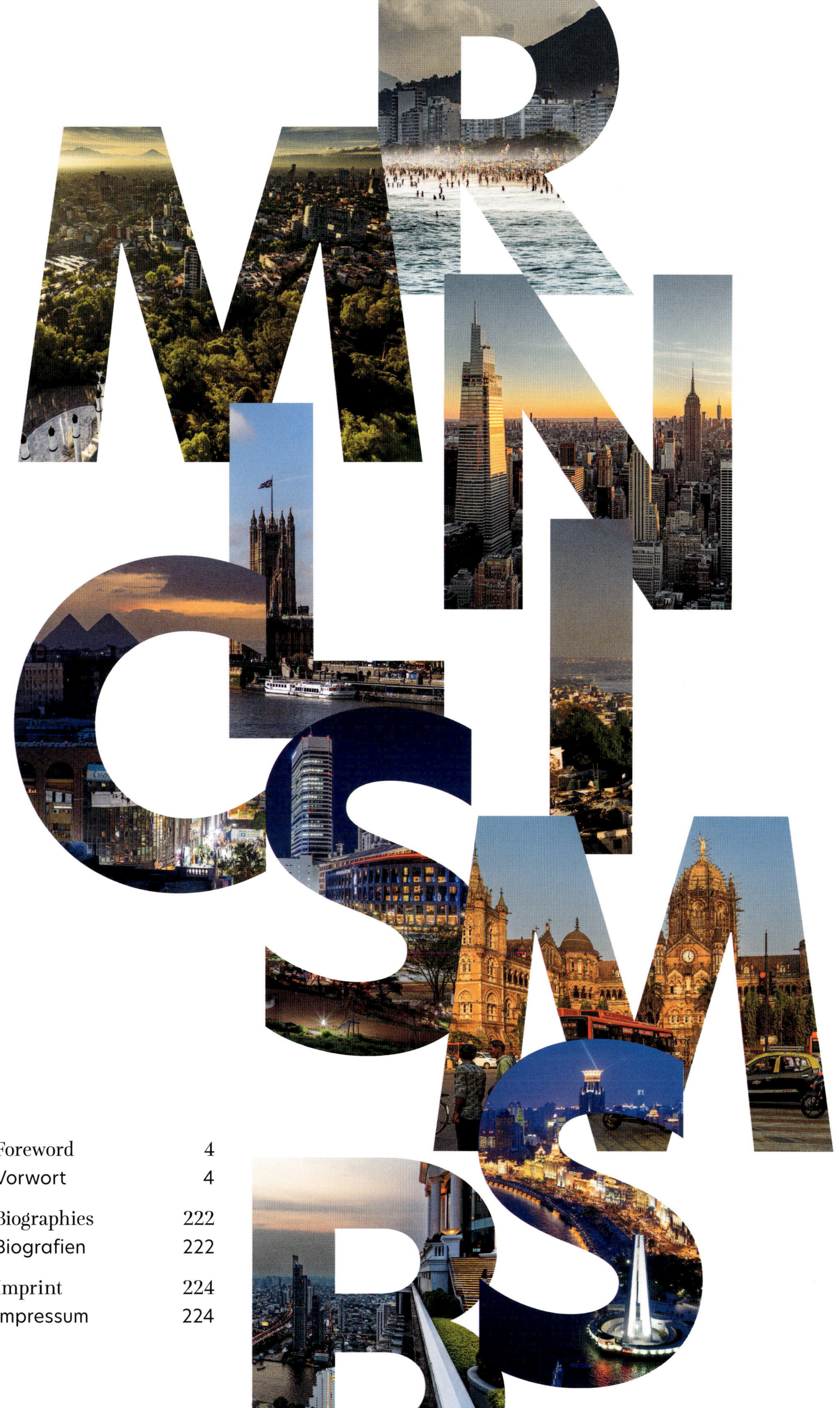

Megacities – A Wonderful "Catastrophe"

Megacities – Eine wunderbare „Katastrophe"

You hear a lot of preconceptions when it comes to megacities: They are too noisy, too dirty, too crowded, there are too many people, the streets are congested, there is a lot of crime, the quality of life is low... Did we forget anything? Oh yes, poverty, slums, shattered dreams—none of that rags-to-riches business. Megacities trigger mixed feelings in many people, but these often-vague notions are generated almost exclusively by frequently one-sided media coverage.

People who don't live in a megacity often imagine them as worlds devoid of any quality of life. They visit them, perhaps with a somewhat queasy feeling, to see prominent attractions or attend popular events, but to live there? Yet megacities are not an invention of modern times. They already exerted their pull and fascination at a time when there were no cities at all on European soil. According to the ancient Greek historian Herodotus, Babylon, with a population of almost 200,000, was already "huge and beautifully built" 4,000 years ago. Carthage was probably the first city in the world to reach half a million residents. In China, the capital Chang'an grew into a city with a population of one million+ about the same time as Rome did.

While the Christian West was experiencing the Middle Ages, the Golden Age of Islam dawned in the Orient. This was also reflected in the size of its cities: Baghdad was probably the world's largest city as of the year 900. But in Central America, too, numerous Mayan settlements grew into extensive cities, including Tikal, whose boundaries were home to as many as a million people in the 7th and 8th centuries. And as late as the 15th century, Spanish conquistadors were overwhelmed by the size and splendor of Aztec cities like Tenochtitlán, present-day Mexico City.

It would take a full 1400 years after the collapse of ancient Rome before another European city had more than a million people living in it, and that was London, with a population of around six million in the early 19th century. London remained the largest city in the world until 1914, when New York caught up with it, after which record population sizes were beaten one after the other at an ever-increasing pace. There seems to be a certain natural order that makes large cities, and ultimately megacities, almost inevitable. They magically attract us, they

Über Megacities kursieren viele Vorurteile: zu laut, zu schmutzig, zu eng, zu viele Menschen, verstopfte Straßen, Kriminalität... etwas vergessen? Ach ja die Armut, Slums, geplatzte Träume – nichts da vom Tellerwäscher zum Millionär. Megacities lösen bei vielen Menschen gemischte Gefühle aus, aber diese oft diffusen Vorstellungen werden fast ausschließlich über eine oft einseitige Berichterstattung in den Medien erzeugt.

Wer nicht in einer Megastadt wohnt, stellt sie sich oft als eine Welt ohne Lebensqualität vor. Man besucht sie, manchmal verbunden mit einem etwas mulmigen Gefühl, um vielleicht herausragende Sehenswürdigkeiten anzuschauen oder bekannte Events zu erleben, aber dort leben? Dabei sind Megastädte keine Erfindung der Neuzeit. Sie übten bereits einen Sog und eine Faszination aus, als es auf europäischem Boden noch gar keine Städte gab. Laut dem antiken griechischen Historiker Herodot war Babylon mit nahezu 200 000 Einwohnern bereits vor 4000 Jahren „gewaltig und prächtig gebaut". Karthago war vermutlich die erste Stadt der Welt, die eine halbe Million Einwohner erreichte. In China wuchs die Hauptstadt Chang'an etwa zeitgleich mit Rom zu einer Millionenstadt heran.

Während im christlichen Abendland das Mittelalter herrschte, brach im Orient das „Goldene Zeitalter des Islam" an. Das machte sich auch in der Größe seiner Städte bemerkbar: Bagdad war vermutlich ab dem Jahr 900 die weltweit größte Stadt. Doch auch in Zentralamerika wuchsen zahlreiche Siedlungen der Maya zu weitläufigen Städten heran, darunter Tikal, in dessen Einzugsbereich im 7–8. Jahrhundert bis zu 1 Million Menschen lebten. Und noch im 15. Jahrhundert waren die spanischen Konquistadoren überwältigt von der Größe und Pracht der Azteken-Städte wie Tenochtitlán, das heutige Mexico City.

Es sollte ganze 1400 Jahre dauern, bis nach dem Zerfall des antiken Roms wieder eine europäische Stadt mehr als eine Million Einwohner hatte, und zwar London, das Anfang des 19. Jahrhunderts rund 6 Millionen Einwohner zählte. Bis 1914 blieb London die größte Stadt der Welt, bis New York sie einholte. Danach purzelten die Einwohnerrekorde rapide.

are places of hope and opportunity; they generate jobs, money, and new ideas. Megacities are like power plants, energy centers attracting people to them like giant magnets. A megacity quickens the pace of life, becoming an inexhaustible source of communication, inspiration, and creativity. The melting pot of human diversity and the pooled brainpower from the fields of science, academia, and creativity become a breeding ground for forward-looking technologies and solutions. It is not a coincidence that creative people from all walks of life thrive in megacities.

Vibrant urban life reinvents itself every day, and the horizon behind the skyline becomes the symbol of a city that never sleeps. As life, communication, and shopping move online, neighborhoods are starting to be replaced. The result is a hybrid city where physical and virtual, concrete and imaginary worlds intensively blend together. Megacities are changing rapidly, adapting to developments, and creating new models for living that are proving quite successful.

A megacity is not automatically a world city. However, the megacities presented in this book are all also world cities. The most recent development is the emergence of global cities, hubs of the global economy and international politics, including London and New York. Each of the cities presented here has followed its own unique path of development, has found its own solutions to its diverse challenges, and has become a home its residents feel intensely connected to.

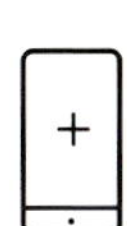

Es scheint also eine gewisse Gesetzmäßigkeit zu geben, die Groß- und schließlich Megastädte fast unausweichlich machen. Sie ziehen magisch an, sind Orte der Hoffnung und der Chancen, generieren Jobs, Geld und neue Ideen. Megacities sind wie Kraftwerke, Energiezentren, die wie riesige Magnete auf die Menschen wirken. Eine Megastadt beschleunigt das Leben. Dadurch wird sie zur unerschöpflichen Quelle von Kommunikation, Inspiration und Kreativität. Der Schmelztiegel menschlicher Vielfalt und der Brainpool aus Wissenschaft und Kreativität werden zum Nährboden zukunftsweisender Technologien und Lösungen. Nicht umsonst fühlen sich Kreative aller Richtungen hier überaus wohl.

Das pulsierende urbane Leben erfindet sich täglich neu und der Horizont hinter der Skyline wird zum Symbol einer Stadt, die nie schläft. Eine Verlagerung des Lebens, der Kommunikation und des Einkaufens ins Netz beginnt die Nachbarschaft zu ersetzen. Das Ergebnis ist eine hybride Stadt, in der sich physische und virtuelle, konkrete und imaginäre Welten intensiv durchmischen. Megastädte verändern sich rasant, passen sich an die Entwicklungen an und erschaffen neue Lebensmodelle, die sich durchaus erfolgreich etablieren.

Eine Megastadt ist nicht automatisch auch eine Weltstadt. Die in diesem Buch vorgestellten Megacitys sind jedoch alle gleichzeitig auch Weltstädte. Die neueste Entwicklung ist dabei die Herausbildung von Global Cities, Knotenpunkte der Weltwirtschaft und internationalen Politik, zu denen London und New York zählen. Jede der hier vorgestellten Städte ist ganz eigene Entwicklungswege gegangen, hat eigene Lösungen für ihre vielfältigen Herausforderungen gefunden und ist für ihre Bewohner zu einer Heimat geworden, der sie sich intensiv verbunden fühlen.

To learn even more about the life in megacities, use the QR code to download the teNeues app. Then, look for this symbol throughout the book.

When you see the symbol, scan that photograph for additional insights. Try it out with the image on the left.

Um noch mehr über das Leben in Megacities zu erfahren, laden Sie sich über den QR-Code die teNeues App herunter und halten Ausschau nach diesem Symbol.

Scannen Sie die entsprechende Fotografie und lassen Sie sich überraschen. Probieren Sie es doch gleich einmal mit dem Bild links aus.

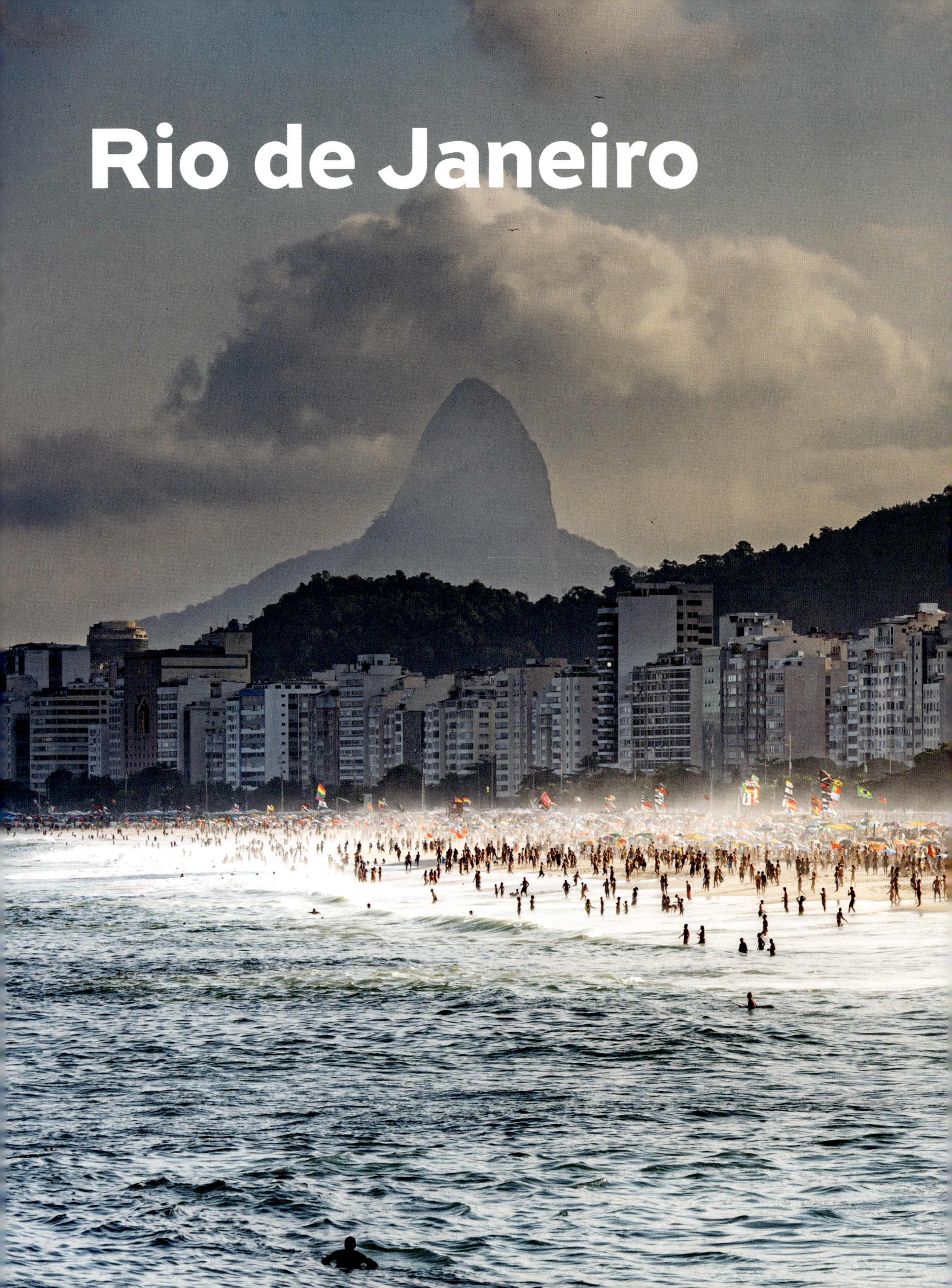

Rio de Janeiro

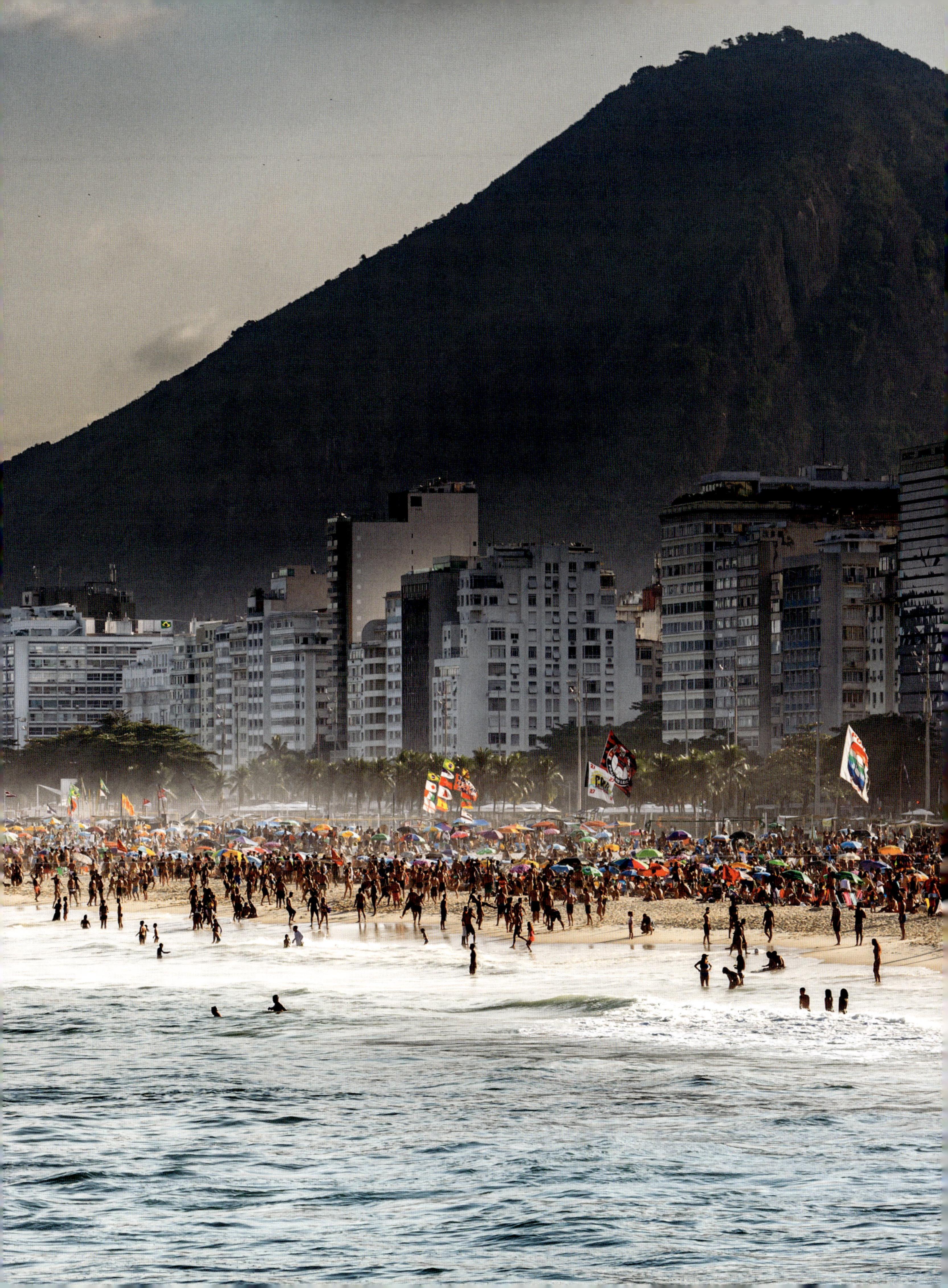

Raw Emotions and Afro-Brazilian Culture

Emotionen pur und afro-brasilianische Kultur

"The whole culture of soccer, samba, and carnival was born in the favelas. They were born with Black people; they were born with marginalized people." (Marcelo)

Rio, a slice of Africa in Brazil: vibrant, colorful, alive with rhythms, whether on one of the countless beaches between the Copacabana or Leblon, at the Pedra do Sal, which quakes every Monday to the sound of the samba rhythms first invented here, or in one of the favelas to usher in the weekend. Hardly any other megacity offers so many easily accessible beaches on its doorstep, a national park with a rainforest and mountains in the midst of the city, lagoons with biking and jogging trails, and a population whose joie de vivre is nothing short of exuberant.

There is no denying that the city struggles with countless major problems and yet, despite all the difficulties, it is still incredibly worth living here. Rio is cosmopolitan and open, but a right-wing city government in power until 2020 is responsible for poisoning its climate. The ancient African religion of Candomblé and the resulting syncretic form of *Umbanda* still have to be practiced in secret, because gangs of criminals were allowed to destroy their sacred sites and meeting places—unpunished and tolerated by the former mayor.

The metropolis boasts a wealth of potential and energy from its residents, but its politics prevent it from achieving a balance between rich and poor, and Black and white. The favelas could be pioneers of inclusive development, but standing in the way of their progress is the disinterest of politicians and the greed of speculators who want to drive the residents out of the settlements, many of which are in prime locations.

"Because there is this culture of community, and everyone helps each other. If you are having a hard moment, you go to your neighbors, you knock on their door, they'll give you flour, sugar, everyone is helping each other." (Marcelo)

„Die ganze Kultur des Fußballs, des Sambas und des Karnevals wurde in der Favela geboren. Sie wurde mit den Schwarzen geboren, sie wurde mit den Ausgegrenzten geboren."(Marcelo)

Rio, das ist ein Stück Afrika in Brasilien: lebensfroh, bunt, voller Rhythmen, sei es an einem der unzähligen Strände zwischen Copacabana oder Leblon, bei der Pedra do Sal, die jeden Montag unter dem Klang der Sambarhythmen, die hier erfunden wurden, erbebt oder in einer der Favelas, wenn das Wochenende eingeleitet wird. Kaum eine andere Megacity bietet so viele schnell zugängliche Strände vor der Haustür, einen Nationalpark mit Regenwald und Bergen mitten im Stadtgebiet, Lagunen mit Rad- und Joggingstrecken und eine Bevölkerung, deren Lebensfreude geradezu überschwänglich ist.

Keine Frage, die Stadt kämpft mit zahllosen gravierenden Problemen und ist doch trotz aller Schwierigkeiten unfassbar lebenswert. Rio ist weltoffen, aber eine bis 2020 rechtsgerichtete Stadtregierung hat das Klima vergiftet. Die urafrikanische Religion des Candomblé und die daraus hervorgegangene synkretistische Form des *Umbanda* müssen noch immer an versteckten Orten ausgeübt werden, weil kriminelle Banden ihre heiligen Orte und Versammlungsstätten – ungesühnt und vom ehemaligen Bürgermeister geduldet –, zerstören durften.

See and be seen 365 days a year: Body worship is part of the local culture in Rio, and when everybody is doing it, well, it takes little more effort to stand out.

365 Tage im Jahr sehen und gesehen werden: Körperkult in Rio ist ein Teil der hiesigen Kultur, und wenn alle mitmachen, muss man eben noch ein bisschen mehr machen, um aufzufallen.

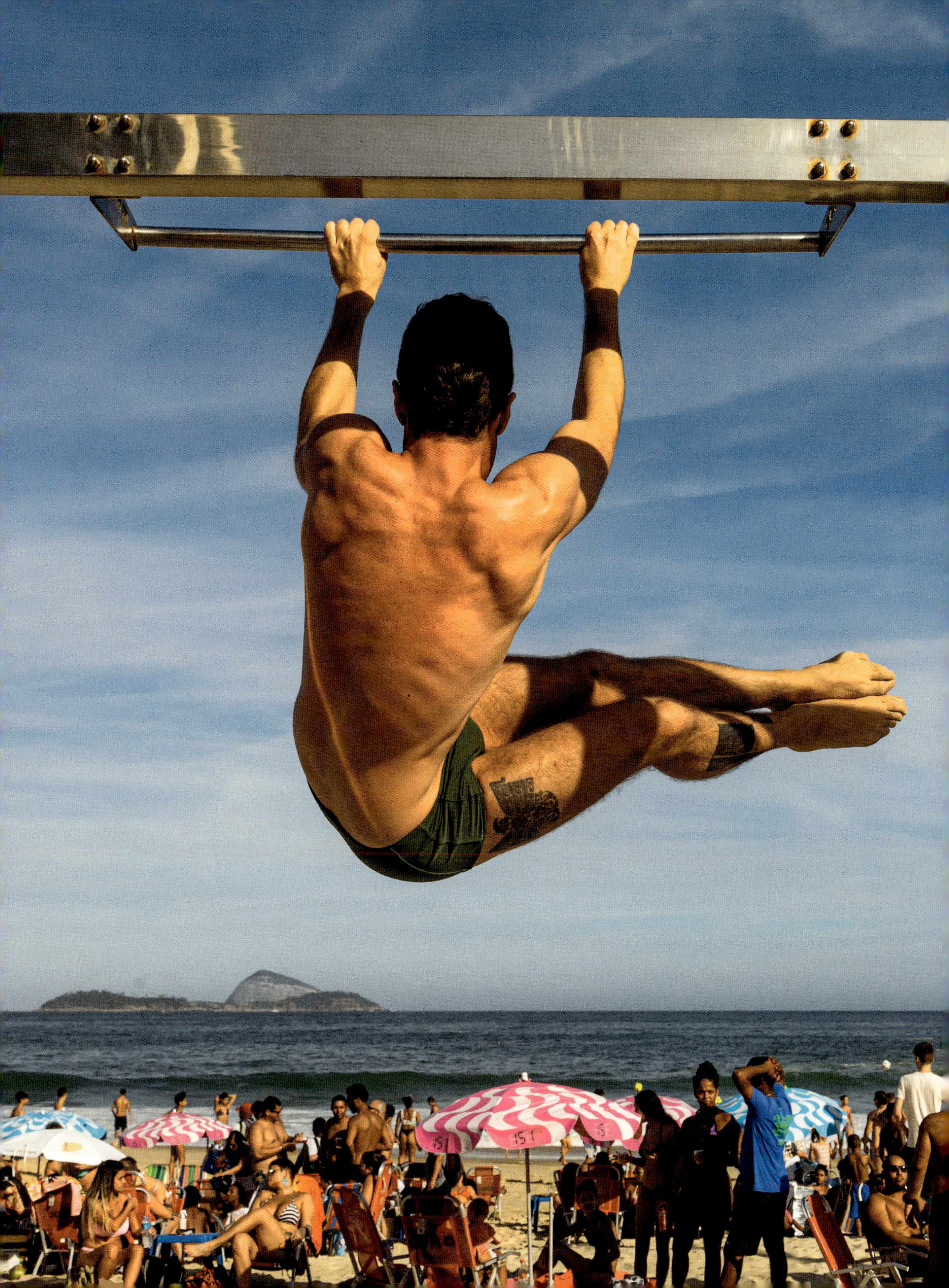

For some, Rio is a failed city whose inhabitants live alongside one another in separate worlds. But this view falls short of the mark. It underestimates the people's ability to improvise and their will to make their city livable and lovable. The need for security may be almost obsessive, whether in the gated communities of the rich or in front of the apartment blocks downtown. But outside, people celebrate together. The preservation of historical sites and land speculation are in a permanent state of conflict, and have transformed the old city into a strangely featureless construct. But Rio is not a static place. The old, decaying port facilities, for example, have been transformed into a cosmopolitan waterfront with museums, parks, and event venues.

And Rio cultivates its African roots. In the bairro da Gamboa, in the immediate vicinity of the old port, where millions of slaves were traded, those who did not survive the hardships were buried. Even today, you can still see traces of slavery throughout the city. In the favelas, founded by freed slaves because they had been cheated out of the land they were promised, in the culture of samba, and in the souls of the Black people, who cannot forget their heritage as descendants of slaves, because they are still disadvantaged and marginalized today.

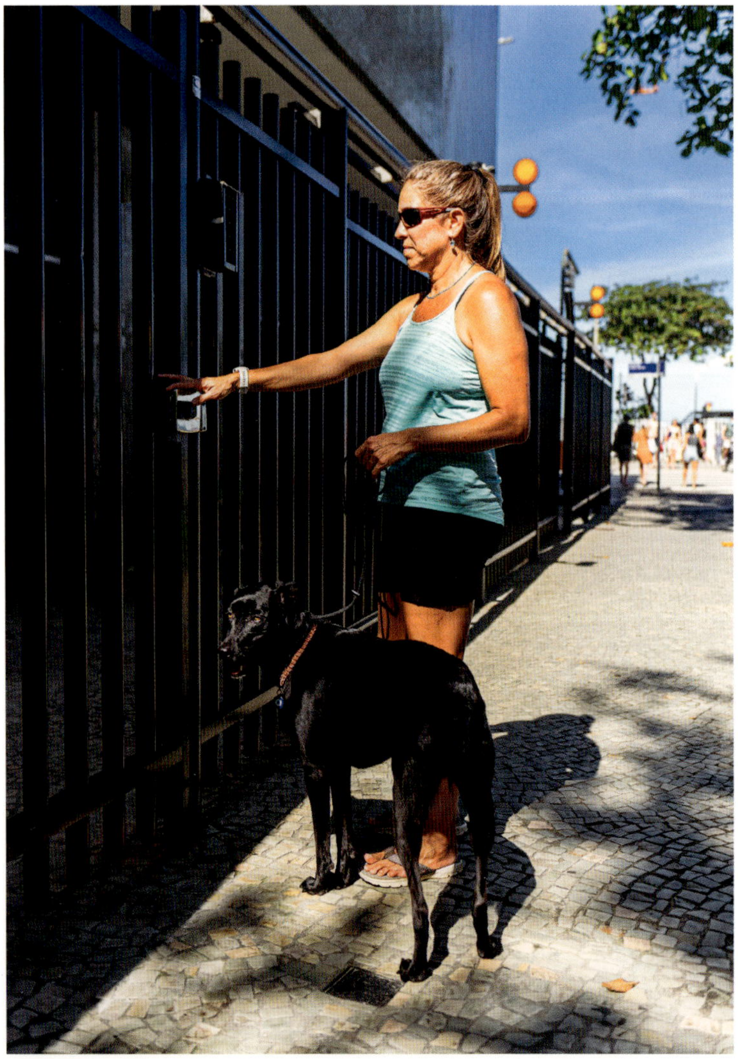

Die Metropole steckt voller Potenzial und Energie ihrer Bewohner, aber die Politik verhindert einen Ausgleich zwischen Arm und Reich, Schwarz und Weiß. Die Favelas könnten Vorreiter einer integrativen Entwicklung sein, aber ihrer Entwicklung steht das Desinteresse der Politik und die Gier von Spekulanten, die die Bewohner aus den oft in Toplagen liegenden Siedlungen vertreiben wollen, im Weg.

„Denn es gibt diese Kultur der Gemeinschaft und jeder hilft dem anderen. Wenn du einen schweren Moment hast, gehst du zu deinen Nachbarn, klopfst an ihre Tür und sie geben dir Mehl, Zucker – jeder hilft einander." (Marcelo)

Für manche ist Rio eine „gescheiterte Stadt", deren Einwohner in Parallelwelten nebeneinander leben. Doch diese Einschätzung greift zu kurz. Sie unterschätzt die Improvisationsfähigkeit und den Willen der Bevölkerung, ihre Stadt lebens- und liebenswert zu machen. Das Sicherungsbedürfnis mag geradezu obsessiv sein, sei es in den *gated communities* der Reichen oder aber vor den Apartmentblöcken im Zentrum. Doch draußen feiert man gemeinsam. Denkmalschutz und Bodenspekulation befinden sich in einem Dauerkonflikt und haben die Altstadt in ein seltsam hüllenloses Konstrukt verwandelt. Aber Rio ist nicht statisch. So sind die alten, verkommenen Hafenanlagen in eine weltstädtische Uferpromenade mit Museen, Parks und Eventstätten verwandelt worden.

Und Rio pflegt seine afrikanischen Wurzeln. Im bairro da Gamboa, in unmittelbarer Nachbarschaft zum alten Hafen, wo Millionen Sklaven umgeschlagen wurden, verscharrte man die Menschen, die die Strapazen nicht überlebten. Überall in der Stadt trifft man auch heute noch auf die Spuren der Sklaverei. In den Favelas, die von freigelassenen Sklaven gegründet wurden, weil man sie um das ihnen versprochene Land betrogen hatte, in der Kultur des Samba, aber auch in den Seelen der Schwarzen, die ihr Erbe als Nachfahren von Sklaven nicht vergessen können, da sie bis heute benachteiligt und ausgegrenzt werden.

Not very attractive, but safe: In most residential areas, the entrances to apartment complexes are protected by iron bars.

Nicht schön, aber sicher: In den meisten Wohngebieten sind die Eingänge der Apartmentanlagen mit Eisengittern gesichert.

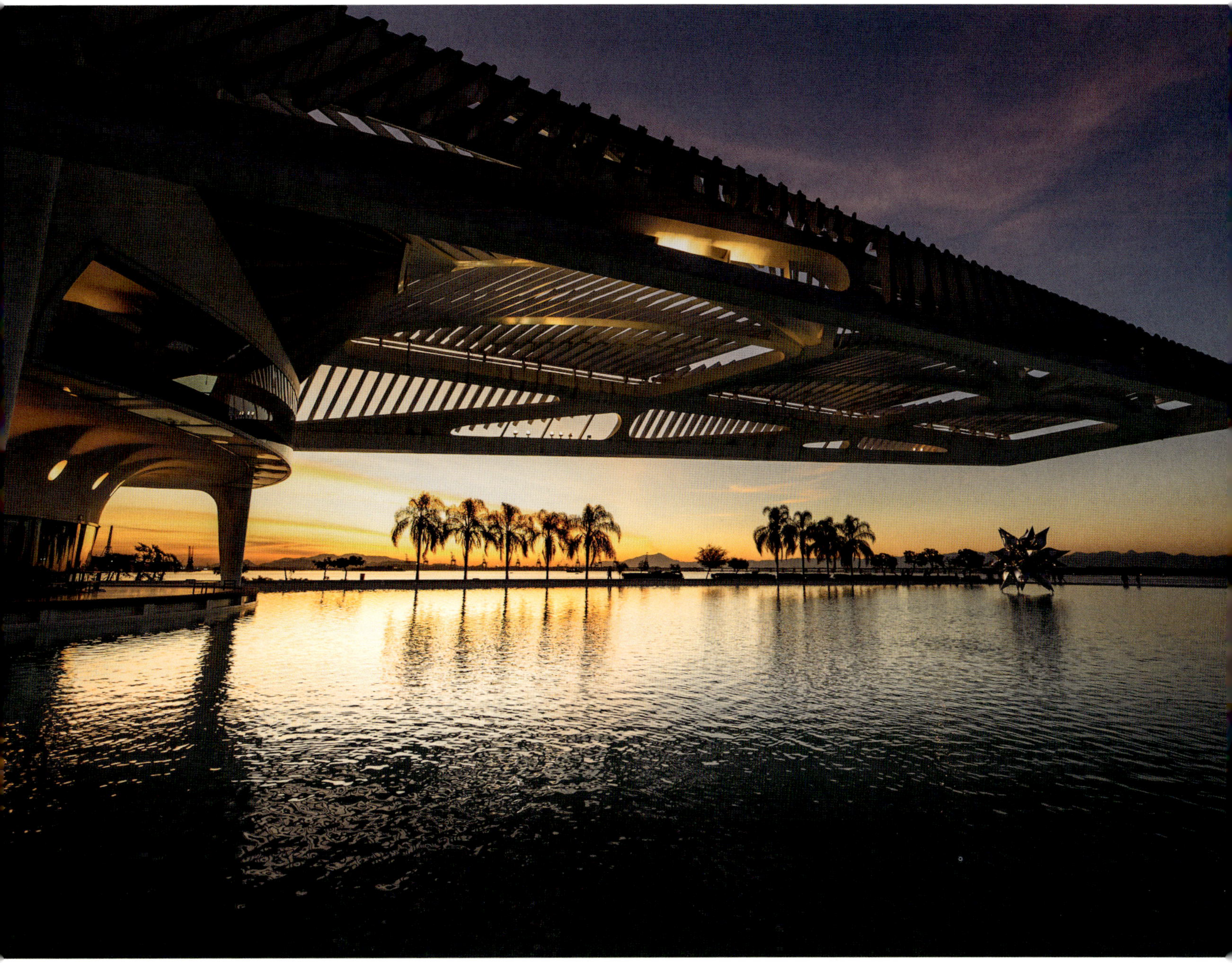

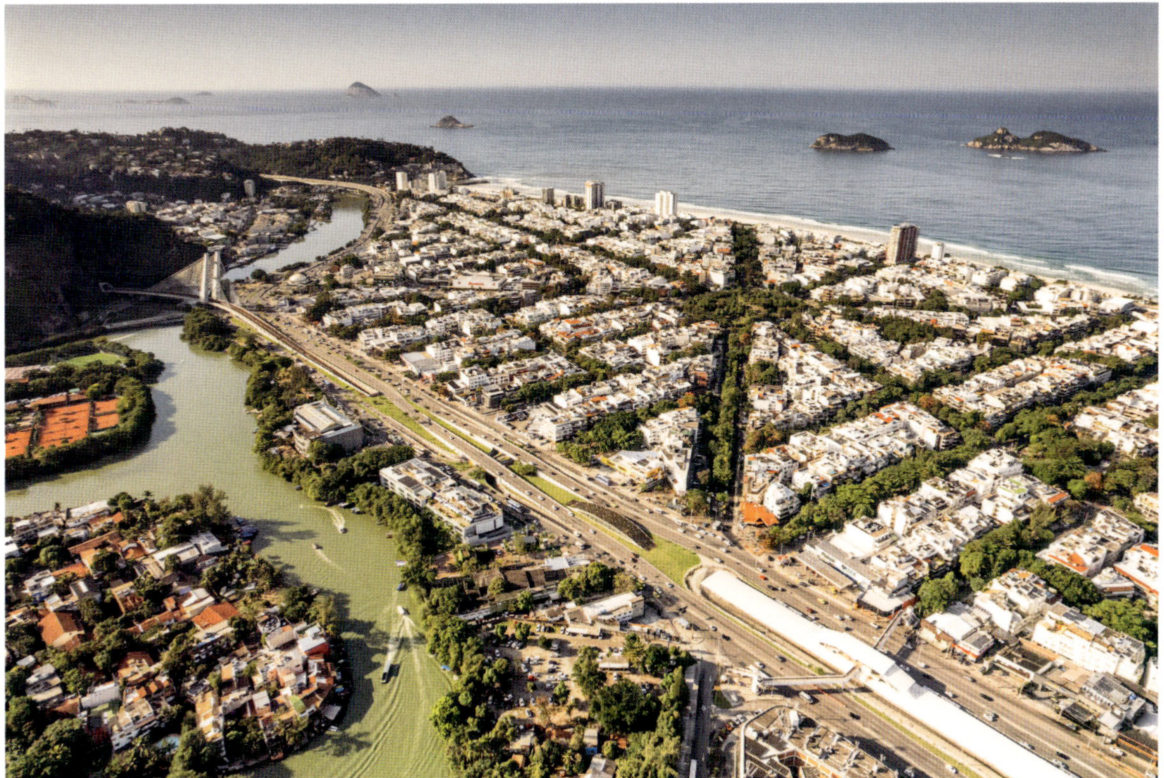

Neo-futurist Spanish architect Santiago Calatrava designed the ultramodern Museu do Amanhã in the old port of the city. Rio's Barra da Tijuca district is also quite glamorous.

Santiago Calatrava, neofuturistischer spanischer Architekt, erdachte das ultramoderne Museu do Amanhã am alten Hafen. Mondän gibt sich auch der Stadtteil Barra da Tijuca.

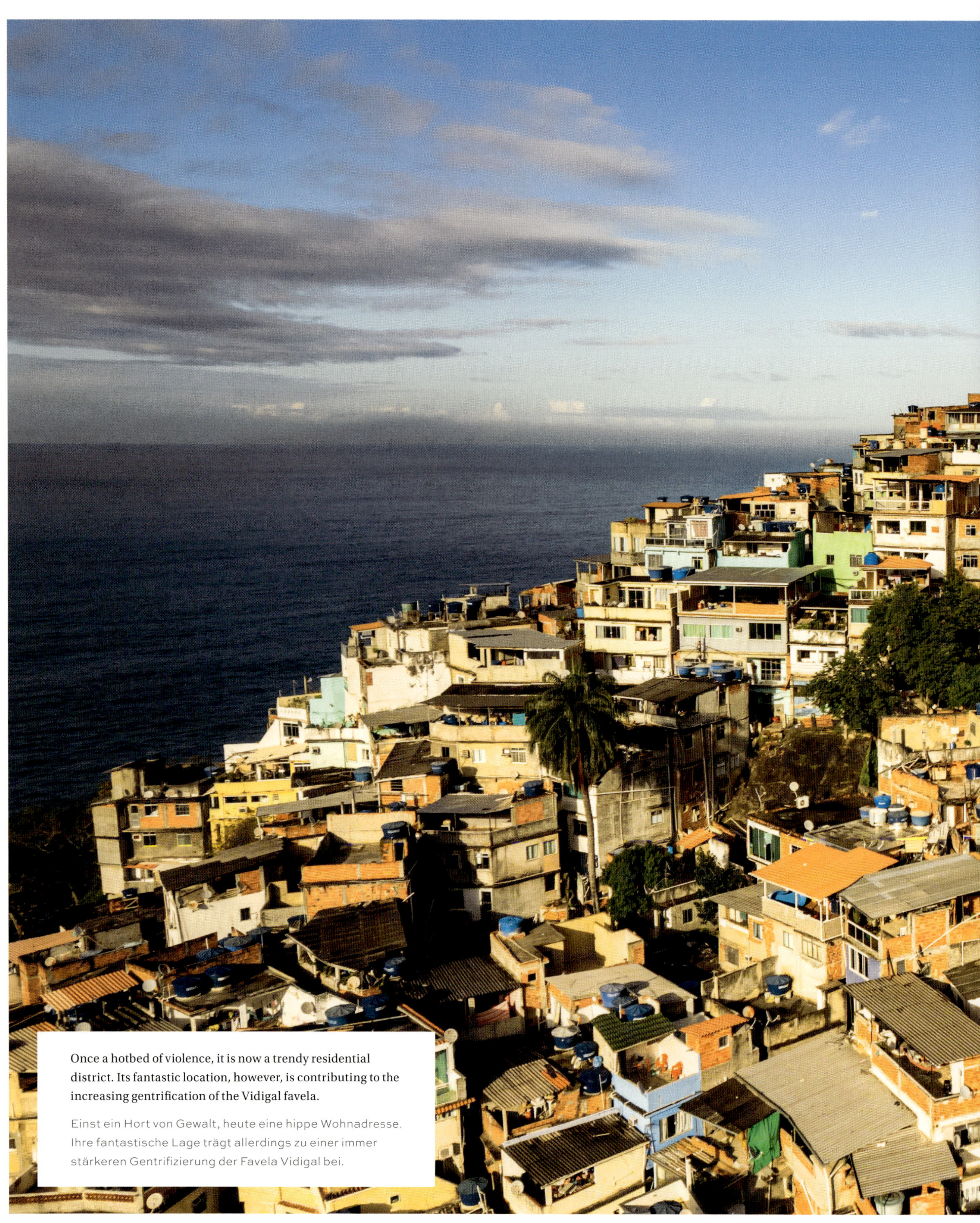

Once a hotbed of violence, it is now a trendy residential district. Its fantastic location, however, is contributing to the increasing gentrification of the Vidigal favela.

Einst ein Hort von Gewalt, heute eine hippe Wohnadresse. Ihre fantastische Lage trägt allerdings zu einer immer stärkeren Gentrifizierung der Favela Vidigal bei.

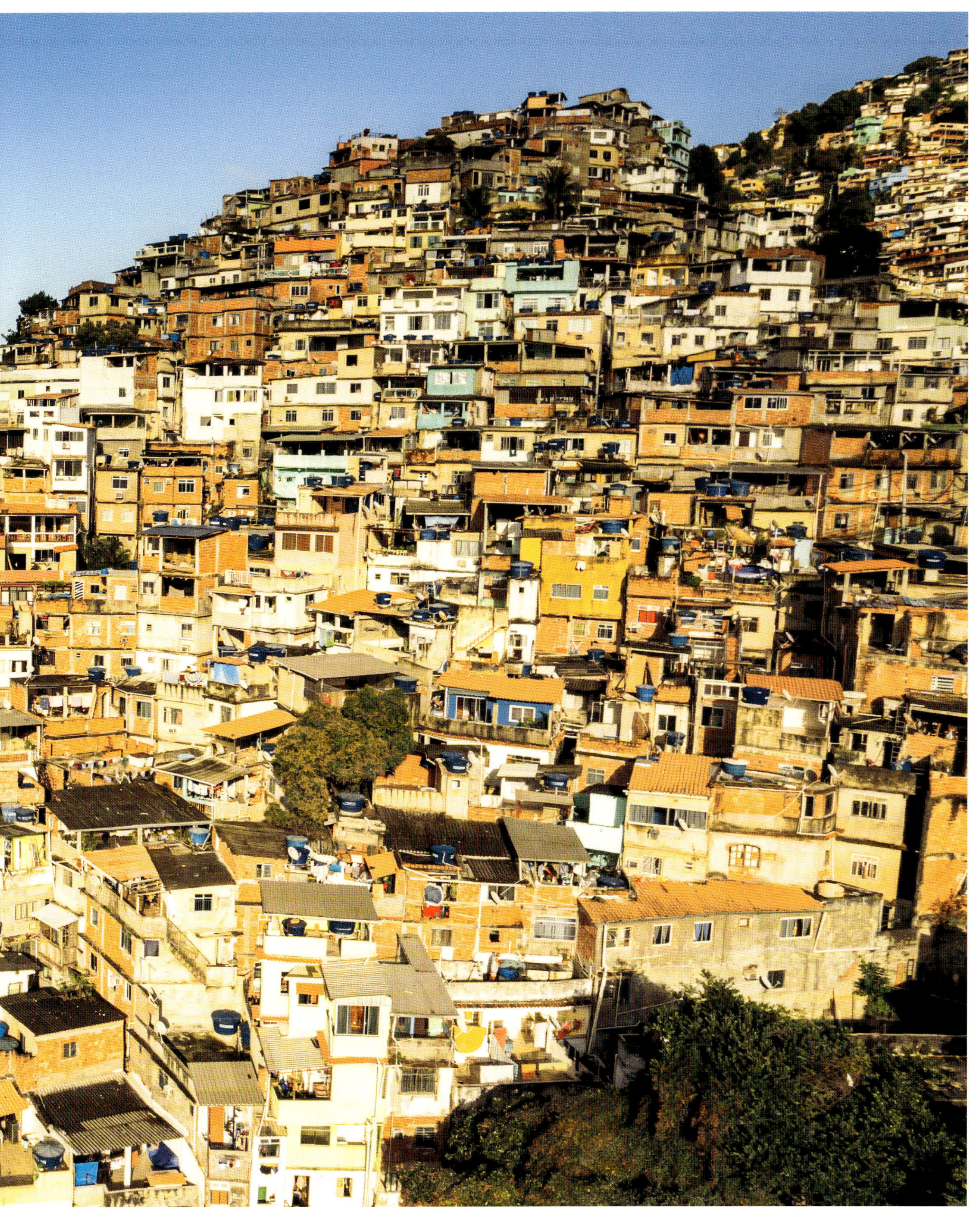

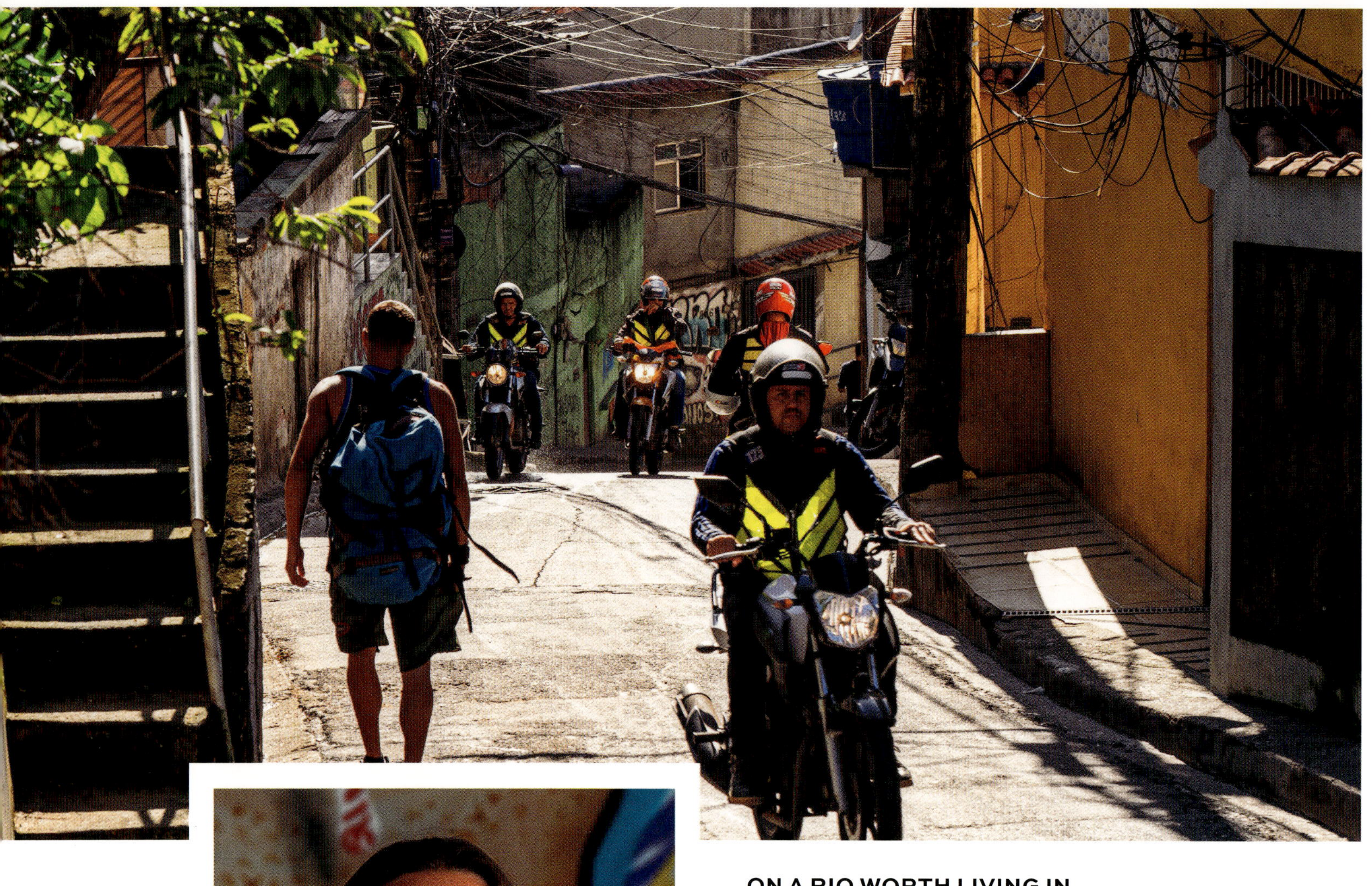

...ON A RIO WORTH LIVING IN

"No, it's not a green city in the sense of being sustainable. We have horrible problems with sewage. We have horrible problems with inequality, lack of resources, right, poverty. But it's green in the literal sense. It's got the largest urban forest in the world. People here love nature, for the most part, feel connected to the beach. (…) Rio is an outdoor city. (…) And people from Rio, they love to be outside. So often people's homes are tiny because they're spending a lot of their free time outside, whether it's on the beach or in the forest."

...ON RIO'S PROBLEMS

"What can we do now? How can we get more community input into the process of planning? Because communities have always known what they needed. In 22 years working with favelas, it's pretty much every meeting I go to, you hear the same three primary demands: health, education, and sanitation. And yet most resources applied are not applied to them. And those are the things that would have saved favelas from being so victimized by the pandemic. It would reduce security problems. It would increase quality of life. It would give people more access to jobs. So those basic investments don't happen. And those are the ones that people know they need."

...ON THE FAVELAS

"Rio has an incredibly rich civil society, a lot of community organizations and favelas doing incredible work, and the government basically uses them, co-ops them, or politicians before an election.

THERESA
CITY PLANNER
STADTPLANERIN

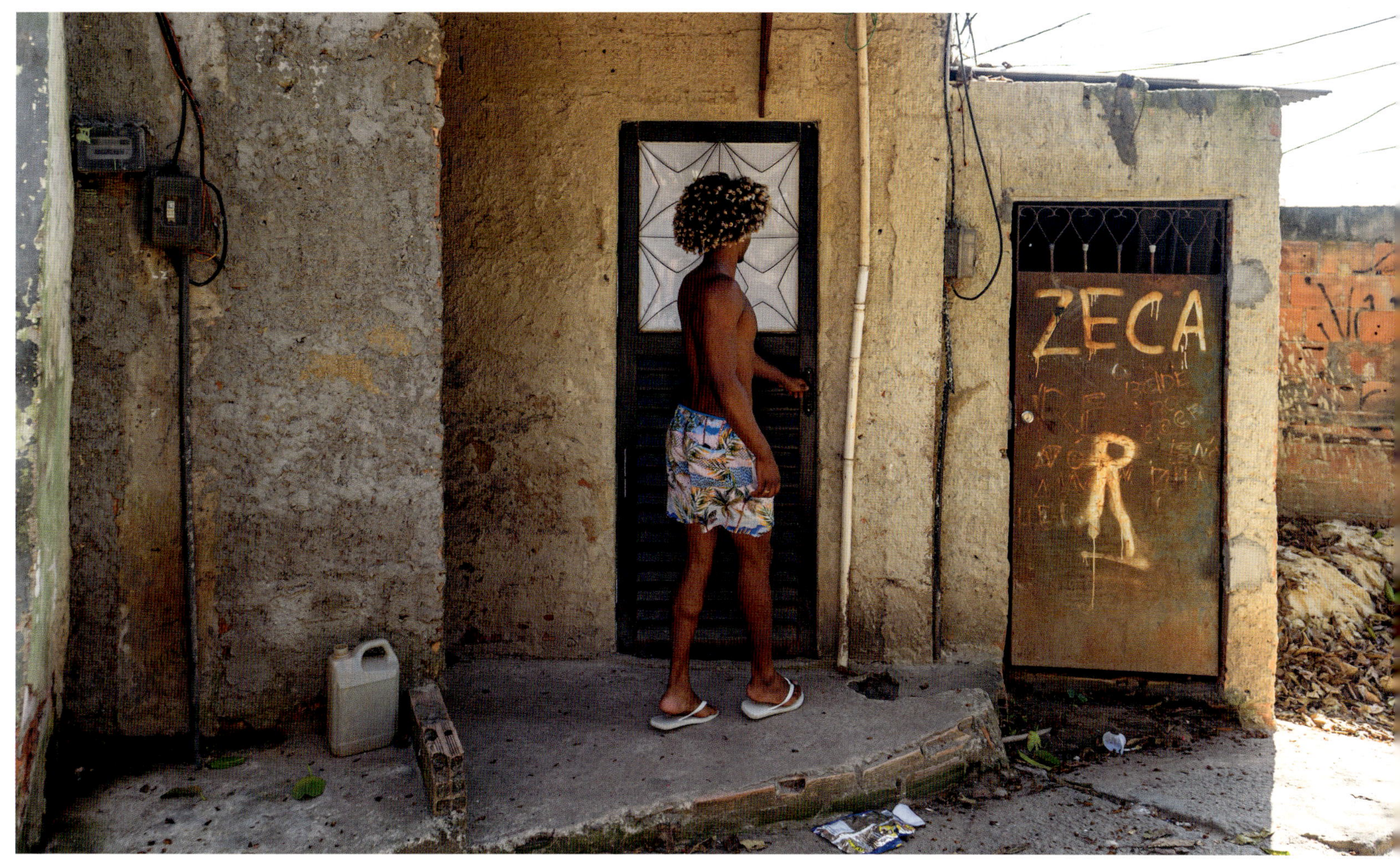

But there's no investment in the organizations, there's no investment in their communities. So, it's really important to try to get past what comes out in the media, past that stereotype that favelas are violent. Favelas are not violent. Violent actors, including drug traffickers, including off-duty police, militias, including police, right. Official police. These violent actors take advantage of the vulnerability of these communities, which is produced through these cycles of repression and neglect by the government. And so we need to dig a lot deeper to understand these communities."

...LEBENSWERTES RIO

„Nein, es ist keine grüne Stadt im Sinne von Nachhaltigkeit. Wir haben schreckliche Probleme mit der Abwasserentsorgung. Wir haben schreckliche Probleme mit der Ungleichheit, dem Mangel an Ressourcen, ja, der Armut. Aber sie ist grün im wörtlichen Sinne. Hier gibt es den größten städtischen Wald der Welt. Die Menschen hier lieben die Natur, fühlen sich größtenteils mit dem Strand verbunden. (...) Rio ist eine Outdoor-Stadt. (...) Und die Menschen aus Rio lieben es, draußen zu sein. Oft sind die Wohnungen der Leute so winzig, weil sie einen Großteil ihrer Freizeit draußen verbringen, sei es am Strand oder im Wald."

...ÜBER PROBLEME RIOS

„Was können wir jetzt tun? Wie können wir die Gemeinschaften stärker in den Planungsprozess einbeziehen? Denn die Gemeinschaften wussten schon immer, was sie brauchen. In den 22 Jahren, in denen ich mit Favelas arbeite, höre ich bei so gut wie jedem Treffen die gleichen drei Hauptforderungen: Gesundheit, Bildung und sanitäre Einrichtungen. Und dennoch werden die meisten Mittel nicht für diese Bereiche eingesetzt. Dabei sind das die Dinge, die die Favelas davor bewahrt hätten, der Pandemie so sehr zum Opfer zu fallen. Sie würden die Sicherheitsprobleme verringern. Es würde die Lebensqualität erhöhen. Es würde den Menschen mehr Zugang zu Arbeitsplätzen verschaffen. Diese grundlegenden Investitionen werden also nicht getätigt. Dabei wissen die Menschen genau, dass sie diese Investitionen brauchen."

...ÜBER FAVELAS

„Rio hat eine unglaublich reiche Zivilgesellschaft, viele Gemeindeorganisationen und Favelas, die unglaubliche Arbeit leisten, und die Regierung oder die Politiker nutzen sie im Grunde nur vor einer Wahl aus. Aber es gibt keine Investitionen in die Organisationen, es gibt keine Investitionen in ihre Gemeinden. Es ist also wirklich wichtig, dass wir versuchen, das Klischee, dass Favelas gewalttätig sind, zu überwinden, das in den Medien verbreitet wird. Favelas sind nicht gewalttätig. Gewalttätige Akteure, einschließlich Drogenhändler, einschließlich Polizisten außer Dienst, Milizen, einschließlich der Polizei, richtig: offizielle Polizei. Diese gewalttätigen Akteure nutzen die Verwundbarkeit dieser Gemeinschaften aus, die durch diese Zyklen der Unterdrückung und Vernachlässigung durch die Regierung hervorgerufen wird. Wir müssen also viel tiefer graben, um diese Gemeinschaften zu verstehen."

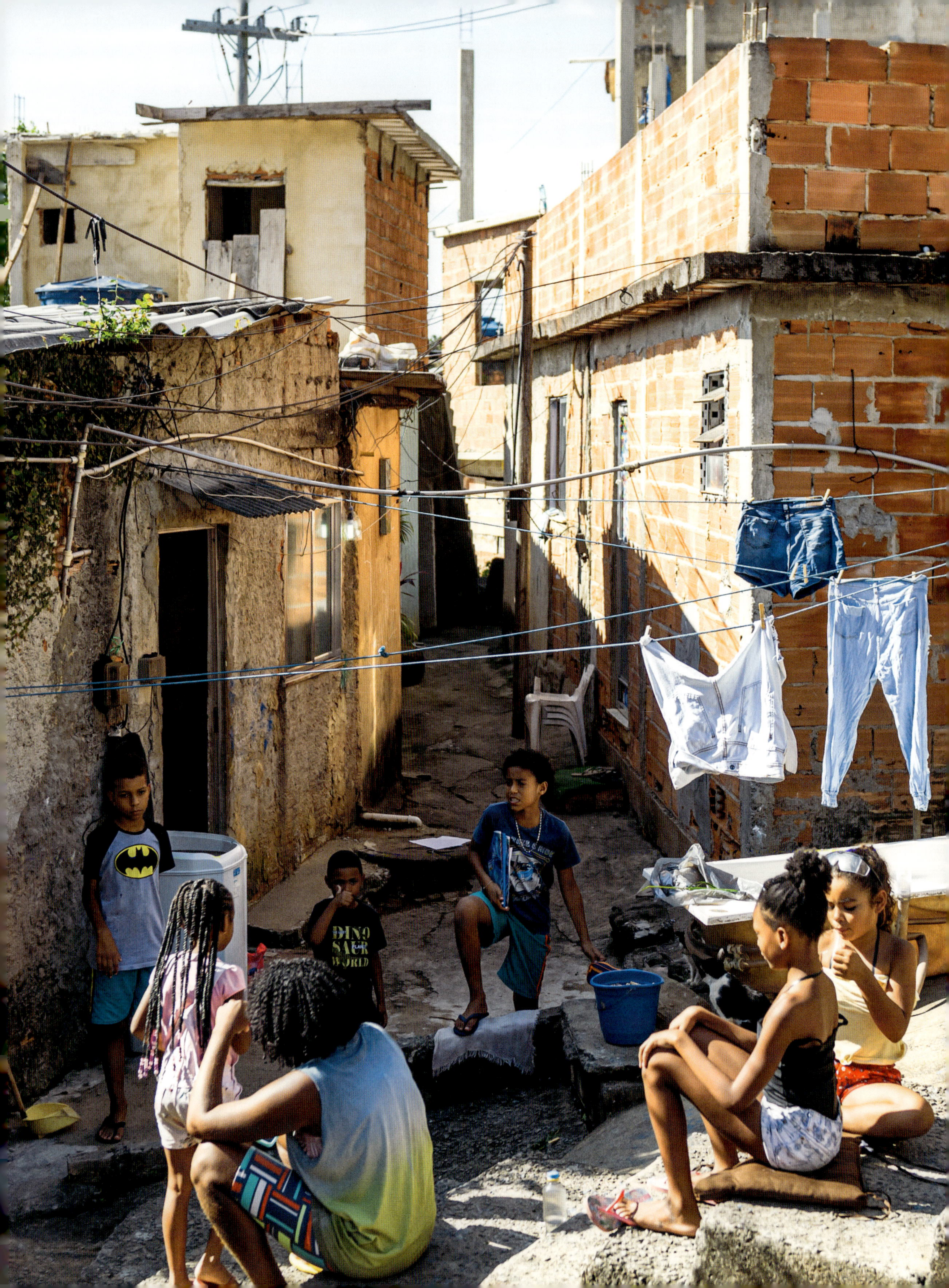

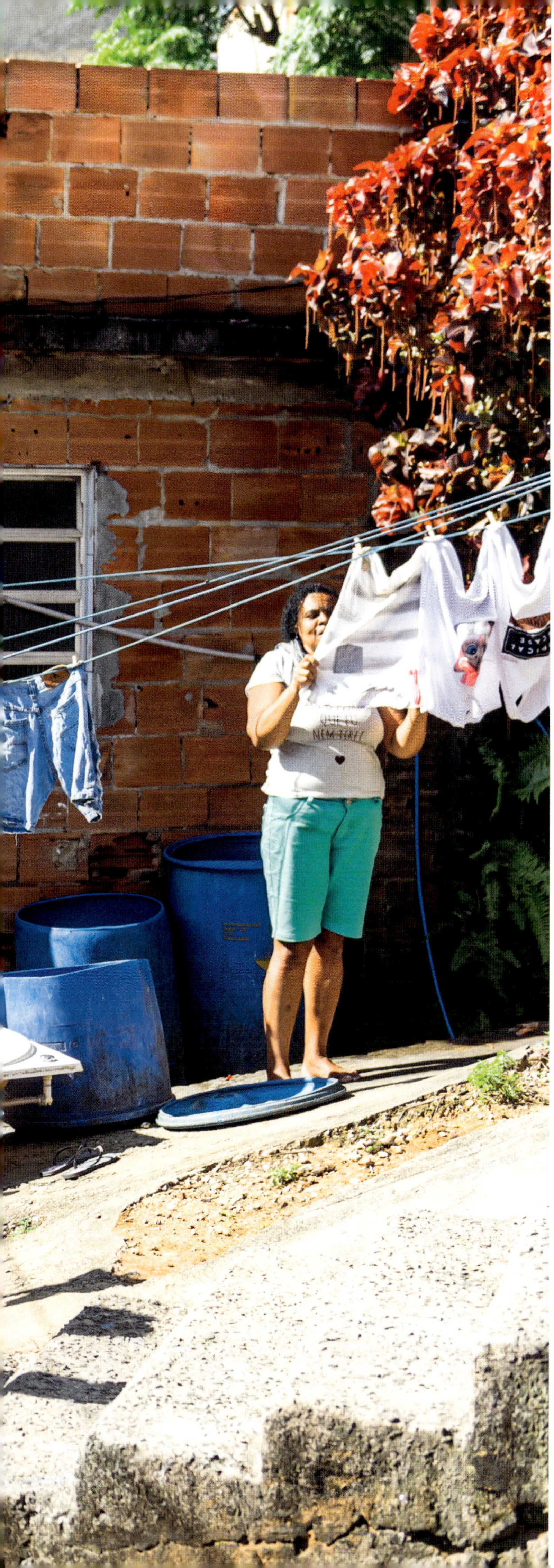

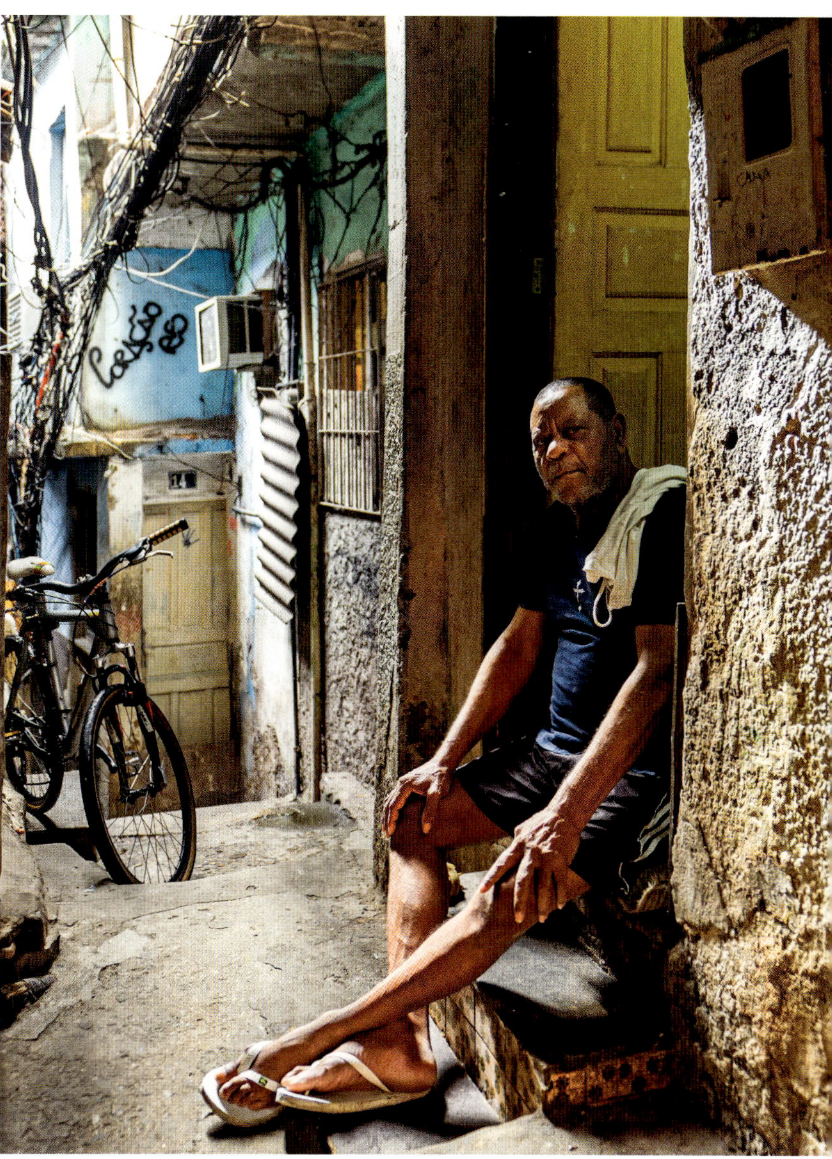

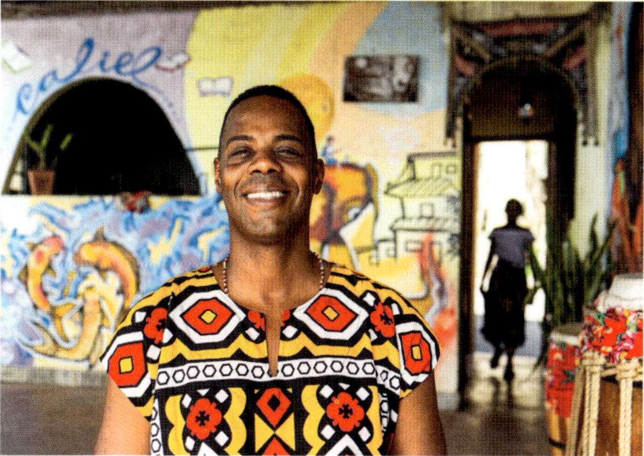

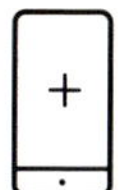

"Salgueiro was one of the first favelas in Rio, and in Brazil overall, so we have a very distinct Black culture here." (Marcelo)

„Salgueiro war eine der ersten Favelas in Rio und in Brasilien überhaupt, daher haben wir hier eine sehr ausgeprägte schwarze Kultur." (Marcelo)

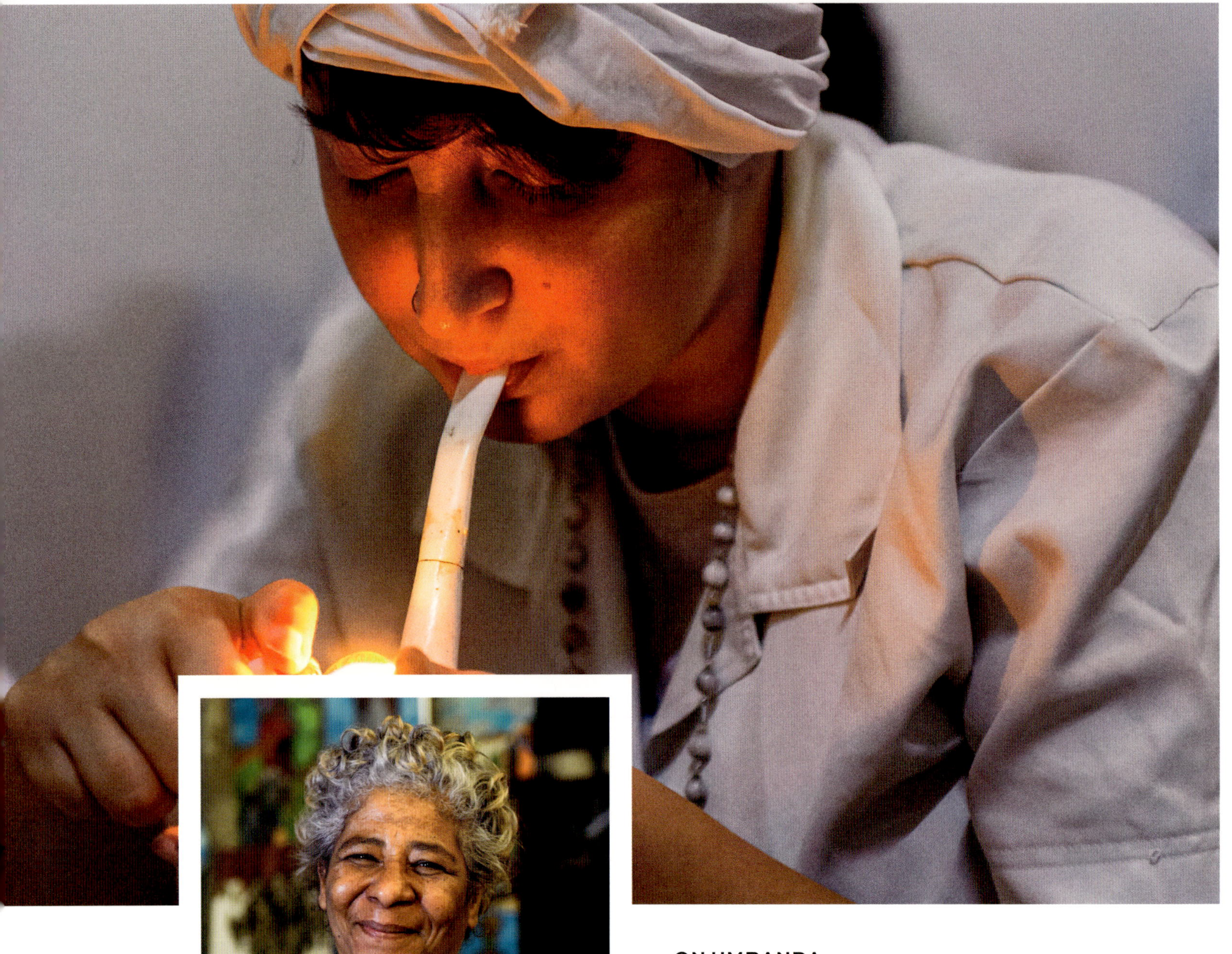

...ON UMBANDA

"Umbanda is one religion that attends to different people from different places with different beliefs. Umbanda is not only the African deity, we have a lot of references from Catholicism, Buddhism, Hinduism. We attend to all these people. And I have a lot of DNA memories from Indigenous people, Black people, European people. (...) So that's Umbanda, so that's why Umbanda is important, because Umbanda attends to everybody. It doesn't matter what you believe. It comes with love and peace. Umbanda is here to attend and give love. (...) Umbanda is a life philosophy. It's not like a religion, it's a life philosophy. So that's the main thing, and the Brazilian people are made by different kinds of beliefs, but this mixture of all these beliefs, it's in some way mystical, so that's why Brazilians come here."

SARA
UMBANDA PRIESTESS
UMBANDA-PRIESTERIN

During rituals, all Umbanda participants are dressed in white, the color of community and a symbol of all people being equal.

Alle Teilnehmenden beim Umbanda tragen bei den Ritualen weiße Kleidung, die Farbe der Gemeinschaft und ein Symbol dafür, dass alle Menschen gleich sind.

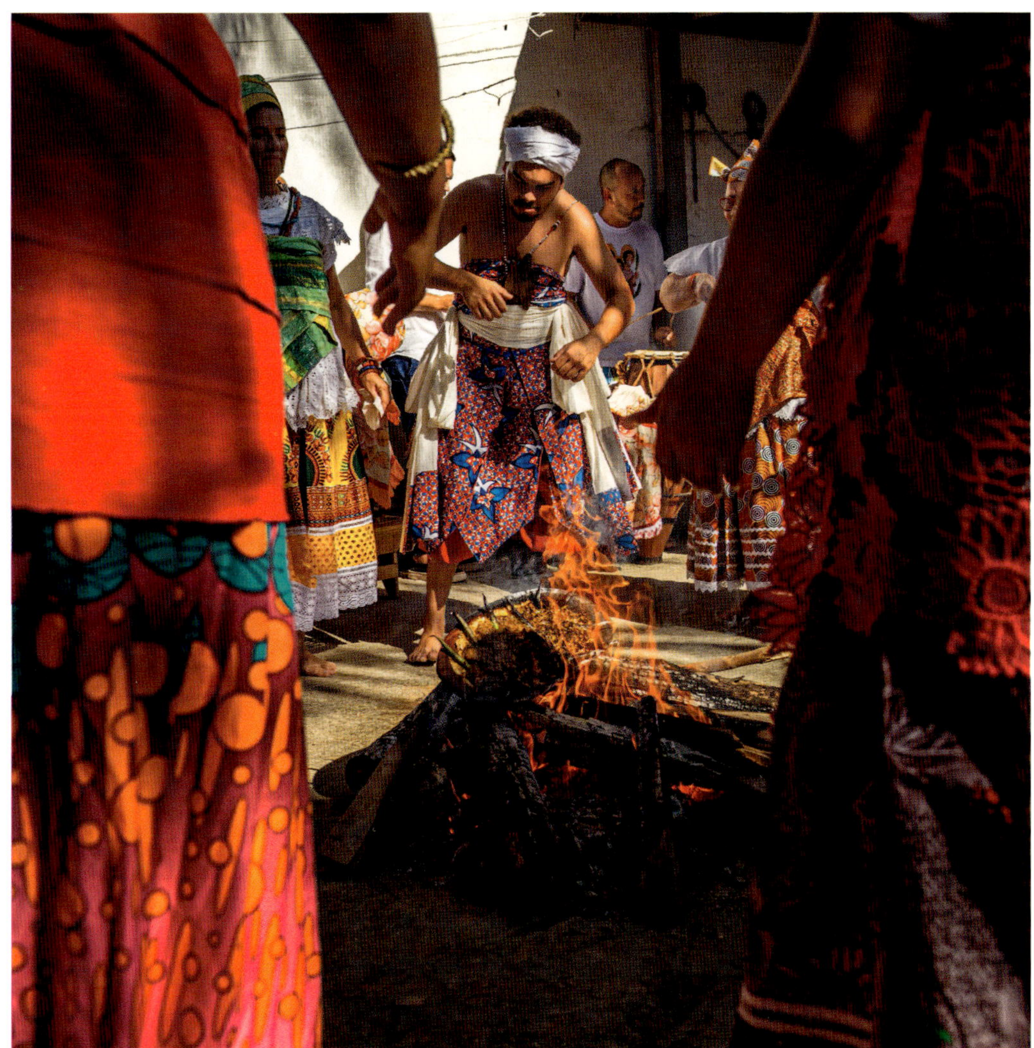

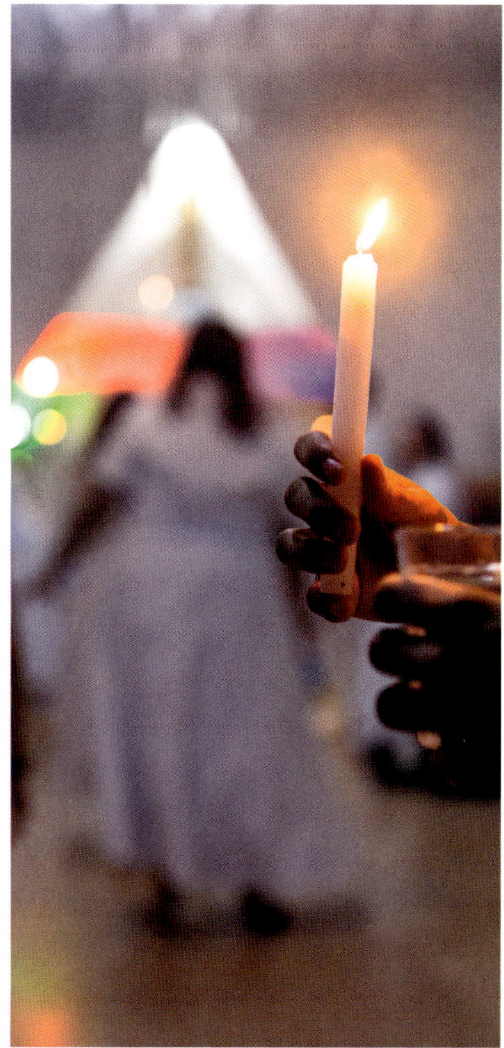

...ÜBER UMBANDA

„(...) Umbanda ist eine Religion, die verschiedene Menschen aus verschiedenen Ländern mit unterschiedlichen Glaubensrichtungen anspricht. Umbanda ist nicht nur die afrikanische Gottheit, und wir haben viele Bezüge zum Katholizismus, Buddhismus, Hinduismus. Wir nehmen also an all diesen Menschen teil. Ich habe eine Menge DNA-Erinnerungen von Ureinwohnern, Schwarzen und Europäern. (...) Das ist also Umbanda, und deshalb ist Umbanda so wichtig, weil Umbanda sich um jeden kümmert, ganz gleich, was man glaubt. Sie kommt mit Liebe und Frieden. Umbanda ist hier, um zu begleiten und Liebe zu geben. (...) Umbanda ist eine Lebensphilosophie, nicht wie eine Religion, es ist eine Lebensphilosophie. Das ist die Hauptsache, und die Brasilianer haben verschiedene Arten von Glauben, aber diese ganze Mischung von Glauben ist auf eine Art mystisch, und deshalb kommen die Brasilianer hierher."

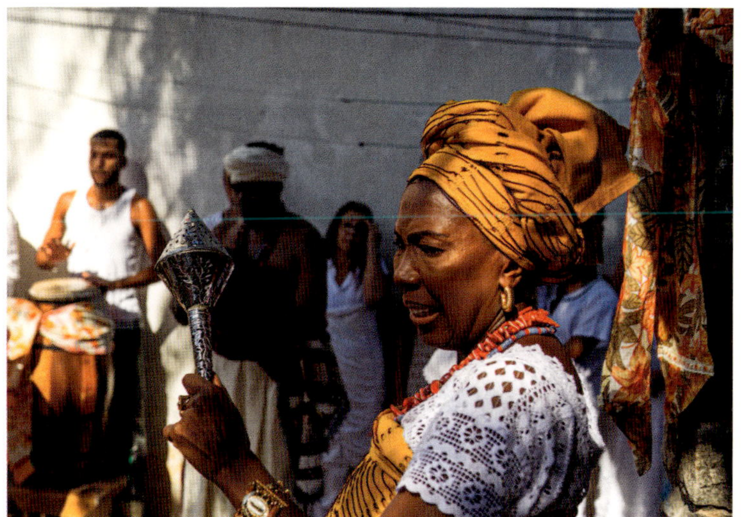

Candomblé is a natural religion with African roots. The power of the orixas, Afro-Brazilian deities, is released during the rituals and dances and is transferred to those present.

Candomblé ist eine Naturreligion mit afrikanischen Wurzeln. Bei den Ritualen und Tänzen wird die Kraft der Orixas, afro-brasilianischer Gottheiten freigelegt und geht auf die Anwesenden über.

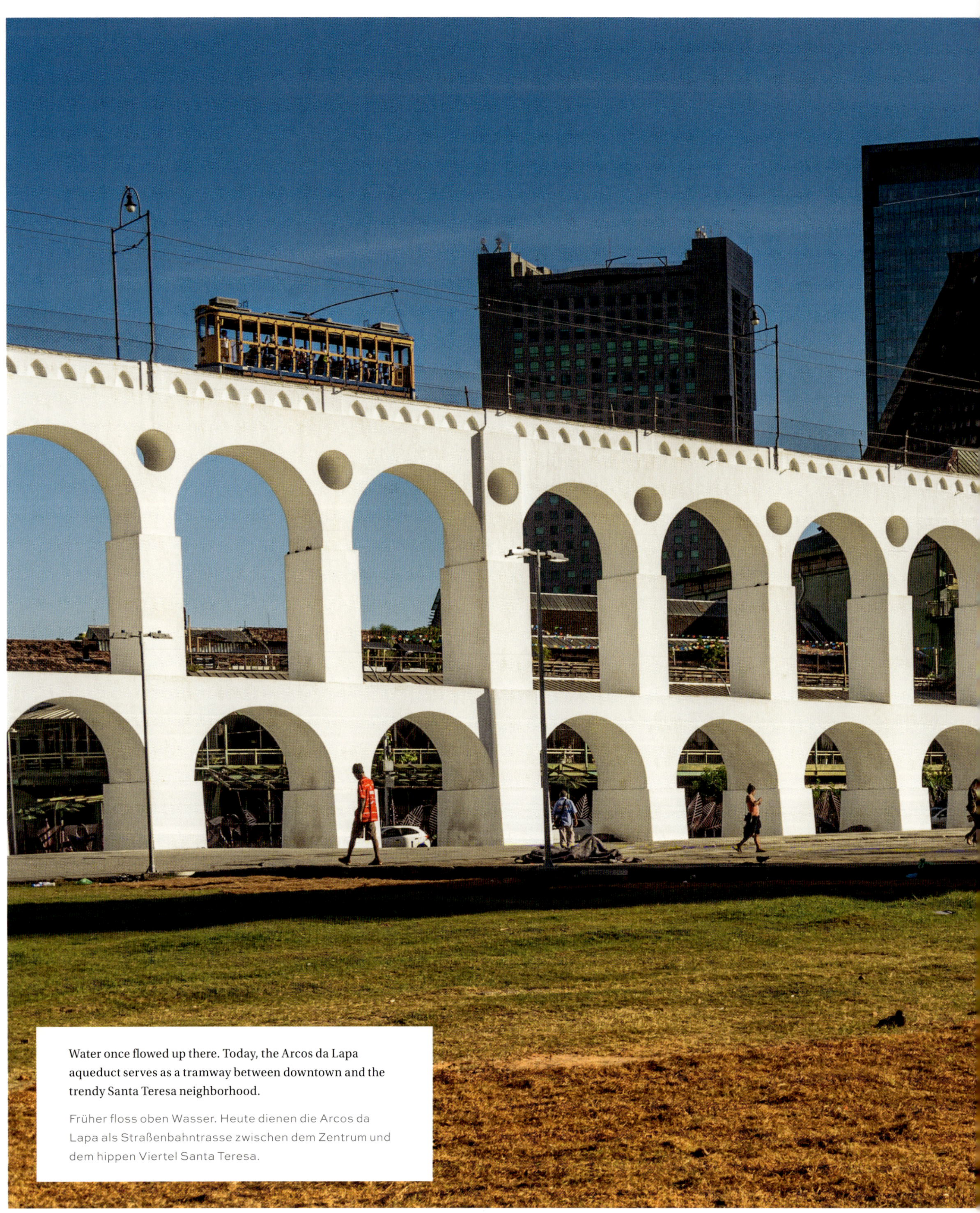

Water once flowed up there. Today, the Arcos da Lapa aqueduct serves as a tramway between downtown and the trendy Santa Teresa neighborhood.

Früher floss oben Wasser. Heute dienen die Arcos da Lapa als Straßenbahntrasse zwischen dem Zentrum und dem hippen Viertel Santa Teresa.

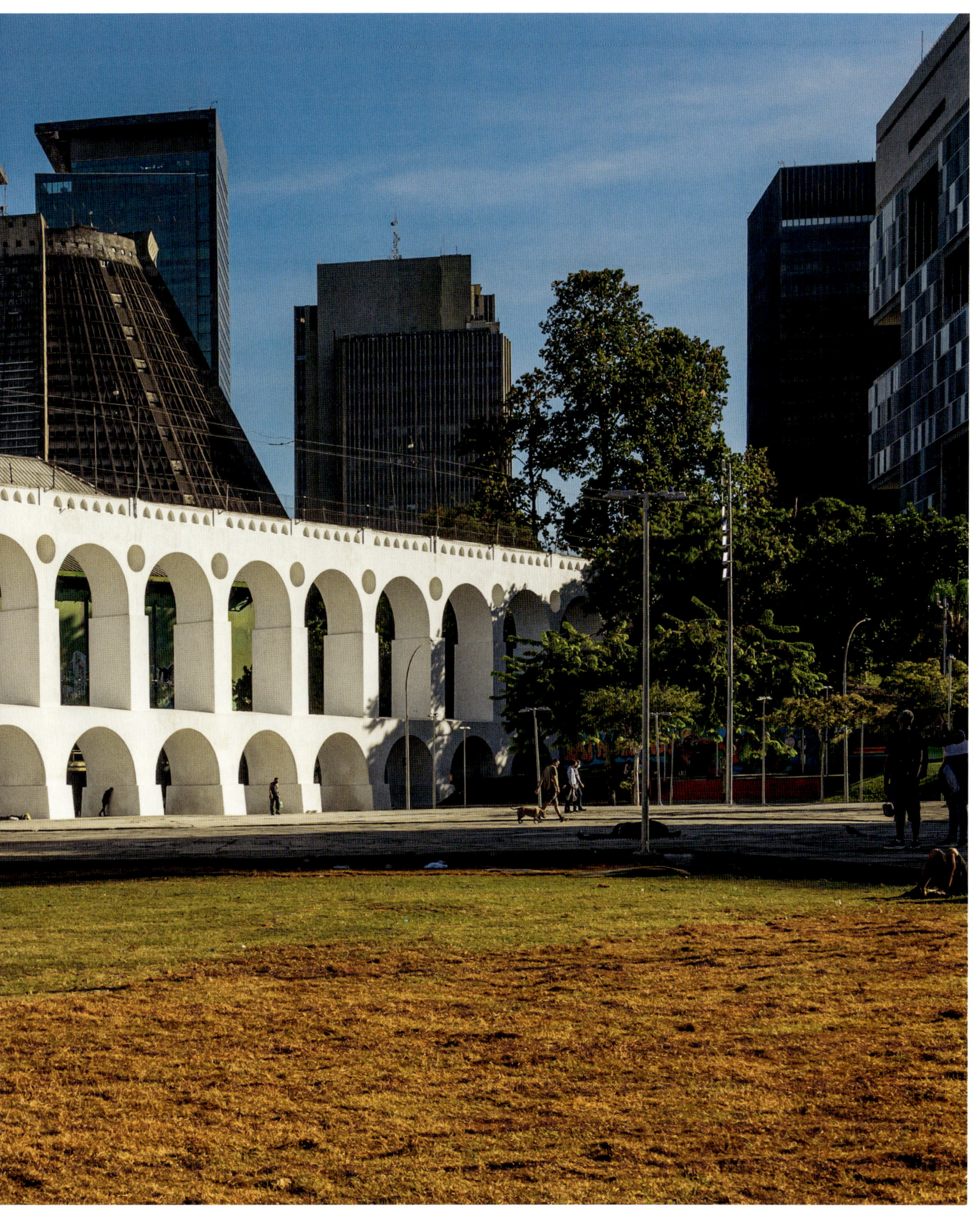

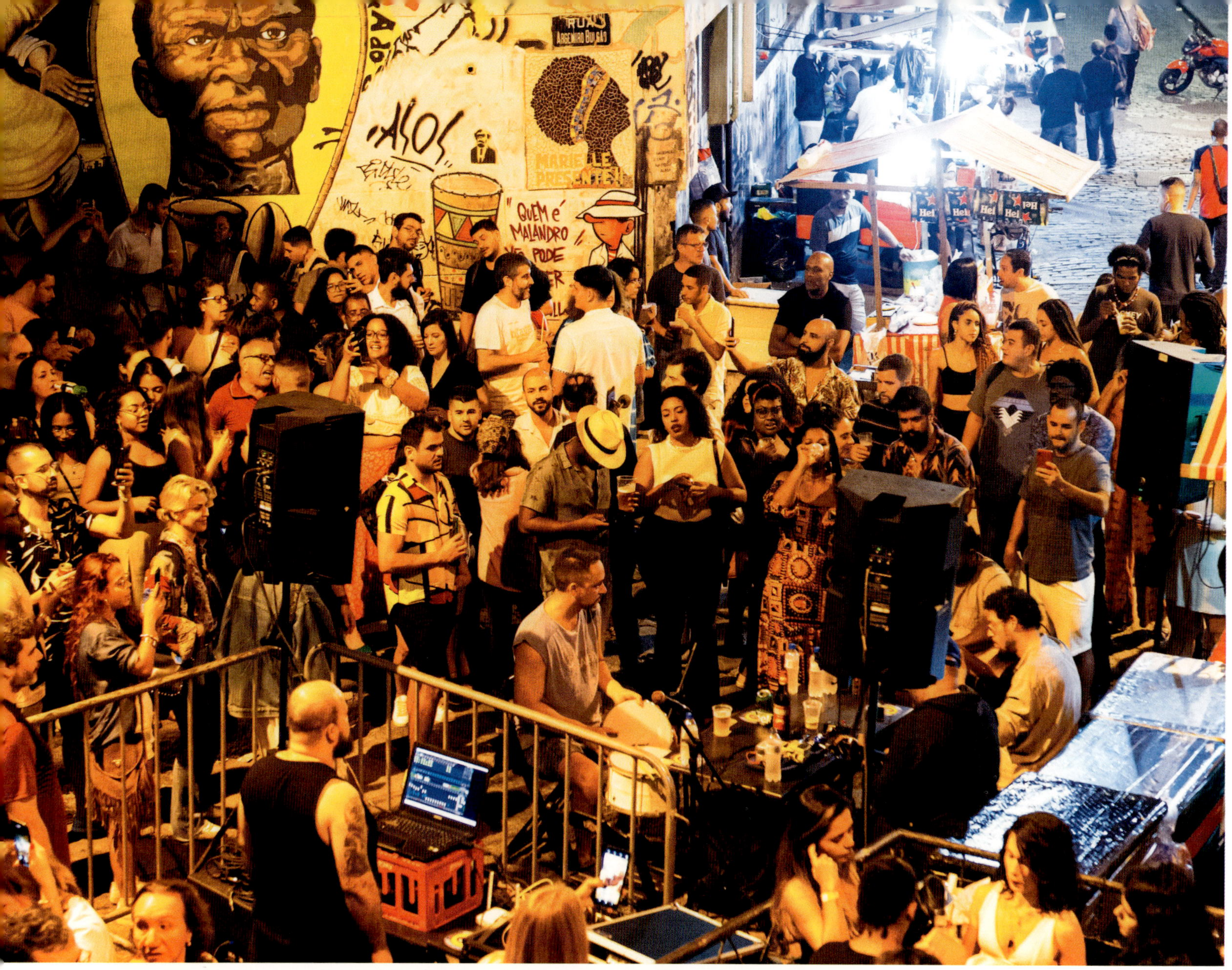

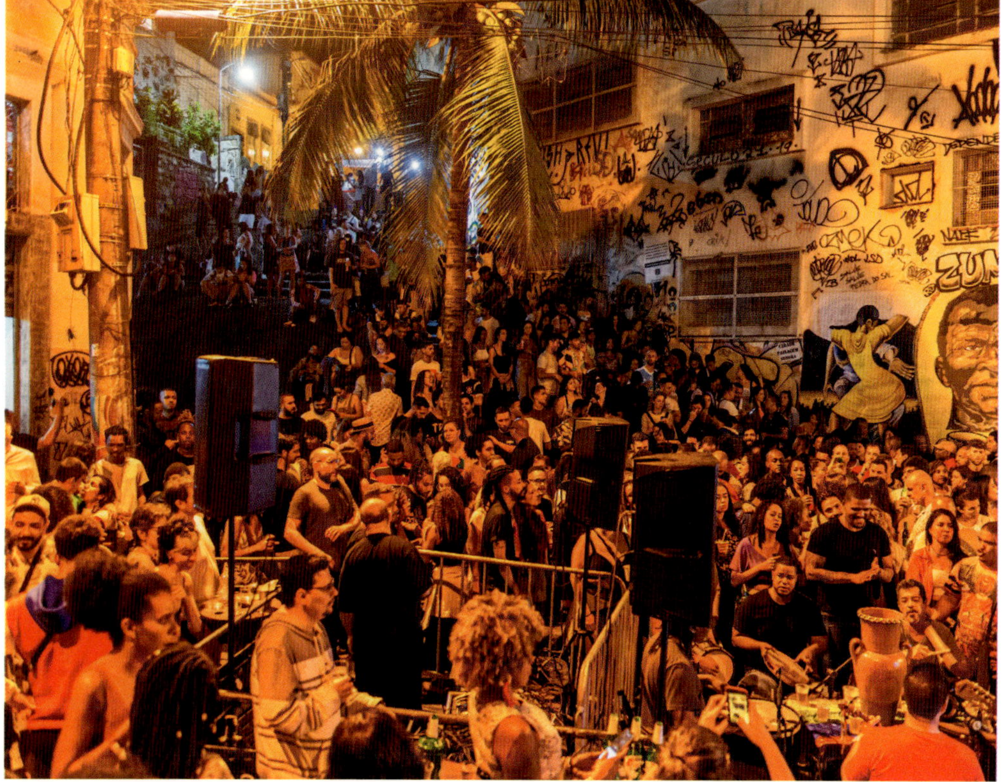

The Pedra do Sal is the birthplace of samba, and to this day it remains a place where samba truly lives.

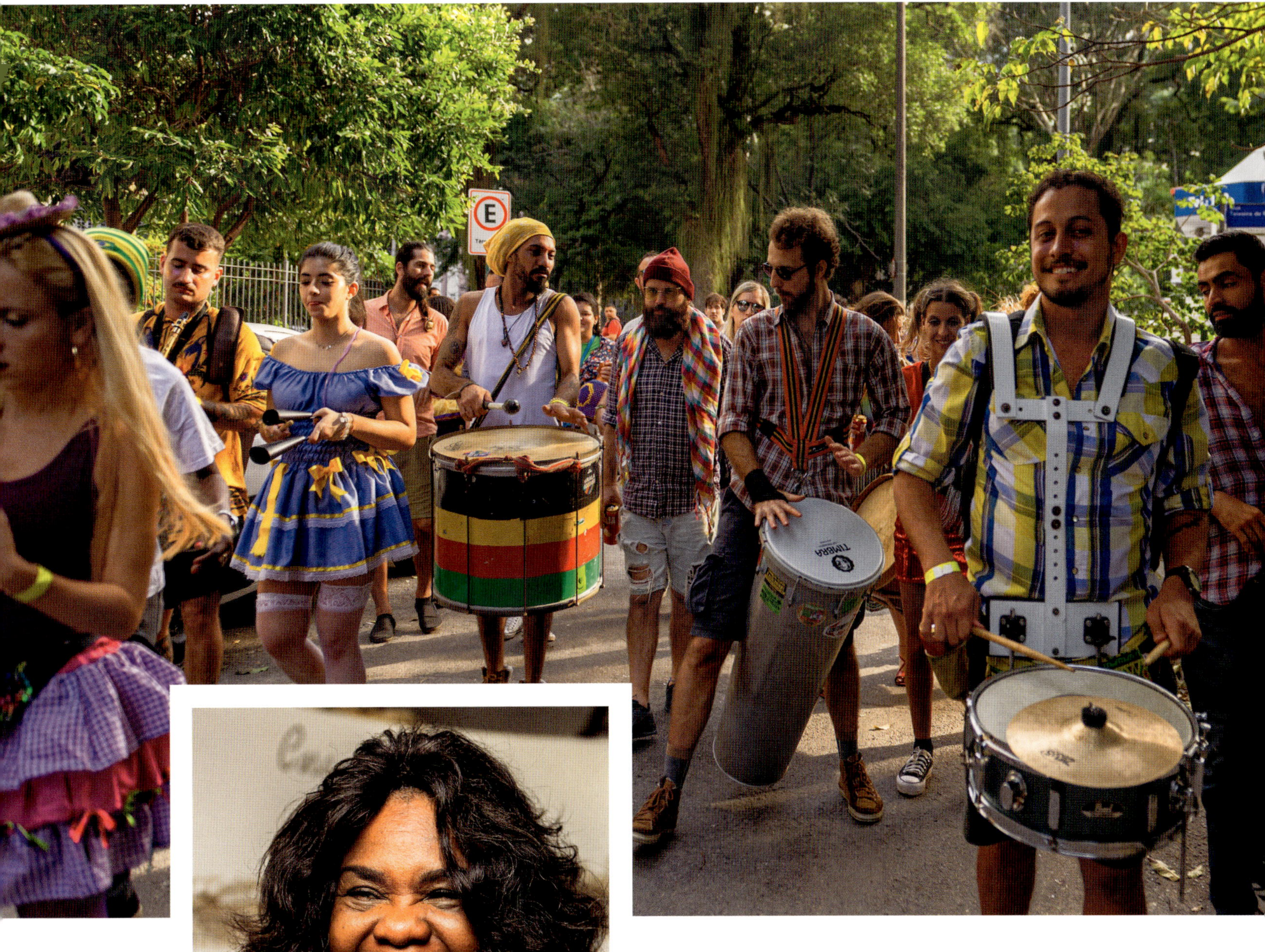

GRACE
GREAT-GREAT-GRAND-
DAUGHTER OF THE
FOUNDER OF SAMBA
TIA CIATA

UR-UR-ENKELIN DER
BEGRÜNDERIN DES
SAMBA TIA CIATA

...ON THE LIFE FORCE OF SAMBA

"Samba doesn't have a specific place. It's a moment when everyone comes together and it's a celebration of life. It's a symbol of
identity and it's a way for all the people, for all the places to be together, celebrating the good things of life. It's, I think, also something like a way to not worry about fixing our problems. Like to
have a way to be together and be happy and celebrate for a time."

...LEBENSELIXIER SAMBA

„Samba hat keinen besonderen Ort. Es ist ein Moment, in
dem alle zusammenkommen, und es ist eine Feier des
Lebens. Es ist ein Symbol der Identität und eine Möglichkeit
für alle Menschen, überall zusammen zu sein und die guten
Dinge des Lebens zu feiern. Ich denke, es ist auch eine
Möglichkeit, Probleme zu vergessen. Es ist ein Weg, um
zusammen zu bleiben und glücklich zu sein und eine Zeit lang
zu feiern.“

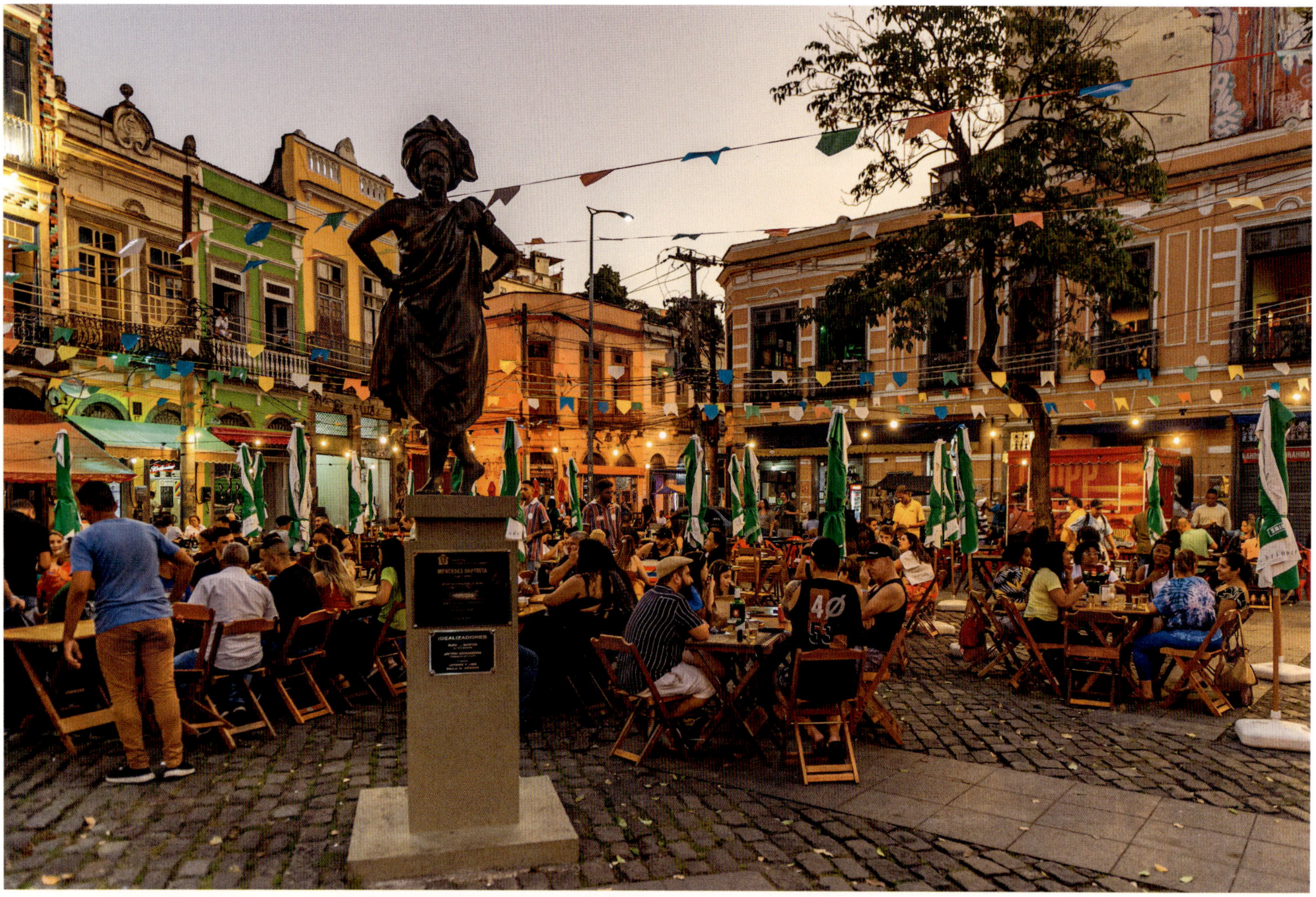

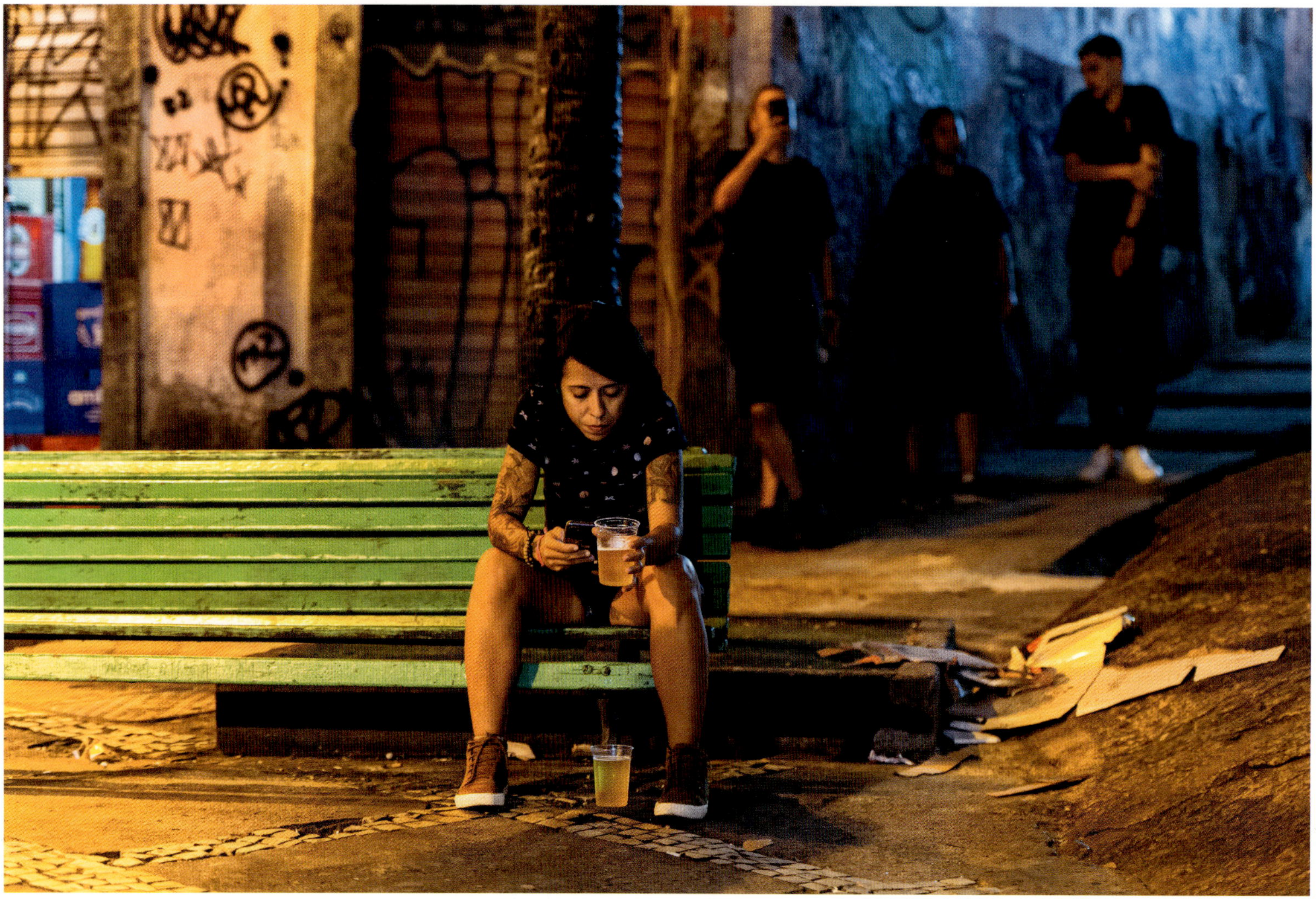

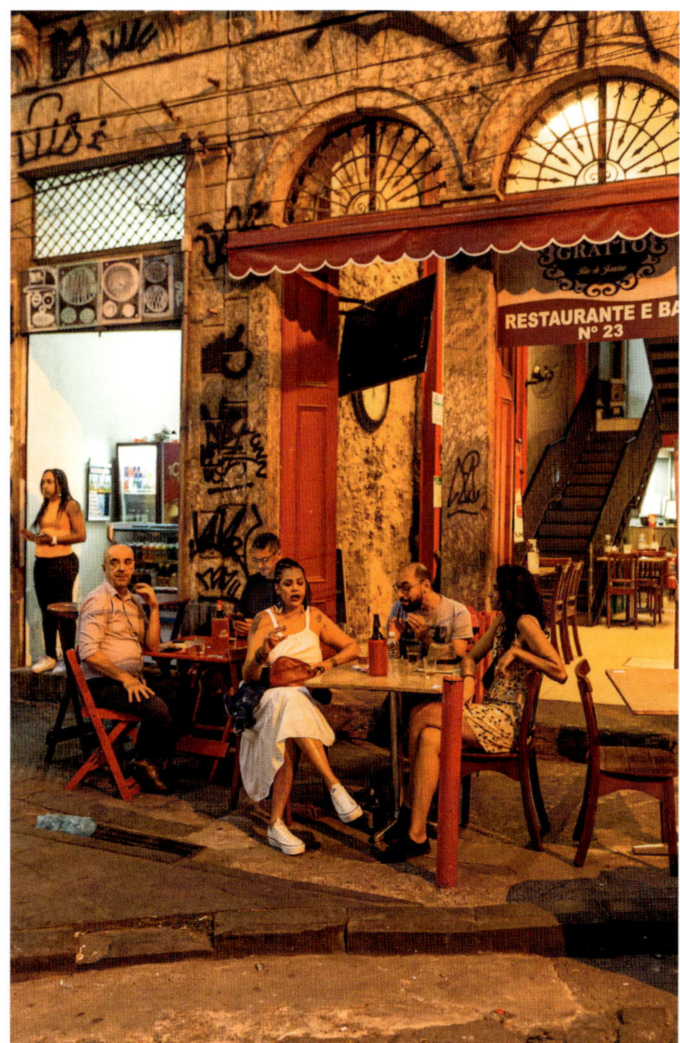

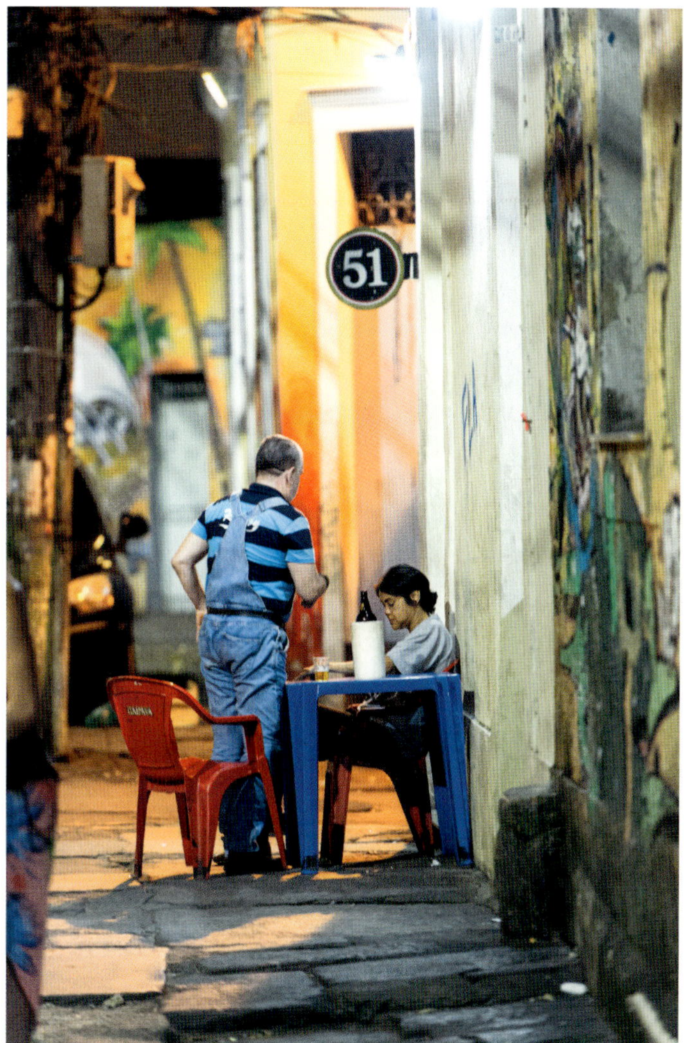

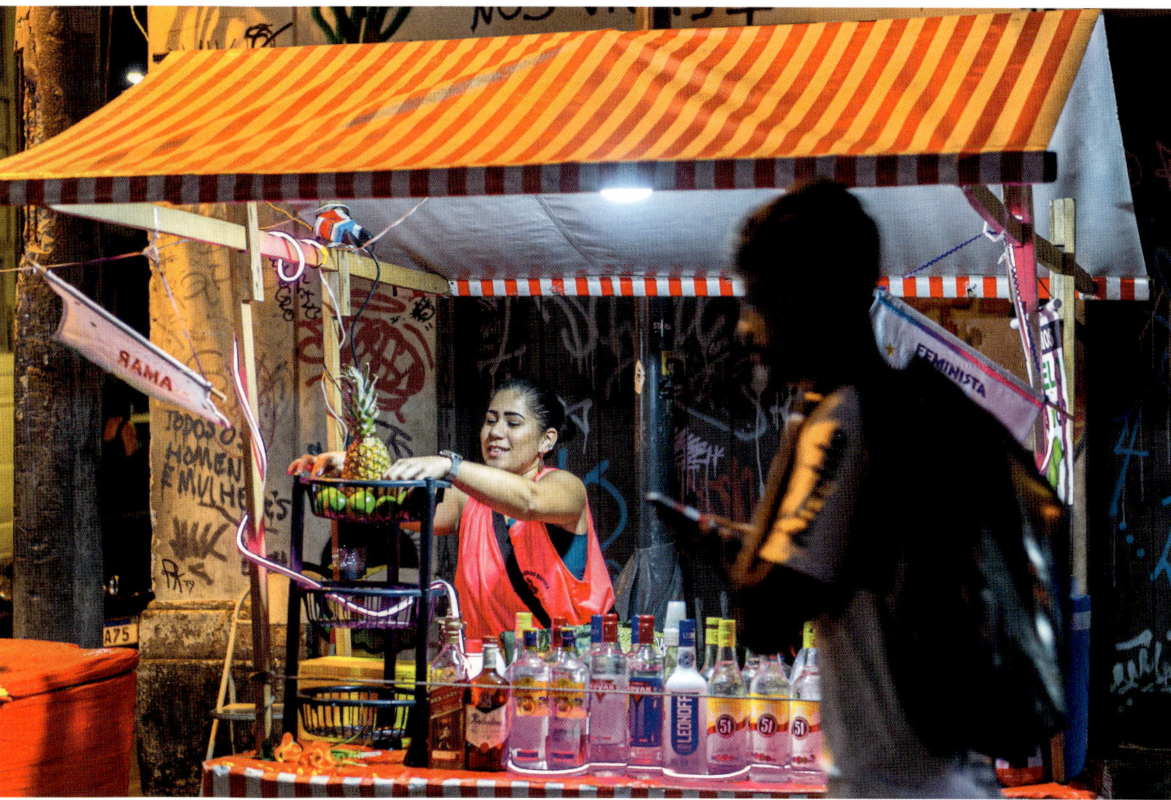

Once a *quilombo*, a settlement of escaped African slaves, the popular neighborhood bairro da Gamboa is also called Pequena África, or "Little Africa".

Einst ein *quilombo*, eine Siedlung geflohener afrikanischer Sklaven, wird das Szeneviertel bairro da Gamboa auch Pequena África „Klein-Afrika" genannt.

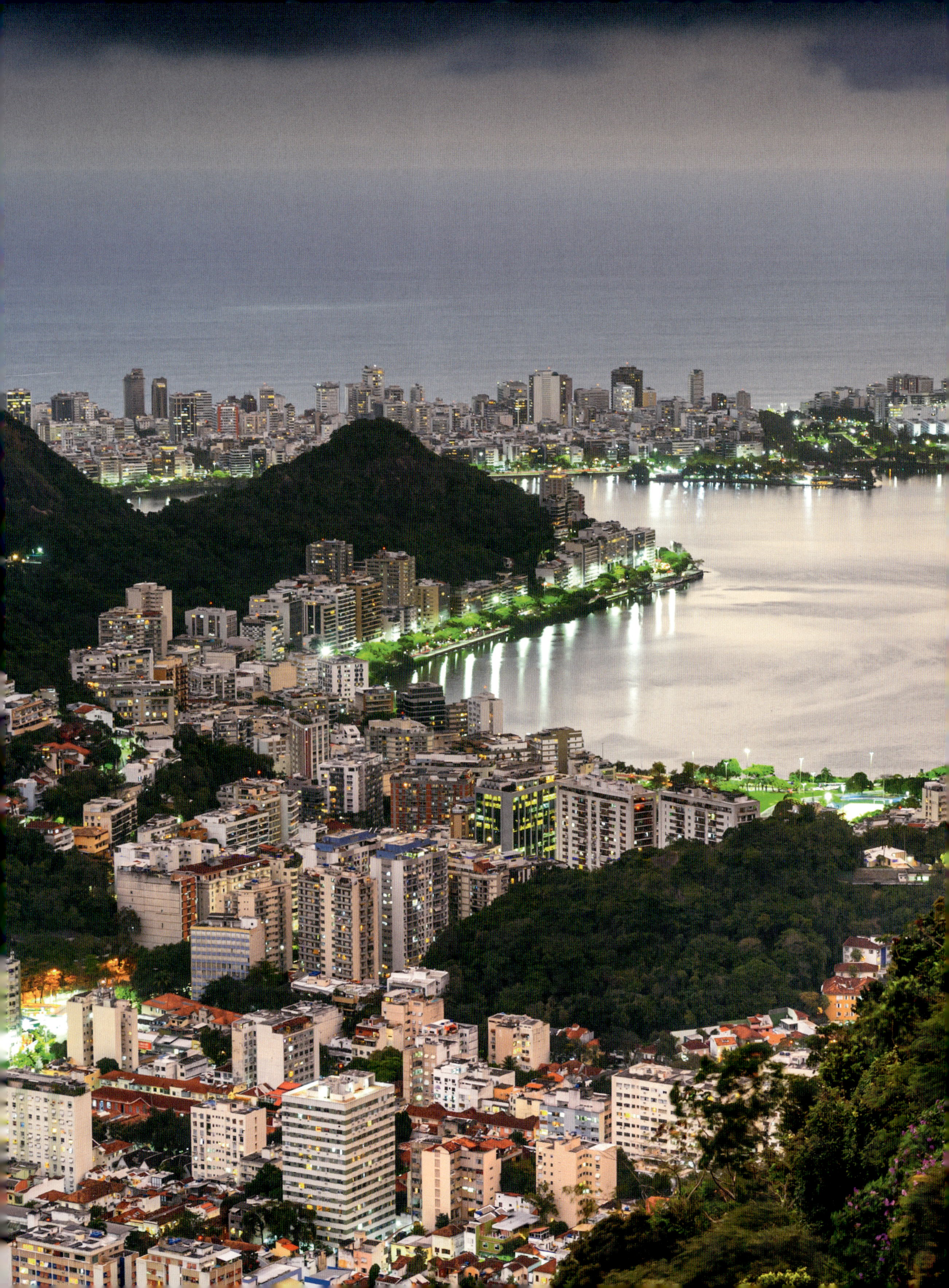

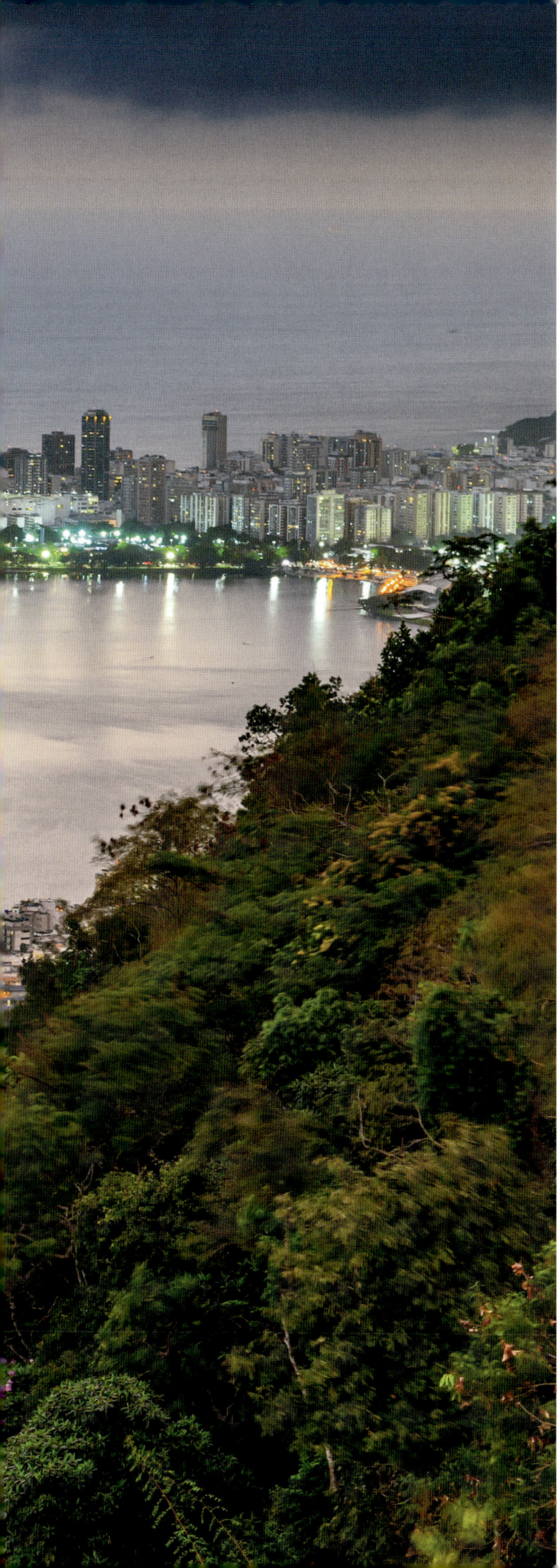

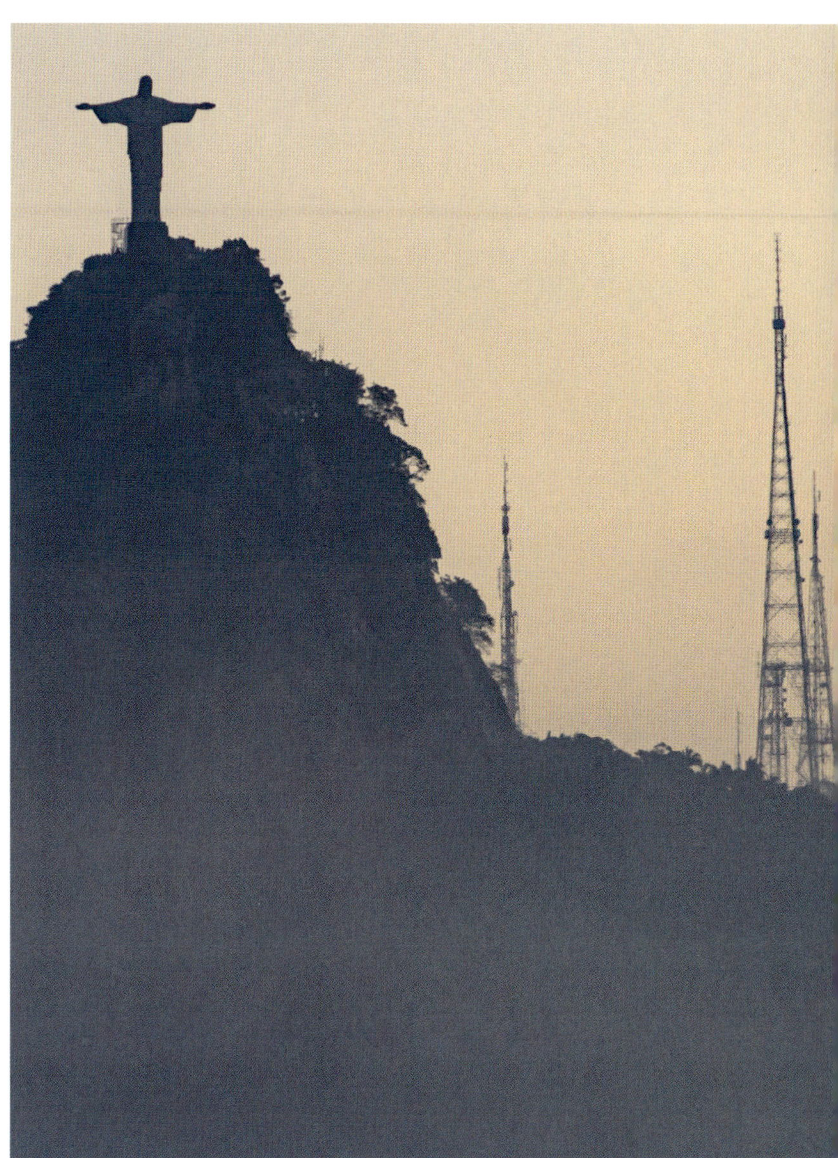

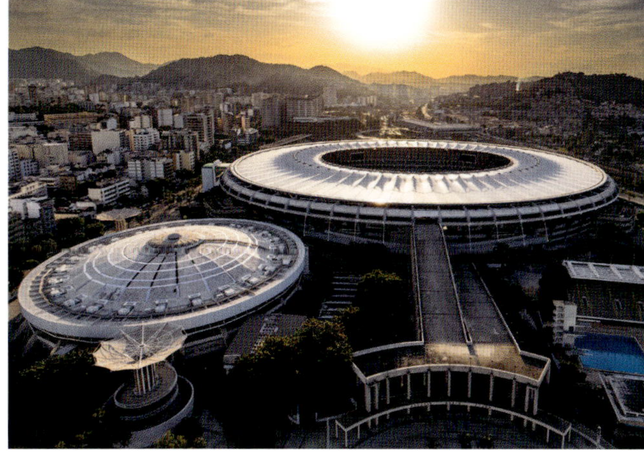

Whether it's Ipanema, Corcovado with its
Christ the Redeemer statue, or Maracana Stadium,
Rio offers breathtaking views for everyone.

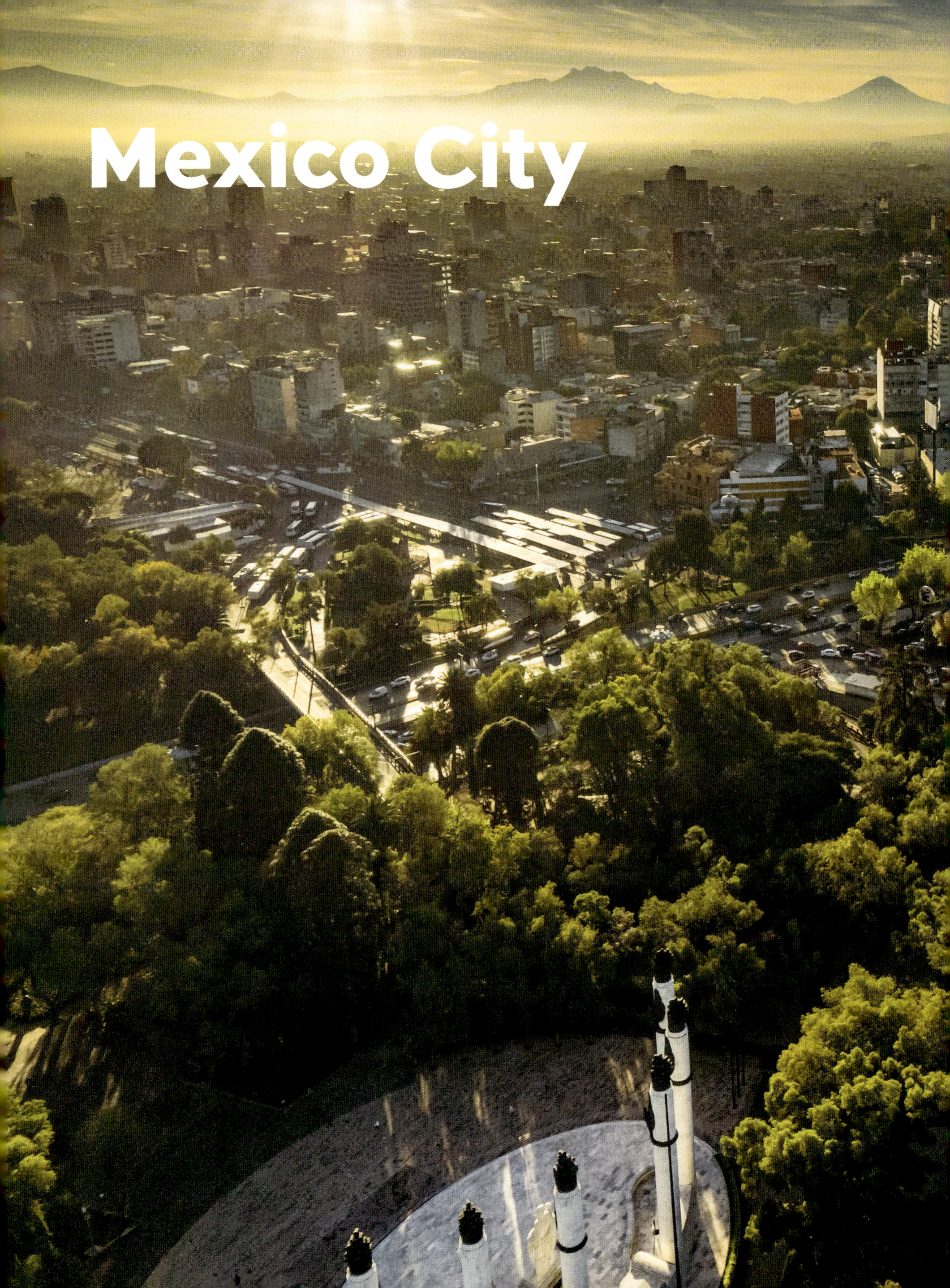

Mexico City

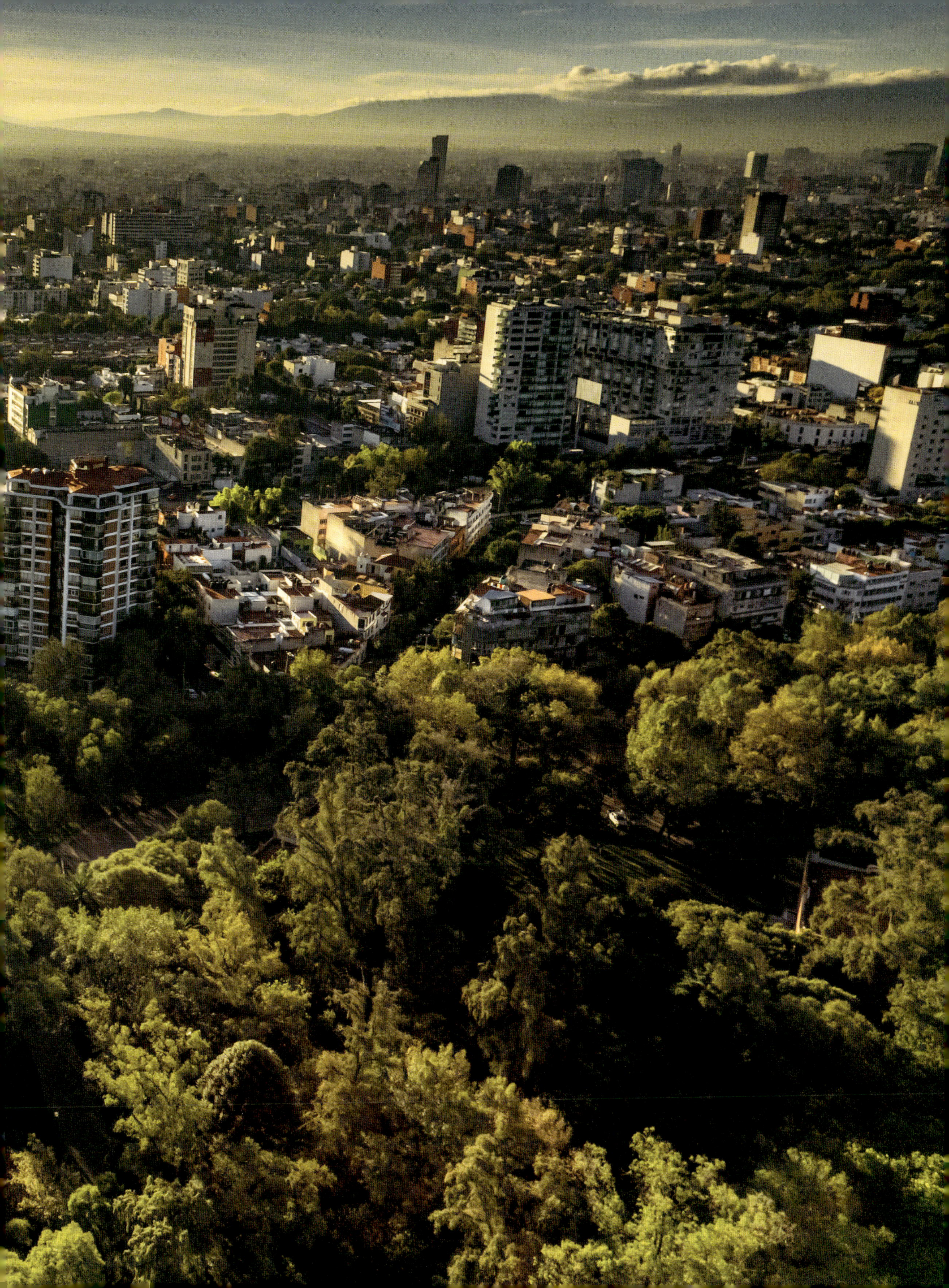

The lightness of Being

Die Leichtigkeit des Seins

I love the warmth of people, (...) no matter what, when you greet someone, they greet you back with "ola". And yes, we are very affectionate like that as a community. I don't know how to describe it, but it's a … it's a Latin American feeling. Very, very warm." (David)

Surprised? Mexico City was voted one of the top 3 major cities to live in by expats in 2022. To understand this ranking, you have to throw a lot of preconceptions out the window. Our images of Mexico's capital are very much shaped by one-sided reporting that focuses on its negative aspects. The city is considered too big, too poor, too high, too dense, too polluted, too criminal—in other words, too scary.

So much for the prevailing image. Of course, there is crime, and tragically, it often targets those people who do not have much anyway. But the opposite is also true: Mexico City engages its residents, makes them want to live in their city, communicates progress in every subway station and in central public places, speaks to its people. The city's administration has succeeded in creating an authentic metropolis where the synthesis of old and new, market and culture, native and foreign, stability and mobility is actually highly fruitful.

One particular aspect receiving a lot of attention here is mobility. Traditional public transportation options like bus and subway routes are almost impossible to operate in the densely populated suburbs and *colonias*, as the informal settlements in Mexico City are called, so the subways end where they begin. The *colonias* are often located on steep 15-degree slopes, and the streets and alleys there are narrow and winding. *Sistema de Transporte Público Cablebús* is the name of the project offering hope of improved access to public transportation. The aerial tramway shortens transit times from the settlements and connect residents of the suburbs to the metro system.

The cable cars also have the added benefit of slowing down the pace of life. Those coming from the hustle and bustle of the city center can appreciate this. But there are other ways to slow down, too. Every Sunday, for example, the central boulevard Avenida Paseo de la Reforma is closed to motor vehicles. Tens of thousands of people riding bicycles, rollerblading, jogging, and walking populate the six-lane thoroughfare. Magnificent things happen here, when young and old, rich and poor, trendy and traditional come together.

„Ich liebe die Herzlichkeit der Menschen, (...) egal wie, wenn man jemanden grüßt, grüßt er mit „ola" zurück. Und ja, wir sind sehr liebevoll in diesem Sinne als eine Bruderschaft, ich weiß nicht, wie ich es beschreiben soll, aber es ist ein … es ist ein lateinamerikanisches Gefühl. Sehr, sehr herzlich." (David)

Überraschung? Mexico City wurde 2022 von Expatriates auf den dritten Platz der lebenswertesten Großstädte gewählt. Man muss eine Menge Vorurteile über den Haufen werfen, will man diesen Platz verstehen. Unsere Vorstellungen über Mexikos Hauptstadt sind sehr stark durch eine einseitige Berichterstattung mit dem Fokus auf die negativen Seiten geprägt. Die Stadt gilt als zu groß, zu arm, zu hoch, zu dicht, zu verschmutzt, zu kriminell – zum Fürchten eben.

Soweit das vorherrschende Bild. Natürlich, die Kriminalität ist da und tragischerweise richtet sie sich oft gegen die Menschen, die eh schon wenig haben. Doch auch das Gegenteil ist der Fall: Mexico City nimmt seine Bewohner mit, macht ihnen Lust auf ihre Stadt, kommuniziert den Fortschritt in jeder U-Bahnstation und an zentralen Orten, spricht die Menschen an. Die Stadtverwaltung hat es geschafft, eine authentische Metropole zu schaffen, in der die Synthese aus Alt und Neu, Markt und Kultur, Eigenem und Fremdem, Stabilität und Mobilität tatsächlich in hohem Maße gelingt.

High spirits are guaranteed. Plaza Garibaldi is a popular meeting place for mariachi bands, Mexican folk musicians who are also available for hire here.

Gute Laune ist garantiert. Die Plaza Garibaldi ist ein beliebter Treffpunkt der Mariachis, mexikanischer Volksmusikanten, die man hier auch gleich für Auftritte engagieren kann.

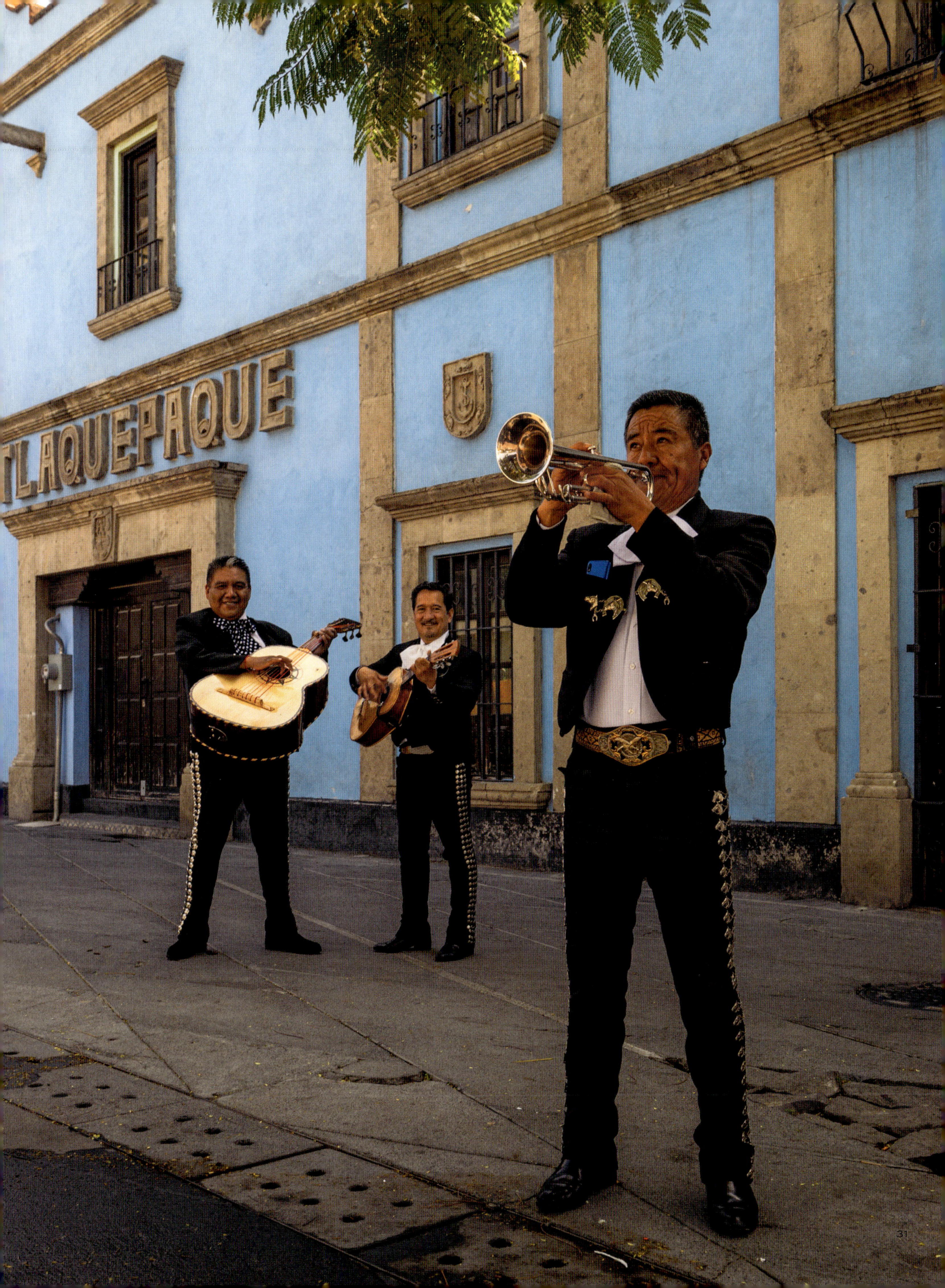
TLAQUEPAQUE

"I think you can visit any part. We have magical neighbor-hoods everywhere, for example the neighborhood of Tlalpan, the neighborhood of Coyoacán, the neighborhood of Romita (...), essentially, it's nice to just be there." (David)

Mexico City is a blend of contradictory attributes like fascinating history and contemporary spirit, sheer size and little neighborhoods, good infrastructure and chaotic suburbs, innumerable green oases and densely populated squares, trendy neighborhoods to unwind and linger in and business districts packed with skyscrapers, developed colonias that are also infiltrated by street gangs involved in drugs. What is particularly striking, however, is the ever-present extraordinary friendliness of the people to one another.

And who would have guessed that Mexico City was built on the water. Even the Aztec capital Tenochtitlán, completely destroyed by the Spaniards, was situated on a giant canal system, which even the colonial center, the zocalo, was once connected to. On a boat trip along the canals here, you can feel why this megacity is so livable and lovable.

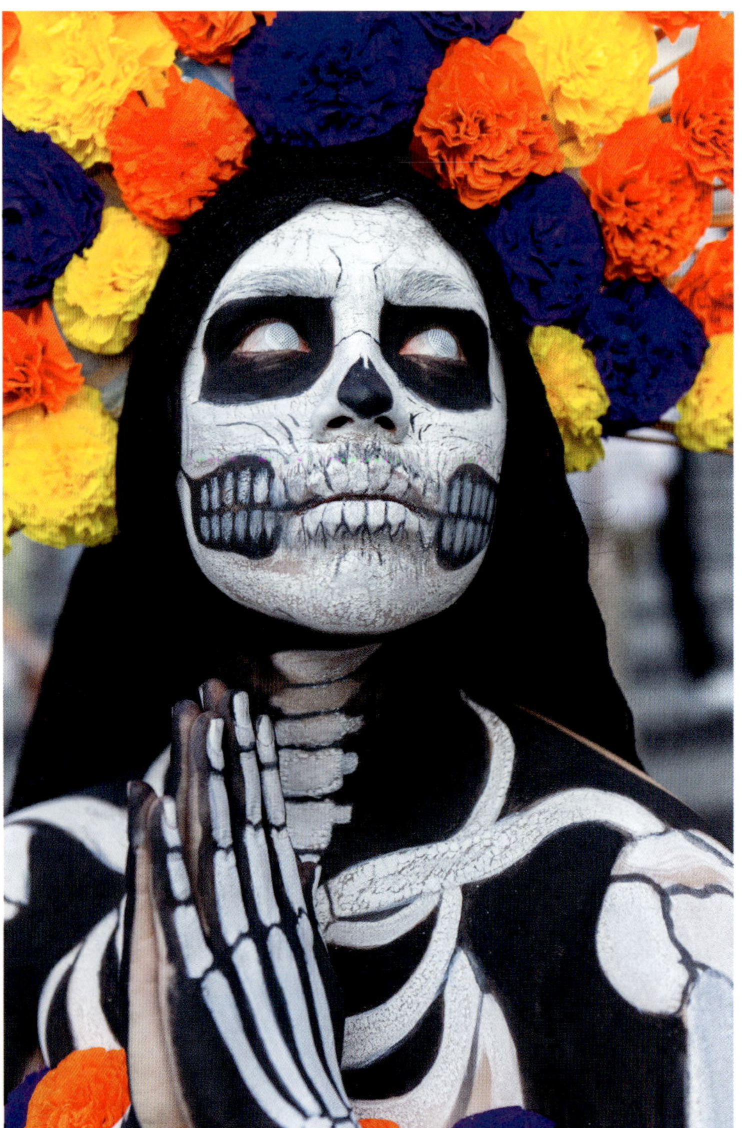

Ein besonderes Augenmerk liegt dabei auf der Mobilität. Traditionelle Transportlösungen wie Bus- oder U-Bahnlinien sind in den dicht gedrängten Vororten und *colonias*, wie die informellen Siedlungen in Mexico City genannt werden, fast unmöglich, also enden die U-Bahnen an ihren Rändern. Die Colonias befinden sich oft an steilen 15-Grad-Hängen und die Wege dort sind eng und verwinkelt. „Sistema de Transporte Público Cablebús" nennt sich der Hoffnungsträger zur Verbesserung der Verkehrsanbindung. Seilbahnen verkürzen die Transportzeiten aus den Siedlungen und binden die Anwohner der Vororte an das Metro-System an.

Die Gondeln bieten noch einen Nebeneffekt: Sie entschleunigen. Wer aus der Hektik der Innenstadt kommt, wird das zu schätzen wissen. Entschleunigung findet aber auch auf anderen Ebenen statt. Jeden Sonntag beispielsweise wird die zentrale Magistrale Avenida Paseo de la Reforma für den Autoverkehr gesperrt. Dann bevölkern zehntausende Radfahrer, Inlineskater, Jogger und Spaziergänger die sechsspurige Straße. Es ist ein grandioses Happening, wenn sich hier Jung und Alt, reich und arm, hip und traditionell treffen.

„Ich glaube, dass man jeden Ort besuchen kann. Wir haben überall magische Viertel, zum Beispiel das Viertel von Tlalpan, das Viertel von Coyoacán, das Viertel von Romita (…), im Grunde ist es schön, einfach nur da zu sein." (David)

Mexico City ist eine Mischung aus gegensätzlichen Attributen wie faszinierender Geschichte und modernem Zeitgeist, schierer Größe und kleinen Nachbarschaftsvierteln, guter Infrastruktur und chaotischen Vorstädten, unzähligen grünen Oasen und dicht bevölkerten Plätzen, Szenevierteln zum Verweilen und Businessvierteln voller Wolkenkratzer, entwickelten, aber auch von Drogenbanden unterwanderten Colonias. Besonders auffallend aber ist die allgegenwärtige enorme Freundlichkeit der Menschen untereinander.

Und wer hätte vermutet, dass Mexico City am Wasser erbaut wurde. Schon die von den Spaniern vollständig zerstörte Hauptstadt der Azteken Tenochtitlán, lag an einem gigantischen Kanalsystem, an das einst sogar das koloniale Zentrum, der Zocalo, angeschlossen war. Hier, auf einer Bootsfahrt auf den Kanälen, spürt man, weshalb diese Megacity so lebens- und liebenswert ist.

Dia de los Muertos is basically Carnival with death as its central theme. Those who can celebrate dying in such a way don't exclude death from everyday life; instead, they view it as a part of their lives. Long live death!

Dia de los Muertos, das ist Karneval mit dem Tod als zentralem Thema. Wer das Sterben so feiern kann, schließt den Tod nicht aus dem Alltag aus, sondern begreift ihn als Teil seines Lebens. Es lebe der Tod!

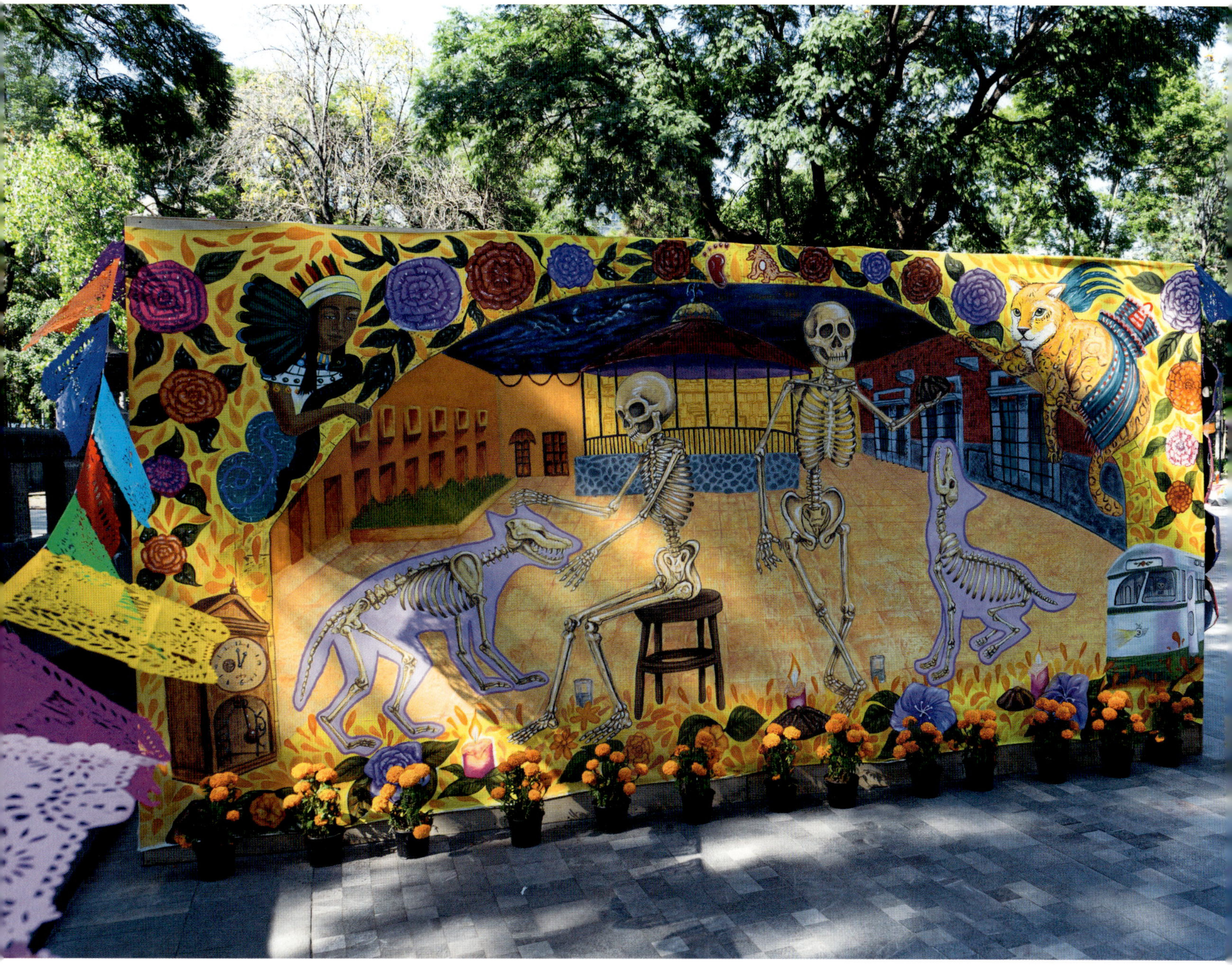

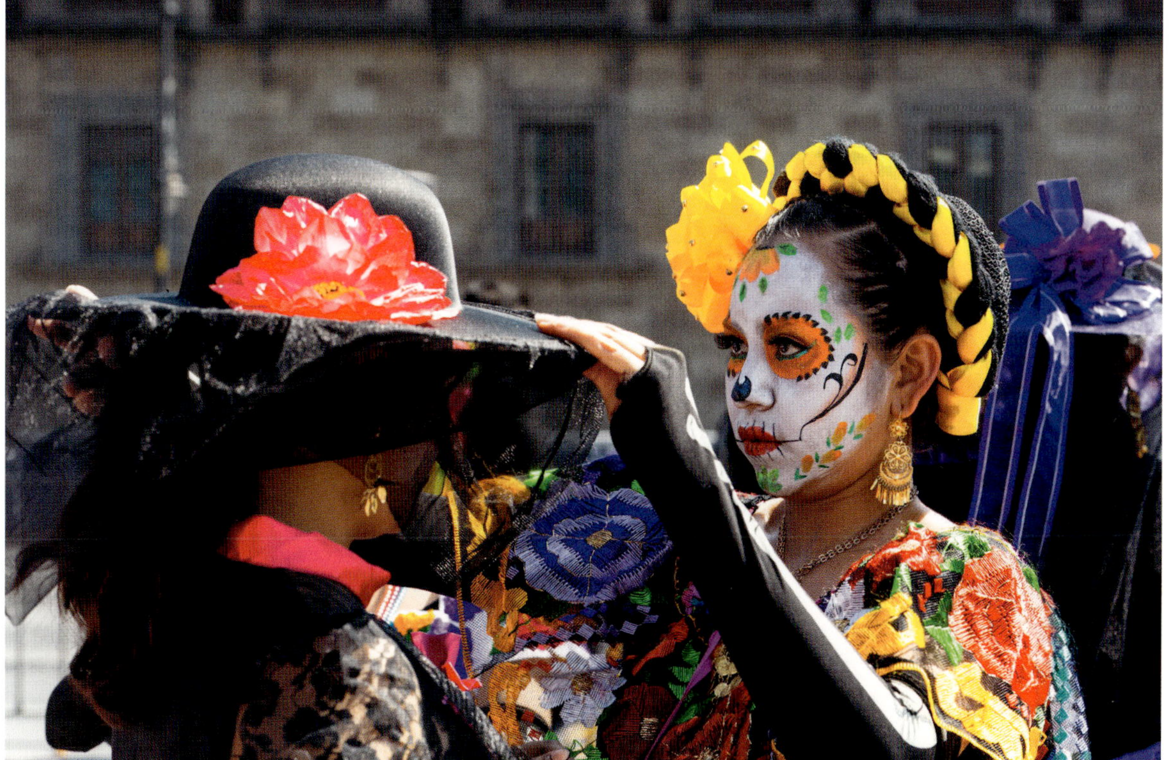

In the days leading up to All Saints'
Day, the city is feverishly decorated,
everyone dons makeup, and all of
Mexico City is in a kind of carniva-
lesque death frenzy.

In den Tagen vor Allerheiligen wird die
Stadt fieberhaft geschmückt, alle
schminken sich und ganz Mexico City
befindet sich in einer Art karnevalisti-
schem Todesrausch.

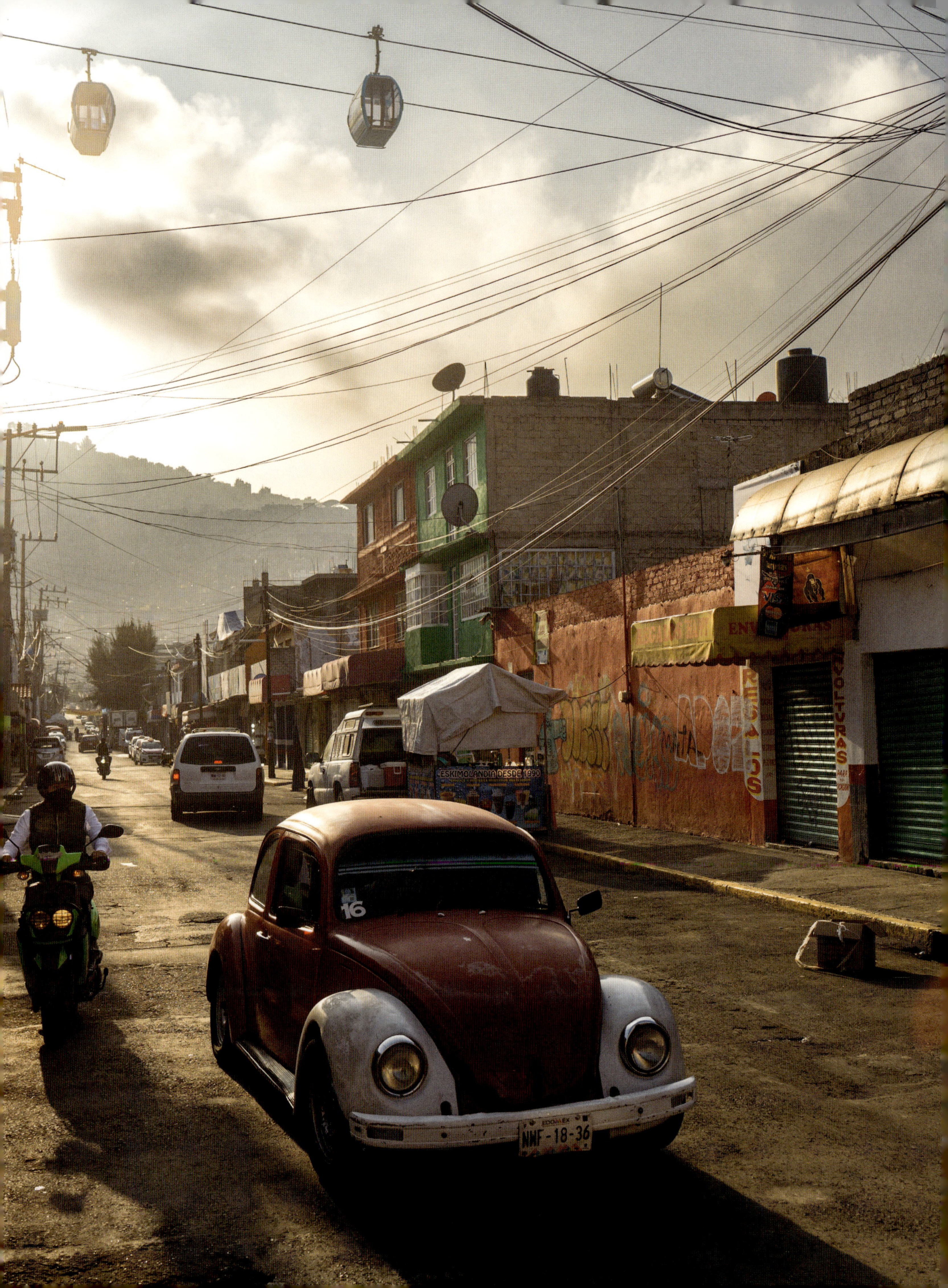

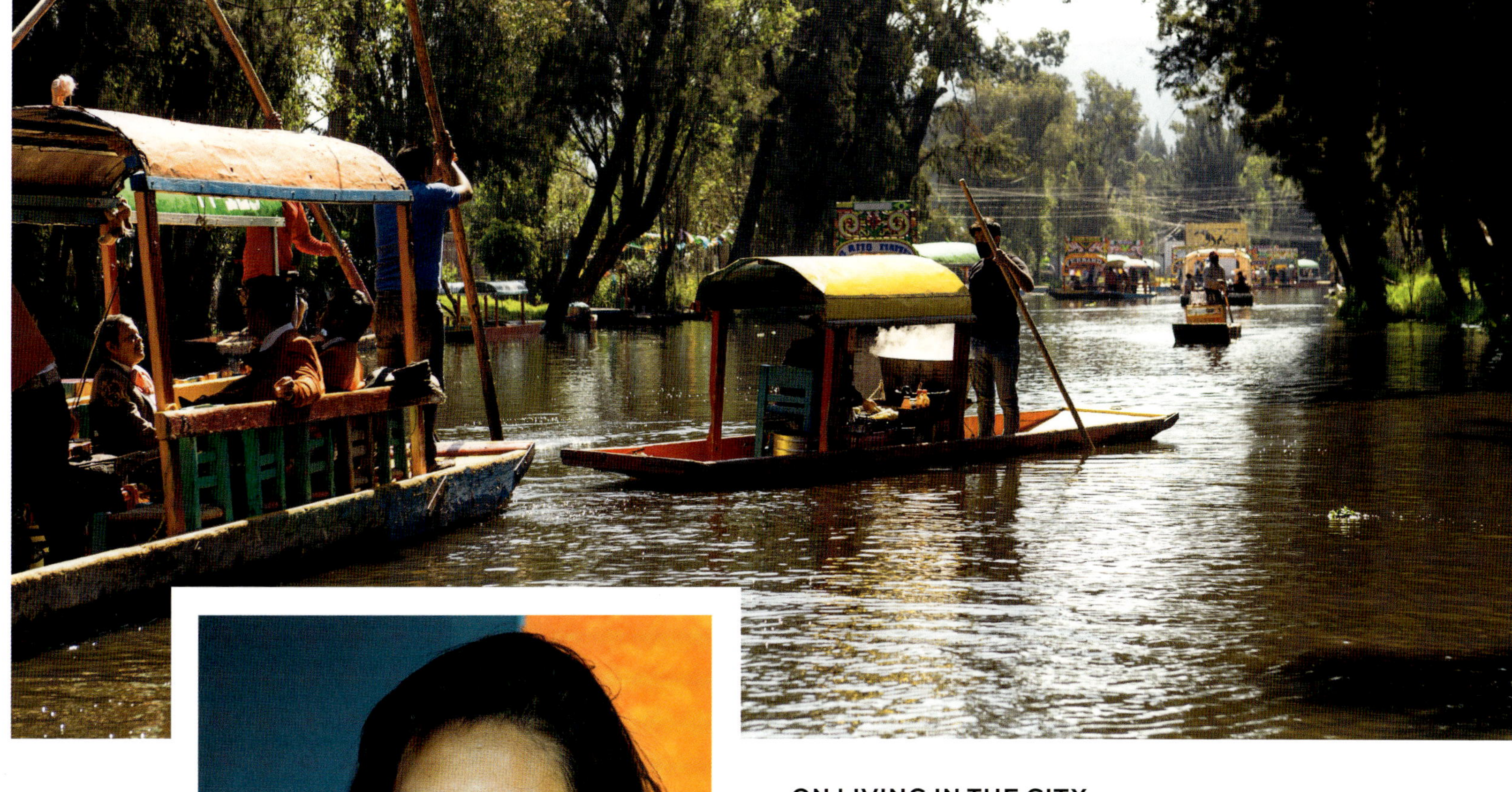

...ON LIVING IN THE CITY

"I think living here has its advantages and disadvantages. An advantage is that you have more opportunities to find work. Transportation is better, it goes faster (...). The cablebús, for example, is very convenient for me because now I can get to the end station of the metro much faster. I used to have to take a bus for an hour or more to get there, now it's just 20 minutes. I used to work in Campeche, and the fact is that public transit was very scarce there, everything was more expensive, transportation, food is more expensive, there was less food than here, so it has its disadvantages in small areas. The advantage is that it is quieter there than here in the city. The disadvantage in the city is crime, garbage, and it's often noisy."

ANNA
EMPLOYEE
ANGESTELLTE

Step aboard and enjoy the peace and quiet as the cablebús floats over Colonia Cuautepec. Take a boat ride along the canals of Xochimilco, and treat yourself to some real downtime.

Einsteigen und die Ruhe genießen, während der Cablebús über die Colonia Cuautepec schwebt. Eine echte Auszeit gönnt man sich dagegen bei einer Bootsfahrt auf den Kanälen von Xochimilco.

...ZUM LEBEN IN DER STADT

„Ich denke, das Leben hier hat seine Vor- und Nachteile. Vorteil ist, dass man mehr Möglichkeiten hat, Arbeit zu finden. Die Transportmittel sind besser, es geht schneller (...). Der Cablebús kommt mir zum Beispiel sehr entgegen, weil ich jetzt sehr viel schneller zur Endstation der Metro komme. Früher musste ich eine Stunde und länger mit dem Bus dorthin fahren, jetzt nur noch 20 Minuten. Ich habe in Campeche gearbeitet und Tatsache ist, dass die Transportmittel dort schon sehr knapp waren, alles war teurer, Transport, Lebensmittel sind teurer, es gab weniger Lebensmittel als hier, also hat es seine Nachteile in kleinen Orten. Der Vorteil ist, dass es dort ruhiger ist als hier in der Stadt. Der Nachteil in der Stadt ist die Kriminalität, der Müll und oft der Lärm."

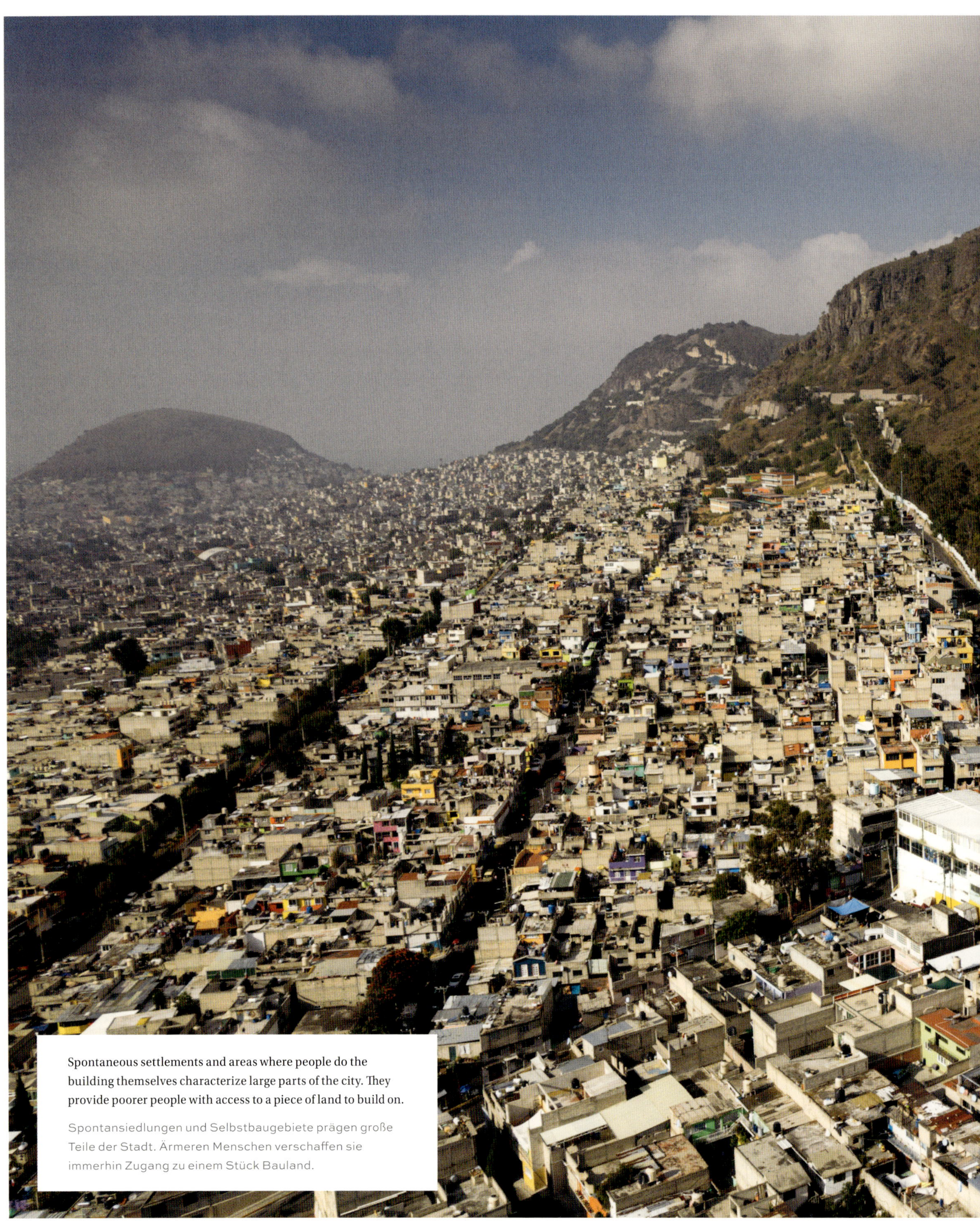

Spontaneous settlements and areas where people do the building themselves characterize large parts of the city. They provide poorer people with access to a piece of land to build on.

Spontansiedlungen und Selbstbaugebiete prägen große Teile der Stadt. Ärmeren Menschen verschaffen sie immerhin Zugang zu einem Stück Bauland.

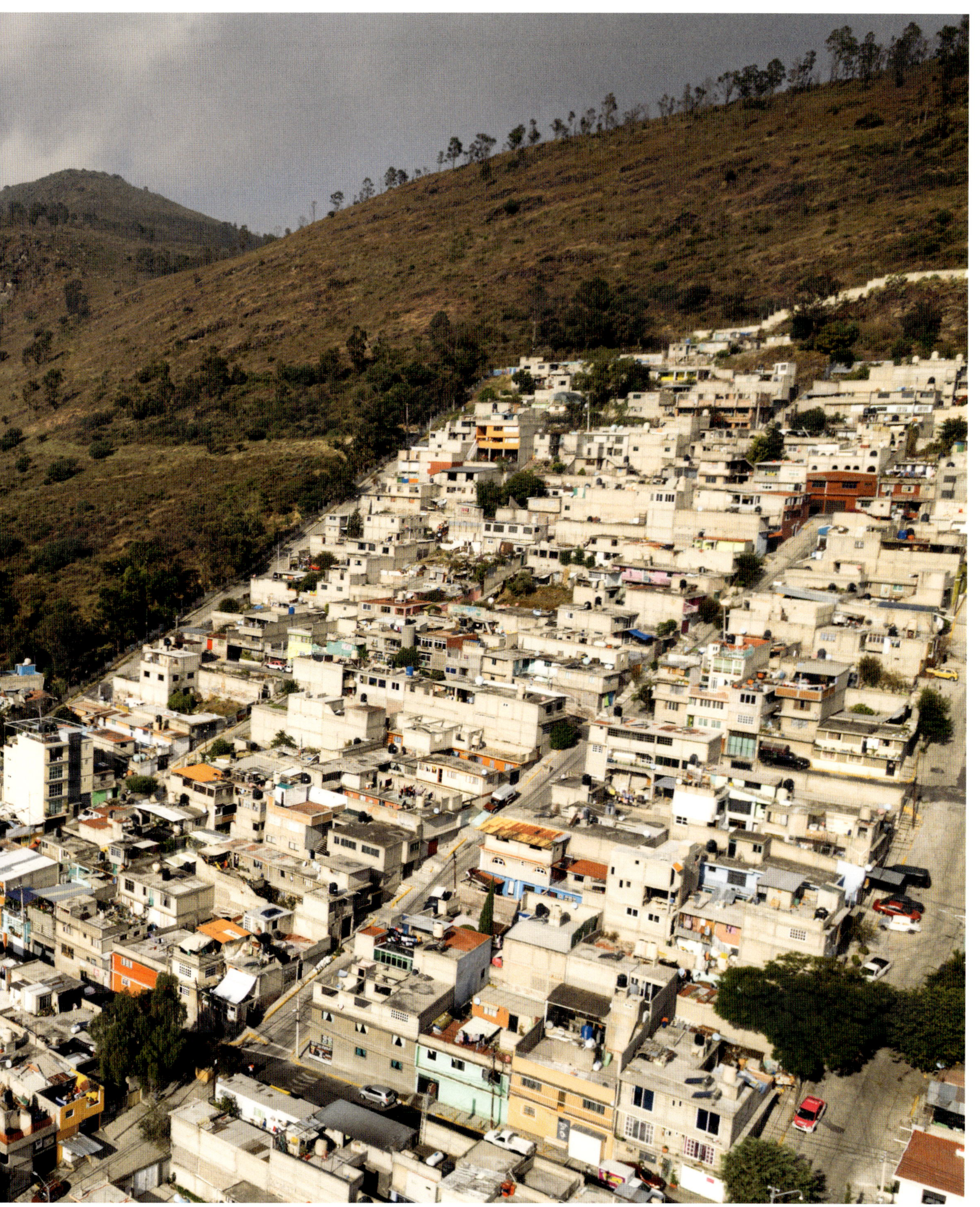

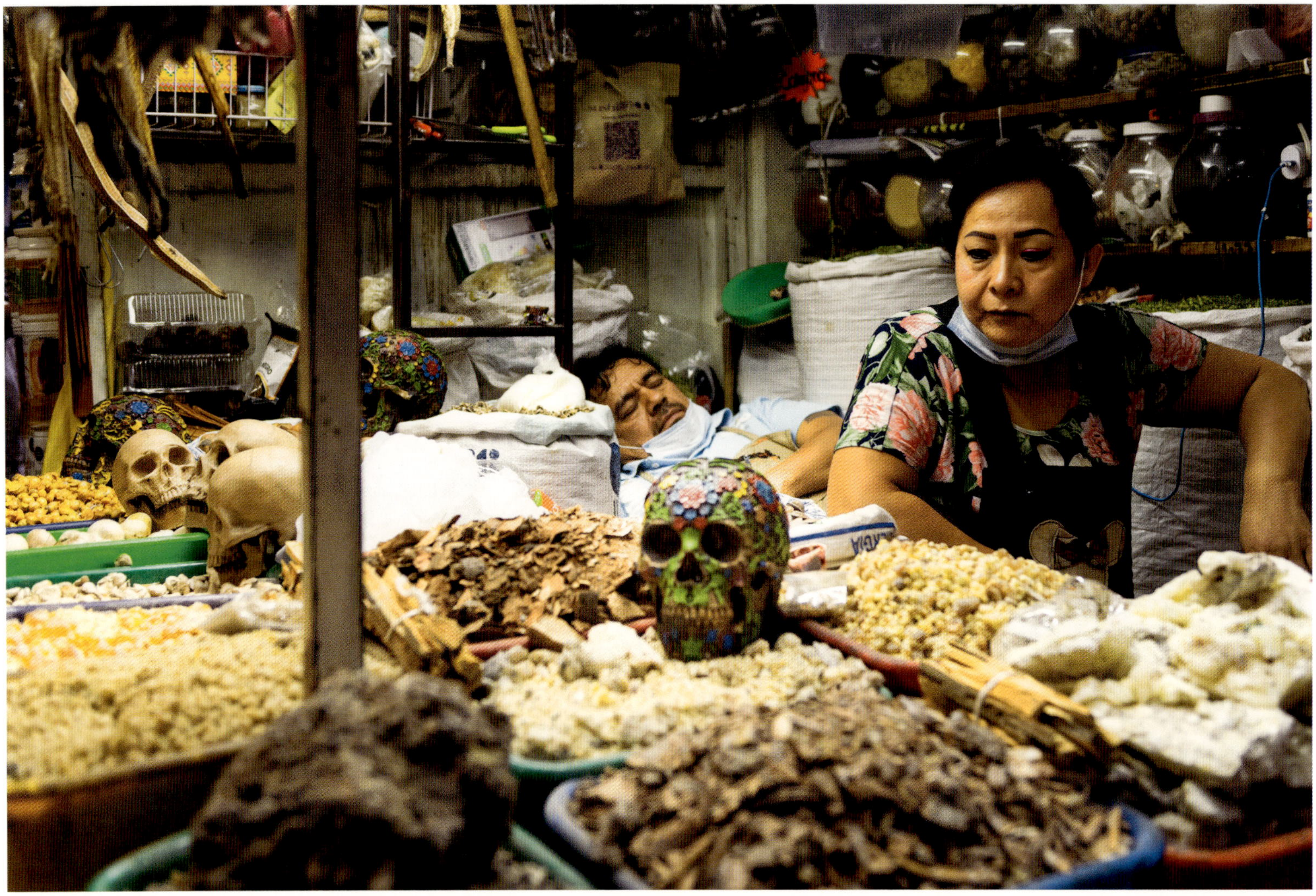

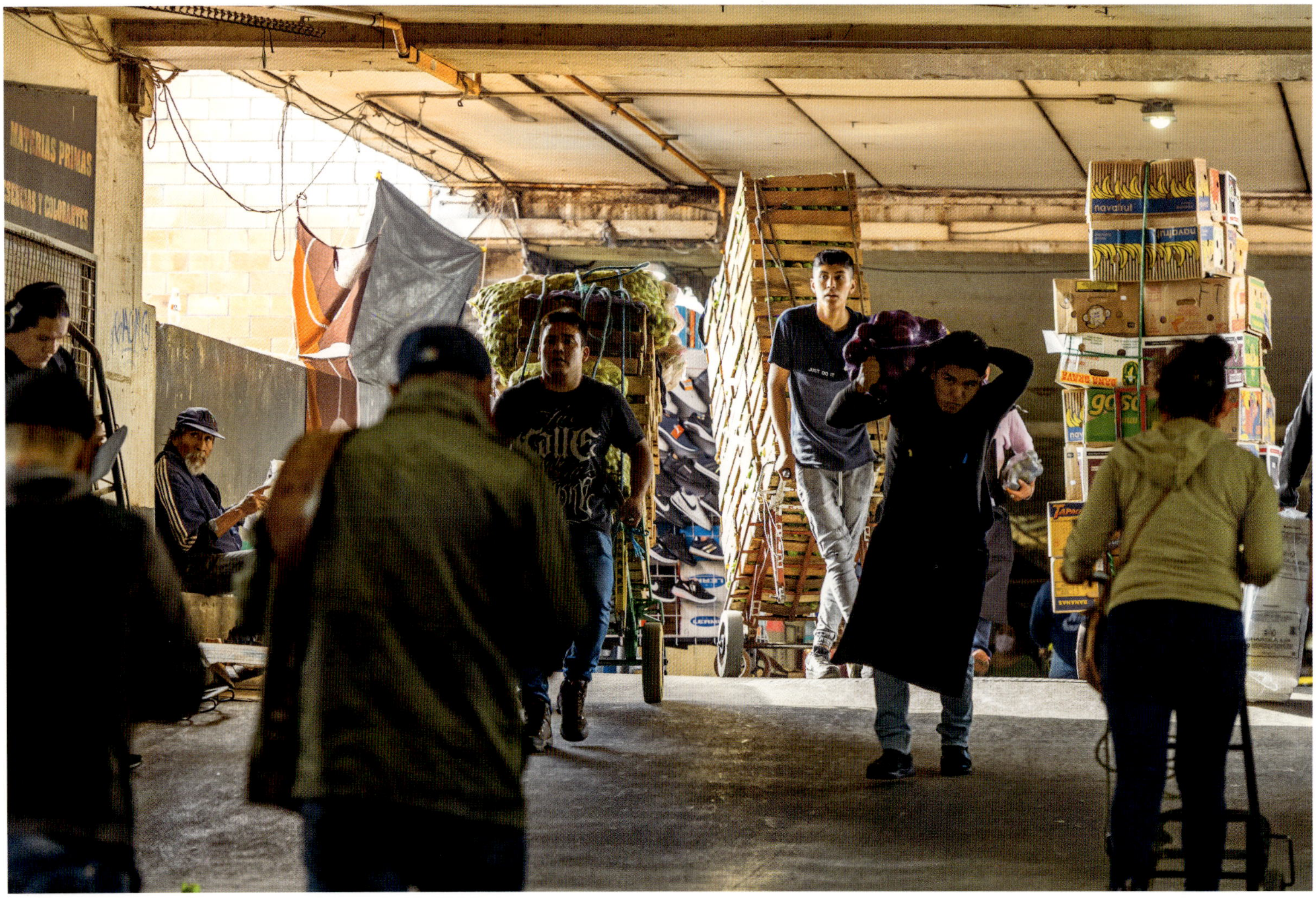
MATERIAS PRIMAS
navafrut

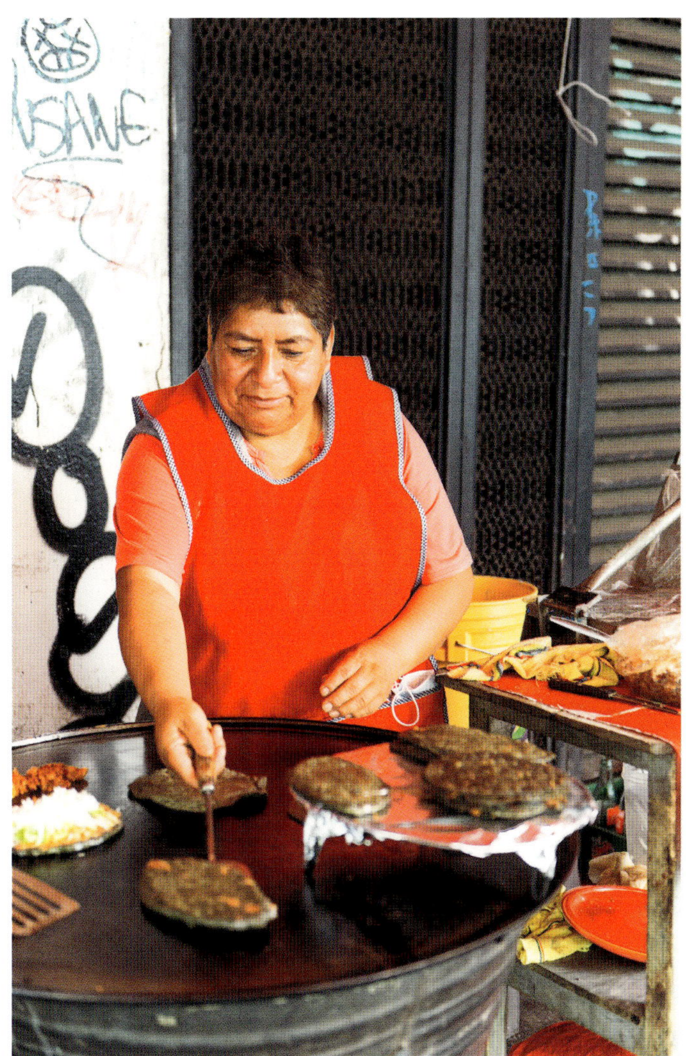
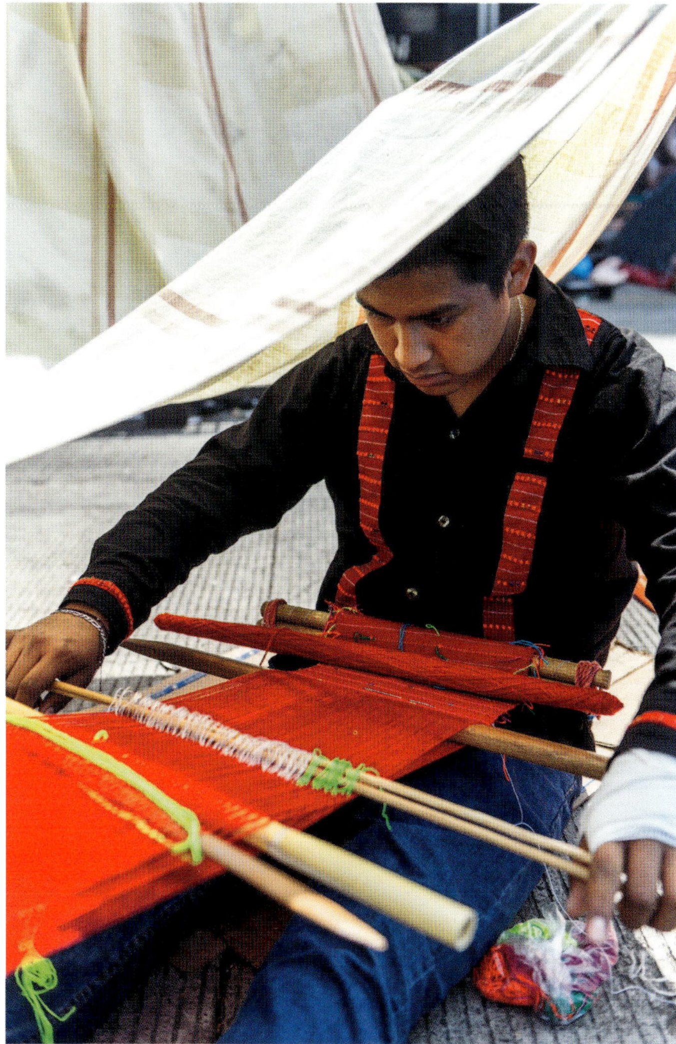
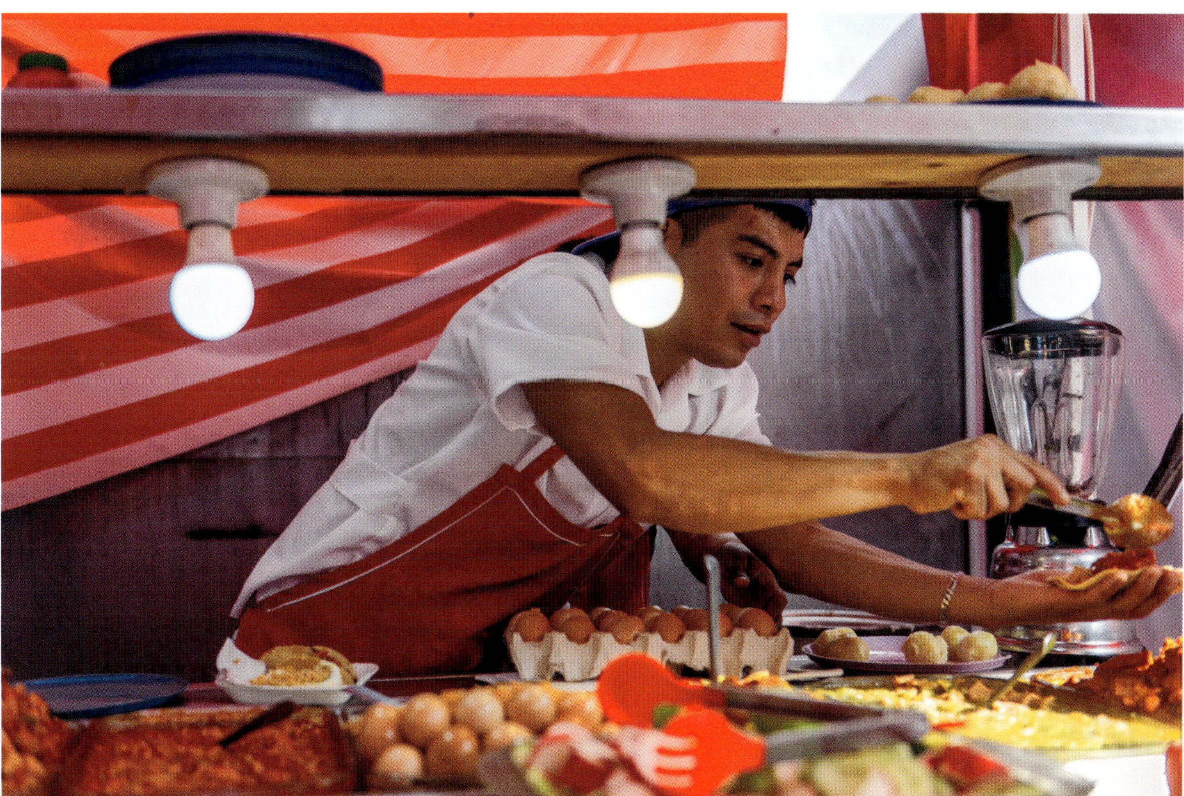

Markets, merchants, food stalls everywhere:
They serve the needs of millions of people
day and night.

Märkte, Händler, Garküchen allerorten:
Sie versorgen Millionen von Menschen
Tag und Nacht.

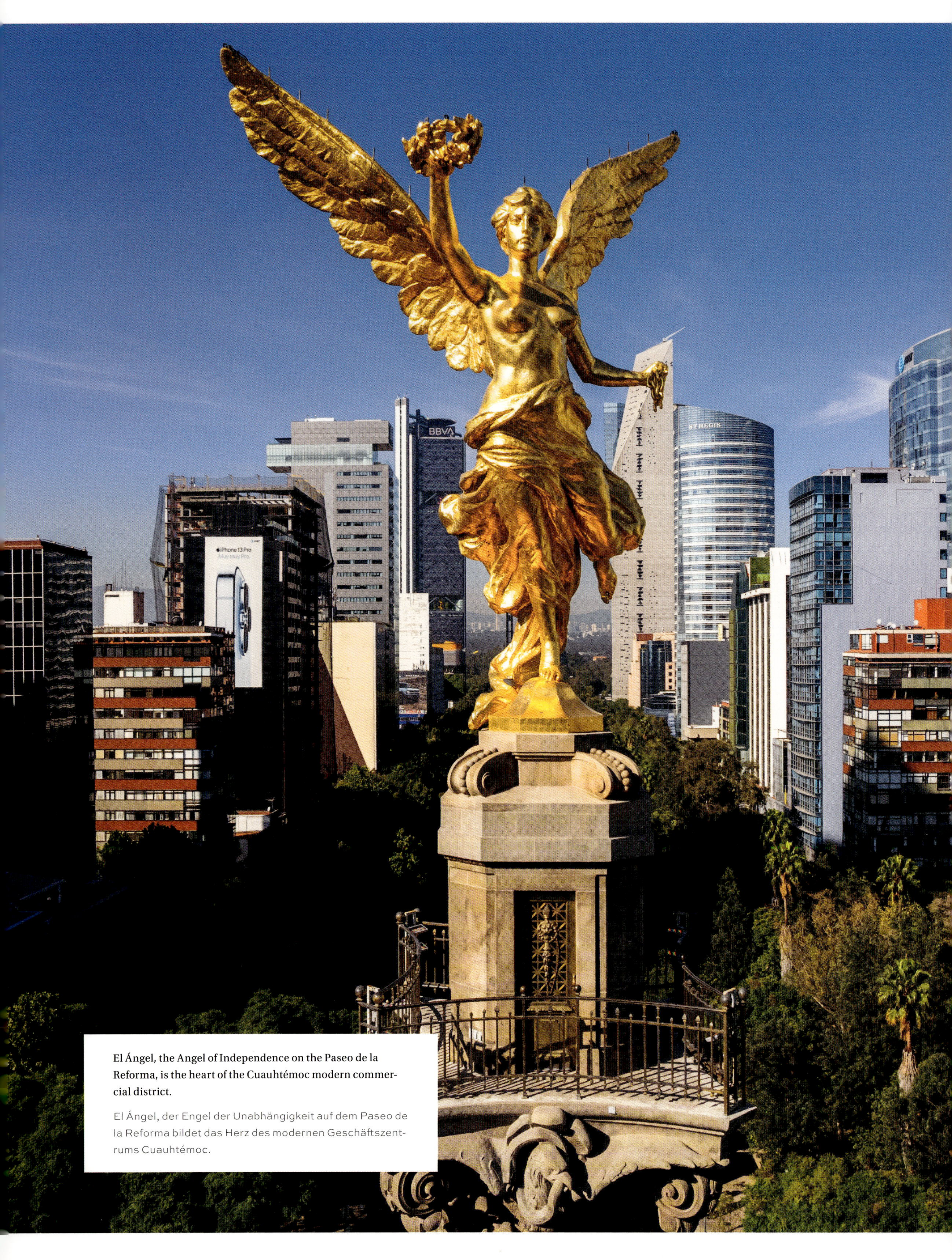

El Ángel, the Angel of Independence on the Paseo de la Reforma, is the heart of the Cuauhtémoc modern commercial district.

El Ángel, der Engel der Unabhängigkeit auf dem Paseo de la Reforma bildet das Herz des modernen Geschäftszentrums Cuauhtémoc.

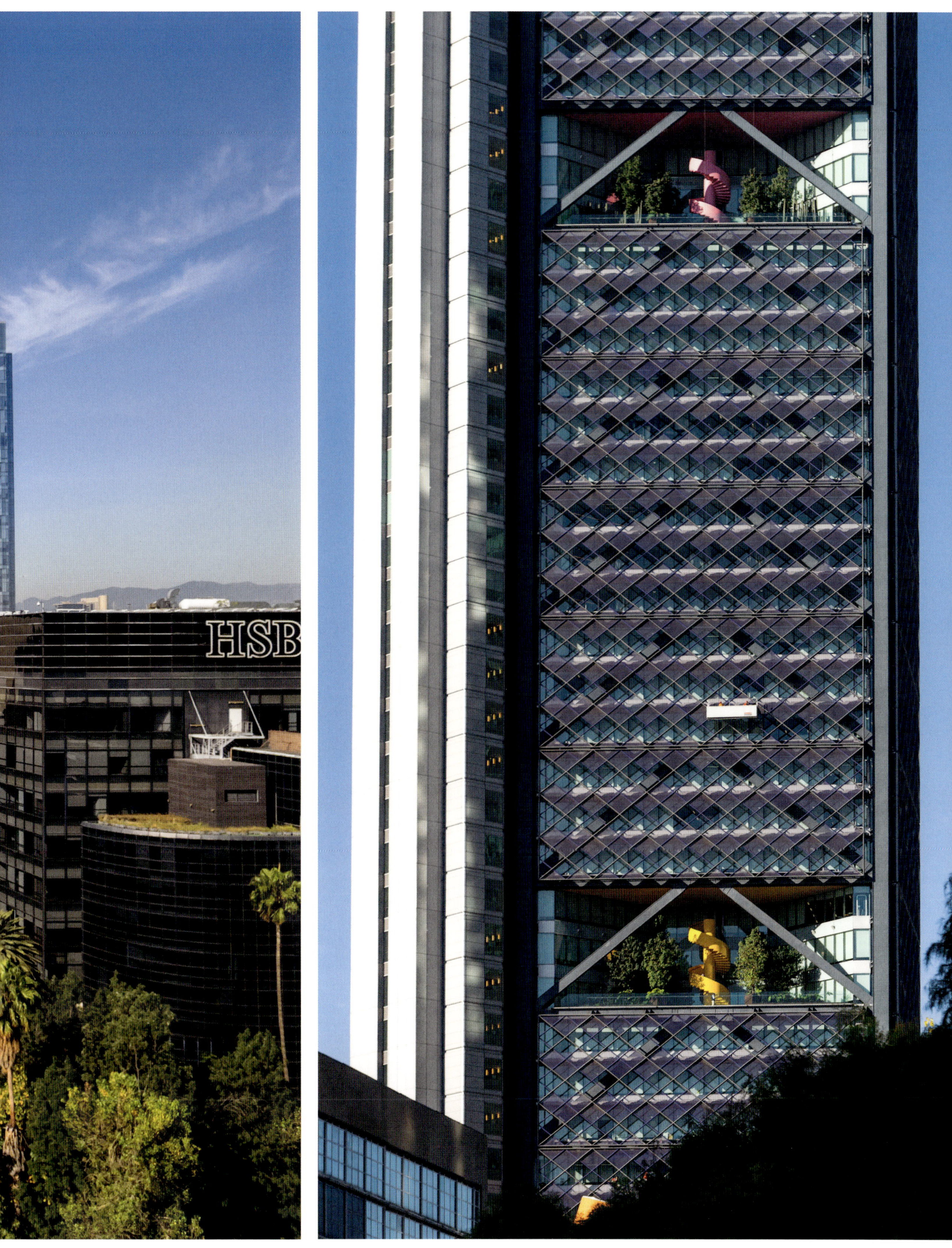

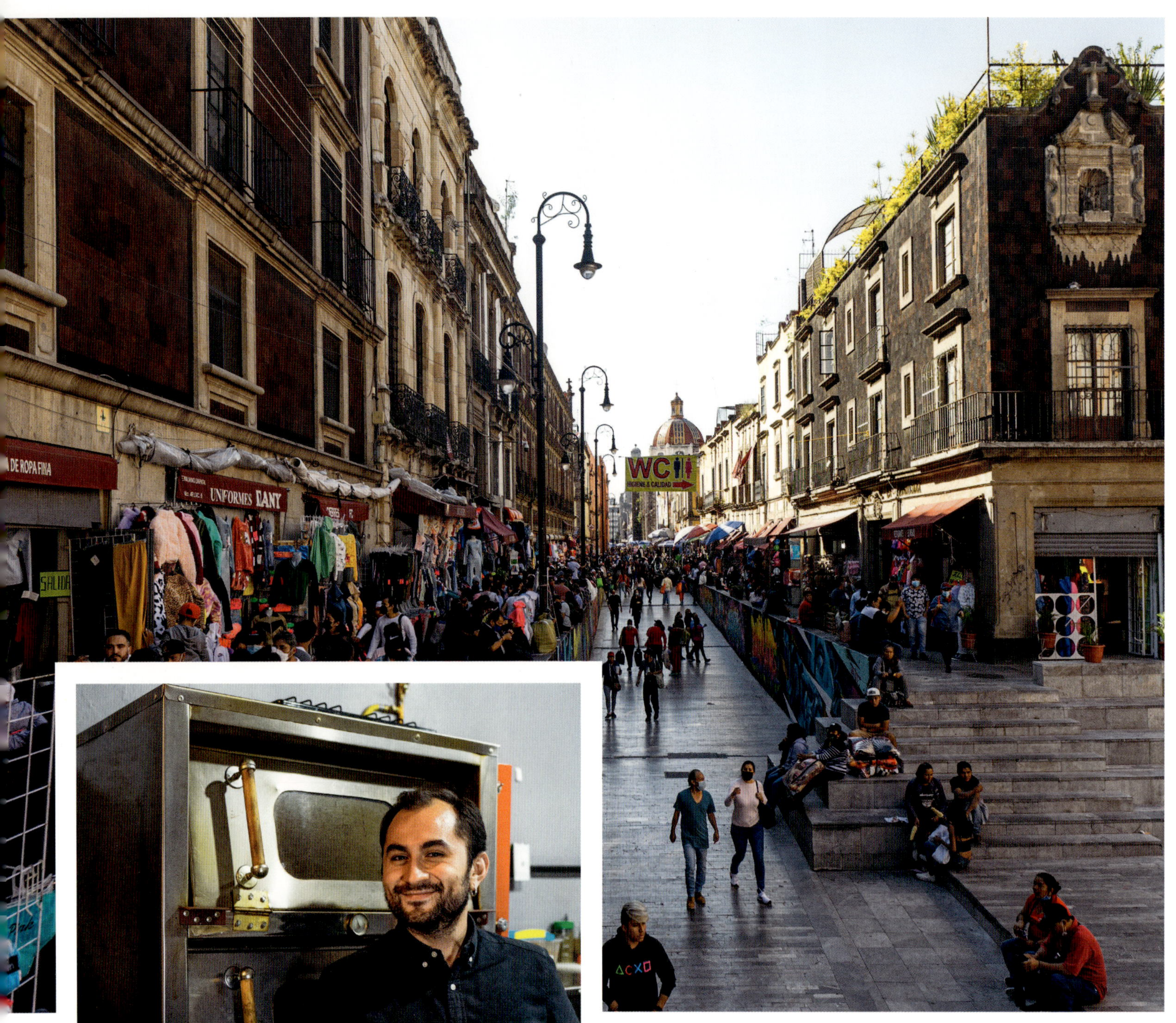

ALAN
PIZZERIA OPERATOR
BETREIBER EINER PIZZERIA

Where have they gone? To this day, relatives at Alameda Park (right) in front of the historic Old Town (above) are fighting for answers about the murders of 43 students.

Wo sind sie geblieben? Bis heute kämpfen Angehörige am Alameda-Park (Bild rechts) vor der historischen Altstadt (Bild oben) für die Klärung der Morde an 43 Studenten.

...ON THE CITY'S TRANSFORMATION

"I was born in the nineties, for example, and I know that we are in a state of transition. (...) Everything used to be manual, now everything is digital. We used to listen to records and cassettes, and now everything is on a flash drive. We are experiencing a technological transformation, and the infrastructure is also good (...). Houses used to be very big, very spacious, and now the more people we are, the smaller the houses are, the smaller the apartments are, where you have to fit, I don't know, a whole family into 60 square meters, and that's crazy (...).

...ON INJUSTICE

"On three or four days a week there are demonstrations on the main streets (...). And so I do feel like something is happening, but the demonstrators aren't really recognized because, for example, they're holding up traffic, people are late for work, they're creat-

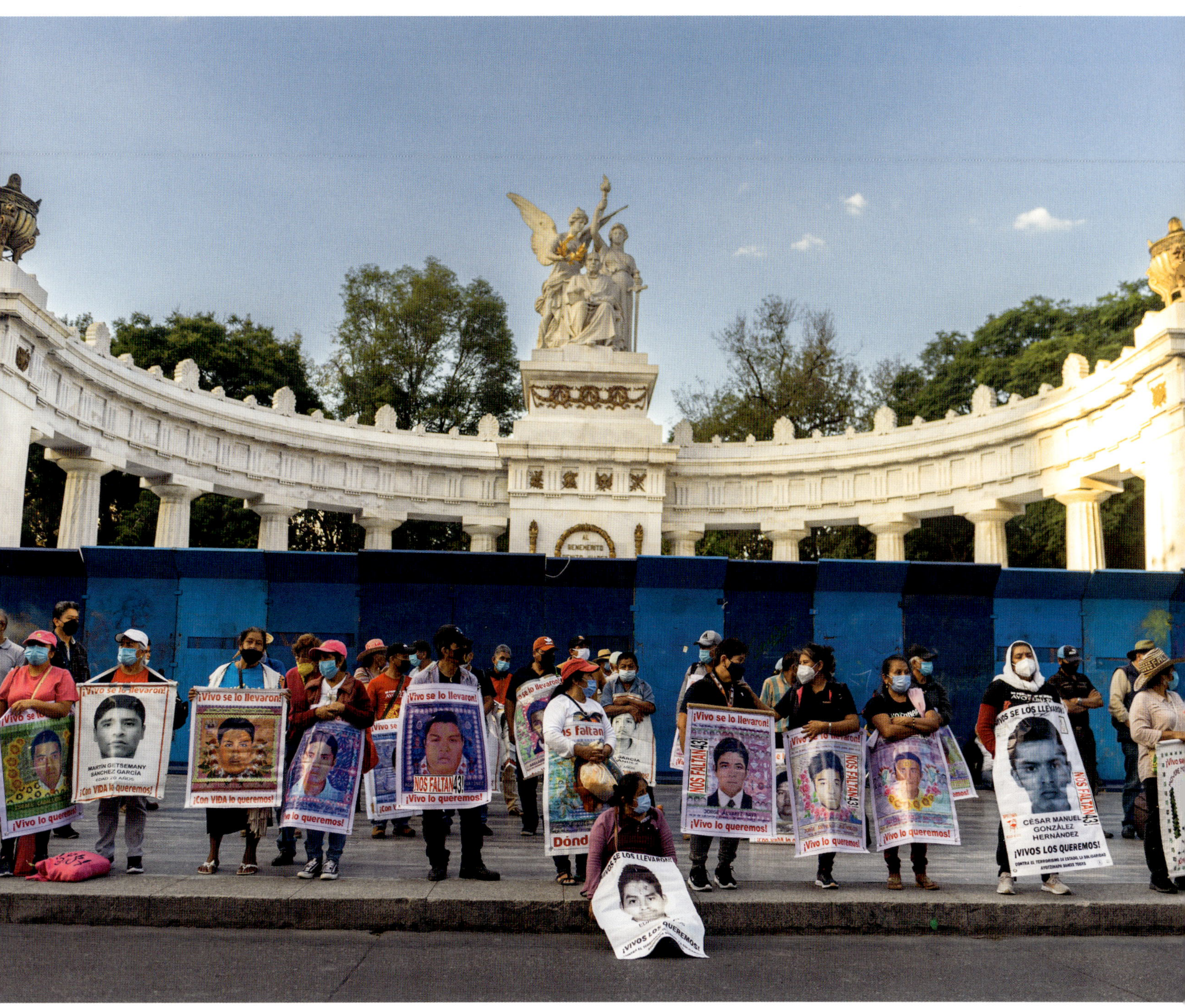

ing chaos, but they're not really reaching their goal or the government is turning a blind eye. So as long as the powerful stay in power and the rich stay rich, the poor are not really heard."

...ZUM WANDEL DER STADT

„Ich bin zum Beispiel in den neunziger Jahren geboren, und ich weiß, dass wir uns im Übergang befinden. (...) Früher war alles manuell, heute ist alles digital. Früher haben wir Schallplatten und Kassetten gehört, und jetzt ist alles auf einem Speicherstick. Wir erleben also einen technologischen Wandel, und die Infrastruktur ist auch gut (...). Früher waren die Häuser sehr groß, sehr geräumig, und jetzt, je mehr Menschen wir sind, desto kleiner sind die Häuser, desto kleiner sind die Wohnungen, wo man, ich weiß nicht, eine ganze Familie auf 60 Quadratmetern unterbringen muss, und das ist Wahnsinn (...)."

...ÜBER UNGERECHTIGKEITEN

„An drei oder vier Tagen in der Woche finden also Demonstrationen auf den Hauptstraßen statt (...). Ich habe also das Gefühl, dass etwas passiert, aber die Demonstranten werden nicht wirklich wahrgenommen, weil sie zum Beispiel den Verkehr aufhalten, die Leute zu spät zur Arbeit kommen, ein Chaos anrichten, aber sie erreichen nicht wirklich ihr Ziel oder die Regierung schaut weg. Solange also die Mächtigen an der Macht bleiben und die Reichen reich bleiben, wird den Armen nicht so viel Gehör geschenkt."

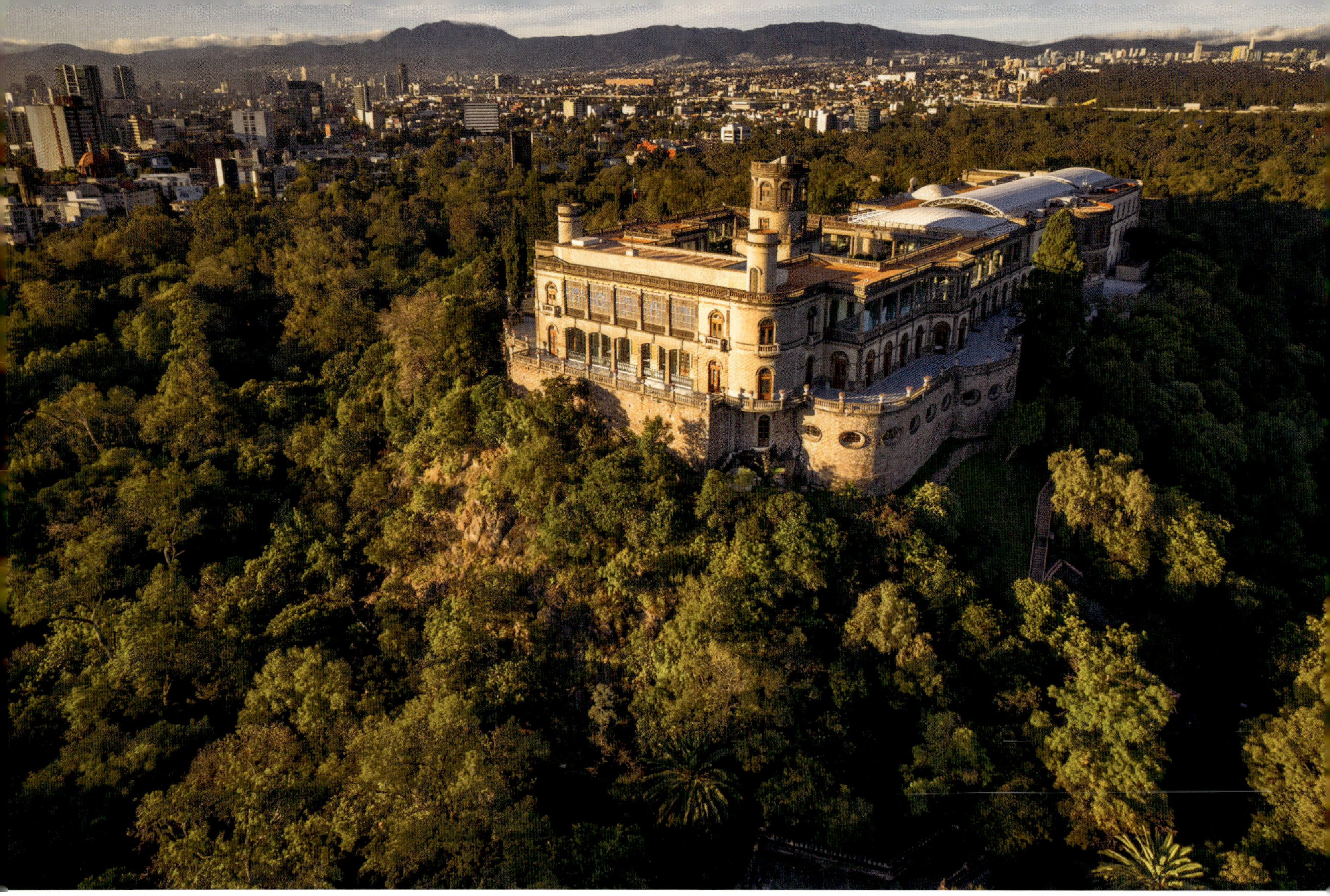

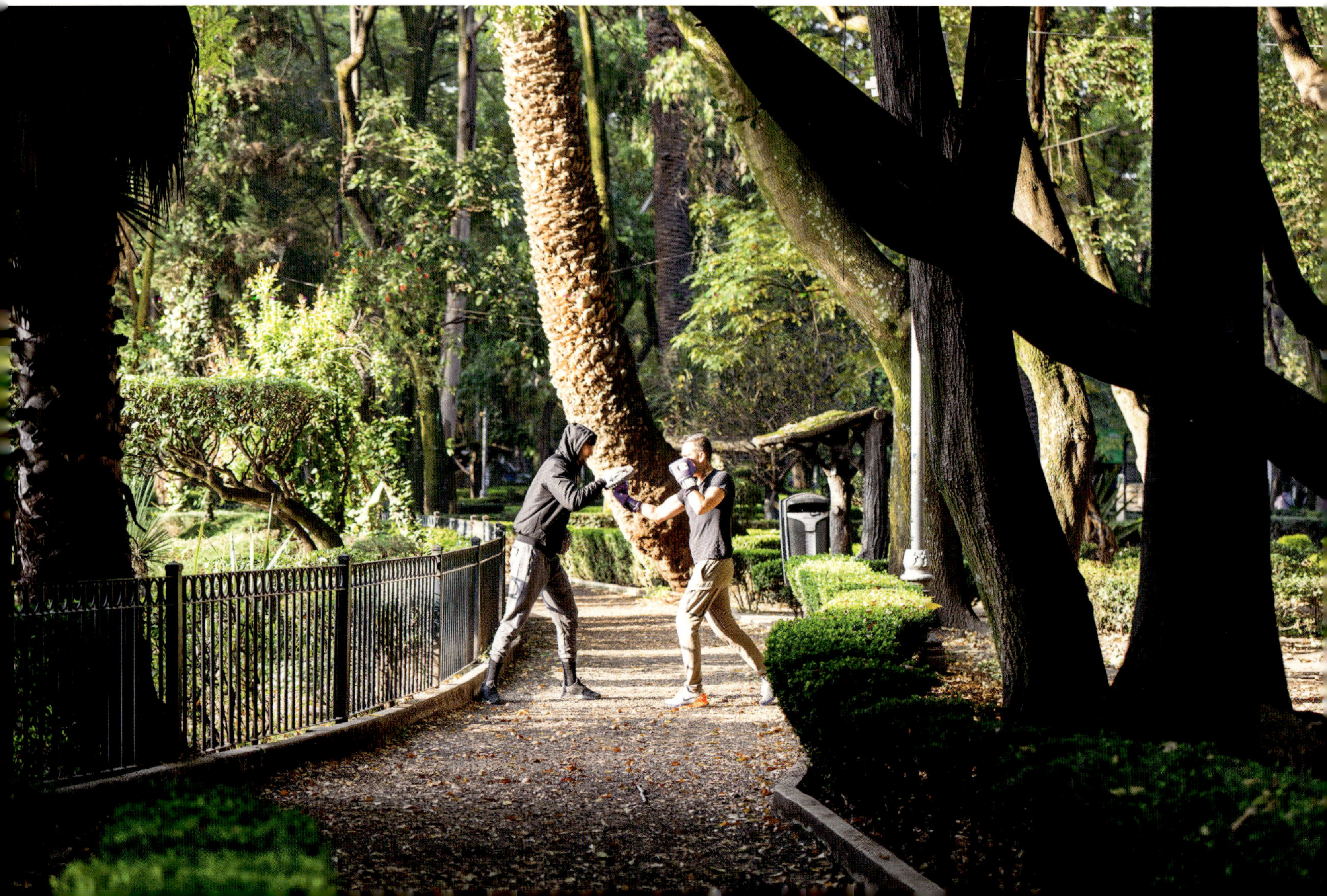

"We have now created more awareness about nature. My advice (...) use your bike, use your feet (...), that doesn't create pollution." (Alan)

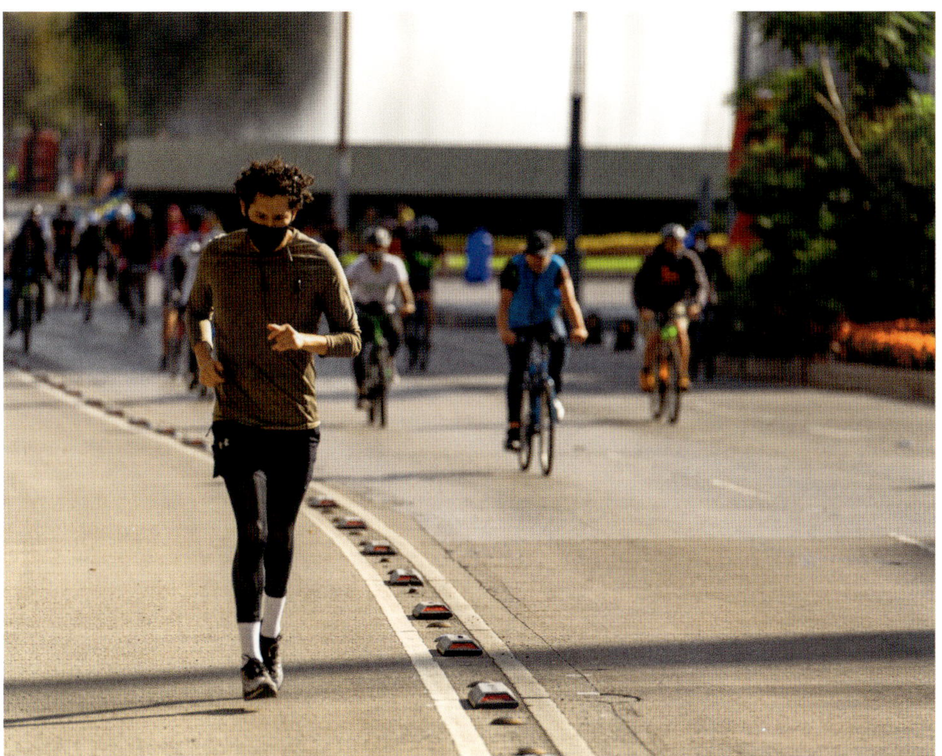

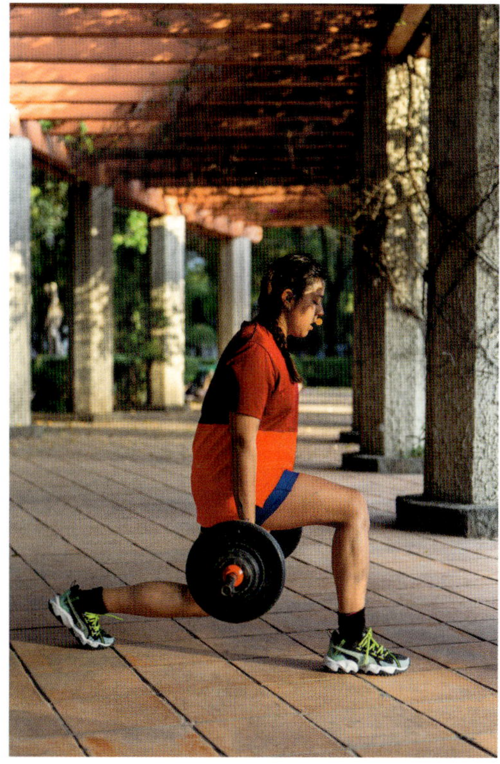

„Wir haben jetzt mehr Bewusstsein für die Natur geschaffen. Mein Ratschlag (…) Benutzen Sie das Fahrrad, benutzen Sie ihre Füße (…), das verursacht keine Umweltverschmutzung." (Alan)

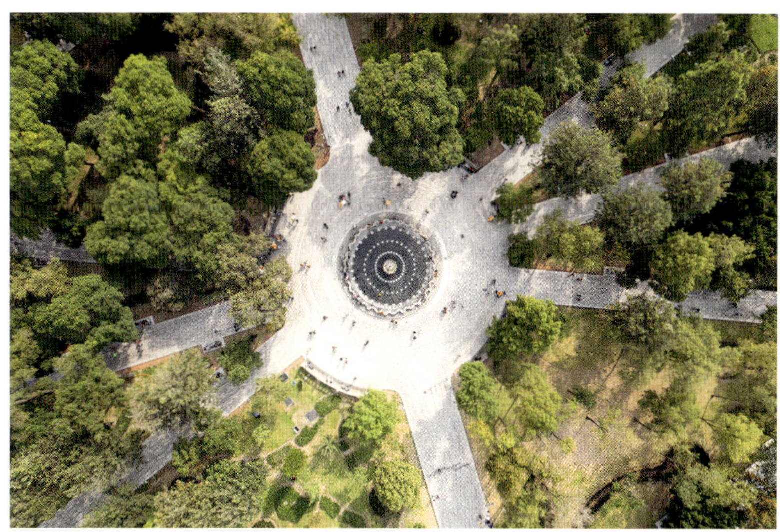

The lungs of the city, Chapultepec Park (left) and Alameda Park (right), and the Paseo de la Reforma, which is closed to cars on Sundays, are used intensively for various activities.

Die grünen Lungen der Stadt Chapultepec- (li.) oder Alameda-Park (re.) und der sonntags für Autos gesperrte Paseo de la Reforma werden intensiv für Aktivitäten genutzt.

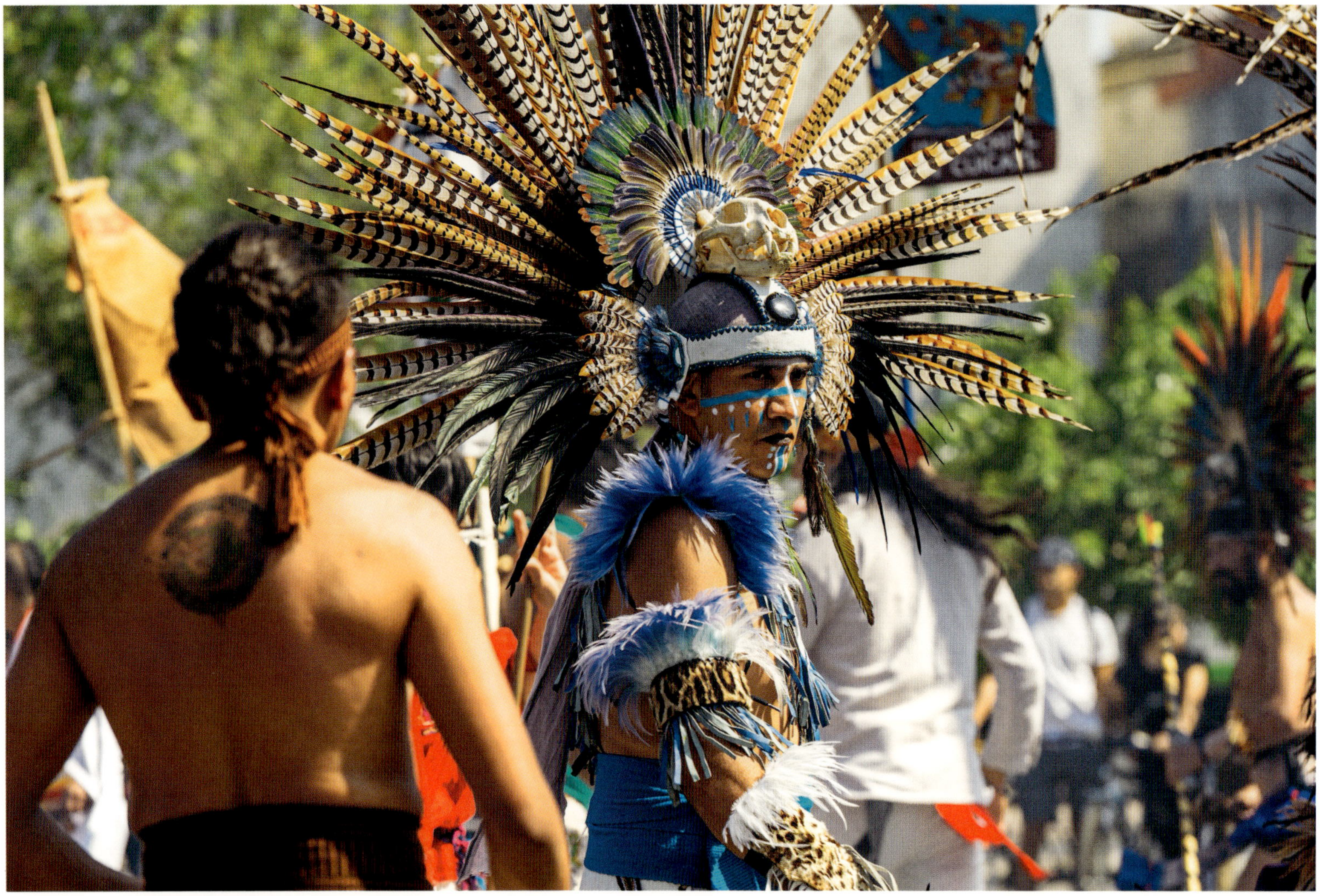

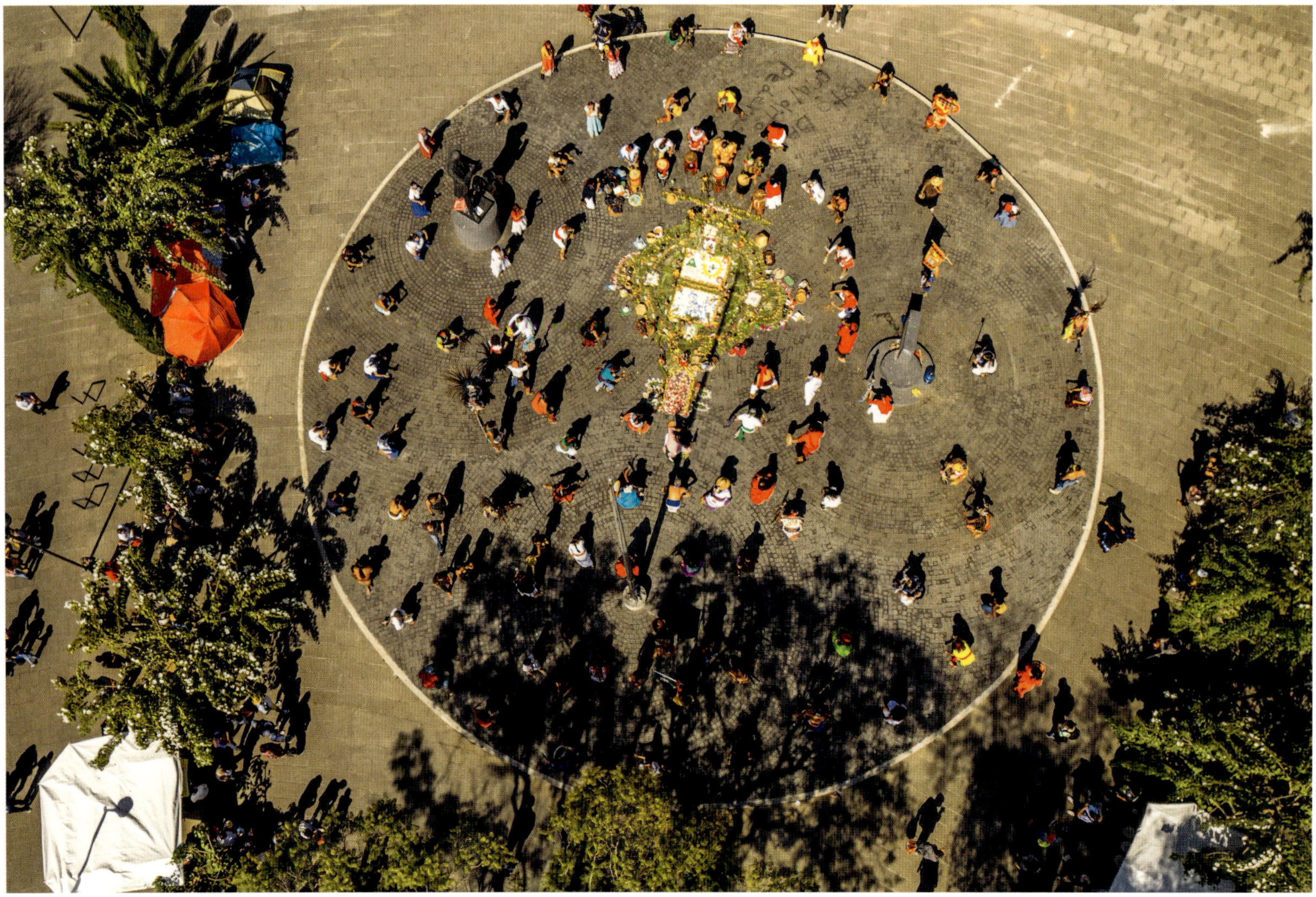

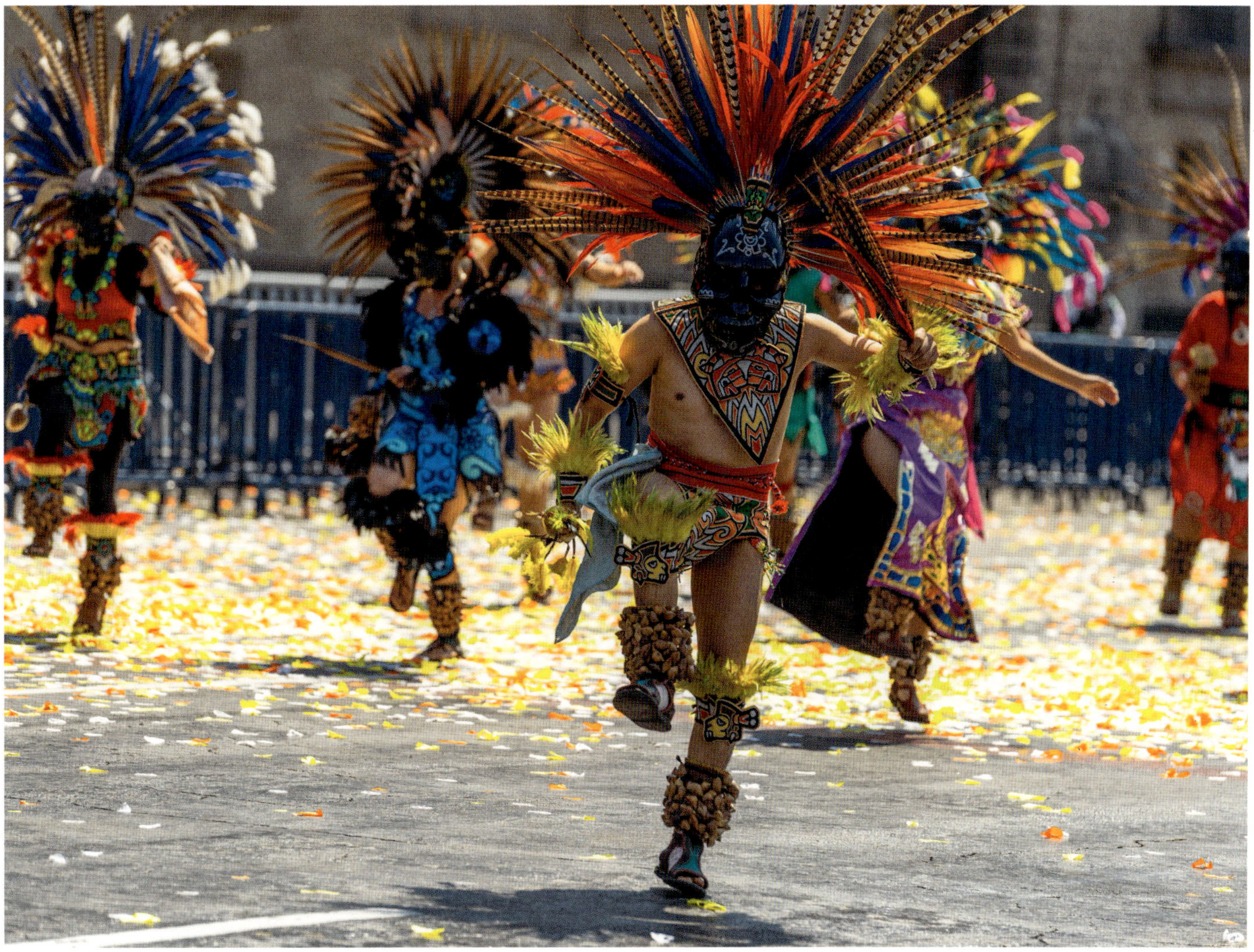

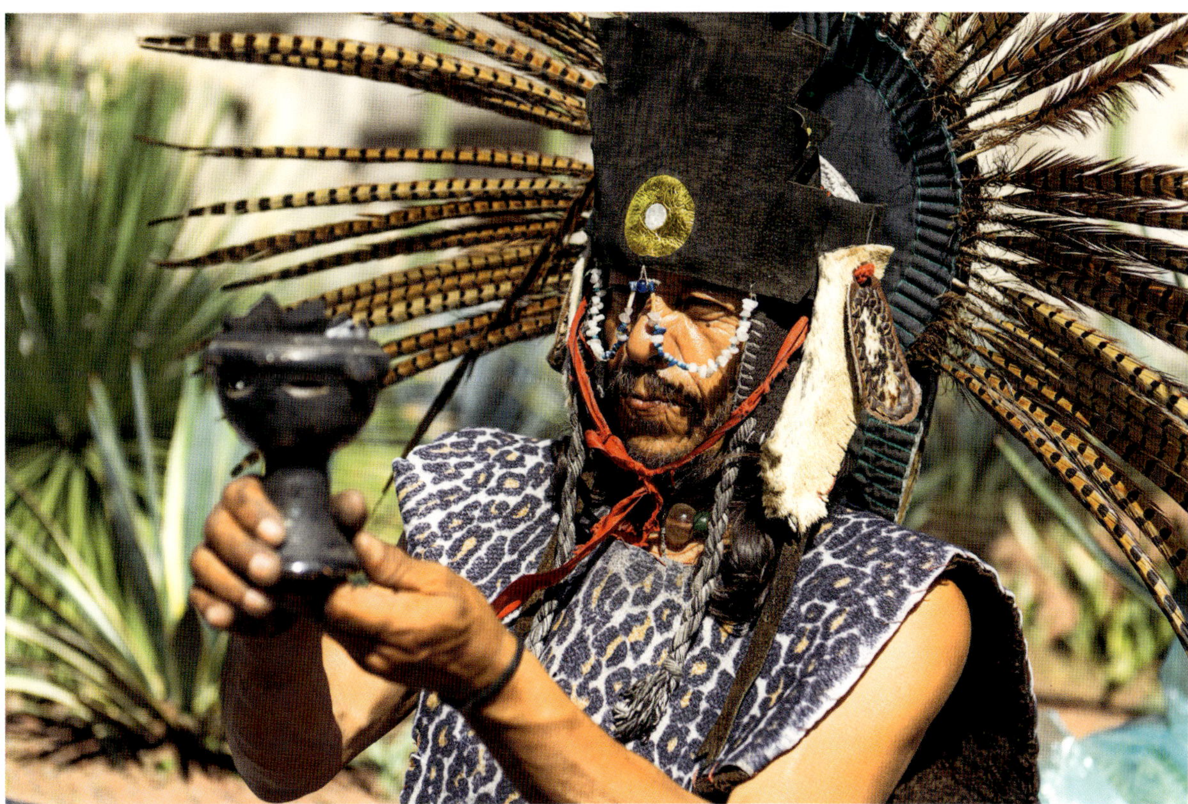

Mexico City is an important site for *Concheros*, or shell dancers, whose traditional dance is embraced here as an expression of ethnic and cultural identity.

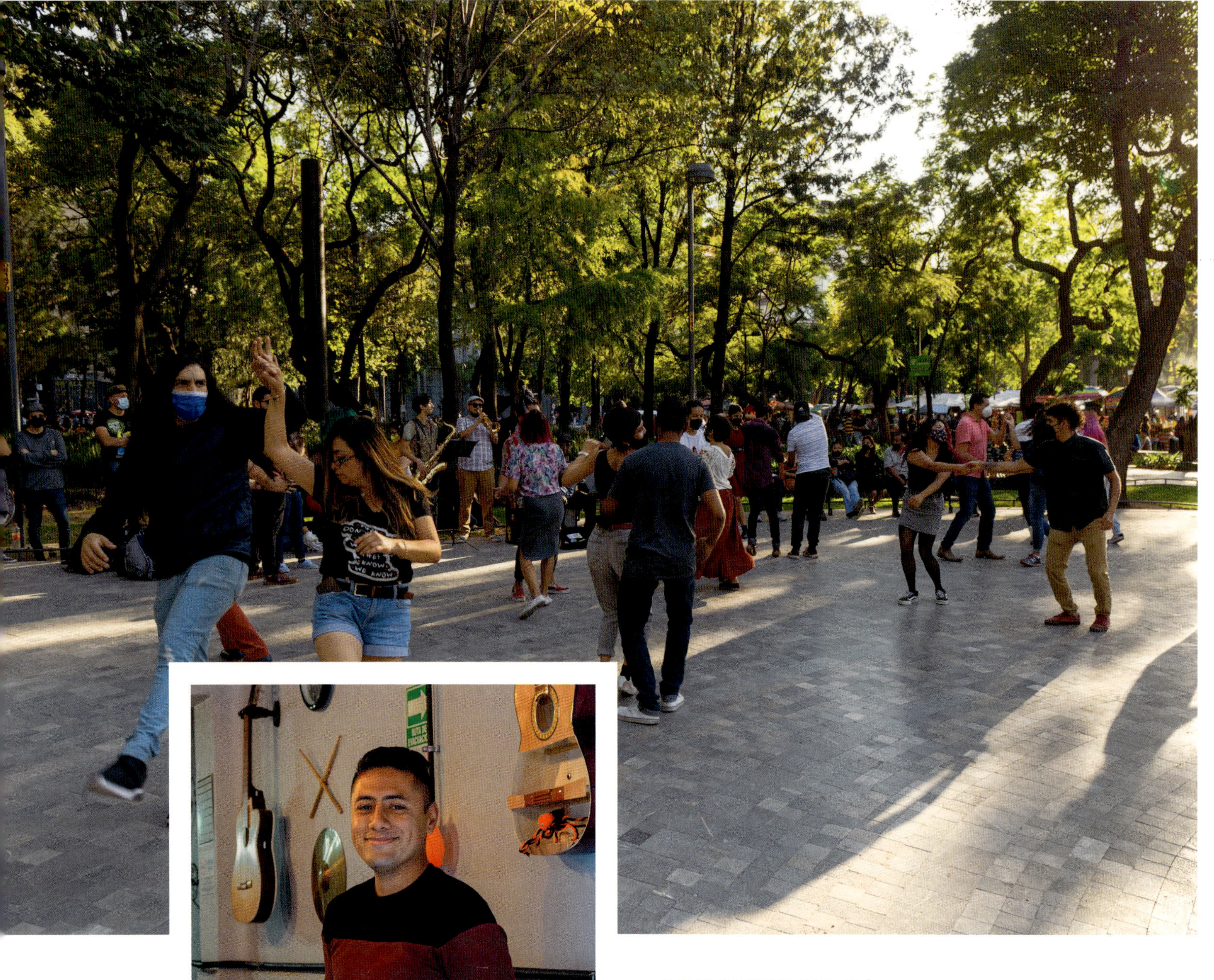

DAVID
EMPLOYEE
ANGESTELLTER

Alameda Park in the heart of the city is an important venue for recreation and interaction.

...ON THE FEELING OF JOIE DE VIVRE

"I would like to share a sentence I heard at some point (…) A people that sings and dances is happy (…). This is true for Mexico, and South America in general. We must enjoy, live in the here and now and not worry, like the Asian people, for example, who say, 'I have to be the best, I have to be perfect.' Here with us you can make mistakes (…) because sometimes we started with a mistake from the beginning, which was maybe that my parents didn't want to have a baby (…). So, you are already born from a mistake that became something magical, and you have to accept the mistake, because the more you accept something, a failure that may be good, as I see it, the more you evolve."

...ON REASONS TO MOVE TO THE CITY

"What brings people here is hope. The hope of getting something more than they already have in their reality. And a reality is often idealized. Even on social media, it's always perfect. Nothing in

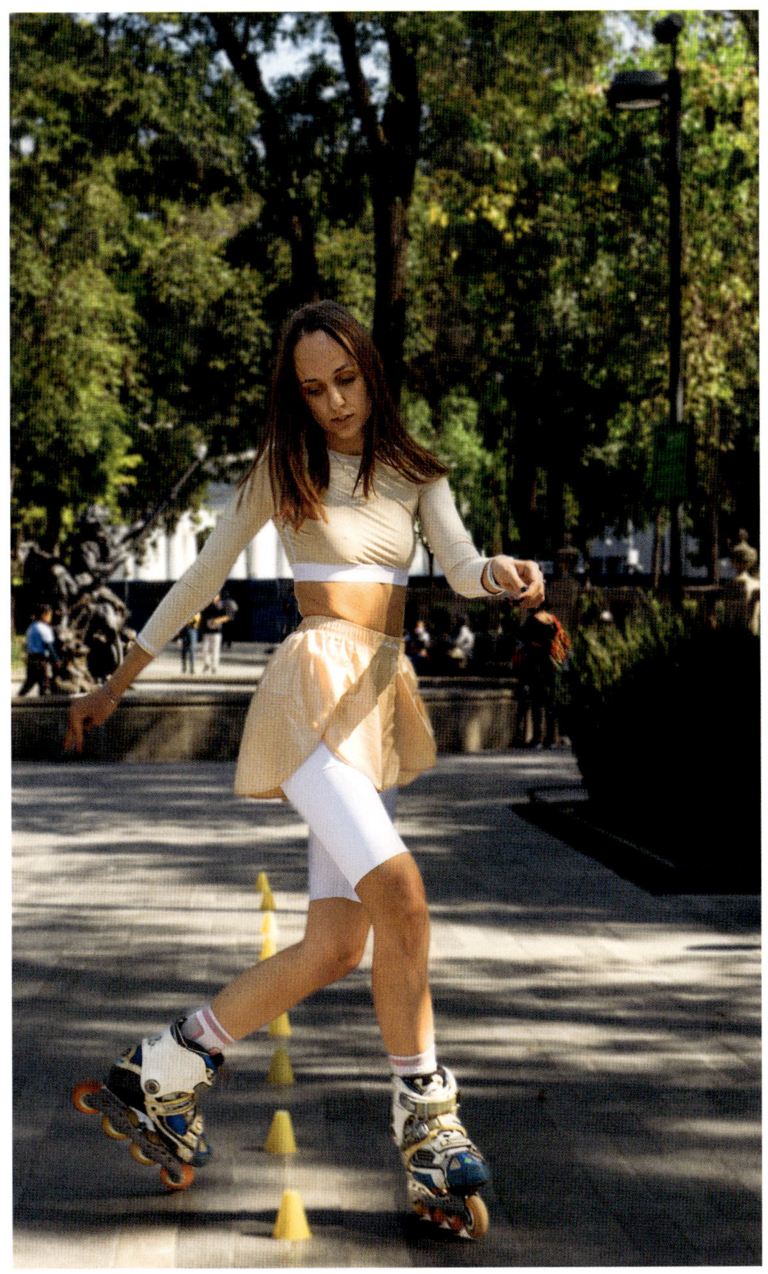

life is perfect, and I think that people in the city live every day with the fact that it's not perfect, that you're not going to make millions (...)."

...ZUM LEBENSGEFÜHL

„Ich würde gerne einen Satz sagen, den ich irgendwann einmal gehört habe: (...) Ein Volk, das singt und tanzt, ist glücklich (...). Das gilt für Mexiko und Südamerika im Allgemeinen. Wir sollen genießen, im Hier und Jetzt leben und uns keine Sorgen machen, wie zum Beispiel bei den Asiaten, wo es heißt, ich muss der Beste sein, ich muss perfekt sein. Bei uns kann man Fehler machen (...), weil wir manchmal von Anfang an mit einem Fehler begonnen haben, der vielleicht darin bestand, dass meine Eltern mich nicht wollten (...). Du bist also bereits aus einem Fehler geboren, der zu etwas Magischem geworden ist, und du musst den Fehler annehmen, denn je mehr du etwas annimmst, ein Scheitern, das vielleicht gut ist, wie ich es sehe, desto mehr entwickelst du dich."

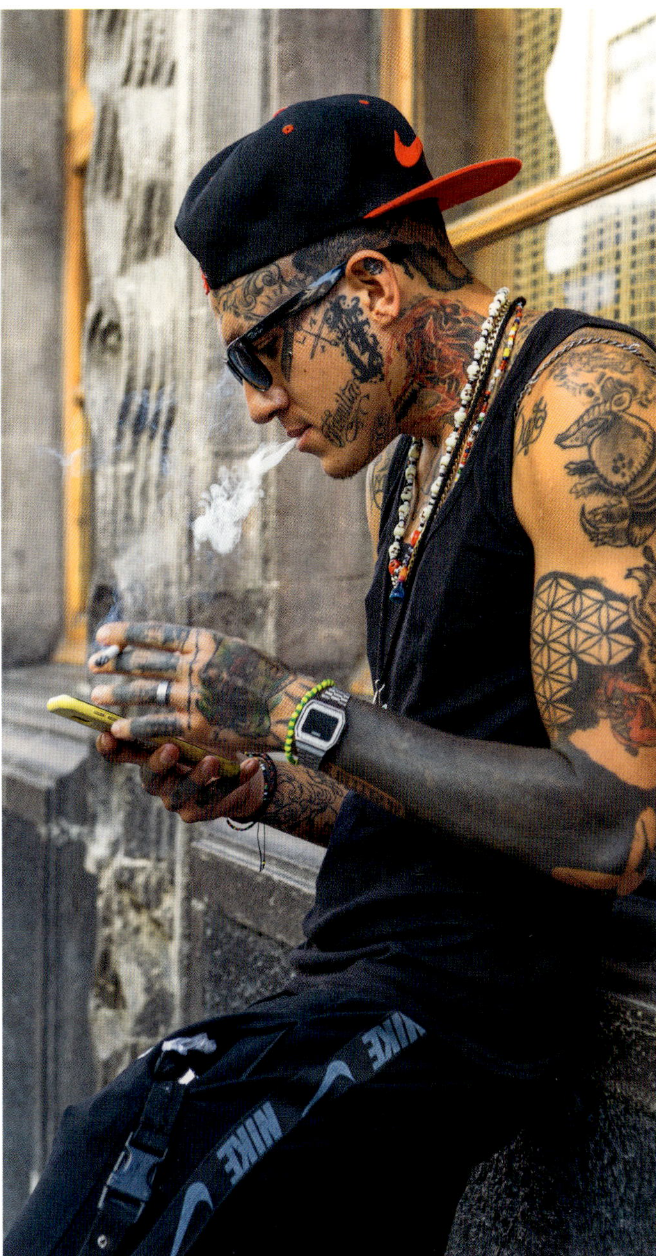

...ZU DEN GRÜNDEN,
IN DIE STADT ZU ZIEHEN

„Was die Menschen dazu bringt, herzukommen, ist die Hoffnung. Die Hoffnung, etwas mehr zu bekommen als das, was sie in ihrer Realität bereits haben. Und oft wird eine Realität idealisiert. Auch in den sozialen Netzwerken ist sie bereits perfekt. Nichts im Leben ist perfekt, und ich denke, dass die Menschen aus der Stadt Tag für Tag damit leben, dass es nicht perfekt ist, dass man keine Millionen verdienen wird (...)."

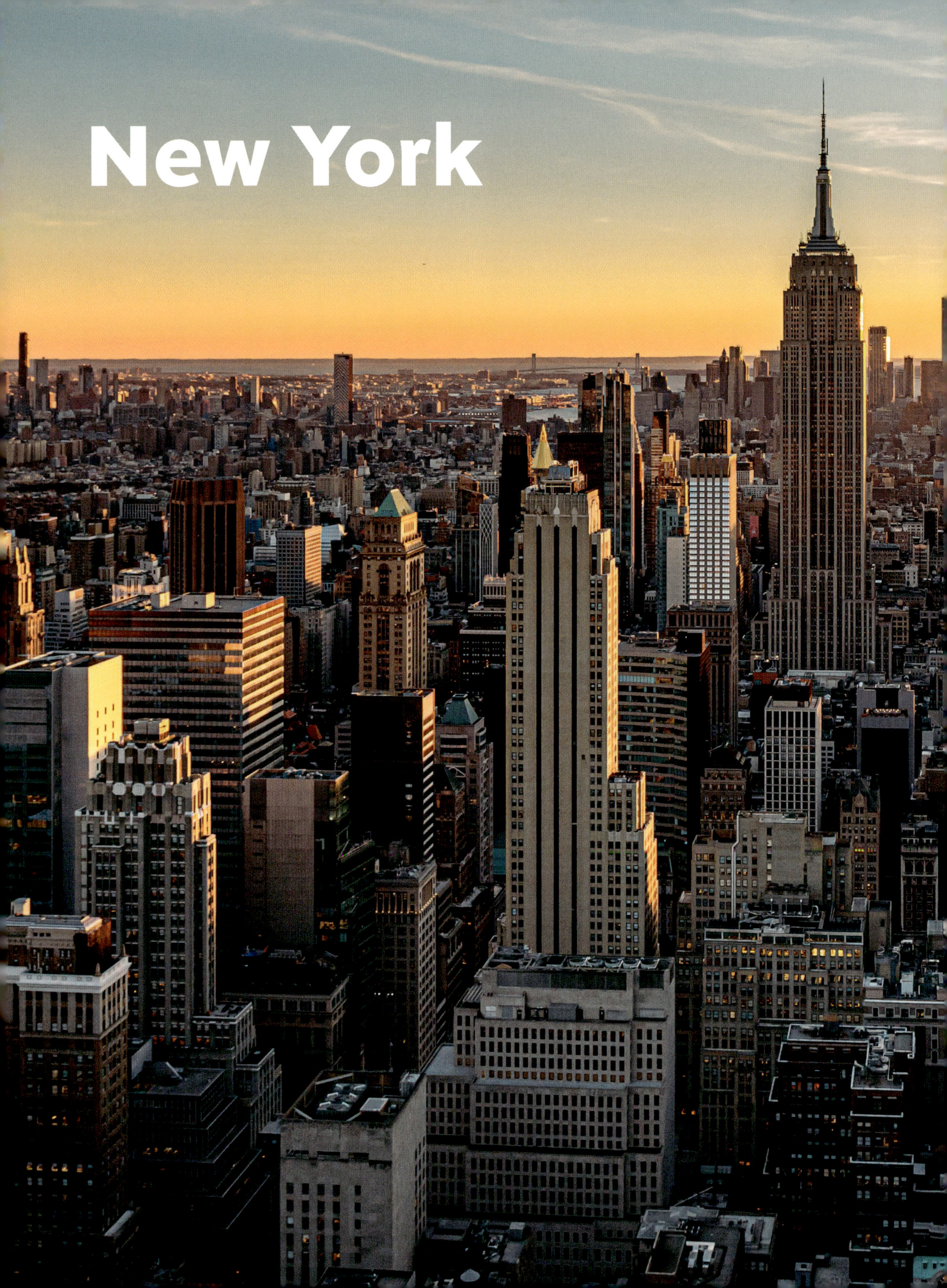
New York

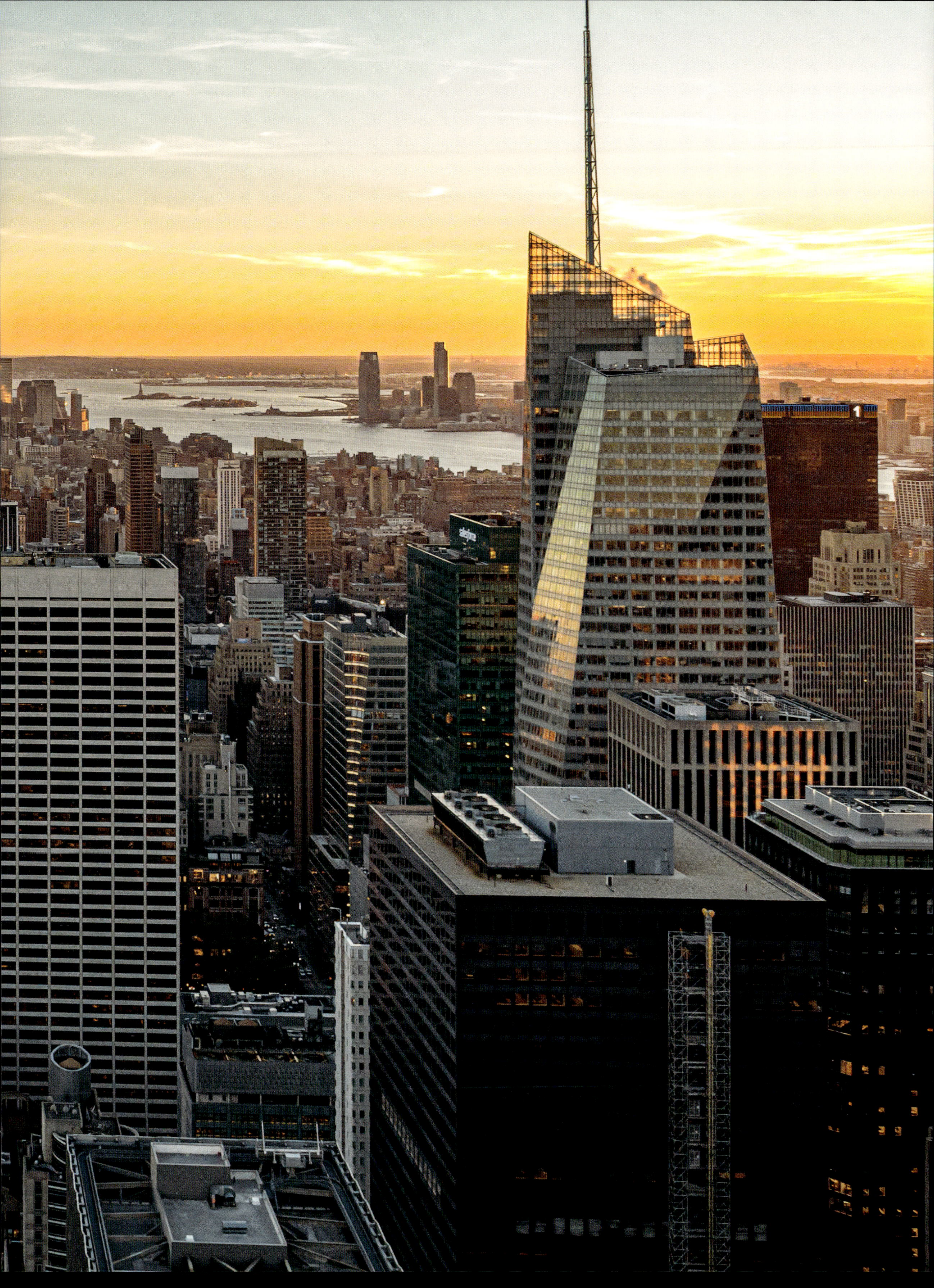

The Powerhouse for Creatives

Kraftzentrum der Kreativen

"What's special about New York? I think it's just the energy, man. You know, everywhere you go, the diversity, the different cultures, it's just everything here, man." (Fernando Carlo, Jr | Cope2)

A city that never sleeps? Yes, it does, at least in the morning, and then for quite a long time. If you want to be creative and productive, you need sleep. But as soon as you set foot out of the door, New York is pure inspiration, only allowing you to relax and disconnect when you get home in the evening. Because New York is electrified, and it has to be, the energy of its creative people, no matter their profession, has to constantly be recharged.

New York is exhausting, often noisy, a veritable barrage of impressions. That requires spaces where you can retreat, and there are plenty of them. Central Park is the most famous, but with the transformation of Brooklyn's old docks where the East and Hudson Rivers meet, the city has created an enormous recreational area with sports facilities for everyone, bike paths, parks, spaces for reading, picnic areas, and much more. Sports and life just as they should be—and right in front of the perfect skyline.

Manhattan, admittedly, takes some getting used to. Here, the modern service metropolis spawned an architecture that knows nothing but the unrestrained market. Its economic focus has given rise to large, insular buildings and consumer worlds that defy conventional urban planning. The Financial District in particular appears rather cold, almost forbidding, but perhaps motivating and inspiring for the bankers, who can feel they are part of the economic success up in their glass palaces.

Anyone strolling through the urban canyons between skyscrapers can't help but wonder, "How can you live in this megacity?" You can, and that's exactly what makes New York so appealing. All you have to do is change sides. For example, take the subway across the East River to Williamsburg, where you get the full range of the metropolis's cultures in one place.

"But everyone has different cultures in a sense, with their religions and food. So it's cool when you meet different cultures, because you can share that." (Fernando Carlo, Jr | Cope2)

„Was ist das Besondere an New York? Ich denke, es ist einfach die Energie, hey. Überall, wo man hinkommt, die Vielfalt, die verschiedenen Kulturen, einfach alles hier." (Fernando Carlo, Jr | Cope2)

Eine Stadt, die niemals schläft? Doch, tut sie, zumindest morgens und dann auch recht lange. Wer kreativ und produktiv sein will braucht Schlaf. Aber kaum tritt man aus der Tür, ist New York pure Inspiration, lässt einen erst wieder entspannen und abschalten, wenn man abends heimkommt. Denn New York steht unter Strom, muss es auch, die Energie der Kreativen, egal aus welchem Metier, muss beständig geladen werden.

New York ist anstrengend, oft laut, ein Feuerwerk an Eindrücken. Das erfordert Rückzugsräume, und die gibt es zuhauf. Der Central Park ist nur der berühmteste, aber mit der Umwandlung der alten Hafenanlagen Brooklyns am Zusammenfluss von East und Hudson River hat sich die Stadt ein gigantisches Freizeitareal mit Sportanlagen für alle, Radwegen, Parks, Rückzugsräumen zum Lesen, Picknickplätzen und und und geschaffen. Sport pur, Leben pur – vor Skyline pur.

Manhattan ist, zugegeben, gewöhnungsbedürftig. Hier hat die moderne Dienstleistungsmetropole eine Architektur hervorgebracht, die nur noch den ungebremsten Markt kennt. Die ökonomische Konzentration hat inselhafte Großbauten und Konsumwelten entstehen lassen, die sich dem herkömmlichen Städtebau entziehen. Vor allem der Financial District wirkt daher eher kalt, ja fast schon abweisend, aber vielleicht motivierend und inspirierend für die Banker, die sich in den Glaspalästen als Teil des wirtschaftlichen Erfolgs fühlen können.

Who came up with Times Square? Disney, of course. The spectacle of light and architecture is arguably the world's most frequently used backdrop for selfies.

Wer hat den Times Square erfunden? Disney natürlich. Das Licht- und Architekturspektakel dürfte Kulisse für die meisten Selfies weltweit sein.

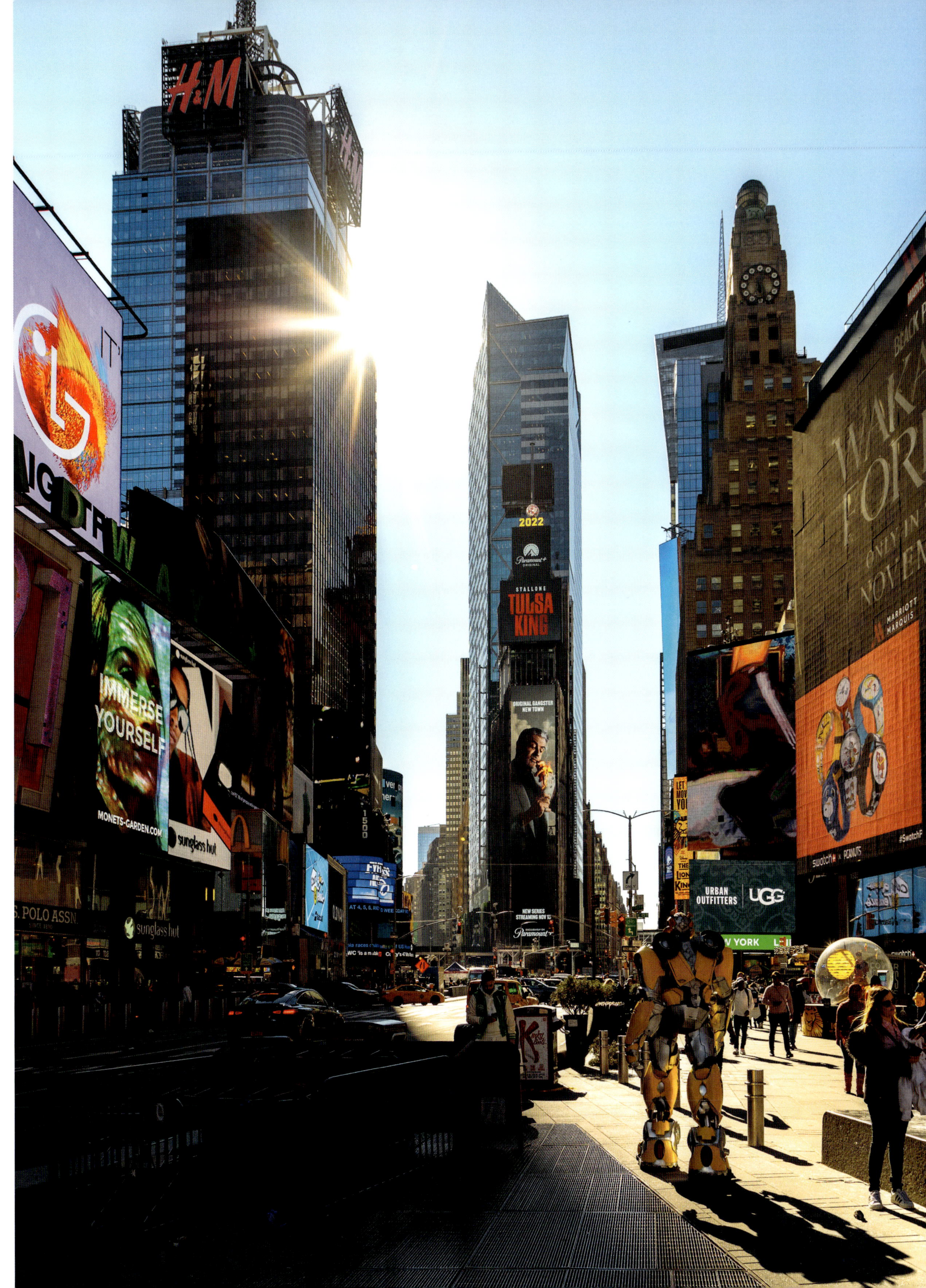

H&M
LG
IMMERSE YOURSELF
MONETS-GARDEN.COM
sunglass hut
S. POLO ASSN.
sunglass hut
2022
Paramount+
ORIGINAL
STALLONE
TULSA KING
ORIGINAL GANGSTER
NEW TOWN
NEW SERIES
STREAMING NOV 13
Paramount+
THE LION KING
URBAN OUTFITTERS
UGG
MARRIOTT MARQUIS
WAKANDA FOREVER
ONLY IN NOVEMBER
#SwatchP
swatch x PEANUTS
NEW YORK

Visitors who come on Saturday, the Jewish Sabbath, enter a different, strange, almost unreal world. This is the center of the Satmars, Hasidic, ultra-Orthodox Jews who reject any assimilation and have created a secluded parallel world in the midst of the pulsating metropolis. Just a few blocks away, you step into the New York of the hipsters, popular with creative, artistic, freedom-loving residents. Over 6,500 artists from all over the world have reportedly settled here. Within just a few miles, you can travel through Puerto Rico, Brazil, China, Italy, and Germany. Each culture has built its own slice of home here, with the world living together peacefully in one city. This is how multiculturalism and survival work in a virtually endless abundance of possibilities. Wait, peacefully? Not always.

The Bronx, too, is very much a world of its own. Here is where people end up who followed their dream of success in New York, but ended up failing for one reason or another. Yet alongside the violence, there has always been hope here in the birthplace of hip hop, break dancing, and graffiti. This, in turn, attracted artists from around the world, sparking a trend of the Bronx emerging as a multicultural borough. The borough's modernization is already clearly visible on its outskirts. You can experience the impressive openness and dynamism that characterizes New York here, along with the related social problems and extremes in architecture and urban development. Its development, however, continues to unfold. Whereas the ghetto was once the center and base for integrating immigrants, its displacement to the fringes of the Bronx risks making it more of an enclave for exclusion and de-integration.

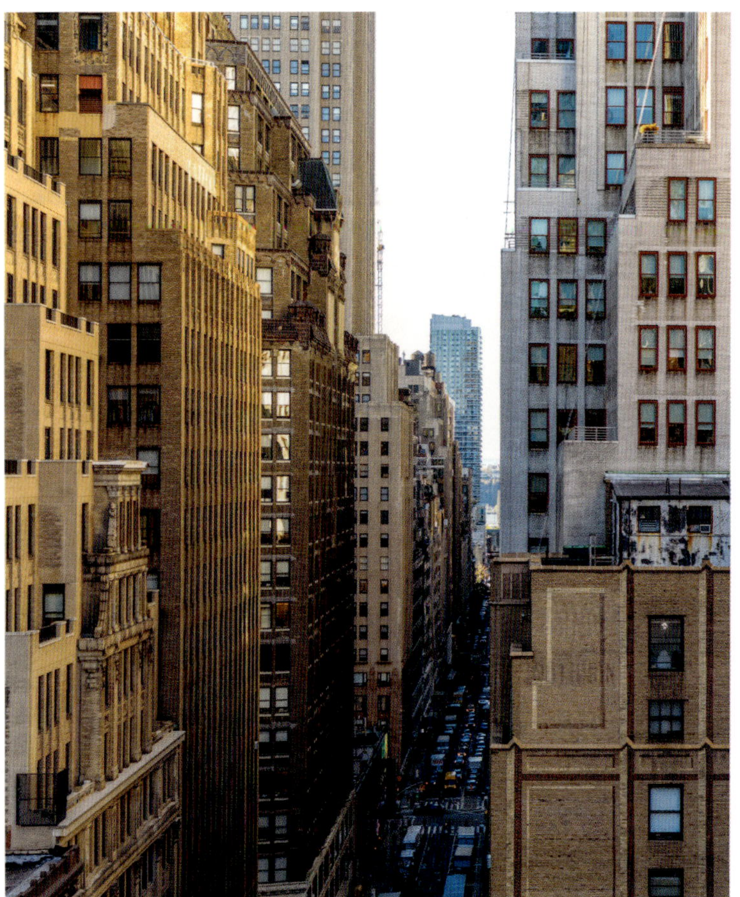

Wer durch die Hochhausschluchten bummelt, fragt sich unwillkürlich: „Wie kann man in dieser Megacity leben?". Man kann, und genau das macht den Reiz New Yorks aus. Dazu braucht man nur die Seiten zu wechseln. Etwa mit der U-Bahn über den East River nach Williamsburg fahren. Hier bekommt man die geballte Kulturenvielfalt der Metropole vorgesetzt.

„Aber jeder hat in gewisser Weise eine andere Kultur, mit seinen Religionen und seinem Essen. Es ist also cool, wenn man verschiedene Kulturen kennenlernt, weil man das teilen kann." (Fernando Carlo, Jr │ Cope2)

Wer am Samstag kommt, dem Sabbat der Juden, fährt in eine andere, fremde, fast schon unwirkliche Welt. Hier ist das Zentrum der Satmarer, chassidischer, ultraorthodoxer Juden, die sich gegen jede Assimilierung stemmen und inmitten der pulsierenden Metropole, eine abgeschottete Parallelwelt erschaffen haben. Nur wenige Blocks weiter betritt man das New York der Hipster, beliebt bei kreativen, künstlerischen, freiheitsliebenden Einwohnern. Über 6 500 Künstler aus aller Welt sollen sich hier niedergelassen haben. Innerhalb von wenigen Kilometern reist man durch Puerto Rico, Brasilien, China, Italien oder Deutschland. Jede Kultur hat sich hier ihre eigenes Stück Heimat aufgebaut – die Welt friedlich zusammen in einer Stadt. Auch so geht Multikulti und Überleben in einer schier unübersichtlichen Fülle an Möglichkeiten. Obwohl friedlich? Nicht immer.

Die Bronx ist ebenfalls eine eigene Welt. Dort landen jene, die dem Traum des Erfolgs in New York gefolgt, aber aus irgendwelchen Gründen gescheitert sind. Doch neben der Gewalt gab es immer auch schon die Hoffnung: Hip-Hop, Breakdance und Graffiti wurden hier geboren. Das wiederum zog Künstler aus aller Welt an und die setzten einen Trend in Gang, sodass sich auch mit der Bronx ein multikultureller Stadtteil zu entwickeln beginnt, dessen Modernisierung an den Rändern bereits deutlich sichtbar wird. Hier erlebt man diese eindrucksvolle Offenheit und Dynamik, die New York auszeichnet, aber auch die damit verbundenen sozialen Probleme und Exzesse in Architektur und Städtebau. Noch ist die Entwicklung offen. War das Ghetto einst Rückhalt und Basis für die Integration von Einwanderern, läuft es mit seiner Verdrängung an die Randgebiete der Bronx Gefahr, eher zum Endpunkt von Ausgrenzung und Desintegration zu werden.

New York is legendary. If you look closely, you will always discover new things along with the old.

New York ist ein Mythos. Wer nur genau hinschaut, entdeckt jederzeit Neues und Altes.

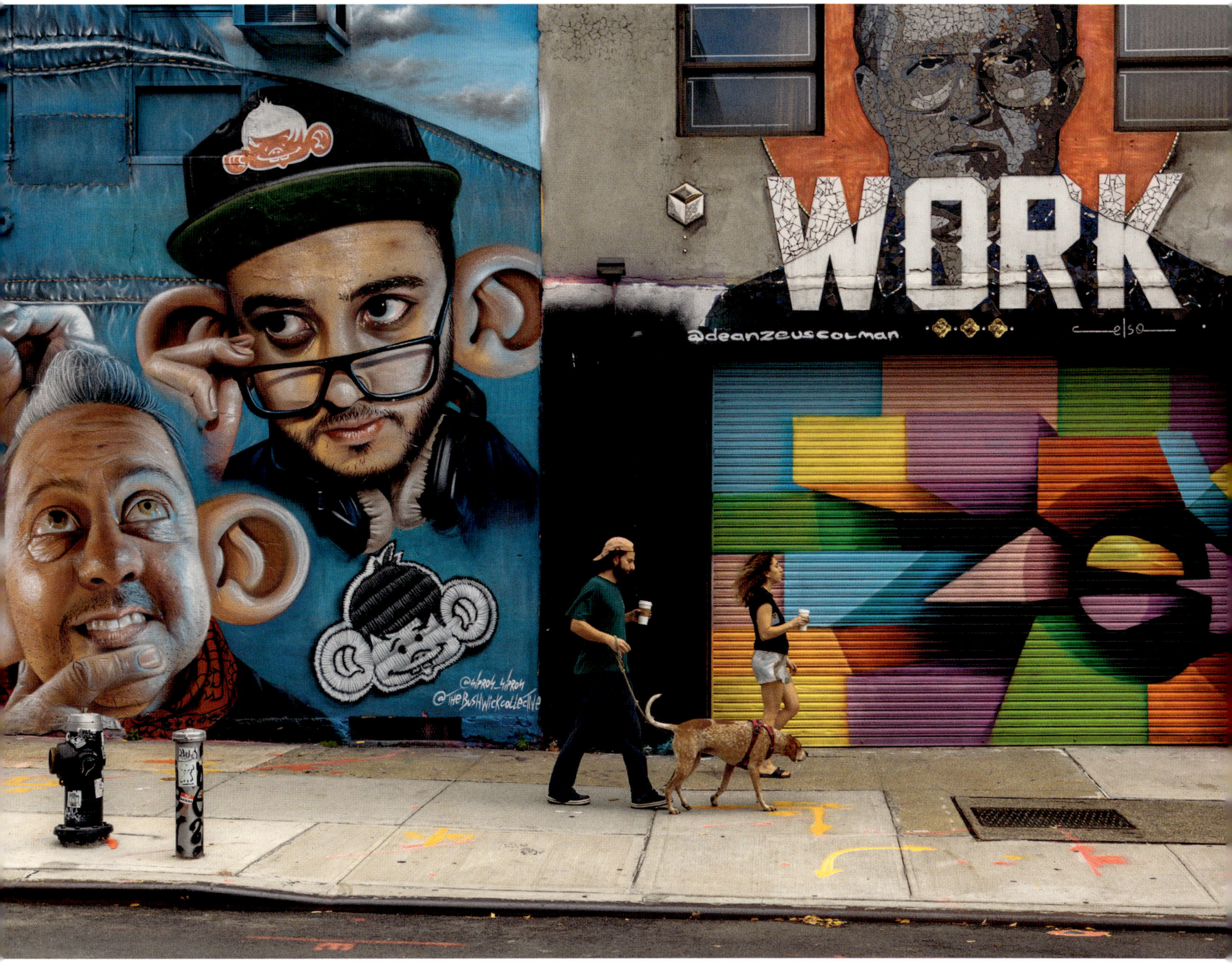

Parallel worlds: Bushwick is a major street art site, while Williamsburg, right next to it, houses the insular world of the Satmar Jews, who resist all forms of assimilation.

Parallelwelten: Bushwick ist ein Zentrum für Street Art, Williamsburg gleich nebenan die abgeschottete Welt der Satmarer-Juden, die sich gegen jede Assimilierung stemmen.

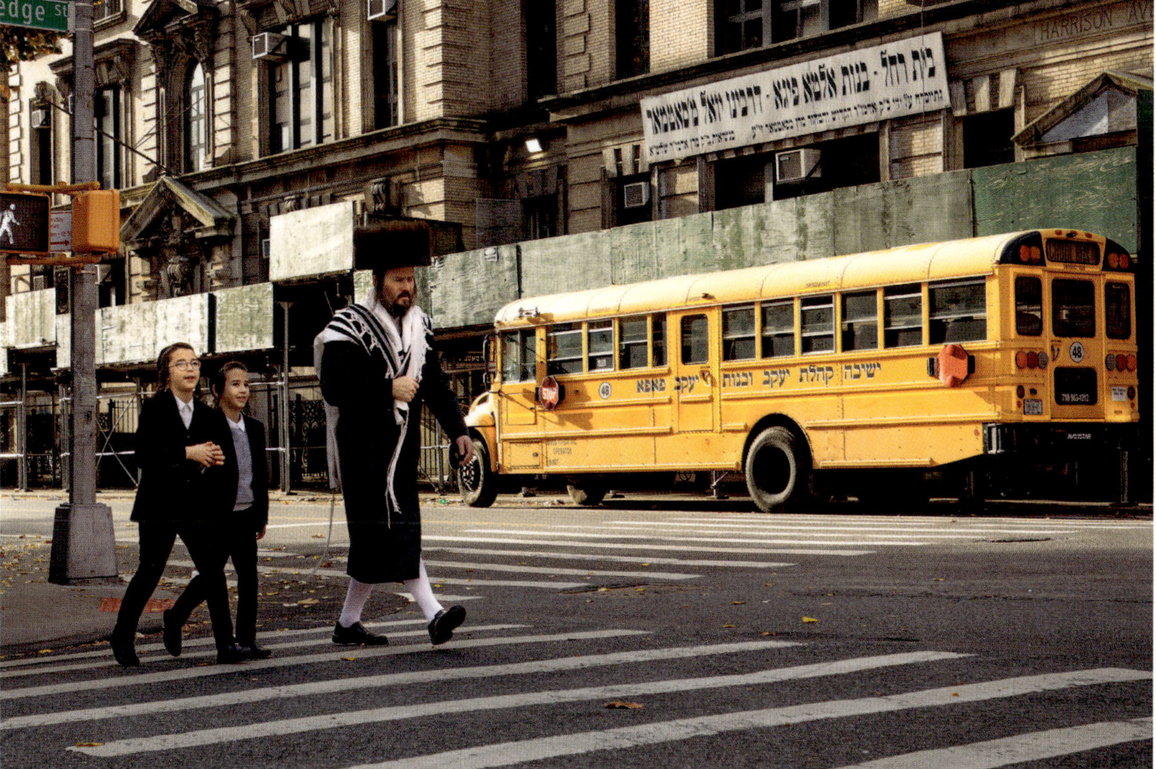

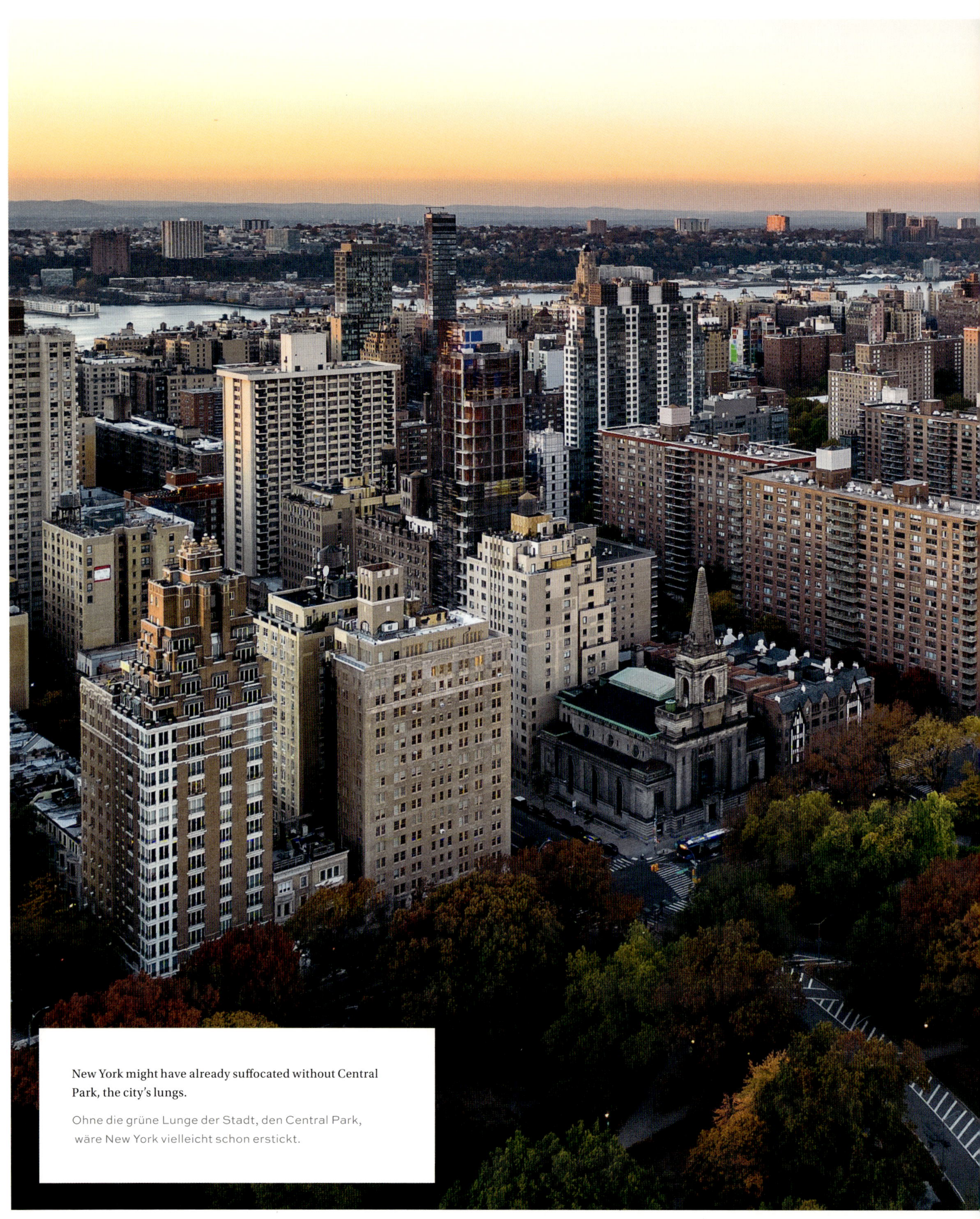

New York might have already suffocated without Central Park, the city's lungs.

Ohne die grüne Lunge der Stadt, den Central Park, wäre New York vielleicht schon erstickt.

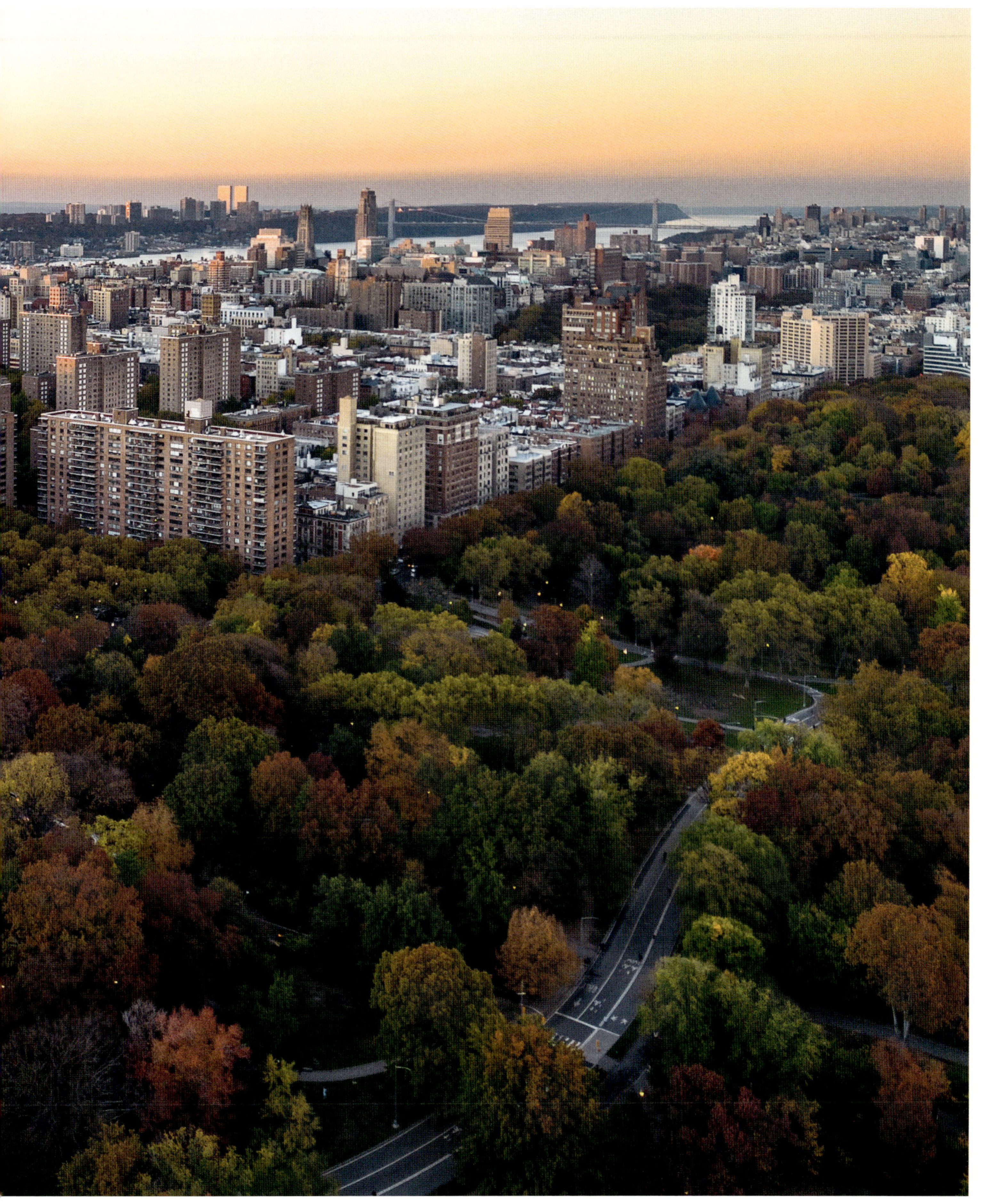

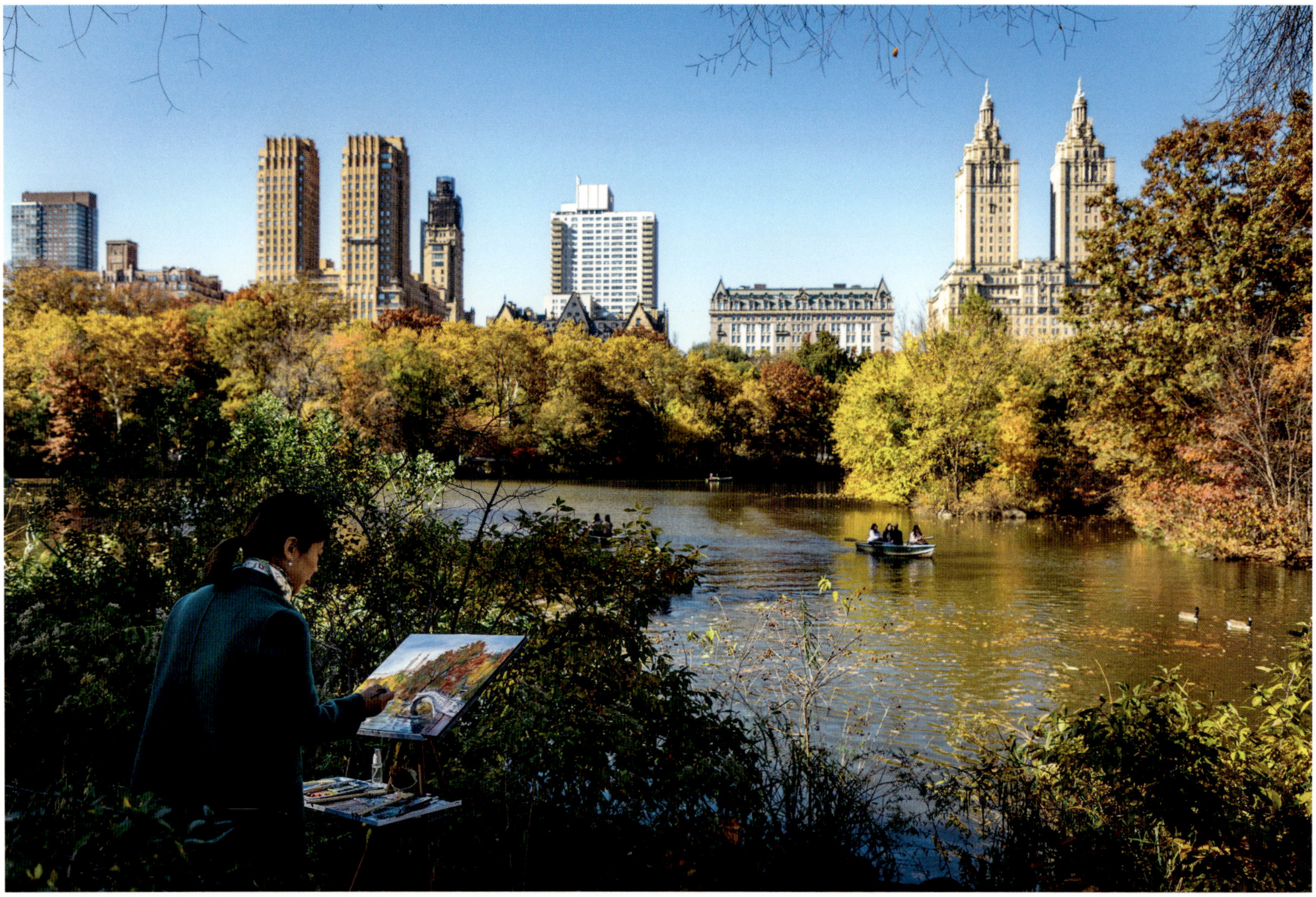

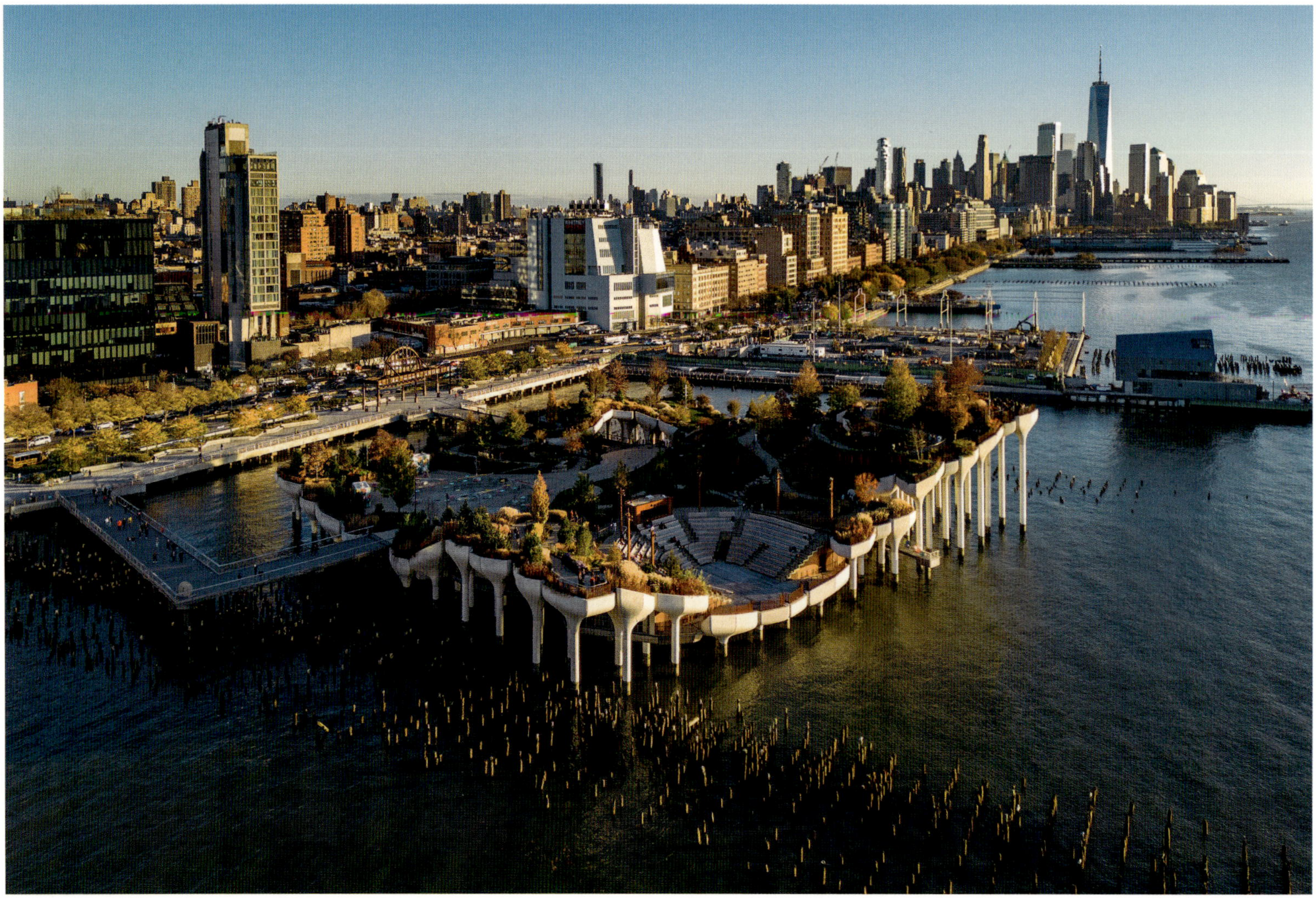

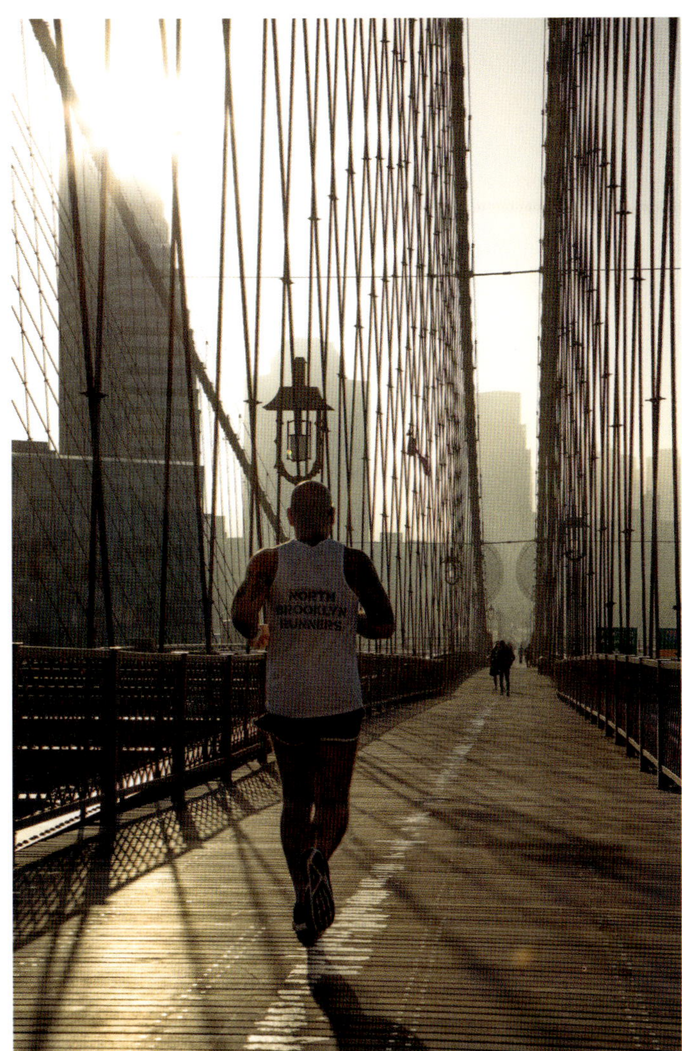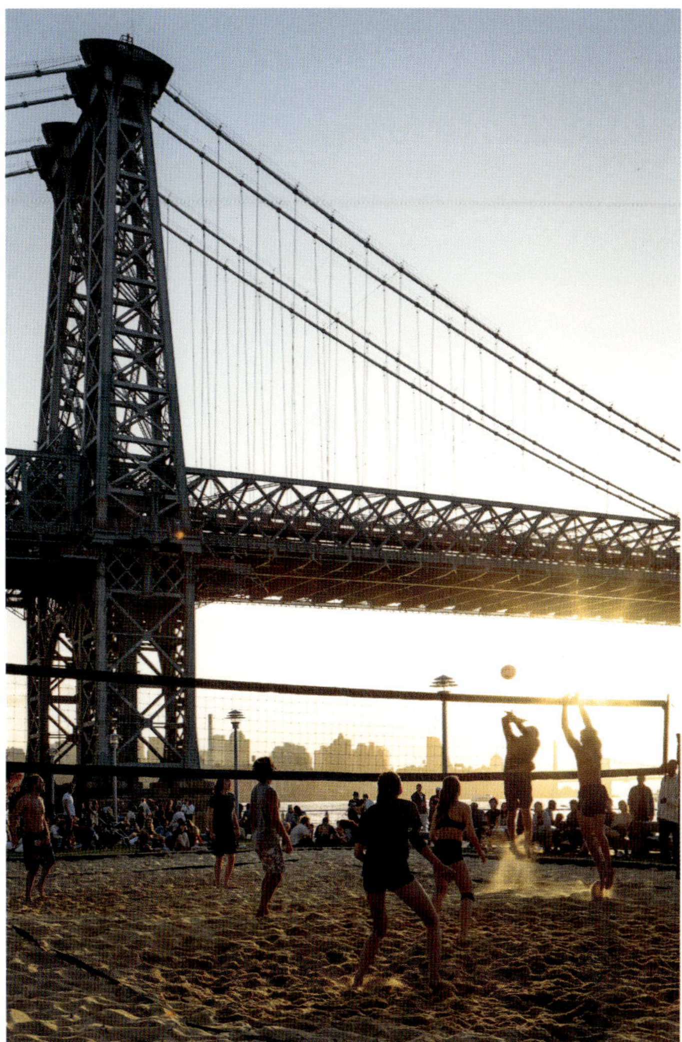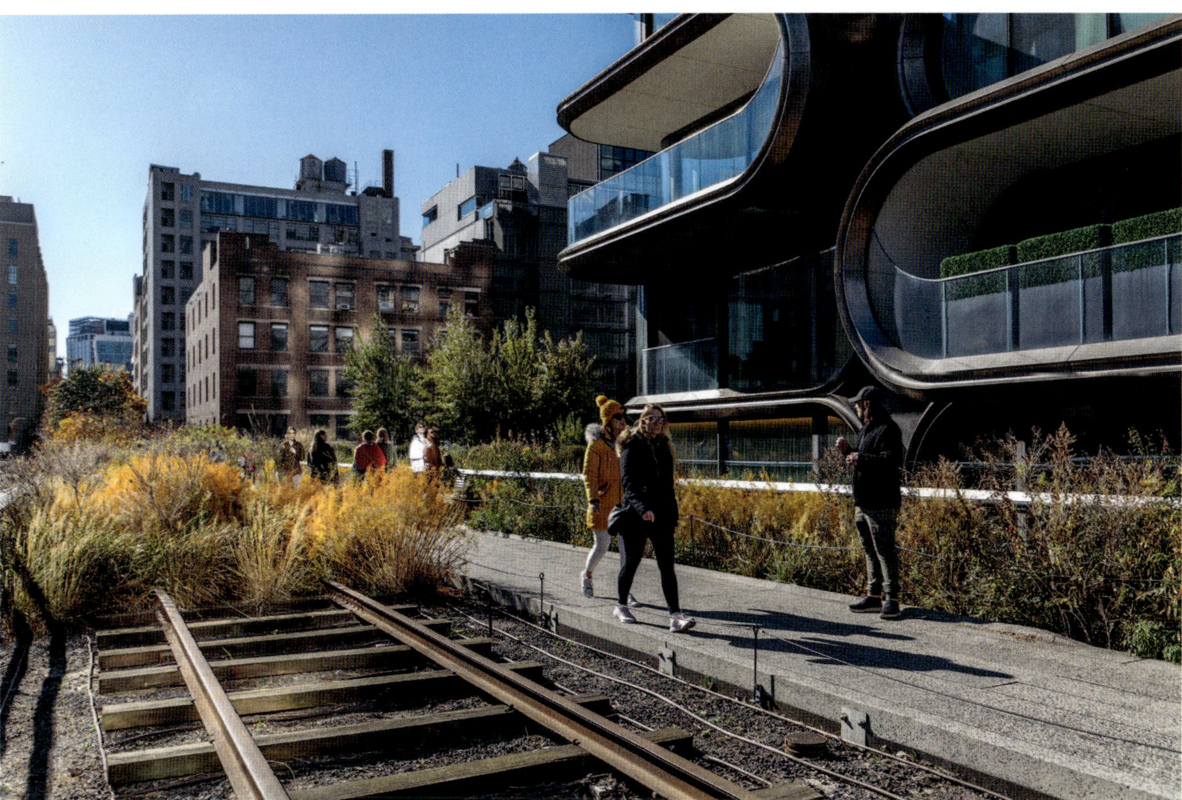

Life in the city's street canyons is as stressful as its skyline is spectacular. And that's supposed to be cool? Yes, it is, because places of refuge and recreational opportunities are also abundant.

So spektakulär die Skyline, so stressig das Leben in den Straßenschluchten. Das soll cool sein? Ja, denn Rückzugsorte und Freizeitmöglichkeiten sind eben auch allgegenwärtig.

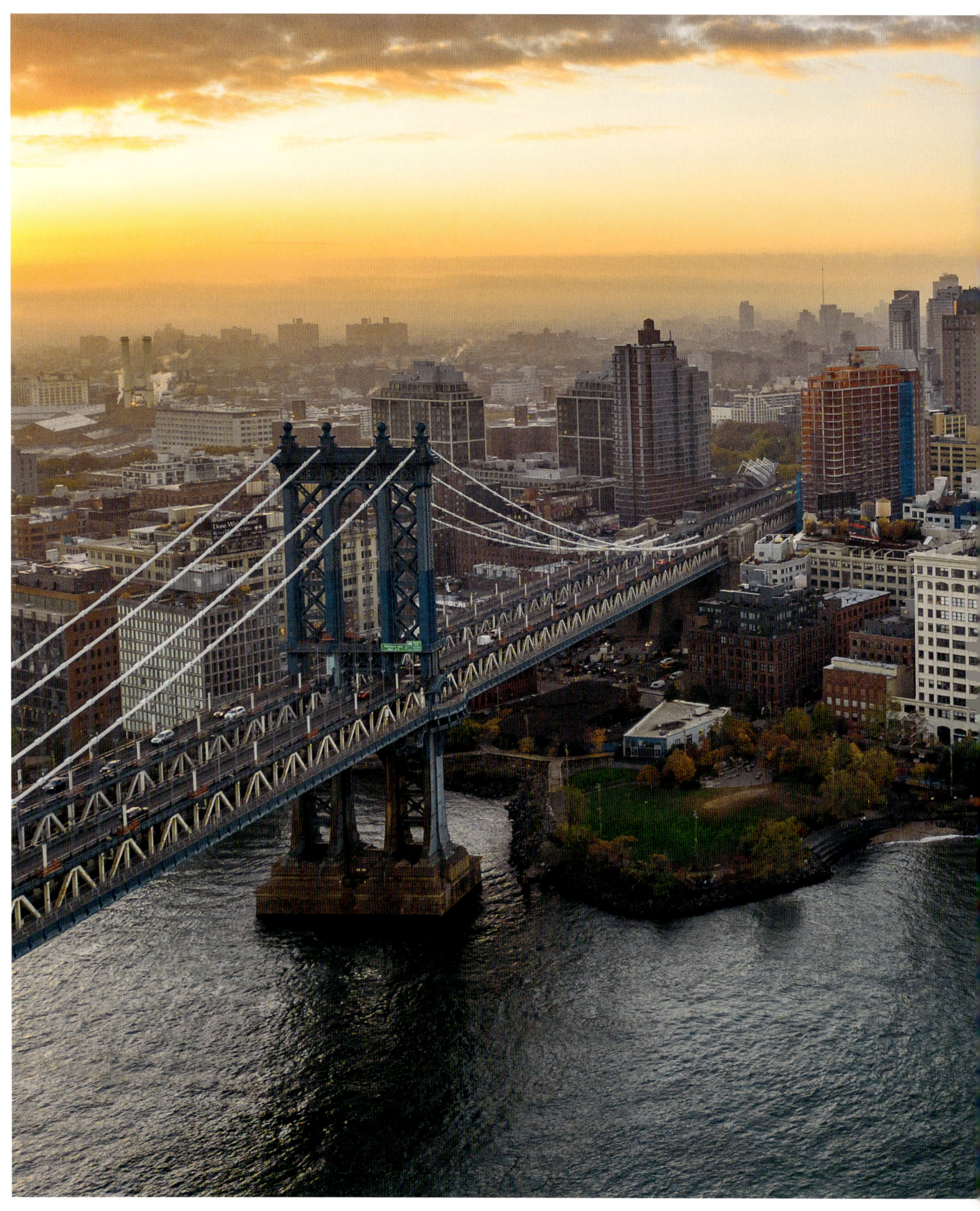

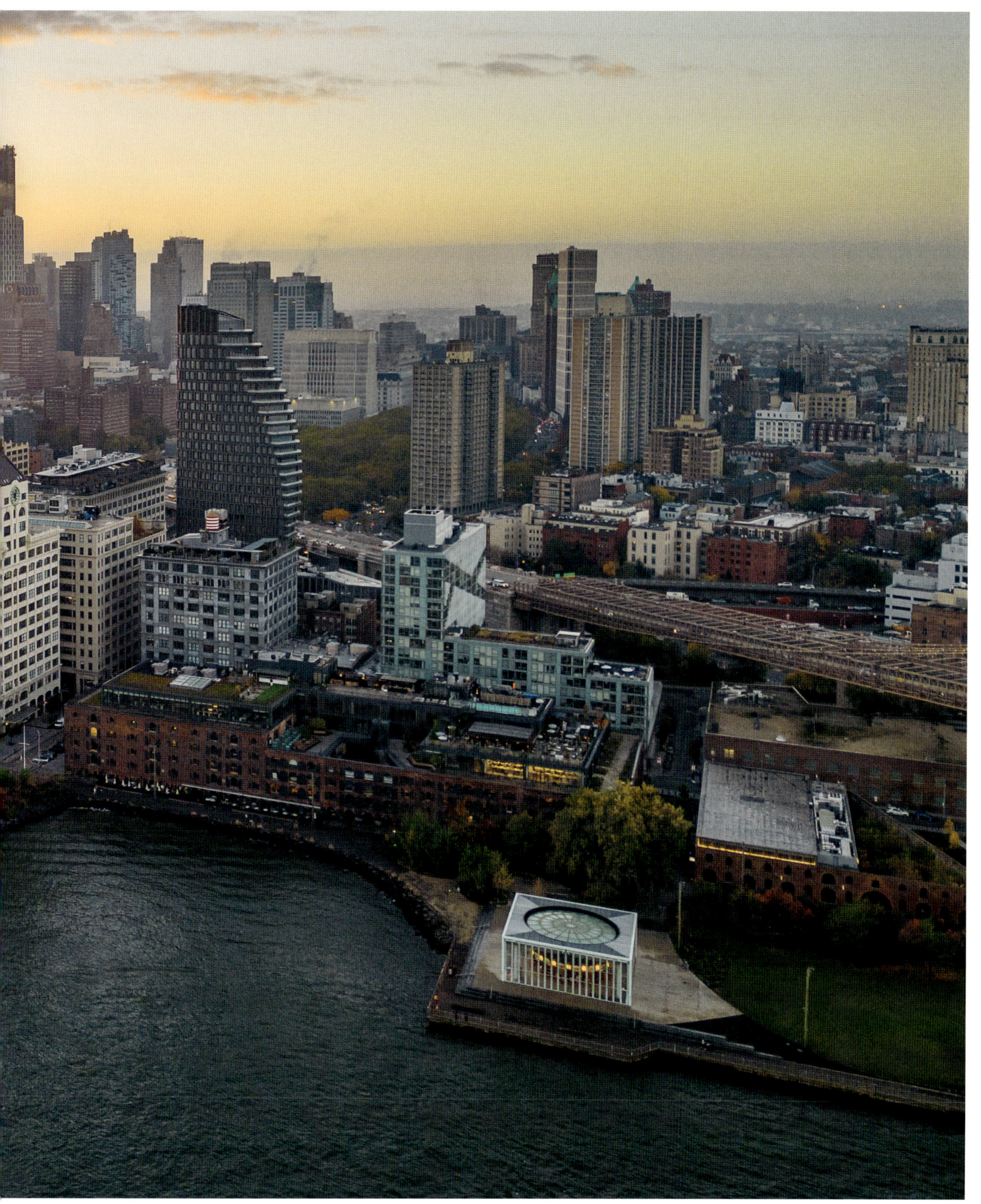

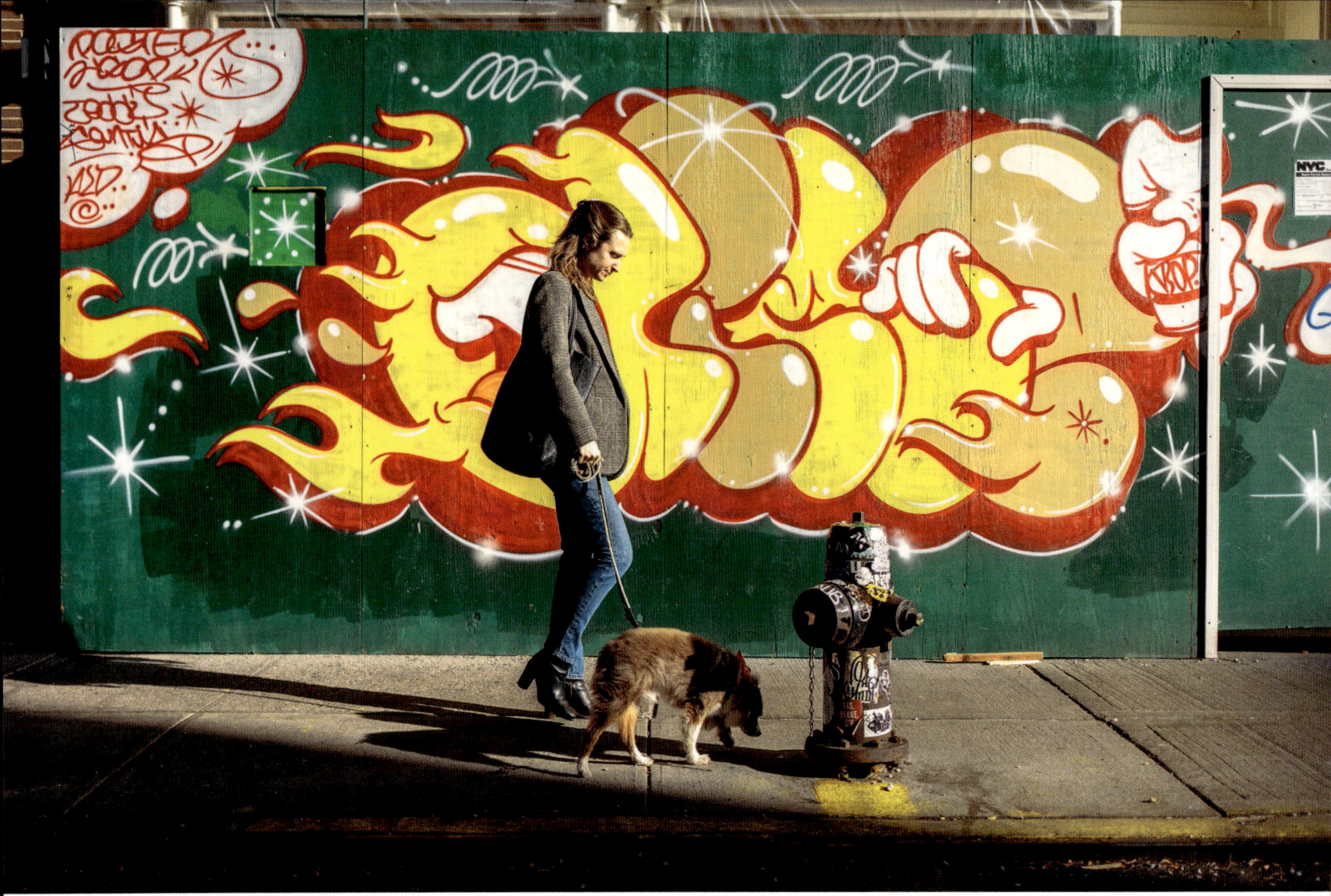

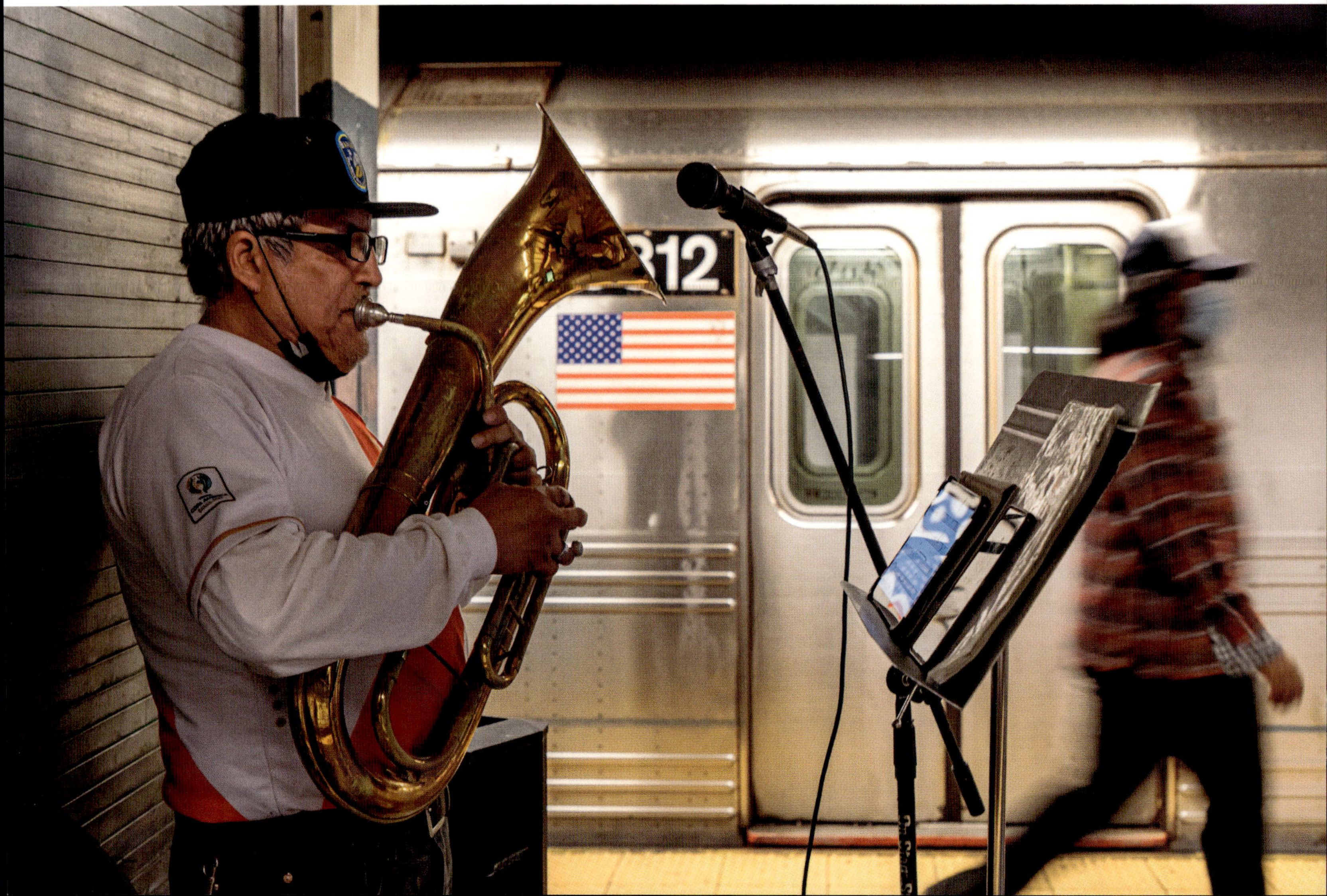

*"It's just you got to try to stay focused and do what you can to try
to live the best life you can, and make your life better.
Because if you make your life better and you're great, if everyone
can do that, eventually everything will be great in time."*
(Fernando Carlo, Jr | Cope2)

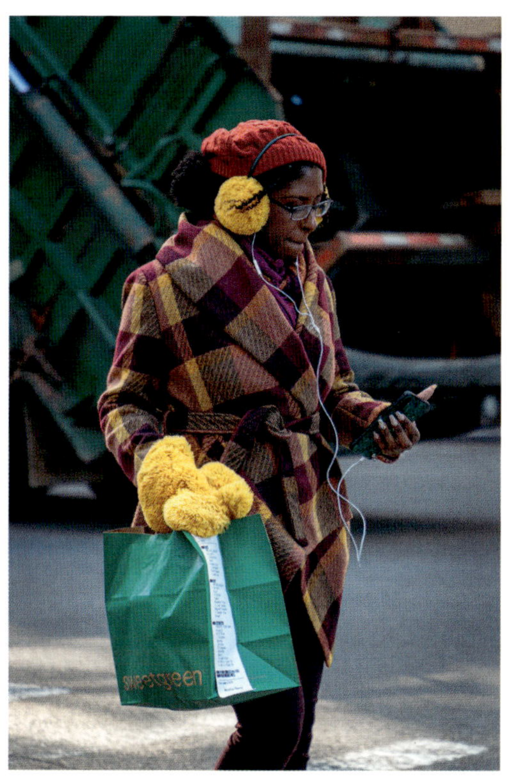

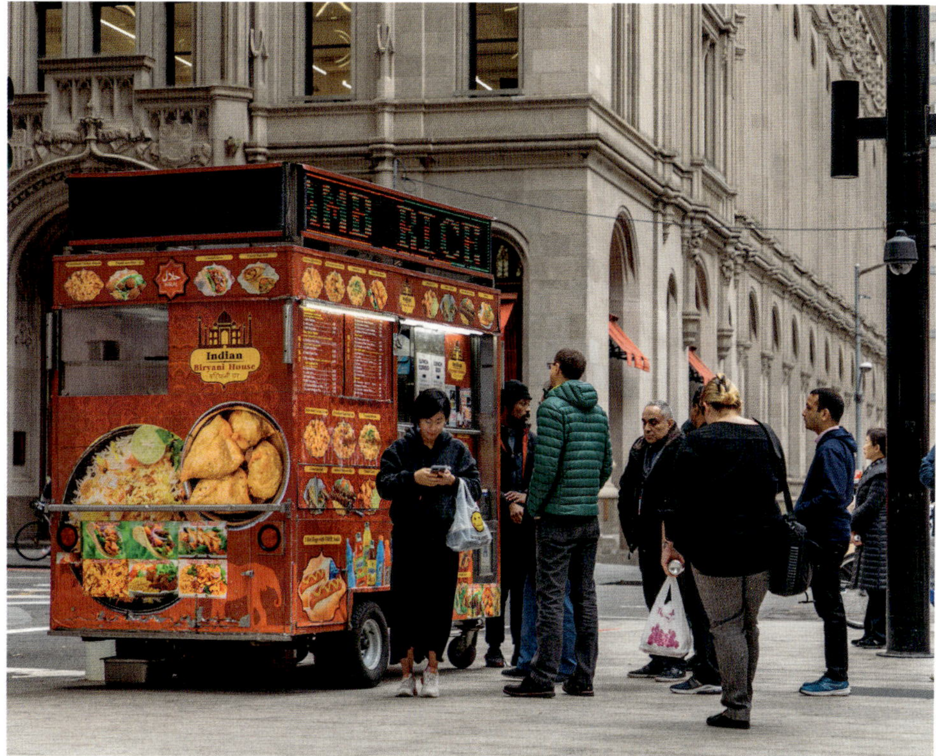

„Man muss versuchen, sich zu konzentrieren und das Beste aus seinem Leben
zu machen und sein Leben zu verbessern. Denn wenn du dein Leben besser
machst und du großartig bist, wenn
jeder das tun kann, wird mit der Zeit
alles großartig sein."
(Fernando Carlo, Jr | Cope2)

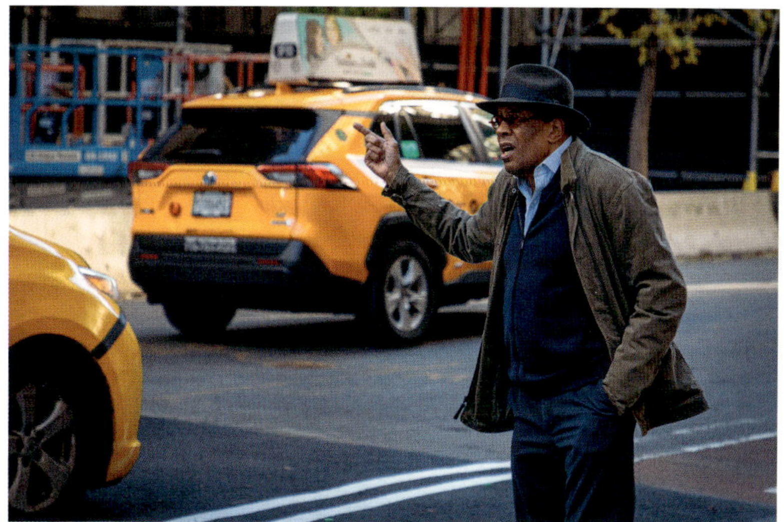

The motto of life in New York is: Don't downplay
yourself and try to celebrate your minor
successes, even if it's just hailing a cab.

In New York gilt: Mach dich nicht klein und
versuche, die kleinen Erfolge zu feiern, auch
wenn es nur darum geht, ein Taxi zu ergattern.

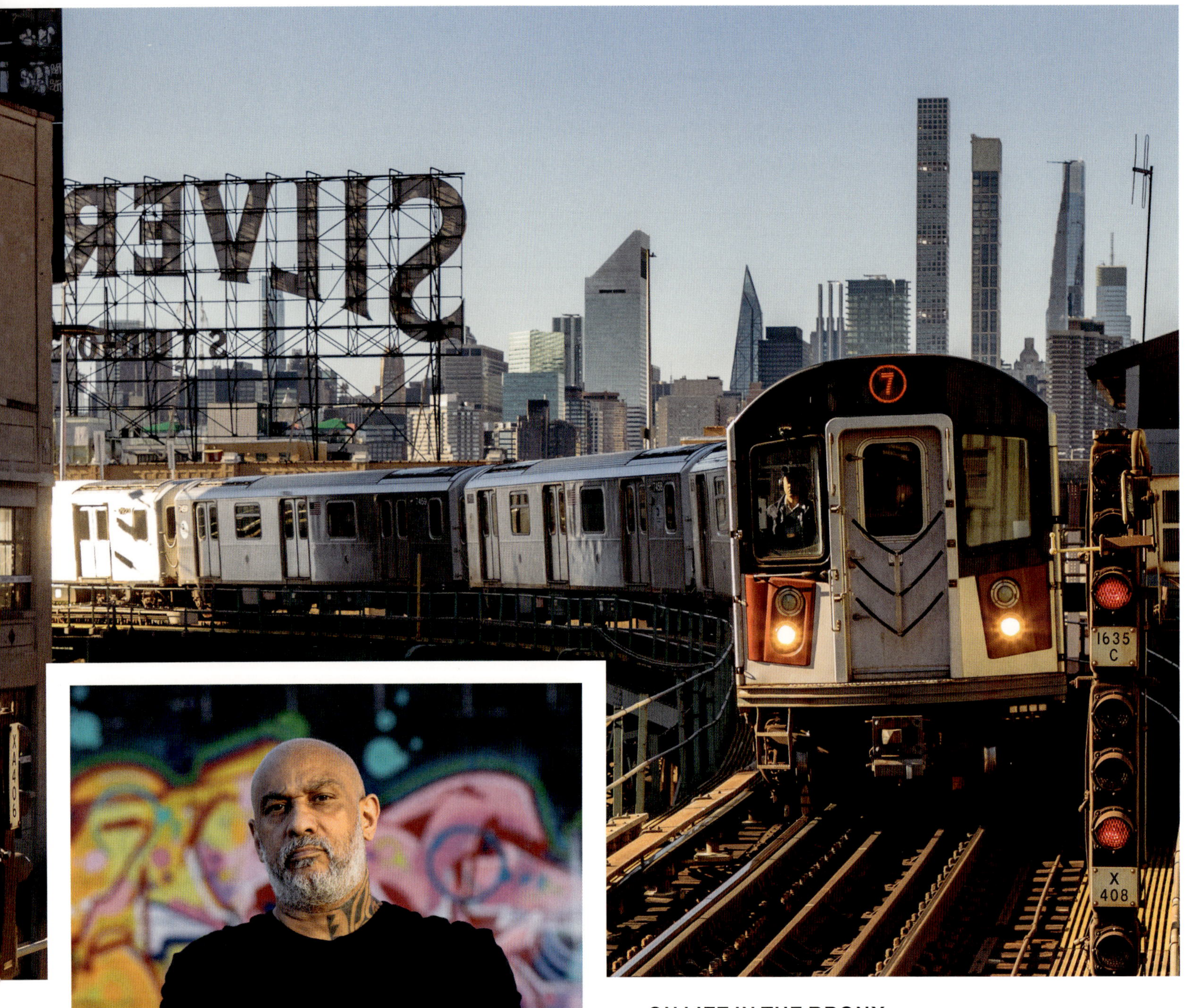

FERNANDO CARLO, JR | COPE2
GRAFFITI ARTIST
GRAFFITI-KÜNSTLER

The subway in New York has a bad reputation. The grid is completely outdated, it's loud, and there are no escalators. All the same, New Yorkers love it.

Der Ruf der New Yorker U-Bahn ist schlecht, das Netz völlig veraltet, sie ist laut und Rolltreppen sind Fehlanzeige. Dennoch, die New Yorker lieben sie.

...ON LIFE IN THE BRONX

"Oh, yeah. I grew up in tough times in the sense that when I had my son in 1985, I had to get an apartment, and me and my daughter, me and my son's mom, we got a furnished room, which is like you rent the room somewhere in the South Bronx town. I was working and selling crack at the same time to pay my bills. (...) And that's how hard it was, crazy, because back then, you had other drug dealers you had to deal with, they were jealous, probably wanted to shoot you or kill you, get you out of the neighborhood because you had some good stuff."

... ON PROJECTS FOR YOUNG PEOPLE

"There's a lot of projects, man. (...) I don't really get into it, but there are projects. There are always community things, always sports and stuff like that. But it's always hard, because it all depends on the person himself. And the kid himself, he wants to change. It's like some kids coming out of the ghetto in the hood, and they become big at basketball, boxing, nutrition. I meet some young kids. You could tell they're crazy, wild little kids. Like, 'Oh, I want to be like you. I want to travel the world and sell paintings.' And I'm like, 'Wow, that's really cool.' So, for me, I feel good that I've touched some young kid's heart, that he's looking up to me."

...ON HIS FAVORITE PLACES

"My favorite place in New York, man, honestly, when I have spare time, is a subway yard. That's like my therapy. If I can get in a subway yard and paint a train, that's my favorite place in New York. (...) But my favorite place really, in New York I like, it's like the city, the Soho area. I like to walk around in the summer, spring, fall, and eat. I really like the downtown Manhattan scene. (...) Sometimes I like to just take a train ride. I take a subway car ride, and I'll take maybe a train ride to Coney Island, go to Coney Island, and have some burgers and hot dogs like we used to do in the late 70s."

...ON GRAFFITI AND HIP HOP

"(...) I was about eleven years old, I started taking more subway cars with my mom, going to visit family members, and seeing the graffiti on the subway cars. The energy of the artwork on the subway cars was insane. So that kind of caught my attention, and it drew me in like a really strong force, like a magnet. (...) My mom's like, 'Oh, it's graffiti. You know, kids do it.' I was like, 'Can I do it?' She was like, 'No, you can't. You can't just do that, it's illegal.' (...) But graffiti still, it's even bigger now. I mean, you go around, it's just killed like walls, murals, throw ups. Everything is just Brooklyn, Queens. It's just bombed and a lot of burners in the street. So that's still saying a lot, if it's harder because you can't paint trains no more. Graffiti [today] is really not much different [than back then]."

...ÜBER DAS LEBEN IN DER BRONX

„Oh, ja. Ich bin in harten Zeiten aufgewachsen, denn als ich 1985 meinen Sohn bekam, musste ich mir eine Wohnung suchen, und meine Tochter, ich und die Mutter meines Sohnes, wir bekamen ein möbliertes Zimmer, das heißt, man mietet irgendwo in der South Bronx ein Zimmer. Ich habe gearbeitet und gleichzeitig Crack verkauft, um meine Rechnungen zu bezahlen. (...) Und es war hart, weil man damals mit anderen Drogendealern zu tun hatte, die eifersüchtig waren und dich vermutlich erschießen oder umbringen wollten, um dich aus der Nachbarschaft zu vertreiben, weil du etwas besseres Zeug hattest."

... ÜBER JUGENDPROJEKTE

„Man, es gibt eine Menge Projekte. (...) Ich bin da nicht wirklich drin, aber es gibt Projekte. Es gibt immer Gemeinschaftssachen, immer Sport und solche Sachen. Aber es ist immer schwierig, weil das alles von der Person selbst abhängt und ob das Kind sich selbst ändern will. Es ist wie bei einigen Kindern, die aus dem Ghetto kommen und bekannt werden im Basketball, im Boxen, bei der Ernährung. Ich treffe einige junge Kinder. Man sieht ihnen an, dass sie verrückt sind, wilde kleine Kinder, die denken: „Oh, ich will so sein wie du. Ich will um die Welt reisen und Bilder verkaufen." Und ich denke: „Wow, das ist wirklich cool. Für mich ist es ein gutes Gefühl, dass ich das Herz eines jungen Kindes in dem Sinne berührt habe, dass es zu mir aufschaut."

...ÜBER LIEBLINGSORTE

„Mein Lieblingsort in New York, ehrlich, wenn ich Zeit habe, ist es ein U-Bahnhof. Das ist wie eine Therapie für mich. Wenn ich in einen U-Bahnhof gehen und einen Zug bemalen kann, dann ist das mein Lieblingsort in New York. (...) Aber mein Lieblingsort in New York ist die Stadt, die Gegend um Soho. Ich spaziere gerne im Sommer, im Frühling, im Herbst herum und esse. Ich mag die Szene in Downtown Manhattan sehr. (...) Manchmal fahre ich einfach mit dem Zug. Ich fahre mit der U-Bahn und vielleicht auch mit dem Zug nach Coney Island, um dort Burger und Hot Dogs zu essen, so wie wir es in den späten 70ern gemacht haben."

...ÜBER GRAFFITI UND HIP-HOP

„(...) Ich war ungefähr elf Jahre alt, als ich anfing, mit meiner Mutter mehr U-Bahn zu fahren, um Familienmitglieder zu besuchen, und die Graffiti auf den U-Bahn-Waggons sah. Die Energie der Kunstwerke war wahnsinnig. Das erregte meine Aufmerksamkeit und zog mich mit einer wirklich starken Kraft an, wie ein Magnet. (...) Meine Mutter sagte: ‚Oh, das ist Graffiti. Weißt du, Kinder machen das.' Ich fragte: ‚Kann ich das auch?' Sie sagte: ‚Nein, das kannst du nicht. Das kannst du nicht machen, das ist illegal.' (...) Die Anfänge des Hip-Hops liegen hier in New York. (...) Aber Graffiti ist jetzt sogar noch größer. Ich meine, wenn man herumfährt, das ist heftig: Wände, Wandmalereien, *Throw-ups*. Alles ist wie in Brooklyn, Queens, es ist alles zerbombt und es gibt eine Menge Waffen auf der Straße. Das ist immer noch ziemlich viel, wenn man bedenkt, dass es schwieriger geworden ist, weil man keine Züge mehr bemalen kann. Also Graffiti ist (heutzutage) wirklich kein Unterschied (zu damals)."

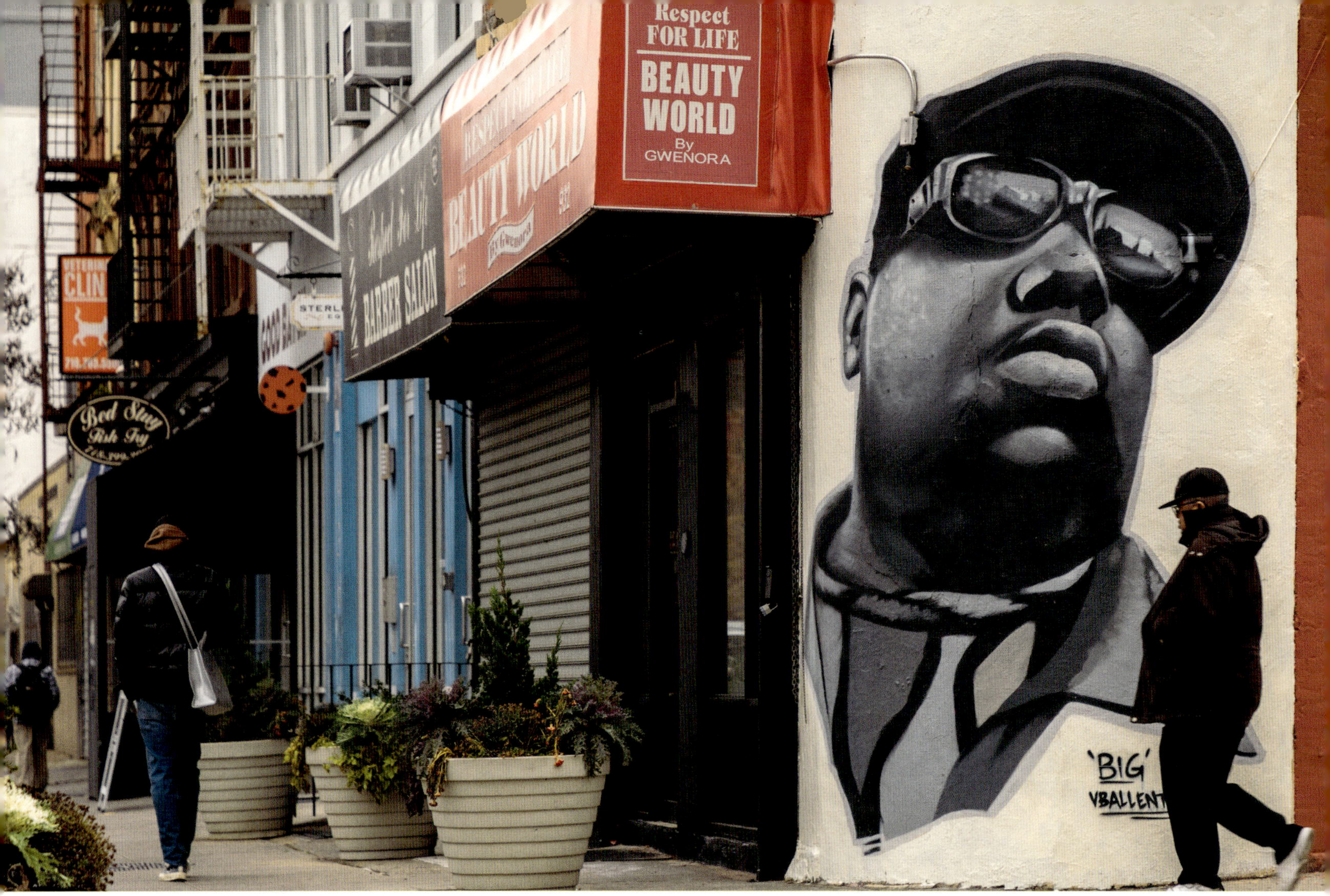

Respect
FOR LIFE
BEAUTY
WORLD
By
GWENORA
BEAUTY WORLD
BARBER SALON
VETERIN
CLIN
Bed Stuy
Fish Fry
'BIG'
VBALLENT

NY

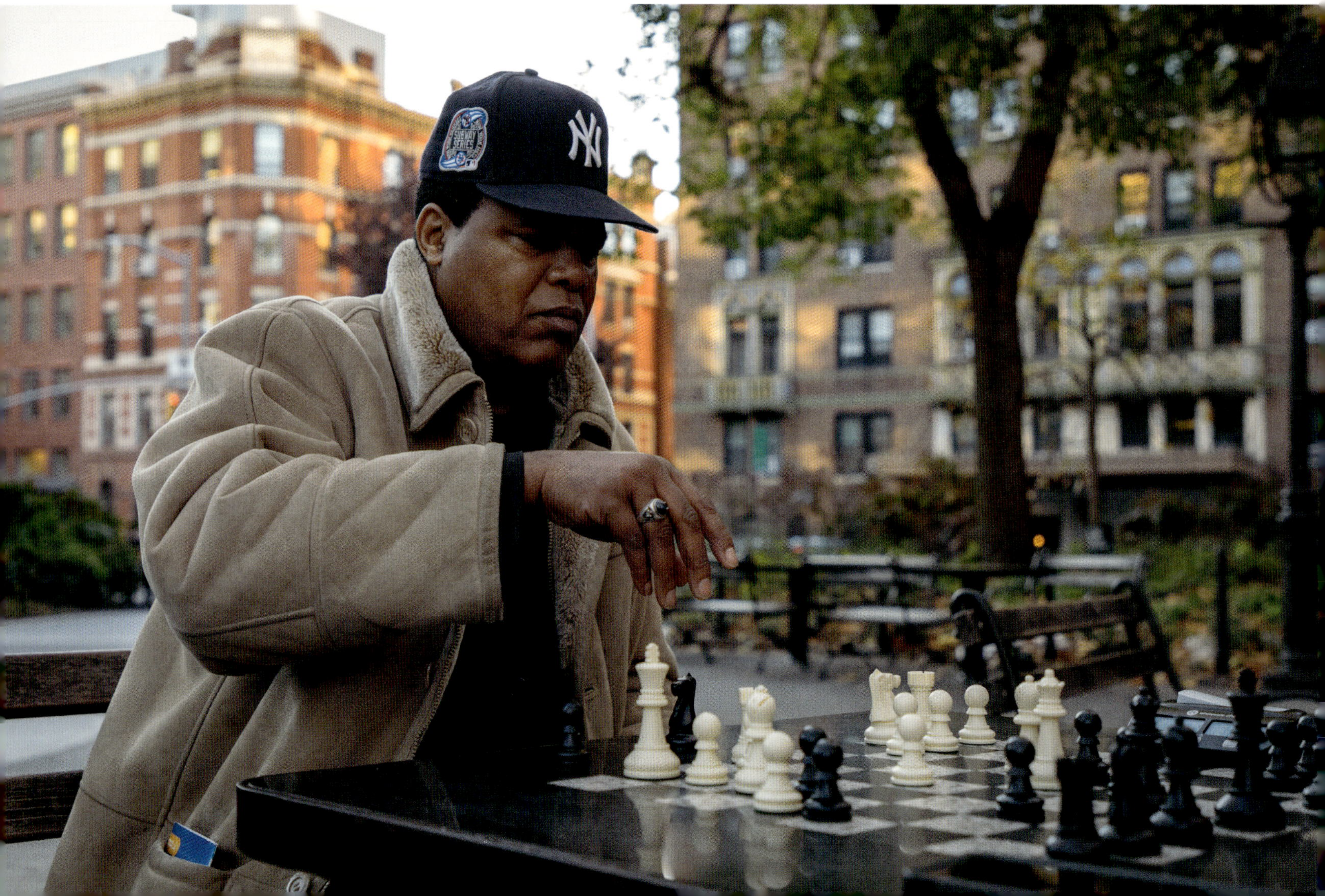

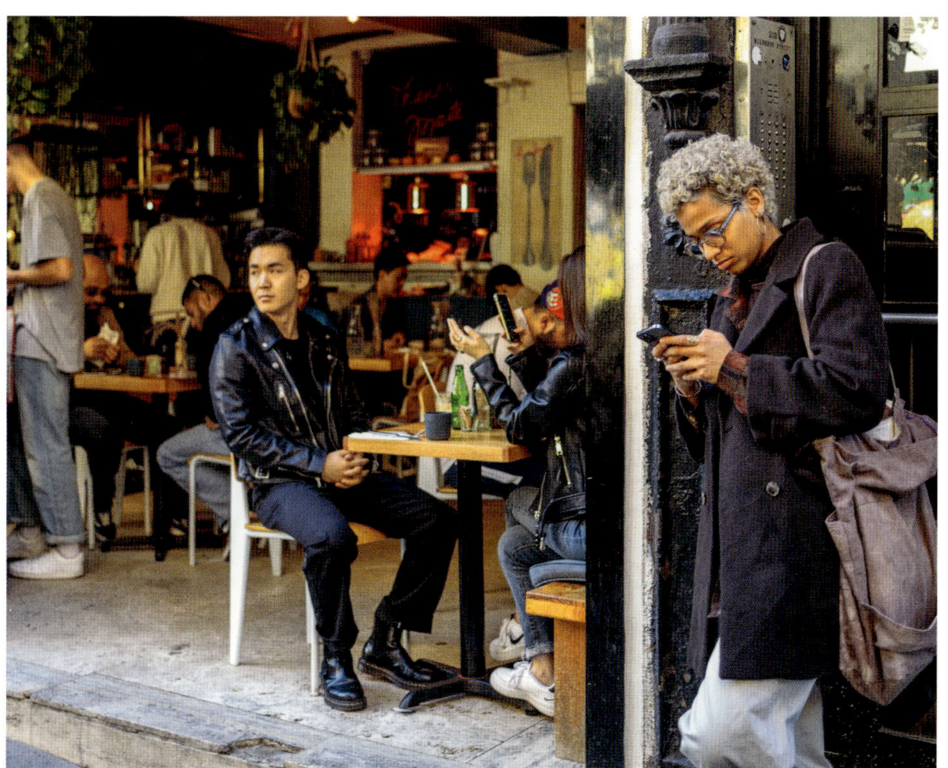

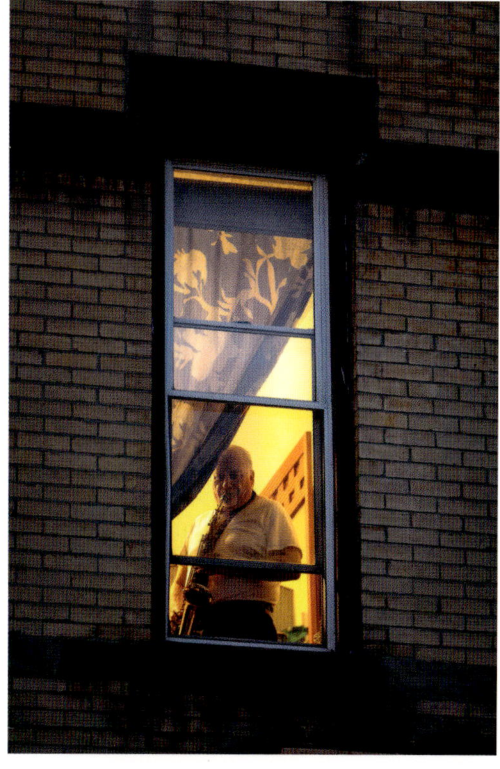

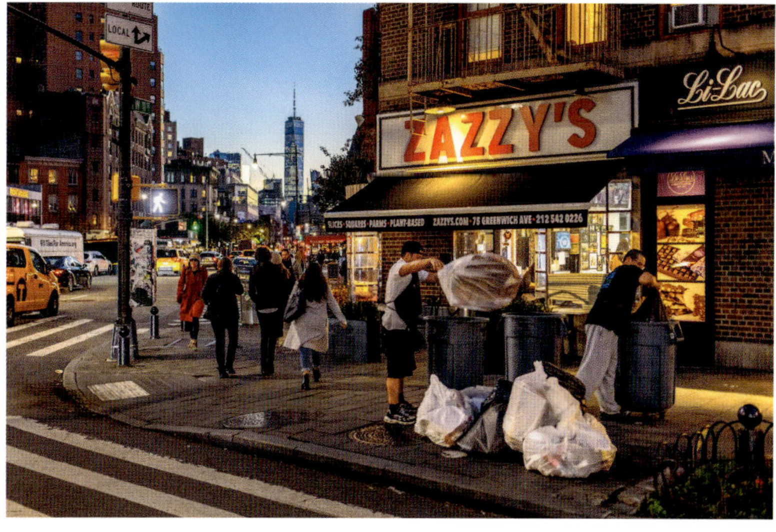

„Manchmal ist es also ziemlich cool,
wenn man ein schönes buntes Stück an
die Wand malen kann. Die Leute in der
Nachbarschaft mögen es, im Gegensatz
zu anderen Spots, wo man nur härteres
Graffiti sieht, das die Gegend kaputt
aussehen lässt."
(Fernando Carlo, Jr | Cope2)

People may be rushed in the Financial District,
but otherwise New Yorkers like to
appear relaxed.

Gehetzt wird vielleicht im Financial District,
ansonsten geben sich die New Yorker
gerne entspannt.

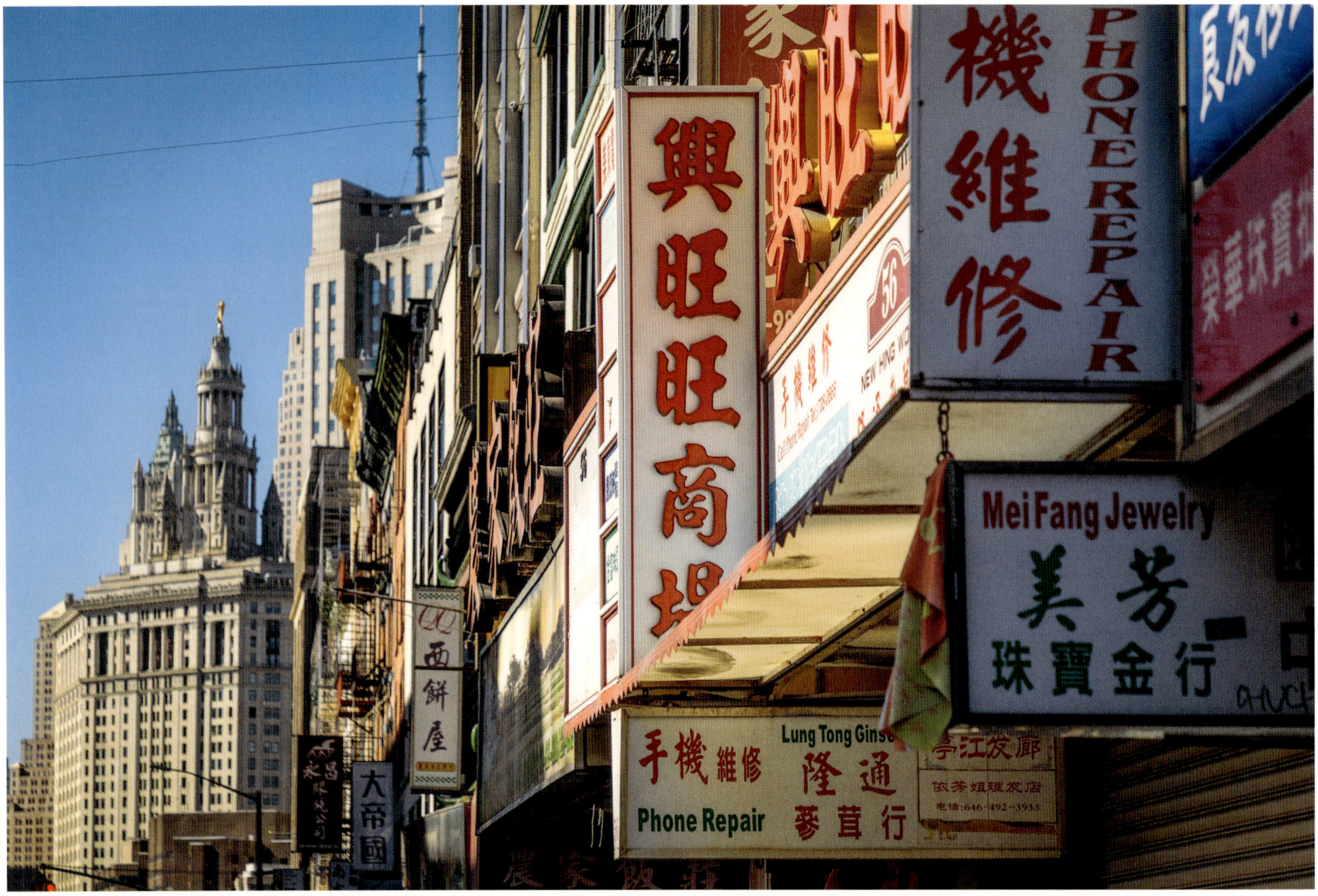

興旺商場
機維修
PHONE REPAIR
機維修
Mei Fang Jewelry
美 芳
珠寶金行
手機維修
Phone Repair
Lung Tong Ginseng
隆 通
蔘茸行
大帝國
西餅屋

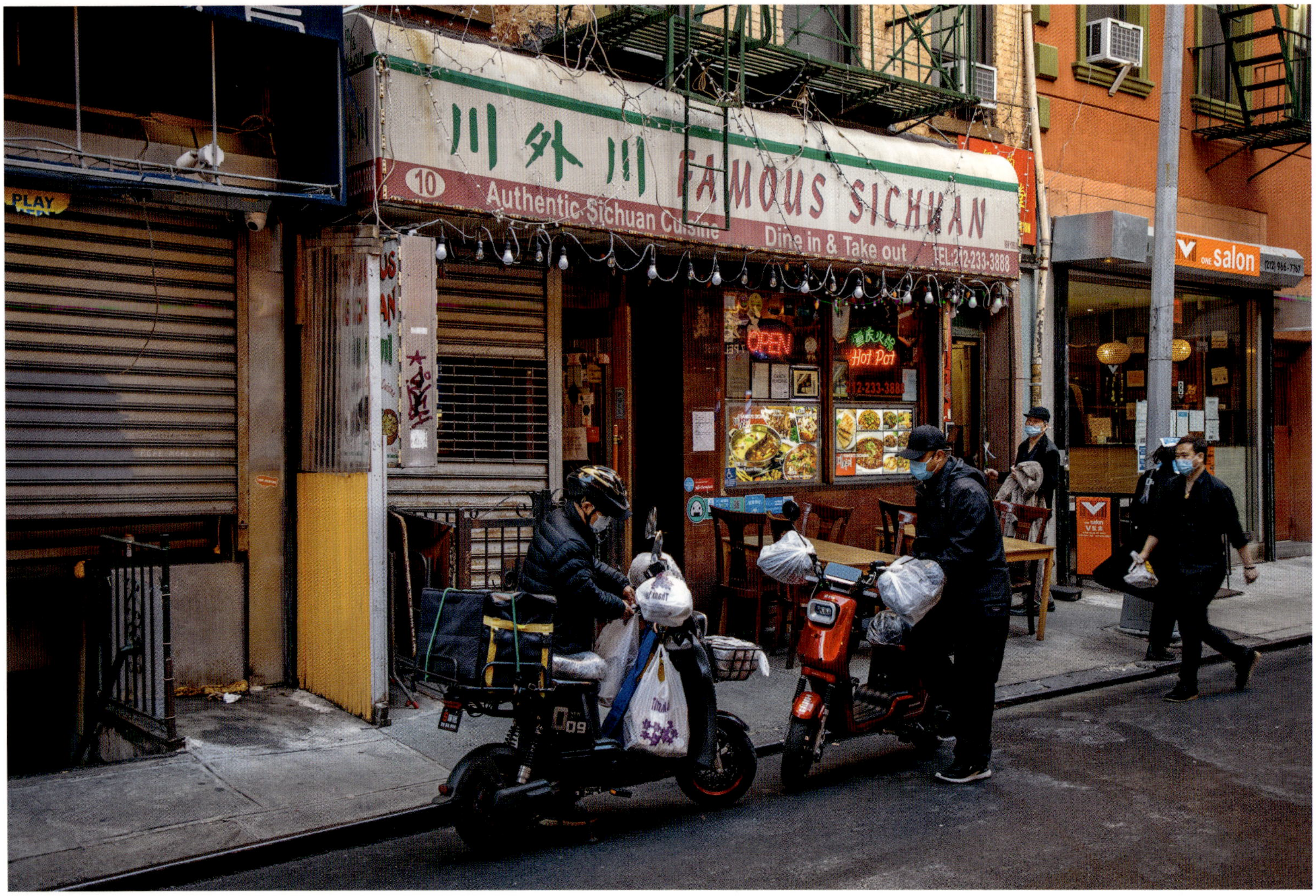

川外川 FAMOUS SICHUAN
10 Authentic Sichuan Cuisine
Dine in & Take out TEL 212-233-3888
OPEN
Hot Pot
PLAY
Salon

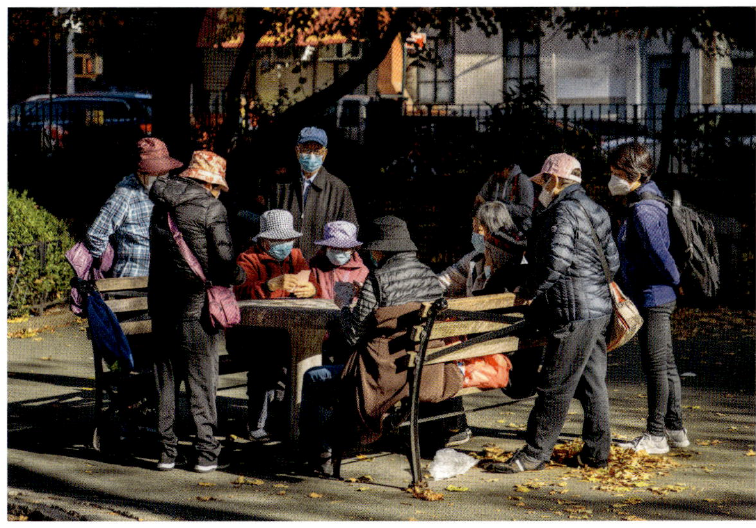

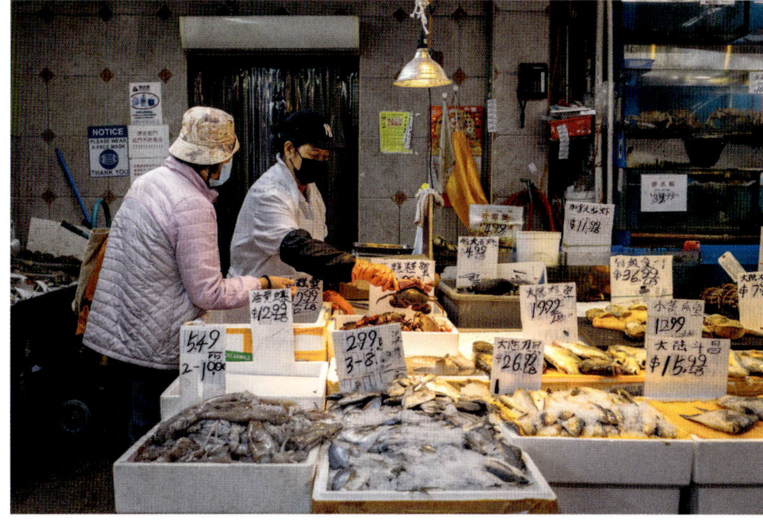

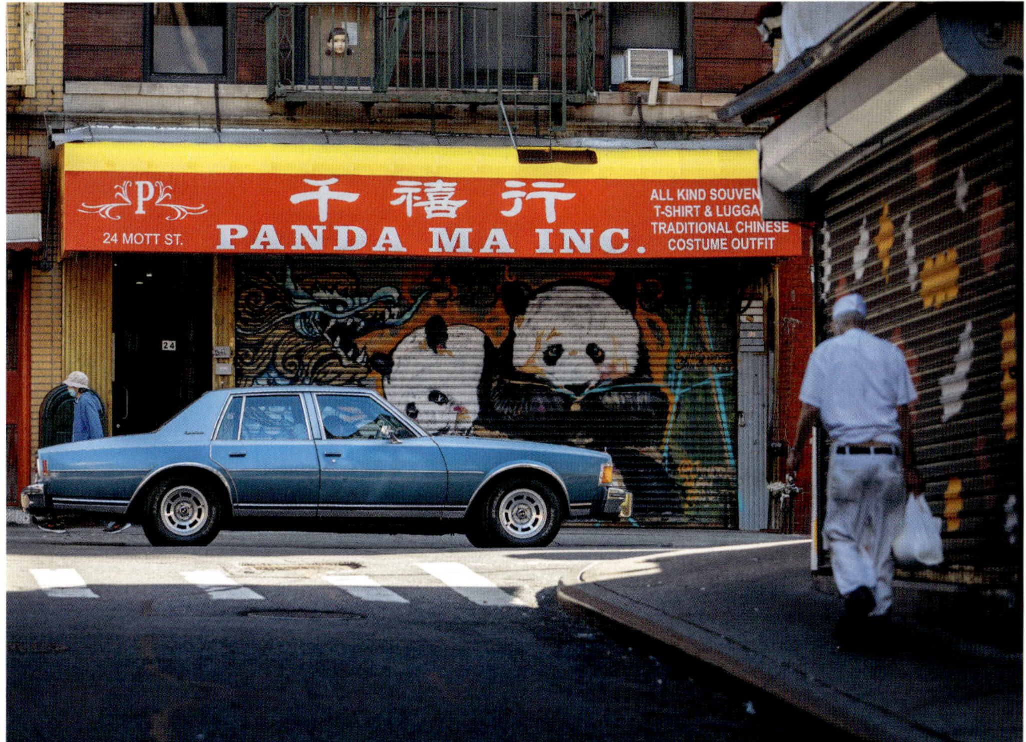

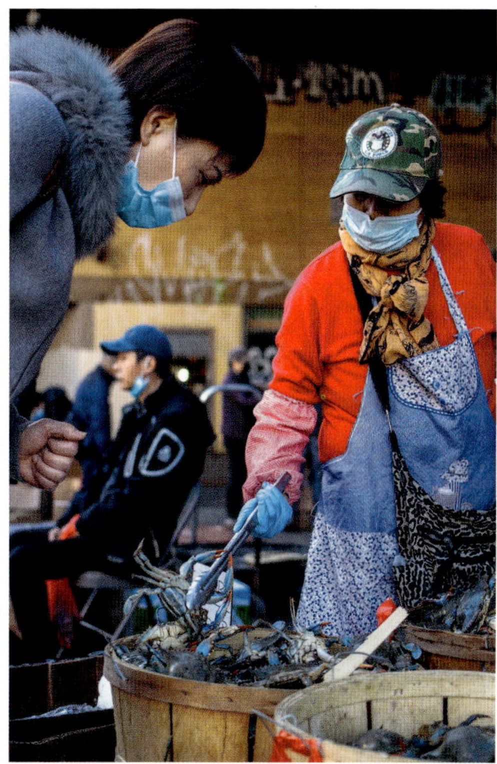

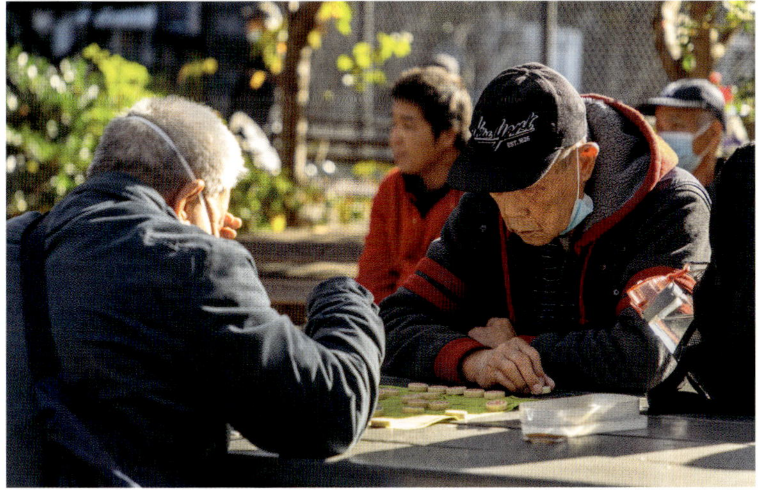

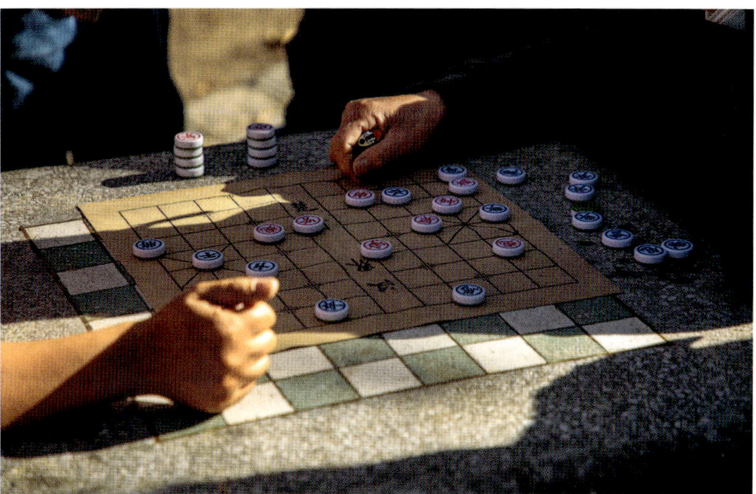

欢迎在中国城 Don't know what it says? Welcome to New York's Chinatown. Typical New York on the outside, but the Middle Kingdom on the inside.

欢迎在中国城 Keine Peilung, was da steht? Dann willkommen in New Yorks Chinatown. Außen typisch New York, aber innen ganz das Reich der Mitte.

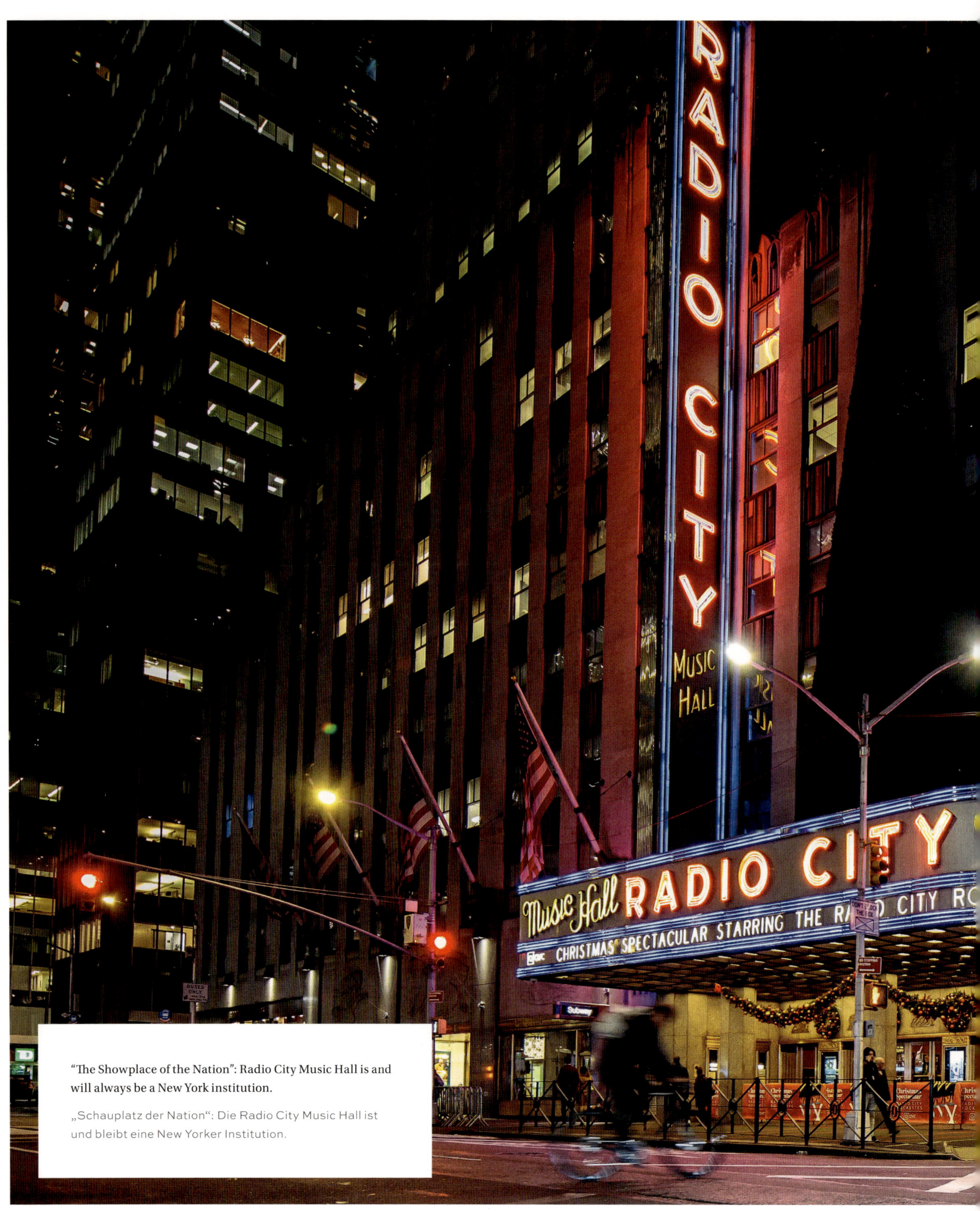

"The Showplace of the Nation": Radio City Music Hall is and will always be a New York institution.

„Schauplatz der Nation": Die Radio City Music Hall ist und bleibt eine New Yorker Institution.

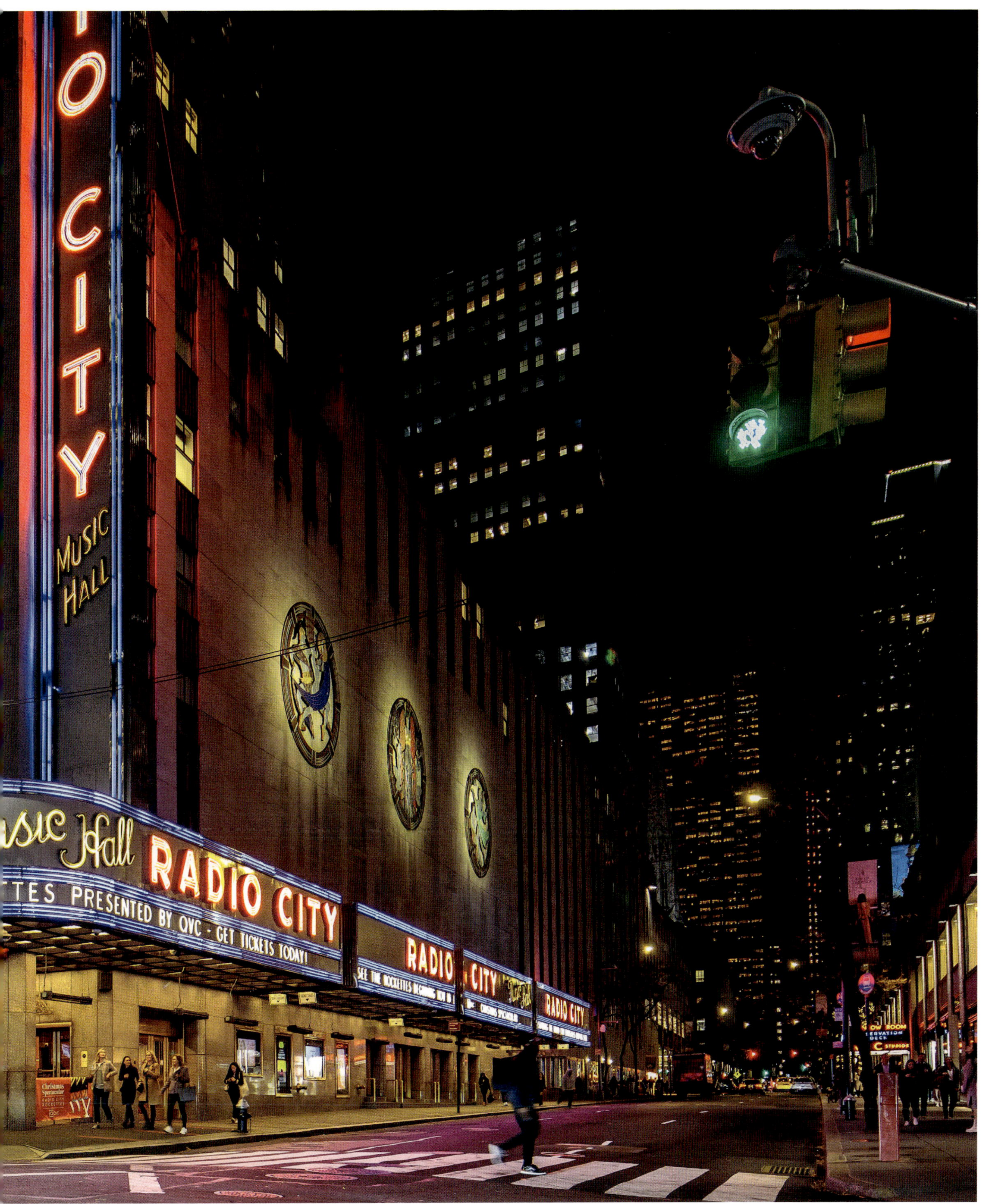
RADIO CITY
MUSIC HALL
MUSIC HALL RADIO CITY
PRESENTED BY QVC · GET TICKETS TODAY!
RADIO CITY
RADIO CITY

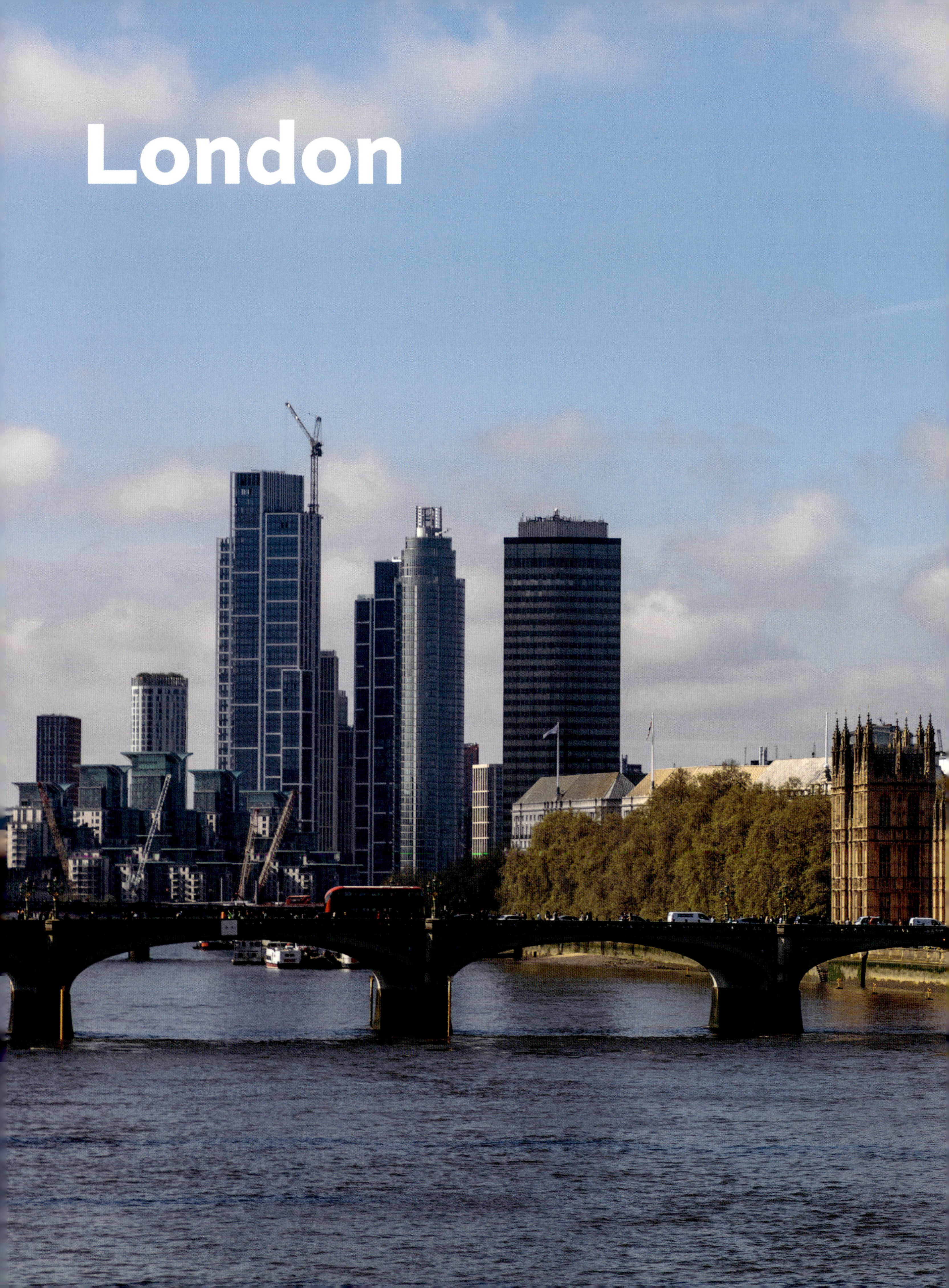
London

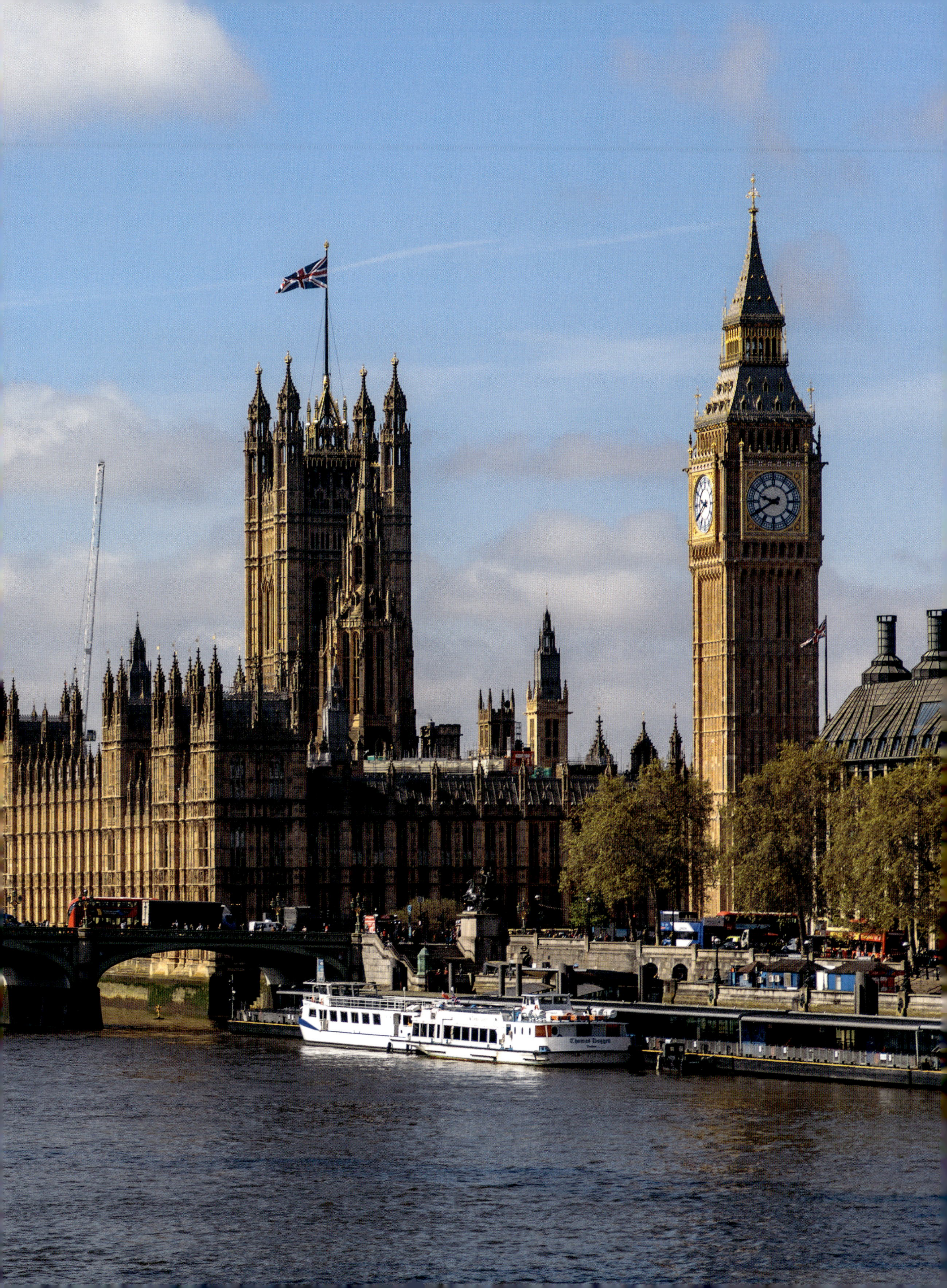

The Heart of the World

Das Herz der Welt

"London has, for its entire history, been built on successive waves of immigration. There was really very little or nothing here before the Romans came. And then on top of that, we have had the Anglo Saxons and the Danes and the Normans and et cetera, et cetera, et cetera, for hundreds of years." (Tom Hall)

London calling! Or did London hang up? The shock of Brexit still runs deep. But Londoners wouldn't be Londoners if they just gave up now. After all, their city was the world's first megacity: huge, innovative, bursting with energy, and multicultural before the word was even invented. And London was already international at the time of its founding under Claudius, ruler of the mighty Roman Empire. But it was not until Great Britain had built up its own empire based on the Roman model, with many different peoples, languages, and religions, and the embodiment of the idea of an *imperium sine fine*, an empire without end, that the combination of global trade and the Industrial Revolution contributed to London's rise as the world's first and, by 1925, largest megacity.

"When it became possible for people to live outside the immediate center of London and come in, that was when, in the 19th century, the population exploded all through that century, when London was really at the heart of the British Empire (…)." (Tom Hall)

Starting in the mid-19th century, more and more people from around the world flocked to the city in search of work, happiness, and wealth. In just a few decades, the population of 2.5 million grew to 6.7 million people in 1900. London was growing at an increasingly unchecked rate. Poverty, homelessness, pollution, epidemics, and crime came along with this expansion. Various waves of immigration had already occurred earlier, including Huguenots from France and Jews who settled in the East End, an area that had been the gateway for refugees and immigrants, first from Europe and later from other parts of the world, to the metropolis since the early modern era. After them came immigrants from the Caribbean, who settled in Brixton in South London, and then above all from South Asia, where they now characterize the streetscape in Whitechapel, Shoreditch, and the surrounding area.

„London ist in seiner gesamten Geschichte auf einander folgenden Einwanderungswellen aufgebaut worden. Bevor die Römer kamen, gab es hier nur sehr wenig oder gar nichts. Und dann kamen die Angelsachsen, die Dänen, die Normannen und so weiter und so fort, und dass seit Hunderten von Jahren." (Tom Hall)

London calling! Oder hat London aufgelegt? Zumindest sitzt der Schock des Brexits noch immer tief. Doch die Londoner wären keine Londoner, gäben sie jetzt einfach auf. Schließlich war ihre Stadt die erste Megacity weltweit: gigantisch, innovativ, voller Energie und multikulti, bevor es das Wort überhaupt gab. Und international war London bereits Zeit seiner Gründung unter Claudius, dem Herrscher über das gewaltige Imperium Romanum. Doch erst als Großbritannien nach dem Muster der Römer ein eigenes Empire mit vielen unterschiedlichen Völkern, Sprachen und Religionen und einer Verkörperung der Idee eines *imperium sine fine*, eines „grenzenlosen Reiches", aufgebaut hatte, boosterte der weltweite Handel im Verbund mit der industriellen Revolution die Entwicklung Londons zur ersten und bis 1925 größten Megacity der Welt.

„Als es den Menschen möglich wurde, außerhalb des unmittelbaren Zentrums zu leben und zum Arbeiten nach London hineinzufahren, explodierte die Bevölkerung im 19. Jahrhundert. Zu jener Zeit war London mit so vielen Menschen wirklich das Herz des British Empire (…)." (Tom Hall)

In downtown London, Georgian, Victorian, and Edwardian buildings are struggling to keep from disappearing, yet at the time they were also an expression of London becoming a cosmopolitan city, as they too replaced the old.

In der City kämpfen georgianische, viktorianische und edwardische Bauwerke gegen ihr Verschwinden und waren doch ihrerzeit auch Ausdruck der Entwicklung Londons zur Weltstadt, indem auch sie Altes verdrängten.

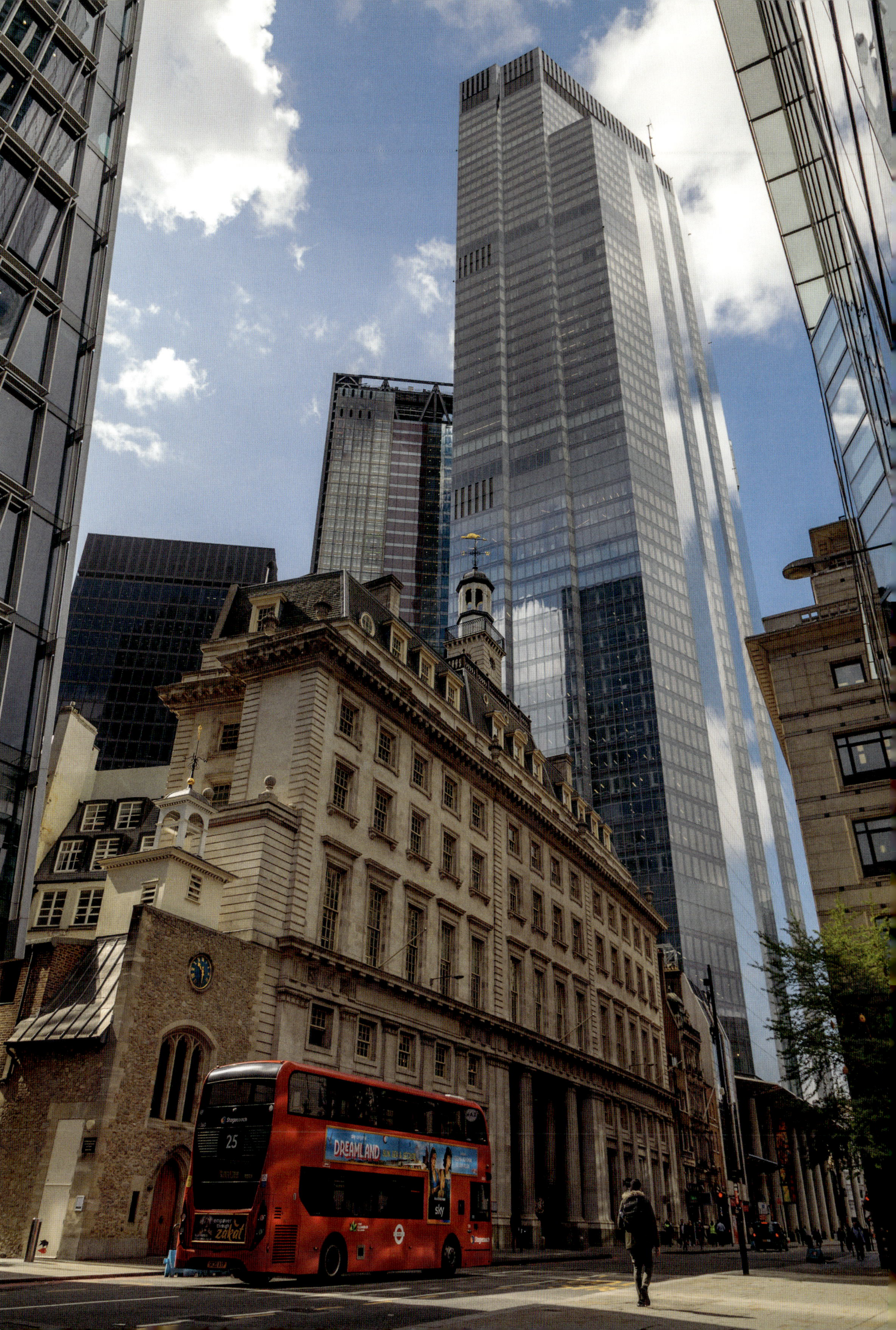

And then the unthinkable happened: On December 31, 2020, the United Kingdom closed its doors. Immigration is no longer welcome. Will the city now sink to a provincial level? Hardly. For over 2,000 years, London has always found a way out of crises: Brexit? There's no sign of it in Bishopsgate, the dynamic heart of the city, that indefinable element that makes world cities what they are: tirelessly hustling, innovative, full of drive, trendsetters, and everything that makes a true metropolis. In the skyscrapers of this district, people are working non-stop to reinvent the city.

The people of London have, after all, always taken unusual paths. A trip to the Barbican is enough to show that. The English invented their own term for what you see here: Brutalist Architecture. 2,000 apartments are housed in this monstrosity, which looks forbidding and inaccessible as though it were a gigantic defensive fortress. Built between 1965 and 1976, it is nevertheless, or perhaps precisely because of this, an expression of the power that keeps London running.

Ab Mitte des 19. Jahrhunderts strömten immer mehr Menschen aus aller Welt auf der Suche nach Arbeit, Glück und Reichtum in die Stadt. In nur wenigen Jahrzehnten wuchs die Einwohnerzahl von 2,5 Millionen auf 6,7 Millionen Menschen im Jahr 1900. London begann, sich immer unkontrollierter auszudehnen. Armut, Obdachlosigkeit, Umweltverschmutzung, Epidemien und Kriminalität waren die Begleiterscheinungen dieser Entwicklung. Schon früher hatte es verschiedene Einwanderungswellen gegeben, beispielsweise von Hugenotten aus Frankreich oder Juden, die sich in East End niederließen, das schon seit der frühen Neuzeit das Einfallstor für Flüchtlinge und Migranten, zunächst aus Europa, später aus der ganzen Welt in die Metropole war. Ihnen folgten Einwanderer aus der Karibik, die sich in Brixton im Süden Londons niederließen, und dann vor allem aus Südasien, wo sie heute das Straßenbild in Whitechapel, Shoreditch und Umgebung beherrschen.

Doch dann geschah das Unfassbare: Am 31.12.2020 schloss Großbritannien die Tür. Einwanderung ist nicht mehr erwünscht. Wird die Stadt nun auf Provinzniveau sinken? Wohl kaum. Über 2000 Jahre lang hat London immer wieder einen Weg aus Krisen gefunden: Brexit? In Bishopsgate ist davon nichts zu spüren. Hier befindet sich das Energiezentrum der Stadt, jenes undefinierbare Element, das Weltstädte ausmacht: unermüdlich am Schlagen, innovativ, voller Tatendrang, Trendsetter und allem, was eine echte Metropole ausmacht. In den Wolkenkratzern dieses Viertels wird ohne Unterlass an einer Neuerfindung der Stadt getüftelt.

Die Londoner sind schließlich schon immer ungewöhnliche Wege gegangen. Man braucht nur einmal nach Barbican zu fahren. Die Engländer haben für das, was man hier sieht, einen eigenen Begriff erfunden: Brutalist Architecture. 2 000 Wohnungen sind in dem Monstrum, das wie eine gigantische Wagenburg abweisend und unzugänglich wirkt, untergebracht. Zwischen 1965 und 1976 erbaut, ist es dennoch oder gerade deshalb Ausdruck von der Kraft, die London am Laufen hält.

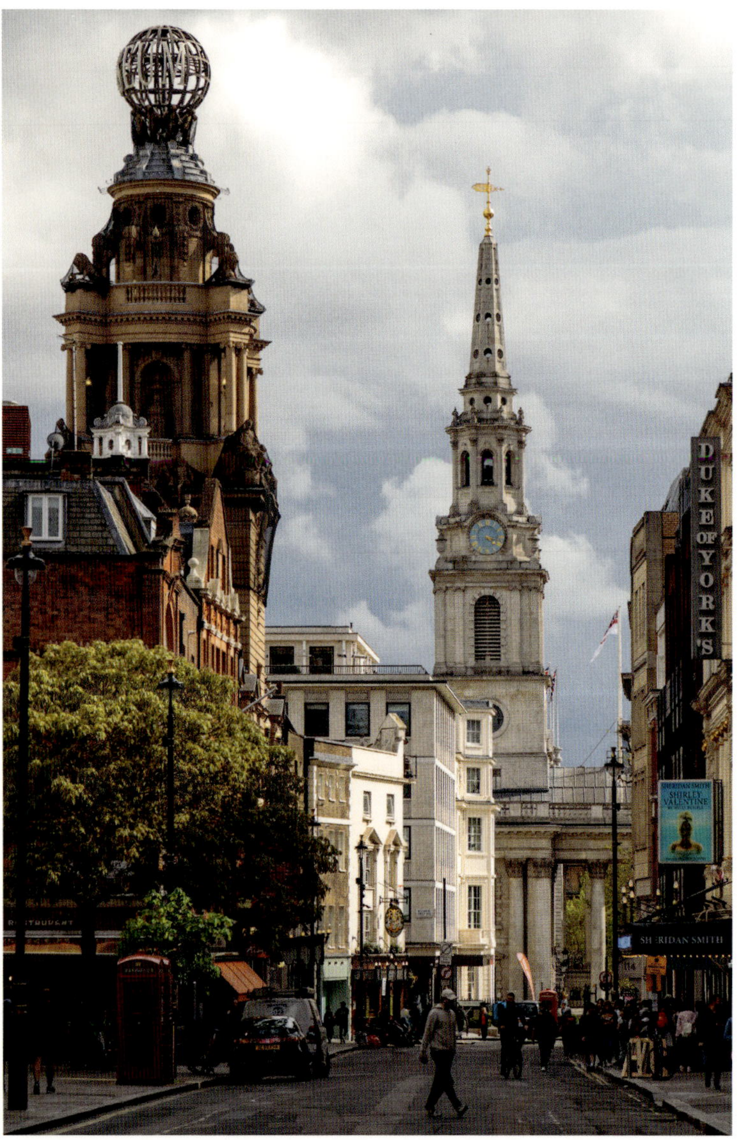

Once criticized for being too modern, then often imitated, the Church of St. Martin-in-the-Fields also stands for London's innovativeness.

Oft nachgeahmt, einst als zu modern kritisiert, steht auch die Kirche St.-Martin-in-the-Fields für die Innovationskraft Londons.

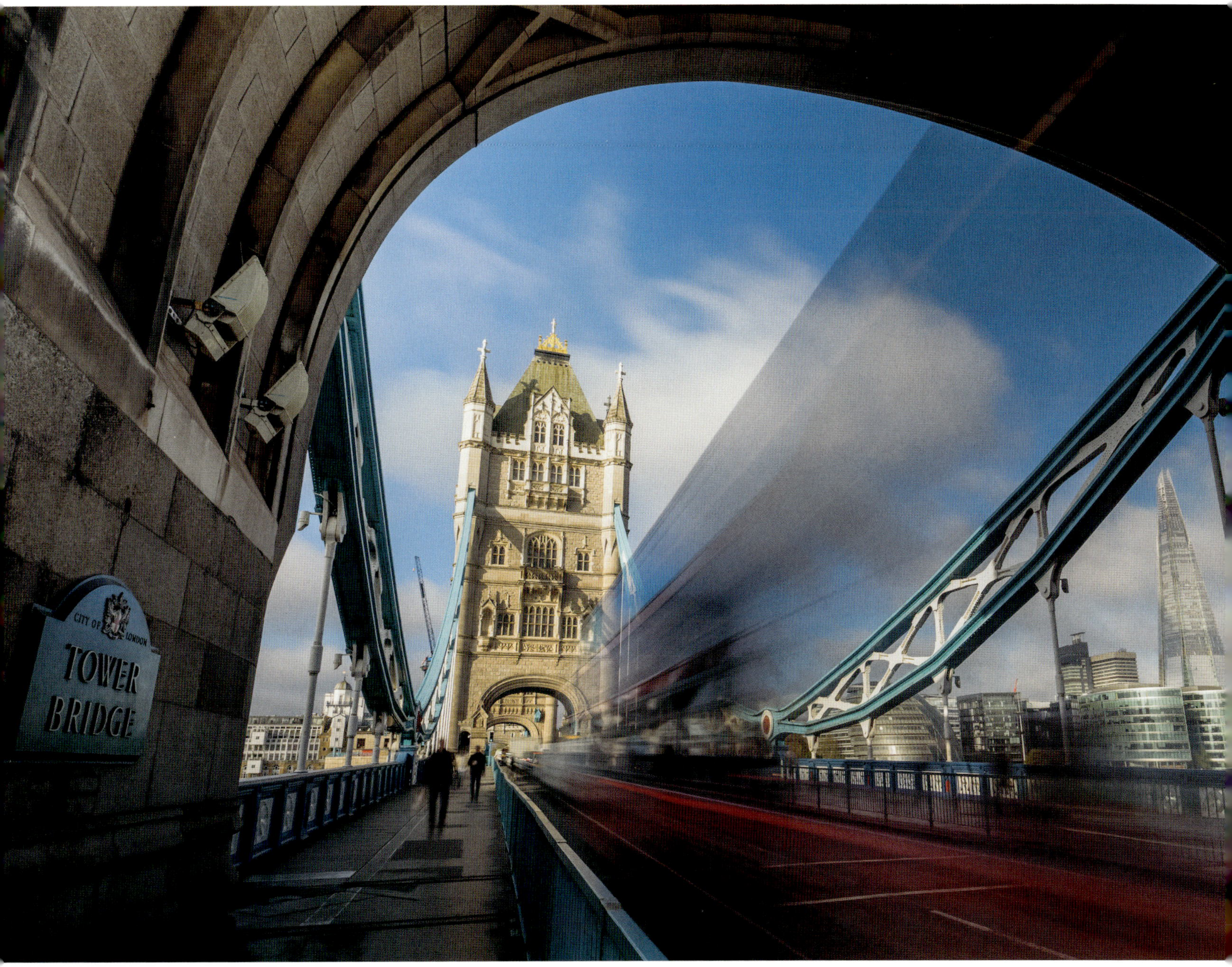

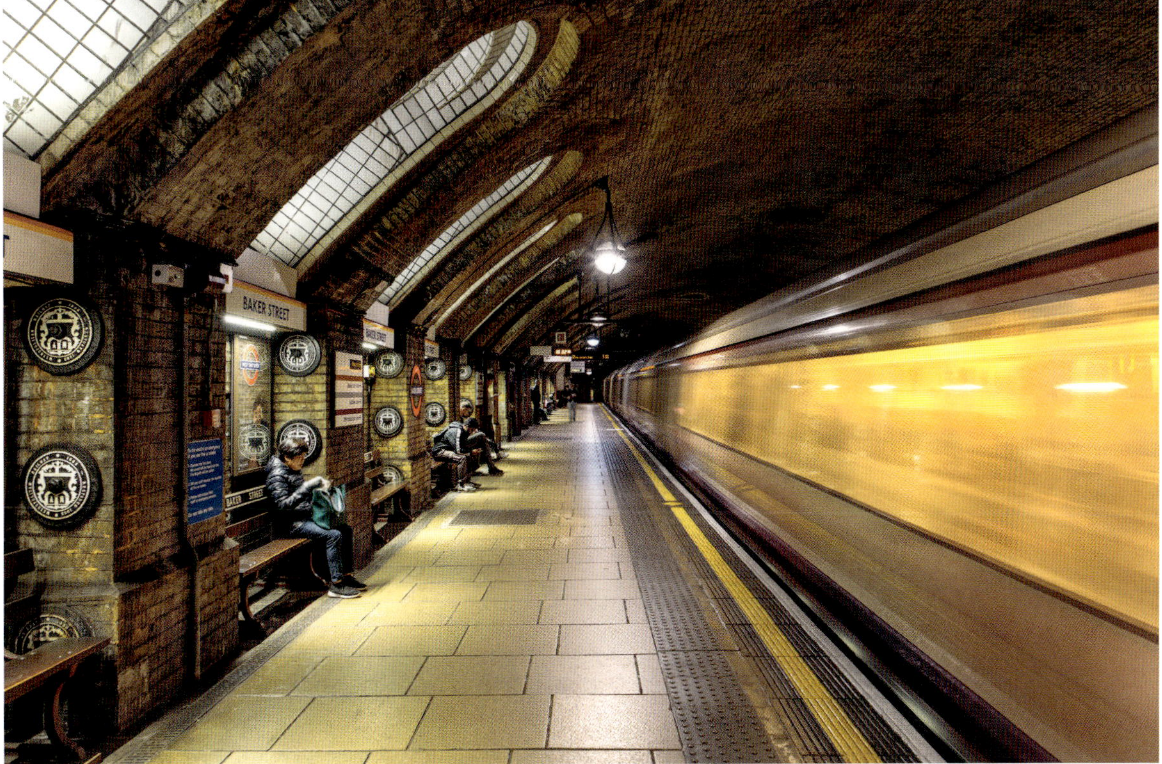

Sherlock Holmes never lived here, yet Baker Street Underground Station, along with the venerable Tower Bridge, represents that nostalgic London feeling.

Sherlock Holmes hat hier nie gewohnt, dennoch stehen der U-Bahnhof Baker Street, aber auch die altehrwürdige Tower Bridge für nostalgisches London Feeling.

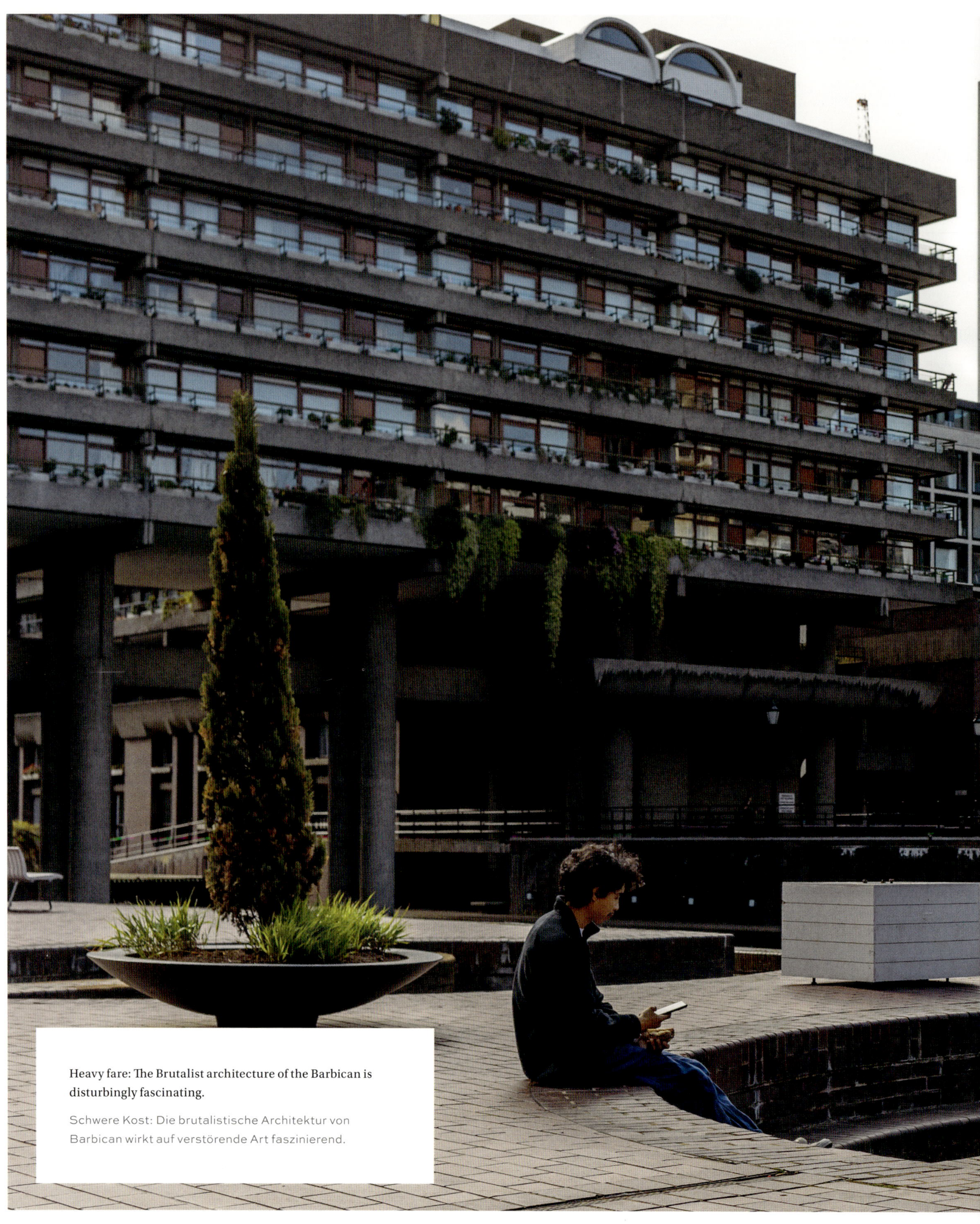

Heavy fare: The Brutalist architecture of the Barbican is disturbingly fascinating.

Schwere Kost: Die brutalistische Architektur von Barbican wirkt auf verstörende Art faszinierend.

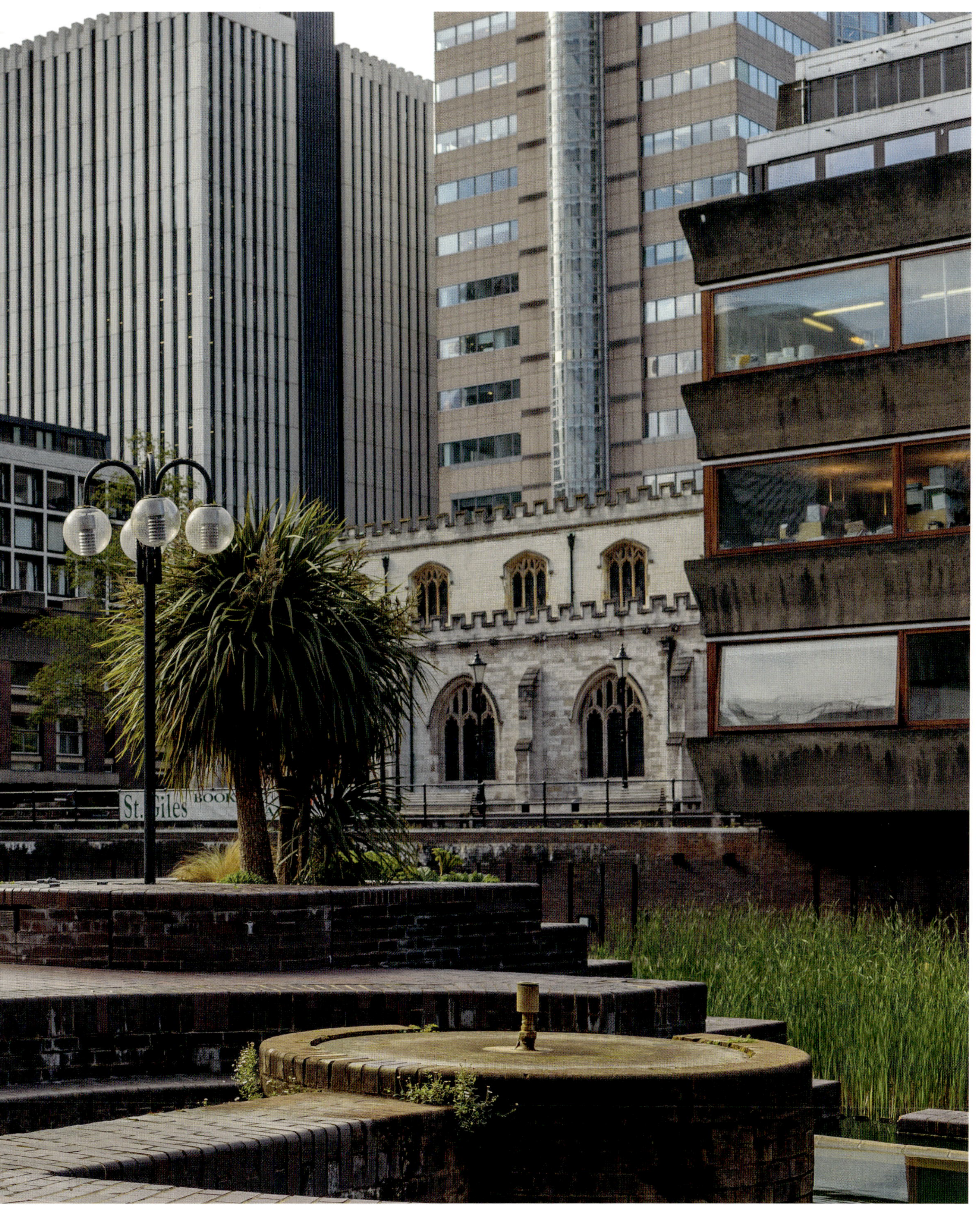

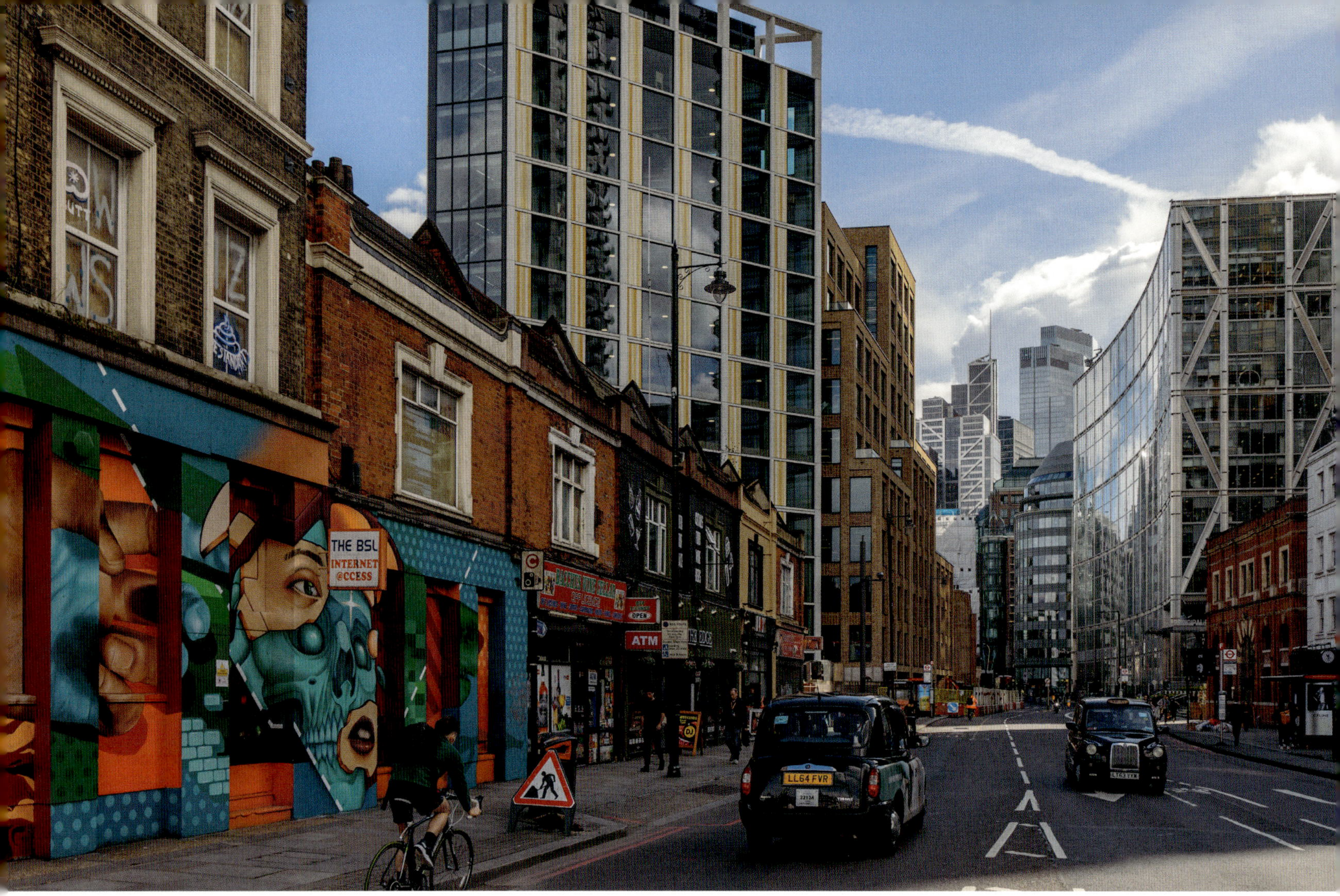

THE BSL
INTERNET
@CCESS
OPEN
ATM
LL64 FVR

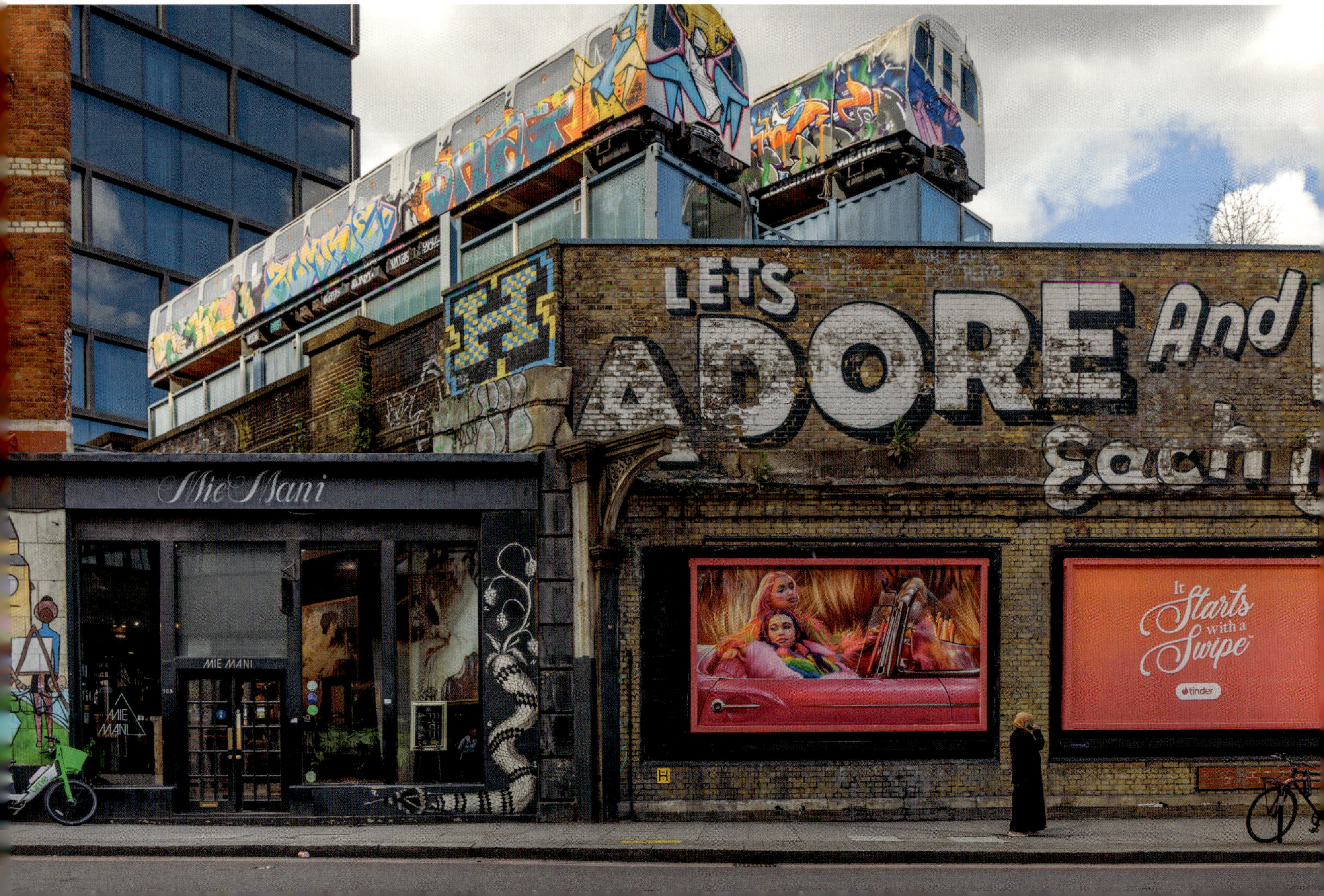

Mie Mani
MIE MANI
LETS
ADORE And
Each
It
Starts
with a
Swipe
tinder

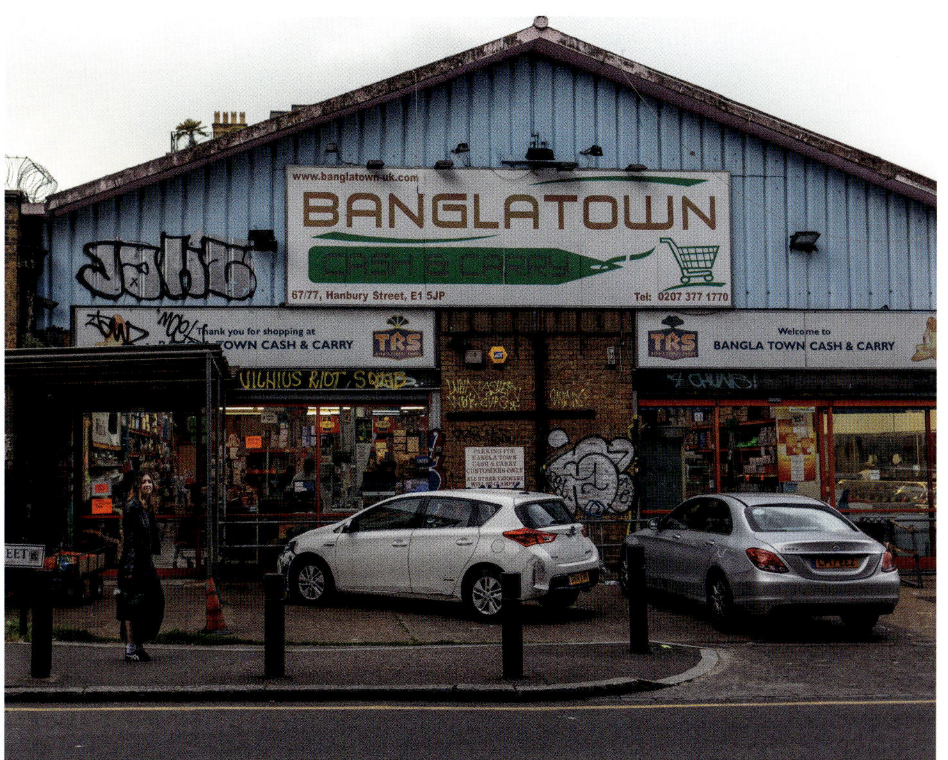

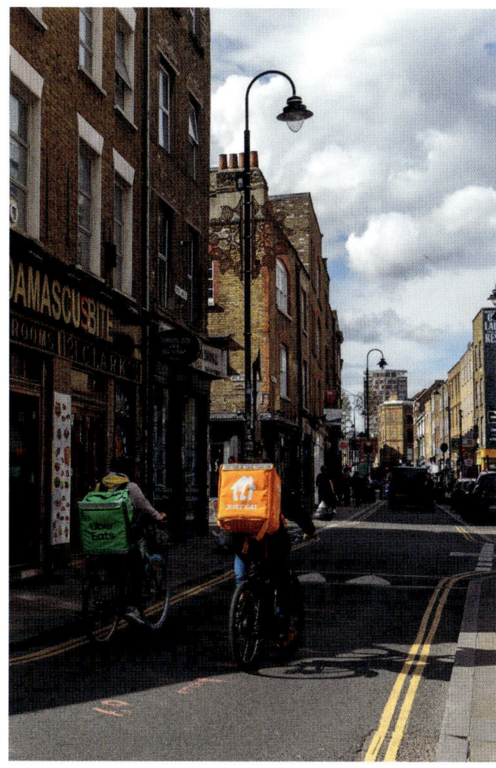

„Wenn man (...) in Shoreditch (...) wohnt, findet man eine große Anzahl von Menschen mit sehr unterschiedlichem Hintergrund. (...) Menschen, die (...) sich gerne in Gegenden aufhalten, in denen etwas los ist und das Gefühl besteht, dass etwas anders ist." (Tom Hall)

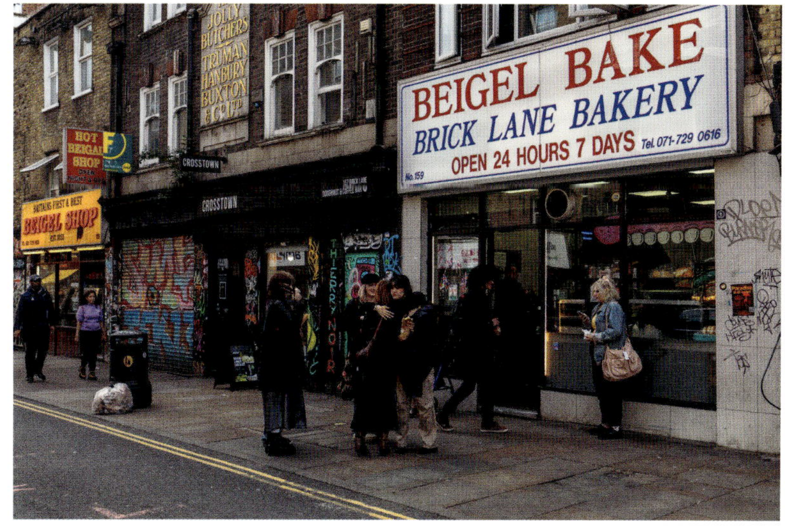

Where is London cool? That's easy to answer: In the East End in the boroughs of Shoreditch (left) and Tower Hamlets (right).

Wo ist London cool? Die Antwort fällt leicht: In East End in den Stadtbezirken Shoreditch (li.) und Tower Hamlets (re.).

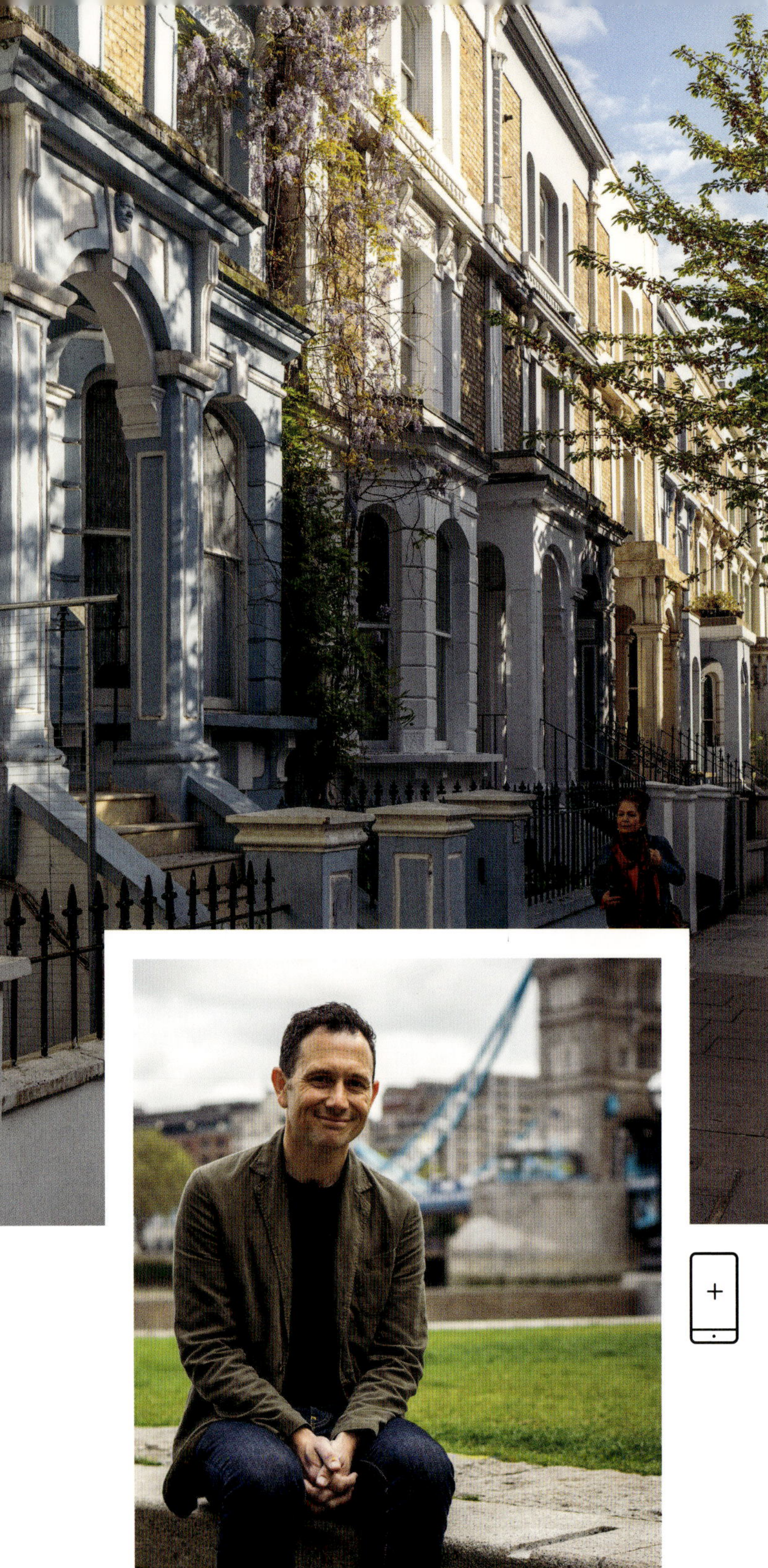

TOM HALL

AUTHOR, EDITOR, AND HISTORIAN
AUTOR, REDAKTEUR UND HISTORIKER

Trendy and rich in flair: But in districts like Notting Hill,
only those who are able to afford it actually live there.

Trendig und voller Flair: Doch in Bezirken wie Notting Hill
wohnt nur, wer es auch bezahlen kann.

…ON IMMIGRATION

"I think any megacity has a very strong multicultural element to
it, or at least an international element to it, an outward-looking
element to it. And London has been doing that for a really long
time. In fact, some of the things that you can see in London now
… we have a mayor who has a Pakistani background. We have a
prime minister who causes a huge amount of our discussions
about the identity of London, I think, this surrounds how we
continue to … particularly as gentrification occurs, as there's
pressure on housing, there's competition for jobs, and where we
go with all of that. But the good news, I think, about jobs missing
is that this is what London is. We are a city, as I said, built on successive waste immigration. We're very used to it. It's part of our
DNA (…)."

…ON BREXIT

"(…) Brexit will have and is already having an impact on the
identity of London. The immediate impact is a lack of certain-
ty, I think, about the identity of the city. Just before Brexit you
could have looked at London and said that it was a city whose
ideas were reaching out to the world with great confidence and
really engaging as part of a grander European project. And ob-
viously that is different (…). One of the things that we can see at
the moment is it's harder for people from Europe to come to Britain. (…) The right to come and work here is different. All of that
means there is a substantial impact. But I think we need to look at
this as being a project over maybe ten years or 15 years (…). Particularly younger people feel very strongly that this was the wrong
decision and they want to do something about that. I don't know
what that is, but I think as we go through that, we will see another
change in London's character, maybe to the better."

…ON POVERTY

"There is a huge amount of hidden poverty. It's a subject that
doesn't get talked about very much. We see a large number of
people would not be considered acceptable and appropriate
for a lot of people who live here, particularly around how many
people live in a room, living child poverty. And we've seen a huge
growth in the number of food banks for the distribution of food for
people all through London in a way that actually feels sometimes
like it's something from the 19th century. It is very shocking and
it's proliferating. (…)."

…ON THE ENVIRONMENT

"Environmental issues and environmental pressure groups
are really very fast-emerging influential groups in London.
We've been at the heart of protest groups like Just Stop Oil and
the Extinction Rebellion movement in London, as well as older
groups like the Critical Mass Cycling. I think a lot of these things
are part of an international collective, but we see the ideas and the
energy really emanating from London and a couple of other cities.
I think it's more environmental action and, in particular, direct

action. Things like Just Stop Oil and the Extinction Rebellion are really youth-driven movements that have a huge amount of energetic expression in London and a lot of the ideas and the tactics of these groups coming from London and a few other cities in the UK. This is only really going to intensify."

…ON LONDON'S FUTURE

"My wish for the future of London is that it not only feels like the heart of the world, but it becomes the capital of the world again. And that means that it has to be international, outward looking, creative, with a bit of that alternative which brought things like punk rock."

…ZUM THEMA EINWANDERUNG

„Ich denke, jede Megastadt hat ein starkes multikulturelles Element oder zumindest ein internationales, nach Außen gerichtetes Element. Und London tut dies schon seit langer Zeit. Tatsächlich kann man in London einige Dinge beobachten: Wir haben einen Bürgermeister mit pakistanischem Hintergrund. Wir haben einen Premierminister mit indischem Hintergrund, all das macht einen großen Teil unserer Diskussionen über die Identität Londons aus. Ich denke, es geht darum, wie wir weiter vorgehen werden, um eine multikulturelle, integrative Stadt zu bleiben, insbesondere im Zuge der Gentrifizierung, des Drucks auf den Wohnungsmarkt, des Wettbewerbs um Arbeitsplätze und wie wir mit all dem umgehen (…), denn das ist es, was London ausmacht. Wir sind, wie ich schon sagte, eine Stadt, die auf der sukzessiven Einwanderung aufgebaut wurde. Wir sind sehr daran gewöhnt. Es ist Teil unserer DNA (…)."

…ZUM THEMA BREXIT

„(…) Der Brexit wird sich auf die Identität Londons auswirken und hat dies bereits getan. Die unmittelbare Auswirkung ist meiner Meinung nach ein Mangel an Gewissheit über die Identität der Stadt. Kurz vor dem Brexit hätte man London als eine Stadt bezeichnen können, deren Ideen mit großem Selbstvertrauen in die Welt hinausgehen und die sich wirklich als Teil eines größeren europäischen Projekts engagiert hat. Und das hat sich offensichtlich geändert. (…) Was wir im Moment feststellen können, ist, dass es für Menschen aus Europa schwieriger geworden ist, nach Großbritannien zu kommen. (…) Das Recht, hierher zu kommen und zu arbeiten, ist anders. All das bedeutet, dass es erhebliche Auswirkungen gibt. Aber ich denke, wir müssen dies als ein Projekt über einen Zeitraum von vielleicht 10 oder 15 Jahren betrachten (…). Vor allem jüngere Menschen sind der Meinung, dass dies eine falsche Entscheidung war, und sie wollen etwas dagegen tun. Ich weiß nicht, was das ist, aber ich denke, wenn wir das durchziehen, werden wir eine weitere Veränderung in London erleben."

…ZUM THEMA ARMUT

„Es gibt eine große Menge an versteckter Armut. Es ist ein Thema, über das nicht sehr viel gesprochen wird. Wir sehen eine große Anzahl von Menschen in den Vierteln von Einwanderern, deren Lebensbedingungen für viele Menschen nicht als akzeptabel und angemessen gelten würden, vor allem, wenn es darum geht, wie viele Menschen in einem Zimmer leben und von Kinderarmut betroffen sind. Und wir haben einen enormen Anstieg der Zahl der Tafeln für die Verteilung von Lebensmitteln an Menschen in ganz London erlebt, und zwar in einer Weise, die manchmal an Zustände aus dem 19. Jahrhundert erinnert. Es ist sehr schockierend, und es breitet sich immer weiter aus (…)."

…ZUM THEMA UMWELTSCHUTZ

„Umweltthemen und Umweltgruppen sind wirklich sehr schnell wachsende einflussreiche Gruppen in London. Wir waren das Zentrum von Protestgruppen wie „Just Stop Oil" und der „Extinction Rebellion"-Bewegung in London sowie von älteren Gruppen wie der „Critical Mass Cycling"-Bewegung. Wir denken, dass viele dieser Interessengemeinschaften Teil eines internationalen Kollektivs sind, aber wir sehen, dass die Ideen und die Energie wirklich von London und einigen anderen Städten ausgehen. Ich denke, es geht mehr um Umweltaktionen und insbesondere um direkte Aktionen. Initiativen wie „Just Stop Oil" und „Extinction Rebellion" sind wirklich jugendgetriebene Bewegungen, die in London einen enormen energetischen Ausdruck haben, und viele der Ideen und Taktiken dieser Gruppen kommen aus London und einigen anderen Städten in Großbritannien. Dies wird sich noch verstärken (…)."

…ZUR ZUKUNFT LONDONS

„Ich wünsche mir für die Zukunft Londons, dass es sich nicht nur wie das Herz der Welt anfühlt, sondern dass es wieder zur Hauptstadt der Welt wird. Und das bedeutet, dass es international, weltoffen und kreativ sein muss, mit einem Hauch von Alternative, der Dinge wie Punkrock hervorgebracht hat."

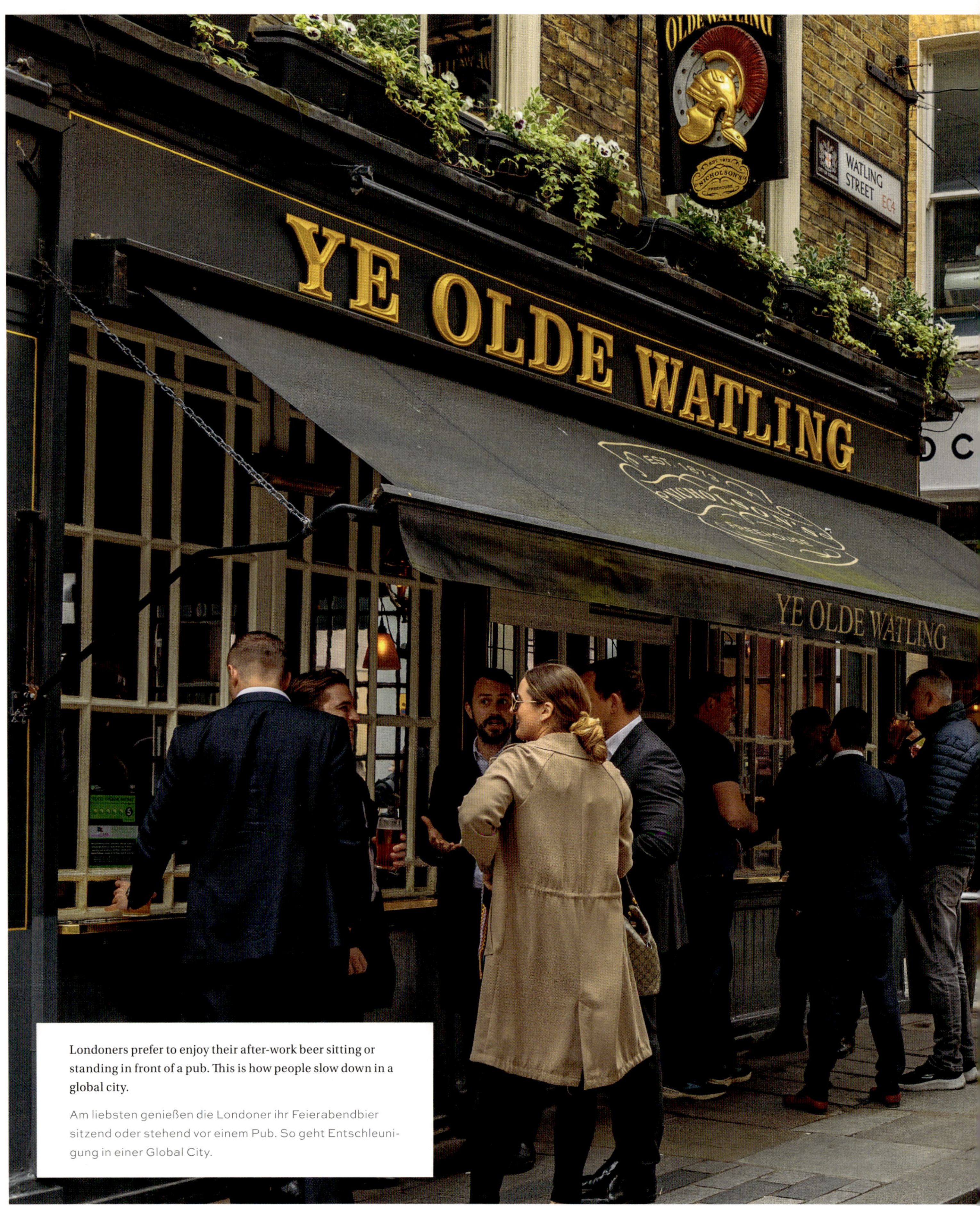

Londoners prefer to enjoy their after-work beer sitting or standing in front of a pub. This is how people slow down in a global city.

Am liebsten genießen die Londoner ihr Feierabendbier sitzend oder stehend vor einem Pub. So geht Entschleunigung in einer Global City.

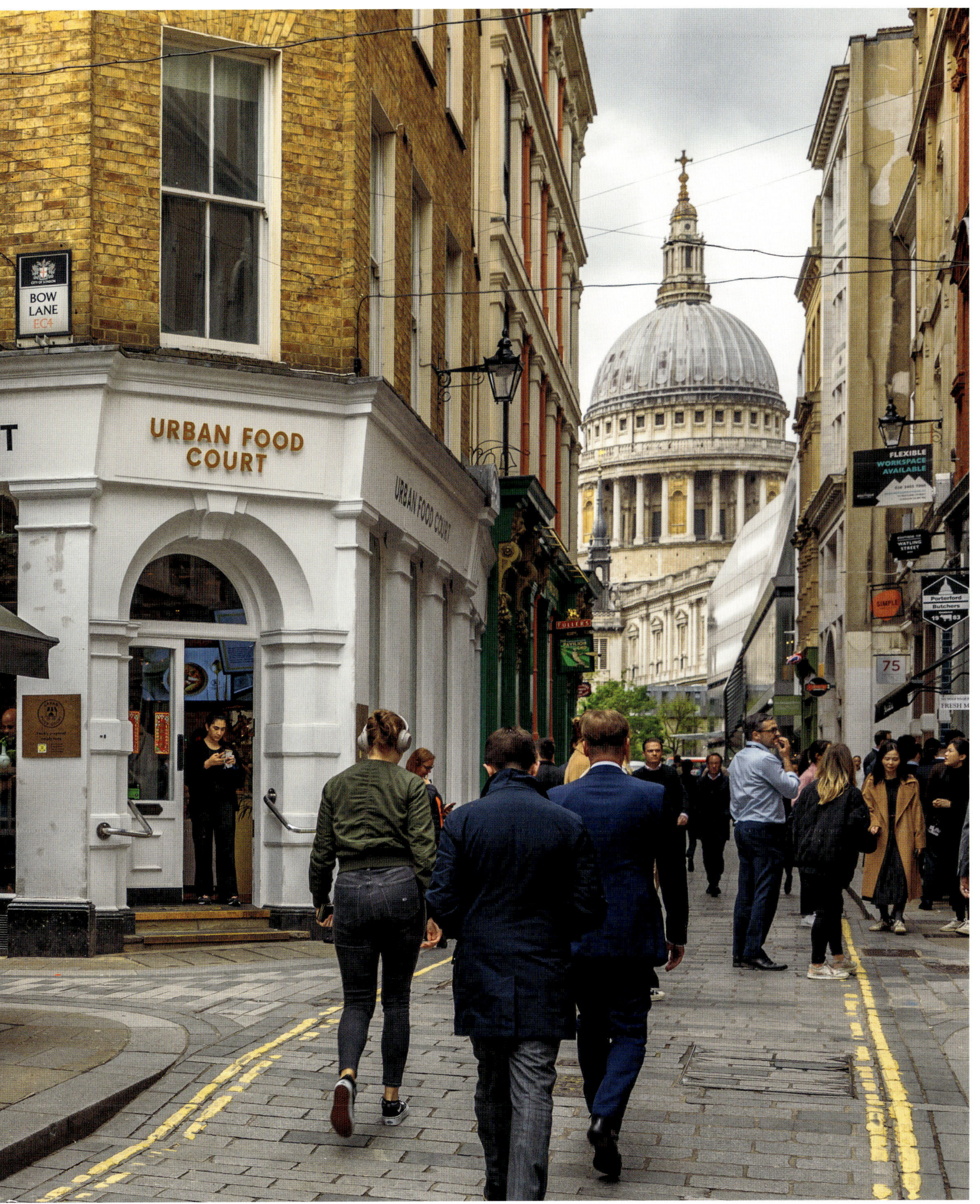
BOW
LANE
EC4
URBAN FOOD
COURT
URBAN FOOD COURT
FLEXIBLE
WORKSPACE
AVAILABLE
WATLING
STREET
Porterford
Butchers
SIMPLE
75

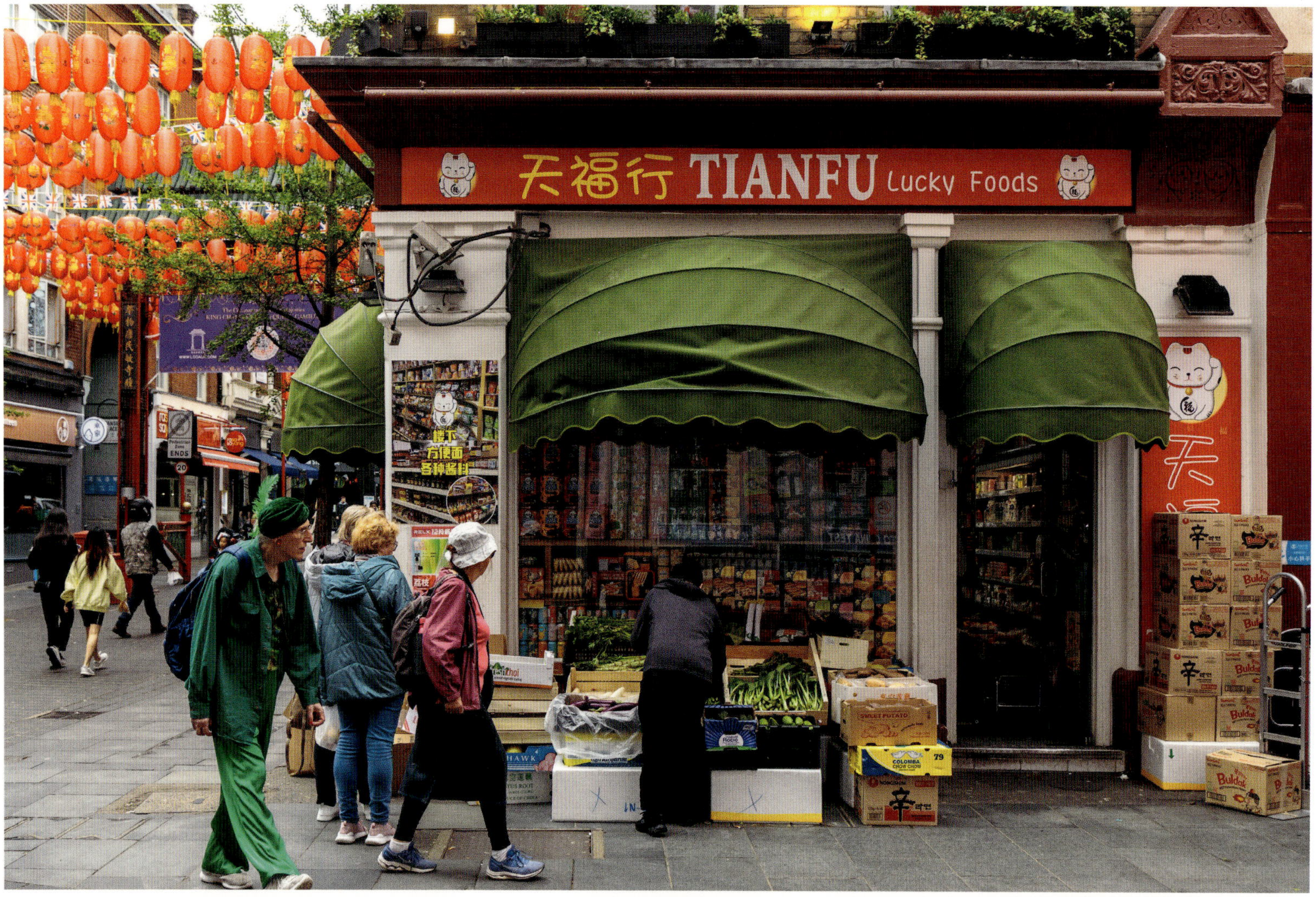

天福行 TIANFU Lucky Foods

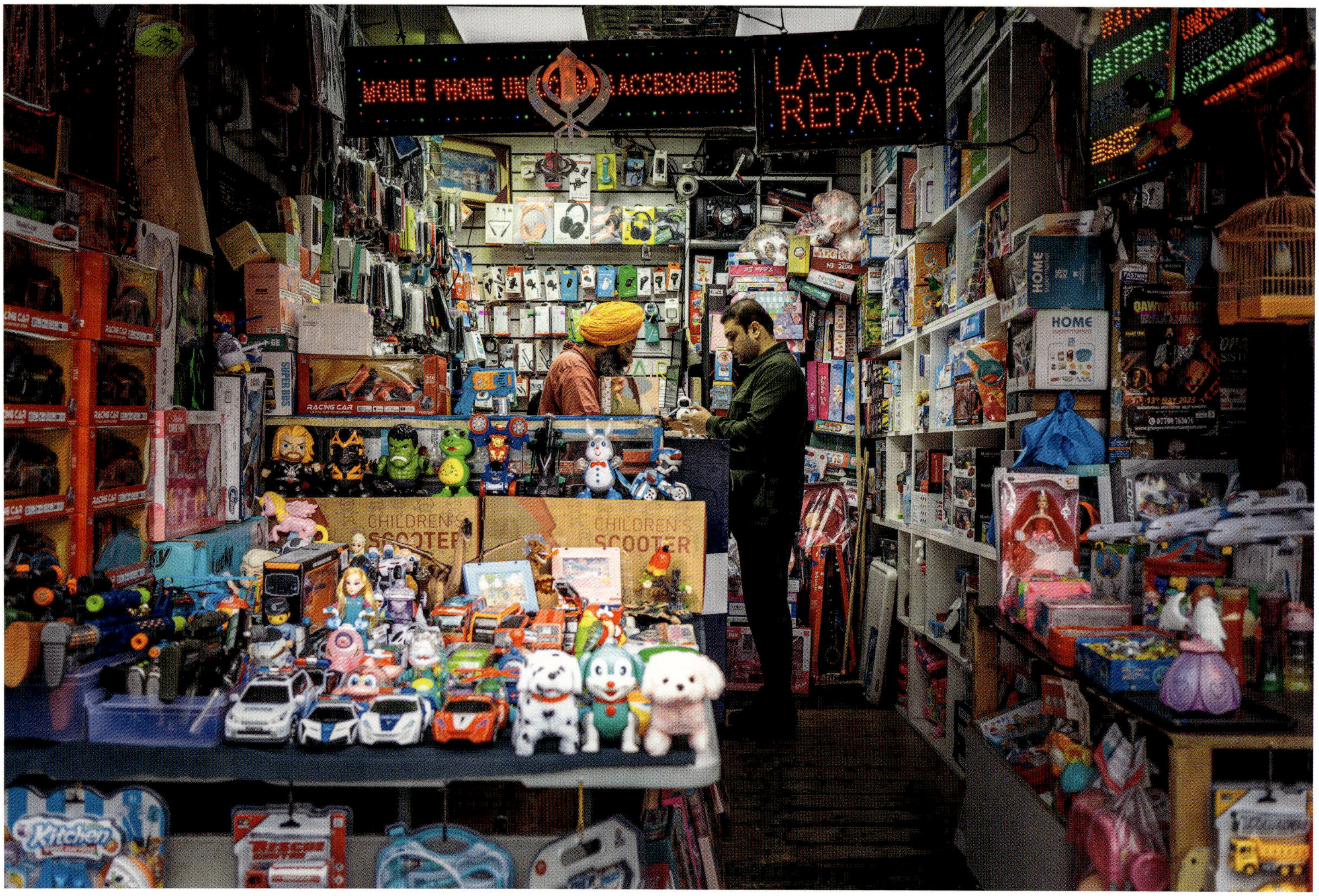

MOBILE PHONE UNLOCKING ACCESSORIES
LAPTOP REPAIR
CHILDREN'S SCOOTER
CHILDREN'S SCOOTER
RACING CAR
Kitchen

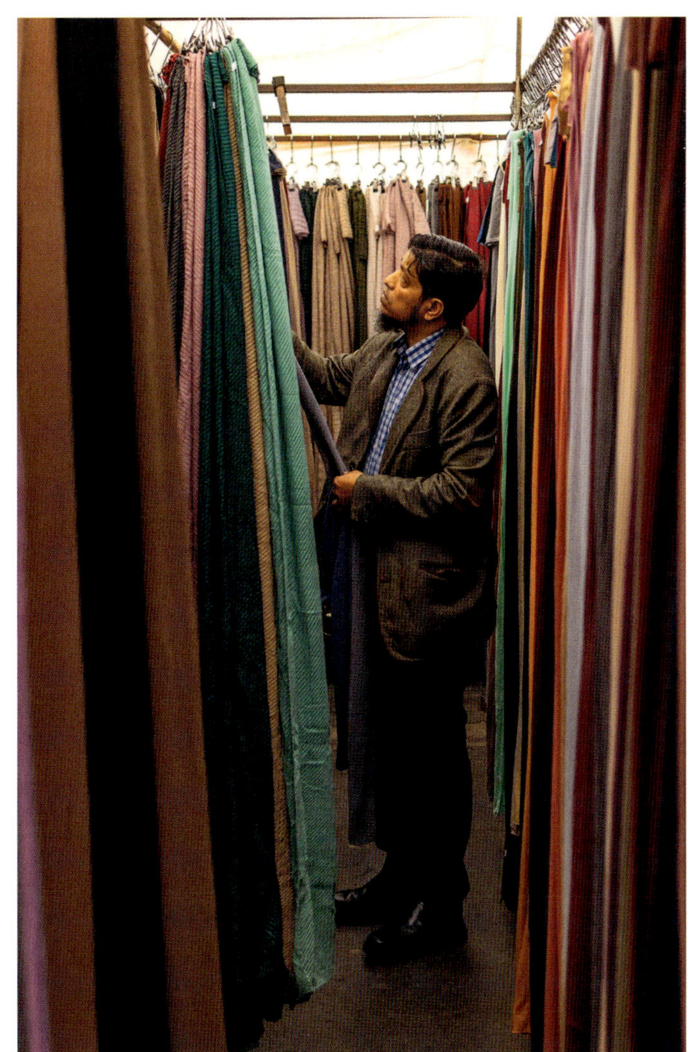
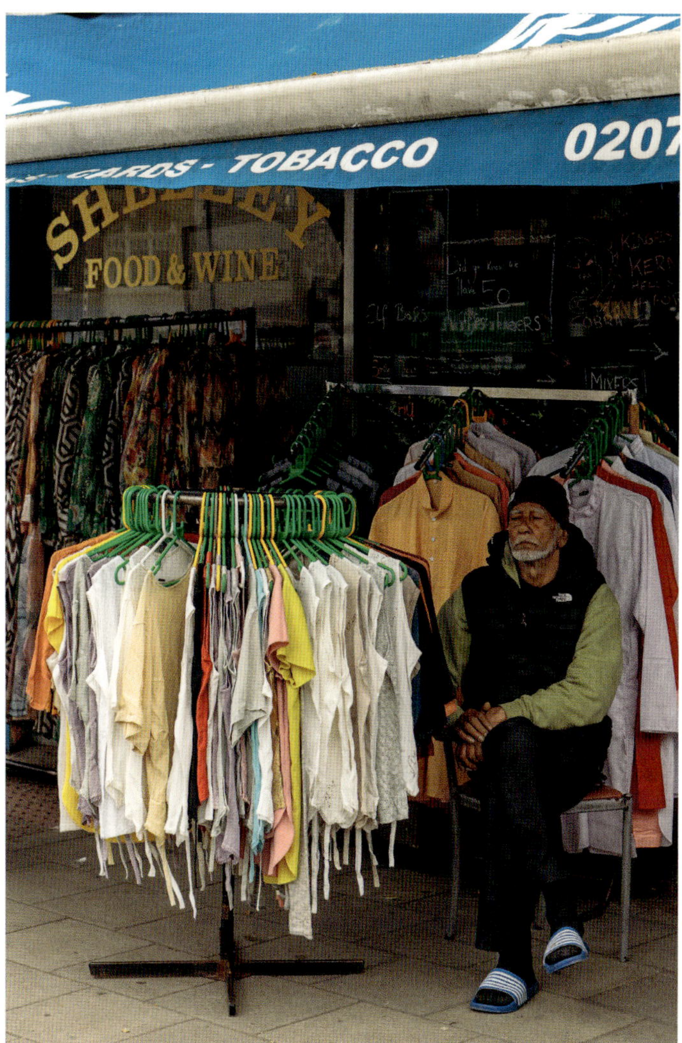
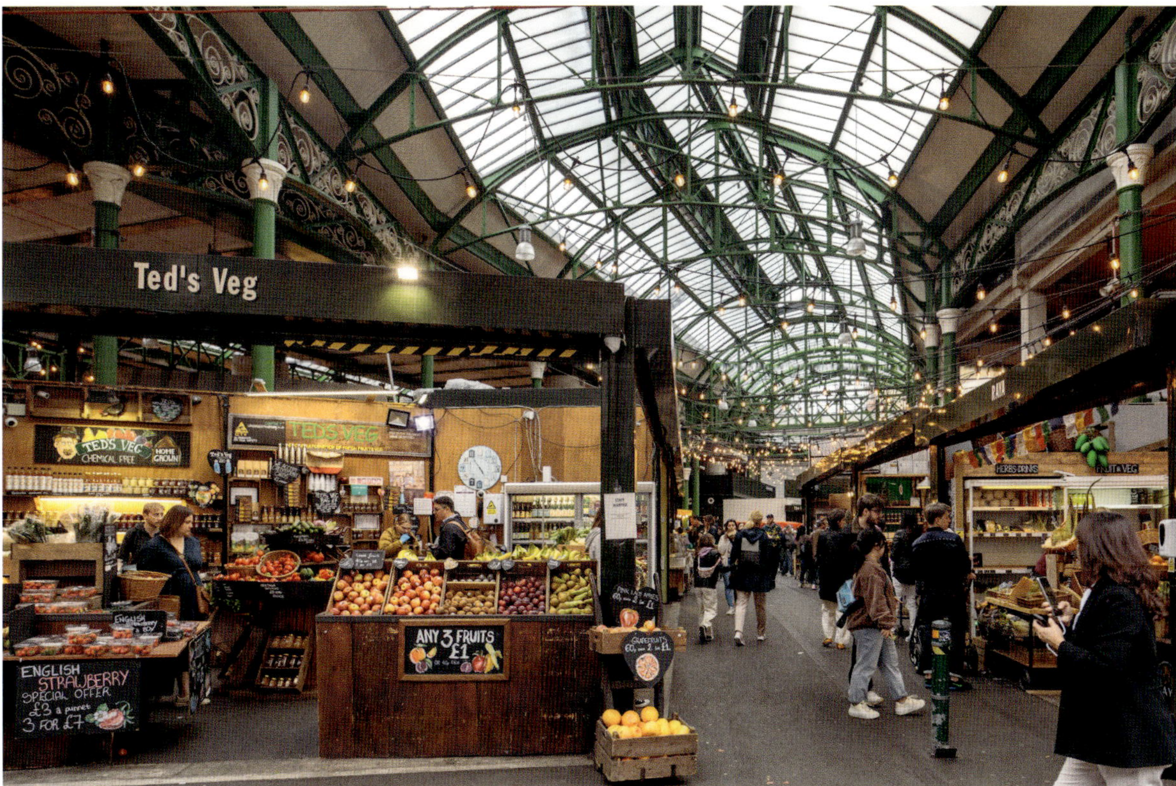

Whether in Chinatown, Little India, Whitechapel, or at the Borough Market, the whole world meets in London.

Ob in Chinatown, Little India, Whitechapel oder auf dem Borough Market, in London trifft sich die ganze Welt.

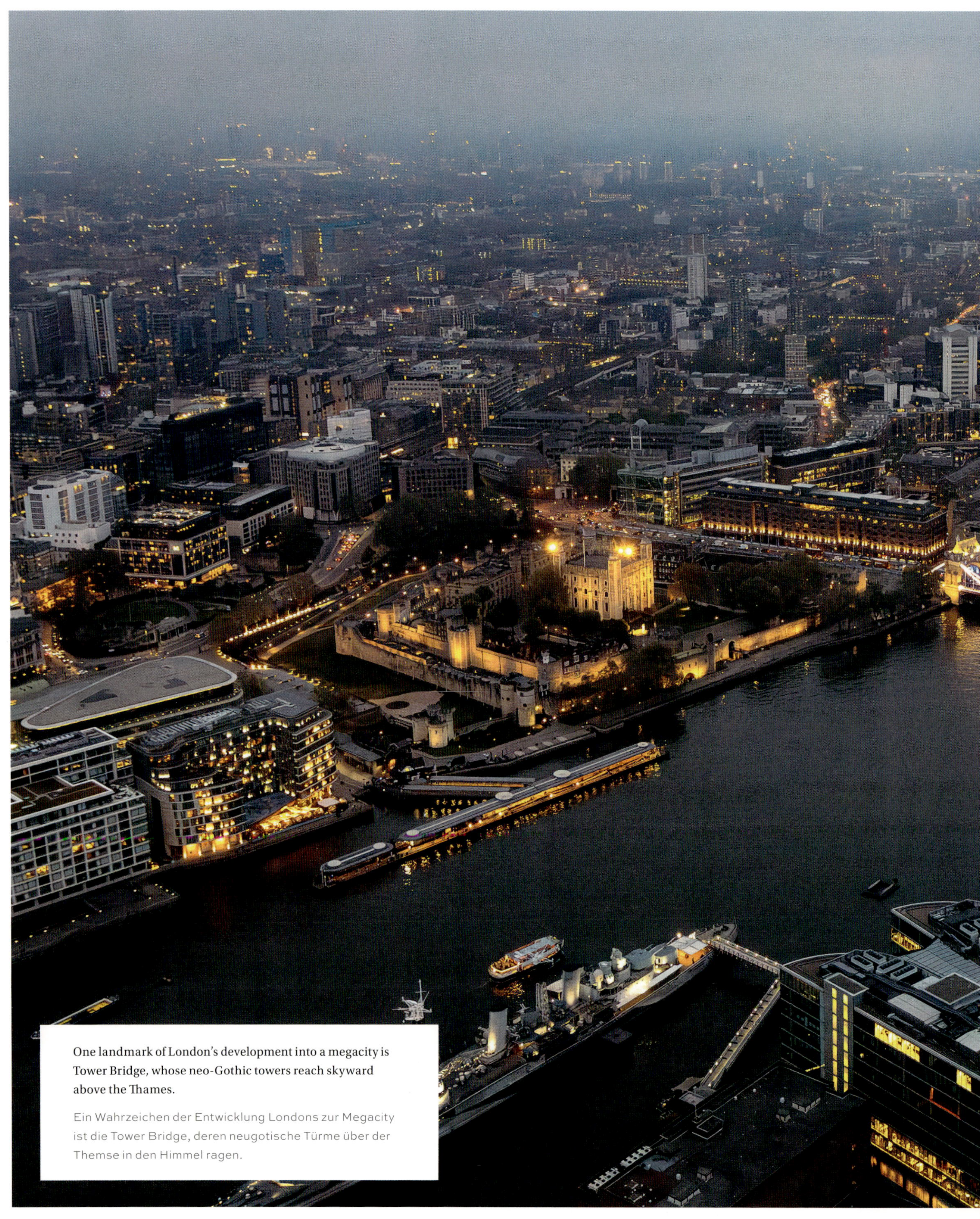

One landmark of London's development into a megacity is
Tower Bridge, whose neo-Gothic towers reach skyward
above the Thames.

Ein Wahrzeichen der Entwicklung Londons zur Megacity
ist die Tower Bridge, deren neugotische Türme über der
Themse in den Himmel ragen.

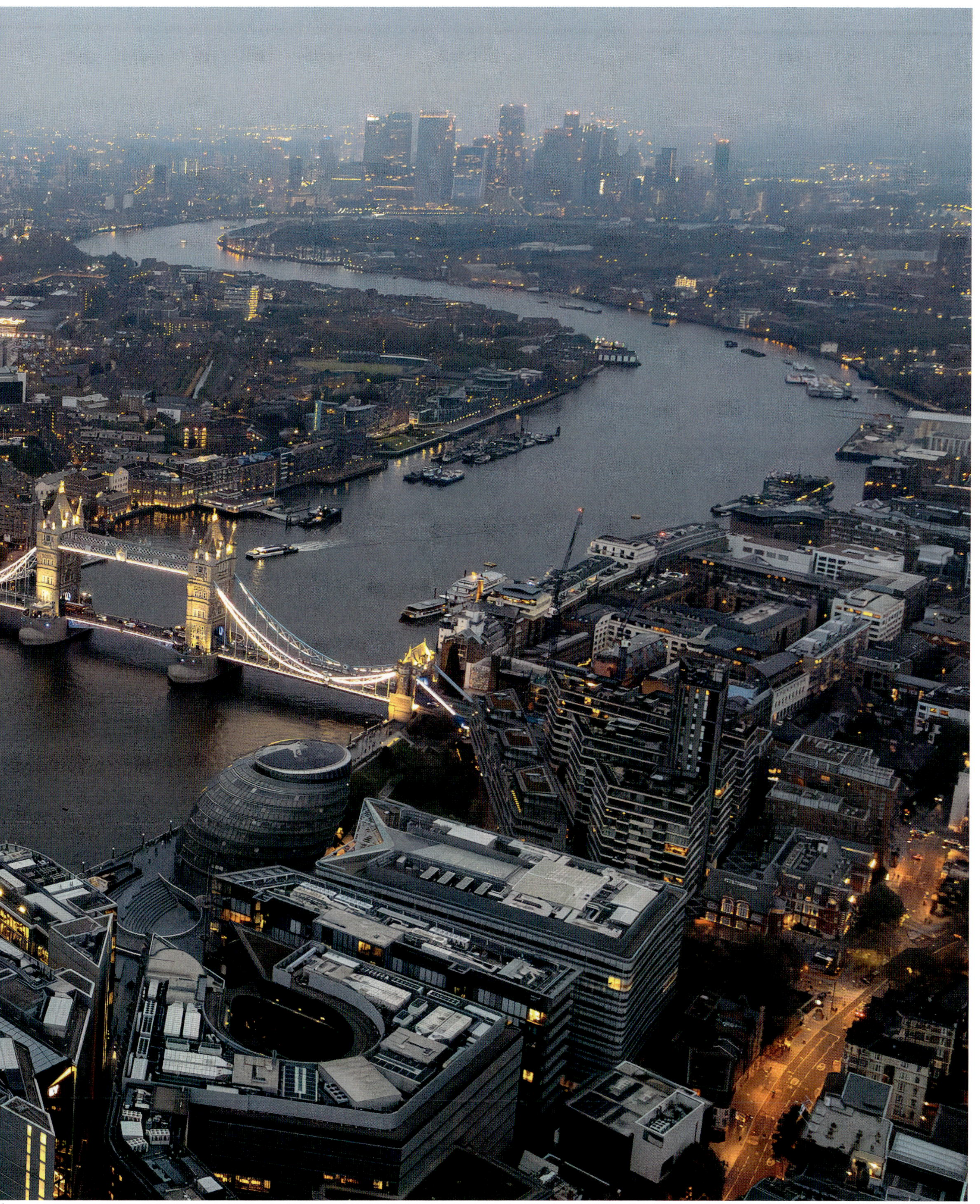

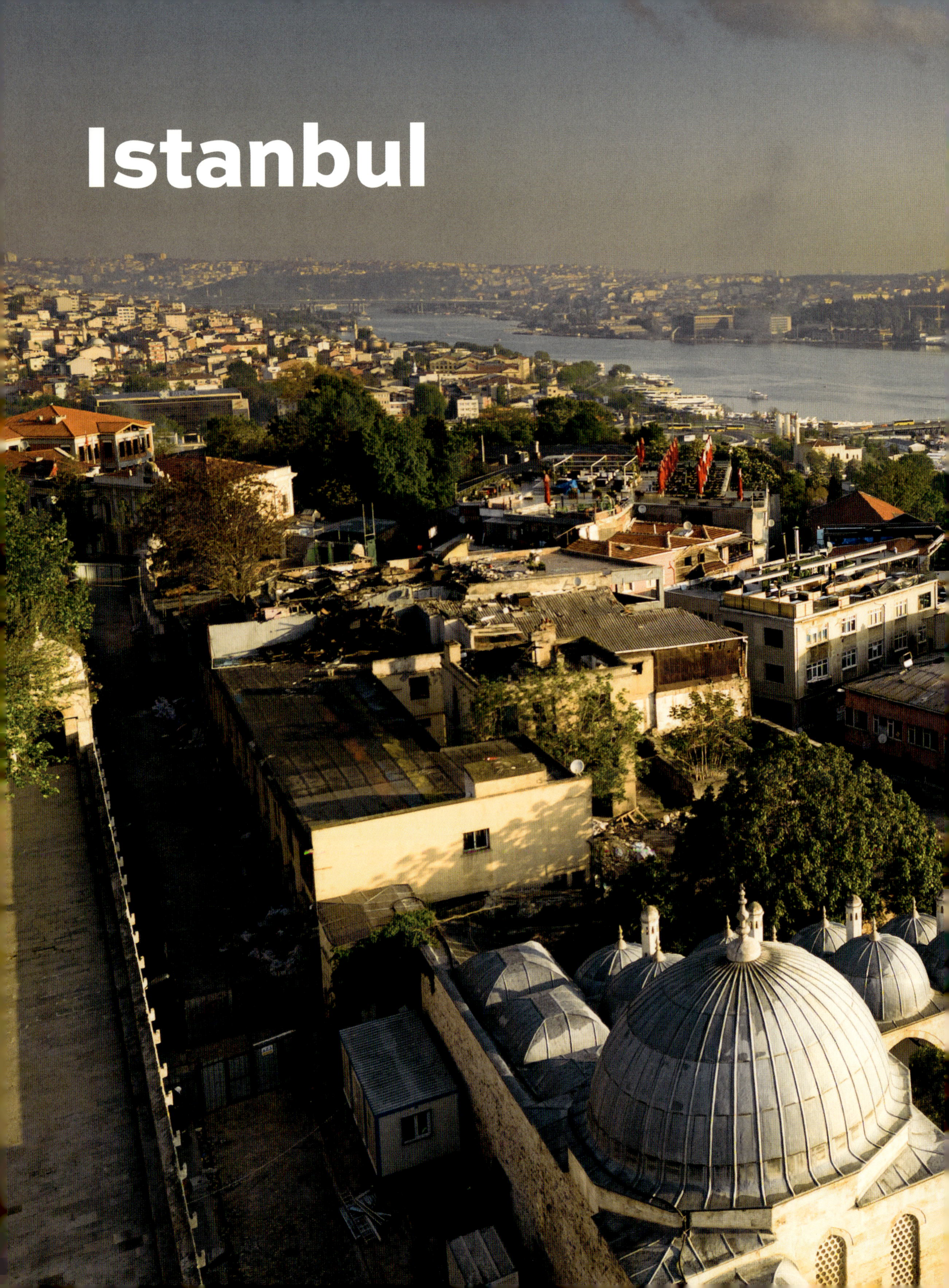

Istanbul

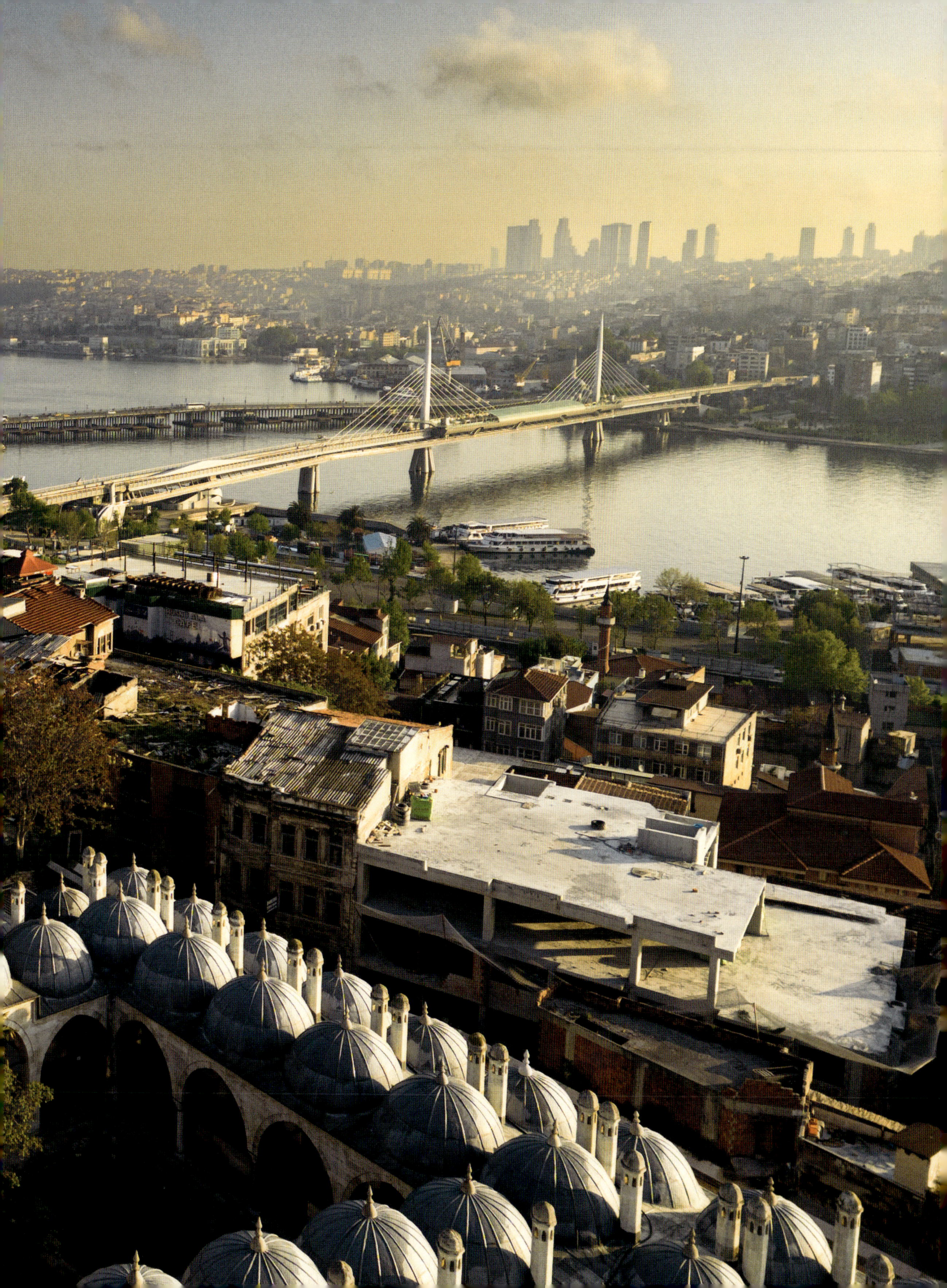

The City of Contradictions

"Istanbul is a multicultural and multireligious city. (...) That is part of the richness of Istanbul, this multicultural and multireligious characteristic of Istanbul. (...) And this tolerance and this culture of living together, it has been a characteristic of Istanbul for centuries, (...) even during the Ottoman times, Istanbul was a multicultural city." (Birgul Demirtas)

Sometimes it is not easy to remain tolerant. No, not because of the religions, or the many different ethnicities, but because of the huge number of people. Istanbul has almost 16 million residents, and almost as many visitors every year. Istanbul is quite simply full. Like a magnet, the city also attracts millions of people, often refugees from Central Asia, Africa, Russia, the Balkans. There seems to be a heyday on the Bosporus for those in exile.

The Bosporus is the soul of Istanbul. It is linked to the city's rich, almost 2700-year-old history under the names of Byzantium, Constantinople, and Istanbul. It is not just the geographical intersection where East meets West, it is also a meeting point for people from all over the world who have fled from crises, wars, and oppression, where rich and poor stroll side by side, where young and old come together. Ferries not only connect the geographical worlds; they also connect people's lives. Together, they all move back and forth between Asia and Europe.

"It is also interesting to note that we have a saying in Turkish. For example, if it snows in any other southern province, it is not big news on Turkey's TV channels most of the time, but when it snows in Istanbul, then you see it on every Turkish channel. It is a big event, because so many people are affected by it." (Birgul Demirtas)

Stadt der Widersprüche

„Istanbul ist eine multikulturelle und multireligiöse Stadt. (...) Das ist einer der Reichtümer Istanbuls, diese multikulturelle und multireligiöse Eigenschaft Istanbuls. (...) Und diese Toleranz und diese Kultur des Zusammenlebens ist seit Jahrhunderten ein Merkmal Istanbuls." (Birgul Demirtas)

Manchmal fällt es schwer, tolerant zu bleiben. Nein, nicht wegen der Religionen, der vielen verschiedenen Ethnien, sondern wegen der vielen Menschen. Istanbul hat fast 16 Millionen Einwohner und jedes Jahr fast genauso viele Besucher. Istanbul ist einfach voll. Wie ein Magnet saugt die Stadt zudem Millionen von Menschen, oft Flüchtlinge aus Zentralasien, Afrika, Russland, dem Balkan an. Es herrscht so etwas wie ein Frühling für Exilanten am Bosporus.

Der Bosporus ist die Seele Istanbuls. Mit ihm verbindet sich eine große und fast 2700 Jahre alte Geschichte der Stadt unter den Namen Byzanz, Konstantinopel und Istanbul. Er ist nicht nur geografisch die Schnittstelle zwischen Orient und Okzident, hier treffen sich die Menschen aus der ganzen Welt, die vor Krisen, Kriegen, Unterdrückung geflohen sind, flanieren Arm und Reich gemeinsam, begegnen sich Jung und Alt. Fähren verbinden nicht nur die geografischen Welten, sondern auch die Lebenswelten. Gemeinsam pendeln alle zwischen Asien und Europa.

A place of assembly and contemplation: The Eyüp Sultan Mosque ranks fourth for Muslims behind Mecca, Medina, and Jerusalem.

Ein Ort der Begegnung und Kontemplation: Die Eyüp Sultan Moschee rangiert für Muslime auf Platz vier hinter Mekka, Medina und Jerusalem.

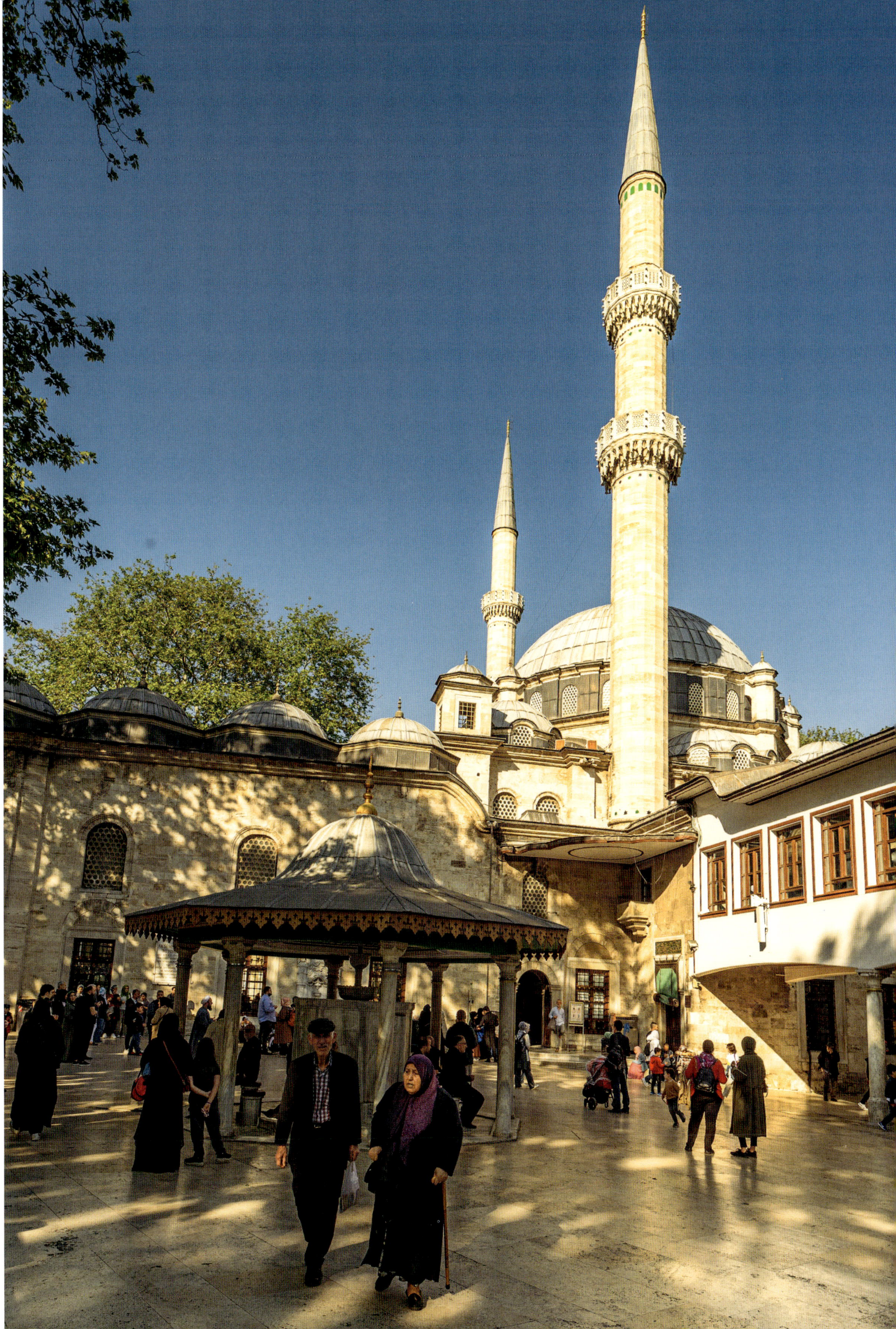

Everything that happens in Istanbul is so dominant that it can affect the entire country. As a result, its vaunted ability to integrate is currently being subjected to a major test of endurance. This is most evident in the central Taksim Square. Once a popular meeting place for Istanbul residents, it has become a center for Syrian and other refugees. The welcoming culture is now on the decline in Istanbul, something that has repercussions for the entire country. Right-wing populists even rant that the Syrian refugees are threatening the solidarity of the Turkish nation.

The weight of this implication is not (yet) affecting ordinary everyday life. Over a drink in one of the cafés on İstiklal Caddesi, browsing in one of the many bookstores at the book market, strolling through the Grand Bazaar, or just fishing on the Bosporus, Istanbul shows what it has always been capable of: being a place for the world to connect.

„Es ist auch interessant, dass wir ein Sprichwort auf Türkisch haben. Wenn es zum Beispiel in einer anderen südlichen Provinz schneit, ist das meistens keine große Nachricht in den türkischen Fernsehkanälen, aber wenn es in Istanbul schneit, dann sieht man es in jedem türkischen Kanal. Es ist ein großes Ereignis, weil so viele Menschen davon betroffen sind." (Birgul Demirtas)

So dominant ist alles, was in Istanbul geschieht, dass es sich auf das ganze Land auswirken kann. So wird die gerühmte Integrationsfähigkeit zurzeit einer hohen Belastungsprobe unterzogen. Sichtbar wird das nicht zuletzt am zentralen Taksim-Platz. Einst ein beliebter Treffpunkt der Istanbuler, ist er zu einem Zentrum für syrische und andere Flüchtlinge geworden. Die Willkommenskultur ist mittlerweile in Istanbul abnehmend und das hat Auswirkungen auf das ganze Land. Rechte Populisten schwadronieren gar, dass der Zusammenhalt der türkischen Nation durch die syrischen Flüchtlinge bedroht sei.

Auf den gewöhnlichen Alltag wirkt sich die Last dieser Bedeutung (noch) nicht aus. Bei einem Drink in einem der Cafés auf der İstiklal Caddesi, beim Stöbern in einer der vielen Buchläden im Büchermarkt, beim Bummel über den Grand Basar oder einfach nur beim Angeln am Bosporus zeigt Istanbul, was es immer schon gekonnt hat: ein Treffpunkt für die Welt zu sein.

During the Ottoman Empire, Gülhane Park functioned as the gardens of Topkapi Palace. It has been a public park since 1912.

Zur Zeit des Osmanischen Reiches war der Gülhane-Park der Garten des Topkapi-Palastes. Bereits seit 1912 dient er als öffentlicher Park.

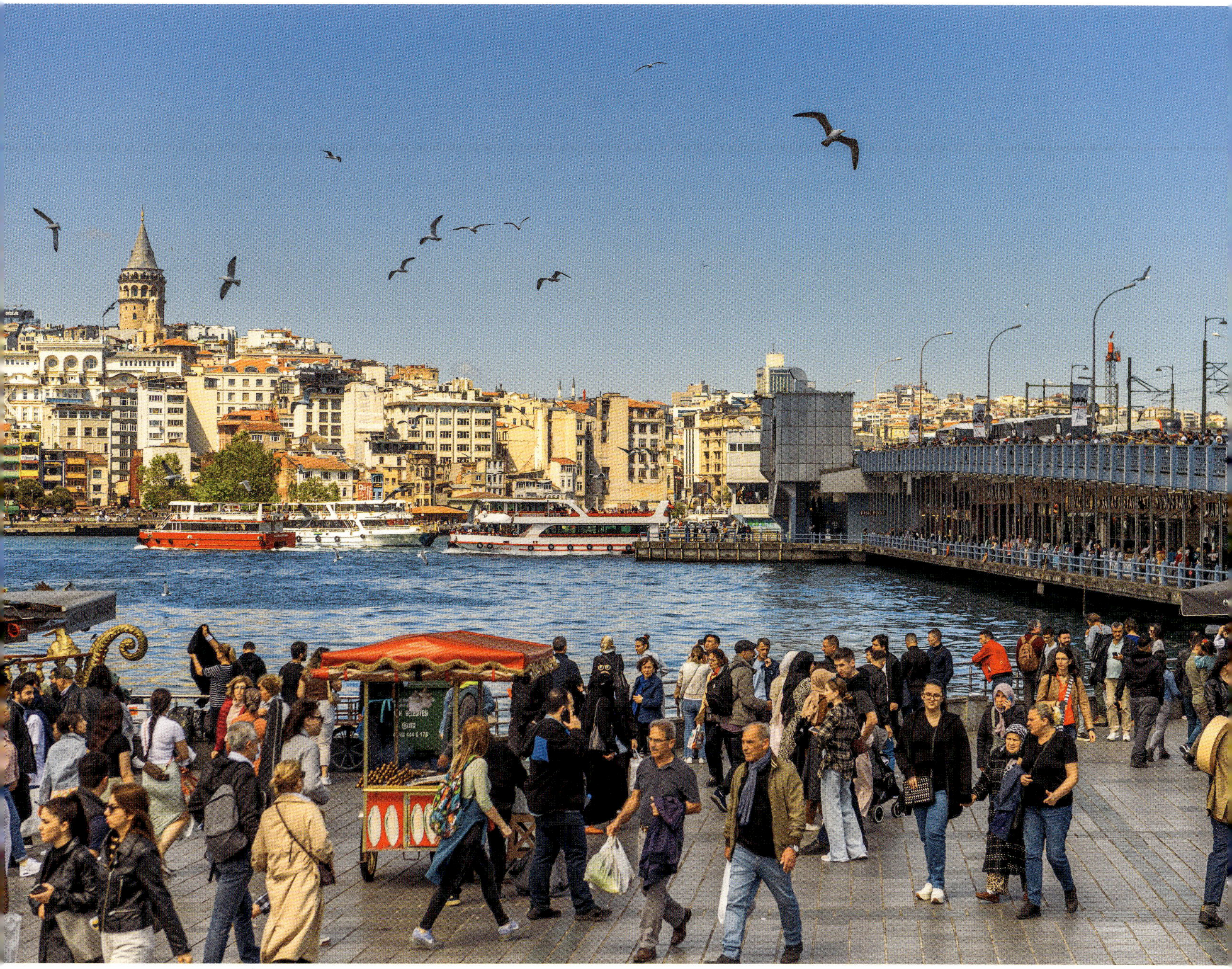

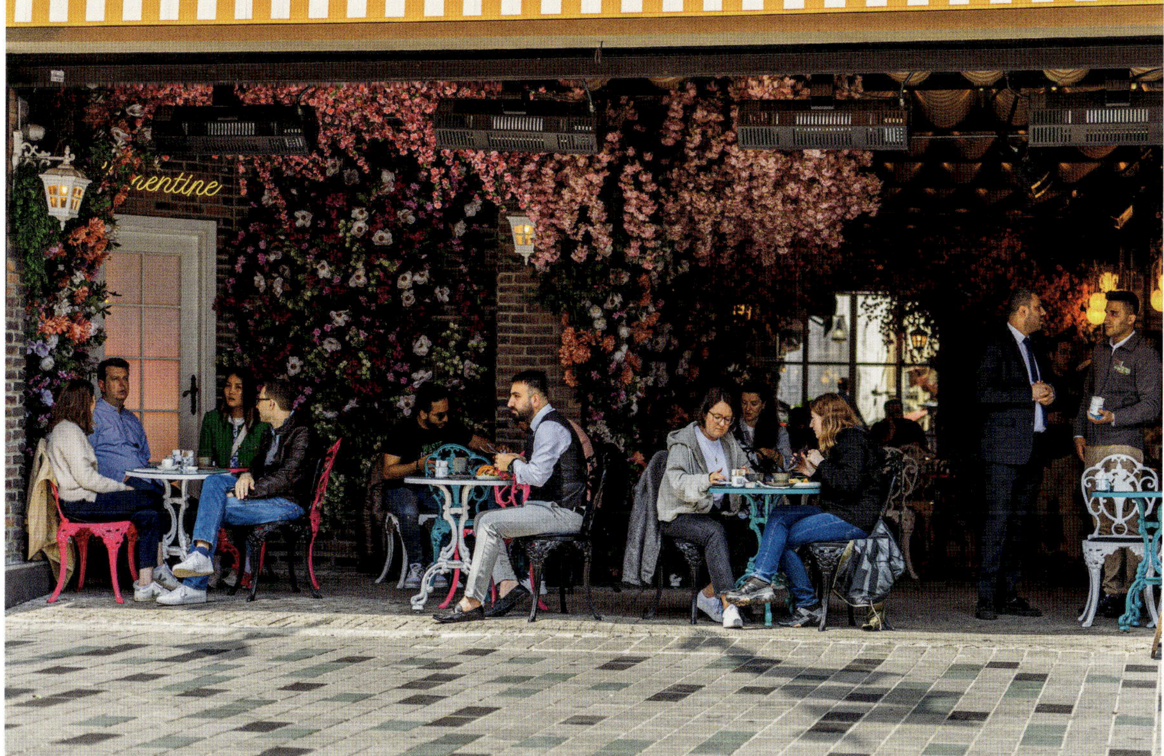

Whether strolling along the Bosporus or in one of the cafés on İstiklal Caddesi, this is where the whole world comes together.

Ob bei einem Bummel am Bosporus oder in einem der Cafés an der İstiklal Caddesi: Hier trifft sich die ganze Welt.

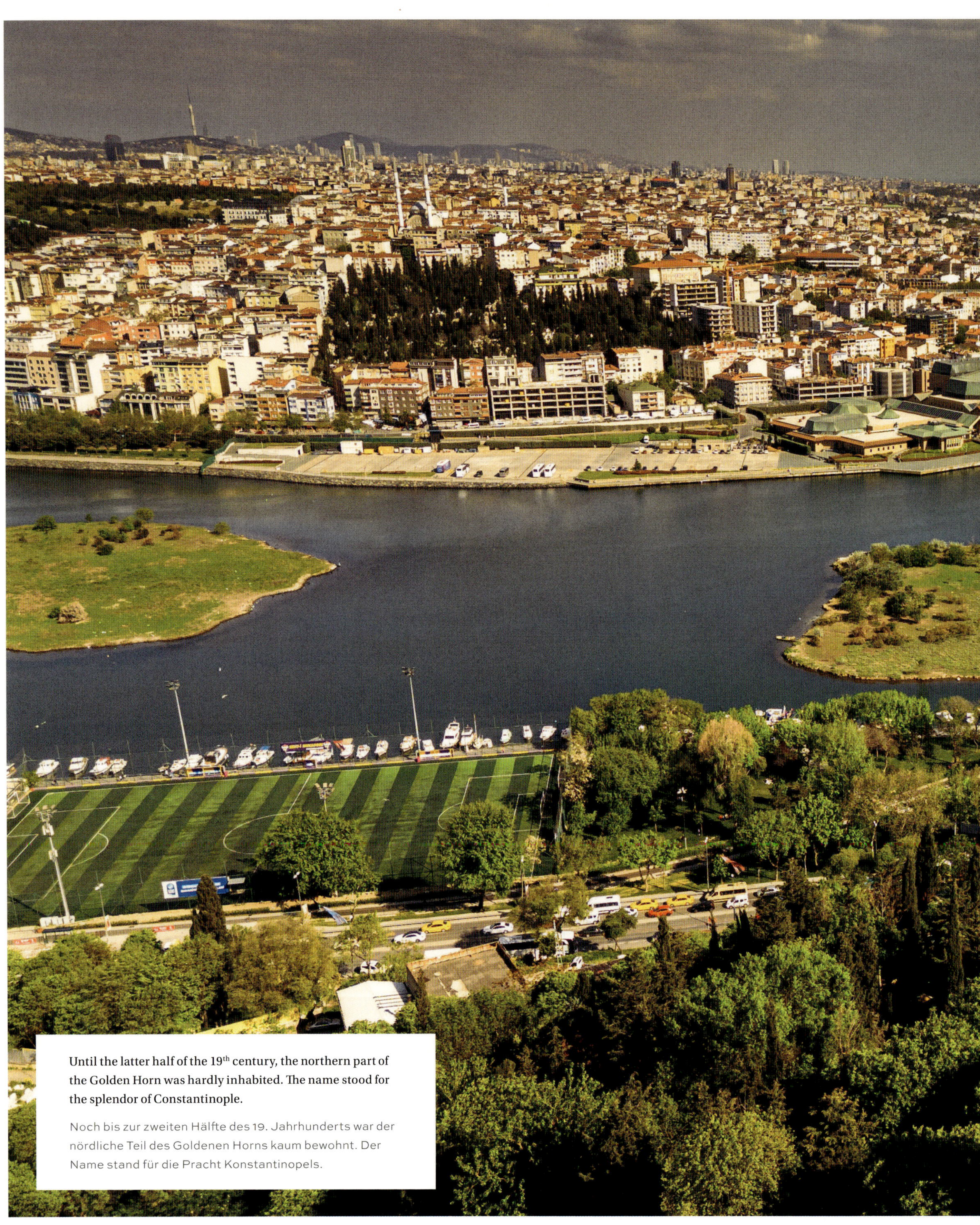

Until the latter half of the 19th century, the northern part of the Golden Horn was hardly inhabited. The name stood for the splendor of Constantinople.

Noch bis zur zweiten Hälfte des 19. Jahrhunderts war der nördliche Teil des Goldenen Horns kaum bewohnt. Der Name stand für die Pracht Konstantinopels.

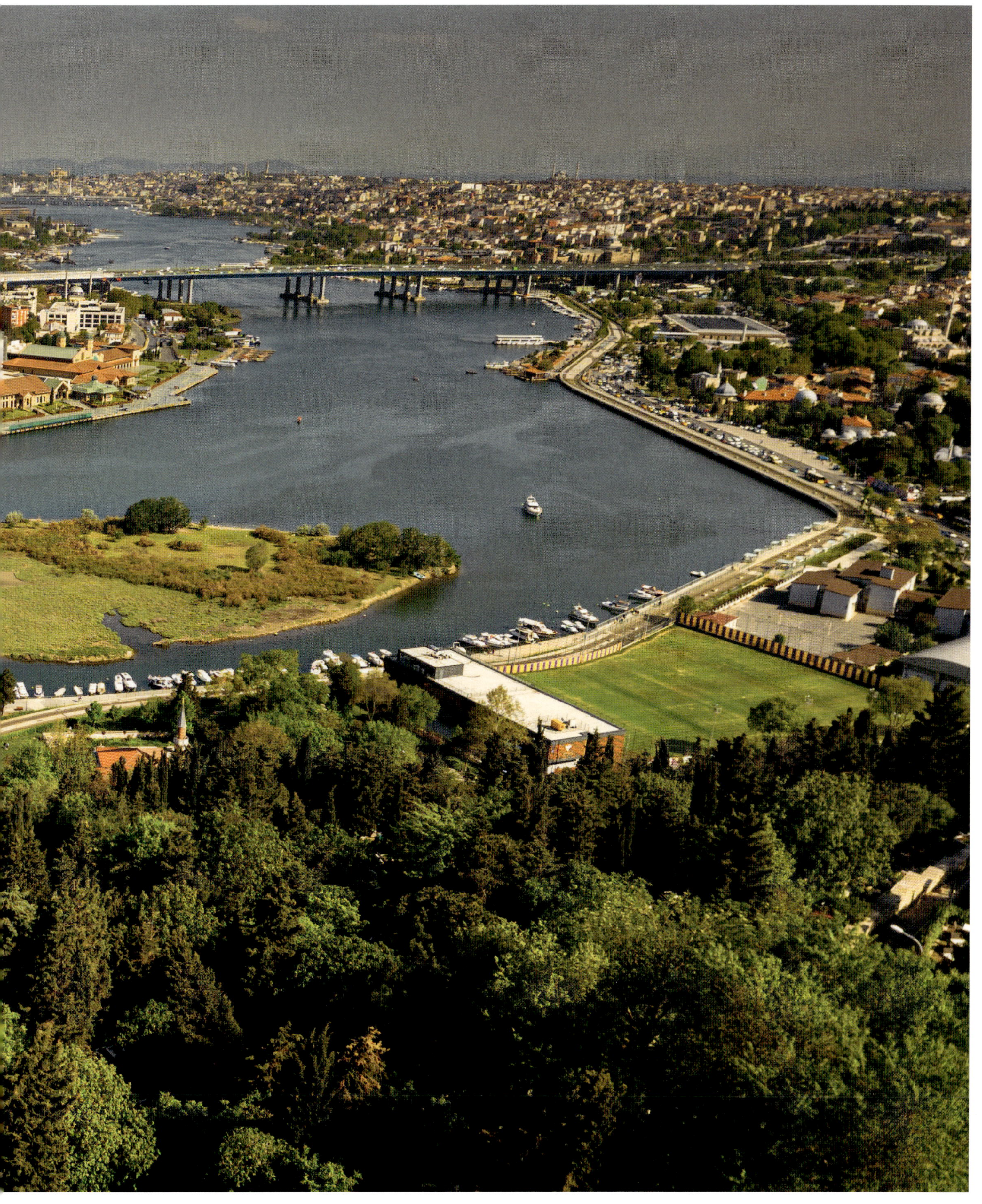

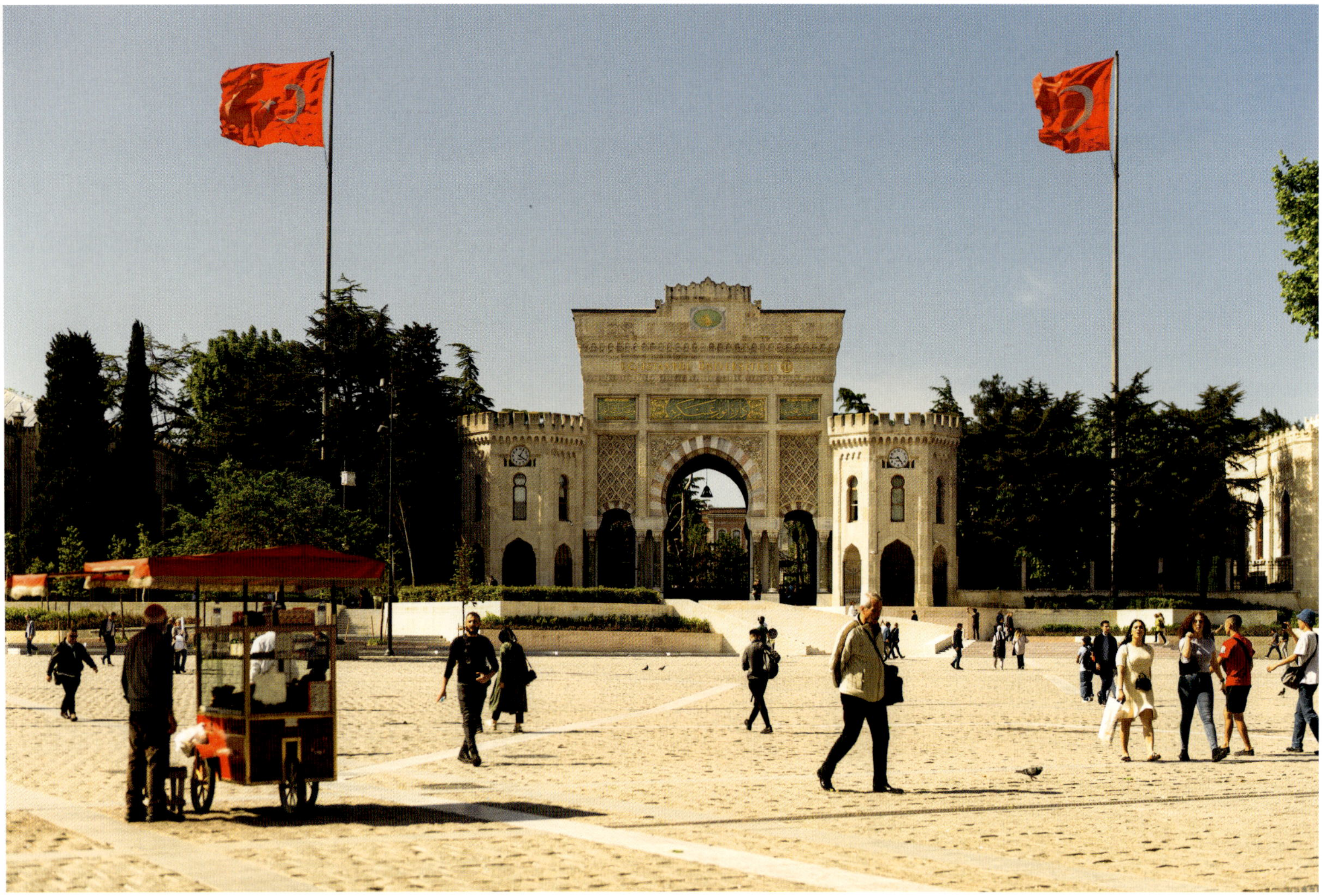

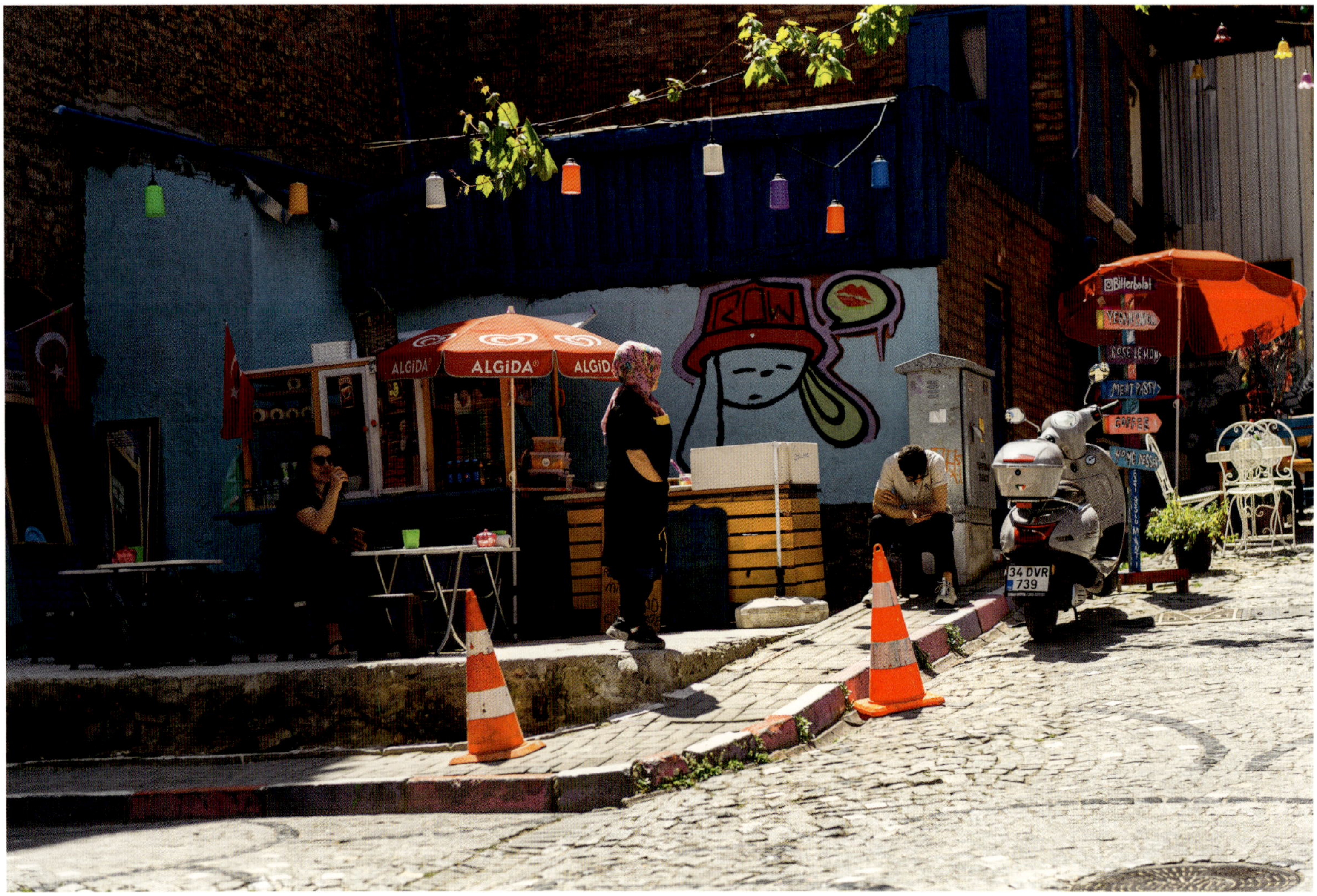

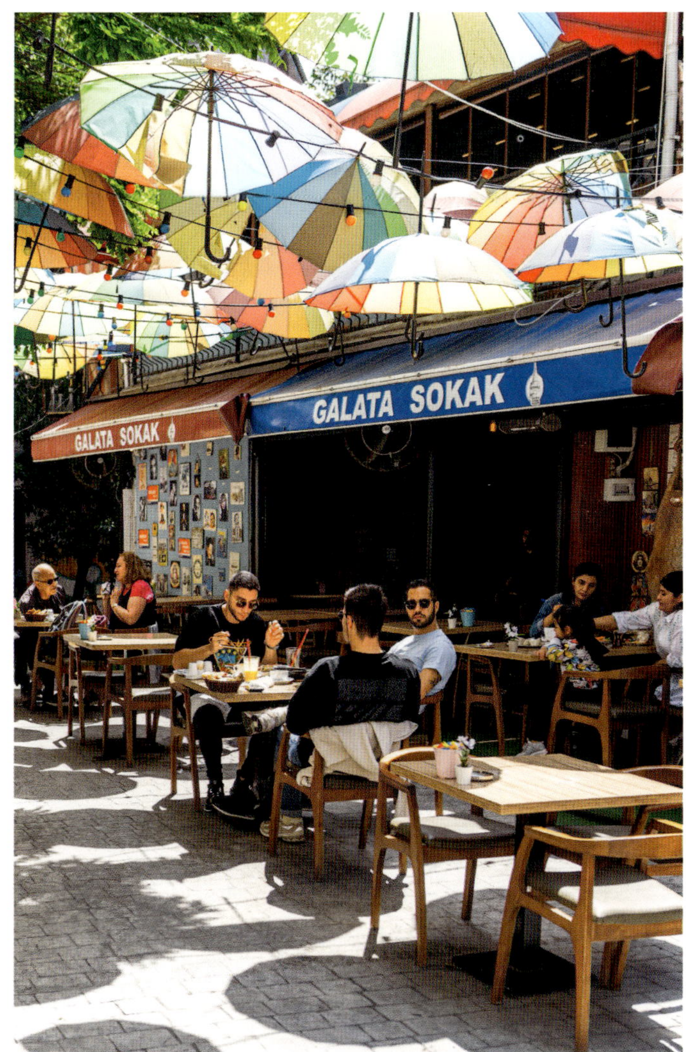

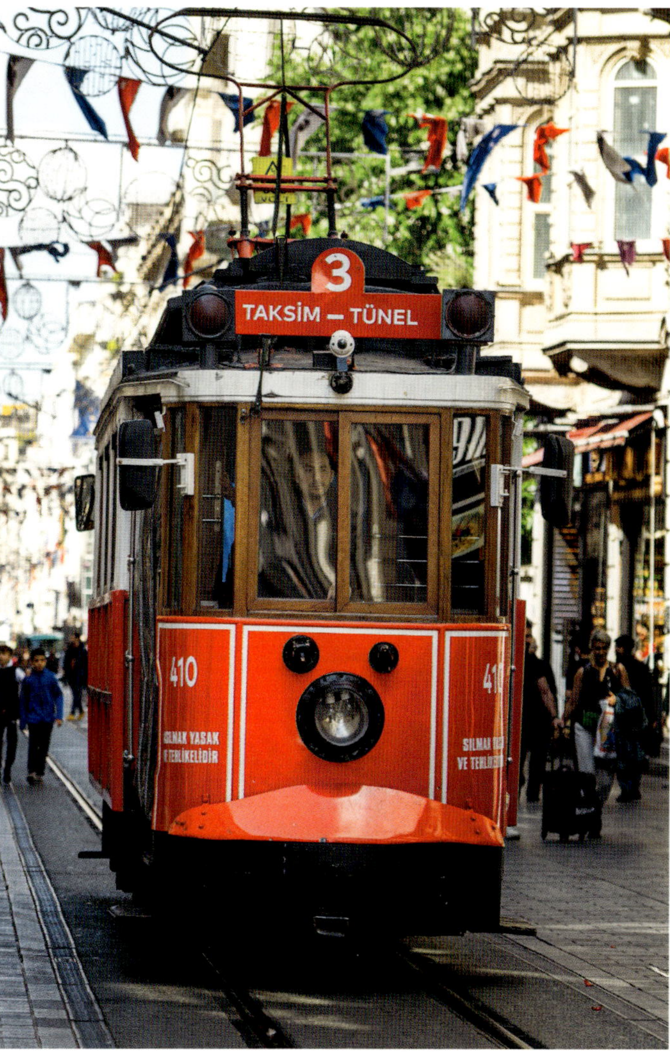

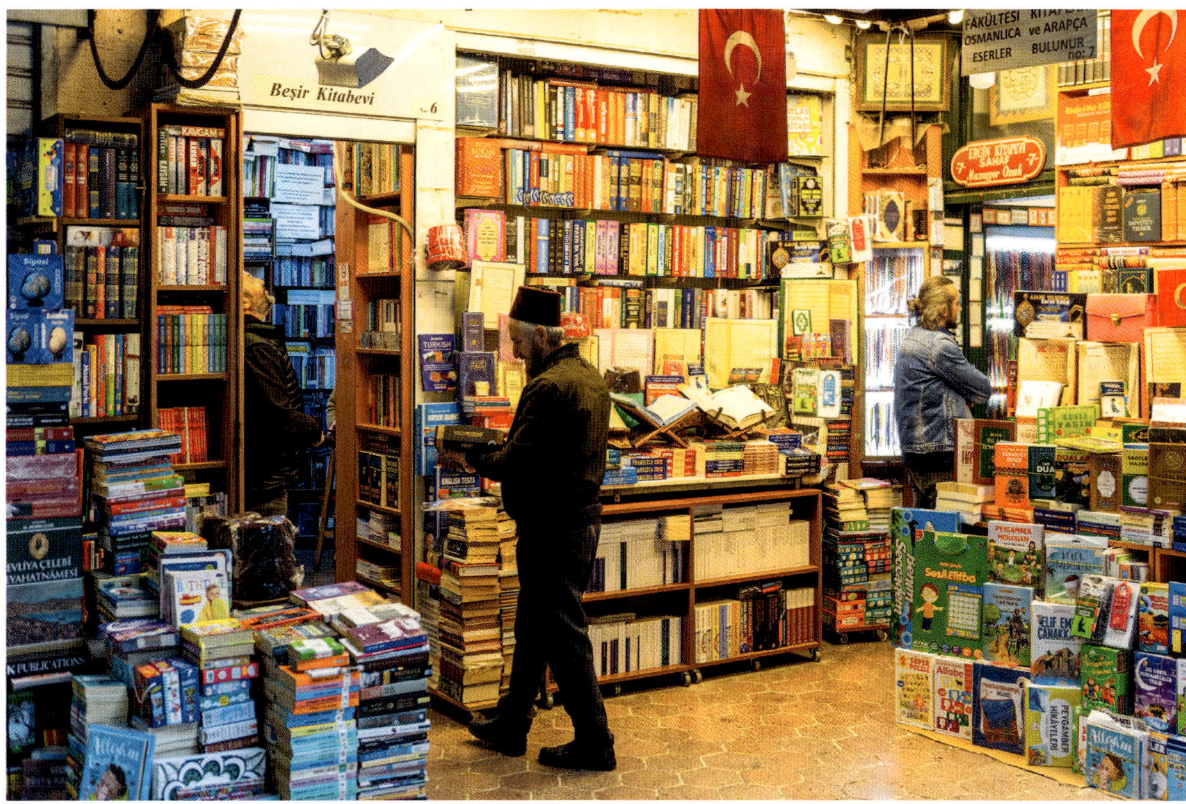

Whether you're walking around the university, in Galata, or on the İstiklal, you tend to forget you're in a megacity here.

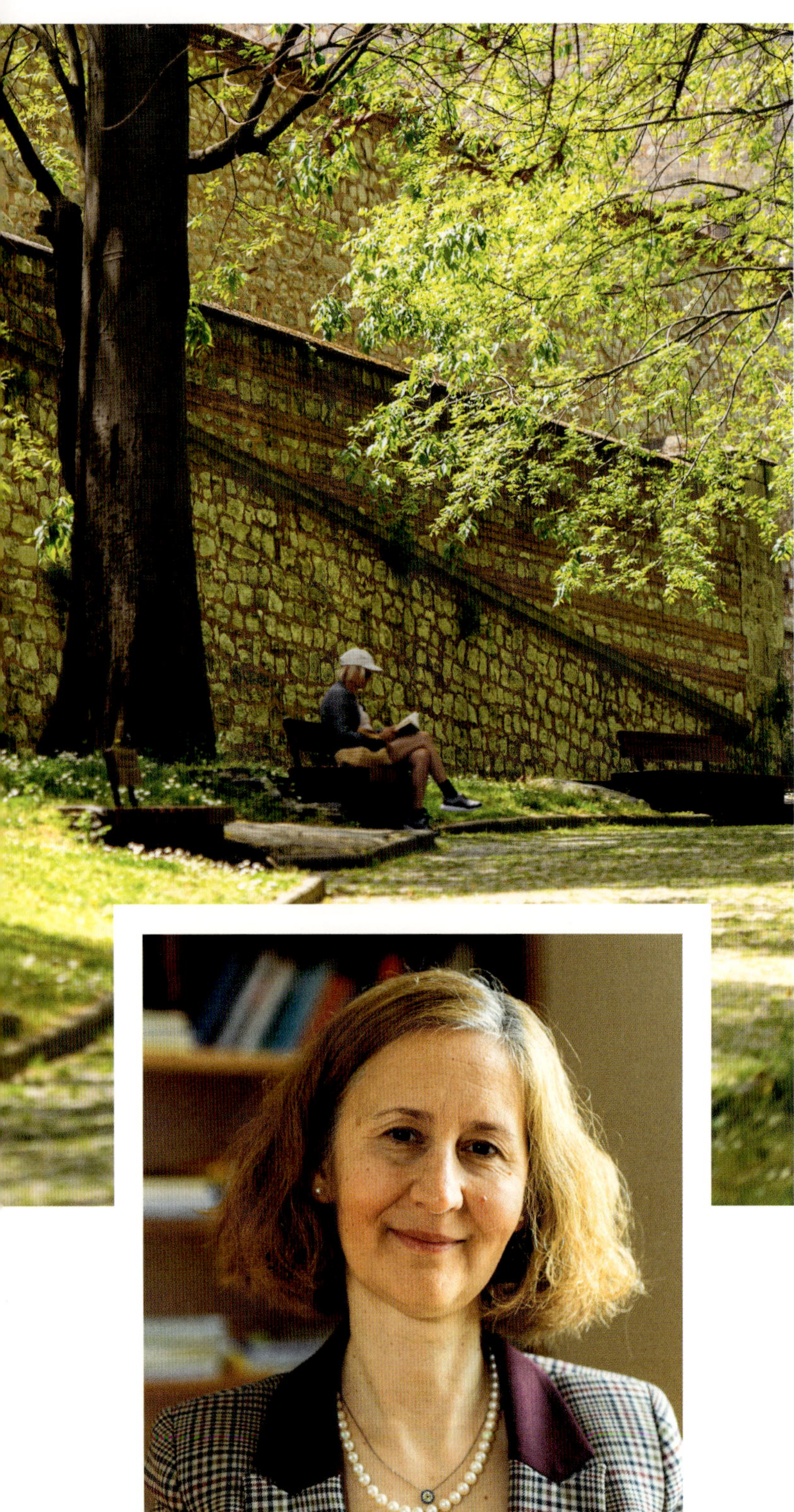

BIRGUL DEMIRTAS
PROFESSOR

Areas of refuge like Gülhane Park are important public spaces and, for many people, the only opportunity for local recreation.

Rückzugsorte wie der Gülhane-Park sind wichtige öffentliche Räume und für viele Menschen die einzige Naherholungsmöglichkeit.

…ON THE CITY'S DEVELOPMENT

"Yes, Istanbul has changed a lot in the recent decades. We can say as the population got bigger and bigger, as so many people from Turkey or from different countries move to Istanbul, it means Istanbul has to invest in infrastructure as well. First of all, it is related to transportation. For example, we have the metro bus and we have new metro lines. That is also quite important. But because of that huge urbanization and because of that huge migration, unfortunately we have fewer forests and fewer parks, fewer green places in Istanbul. Everywhere you see this concrete, these huge buildings, skyscrapers. That was not the case in my childhood. In my youth there were just few skyscrapers in Istanbul. (...) You see a park today or a forest, and tomorrow you see that construction has started in the forest, this deforestation, and this huge construction. It is a big problem in Istanbul."

…ON THE IMPORTANCE OF PARKS

"And Gezi Park has become the symbol. They just tried to destroy the only park, the only green area in the very center of Istanbul. It was the final straw. (...) You know, we are not robots. You know, when you just go to work and then you go to home, if you do not feel nature, then how can you feel your humanity? I think in the megacities we have our right to the city. It means we want to keep these natural places, as long as you are living in a megacity, it means you are spending lots of time in traffic and you already suffer a lot because of the disadvantages of the megacities. It means you need places (...) to go to find quiet."

…ON THE LIMITS OF IMMIGRATION

"Because many of the places like the best universities, best hospitals, whatever, best institutions, they are either in Istanbul, Ankara, or Izmir, they are in big cities. And can you imagine, about one quarter of the Turkish population is living in Istanbul. One quarter. We have in total 81 provinces, 81 cities. But one part of the population is living in just one city. And Istanbul does not have a huge geographical size. Istanbul is a small city compared to many other cities in Turkey as well. But Istanbul has to carry the burden of this huge population. I think we need to change the migration from other cities to Istanbul. (...) We need policies to decrease the population of Istanbul. There should be more infrastructure in other cities, and the companies and people should move to other cities as well. It is also interesting to note that every year at least a few more universities are opened in Istanbul. And one quarter of Turkish universities are located in Istanbul, in just one city. And every year thousands of young people, university students, come to Istanbul to study at the university. And after graduation they just stay here, because they have employment opportunities."

…ON TOLERANCE

"And we also have Christian minorities living in Turkey, Armenian people. We also have a Jewish minority as well. And most of these non-Muslim minorities live in Istanbul. (...) Therefore, when we think of Istanbul, we need to think about of course the historical mosques, but we also need to remember the churches and synagogues as well. (...) We have these differences, having these differences within us, it is important. You have conservative people, but you have the artists as well. (...) If you live in Istanbul and if you work at a big company, for example, or if you are a student from Malawi at a university in Istanbul, then it means you have friends from different ethnicities, from different religions, you come across them and you become friends with all these people. I think that is something quite important."

...ON PROTECTING THE ENVIRONMENT

"I think in some parts of Istanbul there are these young people who got inspired by this Fridays for Future movement, and they have also some small demonstrations. The scale cannot be compared to these huge Fridays for Future demonstrations, but it is kind of growing, I would say. Istanbul is one of the centers of these cultural resistance moments, these demonstrations within the country. It is important to note that it started in Istanbul. (…) But now it has become a countrywide phenomenon. And in many small Anatolian provinces, even in some small villages, people are demonstrating (…) when there are attempts to destroy their villages, (…) And I should note that in these Anatolian provinces and Anatolian towns and villages, women are at the forefront (…), because they say this is my field, I earn my living from this field."

...ÜBER DIE ENTWICKLUNG DER STADT

„Ja, Istanbul hat sich in den letzten Jahrzehnten stark verändert. Wir können sagen, dass die Bevölkerung immer größer wird, da so viele Menschen aus der Türkei oder aus anderen Ländern nach Istanbul ziehen, was bedeutet, dass Istanbul auch in die Infrastruktur investieren muss. Das betrifft in erster Linie das Verkehrswesen. Wir haben zum Beispiel Metrobusse und neue Metrolinien. Auch das ist sehr wichtig. Aber wegen der enormen Verstädterung und der starken Zuwanderung gibt es leider weniger Wälder, weniger Parks und weniger Grünflächen in Istanbul. Überall sieht man diesen Beton, diese riesigen Gebäude, Wolkenkratzer. Das war in meiner Kindheit nicht der Fall. In meiner Jugend gab es nur wenige Wolkenkratzer in Istanbul. (…) Heute sieht man einen Park oder einen Wald, und morgen sieht man, dass in dem Wald ein Bau begonnen hat, diese Abholzung und diese riesige Bautätigkeit. Das ist ein großes Problem in Istanbul."

...ÜBER DIE BEDEUTUNG VON PARKS

„Und der Gezi-Park ist zum Symbol geworden. Sie haben versucht, den einzigen Park, die einzige Grünfläche im Zentrum von Istanbul zu zerstören. Das war der Tropfen der das Fass zum Überlaufen gebracht hat. (…) Wissen Sie, wir sind keine Roboter. Wenn man nur zur Arbeit geht und dann nach Hause, wenn man die Natur nicht spürt, wie kann man dann seine Menschlichkeit spüren? Ich denke, in den Megastädten haben wir ein Recht auf die Stadt. Das bedeutet, dass wir diese natürlichen Orte bewahren wollen, denn wenn man in einer Megastadt lebt, verbringt man viel Zeit im Verkehr und leidet bereits sehr unter den Nachteilen der Megastädte. Das bedeutet, dass man Orte braucht, (…) an denen man zur Ruhe kommen kann."

...ÜBER DIE GRENZEN DER ZUWANDERUNG

„Viele der besten Universitäten, Krankenhäuser und sonstigen Einrichtungen befinden sich entweder in Istanbul, Ankara oder Izmir, also in großen Städten. Und ein Viertel der türkischen Bevölkerung lebt in Istanbul. Ein Viertel. Wir haben insgesamt 81 Provinzen, 81 Städte. Aber ein Viertel der Bevölkerung lebt in nur einer Stadt. Und Istanbul hat keine riesige geografische Ausdehnung. Auch im Vergleich zu vielen anderen Städten in der Türkei ist Istanbul eine kleine Stadt. Aber Istanbul hat die Last dieser riesigen Bevölkerung zu tragen. Ich denke, wir müssen die Migration von anderen Städten nach Istanbul ändern. (…) Wir brauchen eine Politik, die die Bevölkerung von Istanbul verringert. Es sollte mehr Infrastruktur in anderen Städten geben und die Unternehmen und Menschen sollten auch in andere Städte ziehen. Interessant ist auch, dass jedes Jahr mindestens ein paar weitere Universitäten in Istanbul eröffnet werden. Und ein Viertel der türkischen Universitäten befindet sich in Istanbul, in nur einer einzigen Stadt. Und jedes Jahr kommen Tausende von jungen Menschen, Studenten, nach Istanbul, um an der Universität zu studieren. Und nach ihrem Abschluss bleiben sie einfach hier, weil sie hier Beschäftigungsmöglichkeiten haben."

...ÜBER DIE TOLERANZ

„Und wir haben auch christliche Minderheiten in der Türkei, wie z. B. das armenische Volk. Wir haben auch eine jüdische Minderheit. Und die meisten dieser nicht-muslimischen Minderheiten leben in Istanbul. (…) Wenn wir also an Istanbul denken, müssen wir natürlich an die historischen Moscheen denken, aber wir müssen auch an die Kirchen und Synagogen denken. (…) Wir haben diese Unterschiede, und es ist wichtig, diese Unterschiede in uns zu haben. Es gibt konservative Menschen, aber es gibt auch die Künstler. (…) Wenn man in Istanbul lebt und zum Beispiel in einem großen Unternehmen arbeitet oder als Student aus Malawi an einer Universität in Istanbul studiert, dann hat man Freunde aus verschiedenen Ethnien, aus verschiedenen Religionen, man begegnet ihnen und freundet sich mit all diesen Menschen an. Ich denke, das ist etwas ganz Wichtiges."

...ÜBER DEN UMWELTSCHUTZ

„Ich glaube, in einigen Teilen Istanbuls gibt es junge Leute, die sich von der Fridays-for-Future-Bewegung haben inspirieren lassen und die auch kleine Demonstrationen veranstalten. Das Ausmaß ist nicht mit den großen Freitagsdemonstrationen zu vergleichen, aber es wächst, würde ich sagen. Aber Istanbul ist eines der Zentren dieser kulturellen Widerstandsmomente, dieser Demonstrationen im Lande. Aber es ist wichtig zu erwähnen, dass es in Istanbul begonnen hat. (…) Aber jetzt ist es ein landesweites Phänomen geworden. Und in vielen kleinen anatolischen Provinzen, sogar in einigen kleinen Dörfern, demonstrieren die Menschen (…), wenn es Versuche gibt, ihre Dörfer zerstören. (…) Und ich sollte anmerken, dass in diesen anatolischen Provinzen und anatolischen Städten und Dörfern die Frauen an der Spitze stehen (…), weil sie sagen, ‚das ist mein Feld, ich verdiene meinen Lebensunterhalt mit diesem Feld'."

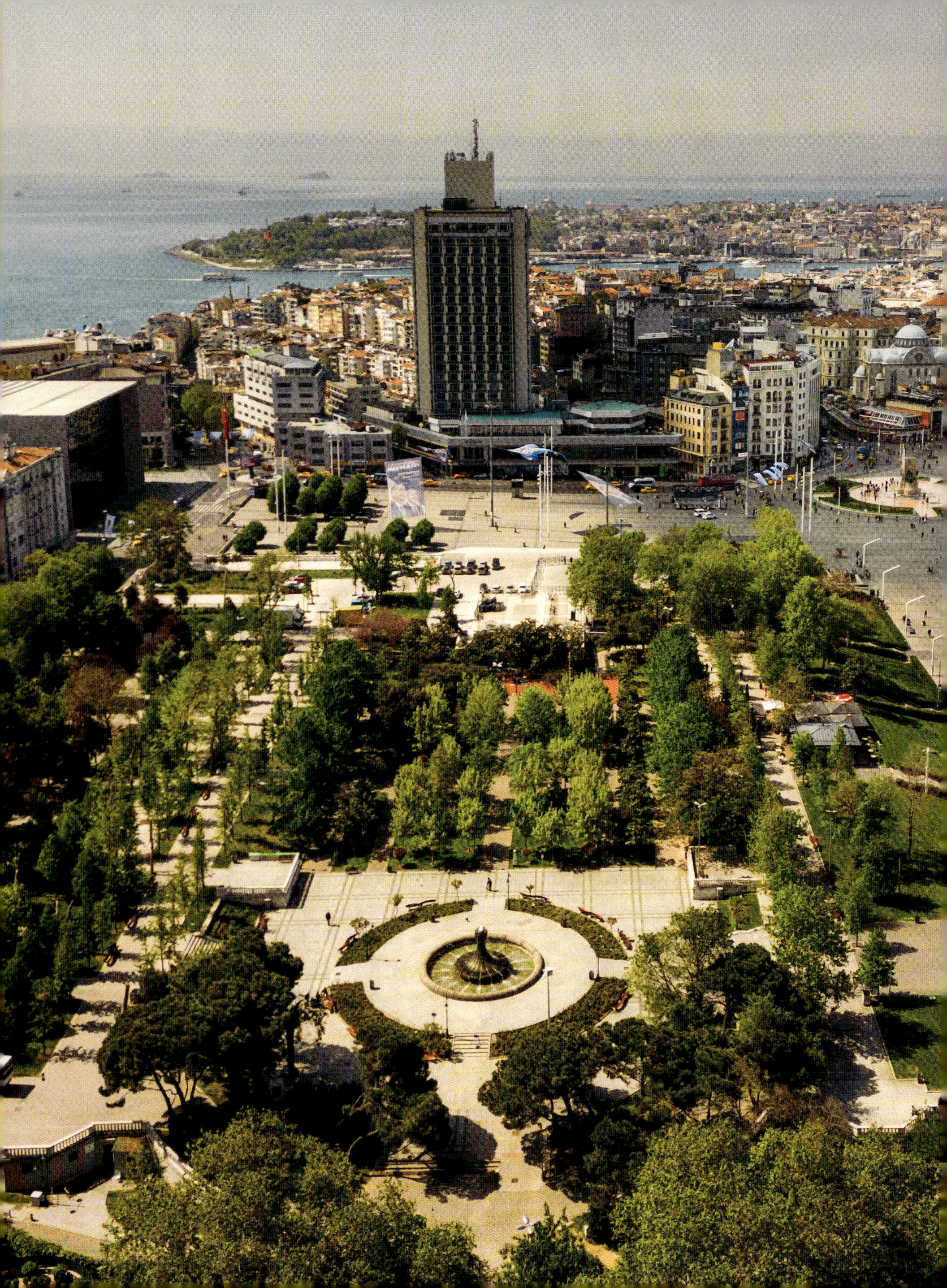

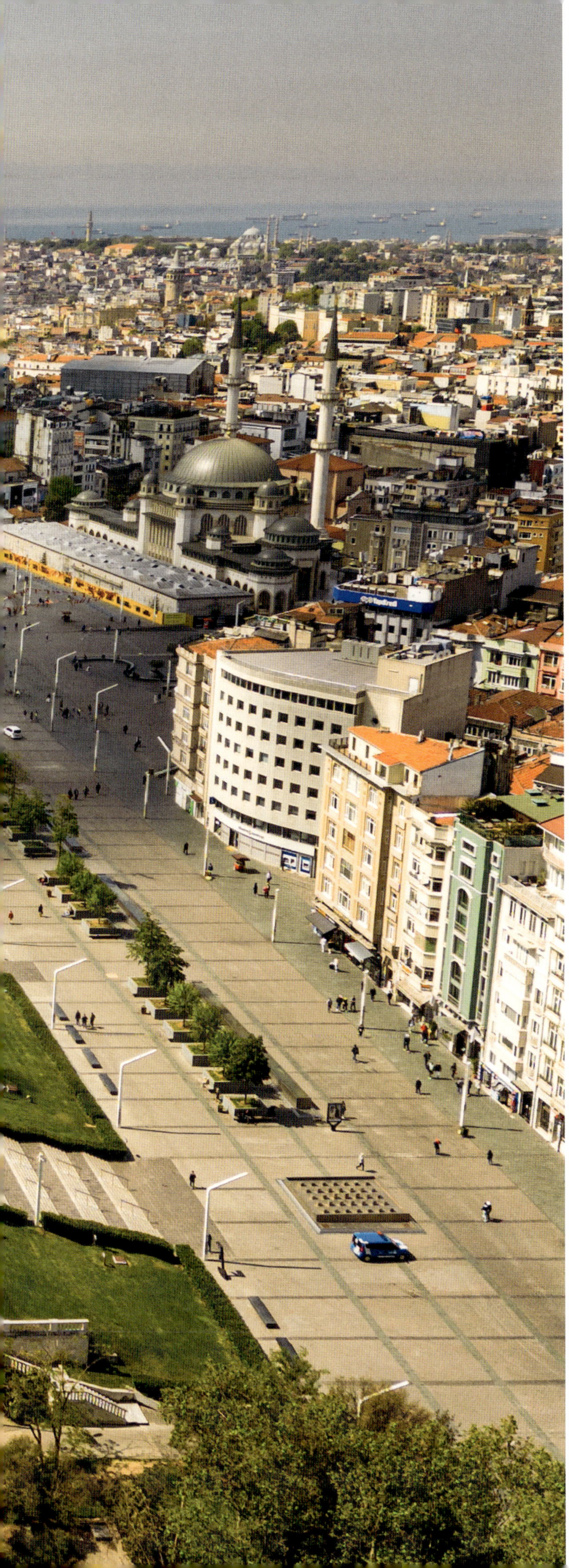

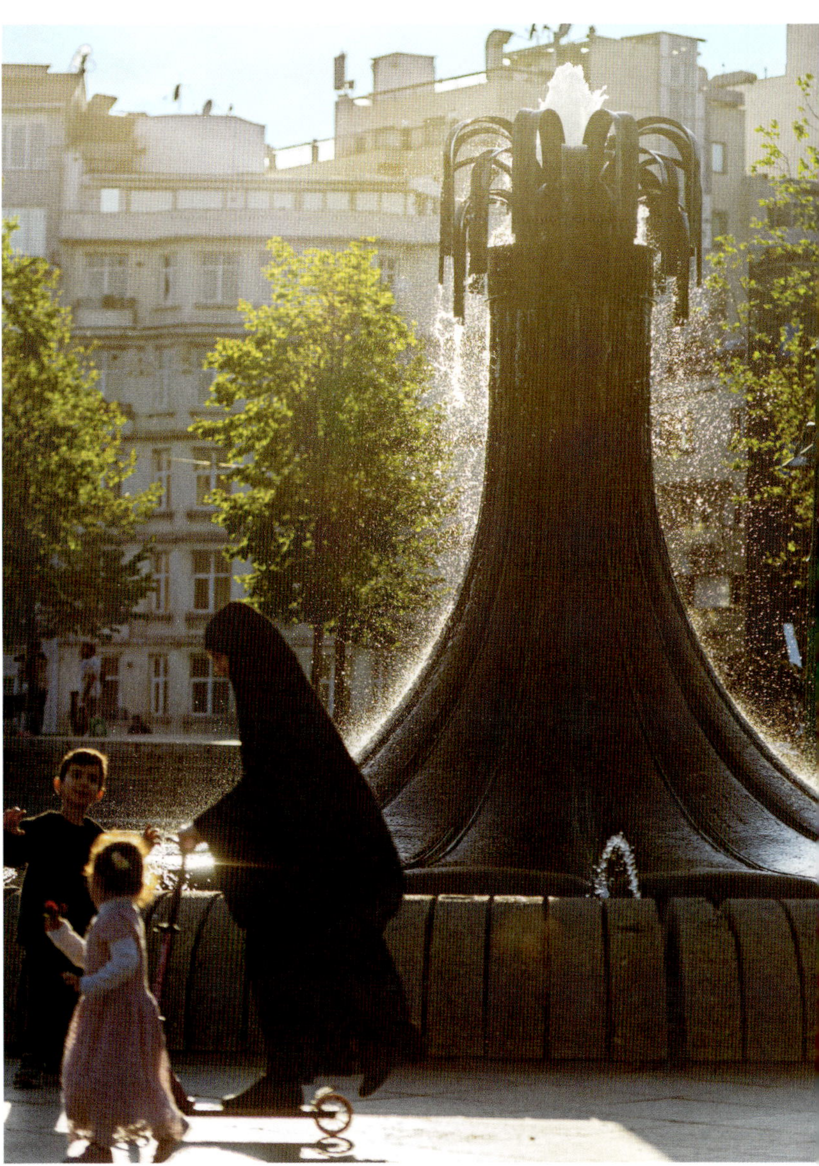

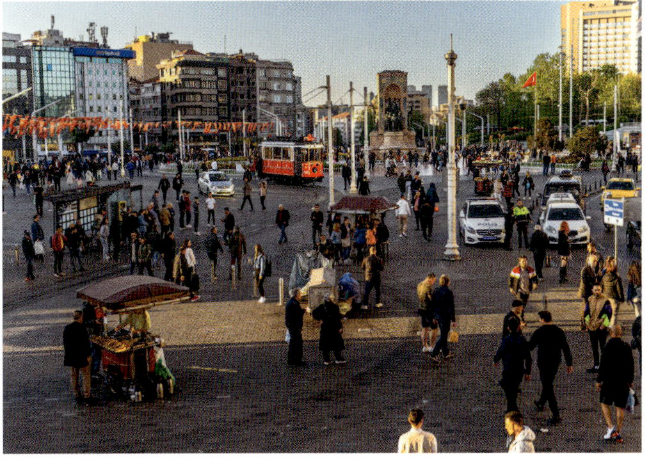

"And Gezi Park has become the symbol.
They just tried to destroy the only park,
the only green area in the very center of Istanbul.
It was the final straw." (Birgul Demirtas)

„Und der Gezi-Park ist zum Symbol geworden,
sie haben tatsächlich versucht, den einzigen
Park, die einzige Grünfläche im Zentrum Istanbuls
zu zerstören. Es war der letzte Tropfen im Glas."
(Birgul Demirtas)

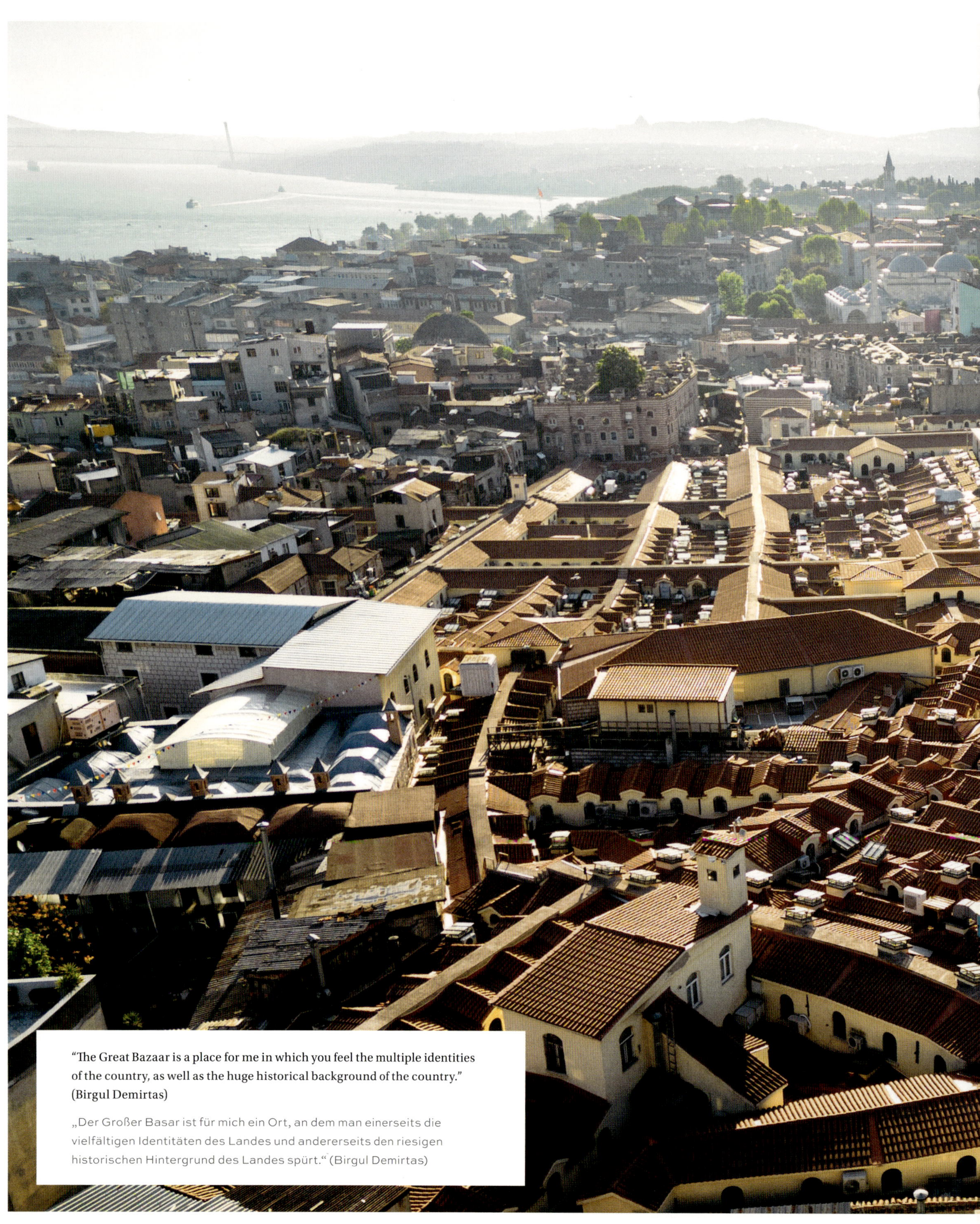

"The Great Bazaar is a place for me in which you feel the multiple identities of the country, as well as the huge historical background of the country." (Birgul Demirtas)

„Der Großer Basar ist für mich ein Ort, an dem man einerseits die vielfältigen Identitäten des Landes und andererseits den riesigen historischen Hintergrund des Landes spürt." (Birgul Demirtas)

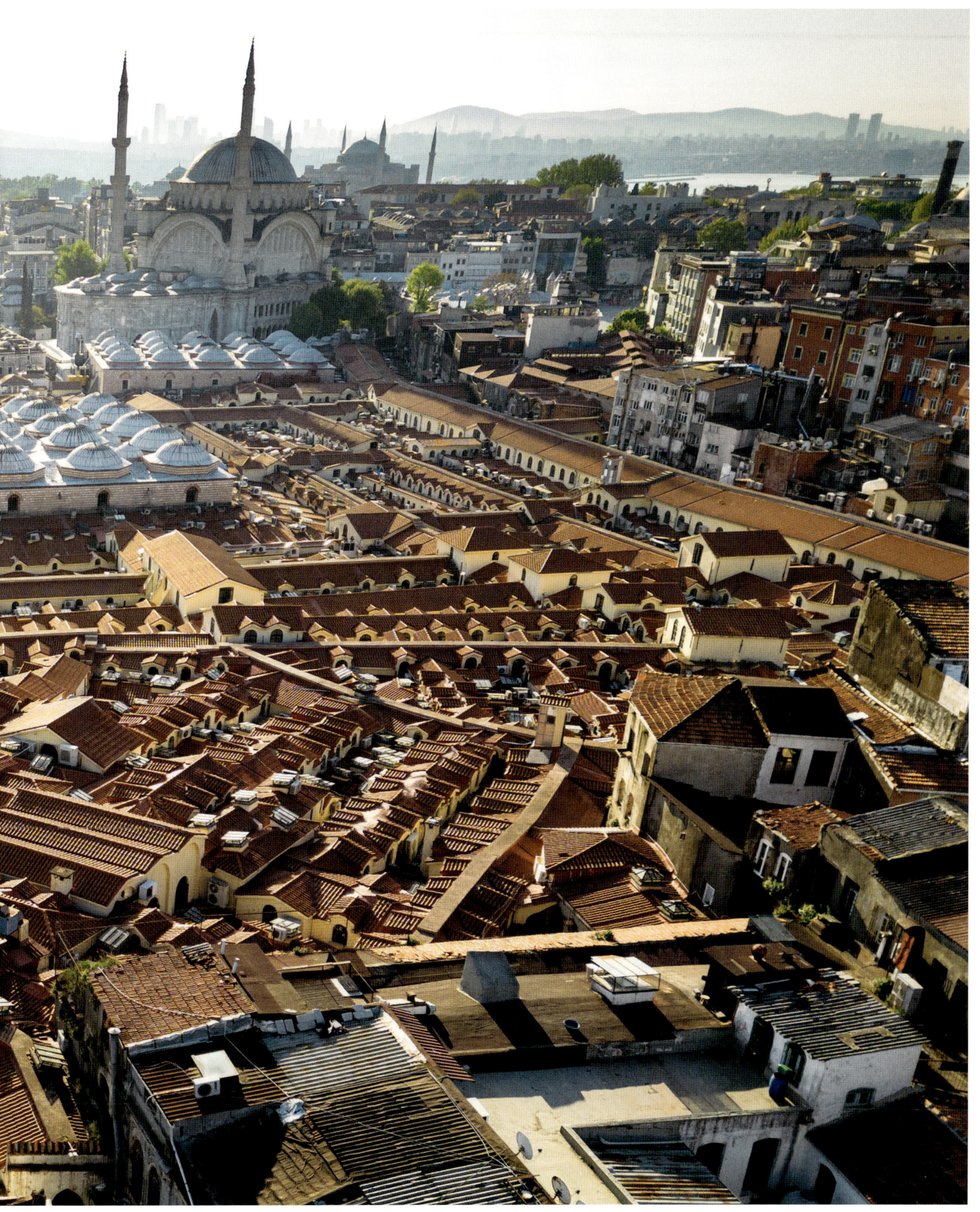

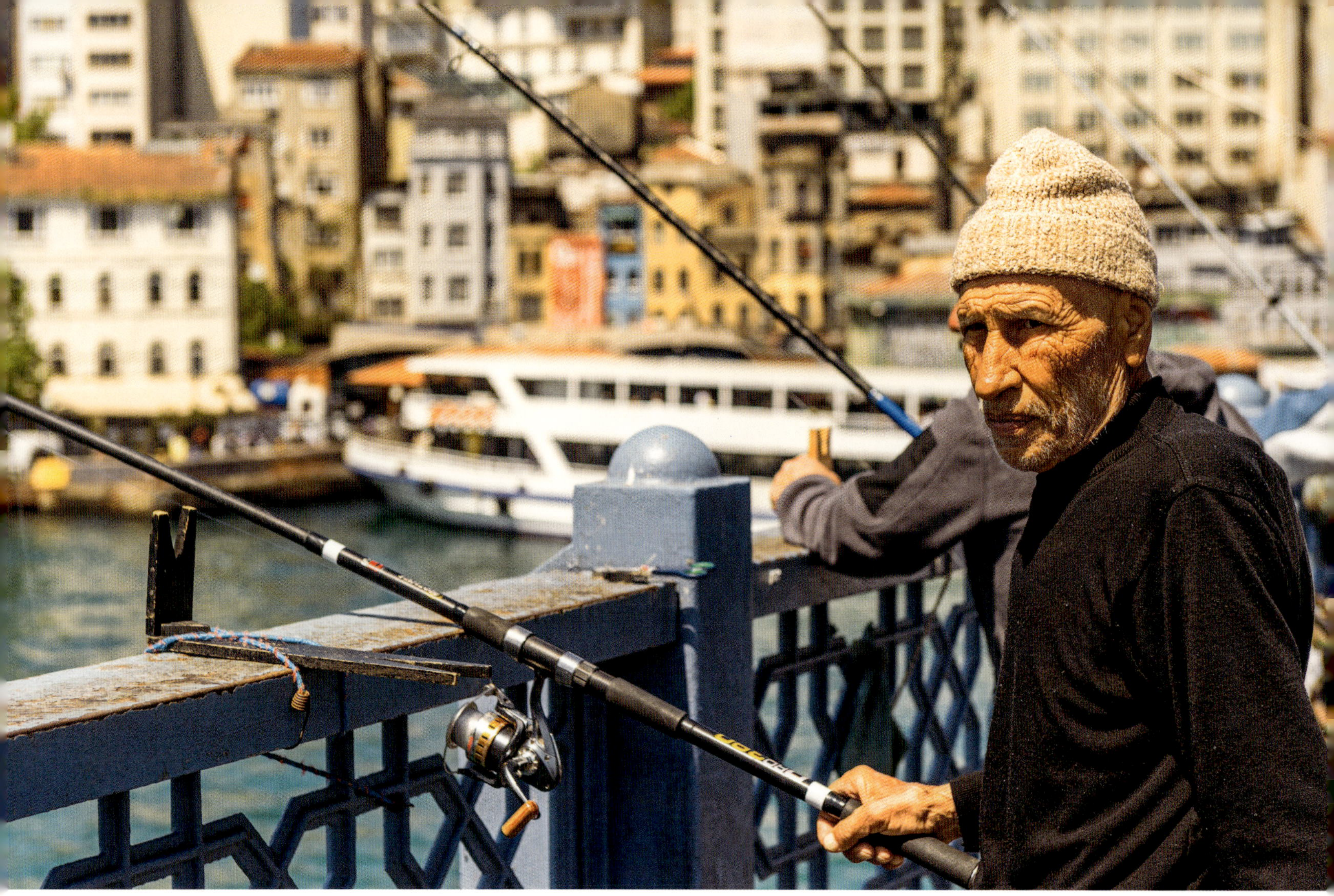

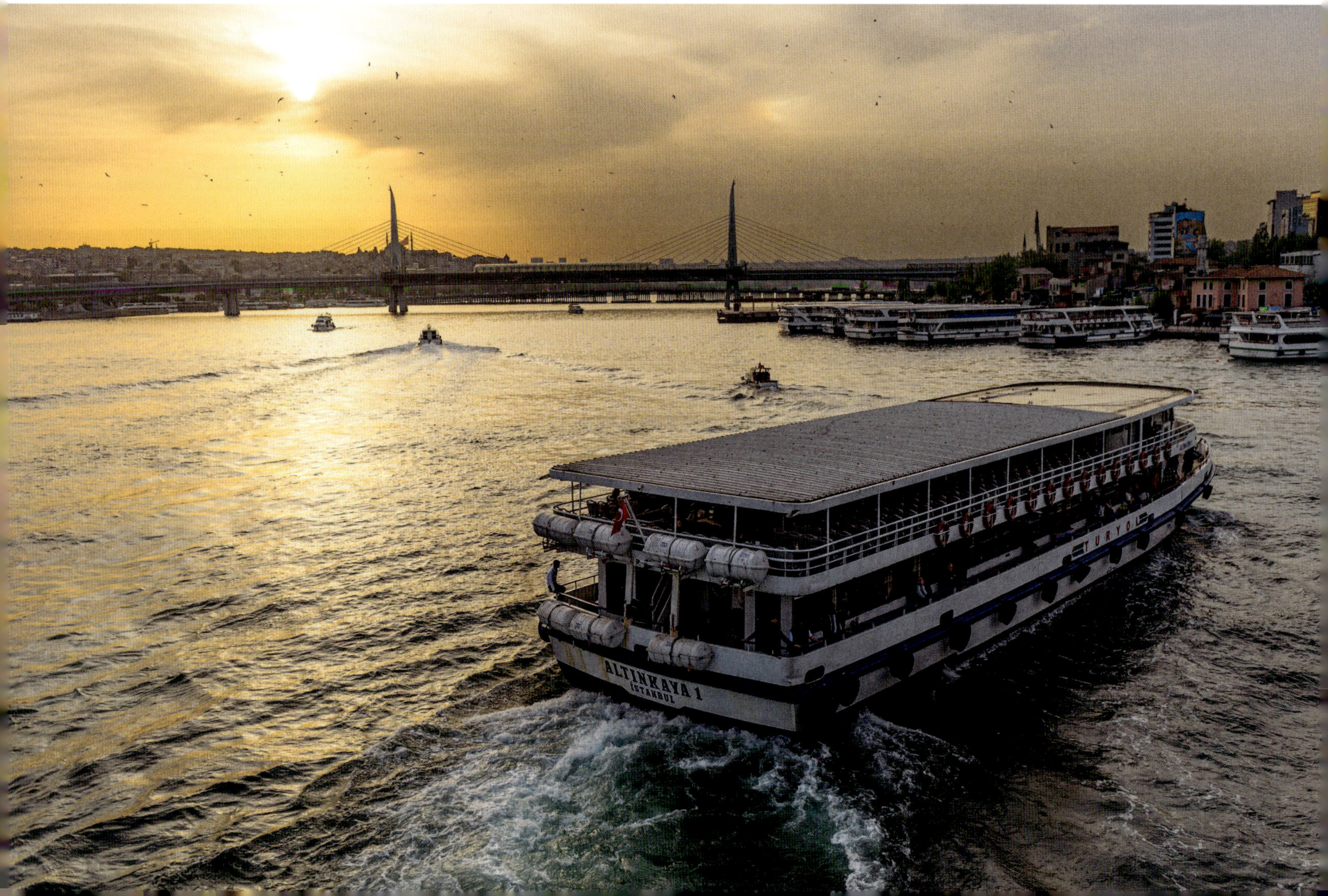

"You suffer from the main disadvantages of Istanbul, but when you go to the Bosporus, you forget about everything. You forget about traffic jams, you forget about the overcrowdedness (…) and you just listen to the Bosporus." (Birgul Demirtas)

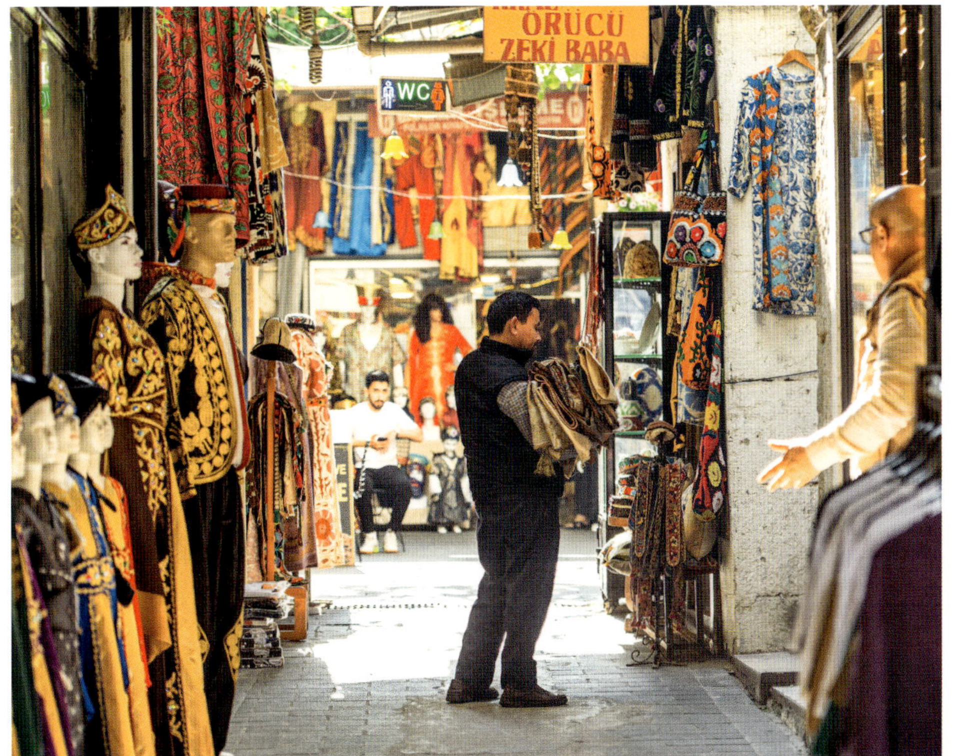

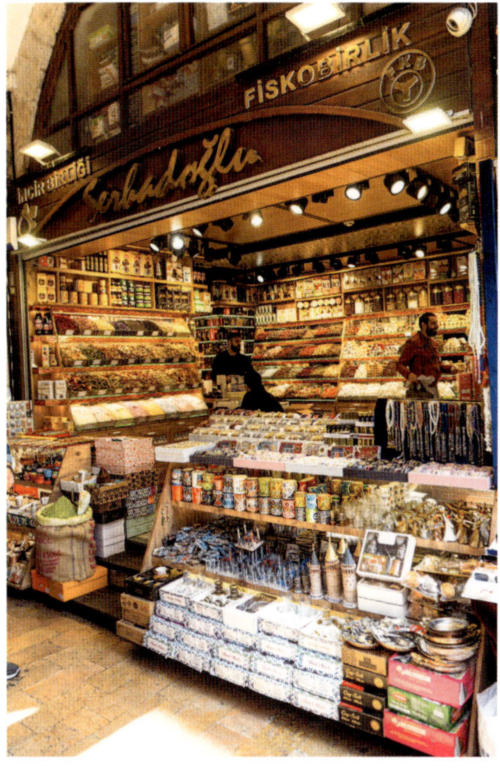

„Man leidet unter den vielen Nachteilen Istanbuls, aber wenn man zum Bosporus fährt, vergisst man alles. Man vergisst den Stau, man vergisst die Überfüllung (…) und man hört nur den Bosporus." (Birgul Demirtas)

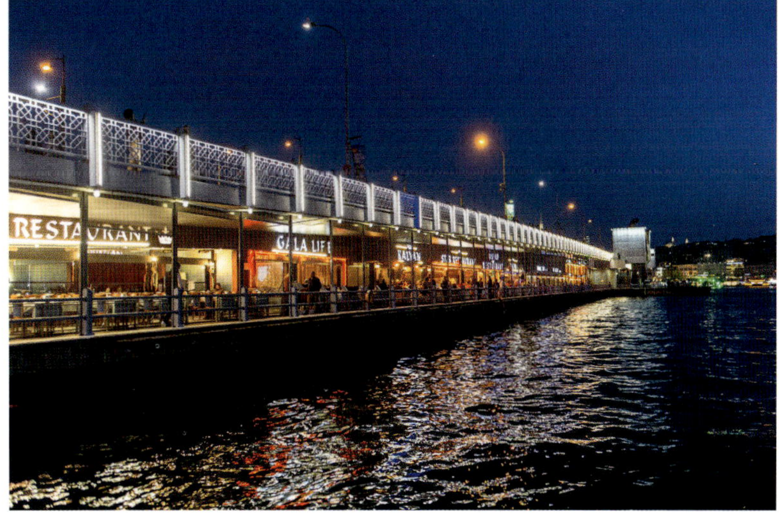

"The Asian part of Istanbul is the more livable part, and the European part is more economic. Many people work in the European part, but prefer to live on the Asian side." (Birgul Demirtas)

„Der asiatische Teil Istanbuls ist der lebenswertere, der europäische eher der ökonomische Teil. Viele arbeiten zwar im europäischen Teil, leben aber lieber auf der asiatischen Seite." (Birgul Demirtas)

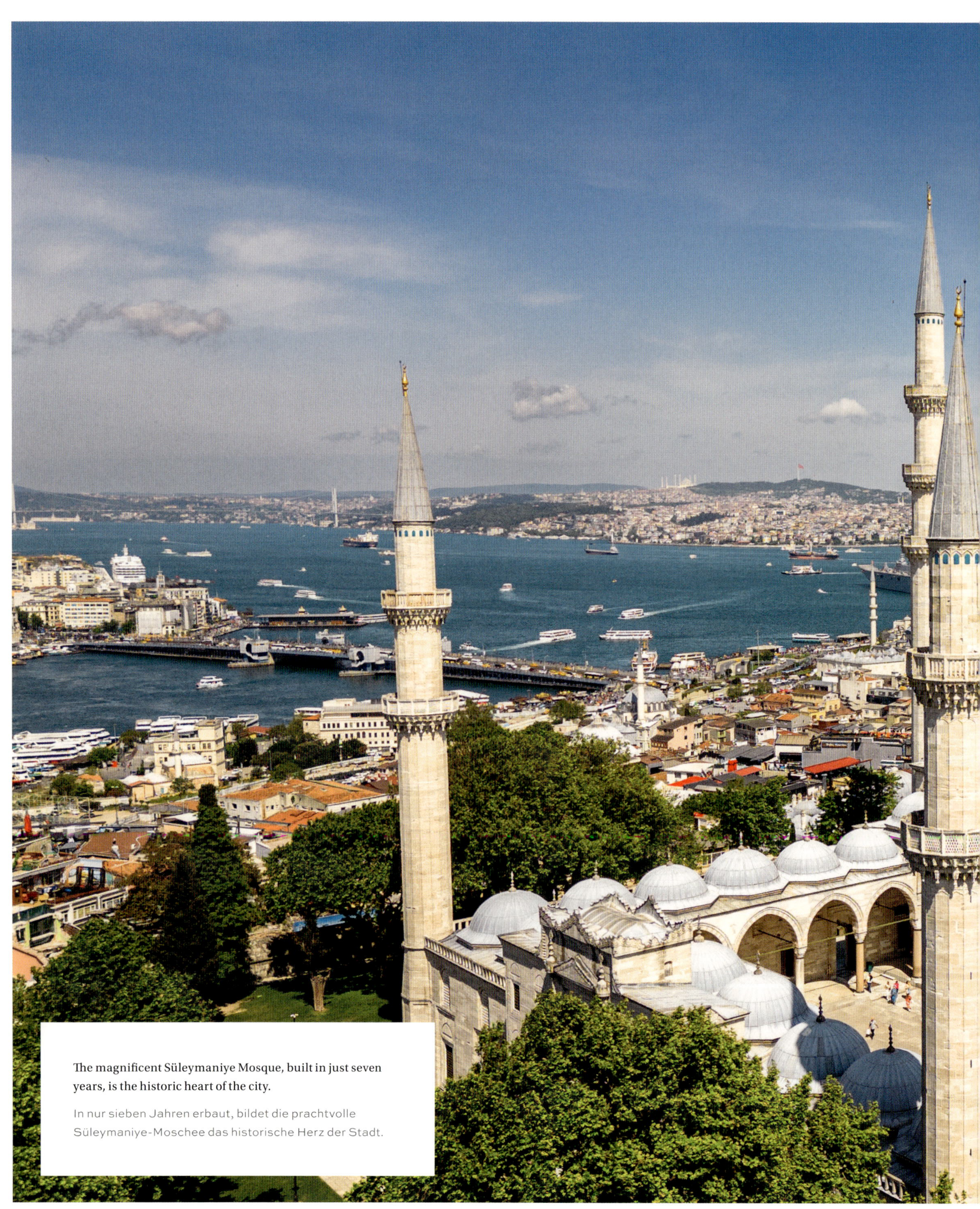

The magnificent Süleymaniye Mosque, built in just seven years, is the historic heart of the city.

In nur sieben Jahren erbaut, bildet die prachtvolle Süleymaniye-Moschee das historische Herz der Stadt.

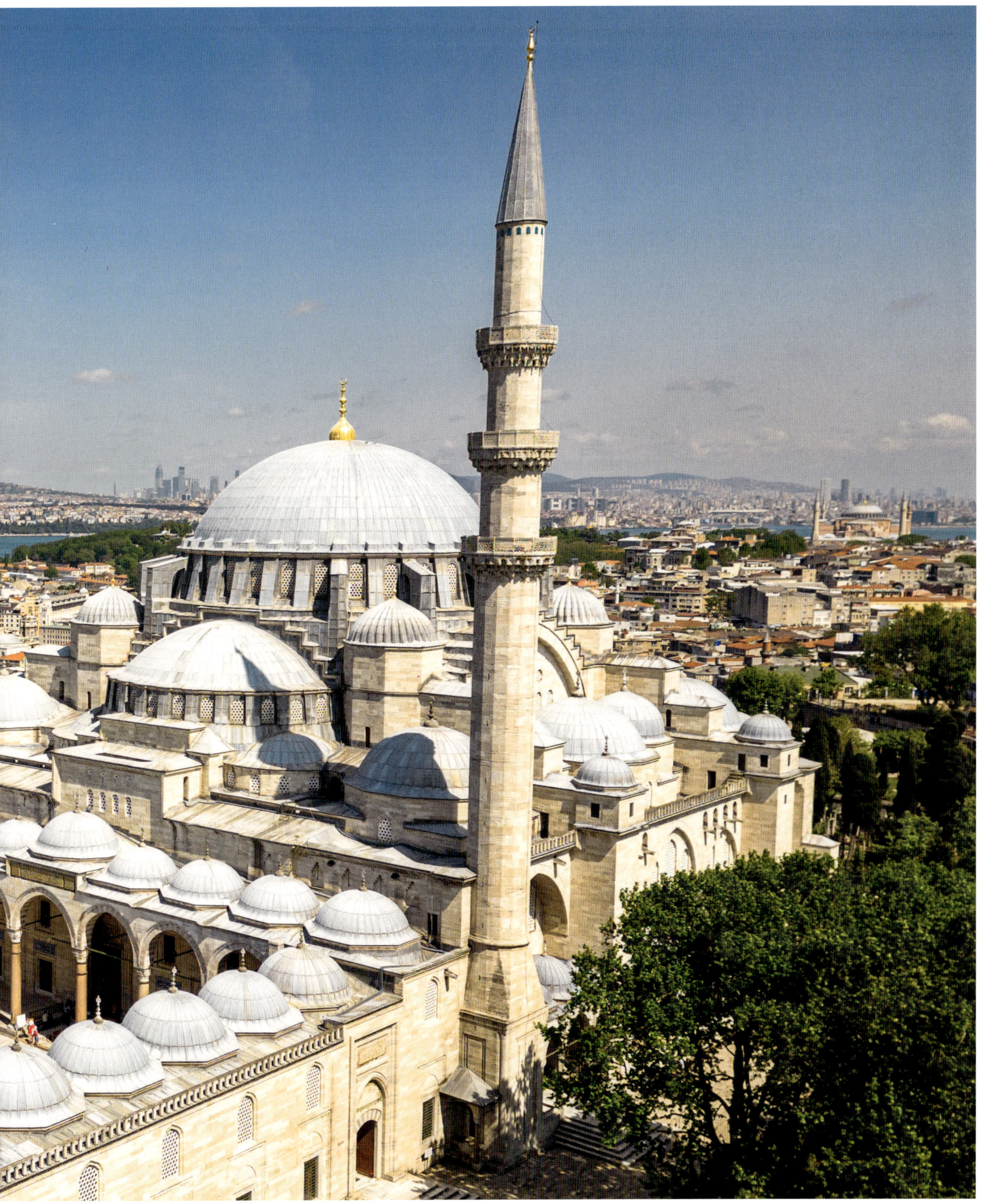

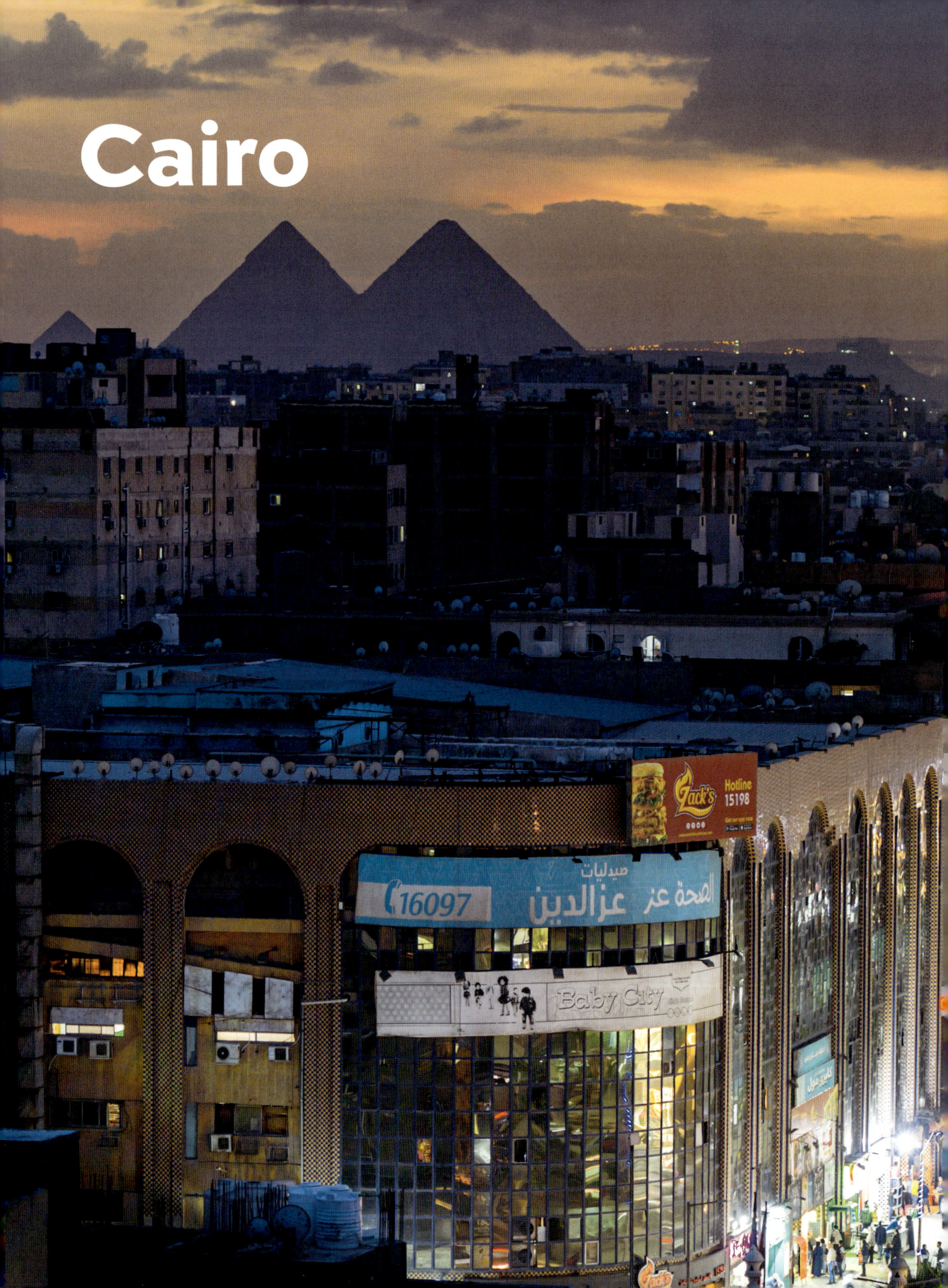

Cairo
Zack's
Hotline
15198
16097
صيدليات الصحة عز عزالدين
Baby City

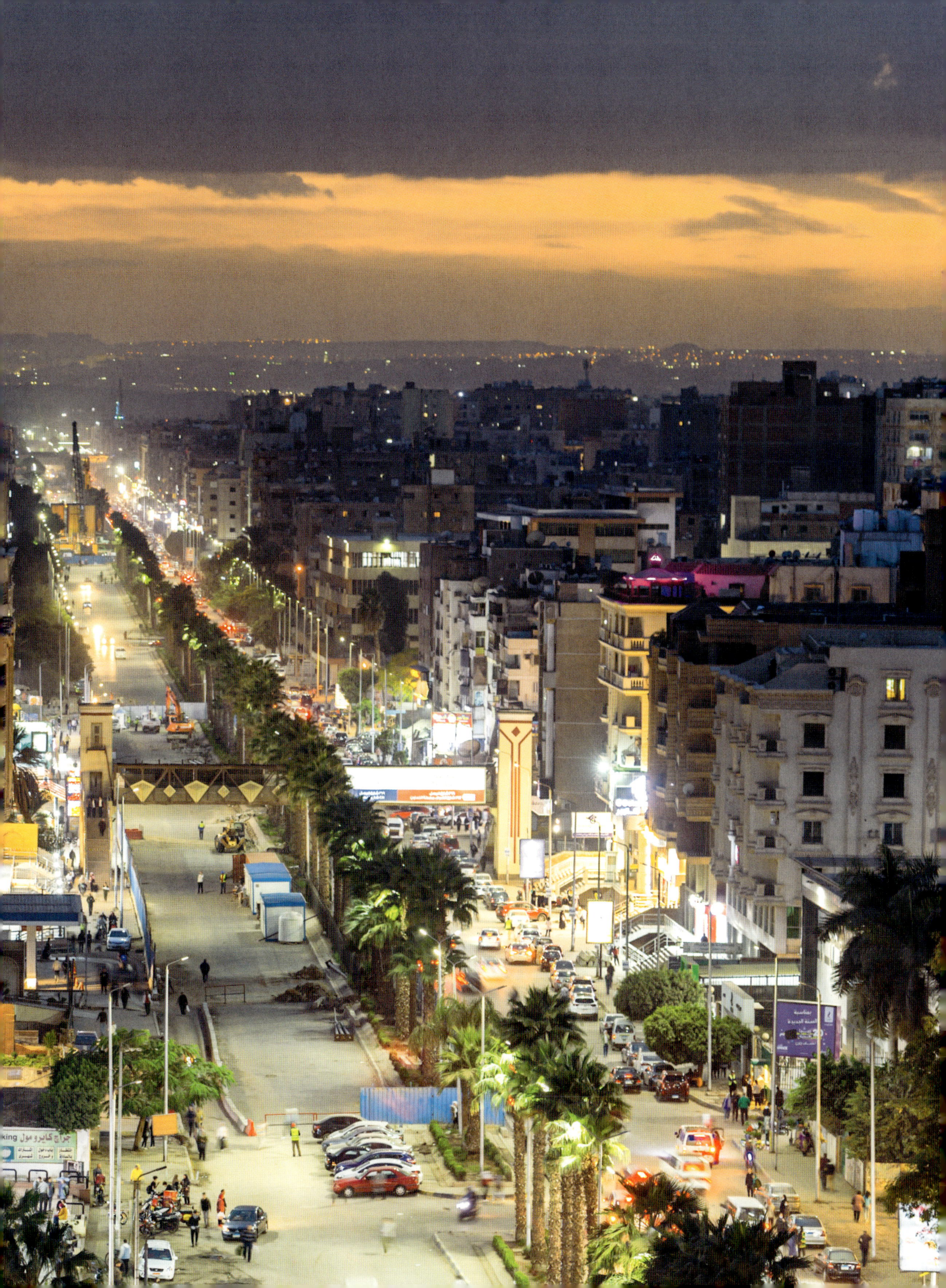

The Unpredictable City

Die unvorhersehbare Stadt

"So the reason for low rates of homelessness (…) may in fact be due to the tremendous importance of the family and familial networks in Egypt. It's very rare for somebody to not be related to anybody. So Egyptians are welcoming to guests in terms of hospitality, but they're extremely welcoming as well to, of course, their own family (…). So if they can't afford their own place, anything like that, you all live together." (Arto)

Only in the early morning hours does Cairo allow itself a little break from the constant din of traffic and throngs of people. This is when it becomes noticeable that, compared to other megacities, you don't see many homeless people here. Family, the social network of support, sticking together–these are the central values of this city. But of course they do exist, the people who fall through the cracks because they have no family, no income, no social support network. They can be found in the City of the Dead, *al-Qarafa*. This vast and sprawling cemetery complex, once located at the gates of the city, now right in its center, has become a refuge for the homeless, who have found humble shelter here in the often roofed tombs and mausoleums.

Outside this necropolis, Egypt's capital is a constructed chaos of high and low, old and new, dingy and attractive—perhaps it's actually unreasonable to expect families, children, the old, and the infirm to live here. Yet every neighborhood pulsates with life. The bazaars like Khan-el-Khalili are among the largest in Africa, unimaginably rich warehouses of goods in a sprawling network of alleyways. On the streets, the wandering commerce of the poor settles into every niche, adding to the strain on an already dismal infrastructure. Running just two or three errands in the city is often sufficient to take up an entire day.

On every corner, teahouses invite you to a brief respite or chat over a cup of tea, or a longer stay with a shisha. Food stalls where you can enjoy a quick *fuul*, puree-like brown beans, are all around, where people are always warmly welcomed and served. In many megacities, people are extremely friendly with one another. In Cairo, however, this warmth is overwhelming. This is how relationship networks are expanded and nurtured. Personal contacts are indispensable in this city, which surprises its inhabitants every day with new impediments, bureaucratic obstacles, and other enigmas.

„Der Grund für die niedrigen Obdachlosenquoten (…) könnte tatsächlich in der enormen Bedeutung der Familie und der familiären Netzwerke in Ägypten liegen. Es ist sehr selten, dass jemand mit niemandem verwandt ist. Die Ägypter sind also sehr gastfreundlich gegenüber Gästen, aber natürlich auch gegenüber ihrer eigenen Familie (…). Wenn sie sich keine eigene Wohnung oder ähnliches leisten können, leben sie alle zusammen." (Arto)

Nur in den frühen Morgenstunden gönnt sich Kairo ein klein wenig Pause vom Dauerlärm des Verkehrs und den Menschenströmen. Dann fällt auf, dass man hier im Vergleich zu anderen Megastädten, nur wenige Obdachlose sieht. Familie, das soziale Netz, und Zusammenhalt sind die zentralen Werte dieser Stadt. Doch es gibt sie natürlich trotzdem, die Menschen, die durch jegliches Raster fallen, weil sie vielleicht keine Familie, kein Einkommen und kein soziales Netzwerk haben. Man findet sie in der Stadt der Toten, *al-Qarafa*. Diese gigantische und weitläufige Friedhofsanlage, einst vor den Toren der Stadt gelegen, heute mitten im Zentrum ist zum Refugium von Obdachlosen geworden, die hier in den oft überdachten Grabanlagen und Mausoleen ein bescheidenes Obdach gefunden haben.

Außerhalb dieser Nekropole ist Ägyptens Hauptstadt ein gebautes Chaos aus Hoch und Niedrig, Alt und Neu, Schmuddelig und Ansprechend – eigentlich eine Zumutung für Familien, Kinder, Alte und Kranke. Dennoch pulsiert das Leben in jedem Viertel. Die Märkte wie Khan-el-Khalili gehören zu den größten in Afrika, unvorstellbar reichhaltige Warenlager in weitverzweigten Gassen. Auf den Straßen setzt sich der ambulante Handel der Armen in jeder Nische fest und belastet die sowieso schon schlechte Infrastruktur weiter. Zwei oder drei Wege in der Stadt sind oft schon ein volles Tagesprogramm.

Below the Cairo Tower, life on the Nile is still unhurried off the island of Gezira, where some of the rare open spaces can be found.

Zu Füßen des Cairo Tower spielt sich vor der Insel Gezira, auf der sich einige der raren Freiflächen befinden, noch heute gemächliches Leben auf dem Nil ab.

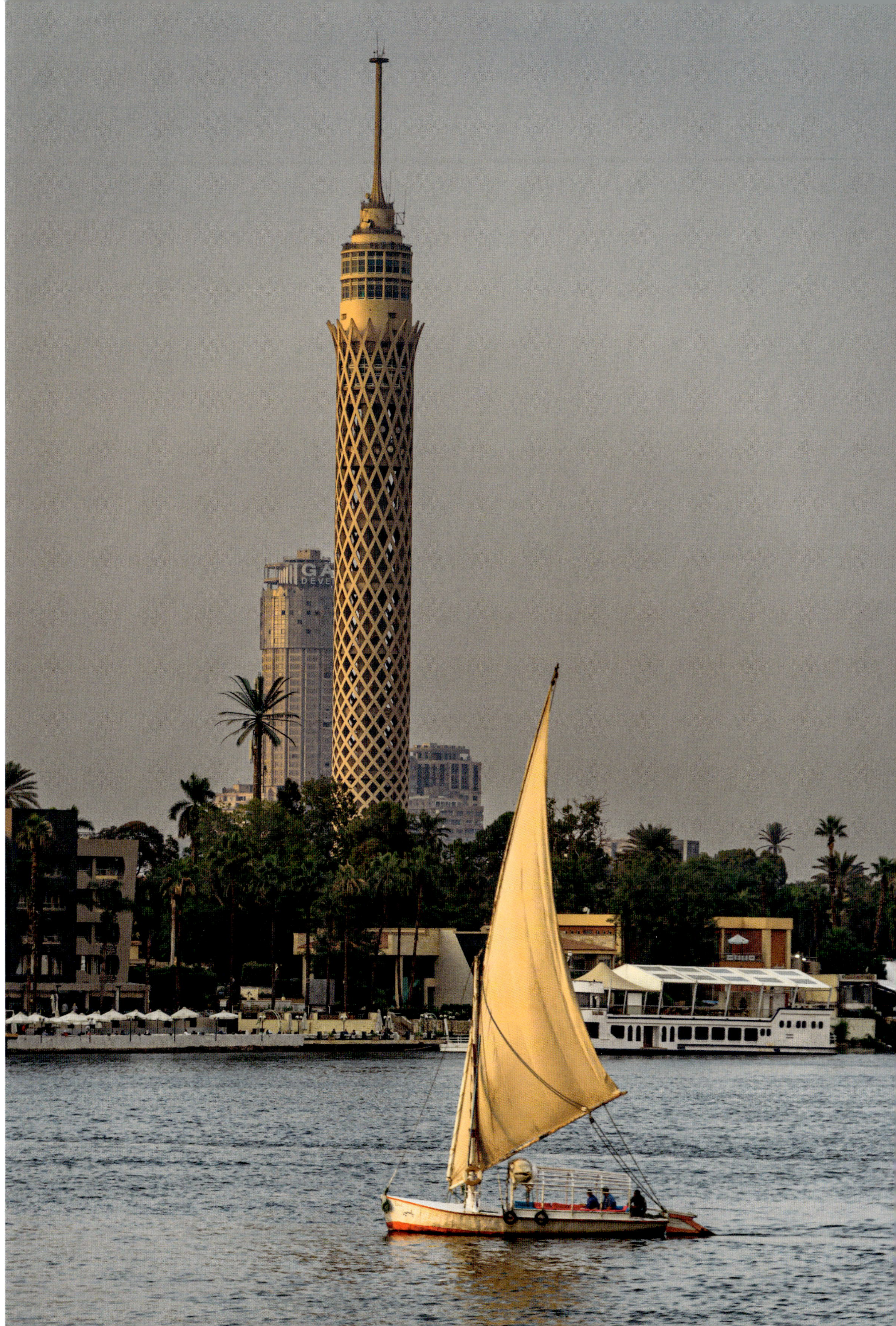

Cairo is strenuous for its residents, but it is also brimming with so much energy that it carries them along. No one can escape its pull, and so the city creates opportunities in every conceivable area. *Manshiyat Naser*, or The Garbage City, is one such case. Once a slum in the center of the city, people here have literally worked their way up from garbage. Small and large trucks full with the refuse of the many millions of residents drive non-stop into the narrow maze of alleys, before departing again loaded with sorted garbage for recycling factories. The *Zabbalin*, as the garbage sorters are called, are predominantly Coptic Christians. 20,000-30,000 Zabbalin live here, with some 40,000-50,000 more living in other parts of the city. Together, they recycle almost 80% of the garbage collected, compared to just 25% in Western industrialized countries.

"I think Cairo has a lot of concrete, and very little greenery and few accessible parks." (Mariam)

Cairo is a desert city. It could be a green city, though, in view of the Nile cutting through it. But city parks? No such thing. Every bit of open space has been developed. Parks are usually the most important retreats and public spaces for people in megacities. But in Cairo, the few green spaces, such as Al Azhar Park, are tourist attractions that charge a fee. Recreation usually takes place in the maze of streets, with people retreating to the rooftops with their increasingly popular rooftop gardens or the characteristic towering pigeon coops. Those who can afford it, however, move to the sprawling suburbs. Here you can enjoy shady boulevards in Heliopolis or cool off in the air-conditioned malls of New Cairo. Urban planners thought they had found their El Dorado here, but the government opted for something else, and is now building its New Administrative Capital east of Cairo in the middle of the desert. This way, the people have it all to themselves, but the new residents are already missing the vibrant energy in this artificial city.

An jeder Ecke laden Teehäuser zum kurzen Verweilen oder Plausch bei einem Tee oder längerem Aufenthalt bei einer Shisha ein. Essensstände, an denen man ein schnelles *fuul*, püreeartige braune Bohnen, bekommt sind allgegenwärtig. Stets wird man herzlich empfangen und bewirtet. In vielen Megacities fällt der überaus freundliche Umgang der Menschen untereinander auf. In Kairo aber ist diese Herzlichkeit überwältigend. So werden Beziehungsnetze ausgeweitet und gepflegt. Denn persönliche Kontakte sind unabdingbar in dieser Stadt, die ihre Bewohner täglich mit neuen Hindernissen, bürokratischen Hemmnissen und sonstigen Unwägbarkeiten überrascht.

Kairo ist anstrengend für seine Bewohner, aber auch voller Energie, die sie mitreißt. Niemand kann sich diesem Sog entziehen und so schafft die Stadt Möglichkeiten in allen nur denkbaren Bereichen. *Manschiyyet Nasser* bzw. „Müllstadt" ist so ein Fall. Einst ein Slum im Zentrum der Stadt, haben sich die Menschen hier buchstäblich aus dem Müll emporgearbeitet. Pausenlos fahren kleine und große LKWs mit den Abfällen der vielen Millionen Einwohner in das enge Gassengewirr und verlassen es wieder mit sortiertem Müll für die Recycling-Fabriken. Die *zabbalin*, wie die Müllsortierer genannt werden, sind überwiegend koptische Christen. 20 000 bis 30 000 Zabbalin leben hier, rund 40 000 bis 50 000 weitere in anderen Stadtteilen. Zusammen recyceln sie fast 80 Prozent des gesammelten Mülls, während westliche Industriestaaten auf gerade einmal 25 Prozent kommen.

„Ich finde, Kairo hat viel Beton und sehr wenig Grün und zugängliche Parks." (Mariam)

Kairo ist eine Wüstenstadt. Dank des Nils, der die Stadt in zwei Teile schneidet, könnte es eine grüne Stadt sein. Aber Parkanlagen? Fehlanzeige. Jede freie Fläche wurde bebaut. Parks sind in den Megastädten meist die wichtigsten Rückzugs- und öffentlichen Räume für die Menschen. In Kairo sind die wenigen Grünflächen wie der Al Azhar-Park Sehenswürdigkeiten und kostenpflichtig. Freizeit findet ansonsten im Gewirr der Straßen statt, Rückzug auf die Dächer mit ihren immer populärer werdenden Dachgärten oder den charakteristischen turmhohen Taubenverschlägen. Wer es sich leisten kann zieht allerdings in die weitläufigen Vororte. Hier genießt man schattige Alleen wie in Heliopolis oder kühlt sich in den klimatisierten Malls von New Cairo ab. Städteplaner fänden ein Dorado für ihre Aktivitäten, aber die Regierung entschied anders. Sie baut ihre Hauptstadt New Administrative Capital östlich von Kairo inmitten der Wüste neu auf. So ist man unter sich, aber die neuen Bewohner vermissen schon jetzt die Energie in dieser künstlichen Stadt.

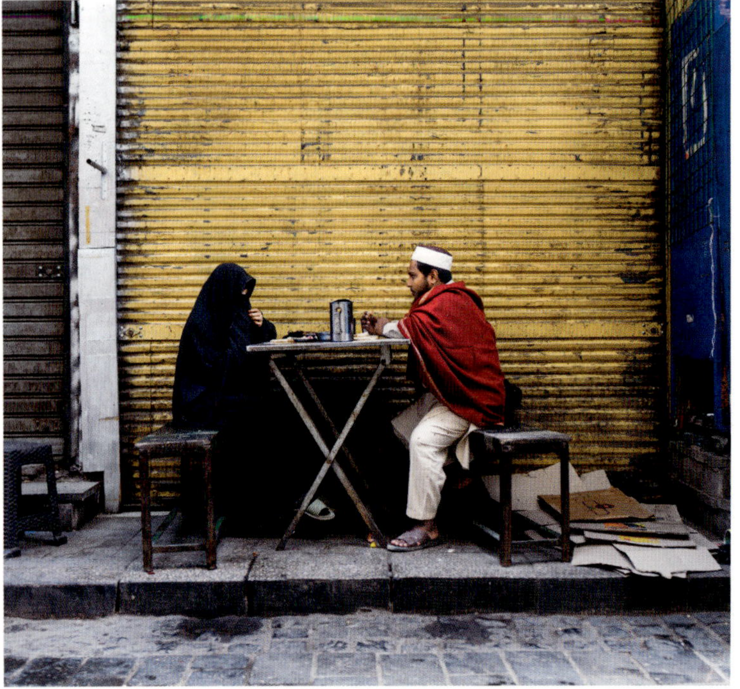

Every bit of available space in the city is used to serve tea or enjoy a break.

Jeder Winkel der Stadt wird genutzt, um Tee zu servieren oder eine Pause einzulegen.

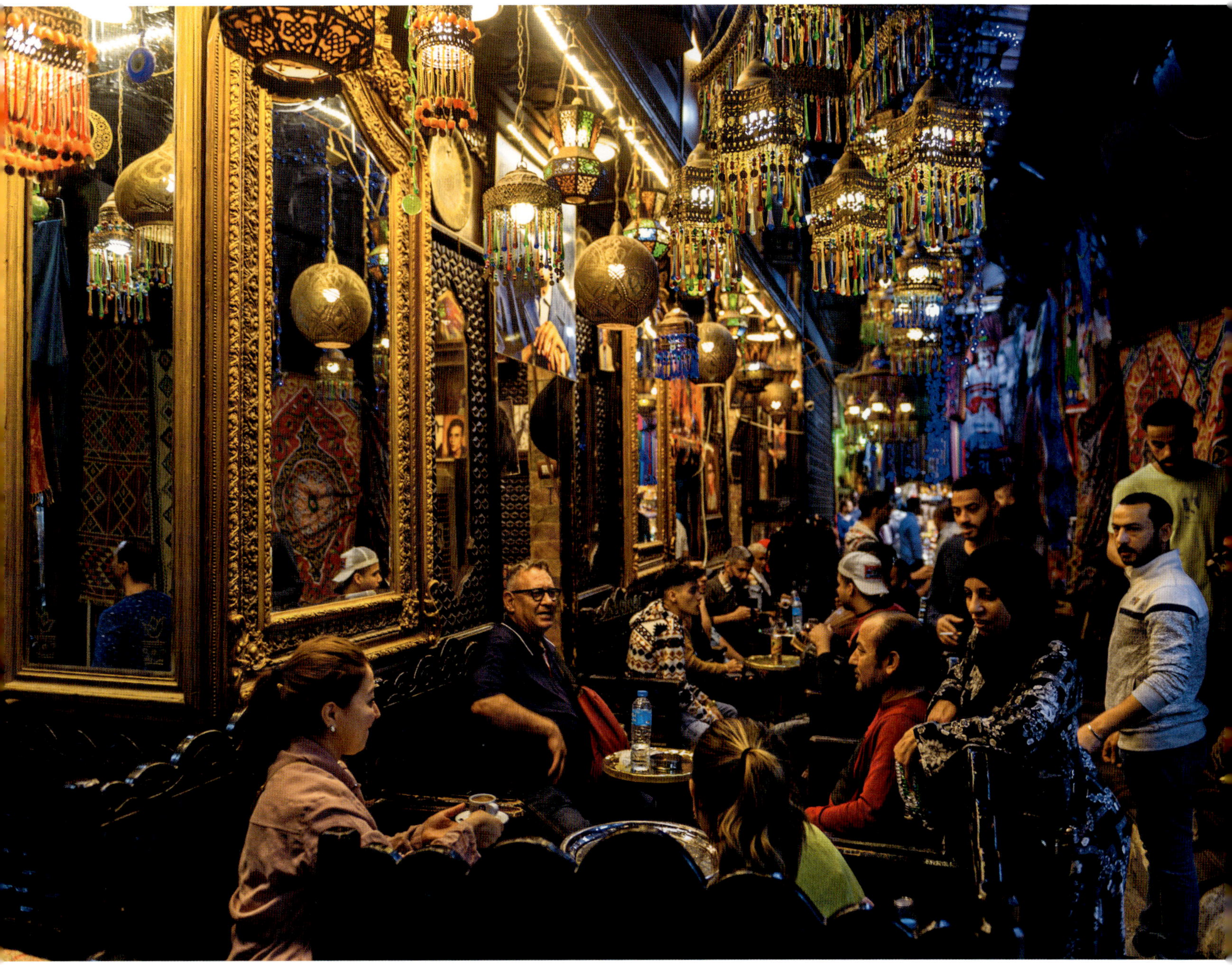

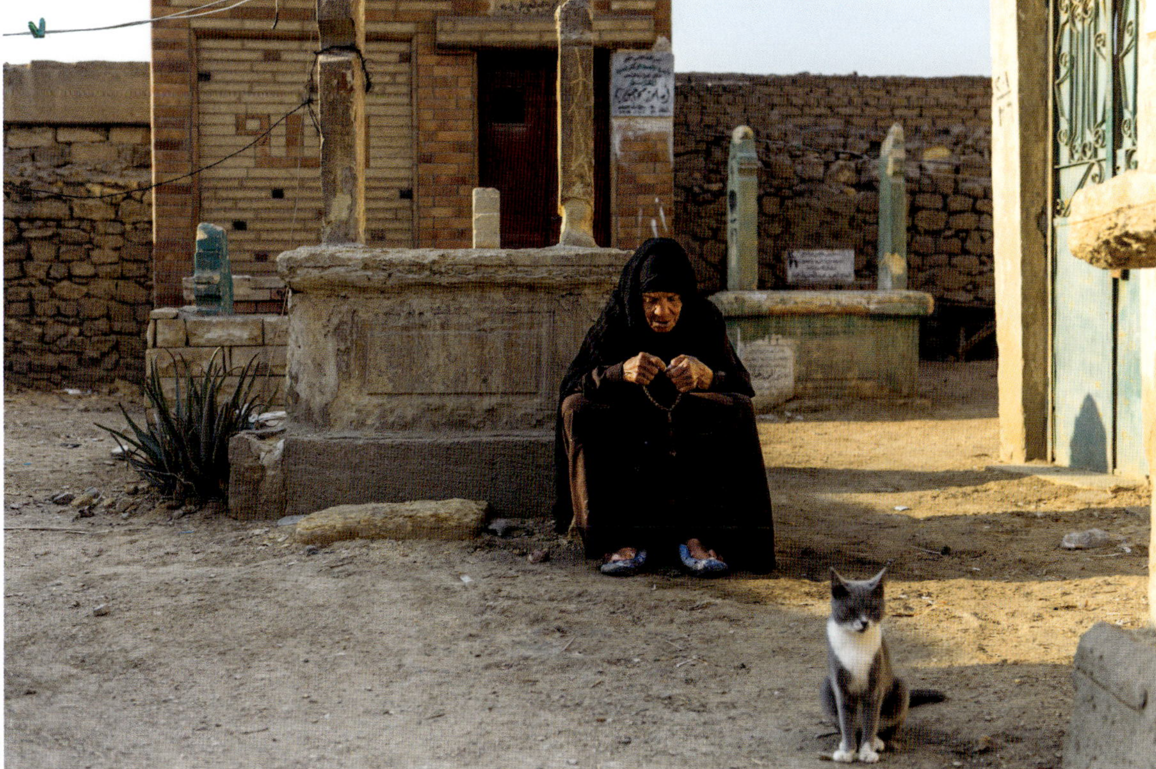

A city of contrasts: While the Islamic Old City is bustling with life, in the nearby City of the Dead live the people on the lowest fringes of society.

Stadt der Kontraste: Während in der islamischen Altstadt das Leben pulsiert, leben nebenan in der Stadt der Toten die Menschen am unteren Rand der Gesellschaft.

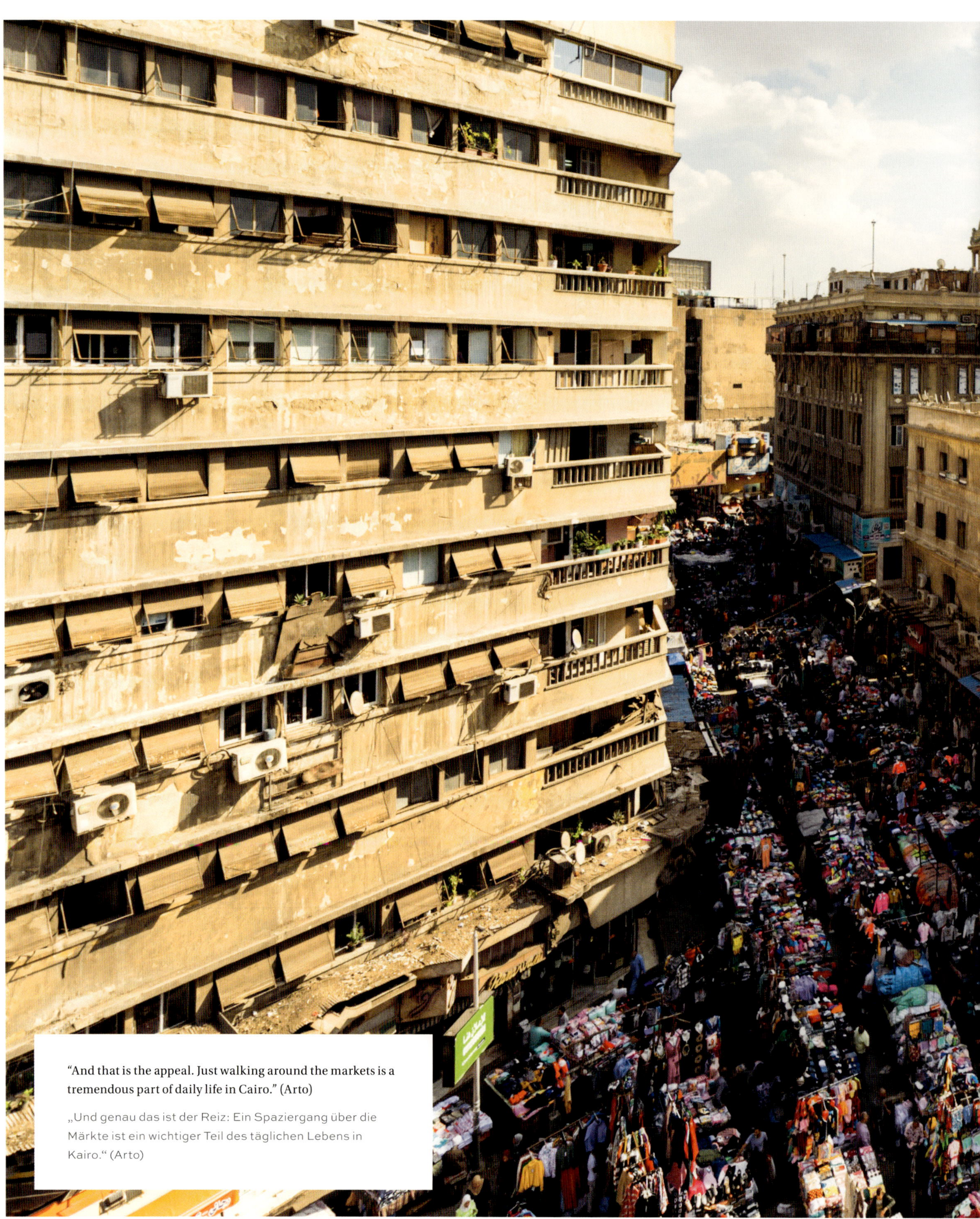

"And that is the appeal. Just walking around the markets is a tremendous part of daily life in Cairo." (Arto)

„Und genau das ist der Reiz: Ein Spaziergang über die Märkte ist ein wichtiger Teil des täglichen Lebens in Kairo." (Arto)

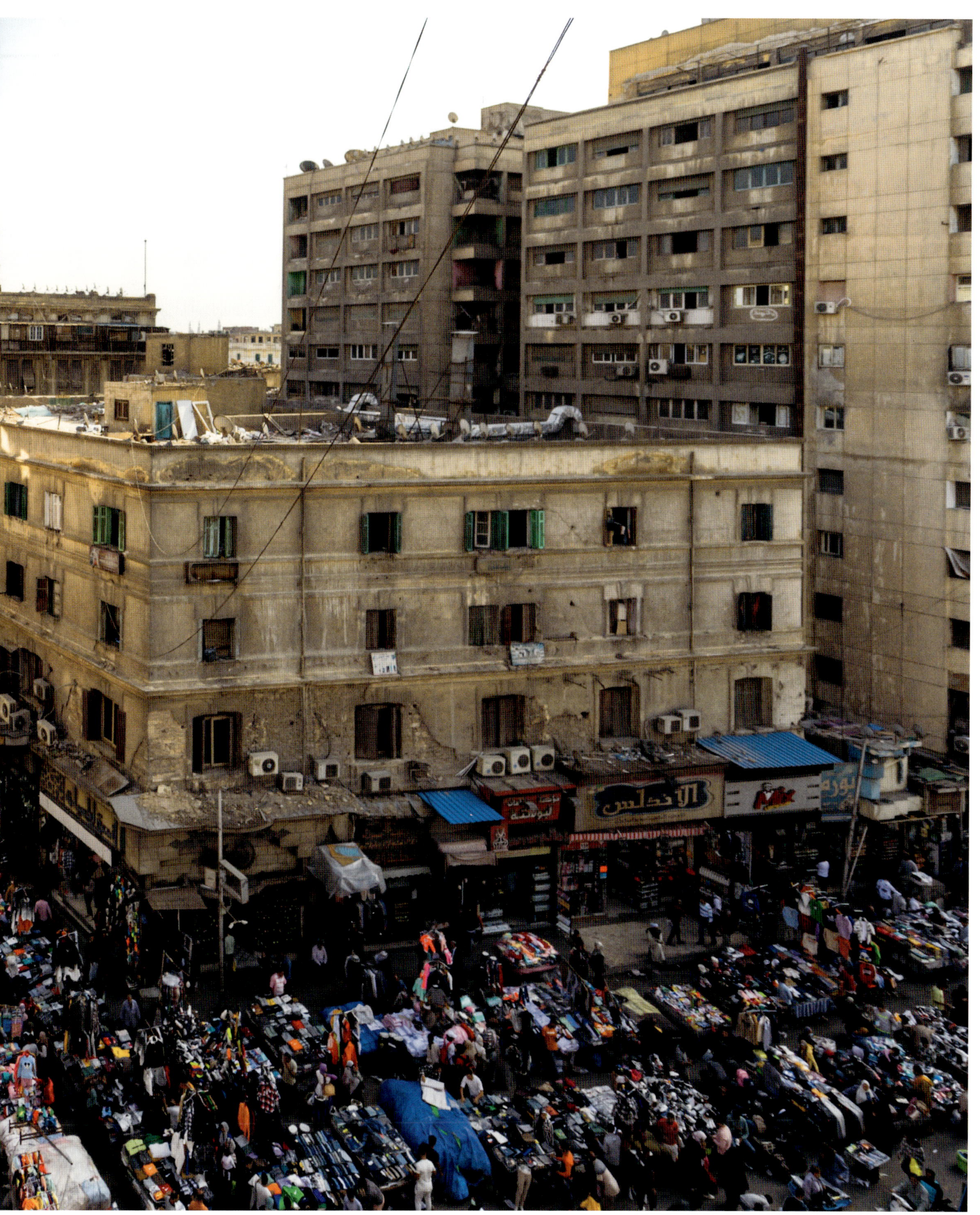

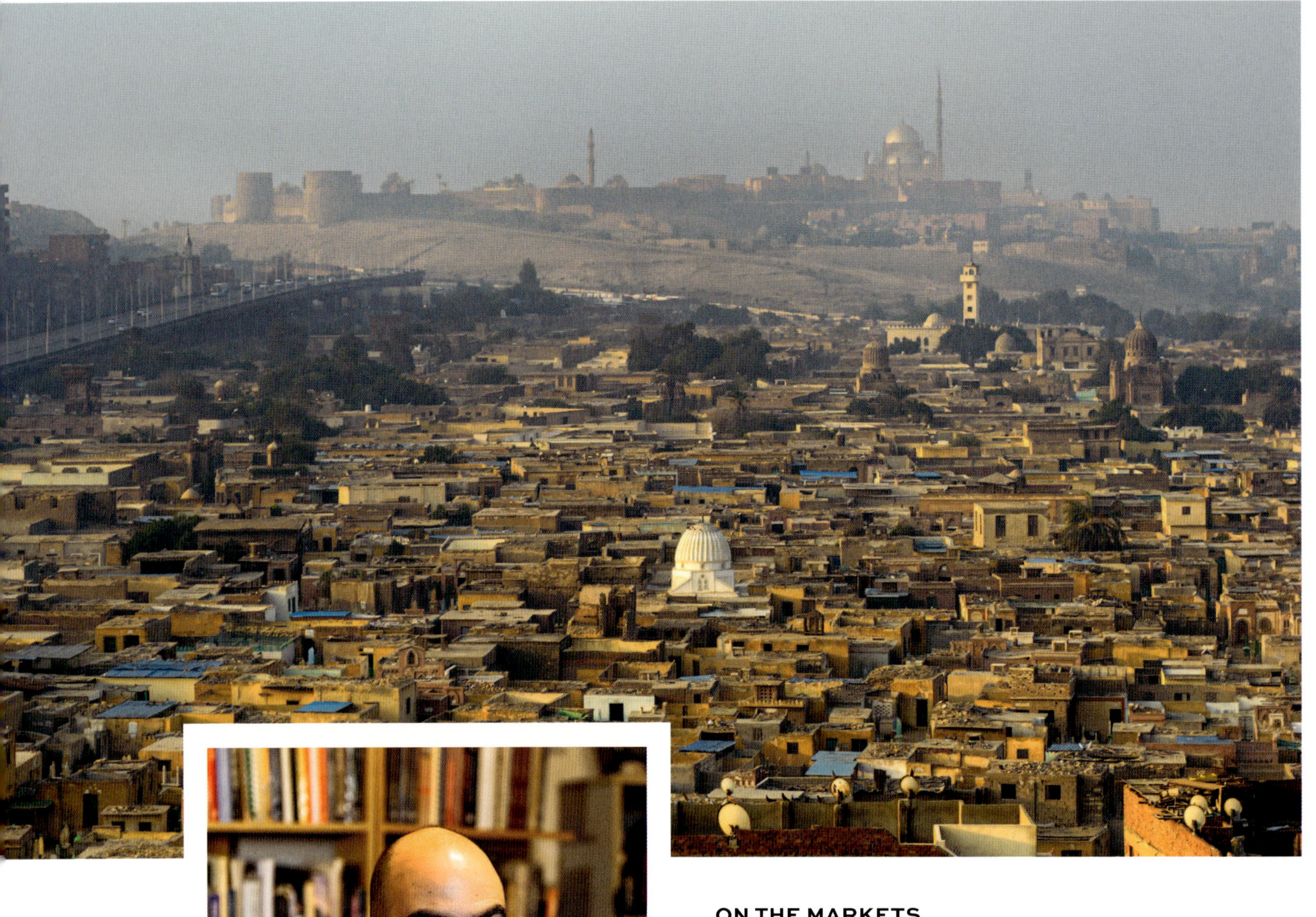

ARTO
EGYPTOLOGIST
ÄGYPTOLOGE

Every day, thousands of bread delivery workers masterfully negotiate the city's alleyways on bicycles or motorcycles.

Täglich kämpfen sich Tausende Brotlieferanten virtuos mit dem Fahrrad oder Motorrad durch die Gassen der Stadt.

...ON THE MARKETS

"I think you can actually call Cairo the city of markets. It is, of course, the city of 1,000 minarets. But on a more, I guess, social level, going to shops and buying something is just such a deeply entrenched part of Egyptian daily life. (...) So downtown Cairo, in a way is kind of like a very large marketplace in and of itself. And then outside of that, in certain areas you get (...) an ad hoc kind of market. Someone sets up a little stall somewhere and then begins selling whatever it is that they're selling. (...) So everywhere you go, there is this activity of somebody looking for something (...)."

...ON THE SIGNIFICANCE OF BREAD

"Bread is incredibly important to Egypt and Cairo. Bread has been around since the dawn of agriculture in Egypt, since the beginning, I don't know, 7000 BCE. (...) It's the main staple of our diet. So much that you get expressions like *aish w malh*, bread and salt. That is your basis, it's your complete basis. (...) But in Egypt in particular, really, it has its own complete dimension (...). You don't necessarily say salary, you don't say income, you say *aisha*, which means eating bread. (...) Bread is life, okay? In fact, the very words in Egypt they use for bread. (...) *Aish* means he lives. So, *aish* is bread, bread is life."

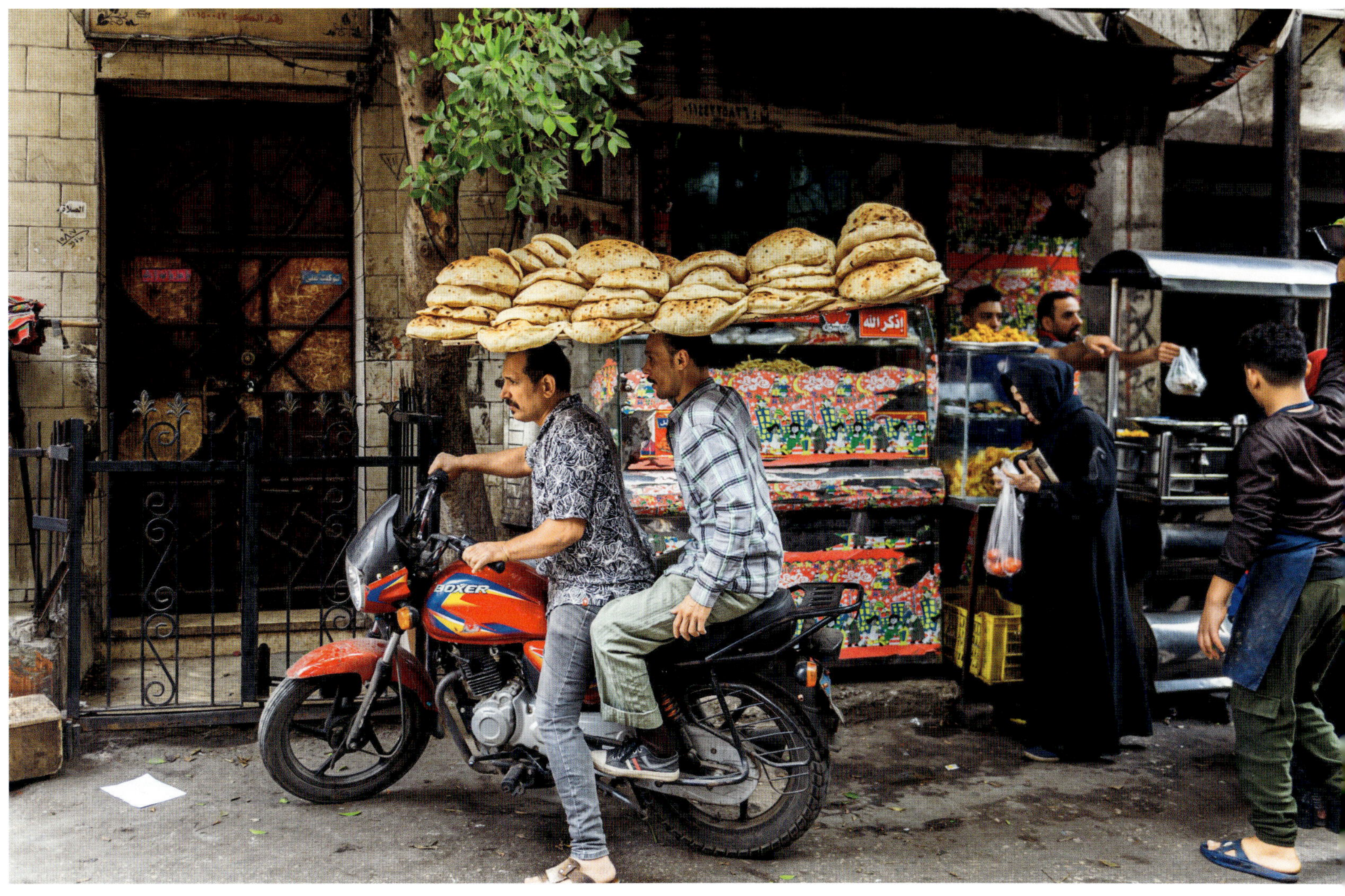

...ON THE NILE

"The importance of the Nile to Egypt and by extension Cairo cannot be underestimated. Of course, Egypt gets very little rainfall. So for water, for agriculture, it's the Nile that is your main source, that is your everything. (…) So the Nile is still, I would say, very important to Egyptians. Then it has led to certain expressions such as where it is said you're not really Egyptian until you've tasted the water of the Nile. It's central to Egyptian identity."

...ÜBER DIE MÄRKTE

„Ich glaube, man kann Kairo tatsächlich die Stadt der Märkte nennen. Es ist natürlich auch die Stadt der 1 000 Minarette. Aber auf einer eher sozialen Ebene ist es ein fester Bestandteil des ägyptischen Alltags, in Geschäfte zu gehen und etwas zu kaufen. (…) Das Stadtzentrum von Kairo ist also in gewisser Weise wie ein sehr großer Marktplatz. Und außerhalb davon gibt es in bestimmten Gegenden (…) eine Art Ad-hoc-Markt. Jemand stellt irgendwo einen kleinen Stand auf und verkauft dann, was immer er verkaufen will. (…) Überall, wo man hinkommt, ist jemand auf der Suche nach etwas (…)."

...ÜBER DIE BEDEUTUNG VON BROT

„Brot ist für Ägypten und Kairo unglaublich wichtig. Brot gibt es seit den Anfängen der Landwirtschaft in Ägypten, seit, ich weiß nicht, 7000 v. Chr. (…) Es ist das wichtigste Grundnahrungsmittel für unsere Ernährung. So sehr, dass man Ausdrücke wie *aish w malh*, „Brot und Salz", kennt. Das ist die Grundlage, die komplette Grundlage. (…) Aber gerade in Ägypten hat das eine ganz eigene Dimension (…). Man sagt nicht unbedingt Gehalt, man sagt nicht Einkommen, man sagt *aisha*, das heißt „Brot essen". (…) Brot ist Leben, okay? Tatsächlich sind es genau die Worte, die sie in Ägypten für Brot verwenden. (…) *Aish* bedeutet „er lebt". Also, *aish* ist Brot, Brot ist Leben."

...ÜBER DEN NIL

„Die Bedeutung des Nils für Ägypten und damit auch für Kairo darf nicht unterschätzt werden. Natürlich gibt es in Ägypten sehr wenig Regen. Für die Wasserversorgung und die Landwirtschaft ist der Nil also die Hauptquelle, er ist alles. (…) Der Nil ist also immer noch sehr wichtig für die Ägypter. Das hat zu bestimmten Ausdrücken geführt, die besagen, dass man erst dann ein echter Ägypter ist, wenn man das Wasser des Nils gekostet hat. Es ist ein zentraler Bestandteil der ägyptischen Identität."

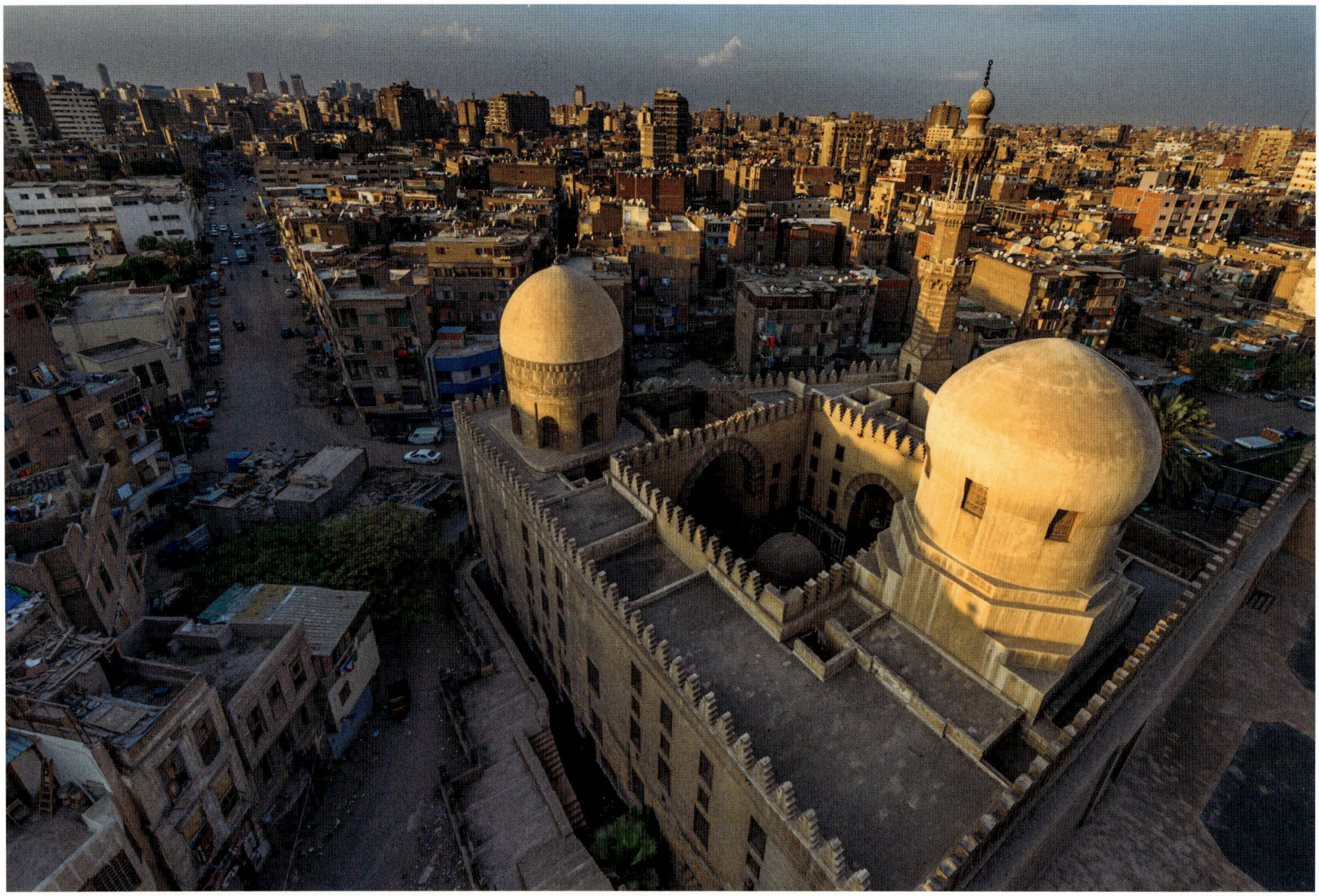

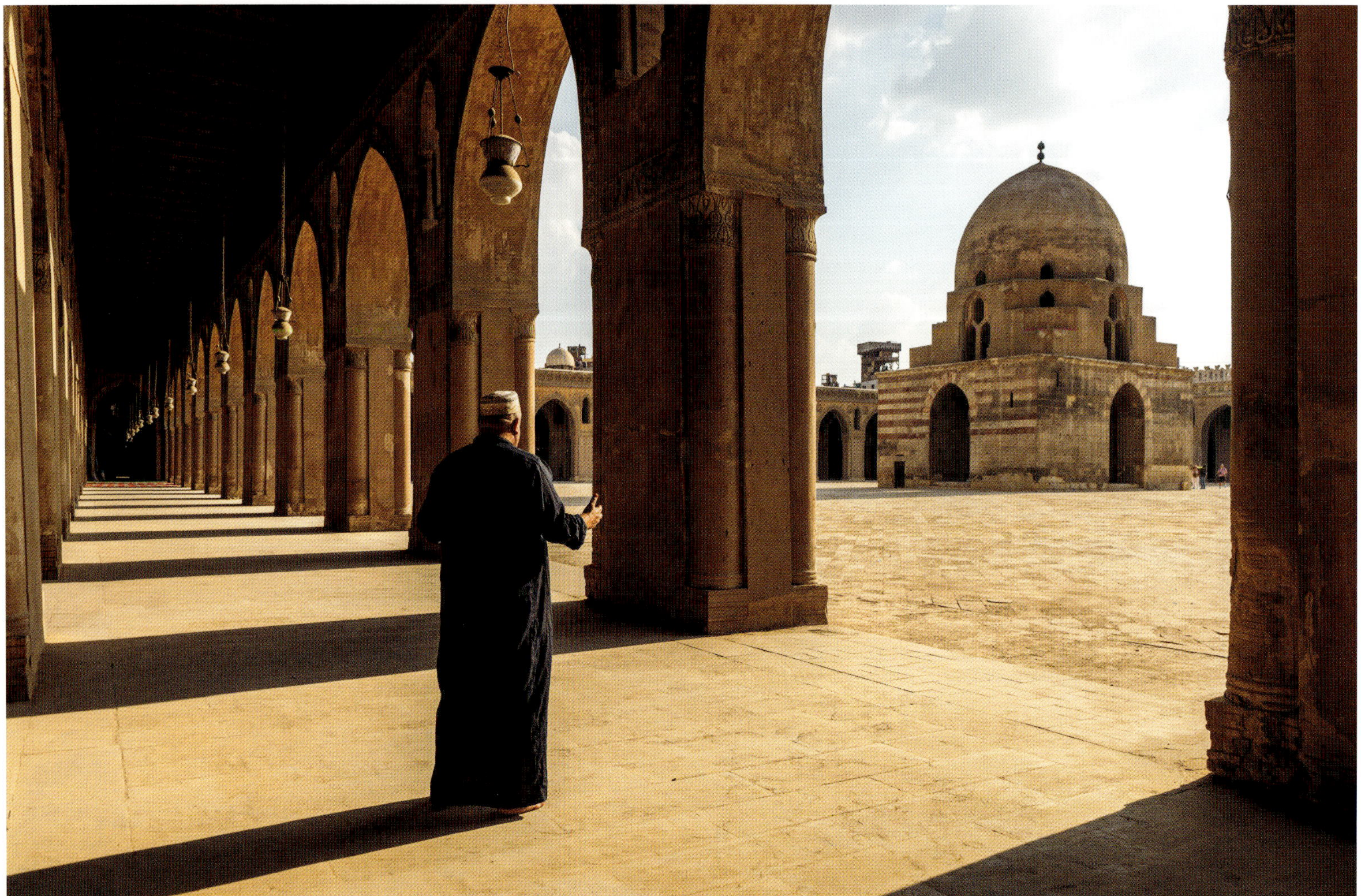

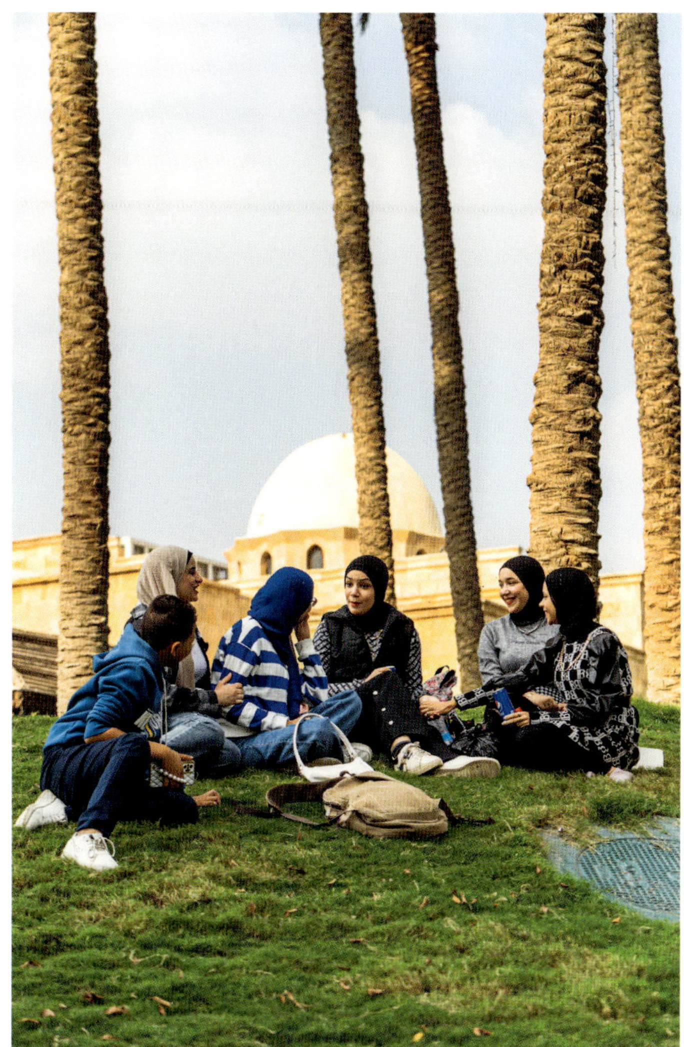

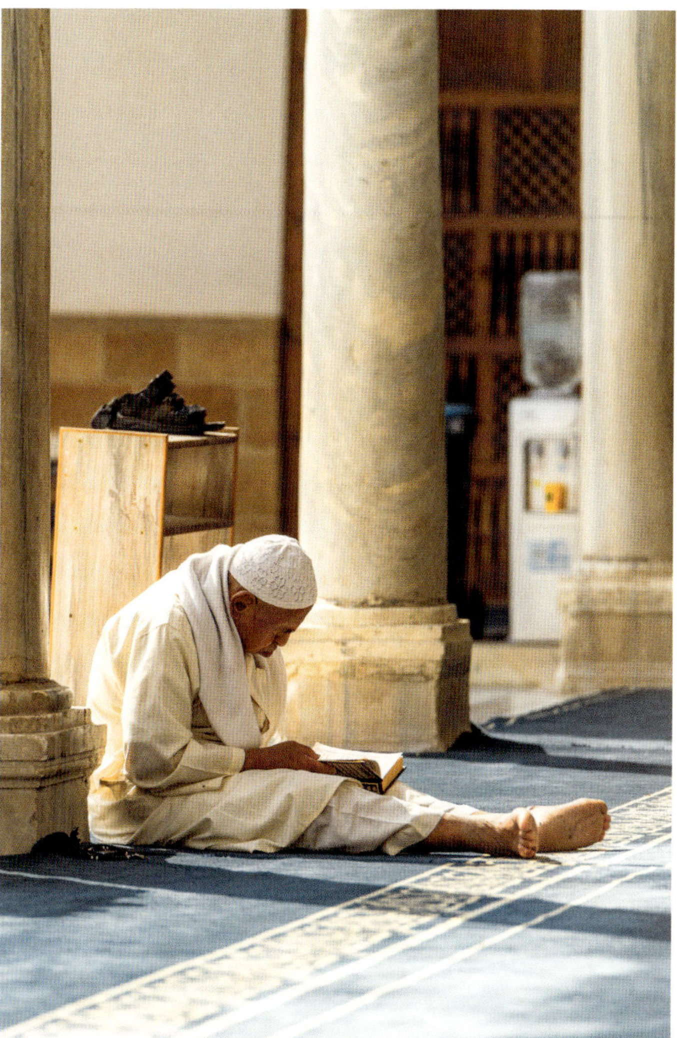

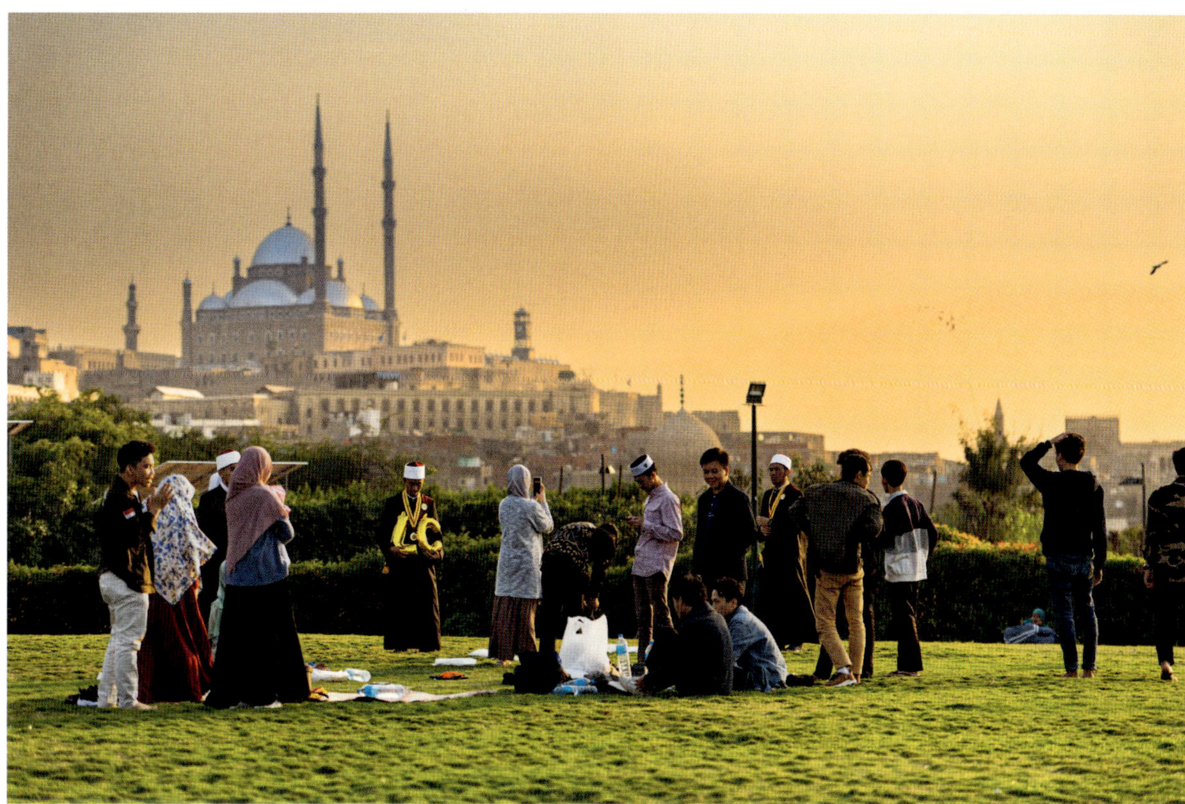

Local recreation is non-existent: Only the mosques or
Al Azhar Park, which charges a fee, provide places of respite
from the stress of everyday life.

Naherholung Fehlanzeige: Nur die Moscheen
oder der kostenpflichtige Al Azhar-Park
bilden Ruhepunkte vom Alltagsstress.

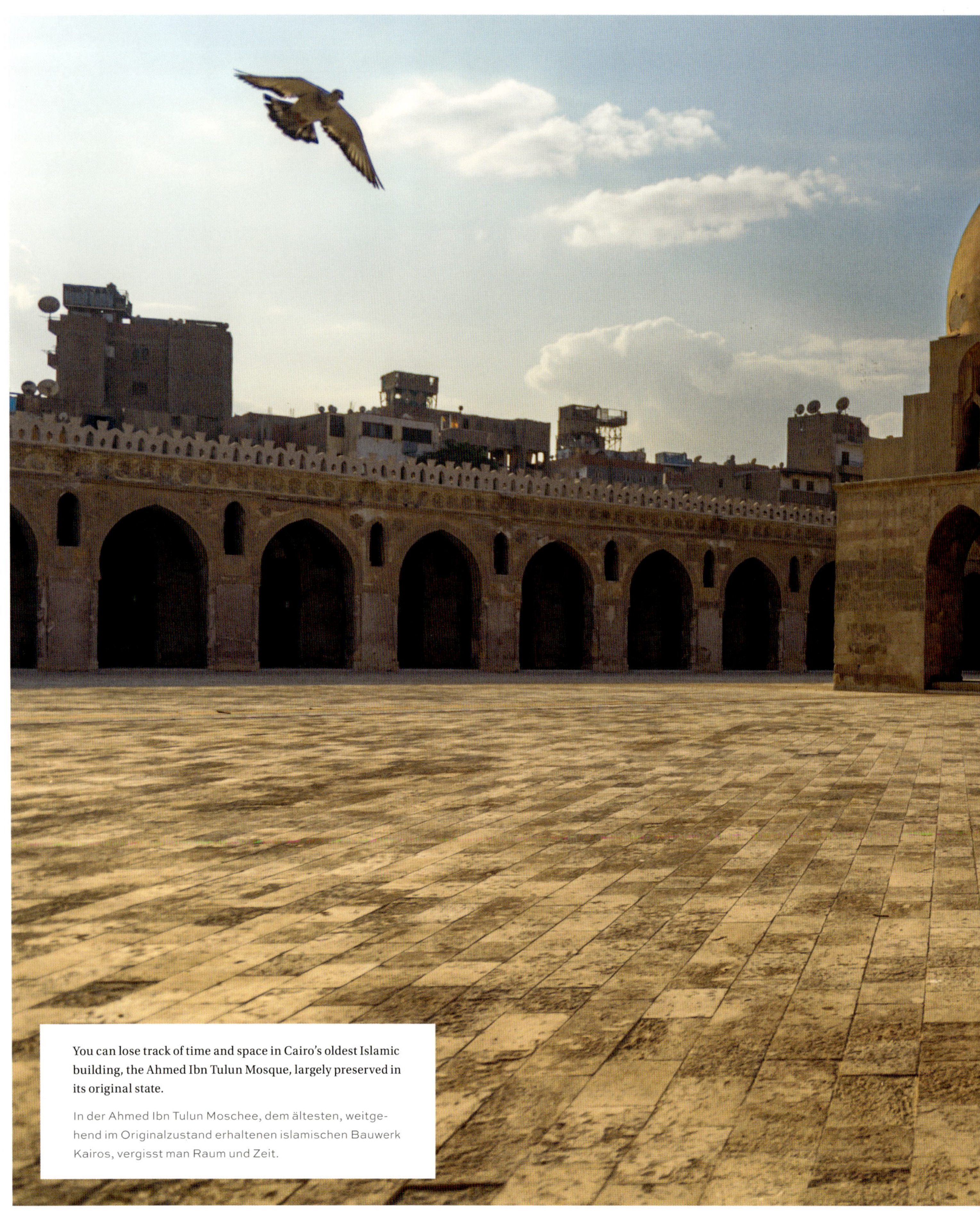

You can lose track of time and space in Cairo's oldest Islamic building, the Ahmed Ibn Tulun Mosque, largely preserved in its original state.

In der Ahmed Ibn Tulun Moschee, dem ältesten, weitgehend im Originalzustand erhaltenen islamischen Bauwerk Kairos, vergisst man Raum und Zeit.

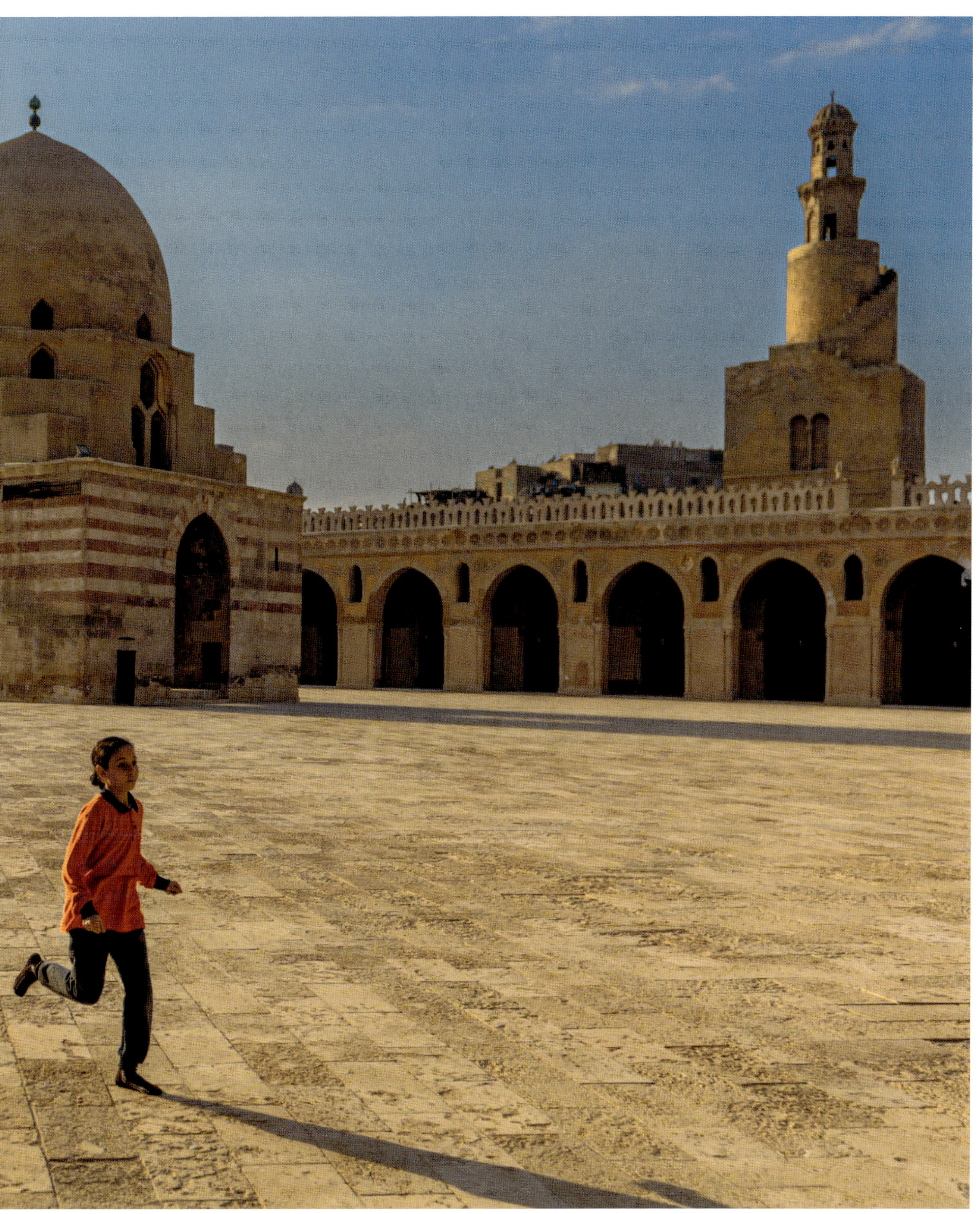

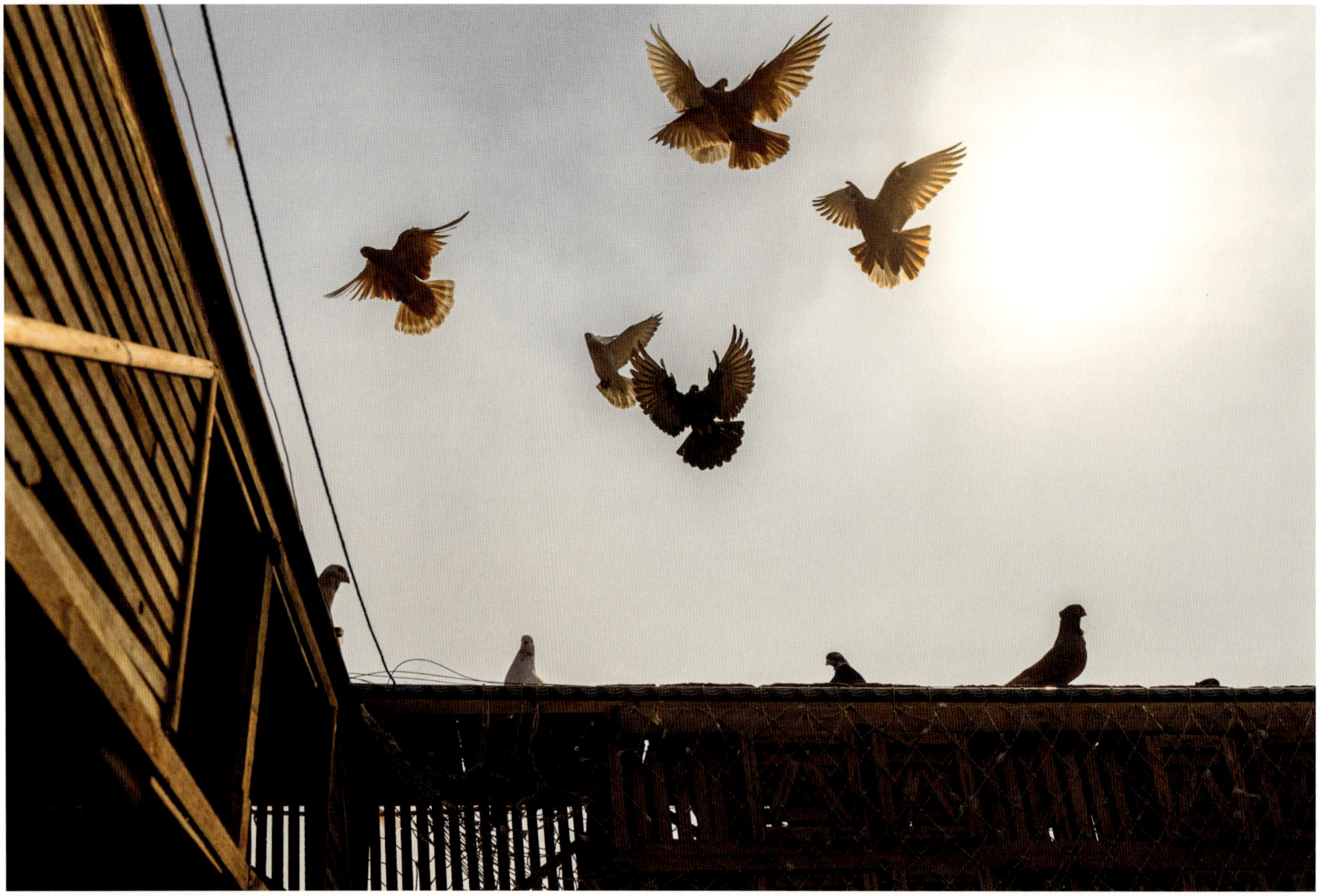

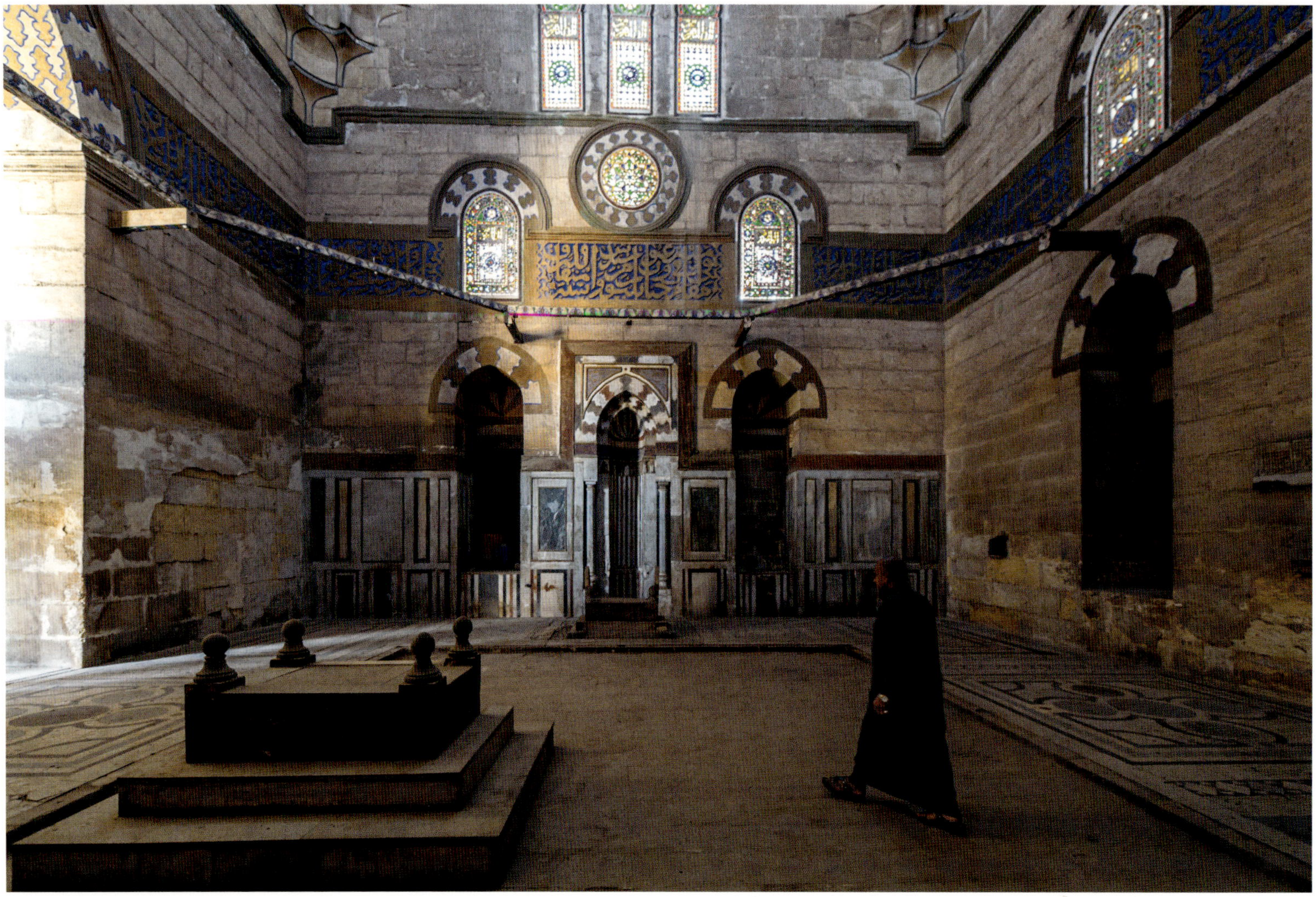

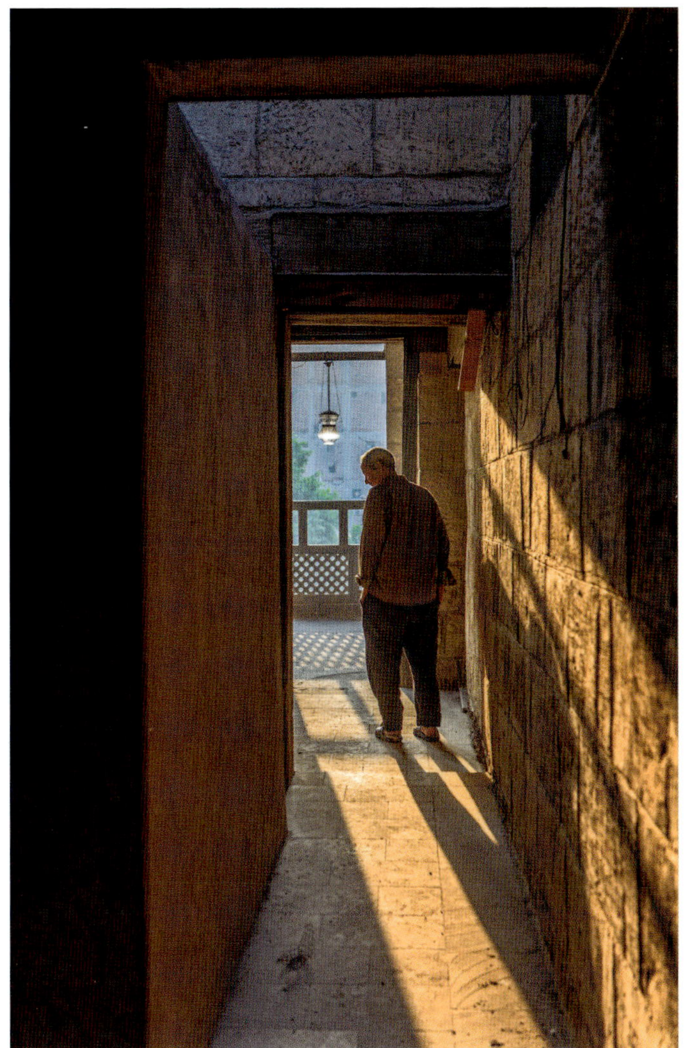
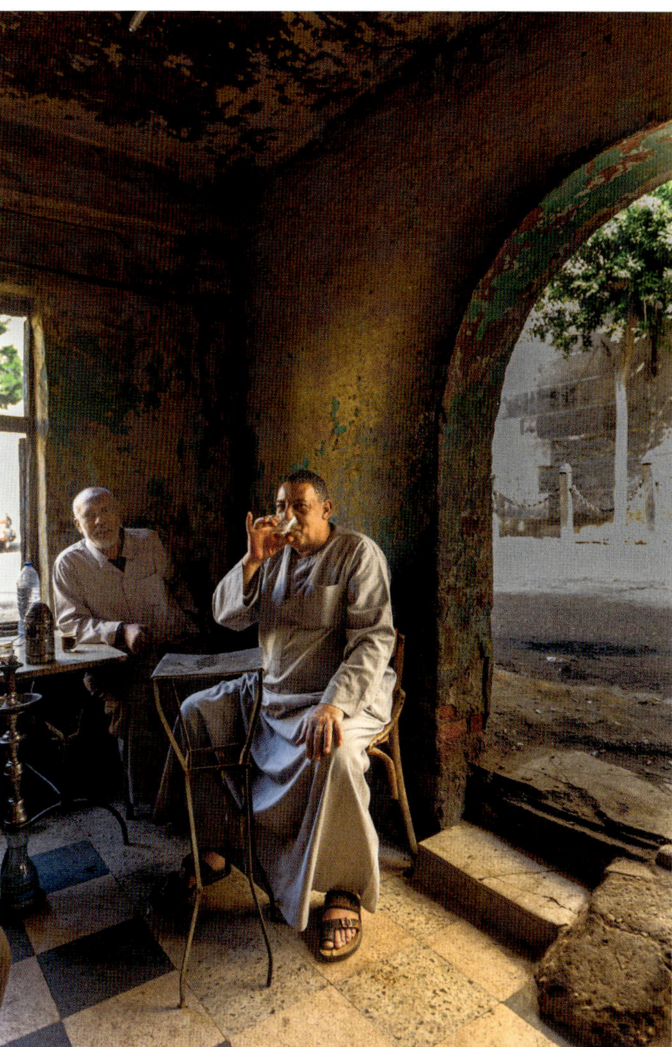
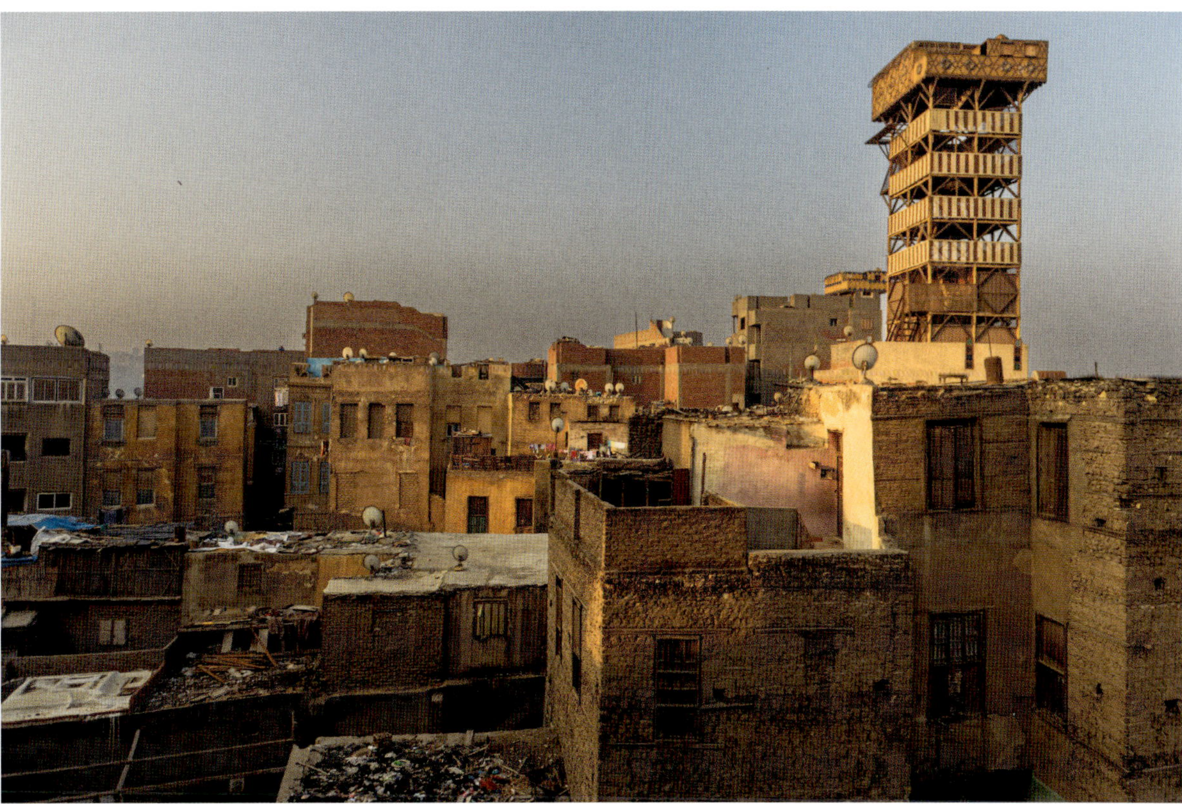

Little getaways: the often-towering pigeon coops on the rooftops, the Faraj Ibn Barquq in the City of the Dead, or a teahouse tucked away in the labyrinthine alleyways.

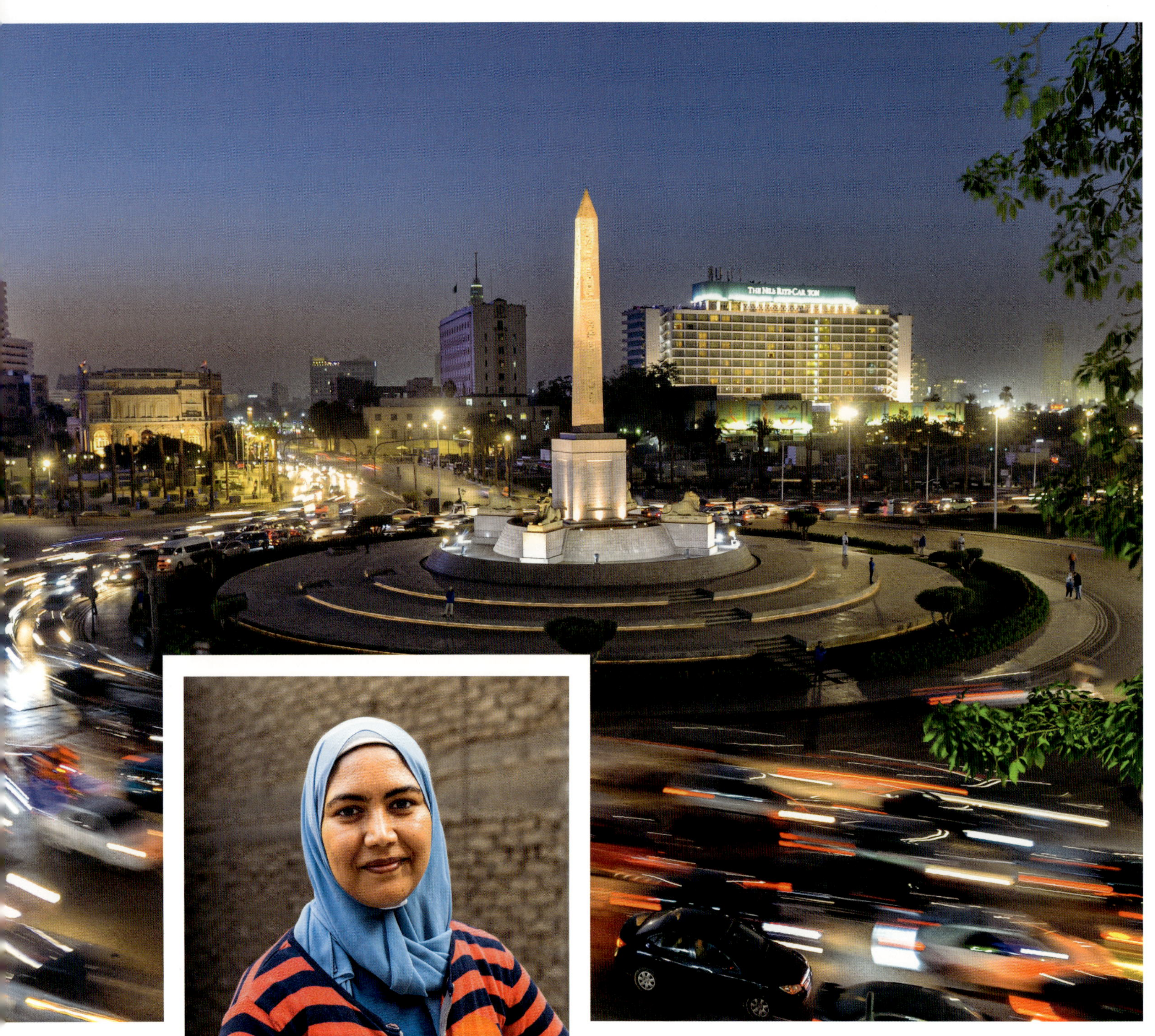

HANAA GAD
ARCHITECT
ARCHITEKTIN

Those who have managed to cross Tahir Square in one piece have quite literally earned a relaxing break at the Nile.

Wer es geschafft hat, den Tahir-Platz heile zu überqueren, hat sich die Entspannungspause am Nil im wahrsten Sinne des Wortes verdient.

...ON THE TRAFFIC

"I wish for the future that I can cross the streets without being afraid. Especially at Tahir Square. Often I think the planners, the road planners, city planners, they just forgot that there are also people living here. Not only cars."

...ÜBER DEN NIL

"Unfortunately, (...) I think the Nile is like the only open artery or open space in Cairo, because it's very claustrophobic and it's full of very dense and full buildings. And it's only the Nile that is kind of flowing in between. If you want some fresh air, if you want some open space, you can go to the river. Yes, it's very important."

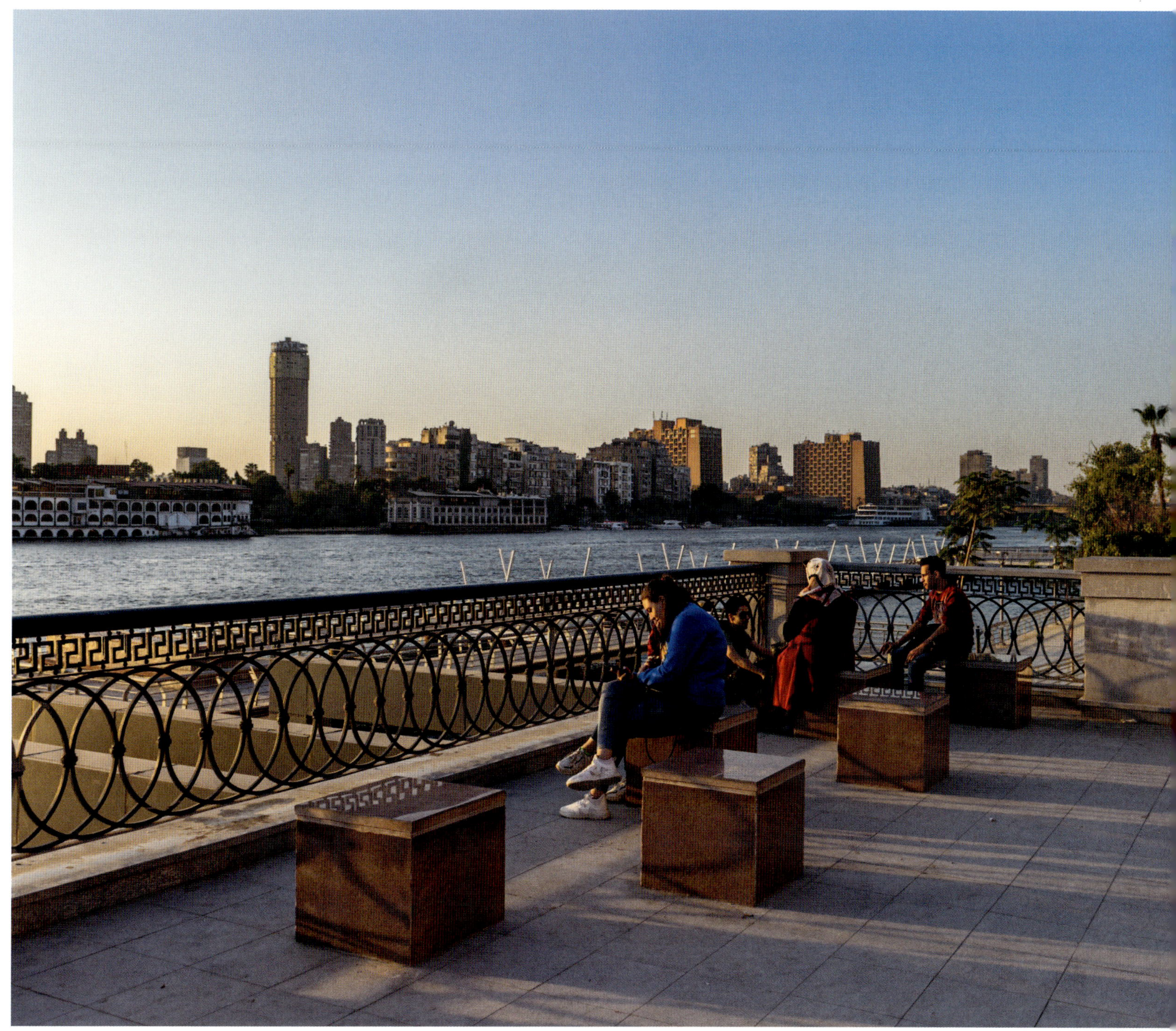

...ÜBER DEN VERKEHR

„Ich wünsche mir für die Zukunft, dass ich die Straße überqueren kann, ohne Angst zu haben. Besonders am Tahir-Platz. Oft denke ich, die Planer, die Straßenplaner, die Stadtplaner, die haben einfach vergessen, dass hier auch Menschen leben, nicht nur Autos."

...ÜBER DEN NIL

„Leider ist (...) der Nil die einzige offene Arterie oder der einzige offene Raum in Kairo, denn die Stadt ist sehr klaustrophobisch und voll von sehr dichten und überfüllten Gebäuden. Und nur der Nil fließt sozusagen dazwischen. Wenn man frische Luft und eine freie Fläche braucht, kann man an den Fluss gehen. Ja, das ist sehr wichtig."

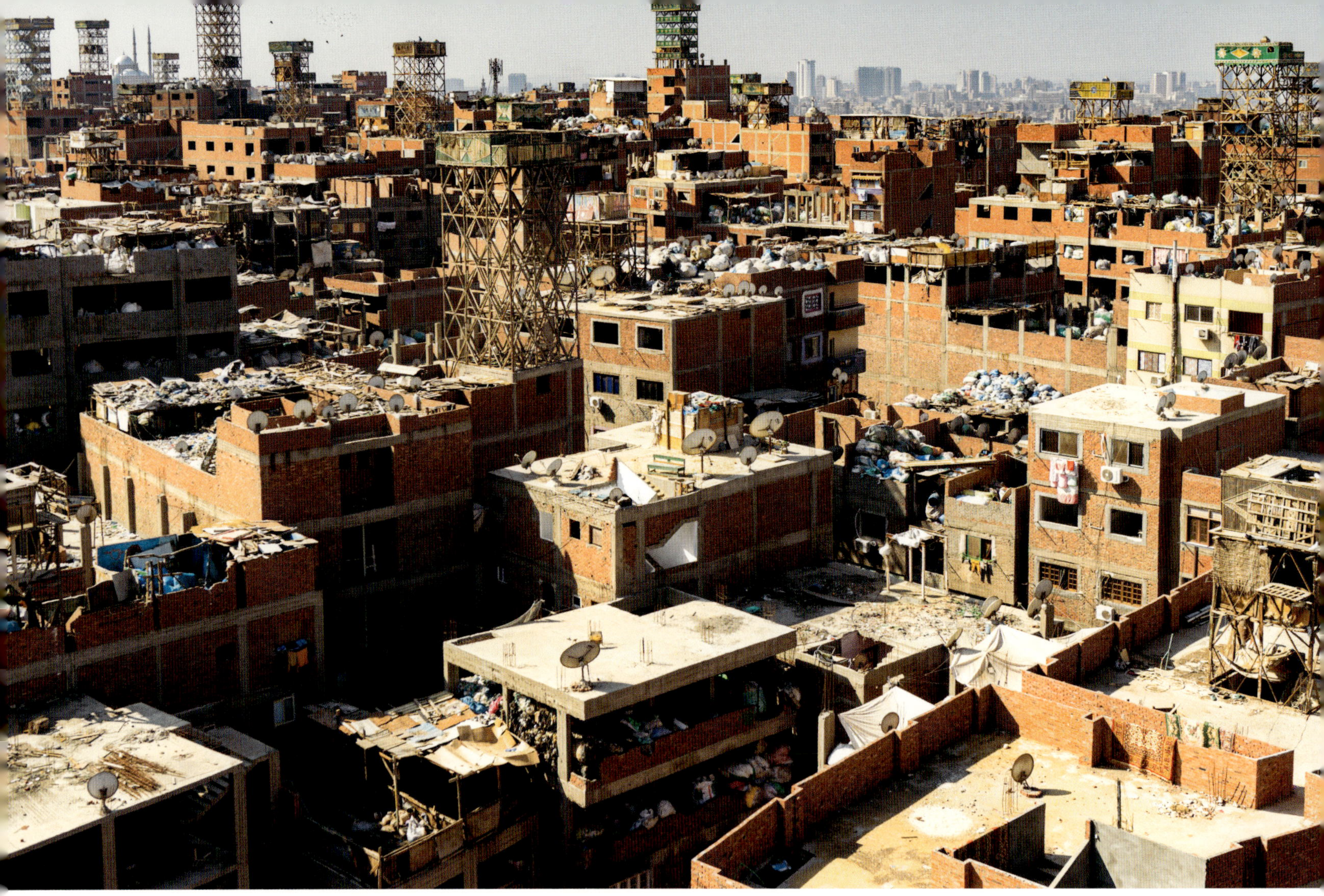

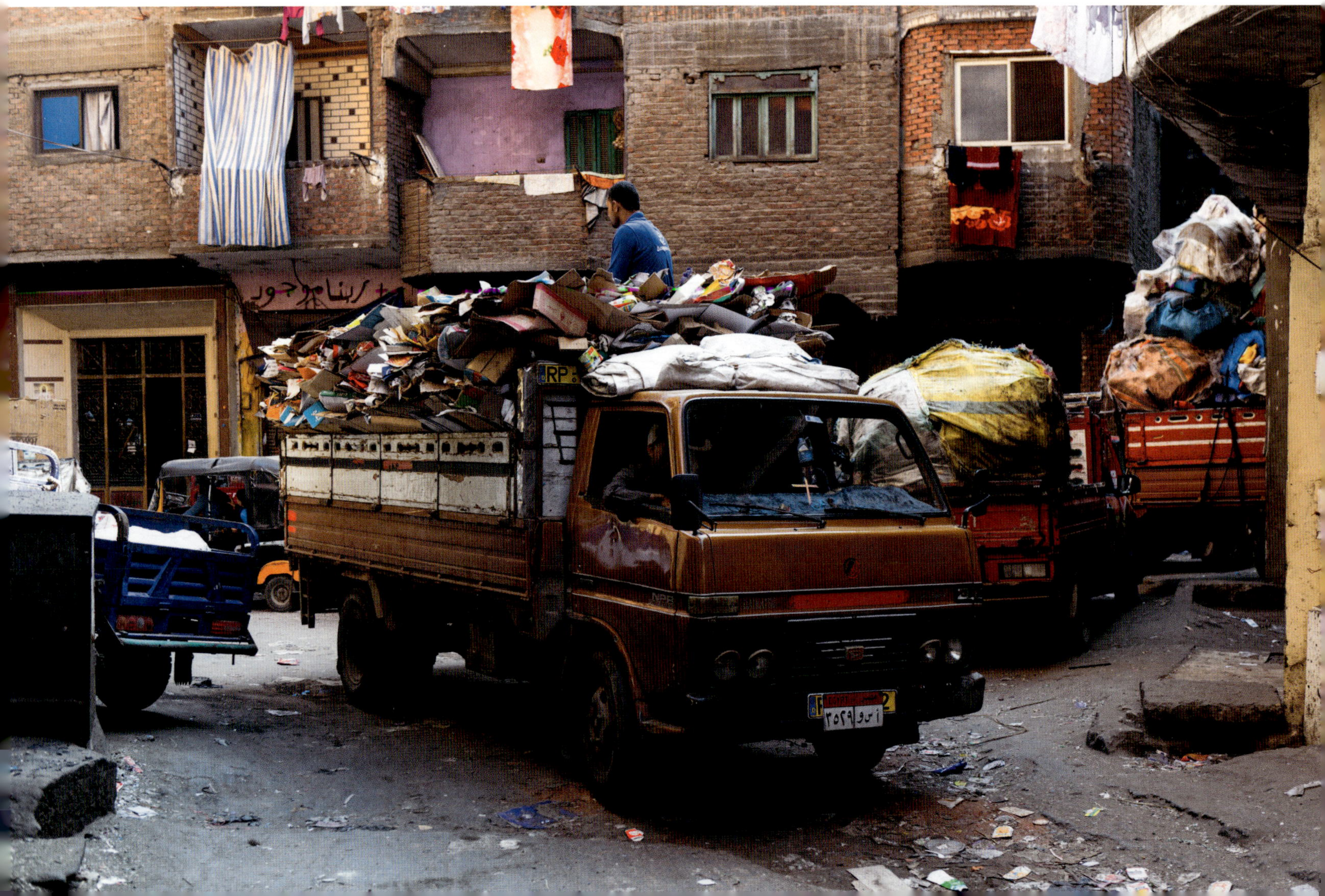

"Cairo is extremely good at collecting everyday trash and litter, extremely good. And (...) in the Garbage City neighborhood, you see how efficient they are at collecting everything." (Arto)

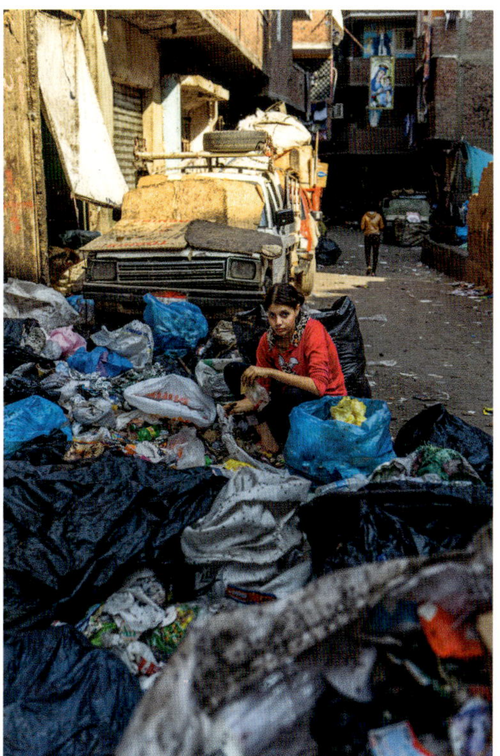

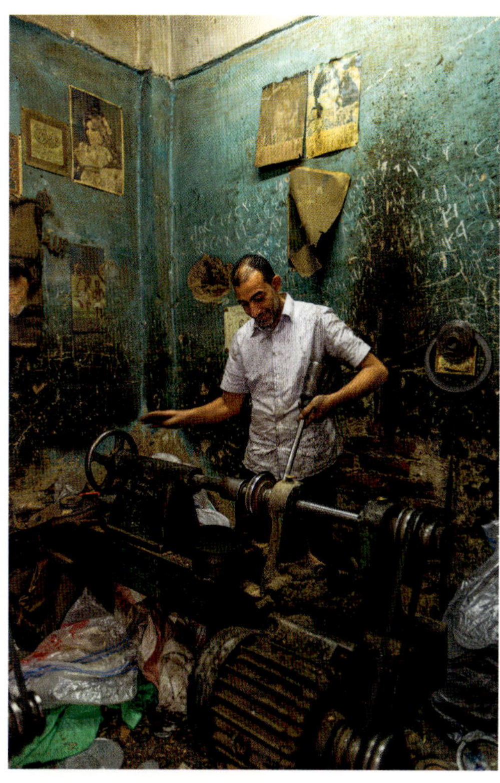

„Kairo ist sehr gut im Einsammeln des täglichen Mülls und der Abfälle, extrem gut. Und (...) im Viertel der Müllstadt sieht man, wie effizient sie alles einsammeln." (Arto)

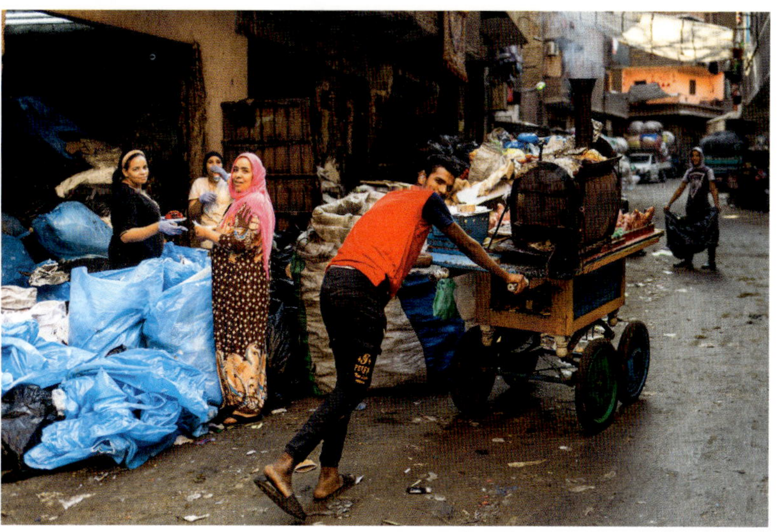

Unusual, yet cleverly devised: Manschiyyet Nasser, the Garbage City, lives in, from, and with the garbage that provides work for tens of thousands of people.

Ungewohnt, doch ausgeklügelt: Manschiyyet Nasser, die „Müllstadt", lebt im, vom und mit dem Müll, der Zehntausenden Menschen Arbeit gibt.

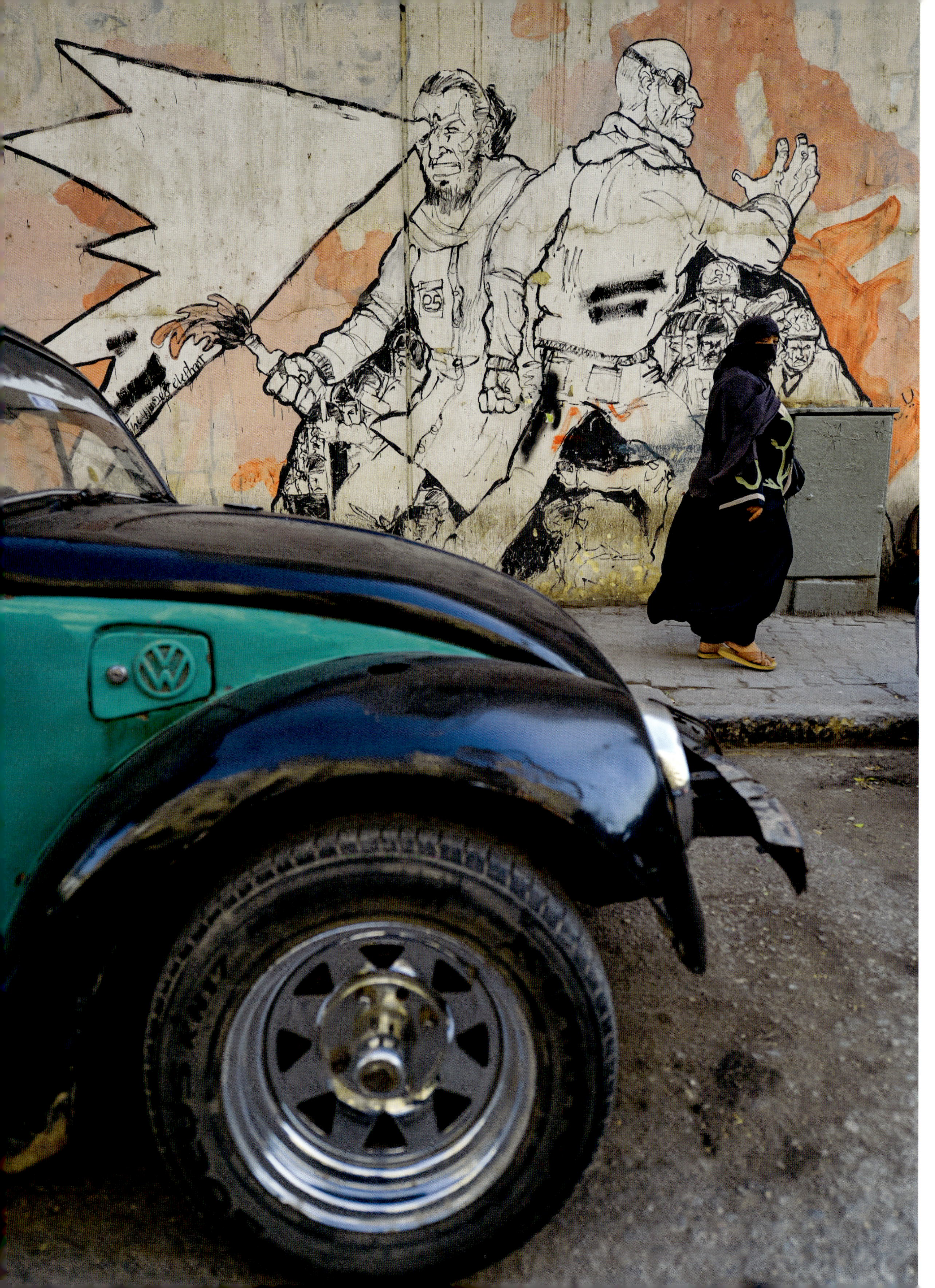

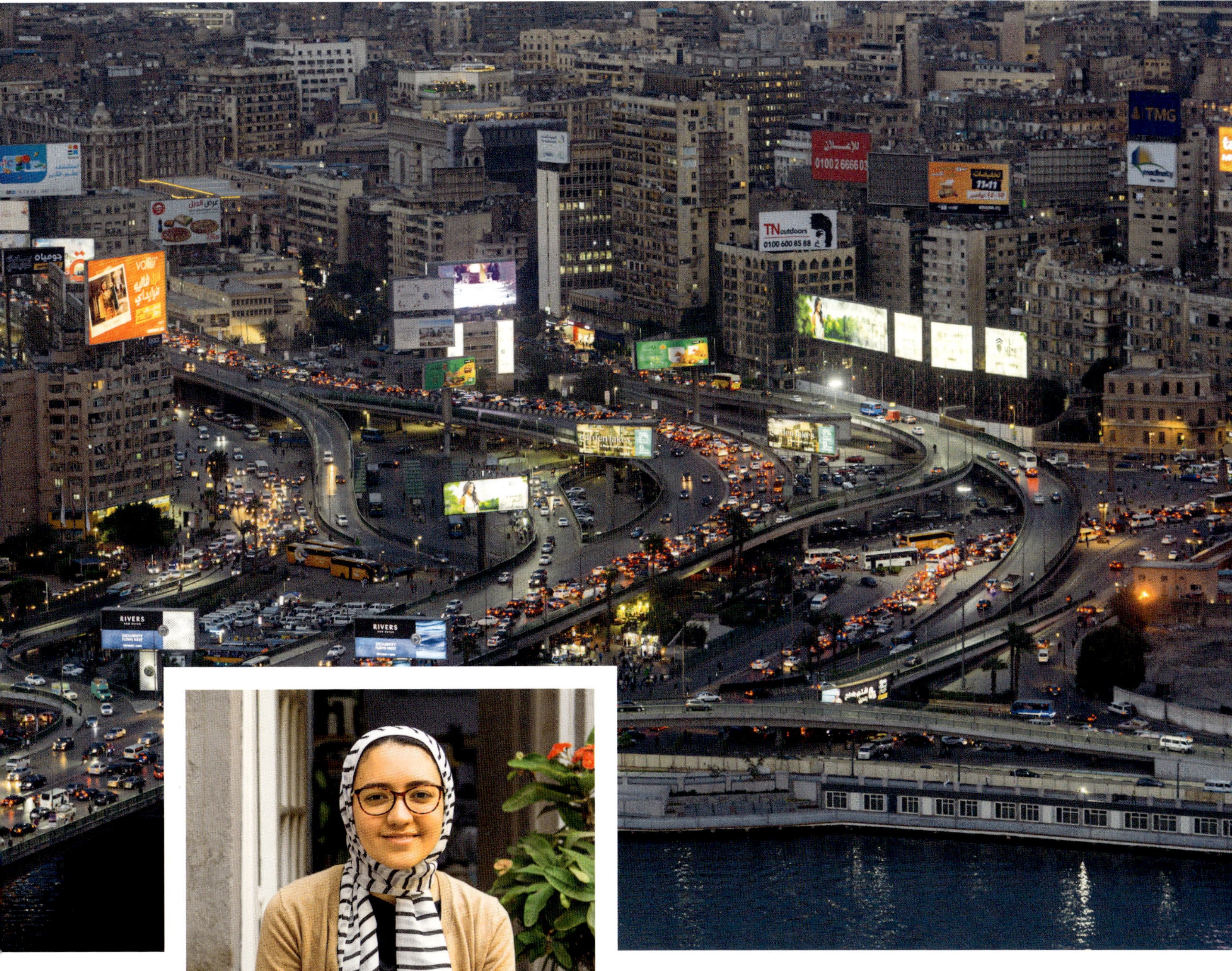

MARIAM
ARCHITECT
ARCHITEKTIN

Graffiti murals, the revolution's newspapers on walls, were the street art scene's expression of a free Egypt. But very few survived the sharp eyes of censorship.

Graffiti, die Wandzeitungen der Revolution, waren der Ausdruck der Street-Art-Szene für ein freies Ägypten. Doch nur ganz wenige haben die scharfen Augen der Zensur überlebt.

...ON THE TRAFFIC

"My main challenge is this daily route to work, the main challenge is mobility, or how we can move in the city, It's hard, whatever your transportation is is a challenge. Now I own a car and I drive a car. I found challenges with it too, but when I was taking public transportation like my boss, it was more challenging than driving."

...ÜBER DEN VERKEHR

„Meine größte Herausforderung auf dem täglichen Weg zur Arbeit ist die Mobilität oder wie wir uns in der Stadt bewegen können. Jetzt besitze ich ein Auto und fahre mit dem Auto. Das ist auch nicht einfach, aber als ich wie mein Chef mit öffentlichen Verkehrsmitteln unterwegs war, war das eine größere Herausforderung als das Autofahren."

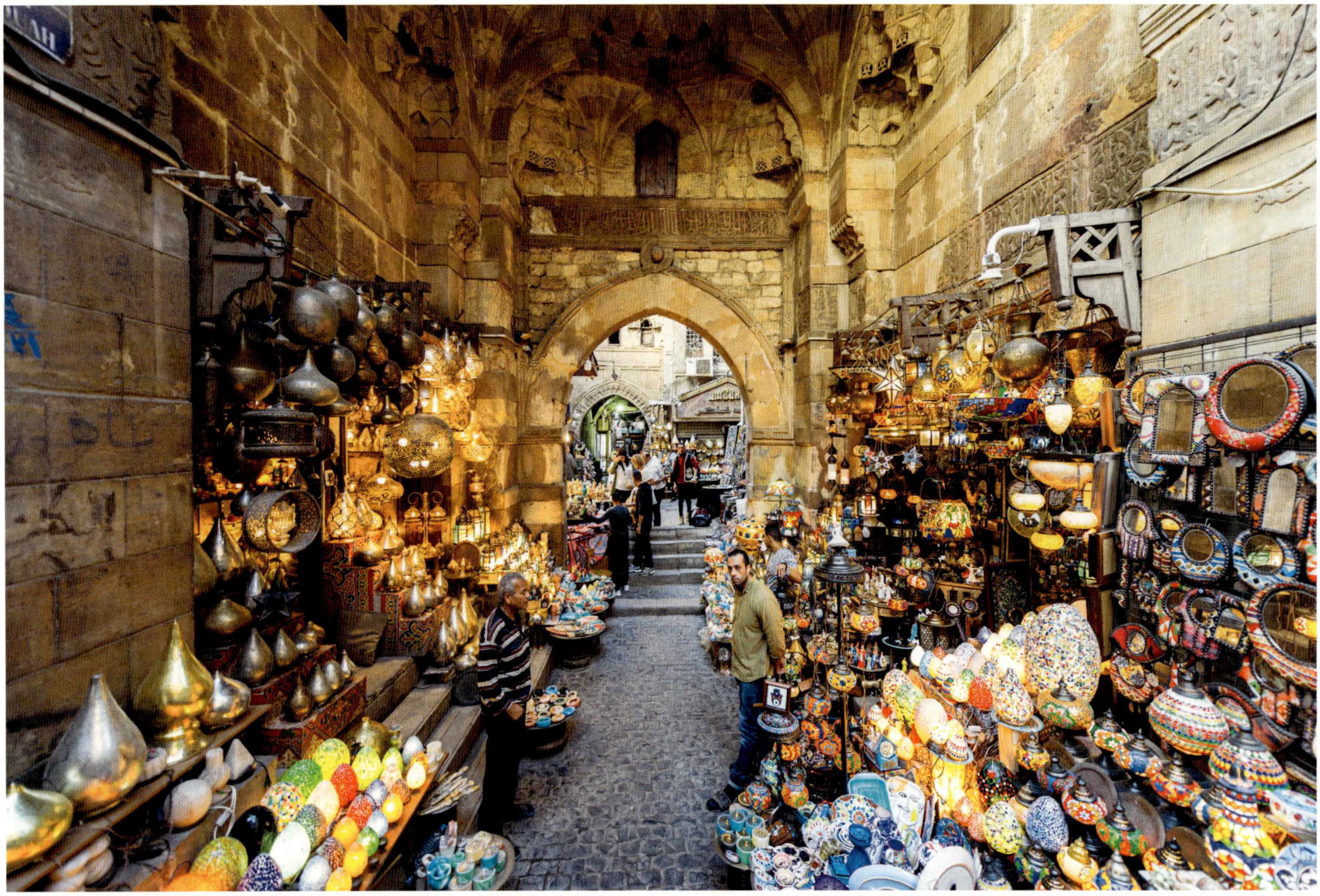

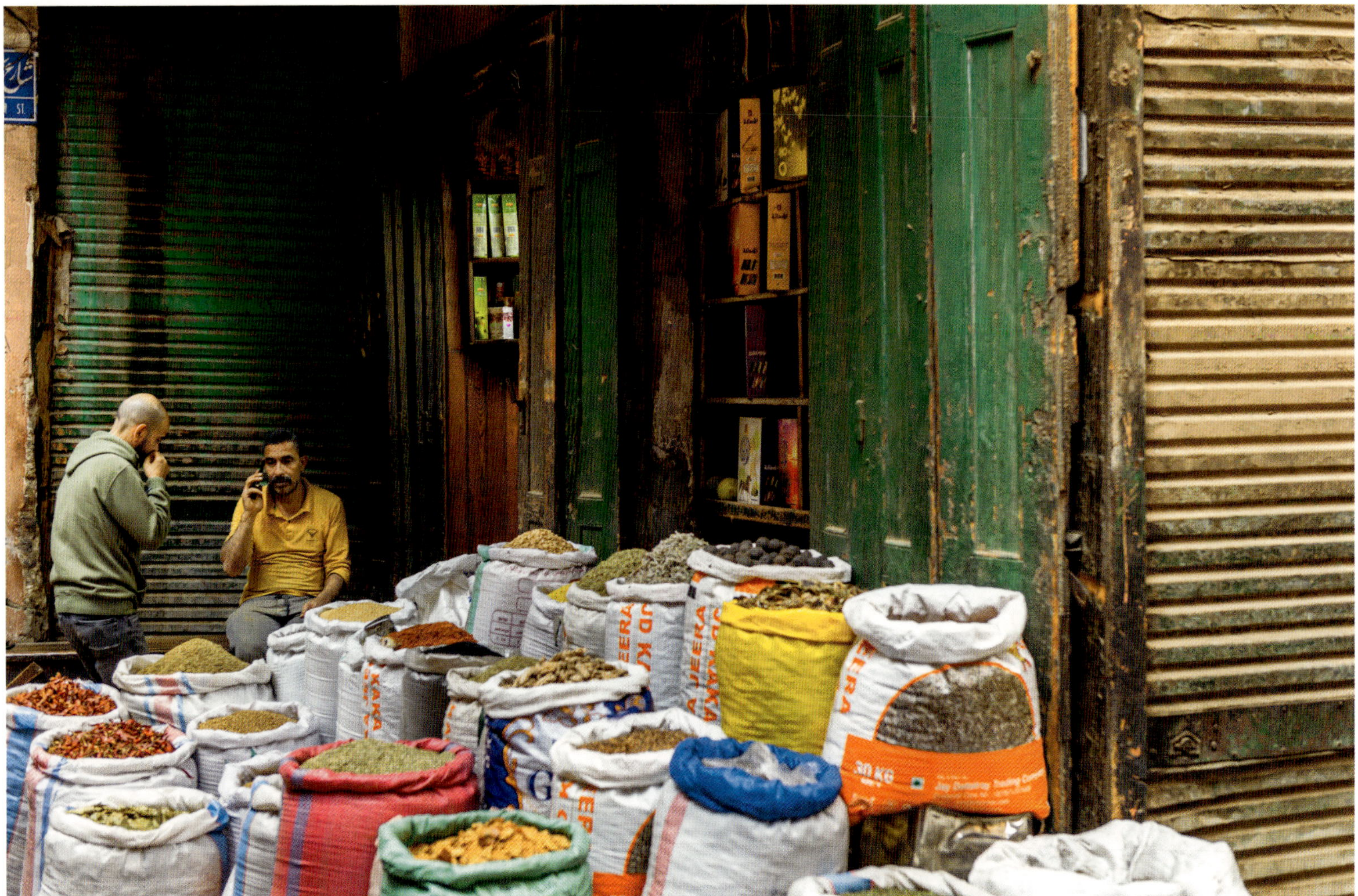

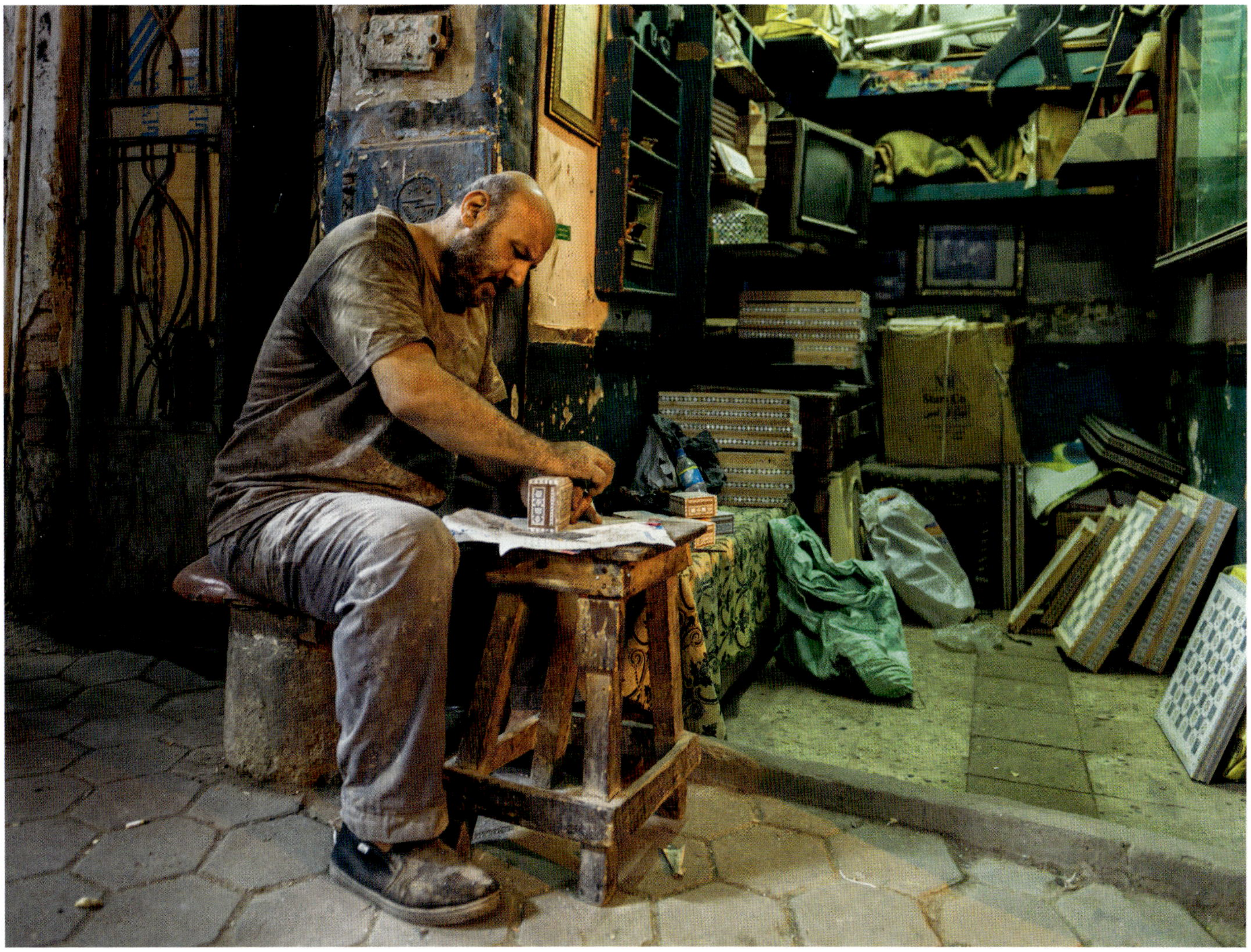

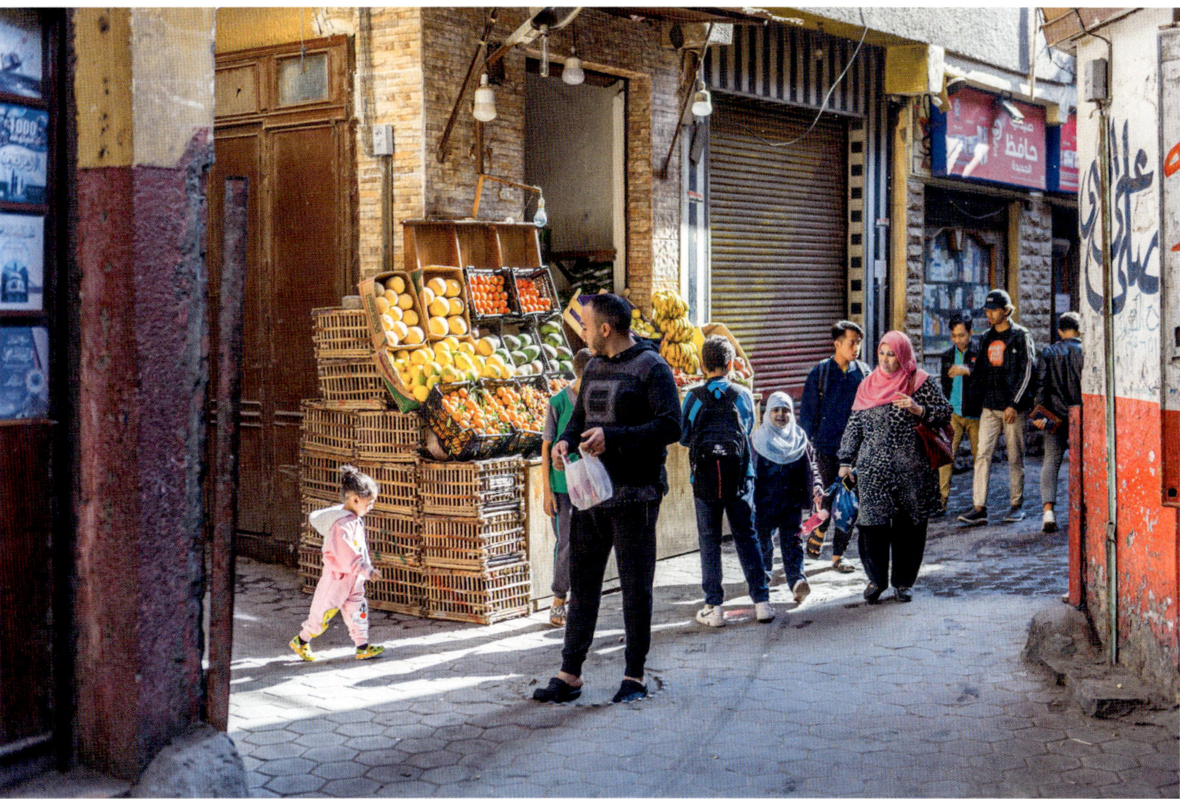

A bazaar with the best of everything: Goods have been offered for sale at the Khan el Khalili since 1382, some of which are still locally made using traditional methods.

Basar der Superlative: Seit 1382 werden auf dem Khan-el-Khalili Waren feilgeboten, die teilweise sogar noch traditionell vor Ort hergestellt werden.

Seoul

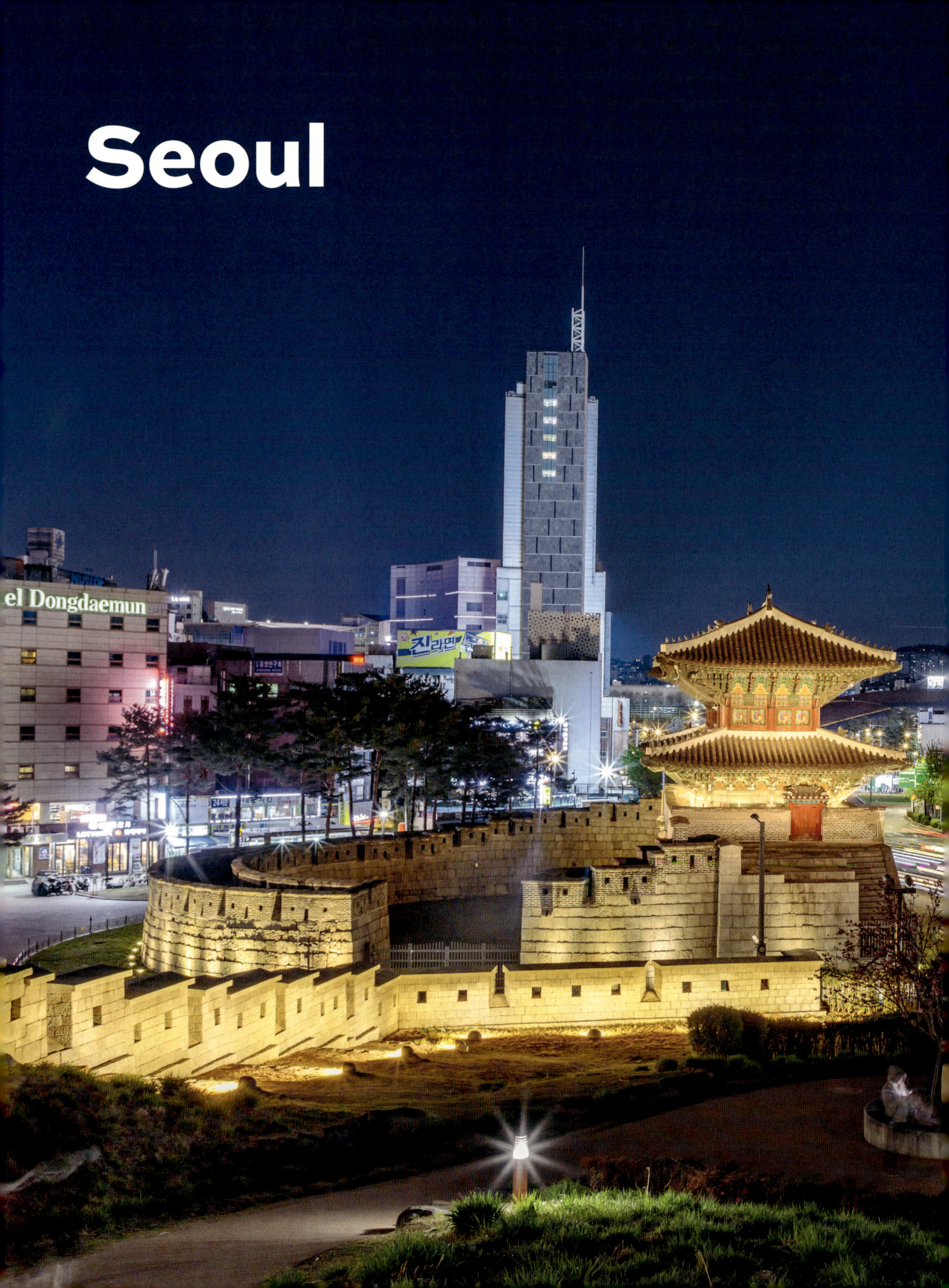

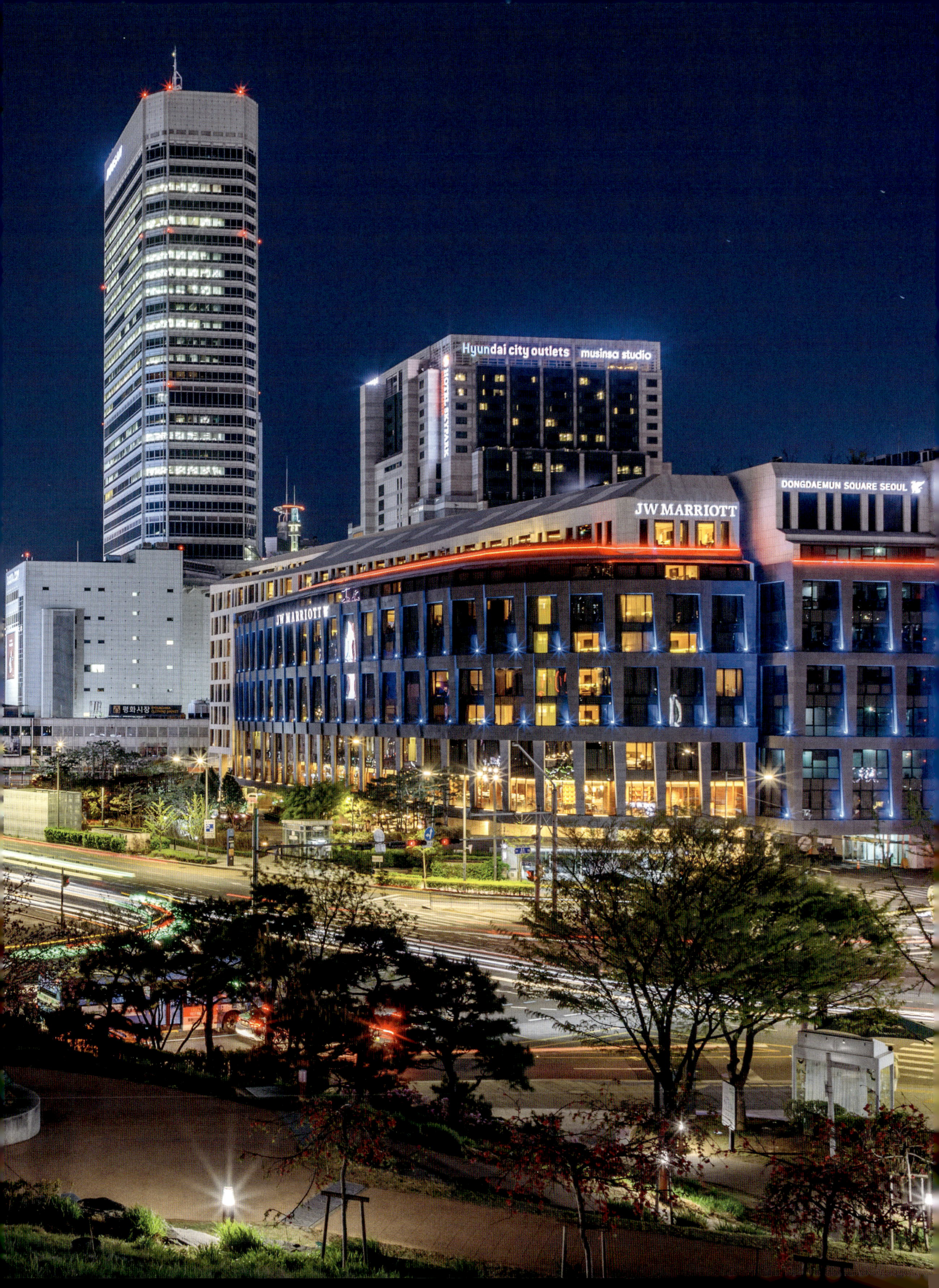

Hyundai city outlets   musinsa studio
JW MARRIOTT
JW MARRIOTT
DONGDAEMUN SQUARE SEOUL
평화시장

Hybrid Parallel Worlds

Hybride Parallelwelten

"(...) And for Koreans, it has a lot of symbolism, like the apartments are a symbol of development, a symbol of having success, of upward mobility. On the social ladder, everything is focused on apartments. So, it's a preferred way of living." (Daniel Tändler)

Seoul is a paradox. The city was once a branching maze of streets with an endless sea of small traditional wooden or stone houses, the *hanok*, built around an open courtyard. Some of these neighborhoods still remain, as tourist attractions, trendy neighborhoods, tolerated remnants of a style of construction considered archaic. Outside the visitor centers, they are considered poor neighborhoods. A *hanok* right in the middle of the city costs much less than one of the apartments in the faceless high-rise complexes blanketing the entire city.

The enormous palace complexes of the Korean kings within the old city walls are the last reminder that Seoul was originally built entirely on the basis of geomantic criteria, and changed its shape very little over the centuries. Then, starting in 1952, it took a mere thirty years to do what it took New York 150 years to do: transform an agricultural administrative city within a city wall into a sprawling megacity.

"But these people don't only come to Deoksu Palace to see the past histories, they want to see what was the past, and what was the implication of the past, and how can we can be inspired by the history, by the history for our present or future." (Park)

It is anachronistic. The people of the capital may love the old, but they prefer the new. Somehow, it has always been that way. Korea had little problem allowing foreign influences and repurposing them for its own needs. Before Korea's own script was developed, Chinese characters were used. Even today, they are often used as a stylistic device. Emperor Gojong commissioned buildings in the neo-Renaissance style in his palace, triggering the development of Western architecture in the country.

Old and new live in a hybrid coexistence. Seoul is ultra-modern, its digitalization turns Europe green with envy, its public transportation system is highly efficient, and Korean modern culture in all its facets, from music to film, is spreading around the world as the Korean Wave, *Hallyu.* But anyone wishing to have something printed has to hand it over to one of the countless mini-print shops still using printing presses from the

„(...) für die Koreaner sind Apartments von hohem symbolischem Wert. Wohnungen sind ein Symbol für Entwicklung, ein Symbol für Erfolg, für den Aufstieg. Auf der sozialen Leiter dreht sich alles um Wohnungen. Es ist daher eine bevorzugte Art zu leben." (Daniel Tändler)

Seoul ist ein Paradoxon. Einst bestand die Stadt aus einem verzweigten Straßengewirr mit einem endlosen Meer aus kleinen traditionellen Holz- oder Steinhäusern, den *hanok*, die um einen offenen Innenhof herum gebaut waren. Einige dieser Viertel gibt es noch, sie sind Touristenattraktion, Szeneviertel, geduldete Reste einer als archaisch empfundenen Bauweise. Außerhalb der Besucherzentren gelten sie als Armenviertel. Ein *hanok* mitten in der Stadt kostet daher deutlich weniger als eines der Apartments in den gesichtslosen Hochhausanlagen, die die gesamte Stadt überziehen.

Die gewaltigen Palastanlagen der koreanischen Könige innerhalb der alten Stadtmauer sind der letzte Hinweis darauf, dass Seoul einst vollständig nach geomantischen Kriterien erbaut worden war und über Jahrhunderte seine Gestalt nur wenig verändert hat. Dann hat es ab 1952 nur dreißig Jahre gedauert, wofür New York 150 Jahre brauchte: aus einer landwirtschaftlich geprägten Verwaltungsstadt innerhalb einer Stadtmauer zu einer ausufernden Megacity zu werden.

„Aber diese Menschen kommen nicht nur (in den Deoksu-Palast), um die Geschichte der Vergangenheit zu sehen, sondern sie wollen sehen, was die Vergangenheit war und welche Auswirkungen sie hatte, und wie wir uns von der Geschichte inspirieren lassen können, von der Geschichte für unsere Gegenwart oder Zukunft." (Park)

Old gazes on new: Maitreya, the Buddha of the future, peers contemplatively from the distant past at the Seoul of tomorrow.

Alt blickt auf Neu: Maitreya, der Buddha der Zukunft, blickt kontemplativ aus ferner Vergangenheit auf das Seoul von morgen.

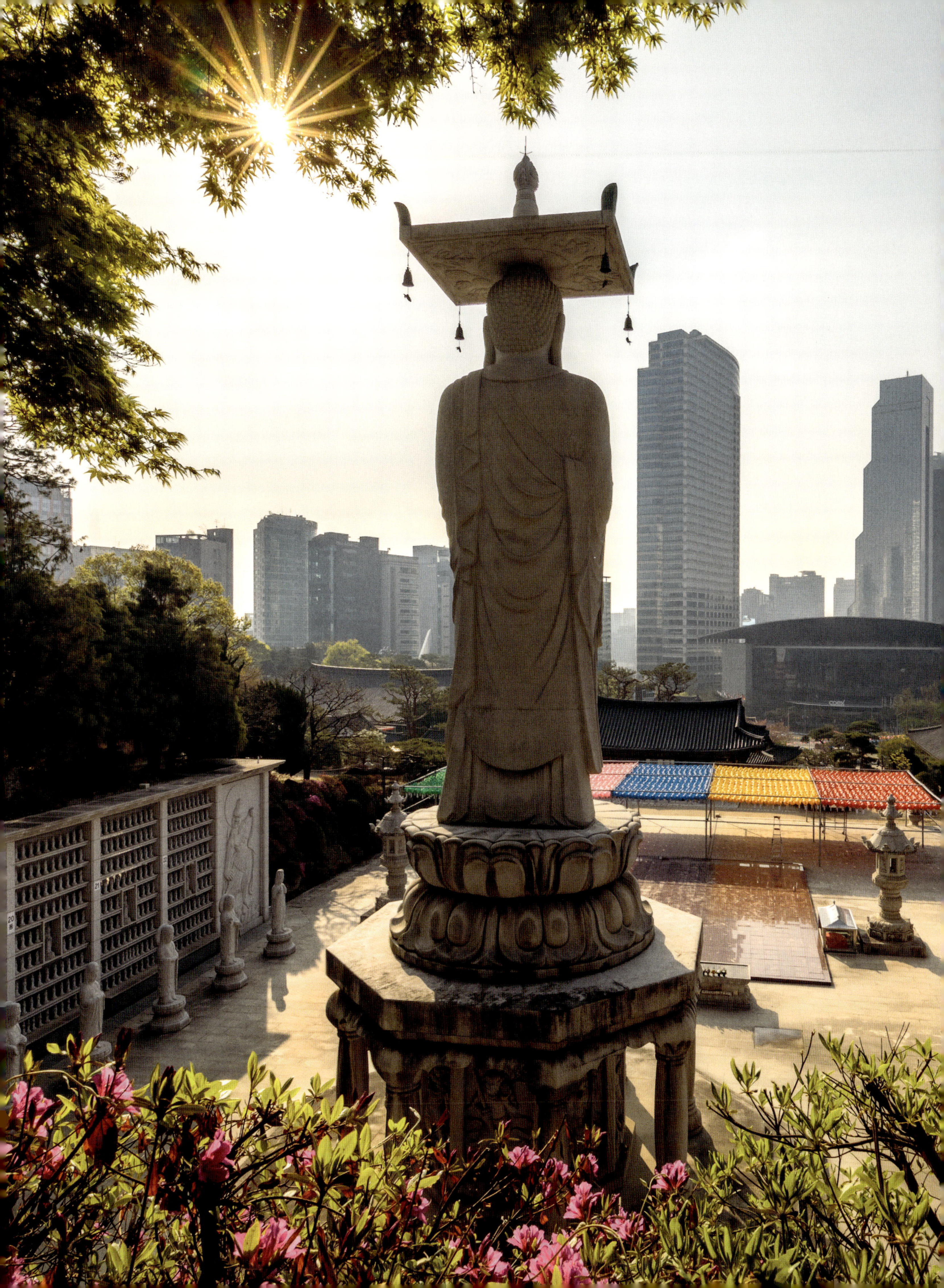

1950s. Online shopping is hot, but strolling through the vast markets is nicer, while the big shopping malls are centers of attraction where people spend their limited free time. Alongside the large esports arenas where Seoul's young people cheer their teams on, men play the game of *Go* in parks. Pay phones and fax machines are as commonplace as Apple Pay.

There is no either/or. Everything is allowed to co-exist. That's what makes this city so livable. Quiet mountain landscapes within the city limits invite visitors to go hiking and view the cherry blossoms, but Seoul itself is also an incredibly quiet city. The pace of life is fast, but the city's residential areas have retained a certain slowness. Anyone who has ever strolled along the 7-mile-long shoreline of the Cheonggyecheon has experienced it. This is how to slow down the pace of life in a megacity.

And this is indeed necessary: Seoul has a certain gravitational pull. Anyone who wants a good education, a good job, a good income, and better opportunities comes to the capital, and it attracts a young demographic in particular. But the trendy and expensive life comes at a high price. The city is beginning to shrink in terms of population. It is too expensive to educate children, people work too much and so, with a declining population, more and more singles or childless couples are found in the city's ubiquitous blocks of apartments.

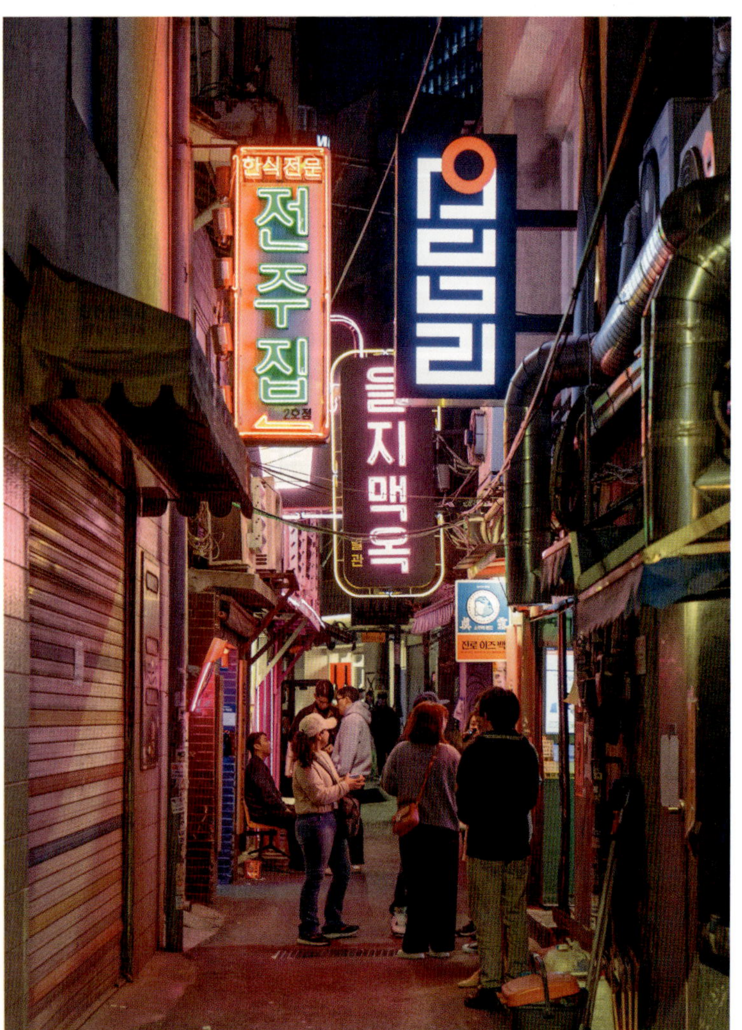

It only seems to be gloomy. The narrow alleys of the Euljiro business district are actually home to countless hip pubs and restaurants.

Nur scheinbar schummrig. In den engen Gassen des Geschäftszentrums Euljiro haben sich unzählige hippe Kneipen und Restaurants angesiedelt.

Es ist anachronistisch. Die Hauptstädter lieben zwar das Alte, aber bevorzugen das Neue. Irgendwie war das schon immer so. Korea hatte wenige Probleme damit, ausländische Einflüsse zuzulassen und für die eigenen Zwecke umzuwidmen. Bevor die kongeniale koreanische Schrift entwickelt wurde, nutzte man die chinesischen Schriftzeichen. Auch heute noch werden sie gerne als Stilmittel benutzt. Kaiser Gojong ließ in seinem Palast Gebäude im Stil der Neo-Renaissance erbauen, und stieß so die Entwicklung westlicher Architektur im Land an.

So leben Alt und Neu in einer hybriden Koexistenz. Seoul ist hochmodern, die Digitalisierung lässt Europa vor Neid erblassen, der öffentliche Nahverkehr ist hocheffizient, koreanische moderne Kultur in allen ihren Facetten von der Musik bis zum Film schwappt als Korean Wave, *hallyu*, in die ganze Welt: Aber wer etwas drucken lassen möchte, überlässt das einer der zahllosen Minidruckereien, die noch Druckmaschinen aus den 1950er-Jahren nutzen. Onlineshopping ist hip, aber über die gigantischen Märkte bummeln ist schöner, während die großen Shopping Malls Erlebniszentren sind, in denen man seine knappe Freizeit verbringt. Neben den großen E-Sports-Arenen, in denen Seouls Jugend ihren Teams zujubelt, spielen Männer in Parks Go. Münztelefone und Faxgeräte sind so selbstverständlich wie Apple Pay.

Es gibt kein Entweder-oder. Alles darf parallel existieren. Das macht die Stadt so lebenswert. Ruhige Bergwelten im Stadtgebiet laden zu Wanderungen und zum Betrachten der Kirschblüte ein, doch auch Seoul selbst ist eine unglaublich leise Stadt. Das Lebenstempo ist hoch, aber die Lebenswelten haben sich eine gewisse Langsamkeit erhalten. Wer einmal am zehn Kilometer langen Ufer des Cheonggyecheon entlang promeniert ist, erlebt es. So geht Entschleunigung in einer Megastadt.

Und die ist notwendig: Seoul ist wie ein Sog. Wer eine gute Ausbildung, gute Jobs, guten Verdienst, bessere Chancen haben möchte, kommt in die Hauptstadt, die dadurch vor allem ein junges Publikum anzieht. Doch das hippe und teure Leben hat einen hohen Preis. Die Stadt beginnt in Bezug auf die Einwohnerzahlen zu schrumpfen. Zu teuer ist die Ausbildung von Kindern, zu viel wird gearbeitet und so leben bei einer schrumpfenden Bevölkerung immer mehr Singles oder kinderlose Ehepaare in den allgegenwärtigen Apartmentblocks.

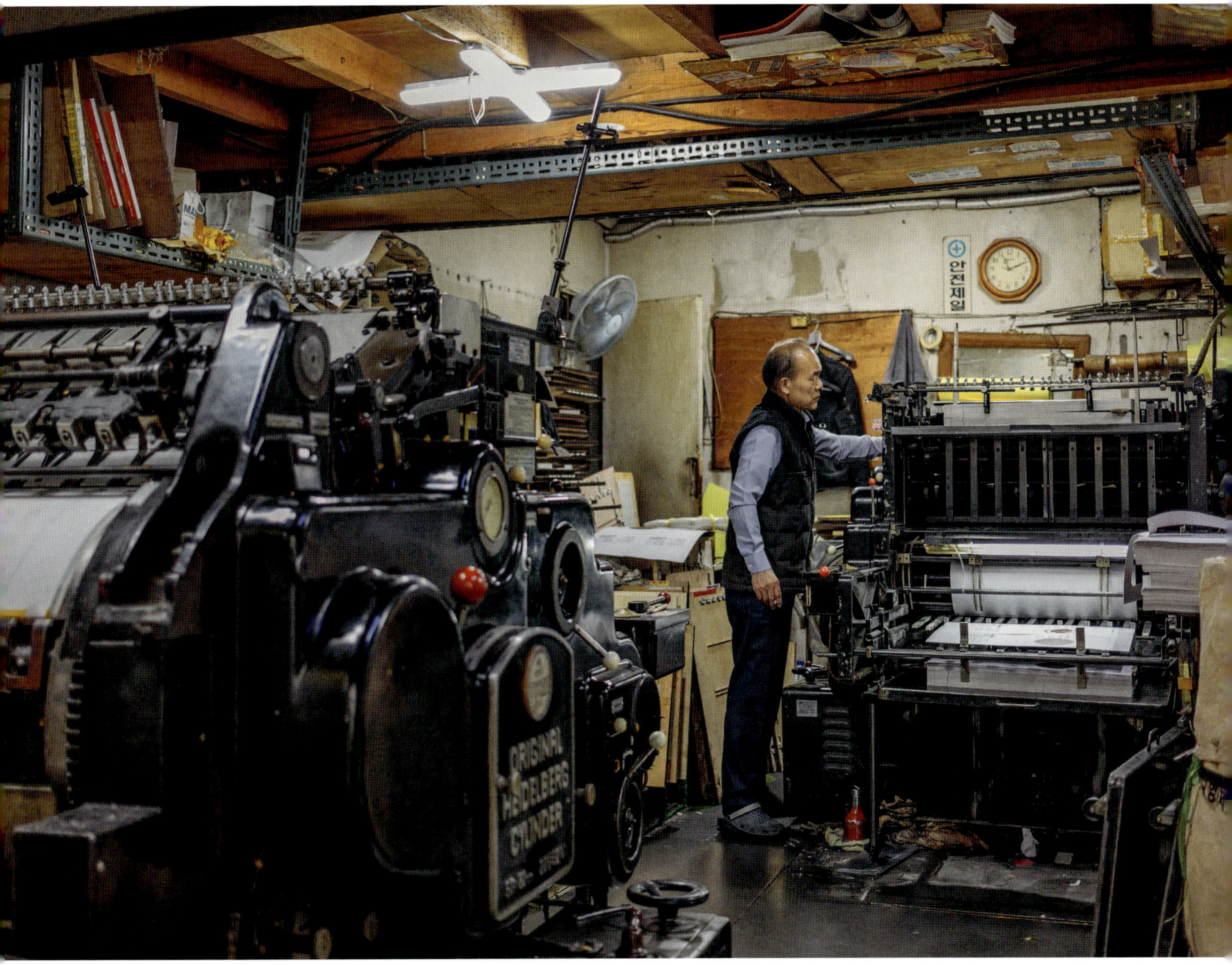

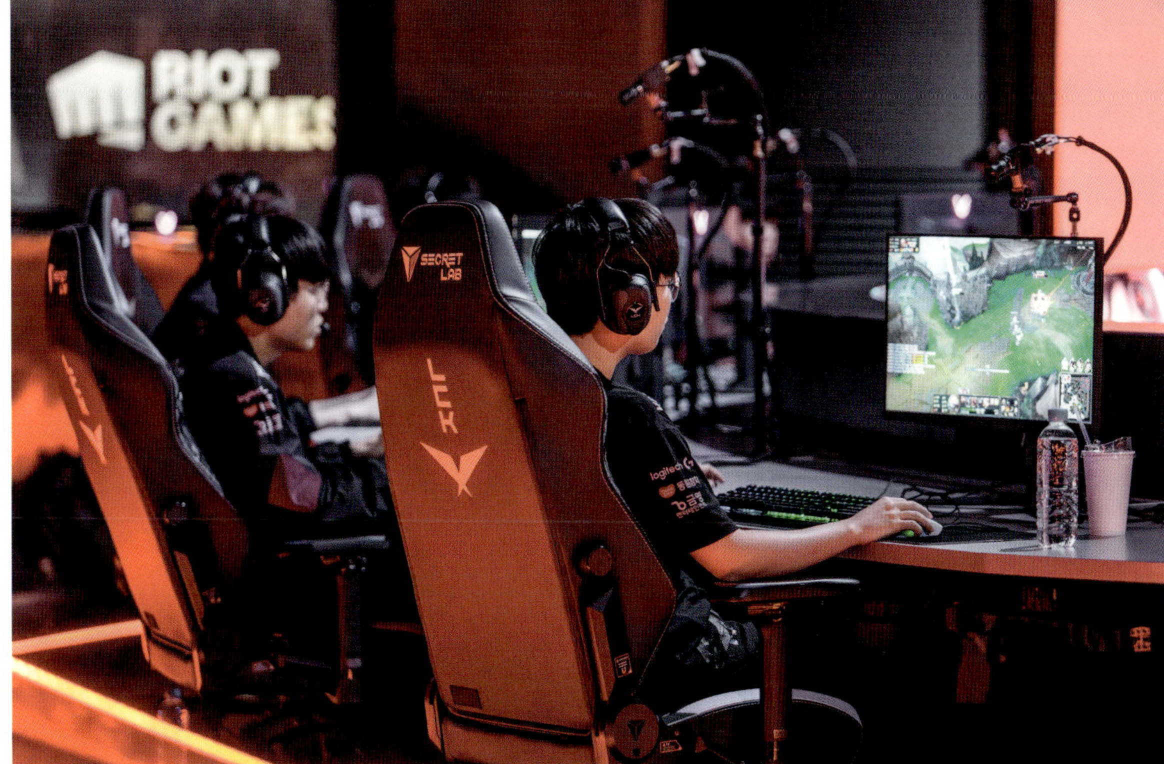

Old versus new? Not in Seoul.
Here, different eras exist alongside
one another.

Alt versus Neu? Nicht in Seoul. Hier
existieren alle Zeitläufe parallel.

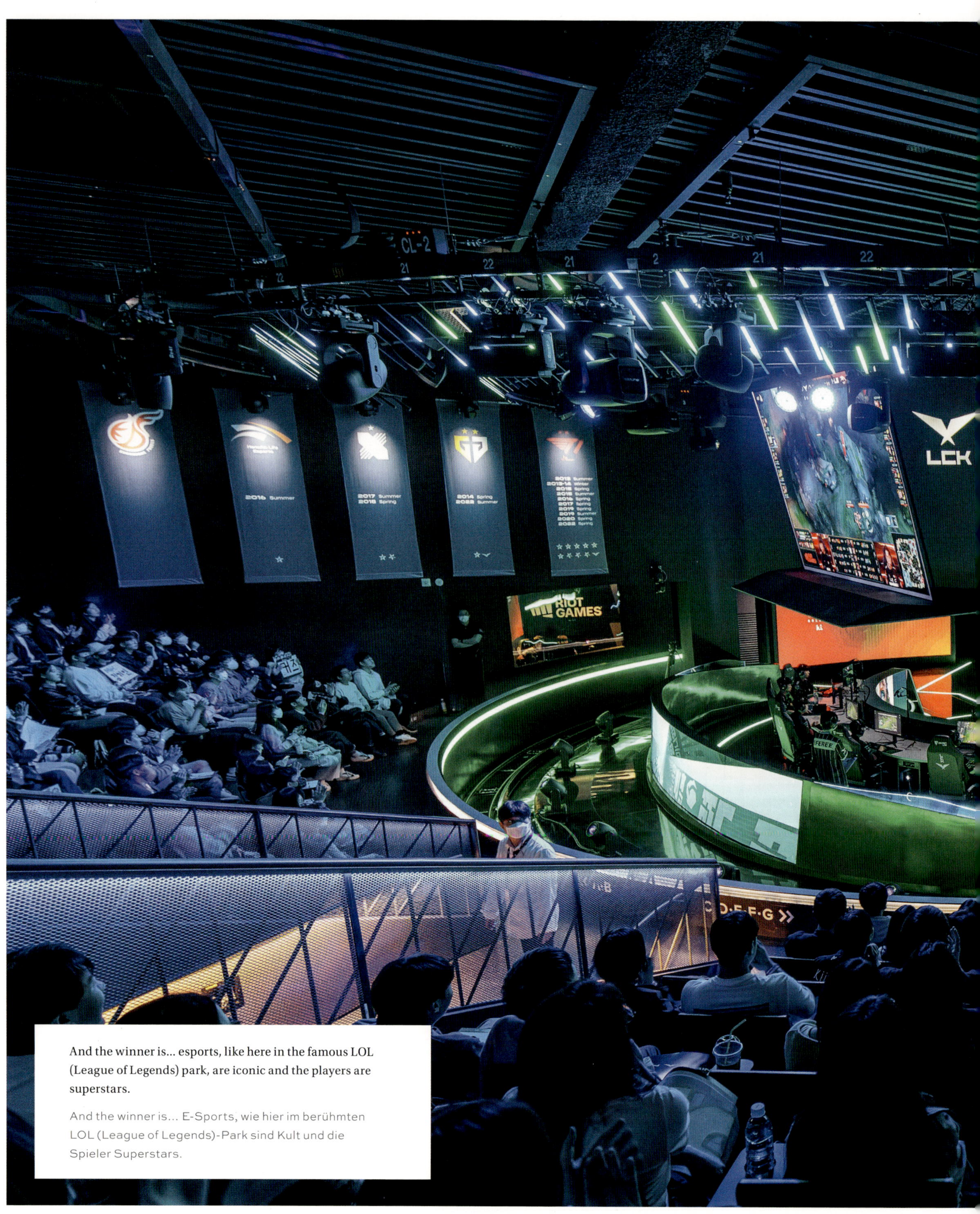

And the winner is… esports, like here in the famous LOL (League of Legends) park, are iconic and the players are superstars.

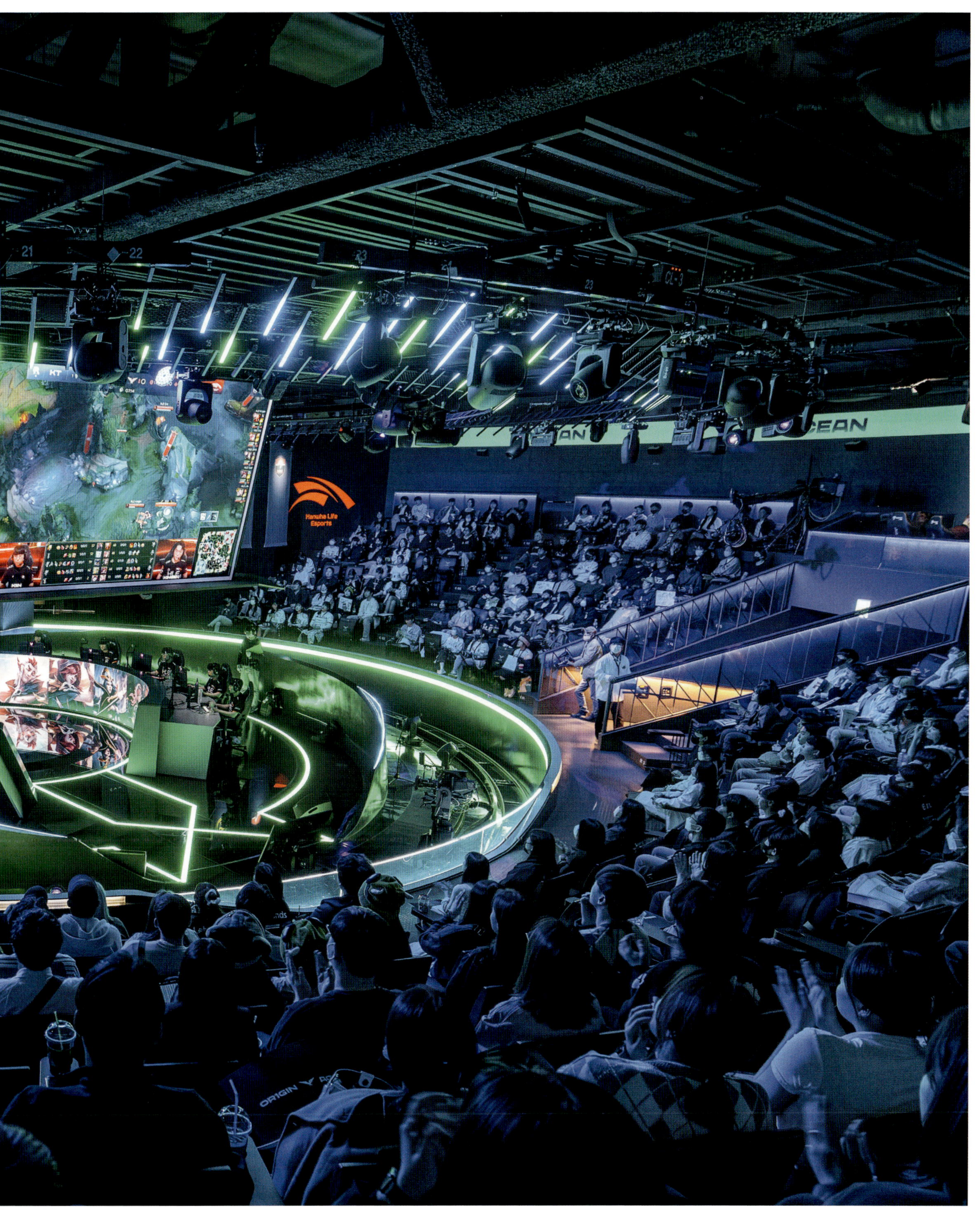

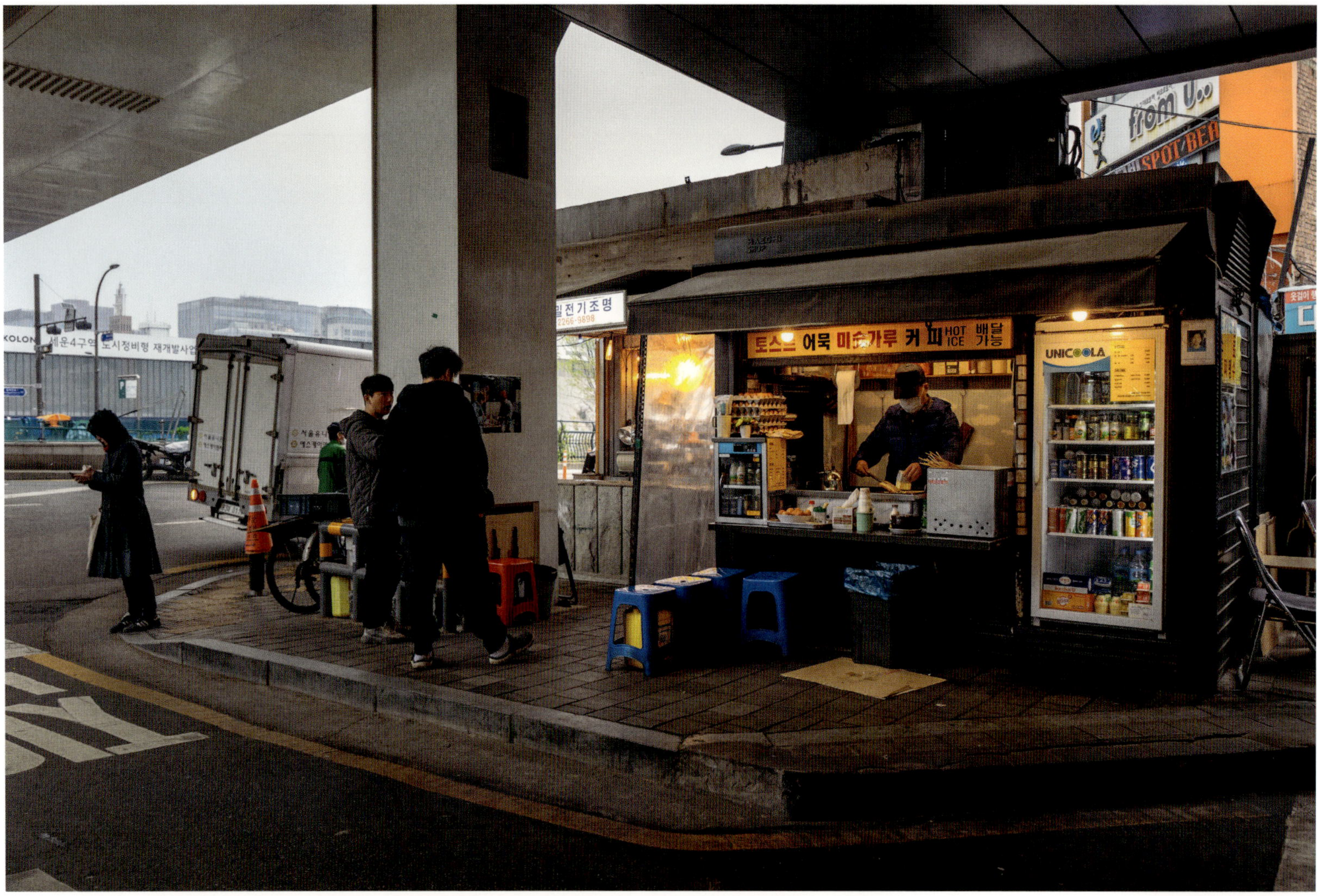

토스트 어묵 미숫가루 커피 HOT ICE 배달 가능
UNICOOLA

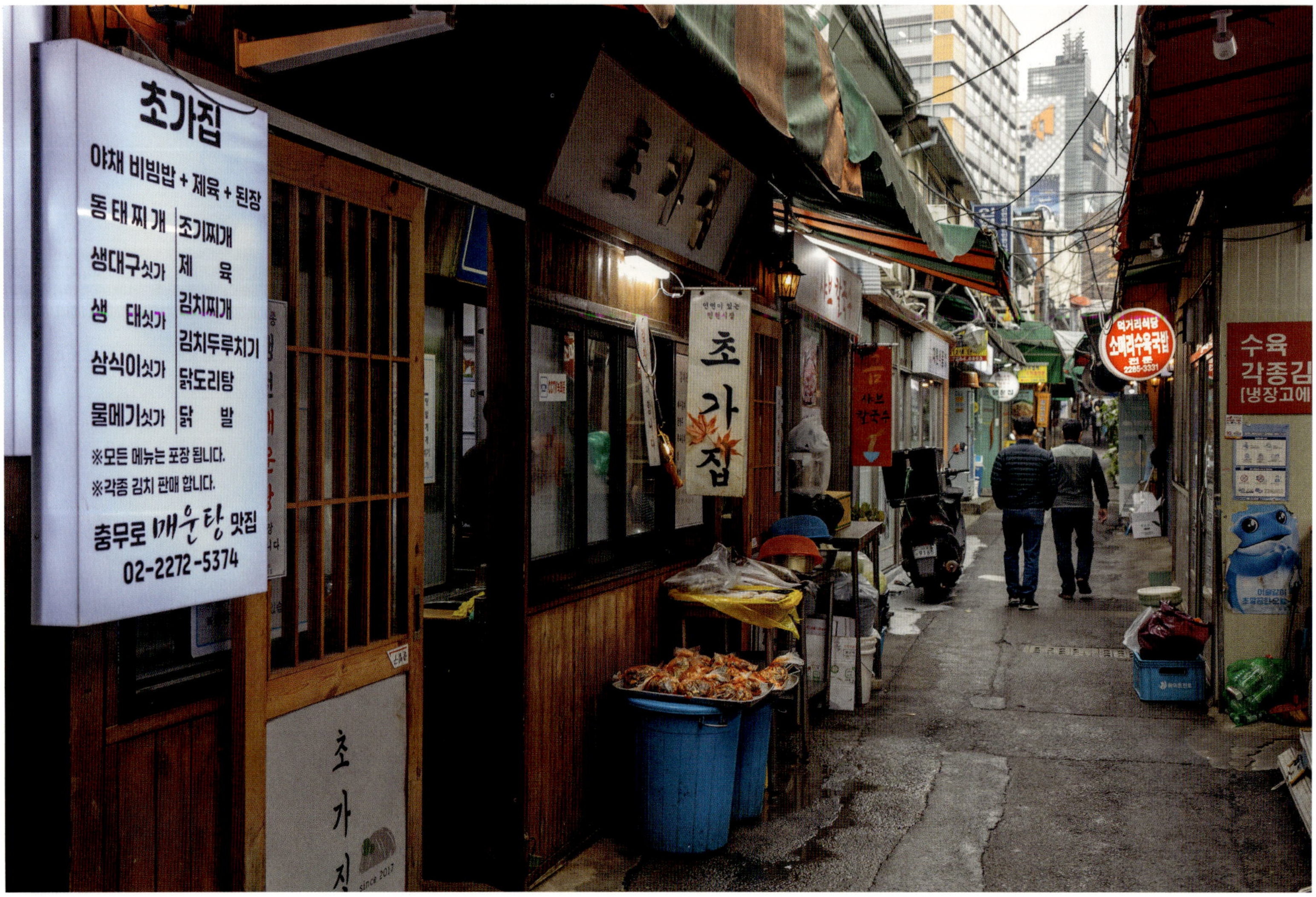

초가집
야채 비빔밥 + 제육 + 된장
동 태 찌 개   조기찌개
생대구싯가   제   육
생   태싯가   김치찌개
삼식이싯가   김치두루치기
물메기싯가   닭도리탕
                     닭   발
※모든 메뉴는 포장 됩니다.
※각종 김치 판매 합니다.
충무로 매운탕 맛집
02-2272-5374
초가집

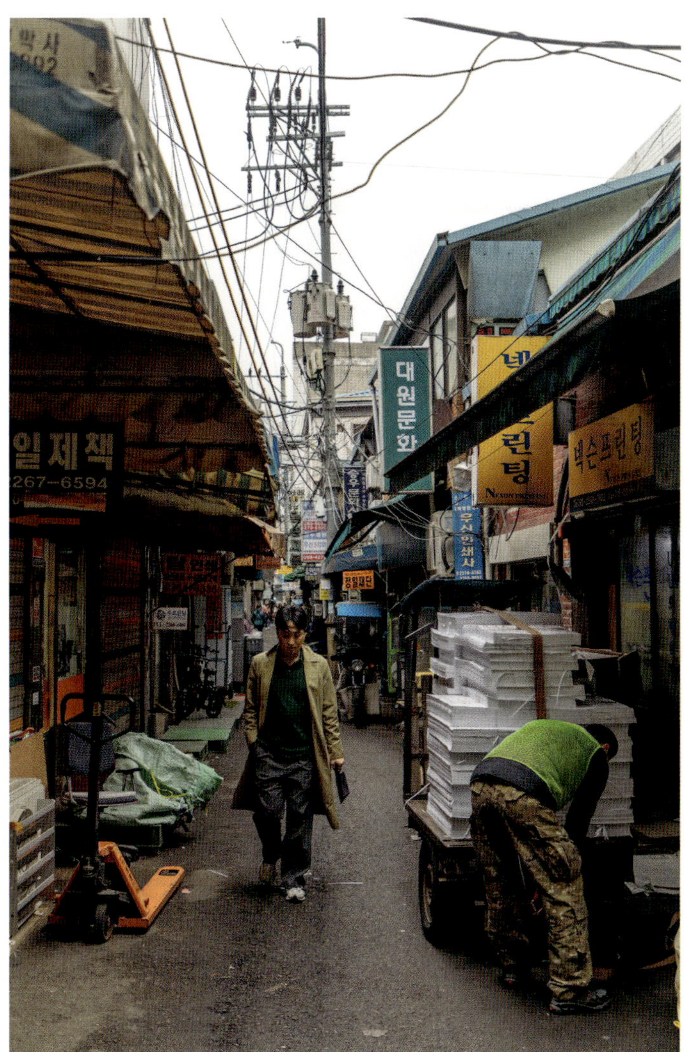

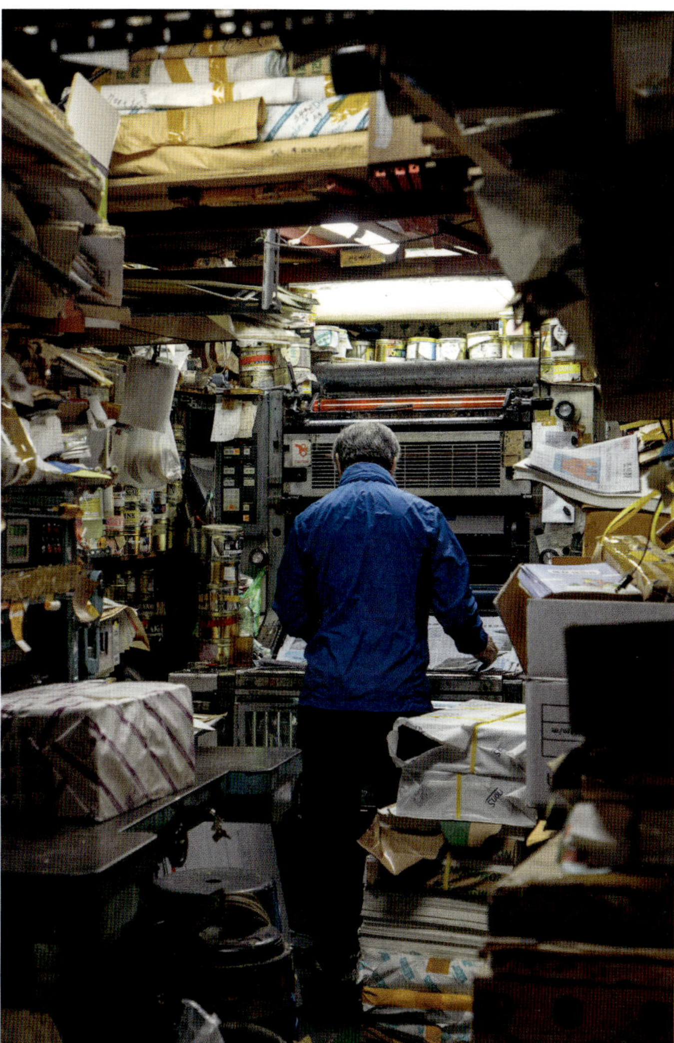

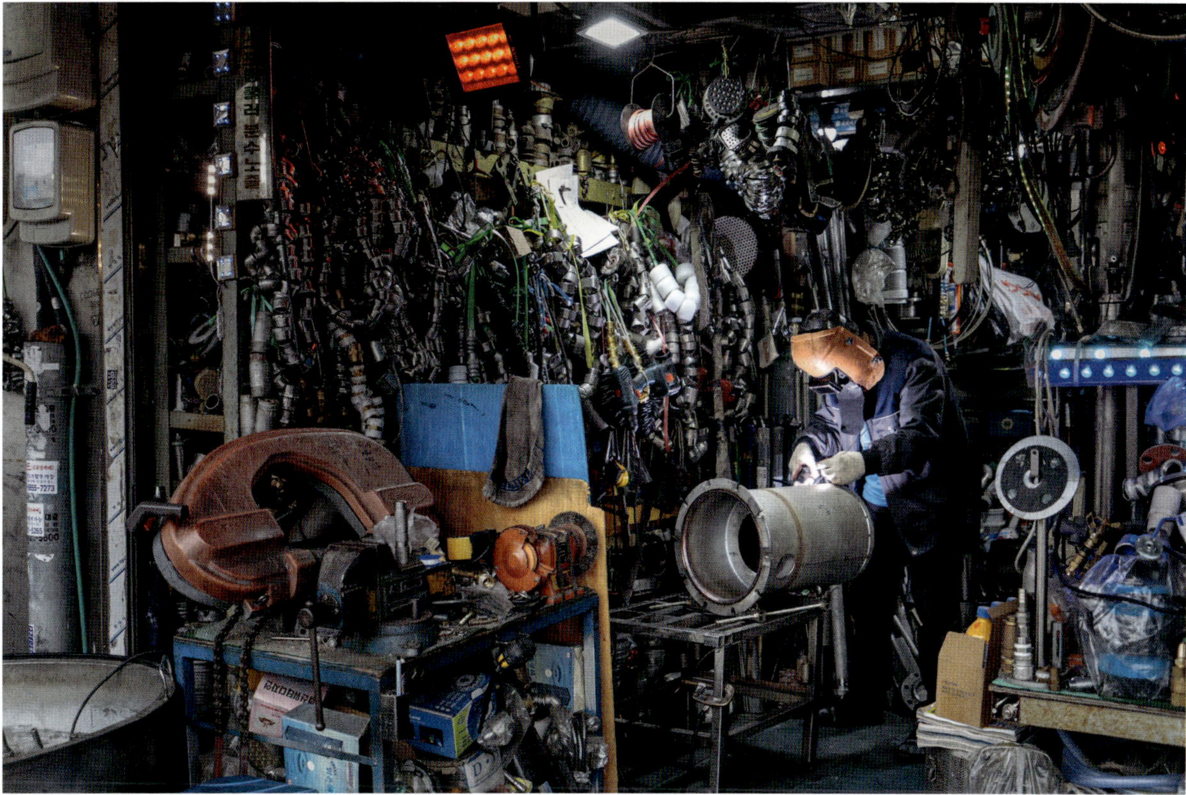

Seoul appears modern on the outside, but in the narrow streets between the skyscrapers it is still delightfully tranquil and old-fashioned.

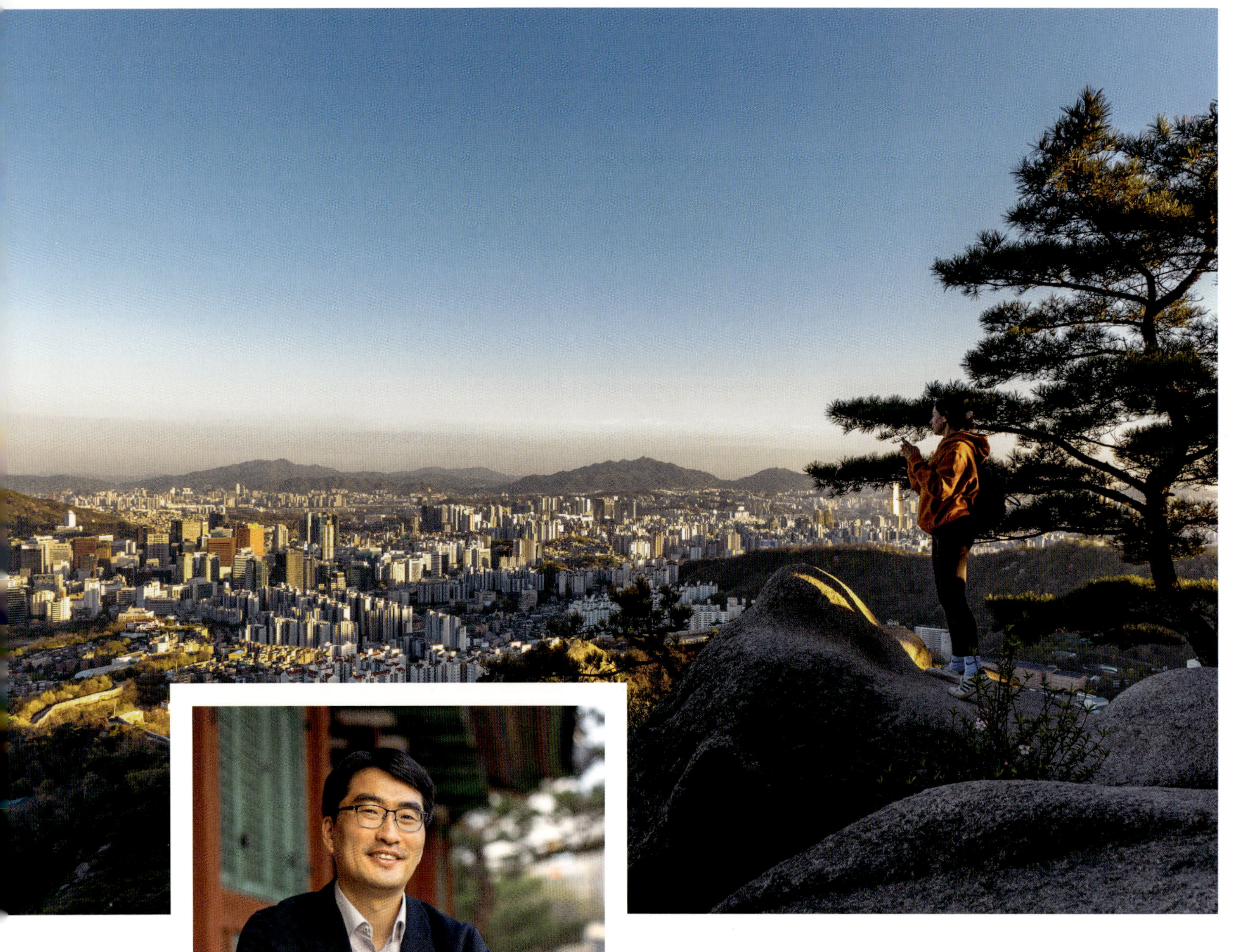

LEE SEOK-MIN
PROFESSOR

Seoul has so much to offer when it comes to recreation. Mountains and forests can be found in the heart of the city, and those who don't like hiking can find a change of scenery in a *hanok* district.

Seoul bietet einen hohen Freizeitwert. Berge und Wälder finden sich mitten in der Stadt und wer nicht wandern möchte, findet Abwechslung in einem *hanok*-Viertel.

...ON THE DYNAMICS OF THE CITY

"Seoul is always changing. I was also in Europe. And I was in America. But I would say Seoul is the fasted-changing city. Every three or five years, you can see the big difference in any part of Seoul. (...) It's very unstable. In a good way, it's very dynamic and also has a sort of energy."

...ON WHY TO MOVE TO SEOUL

"And then during [past] dynasties, people already knew that if they want to have success, they need to come to Seoul. And then if they want to be a politician, they have to come to Seoul. If they want to be successful, they have to come to Seoul. (...) But why do the people just leave local cities for Seoul [today]? There are two reasons. First, the practical reason is the jobs. Jobs here have better salaries. The second reason is, I think, the images. They have lots of preconceptions, etc., which may actually shatter later, but not right now. So, people have some kind of preconception about Seoul, because they think that if they live in Seoul, they will live a better life no matter what the salary, etc."

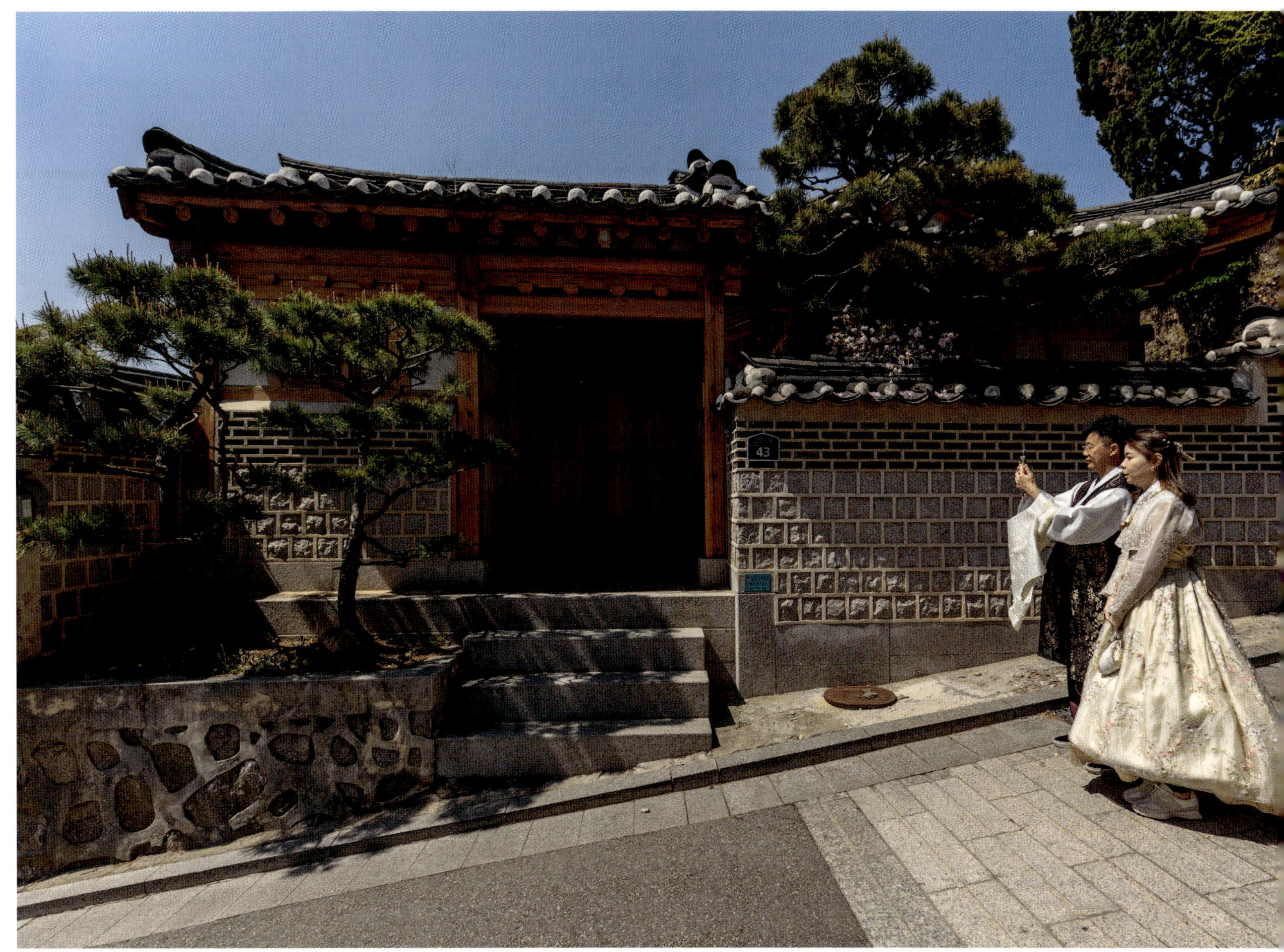

...ZUR DYNAMIK DER STADT

„Seoul ist immer im Wandel. Ich war auch in Europa. Und ich war in Amerika. Aber ich würde sagen, Seoul ist die Stadt, die sich am schnellsten verändert. Alle drei oder fünf Jahre kann man einen großen Unterschied in irgendeinem Teil von Seoul feststellen. Es ist also sehr unbeständig, (...). Auf eine gute Art und Weise ist sie sehr dynamisch und hat eine gewisse Energie.“

...ÜBER DIE GRÜNDE, NACH SEOUL ZU ZIEHEN

„Und während der (vergangenen) Dynastien wussten die Menschen bereits, dass sie nach Seoul kommen müssen, wenn sie Erfolg haben wollen. Und wenn sie Politiker werden wollen, müssen sie nach Seoul kommen, wenn sie erfolgreich sein wollen, müssen sie nach Seoul kommen. (...) Aber warum verlassen die Leute ihre Städte und gehen (heutzutage) nach Seoul? Dafür gibt es zwei Gründe. Der erste, praktische Grund sind die Arbeitsplätze. Die Jobs hier sind besser bezahlt. Der zweite Grund ist, glaube ich, das Image. Sie haben viele Vorurteile und so weiter, die man zwar später abbauen kann, aber nicht jetzt. Die Leute haben also eine Art Vorurteil über Seoul, weil sie denken, dass sie in Seoul ein besseres Leben führen, egal wie hoch das Gehalt ist.“

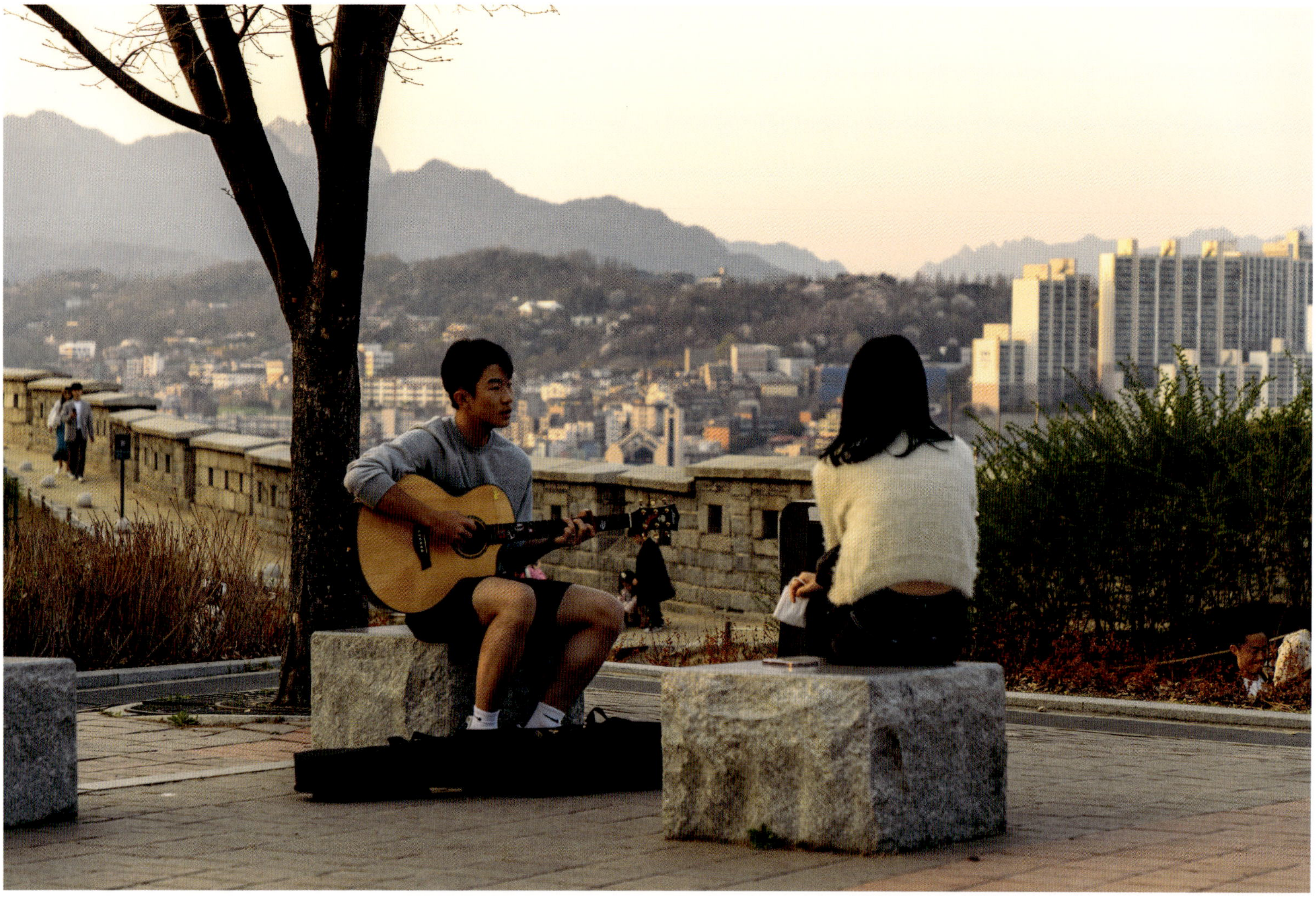

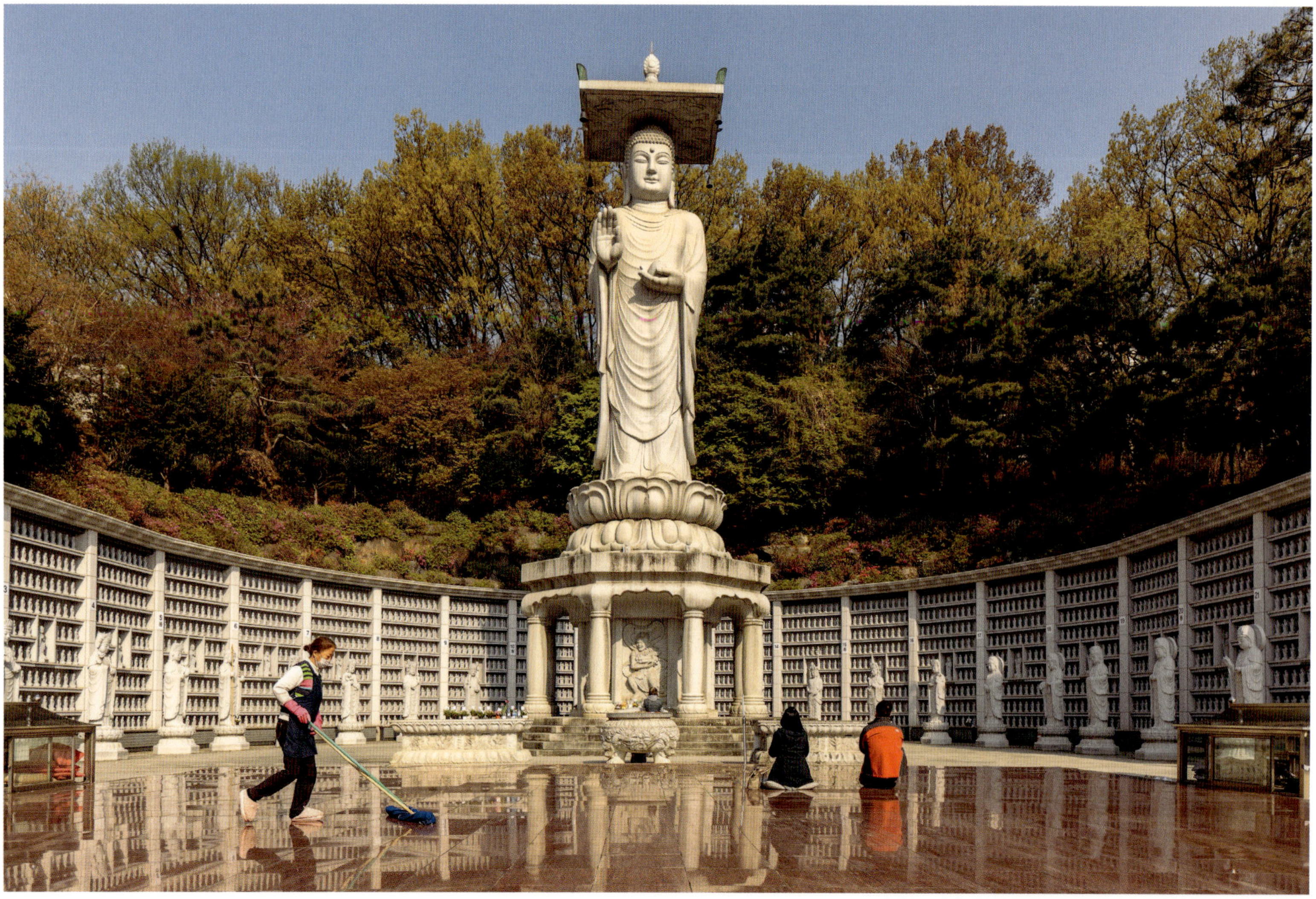

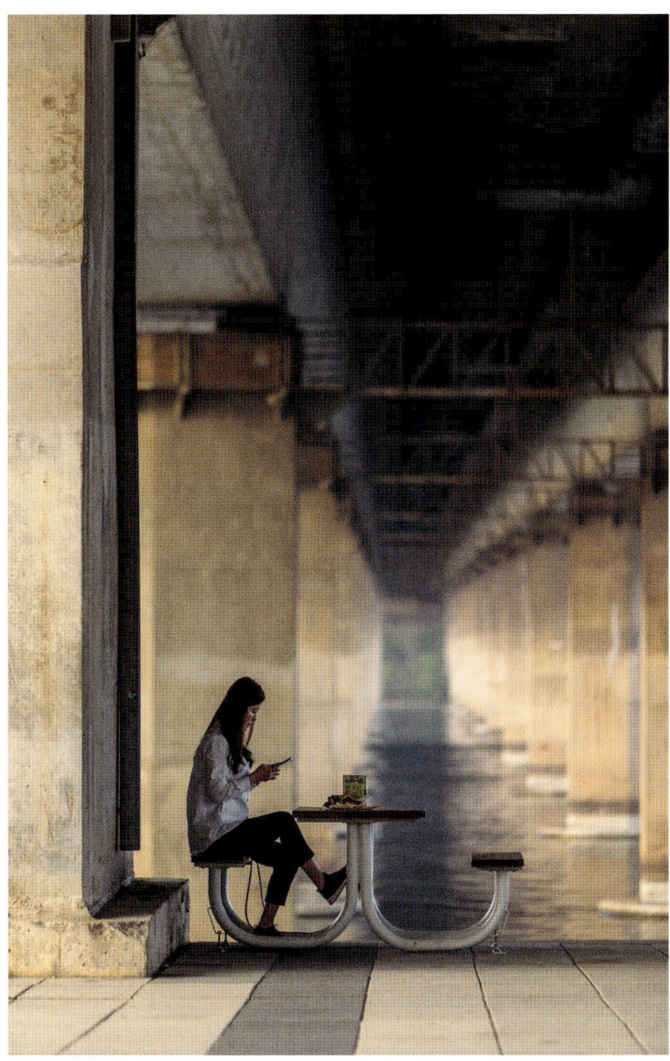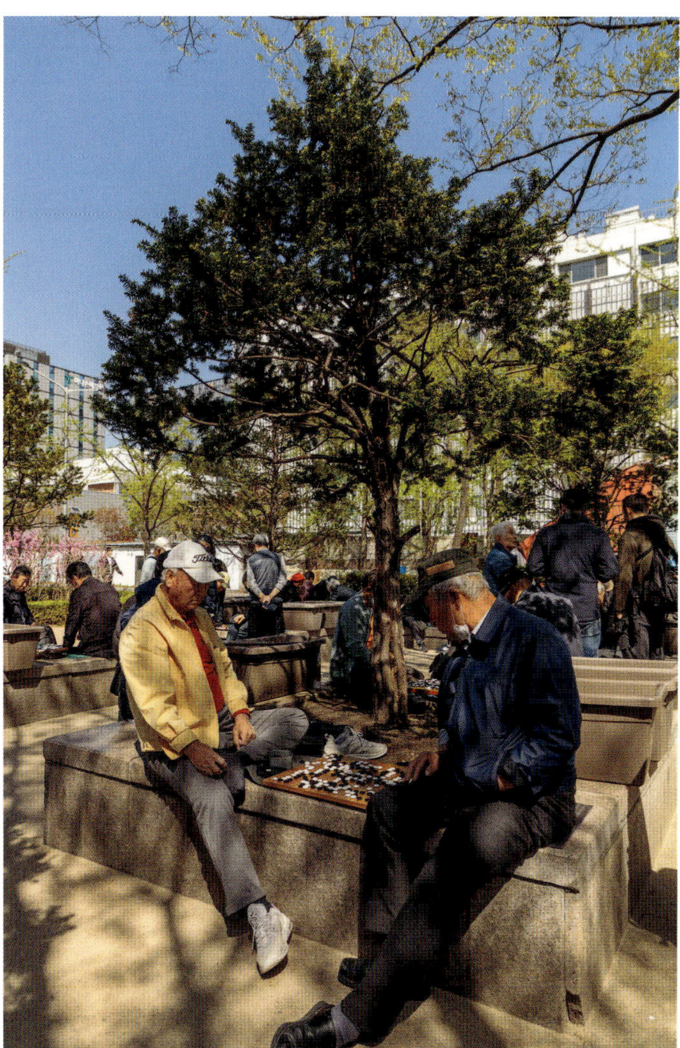

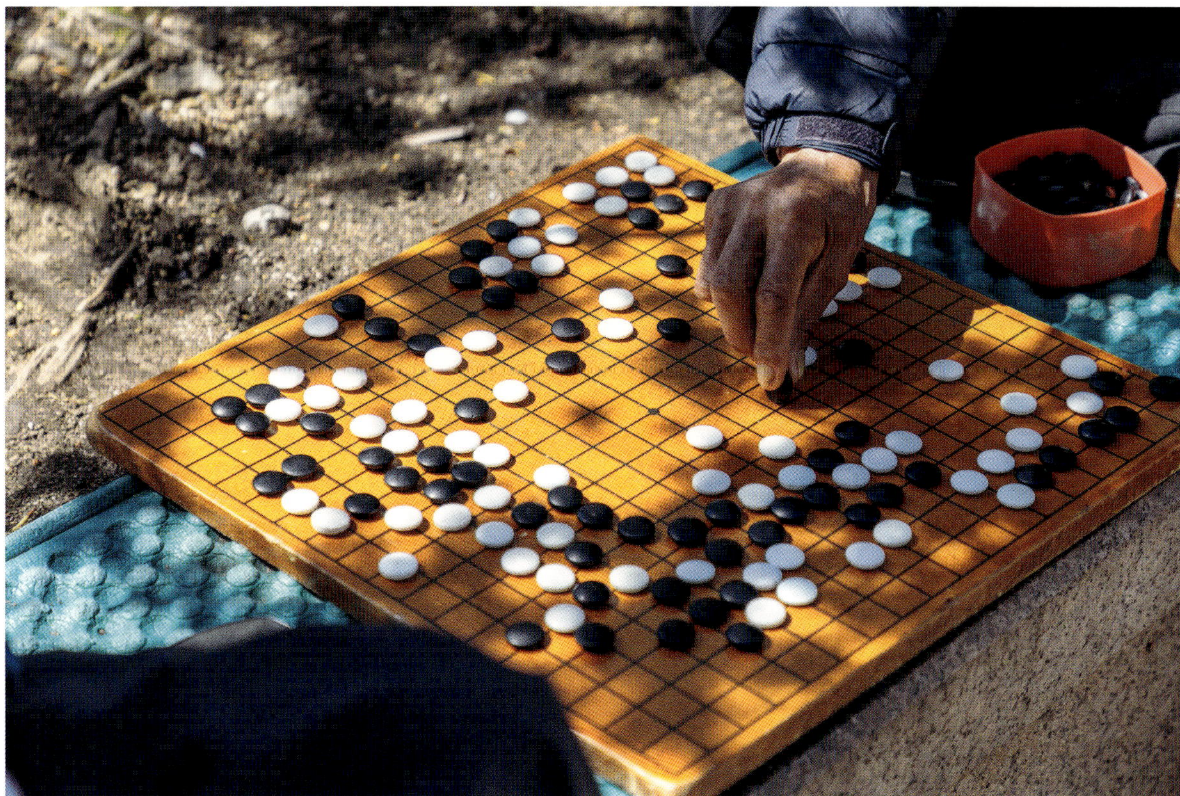

The work week ranges from 52 to 69 hours,
making every moment and every bit of space for
recreation precious.

52 bis 69 Stunden die Woche beträgt die
Arbeitszeit. Da werden jeder Moment und
jeder Raum für etwas Erholung kostbar.

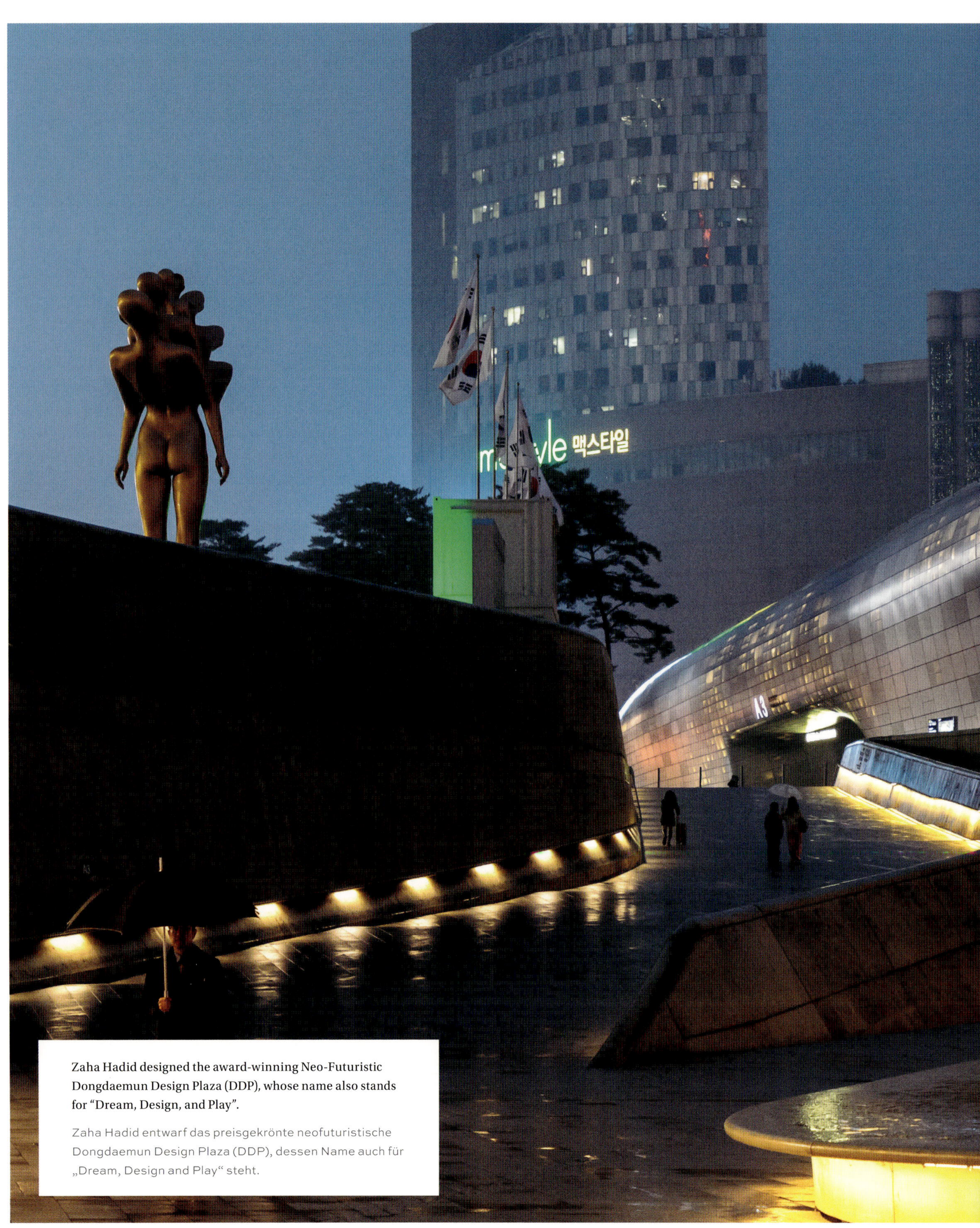

Zaha Hadid designed the award-winning Neo-Futuristic Dongdaemun Design Plaza (DDP), whose name also stands for "Dream, Design, and Play".

Zaha Hadid entwarf das preisgekrönte neofuturistische Dongdaemun Design Plaza (DDP), dessen Name auch für „Dream, Design and Play" steht.

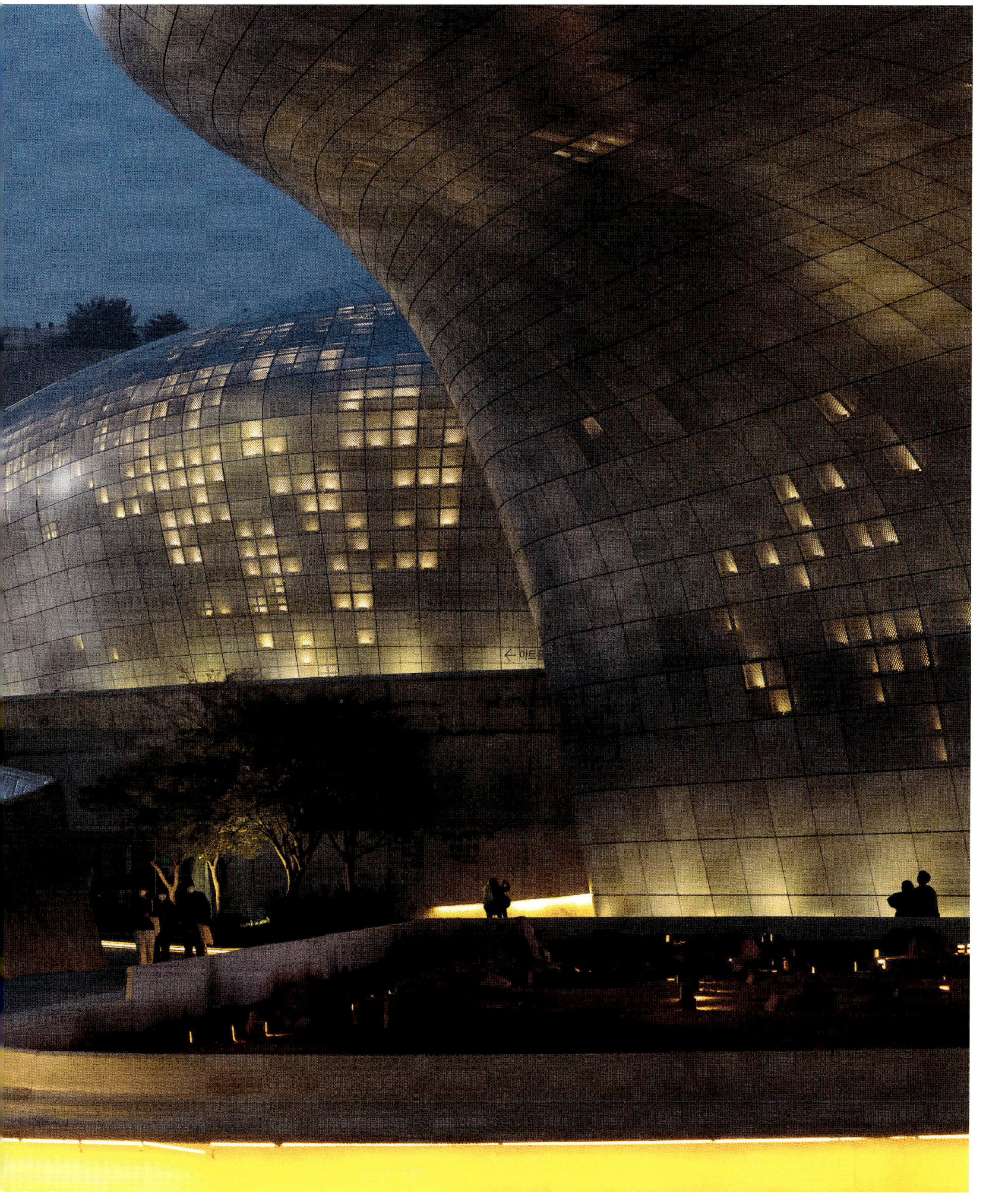
← 아트

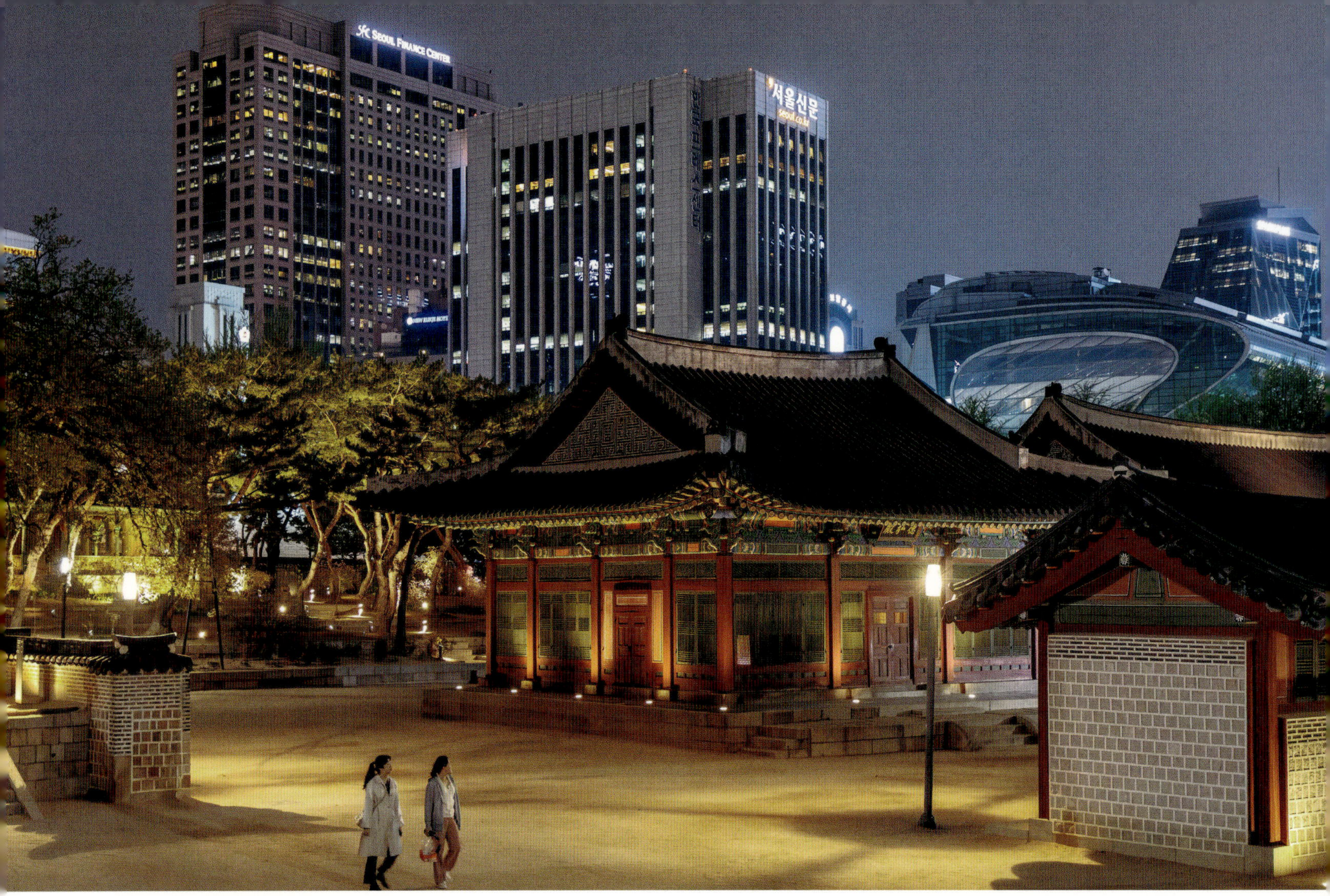
SEOUL FINANCE CENTER
서울신문

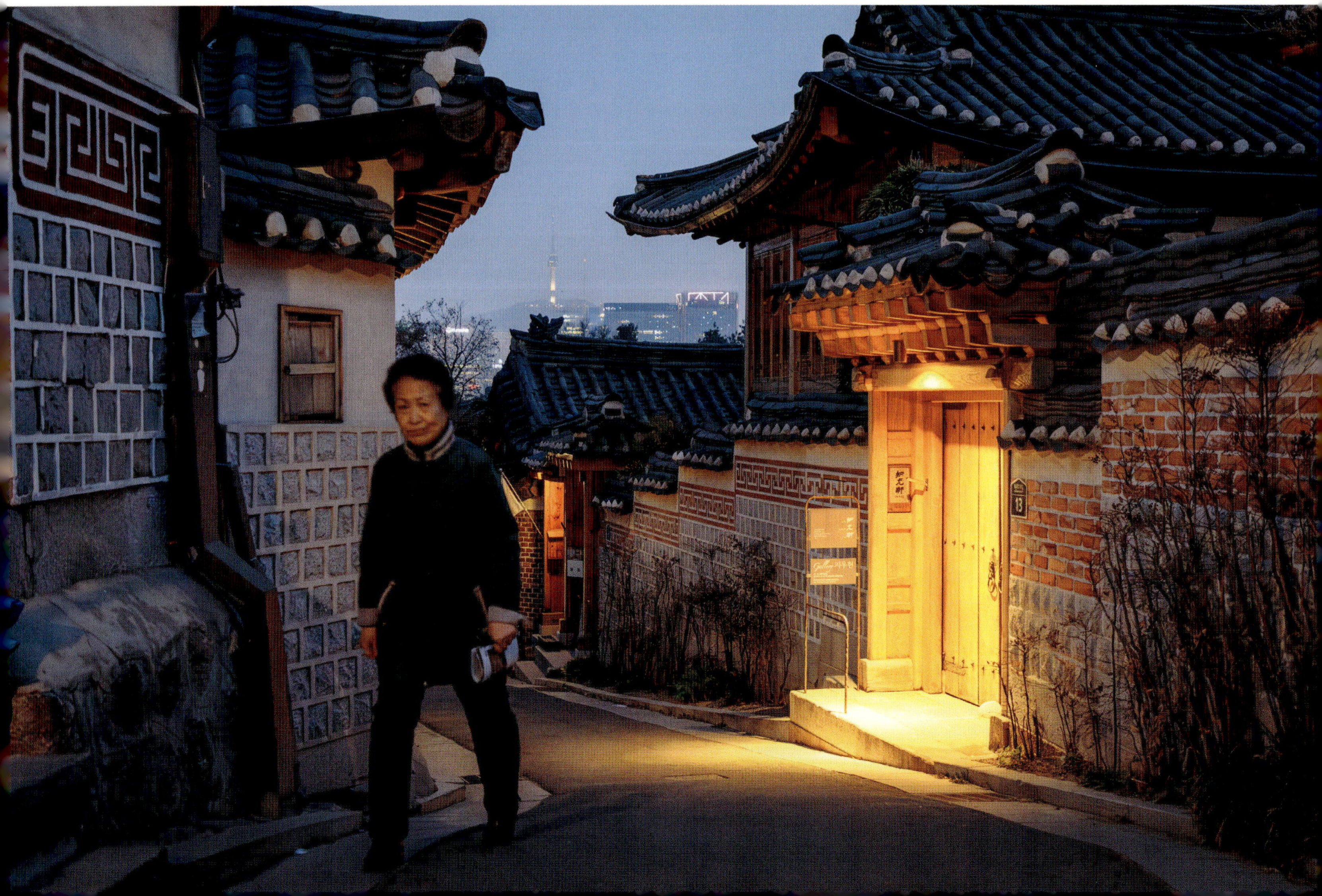

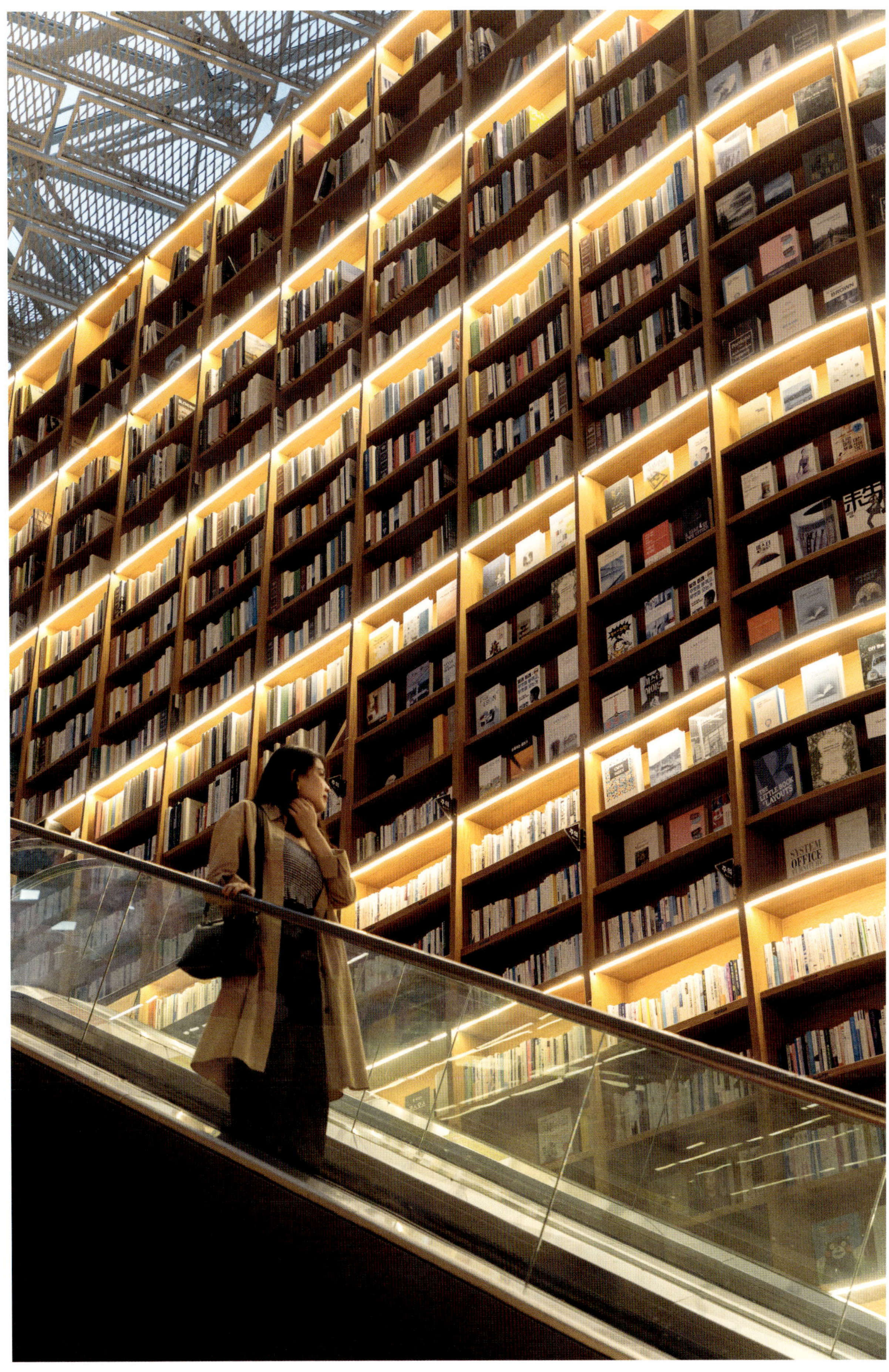

The old, whether it's found in *hanoks* or palaces,
or in the books of Starfield Library, invariably
serves as inspiration for new ideas.

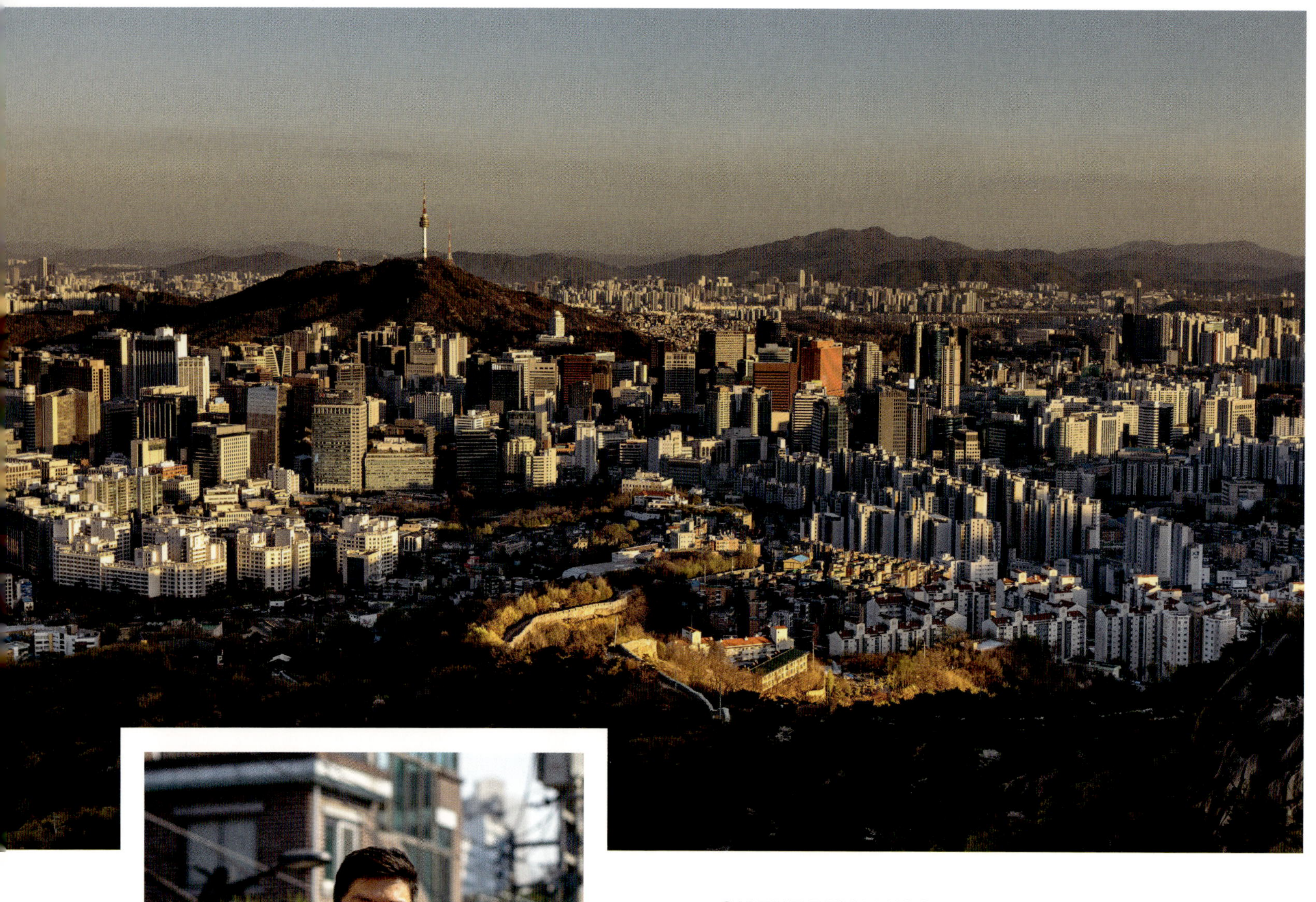

DANIEL TÄNDLER
ARCHITECT
ARCHITEKT

"And the geographical location of Seoul is just stunning.
You cannot get used to the view of the mountains.
It's so stunning and beautiful." (Daniel Tändler)

„Und die geografische Lage von Seoul ist einfach atemberaubend. An die Aussicht auf die Berge kann man sich nicht
gewöhnen. Es ist so atemberaubend und schön."
(Daniel Tändler)

...ON THE DYNAMICS
OF THE CITY

"I remember, it was before the Soccer World Cup took place in
Seoul and in Tokyo. And I remember over the weekend, they had
broadened one of the main roads that would lead to the stadium.
(...) I don't know how long this area was that they demolished, but
within one weekend, they demolished a full row of houses as far
as you could see down the road. And that was so shocking to see.
In that moment, I grasped what kind of dynamic the city has. How
fast it develops, how fast it was changing."

...ON DIGITALIZATION

"It, the whole infrastructure, digital infrastructure, bus system,
everything was overhauled during the past 20 years. We have really reached an unimaginable level of economic and digital development here. Public services offices are all digitalized, the health
sector is all digital, and it's all super-efficient. So, I think, to an
extent it has made the future become today. This is how it feels
sometimes."

...ON ENVIRONMENTAL
AWARENESS

"Fridays for future? I haven't noticed that it has been a thing in
Korea, so I haven't seen a lot of that. In general, I would say environmental issues have been coming up a bit more in recent years,

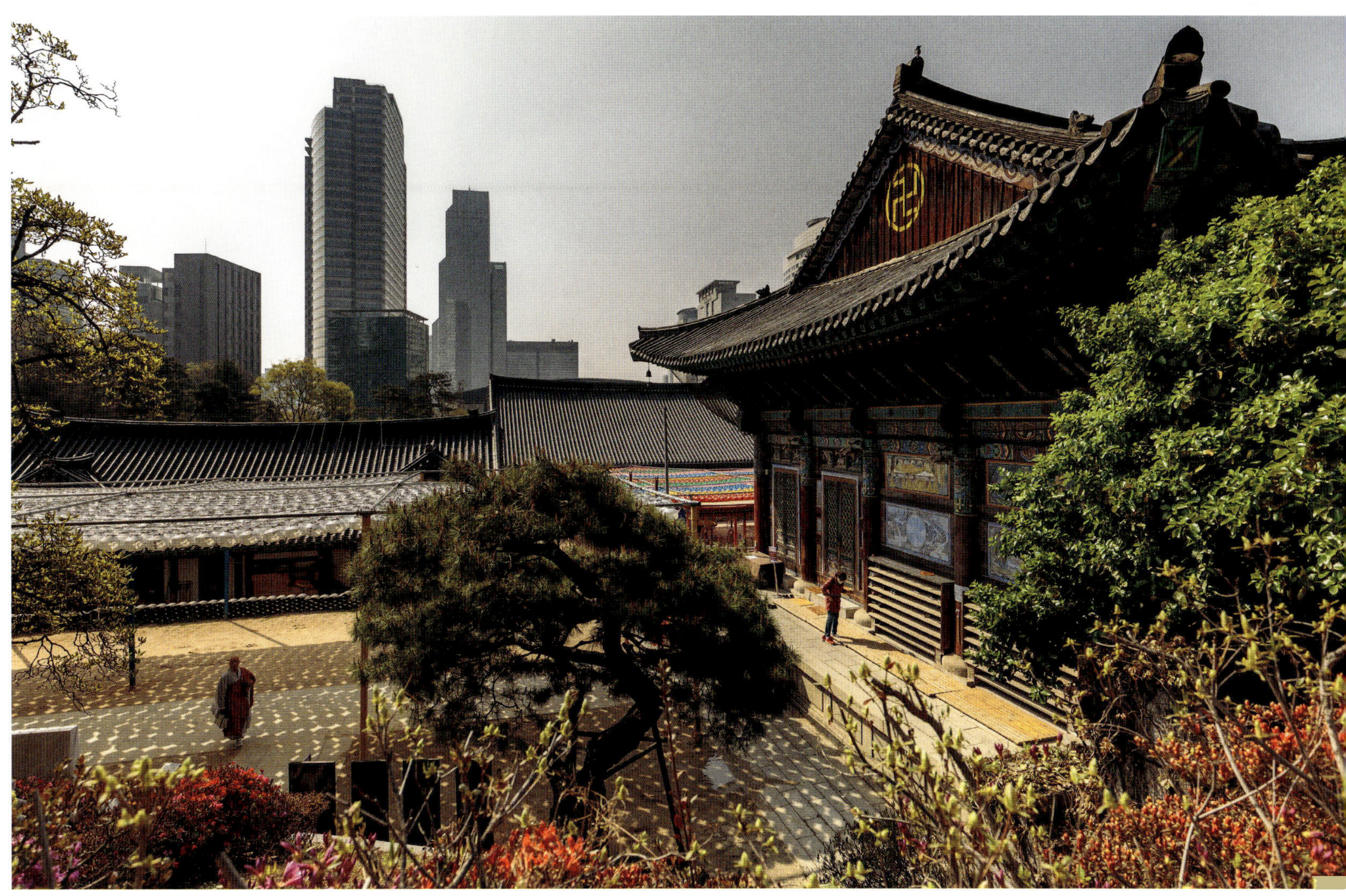

but you can tell that Korea is still in a mindset of a developing country. Even though we've reached a level of a developed nation now, the mindset is still like, oh, we have to sacrifice for the end goal of becoming rich, becoming developed. And I think that's the reason why, in comparison to countries like Germany, the public sentiment is not so much on the side of trying to make the economy more environmentally friendly, but it doesn't mean that it's not happening."

...ZUR DYNAMIK DER STADT

„Ich erinnere mich, dass dies vor der Fußballweltmeisterschaft in Seoul und Tokio geschah. Und ich erinnere mich, dass sie am Wochenende eine der Hauptstraßen, die zum Stadion führen sollten, verbreitert hatten. (…) Ich weiß nicht, wie lang dieses Gebiet war, das sie abrissen, aber innerhalb eines Wochenendes rissen sie eine ganze Reihe von Häusern ab, soweit man die Straße sehen konnte. Und das war so schockierend zu sehen. In diesem Moment wurde mir klar, was für eine Dynamik die Stadt hat. Wie schnell sie sich entwickelt, wie schnell sie sich verändert."

...ÜBER DIE DIGITALISIERUNG

„Die gesamte Infrastruktur, die digitale Infrastruktur, das Bussystem, alles wurde in den letzten 20 Jahren erneuert. Wir haben hier also wirklich ein unvorstellbares Niveau der wirtschaftlichen und digitalen Entwicklung erreicht. Der öffentliche Dienst ist komplett digitalisiert, der Gesundheitssektor ist komplett digital, und das alles ist super effizient. Ich denke also, dass die Zukunft in gewissem Maße heute schon Gegenwart geworden ist. So fühlt es sich manchmal an."

...ÜBER DAS UMWELTBEWUSSTSEIN

„Fridays for Future? Ich habe nicht bemerkt, dass das in Korea ein Thema war, also habe ich nicht viel davon gesehen. Generell würde ich sagen, dass Umweltthemen in den letzten Jahren etwas mehr in den Vordergrund gerückt sind, aber man merkt, dass Korea immer noch die Mentalität eines Entwicklungslandes hat. Auch wenn wir inzwischen das Niveau eines Industrielandes erreicht haben, ist die Einstellung immer noch so, dass wir für das Endziel, reich und entwickelt zu werden, Opfer bringen müssen. Und ich denke, das ist der Grund, warum die öffentliche Meinung im Vergleich zu Ländern wie Deutschland nicht so sehr auf der Seite derjenigen steht, die versuchen, die Wirtschaft umweltfreundlicher zu gestalten, was aber nicht heißt, dass es nicht geschieht."

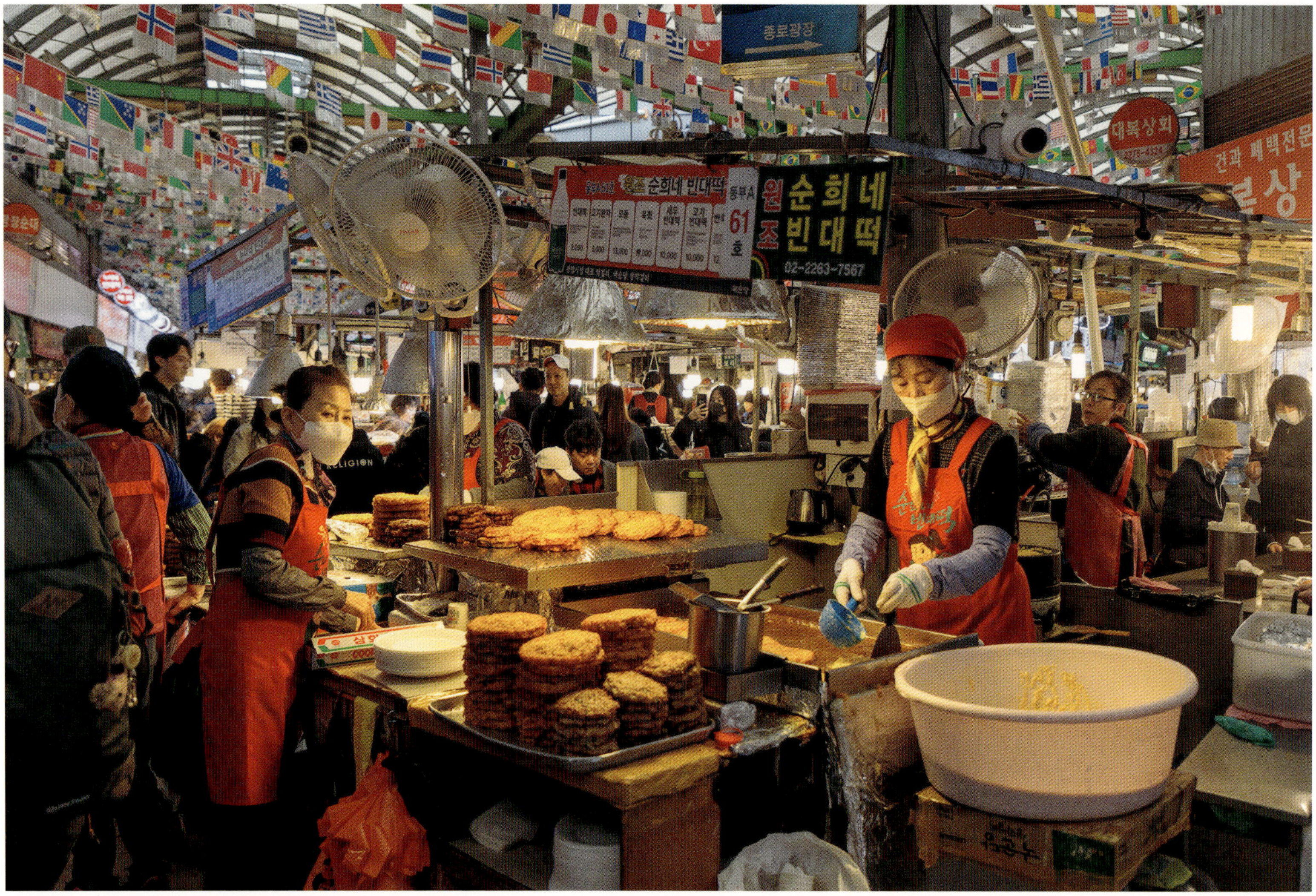
종로광장
순희네 빈대떡
동부A
61
호
원조
순희네
빈대떡
02-2263-7567
대복상회

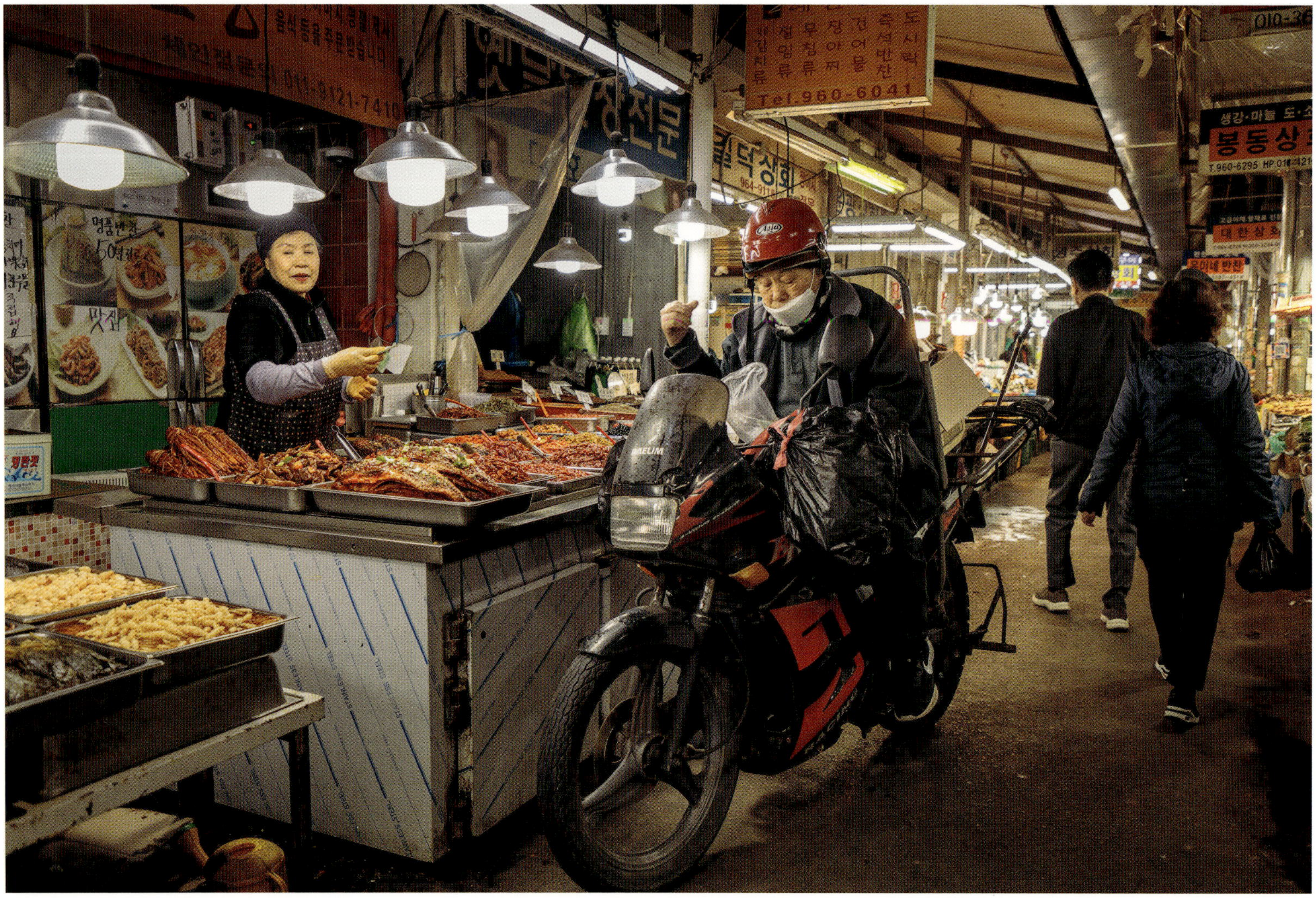
Tel.960-6041

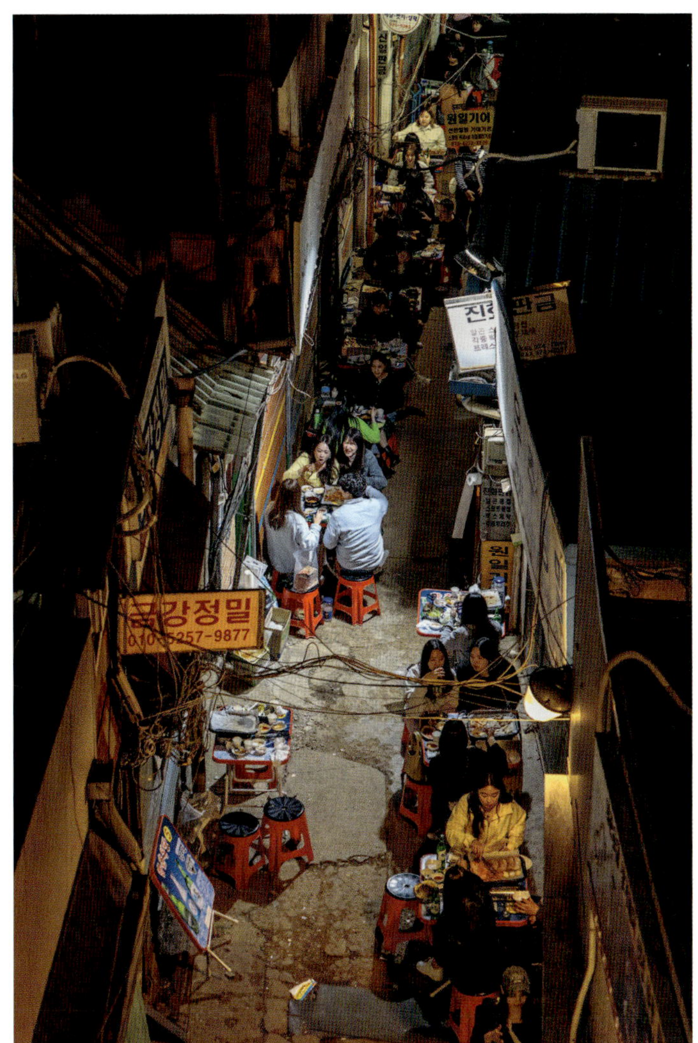

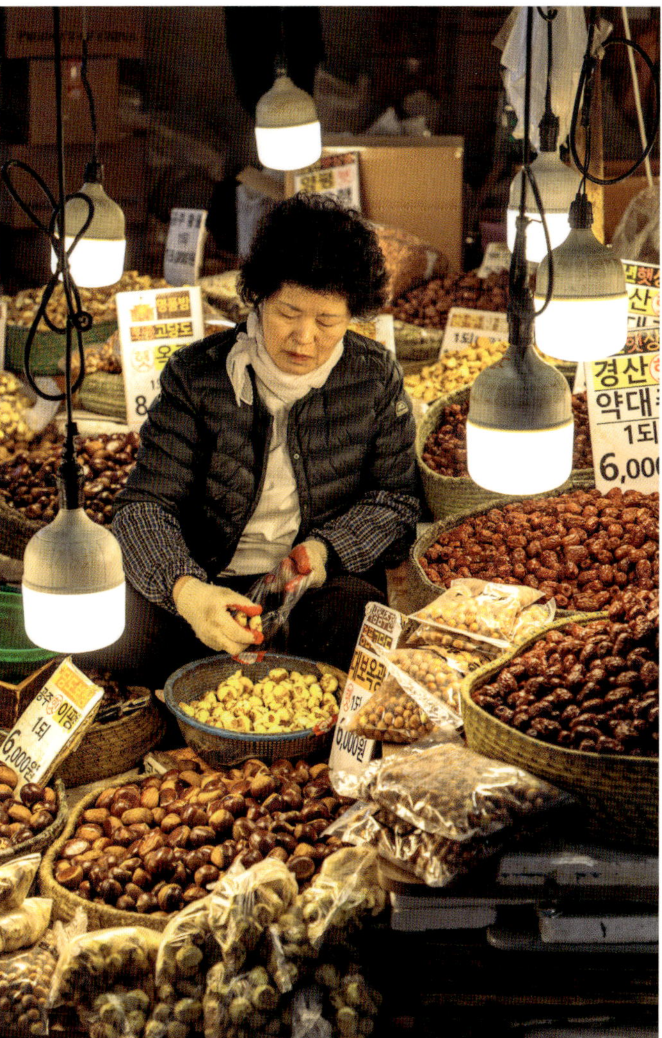

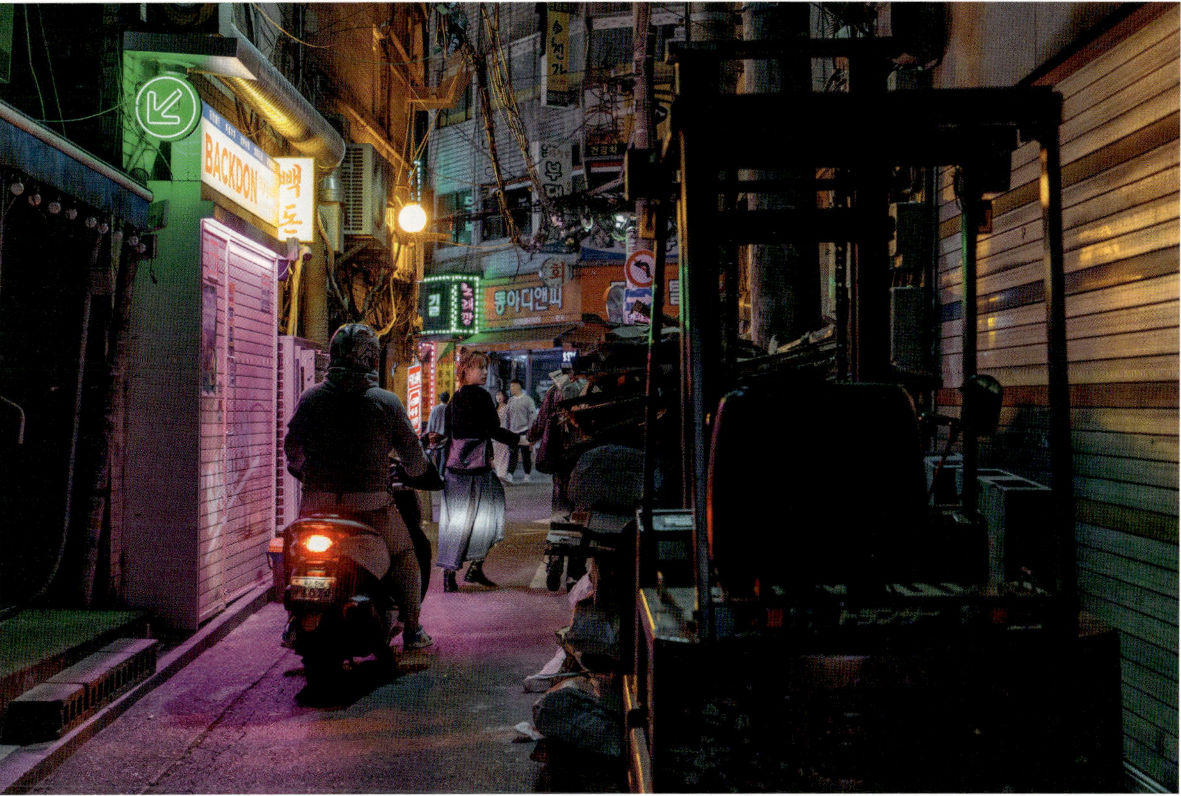

Sprawling markets are the heart of many Seoul neighborhoods, serving as places to meet and to find countless snacks.

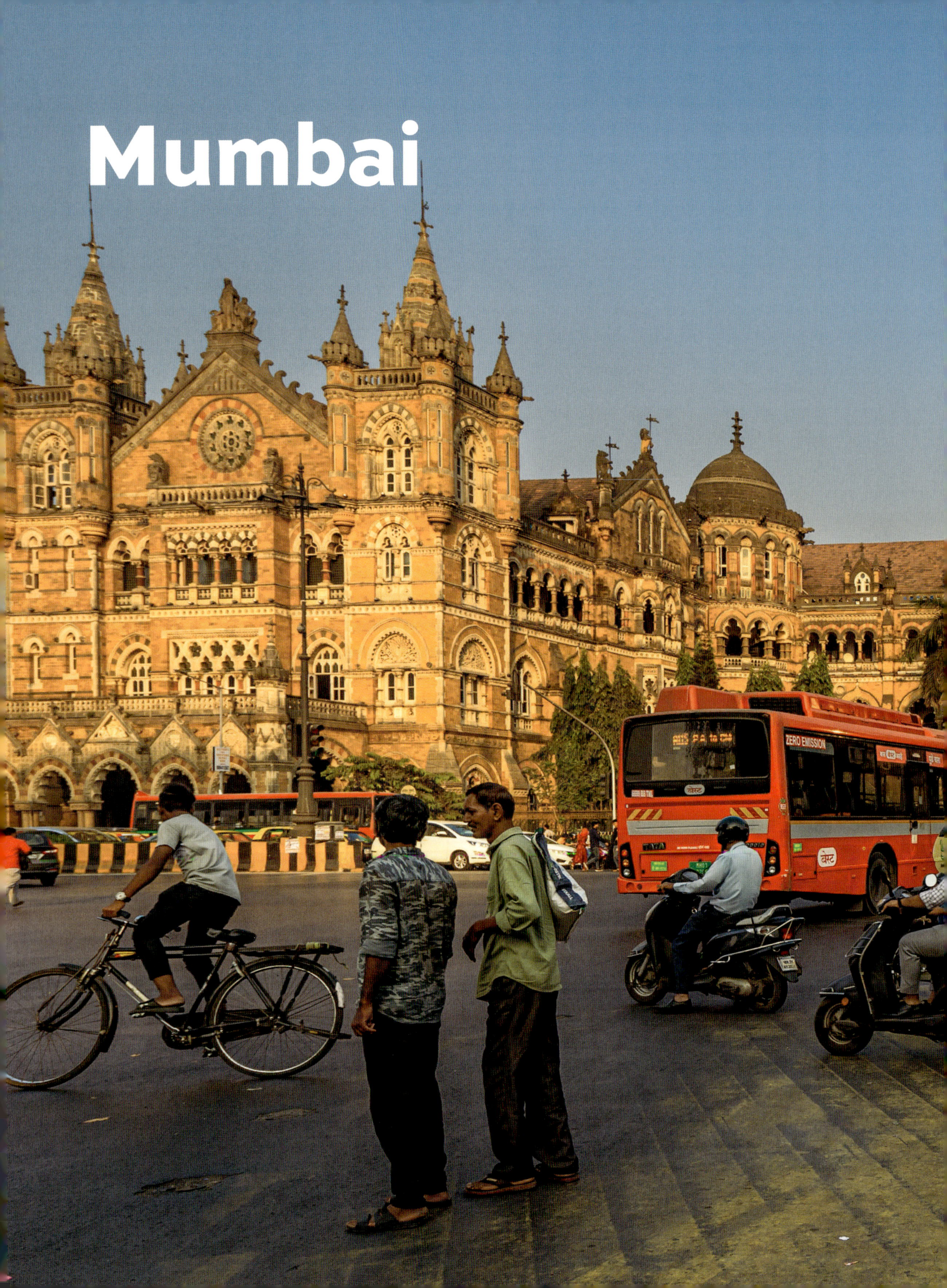

Mumbai

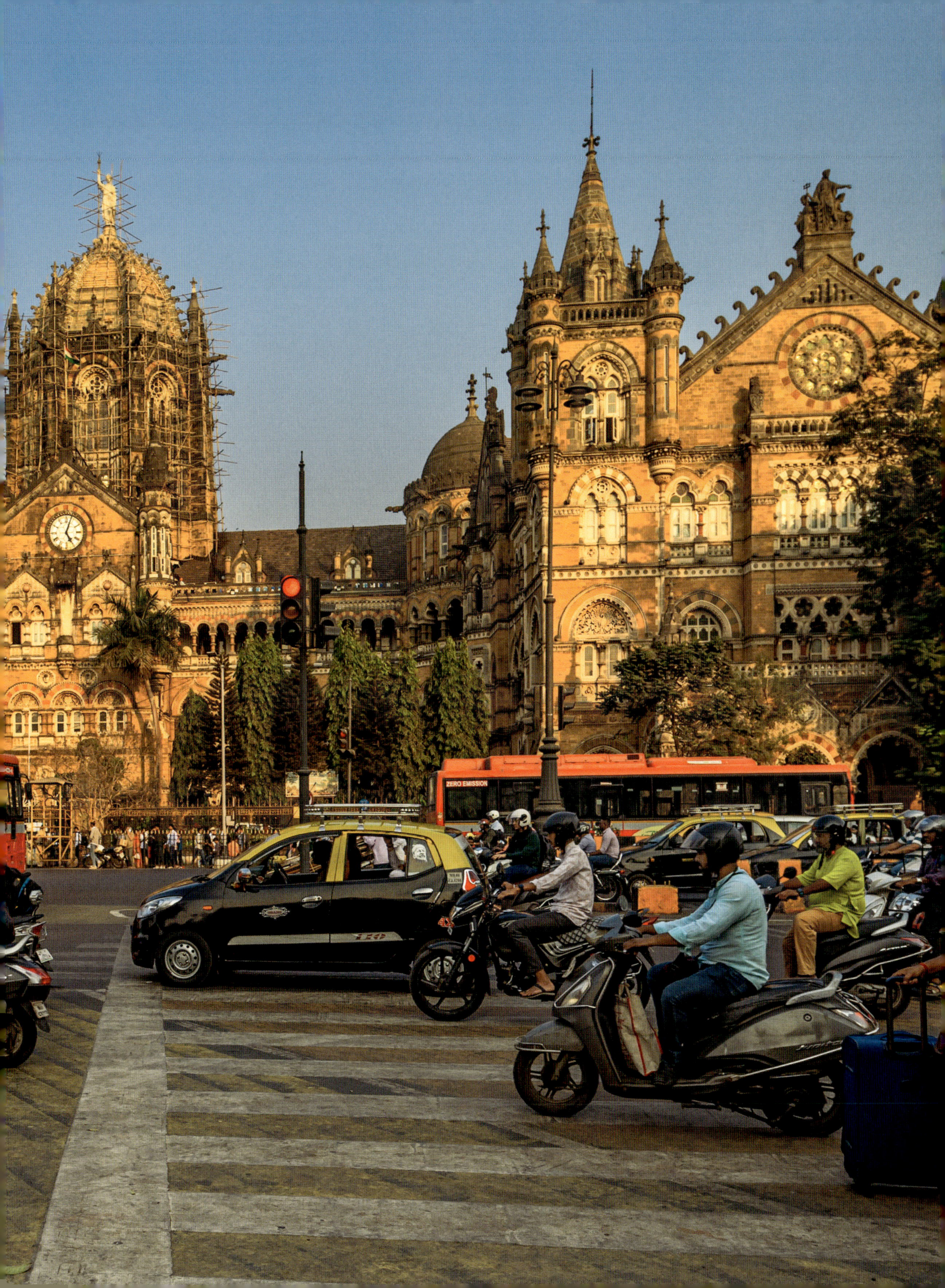

An Indian Dream

Ein indischer Traum

"After the blast, the 1993 blast which happened, entire Mumbai was in chaos and everything had to shut down. (…) I would say that post-blast, people started to be in fact not suspicious of one another, but more caring towards one another. (…) So within the city, within the country, within Mumbai, everybody became friends with each other." (Jatin Wagle)

Mumbai was built on the Seven Islands, and the port on its west coast served as a gateway for the colonial powers and a port to export an endless flow of goods to Europe. The islands separated the people, although they gradually grew together through land reclamation. Hindus, Buddhists, Muslims, Christians, etc. lived in separate neighborhoods, with castes further separating them. That is, until March 12, 1993, when terrorists unleashed their attacks on the city. 257 people were killed and 1,400 injured.

But the attackers did not succeed in achieving their aims; quite the opposite, in fact. The fragmented population, which until then had lived side by side in parallel worlds, did not turn on one another, contrary to the terrorists' intentions. When it became clear that the murderers came from the outside, a previously unprecedented feeling of solidarity gripped the city. Suddenly, people were Mumbaians and no longer Muslims, Hindus, Jains, Dalits, or anything else, and they have been proud to be residents of this metropolis ever since.

The events set the stage for another incredible boom in the city, modeled on nothing less than the development of Singapore. Today, it is money that divides people: into poor, middle class, and rich. Mumbai is gentrified in the old city center, impersonally modern in the sprawling neighborhoods of the wealthy, and chaotically cramped in the slums. Obscene wealth dwells next to crushing poverty; gleaming skyscrapers look down on the gray-blue monotony of the rooftops of the poor districts.

"So this city basically gives courage to people to actually have a dream (…). In other states, you can have a dream, but you don't have the courage to actually know whether it's going to get fulfilled or not. And it just becomes a joke. But in Mumbai, the joke can become a reality." (Jatin Wagle)

It doesn't matter where you are, a tremendous energy is palpable everywhere, the will to be part of the success of this metropolis, which embodies the Indian dream of upward mobility like no other city. You can experience this quite impressively

„Nach dem Terrorakt, der 1993 stattfand, war ganz Mumbai im Chaos und alles musste geschlossen werden. (…) Ich würde sagen, dass die Menschen nach den Anschlägen anfingen, einander nicht mehr zu misstrauen, sondern sich mehr umeinander zu kümmern. (…) In der Stadt, auf dem Land, in Mumbai haben sich also alle miteinander solidarisiert." (Jatin Wagle)

Mumbai wurde auf sieben Inseln erbaut, der Hafen an seiner Westküste diente als Einfallstor für die Kolonialmächte und als Ausfuhrhafen für einen endlosen Warenstrom nach Europa. Die Inseln trennten die Menschen, obwohl sie durch Landgewinnung nach und nach zusammenwuchsen. Hindus, Buddhisten, Muslime, Christen und weitere Religionsgemeinschaften lebten in getrennten Vierteln, Kasten trennten zusätzlich. Bis zum 12. März 1993: Da überzogen Terroristen die Stadt mit ihren Anschlägen. 257 Todesopfer und 1 400 Verletzte waren zu beklagen.

Doch die Attentäter erreichten das genaue Gegenteil. Die fragmentierte Bevölkerung, die bislang in parallelen Welten nebeneinander lebte, ging, anders als von den Terroristen beabsichtigt, nicht aufeinander los. Als man feststellte, dass die Mörder von außen kamen, erfasste ein bisher ungekanntes Gefühl der Solidarität die Stadt. Auf einmal war man Mumbaier und nicht mehr Moslem, Hindu, Jain, Dalit oder sonst etwas und ist seitdem stolz darauf, Bewohner dieser Metropole zu sein.

Die Ereignisse bildeten den Startschuss für einen weiteren unglaublichen Boom der Stadt, die sich nichts Geringeres als die Entwicklung Singapurs zum Vorbild nimmt. Heute ist es das Geld, das die Menschen trennt: in Arme, Mittelschicht und Reiche. Mumbai ist mondän im alten Zentrum, gesichtslos modern in den weitläufigen Vierteln der Wohlhabenden und chaotischeng in den Slums. Obszöner Reichtum residiert neben erdrückender Armut, glanzvolle Wolkenkratzer blicken auf das graublaue Dächereinerlei der Armenviertel.

Dharavi's narrow, dark alleyways are sometimes stifling, but they are interrupted everywhere by small patches full of light and color.

Dharavis enge, dunkle Gassen sind zuweilen bedrückend. Doch überall werden sie von kleinen Plätzen voller Licht und Farben unterbrochen.

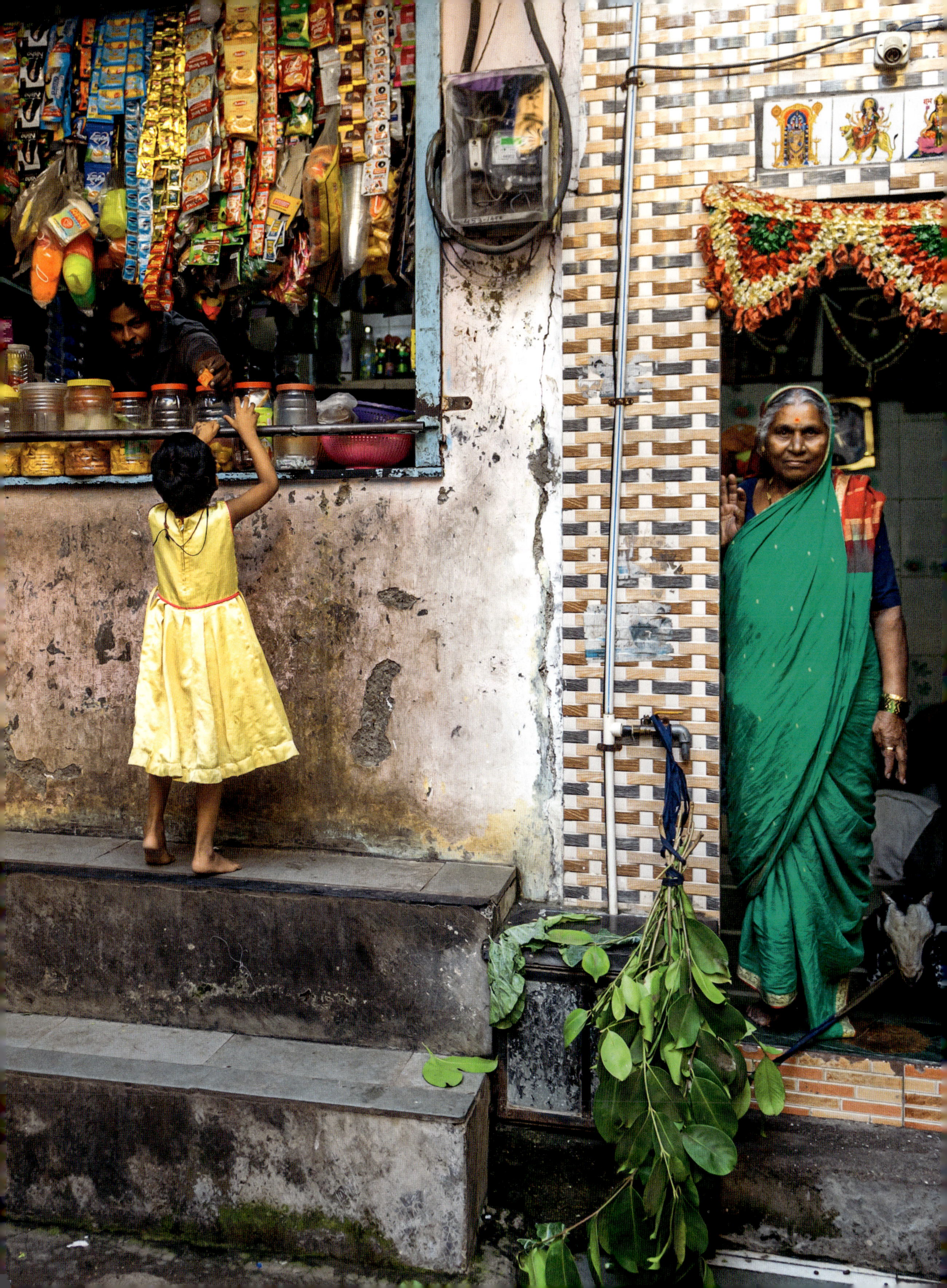

first-hand in the maze of alleys in Dharavi. Between 700,000 and one million people are said to live here. No one knows exactly how many there are. Dharavi is a nerve center of the informal economy, one of the largest slums in Asia, and, at the same time, one of the most densely populated urban districts in the world. Recycling plants, dye factories, garment factories, smelting works, bakeries–in Dharavi, an estimated 20,000 micro-enterprises generate a combined annual turnover of between US$500 million and US$1 billion. The economic energy coming out of Dharavi is in stark contrast to the idea of a slum as the vestibule of hell. The same is true for the city as a whole. It is a tremendous economic powerhouse, an energy hub for all of India.

Mumbai has long ceased to be the India so fondly portrayed in the brochures of the tourism industry. Sacred cows have not wandered the streets for a long time now. You only meet them tethered in a few locations, where you can feed them for a fee to boost your karma. The famed *dabbawallas*, the inventors of the analog just-in-time delivery services for the lunches of hundreds of thousands of office workers, are at risk of losing the battle against the technologically and digitally well-equipped delivery services, and will have to find new fields of business.

Only the huge markets add color to the city. You can still find it here, the loud, colorful, chaotic, richly diverse India teeming with smells and sensory impressions. In the business centers, on the other hand, people in professional attire rush through the streets, and the endless strings of residential neighborhoods lend the city a sometimes stifling anonymity. Yet the people love their city, where every day you can experience, sense, and help shape its immense progress, its forward development, its pulsating energy.

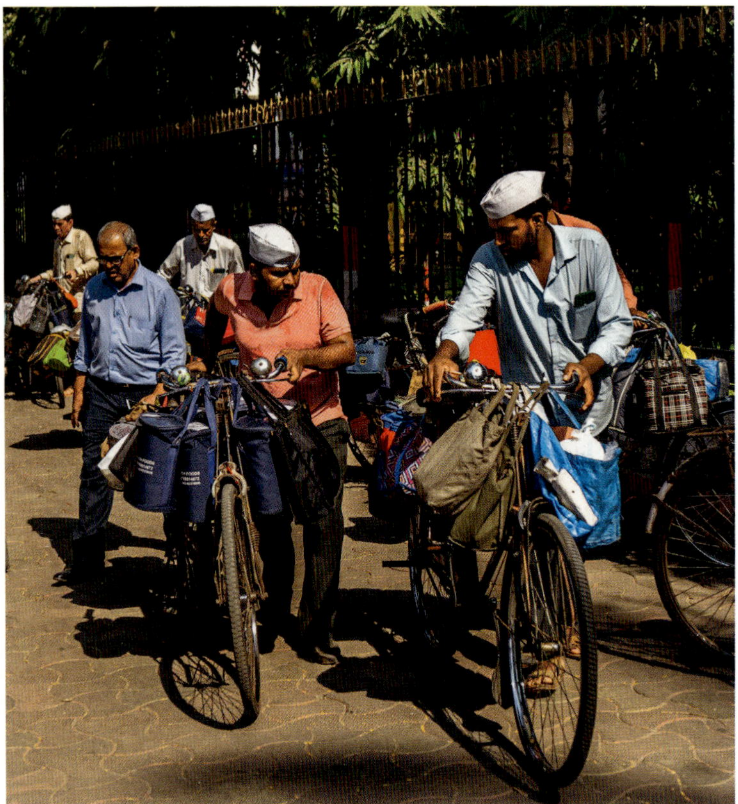

At one time, *dabawallas* by the hundreds set off to deliver the food arriving at Churchgate station. Today there are only a few dozen.

Einst starteten die Dabawallas zu Hunderten, um das am Bahnhof Churchgate eintreffende Essen auszuliefern. Heute sind es nur noch einige Dutzend.

„Diese Stadt macht den Menschen also im Grunde genommen Mut, einen Traum zu leben, einen Traum zu verwirklichen (…). In anderen Staaten kann man einen Traum haben, aber man wird nicht wissen, ob er sich erfüllen wird oder nicht. Dann wird der Traum zu einem Witz. Aber in Mumbai kann der Witz Wirklichkeit werden." (Jatin Wagle)

Doch egal wo, überall pulsiert eine ungeheure Energie, der Wille, Teil des Erfolgs dieser Metropole, die den indischen Traum vom Aufstieg wie keine andere Stadt verkörpert, zu sein. Besonders beeindruckend zu erleben im Gassengewirr von Dharavi. Zwischen 700 000 und 1 Million Menschen sollen hier leben. Wie viele es genau sind, weiß niemand. Dharavi ist ein Nervenzentrum der informellen Wirtschaft, einer der größten Slums in Asien und gleichzeitig einer der am dichtest besiedelten Stadtteile der Welt. Recycling-Werkhöfe, Färbereien, Nähereien, Schmelzhütten, Bäckereien – in Dharavi erwirtschaften geschätzte 20000 Kleinstbetriebe zusammen einen Jahresumsatz zwischen 500 Millionen und 1 Milliarde US$. Die wirtschaftliche Energie, die Dharavi ausstrahlt, steht im krassen Widerspruch zur Vorstellung eines Slums als Vorhof zur Hölle. Gleiches gilt für die ganze Stadt. Sie ist ein ungeheurer Wirtschaftsmotor, eine Energiezentrale für ganz Indien.

Mumbai ist längst nicht mehr das Indien, das die Prospekte der Tourismusindustrie so gerne zeichnen. Heilige Kühe laufen schon lange nicht mehr durch die Straßen. Man trifft sie nur noch angebunden an wenigen Orten und kann sie gegen Bezahlung füttern, was gut für das Karma ist. Die berühmten *Dabbawallas*, die Erfinder analoger Just-in-time-Lieferdienste für das Mittagessen von Hunderttausenden Büroangestellten, sie drohen den Kampf gegen die technologisch und digital hochgerüsteten Lieferdienste zu verlieren und müssen sich neue Geschäftsfelder erschließen.

Einzig die riesigen Märkte bringen Farbe in die Stadt. Hier findet man es noch, das laute, bunte, chaotische, abwechslungsreiche Indien voller Gerüche und Sinneseindrücke. In den Geschäftszentren dagegen hetzen Menschen in Businesskleidung durch die Straßen, die endlos aneinandergereihten Wohnviertel verleihen der Stadt eine zuweilen bedrückende Gesichtslosigkeit. Dennoch, die Menschen lieben ihre Stadt, in der man jeden Tag den immensen Fortschritt, die Entwicklung nach vorn, die pulsierende Energie erlebt, spürt und mitgestaltet.

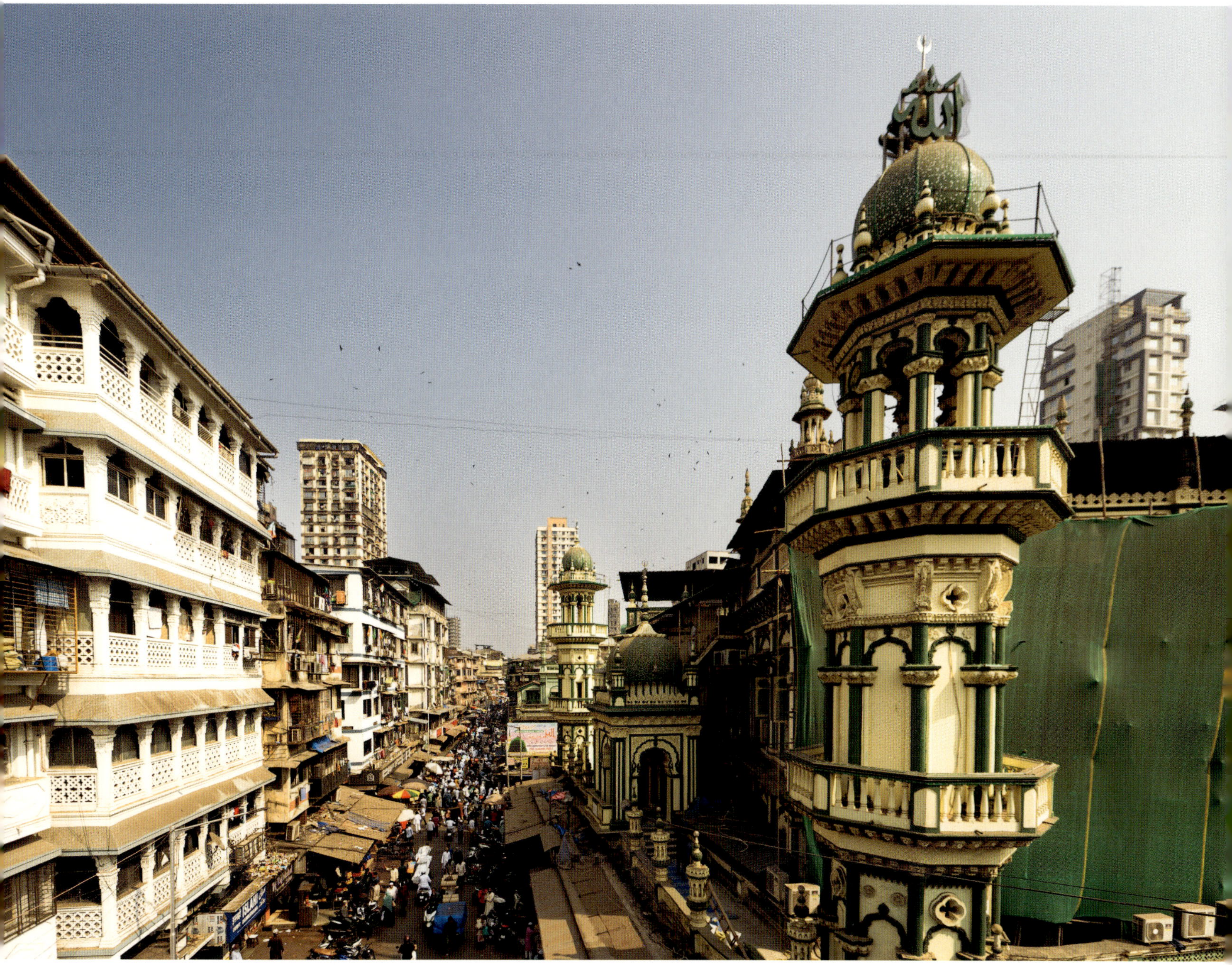

Religious life is directly entwined with everyday life. Sacred places like the Minara Masjid or the last of the sacred cows are usually surrounded by bustling activity.

Religiöses Leben ist unmittelbar mit dem Alltag verwoben. Heilige Orte wie die Minara Masjid oder die letzten heiligen Kühe findet man meist in belebten Umgebungen.

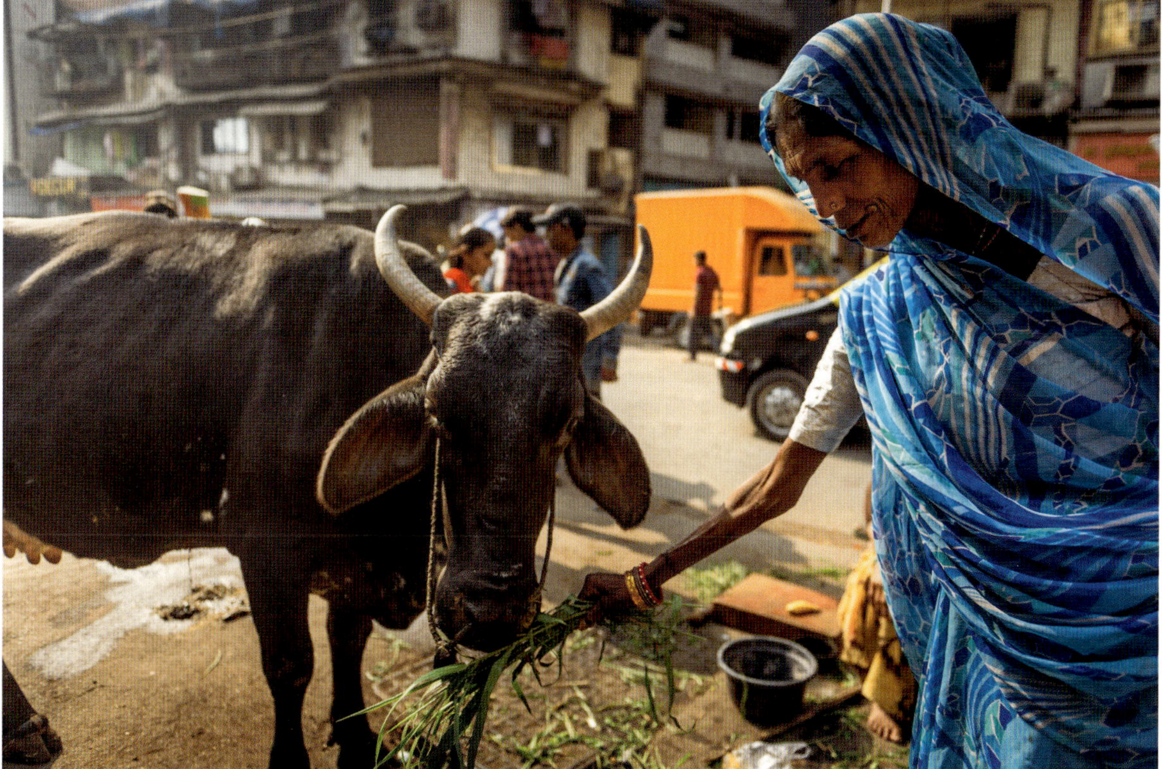

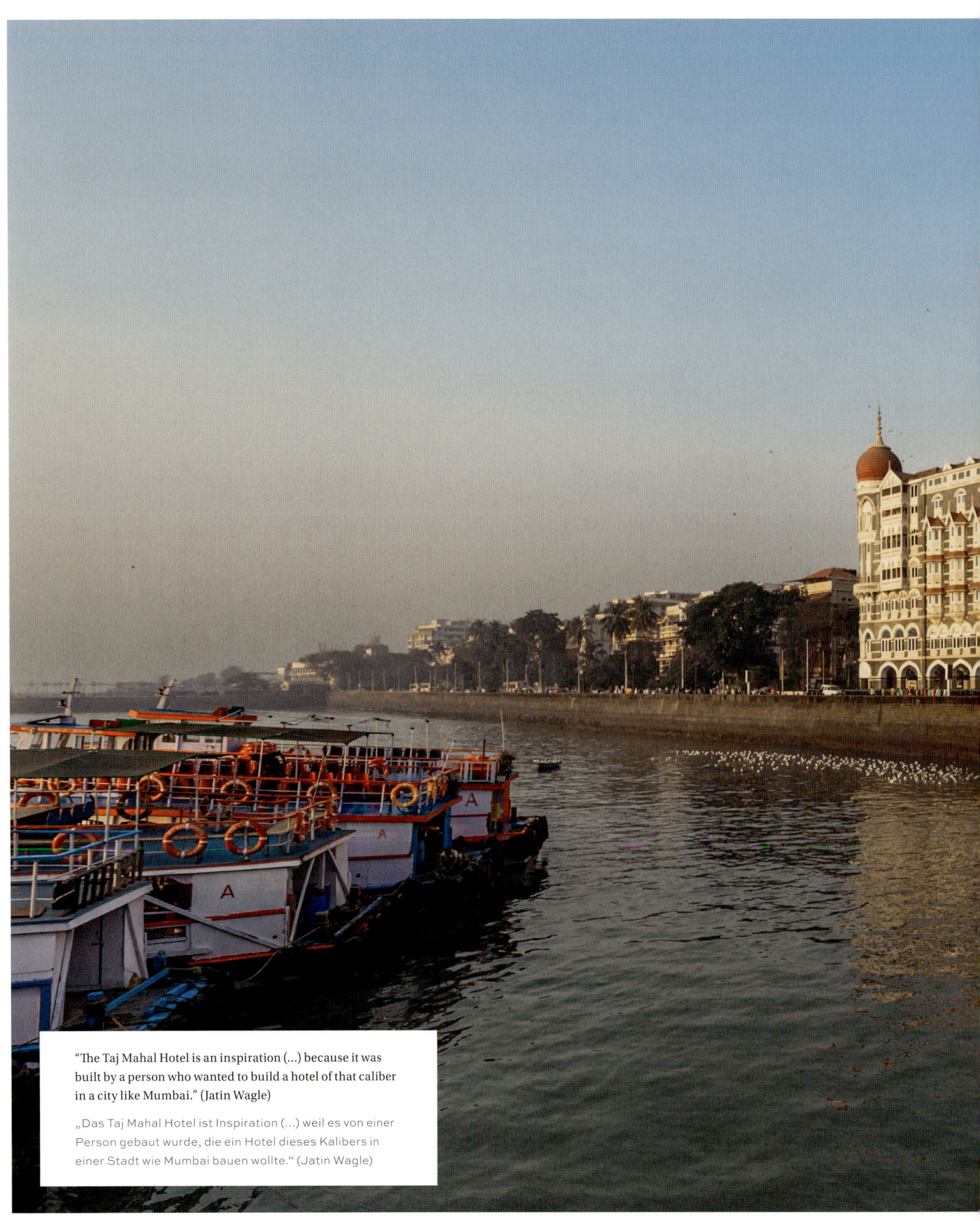

"The Taj Mahal Hotel is an inspiration (...) because it was built by a person who wanted to build a hotel of that caliber in a city like Mumbai." (Jatin Wagle)

„Das Taj Mahal Hotel ist Inspiration (...) weil es von einer Person gebaut wurde, die ein Hotel dieses Kalibers in einer Stadt wie Mumbai bauen wollte." (Jatin Wagle)

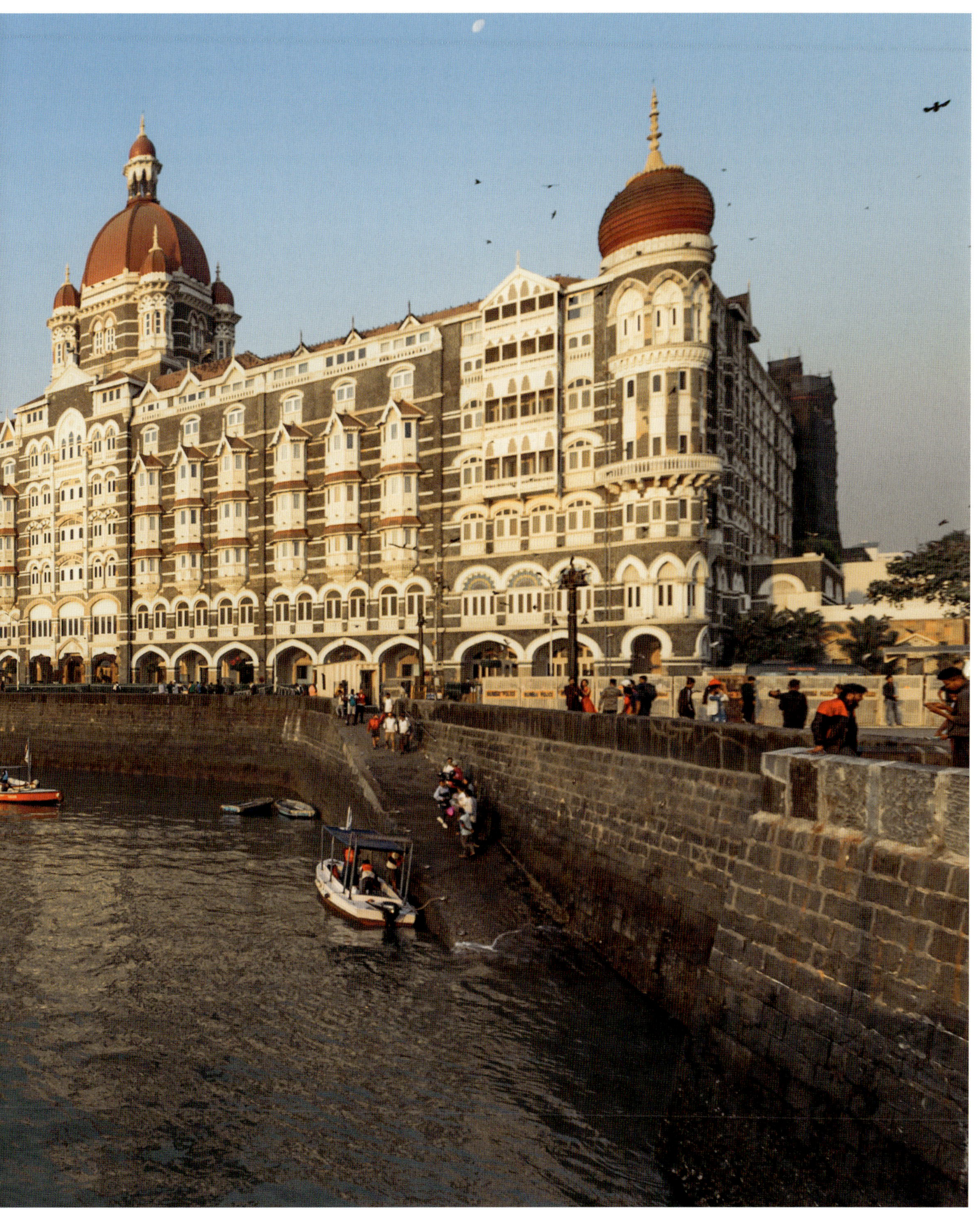

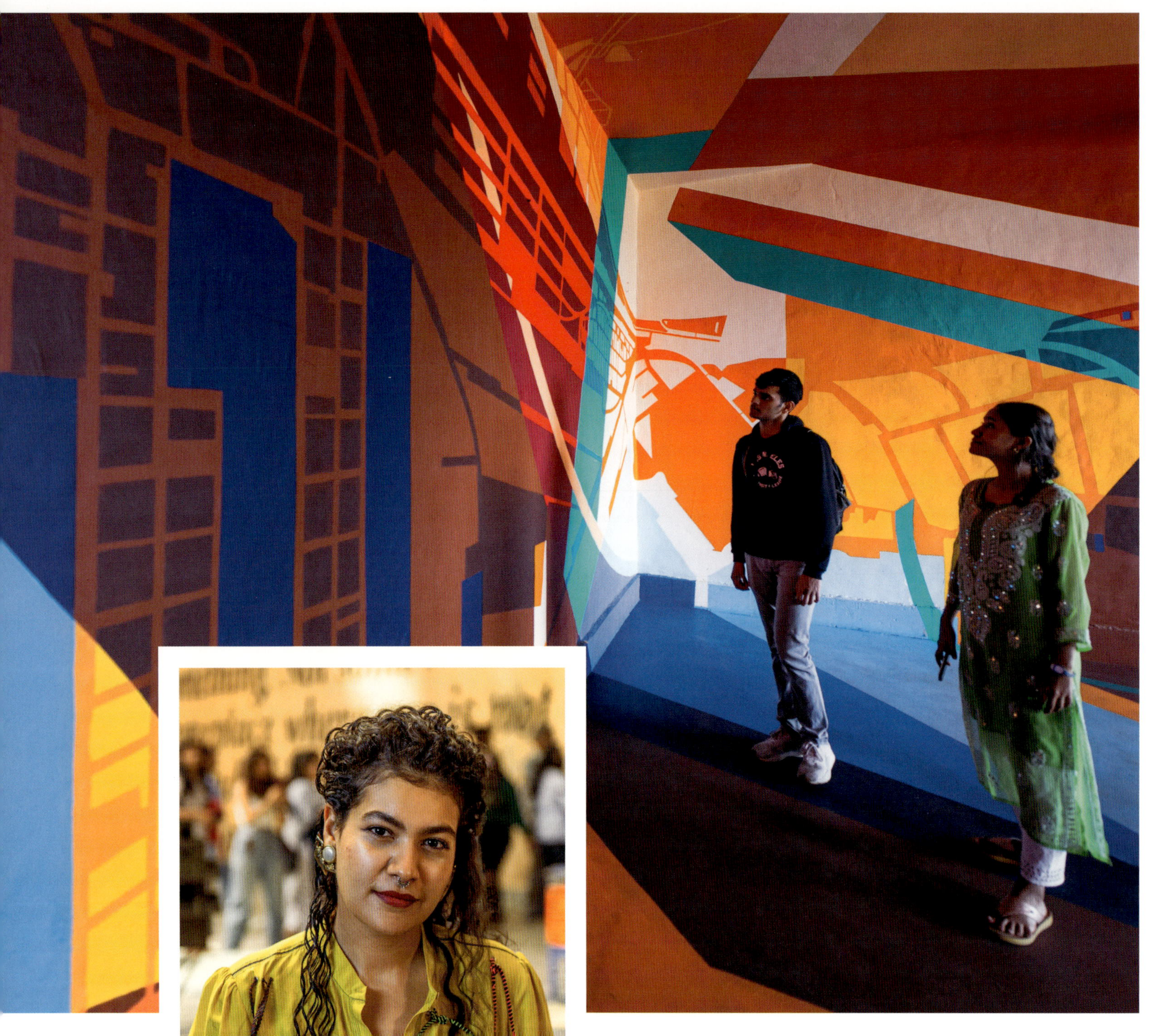

PRIYANSHA JAIN
CURATOR
KURATORIN

Right in the thick of it: The 2023 Mumbai Urban Art Festival took place in the middle of the Sassoon Docks, where fishermen go about their day's work.

Mitten im Leben: Das Mumbai Urban Art Festival fand 2023 inmitten der Sassoon Docks, wo die Fischer ihrem Tagewerk nachgehen, statt.

...ON THE CITY'S ART

"I think having access to public art in Mumbai is a very important thing, because we don't have very many public museums focusing on contemporary and urban art. I also think it is quite important to do these large events where we can take over spaces that are inhabited and have been inhabited by indigenous people and kind of interact with them, and also bring the larger demographics of people to these spaces. I think public art is very important for Mumbai to bring an awareness and a creative stimulation to the minds of a large demographic of people, to facilitate various conversations between them and also engage with it in a cultural way."

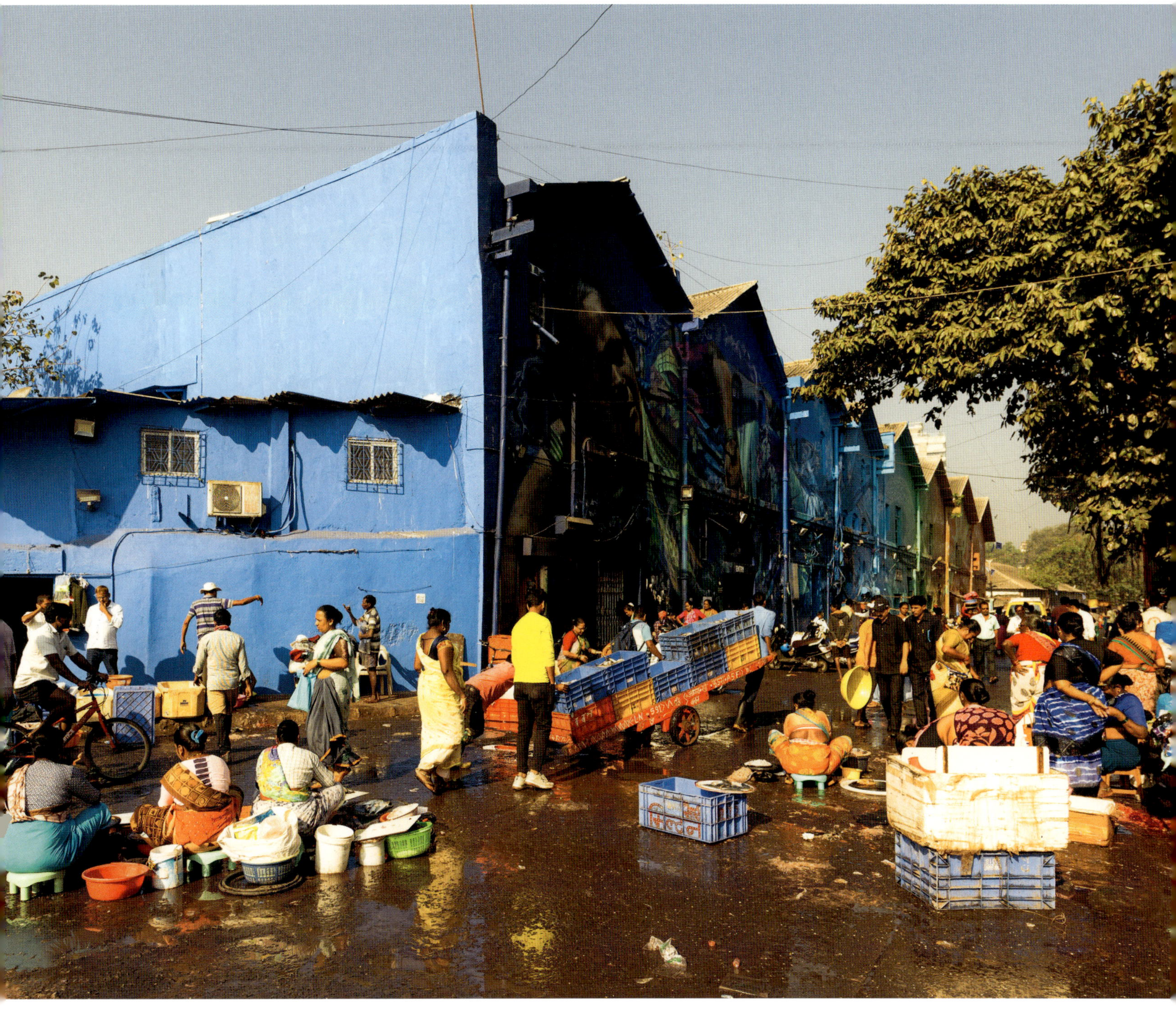

...ÜBER DIE KUNST

„Ich denke, dass der Zugang zu öffentlicher Kunst in Mumbai sehr wichtig ist, weil wir nicht sehr viele öffentliche Museen haben, die sich mit zeitgenössischer und urbaner Kunst beschäftigen. Ich denke auch, dass diese großen Veranstaltungen, bei denen wir Räume einnehmen können, die von der einheimischen Bevölkerung bewohnt werden und wurden, und mit ihnen interagieren und auch eine größere Bevölkerungsgruppe zu diesen Räumen bringen, sehr wichtig sind. Ich denke, dass öffentliche Kunst für Mumbai sehr wichtig ist, um das Bewusstsein und die kreative Stimulierung einer großen Bevölkerungsgruppe zu fördern, um verschiedene Gespräche zwischen ihnen zu ermöglichen und sich auch kulturell mit ihnen auseinanderzusetzen.“

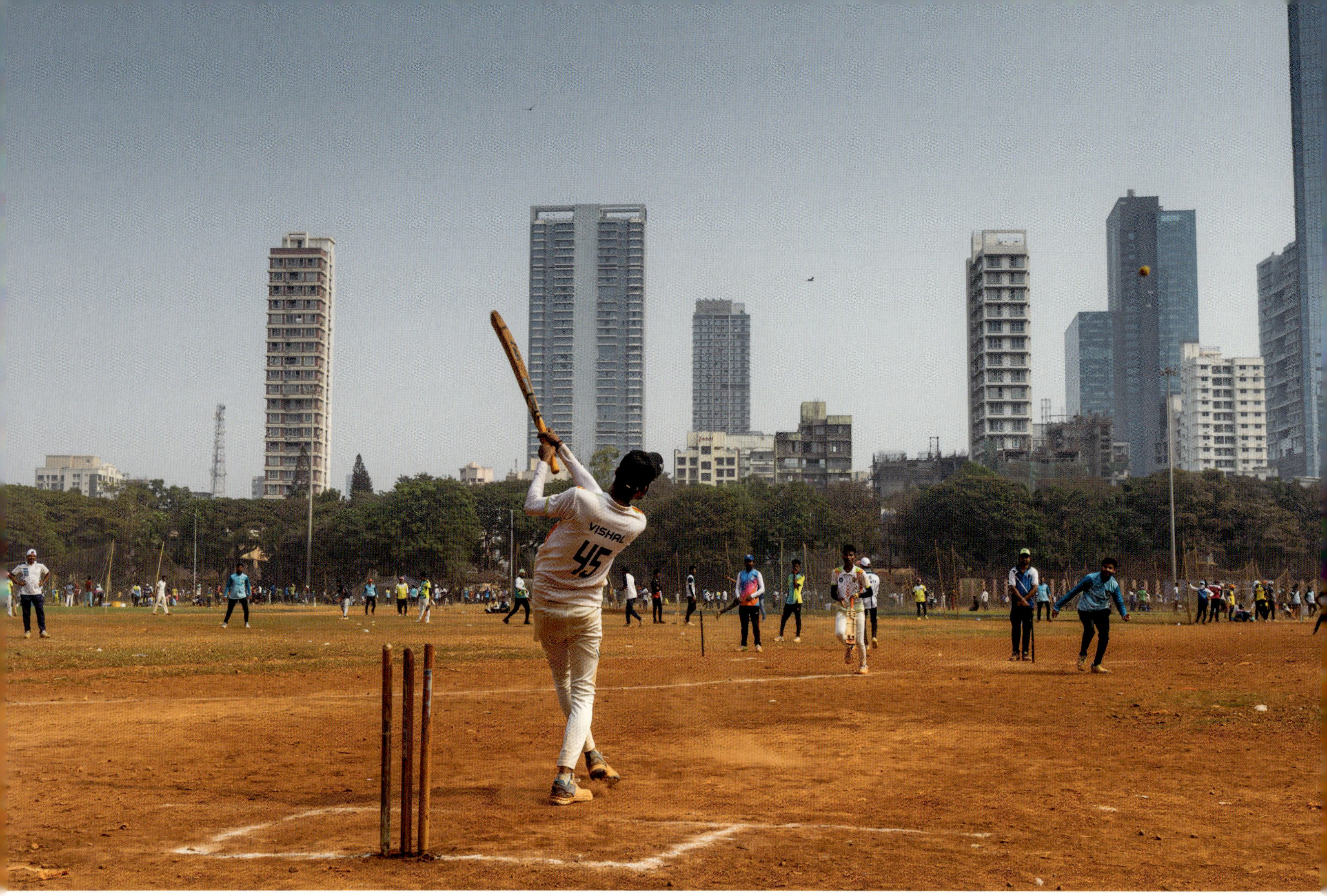

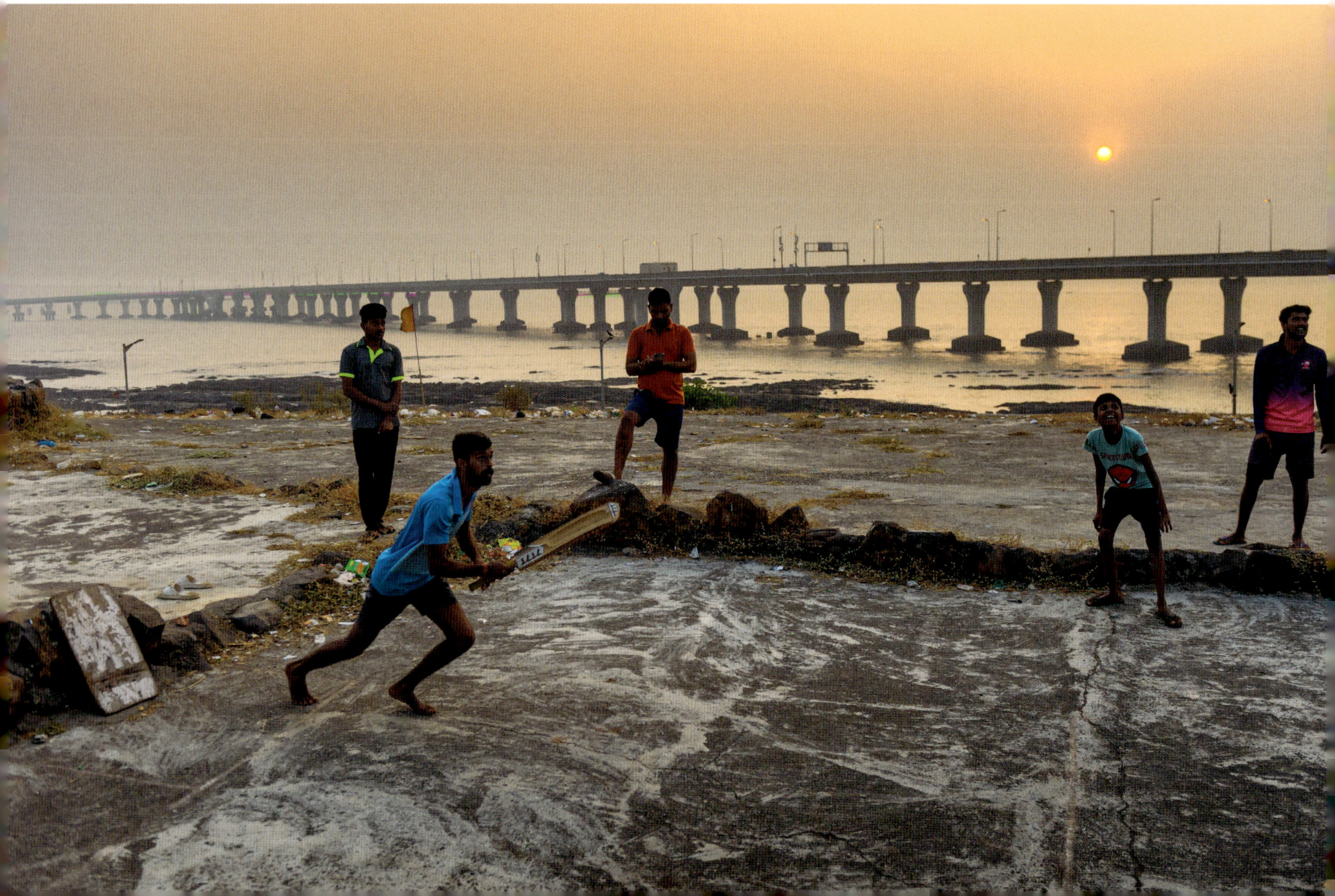

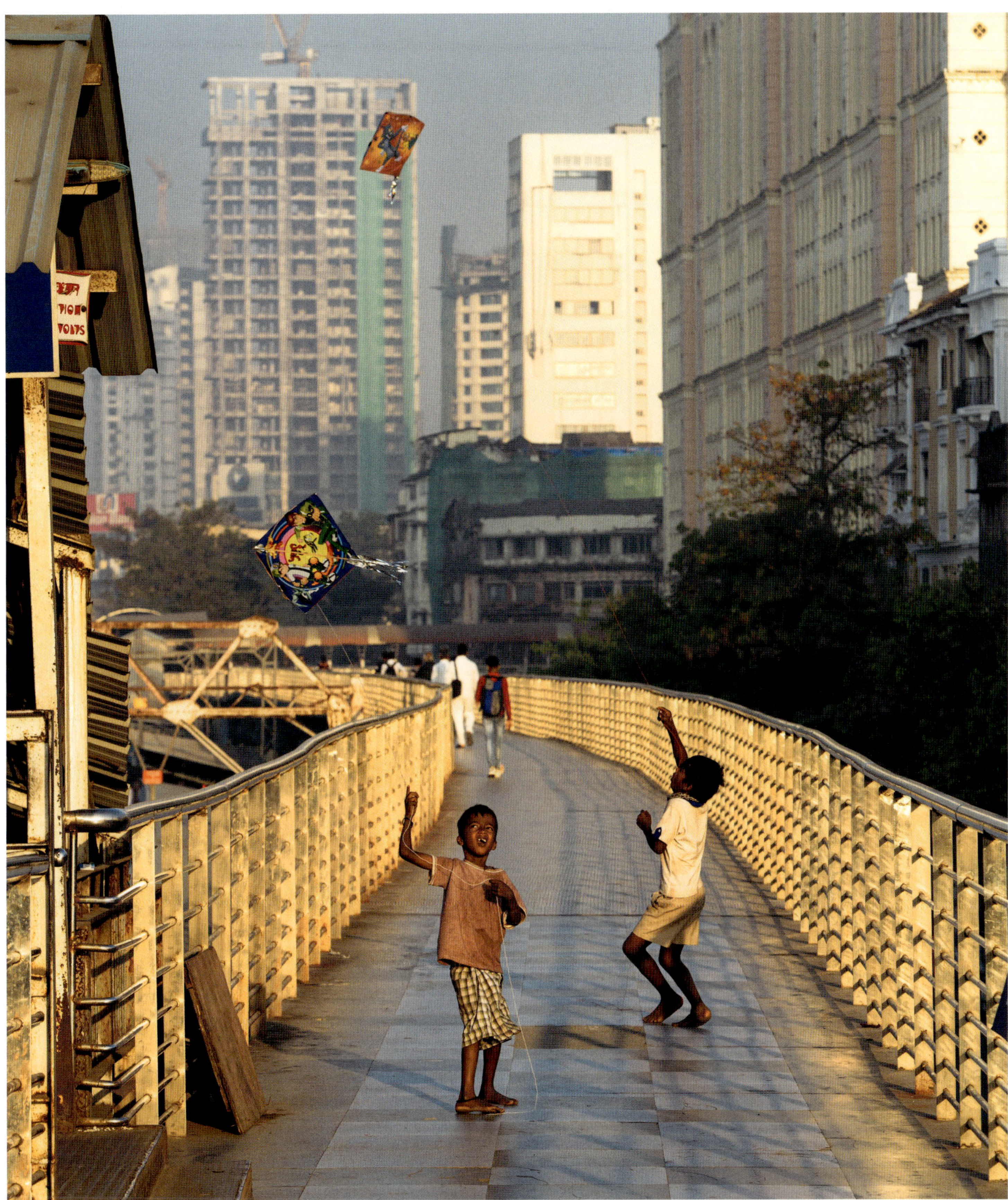

Cricket is a practically a religion in India.
It is played everywhere, from the courts of the
Oval Maidan to the beach at Koliwada.

Kricket ist eine „Religion" in Indien. Gespielt
wird überall, ob auf den Plätzen des Oval
Maidan oder am Strand von Koliwada.

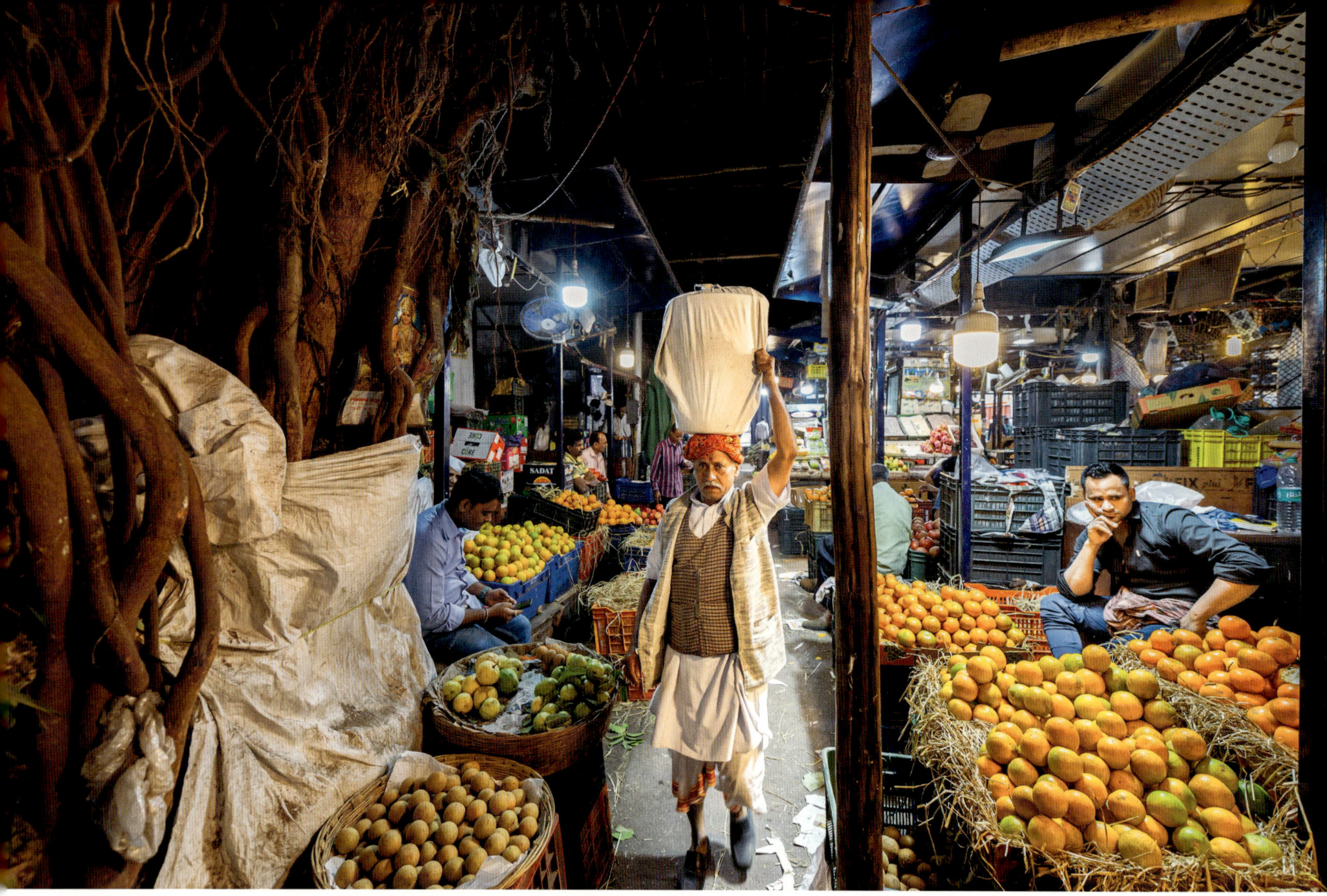

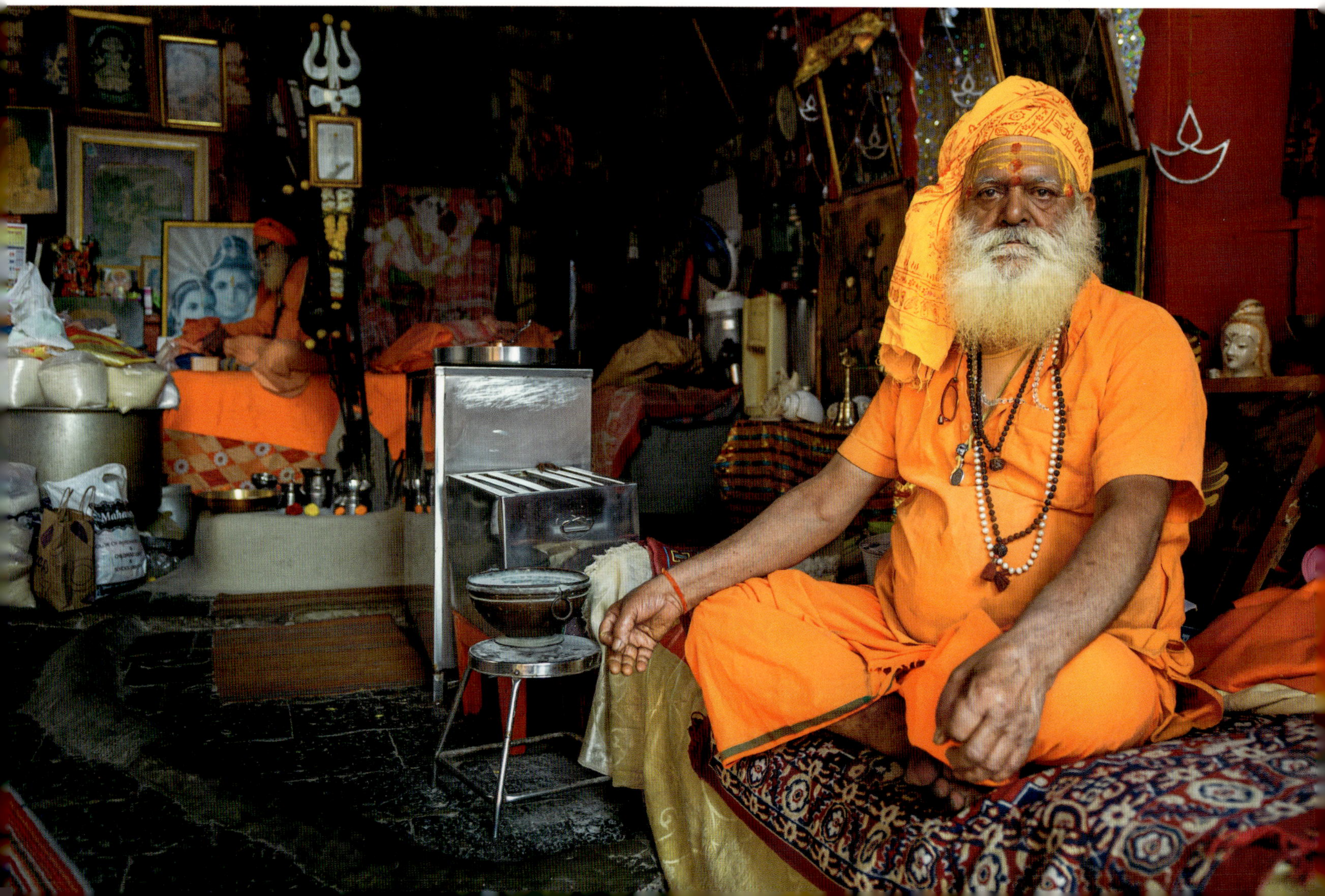

*"Crawford Market is a jumble. It's got everything (…)
there are a lot of things there that we have never seen
before. So you become a child when you go to this
market and buy things." (Jatin Wagle)*

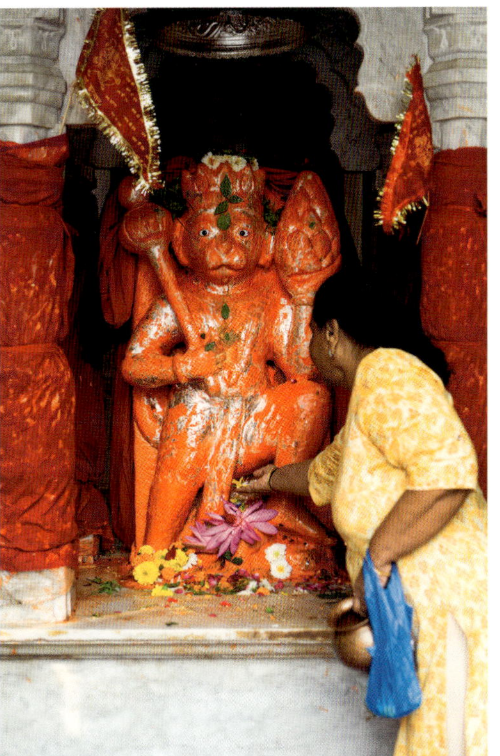

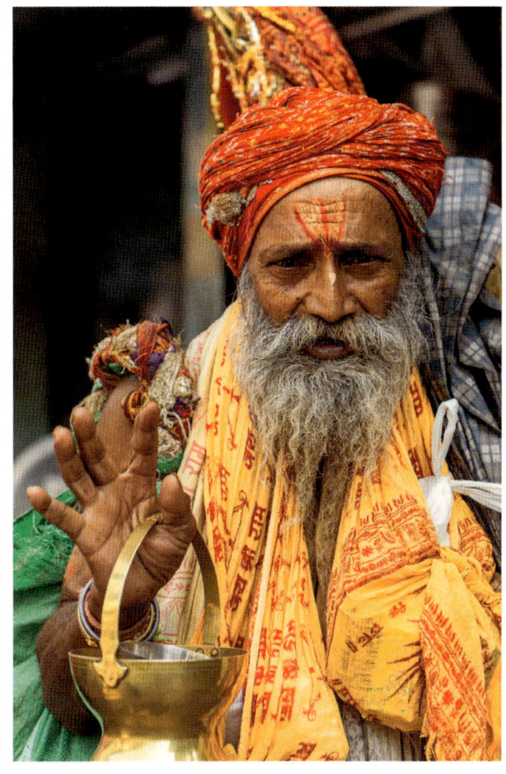

„Der Crawford Market ist ein
einziges Durcheinander. Hier gibt
es alles, (…) eine Menge Sachen,
die wir noch nie gesehen haben.
Man wird zum Kind, wenn man auf
diesen Markt geht und Dinge
kauft." (Jatin Wagle)

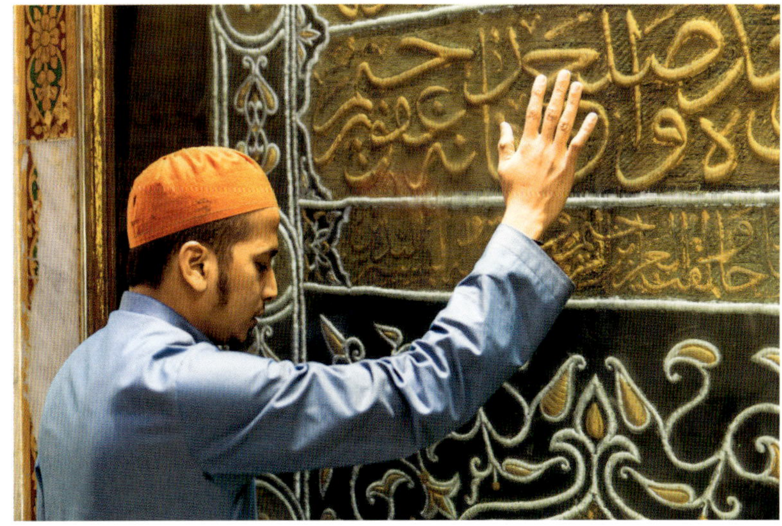

"All these mandirs in Mumbai (…) are not only for the Hindus.
There are so many people who come from different religions,
because it is just peaceful there." (Jatin Wagle)

„All diese Mandirs in Mumbai (…) sind nicht nur für Hindus.
Es gibt so viele Menschen, die aus verschiedenen Religionen kommen, weil es dort einfach friedlich ist." (Jatin Wagle)

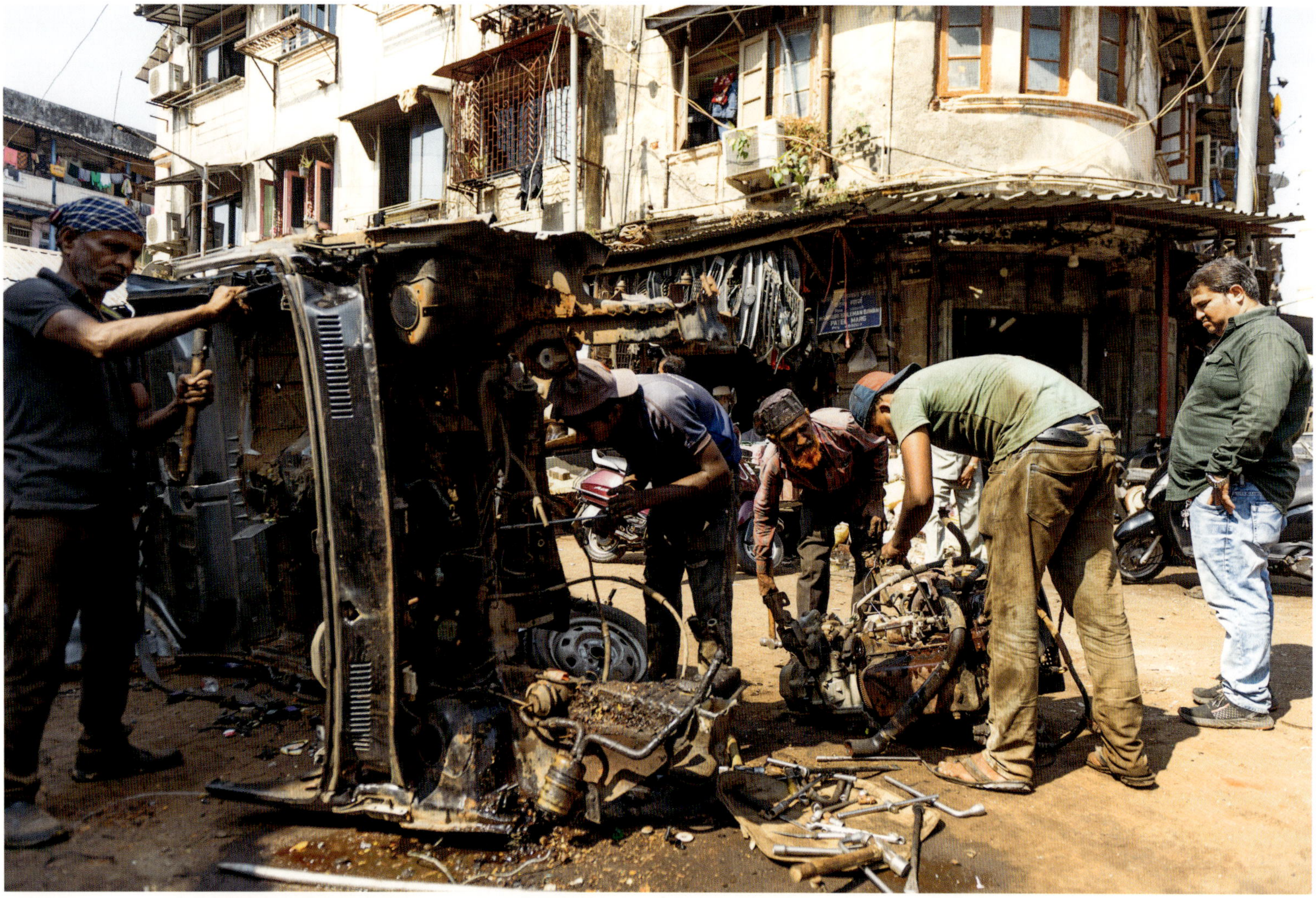

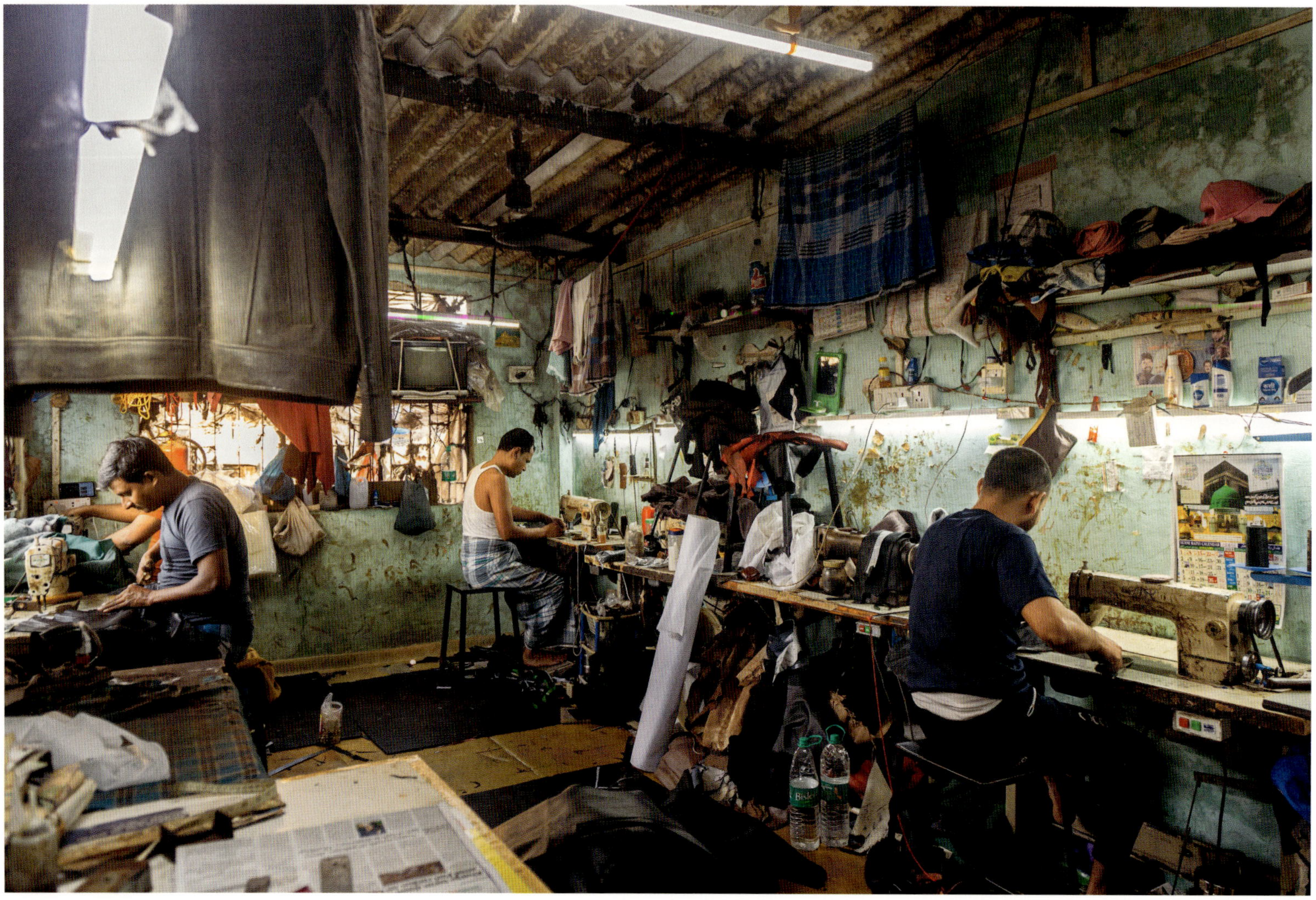

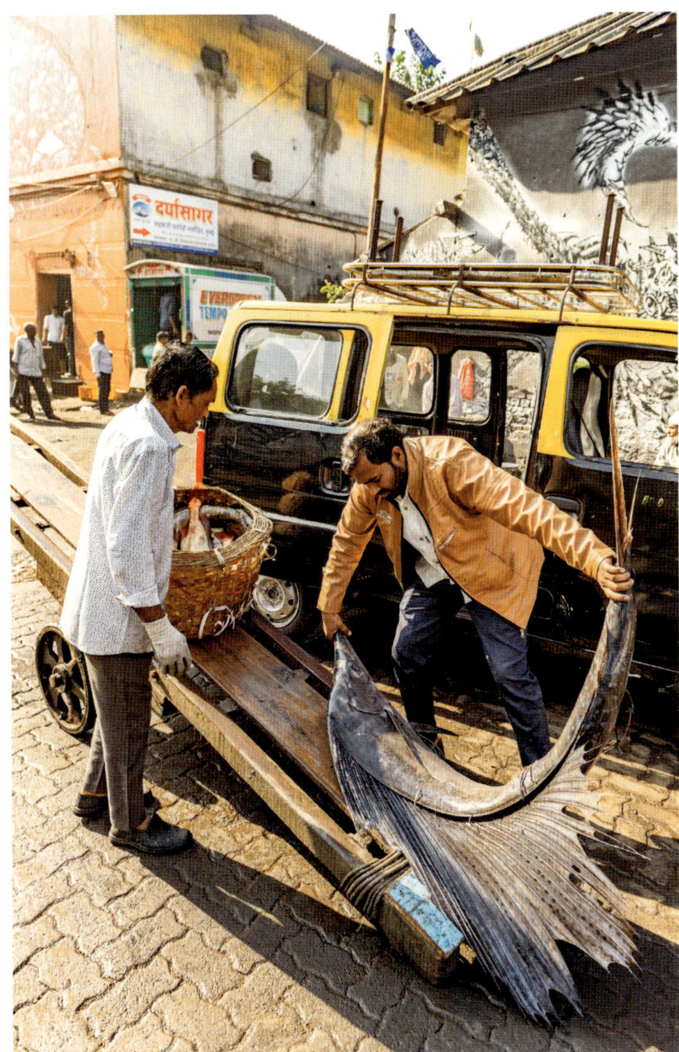

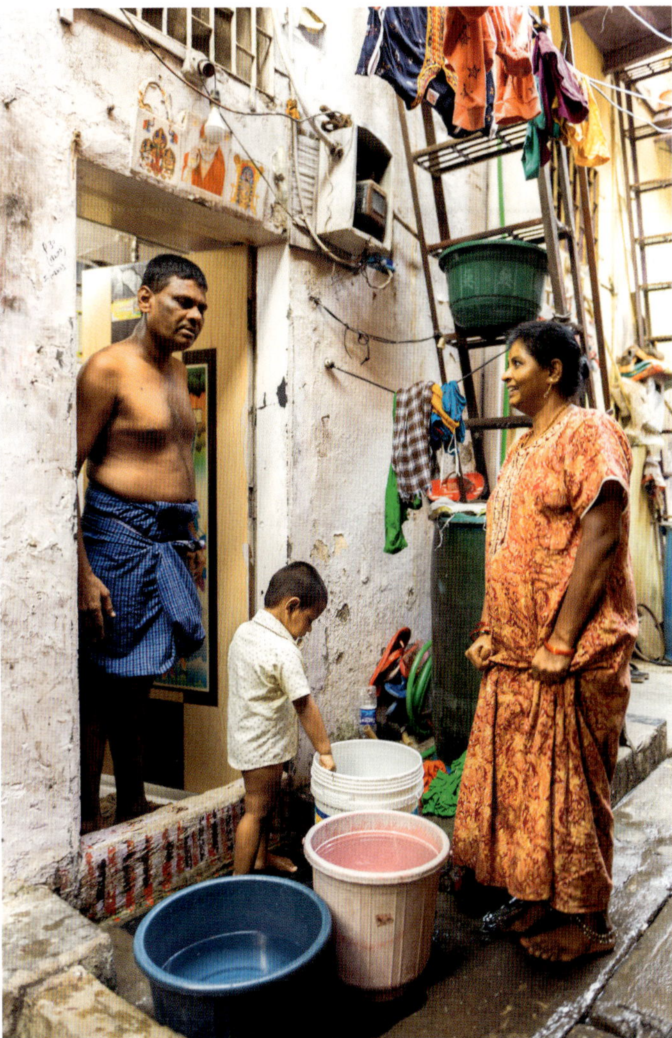

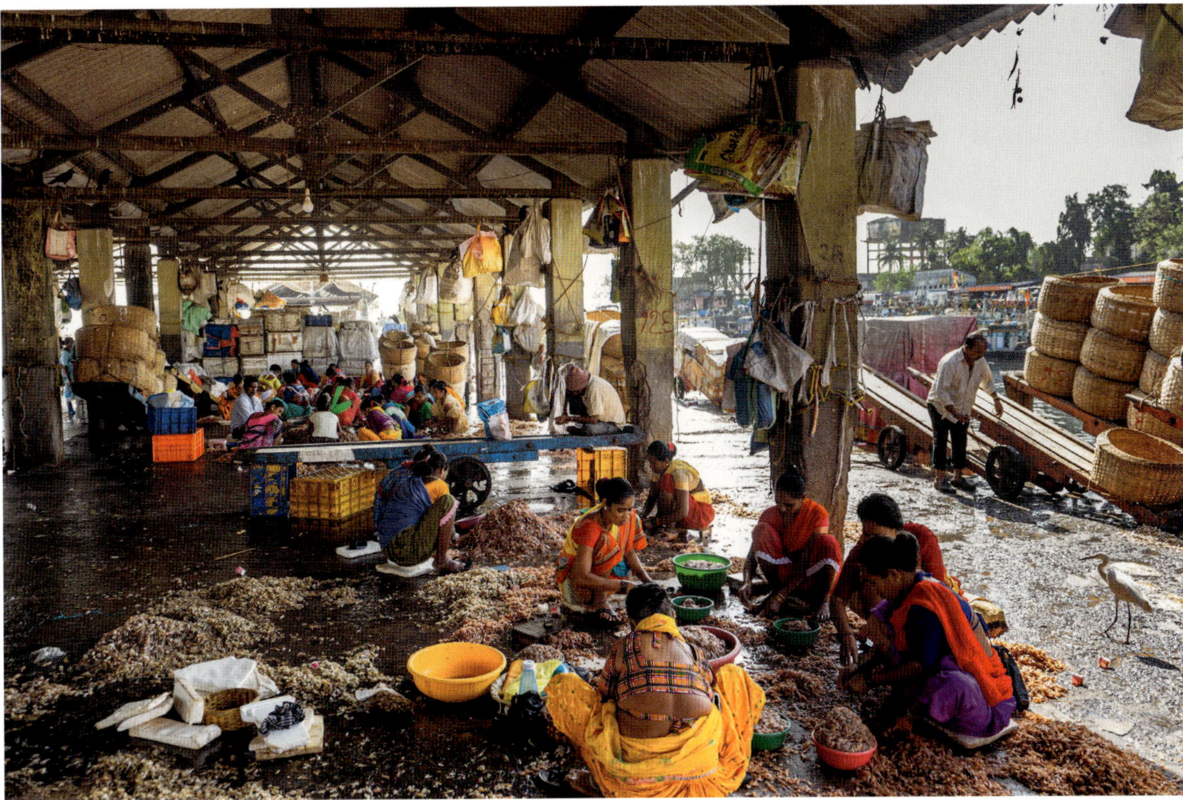

Whether it's at the markets, in the workshops of Dharavi, or at the docks, working hours and conditions are often incredibly grueling.

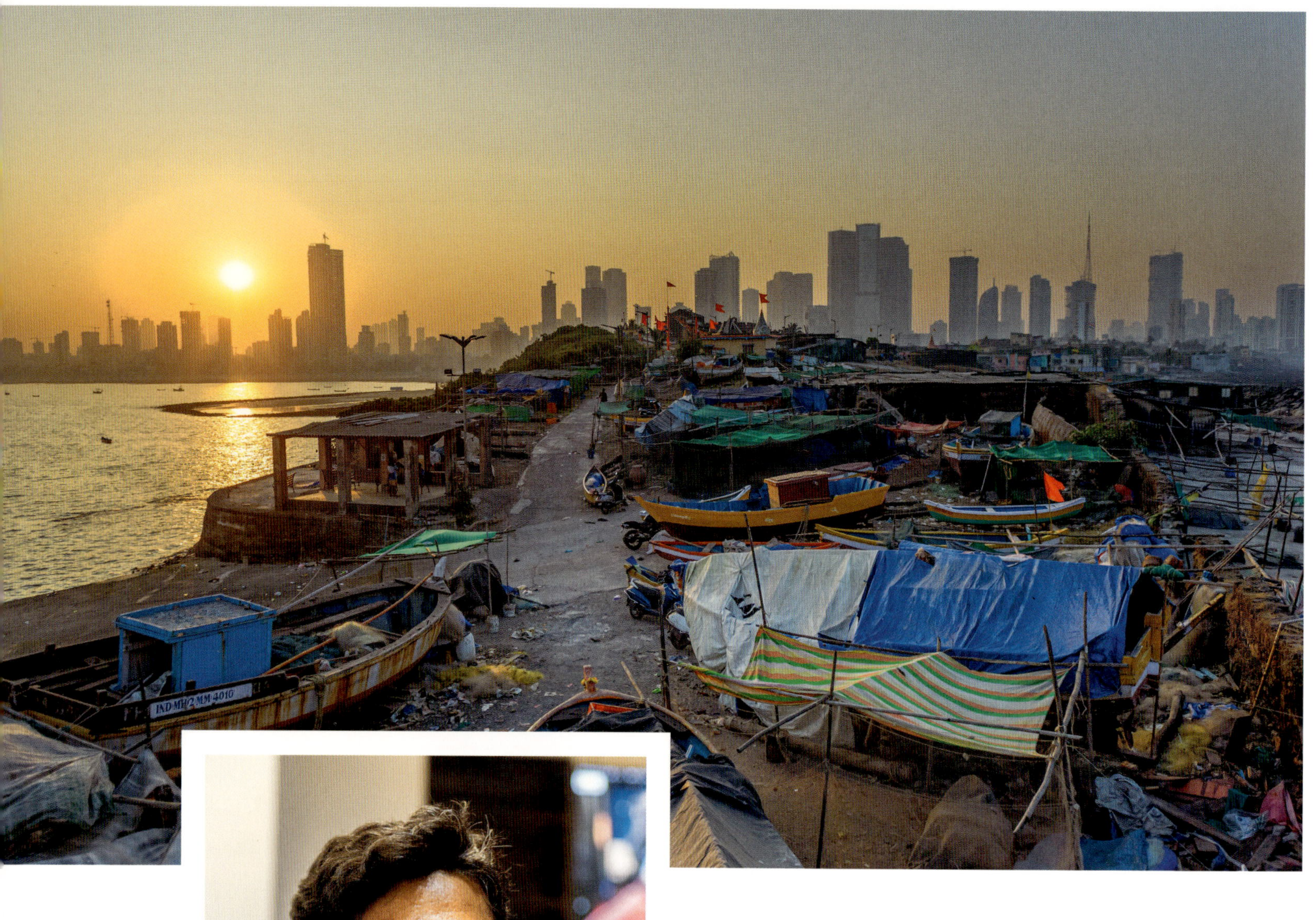

JATIN WAGLE
DIRECTOR
REGISSEUR

Extreme poverty and extreme wealth often exist in close proximity in Mumbai.

In Mumbai existieren extreme Armut und extremer Reichtum oft in unmittelbarer Nachbarschaft.

...ON THE PHENOMENON THAT IS MUMBAI

"As a filmmaker, I've shot all over India, and Mumbai is one city which is very much as if it were a country on its own. It's got its own logic, it's got its own set of rules which do not care about your caste, your community, your economic status, the amount of struggle, the number of years you have put in. It takes everybody equally and it does not differentiate at all. Anybody comes in, you put in your hard work and you grow. (...) Yes, it's a struggle. Everybody has got struggles to go through. It's an expensive city to stay in. The land is quite expensive. The flats are expensive. So a lot of slums are developing. The outskirts of Mumbai are being developed because the rates are cheaper there. That's where there's a burden on transport and everything. But Mumbai is also extremely safe."

...ON INEQUALITY

"The problem in the city right now is not religion. It is, I think, the economic divide, because the richer are becoming better and richer, because they're getting access to the internet, getting access to the international world. They're going abroad, studying. Well, unfortunately, the poor are not able to do that, (...). So the economic divide is something which still is prevalent here."

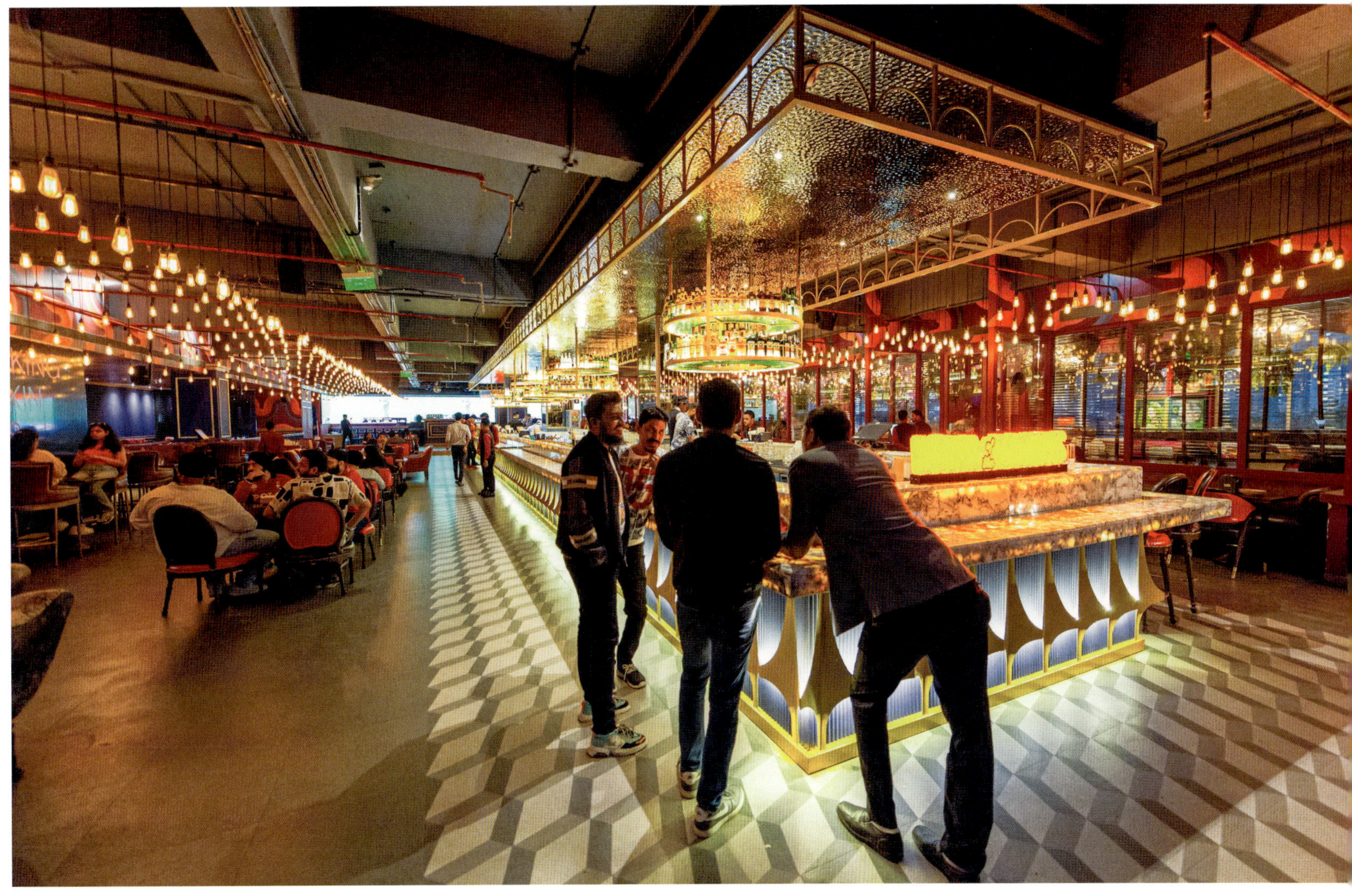

...ON DHARAVI

"It lives. It doesn't require anything from the outside. It's got every-thing within itself. (...) It started as a slum. Asia's biggest slum is probably the Dharavi. But today it's an organization. It's not the kind of slum it was probably 50 or 40 years ago, back when it started. It is just space for living and for hiding and everything. Today, it's got a lot of shops, lot of homemade things (...) and supplying the best of the stores. So it's a living thing on its own. (...) It doesn't require anything from the outside, but it gives a lot of things to the rest of Mumbai."

...ÜBER DAS PHÄNOMEN MUMBAI

„Als Filmemacher habe ich in ganz Indien gedreht, und Mumbai ist eine Stadt, die wie ein eigenes Land ist. Sie hat ihre eigene Logik, ihre eigenen Regeln, die sich nicht um deine Kaste, deine Gemeinschaft, deinen wirtschaftlichen Status oder die Anzahl der Jahre, die du dich abmühst, kümmert. Sie nimmt alle gleichberechtigt auf und macht überhaupt keine Unterschiede. Jeder, der hierherkommt, arbeitet hart und wächst. (...) Ja, es ist ein Kampf. Jeder muss sich durchkämpfen. Es ist eine teure Stadt, um dort zu wohnen. Das Land ist ziemlich teuer. Die Wohnungen sind teuer. Deshalb werden viele Slums gebaut. Die Außenbezirke von Mumbai werden erschlossen, weil die Preise dort günstiger sind. Dort gibt es einen Großteil der Verkehrsmittel und alles andere. Aber Mumbai ist auch extrem sicher."

...ÜBER UNGLEICHHEIT

„Das Problem in der Stadt ist im Moment nicht die Religion. Es ist, denke ich, die wirtschaftliche Kluft, denn die Reicheren haben es immer besser und werden reicher, weil sie Zugang zum Internet und zur internationalen Welt bekommen. Sie gehen ins Ausland und studieren. Leider sind die Armen nicht in der Lage, dies zu tun. (...) Die wirtschaftliche Kluft ist also etwas, das hier immer noch vorherrscht."

...ÜBER DHARAVI

„Es lebt. Es braucht nichts von außen. Es hat alles in sich selbst. Es begann als Slum. (...) Aber heute ist es eine Organisation. Es ist nicht mehr die Art von Slum, die es vor 50 oder 40 Jahren war, als es begann. Es war einfach ein Raum zum Leben und zum Verstecken und so weiter. Heute gibt es viele Läden, viele Dinge werden hier hergestellt (...) und an die besten Geschäfte geliefert. Es ist also ein lebendiger, eigenständiger Organismus. (...) Es braucht nichts von außen, aber es gibt viele Dinge an den Rest von Mumbai weiter."

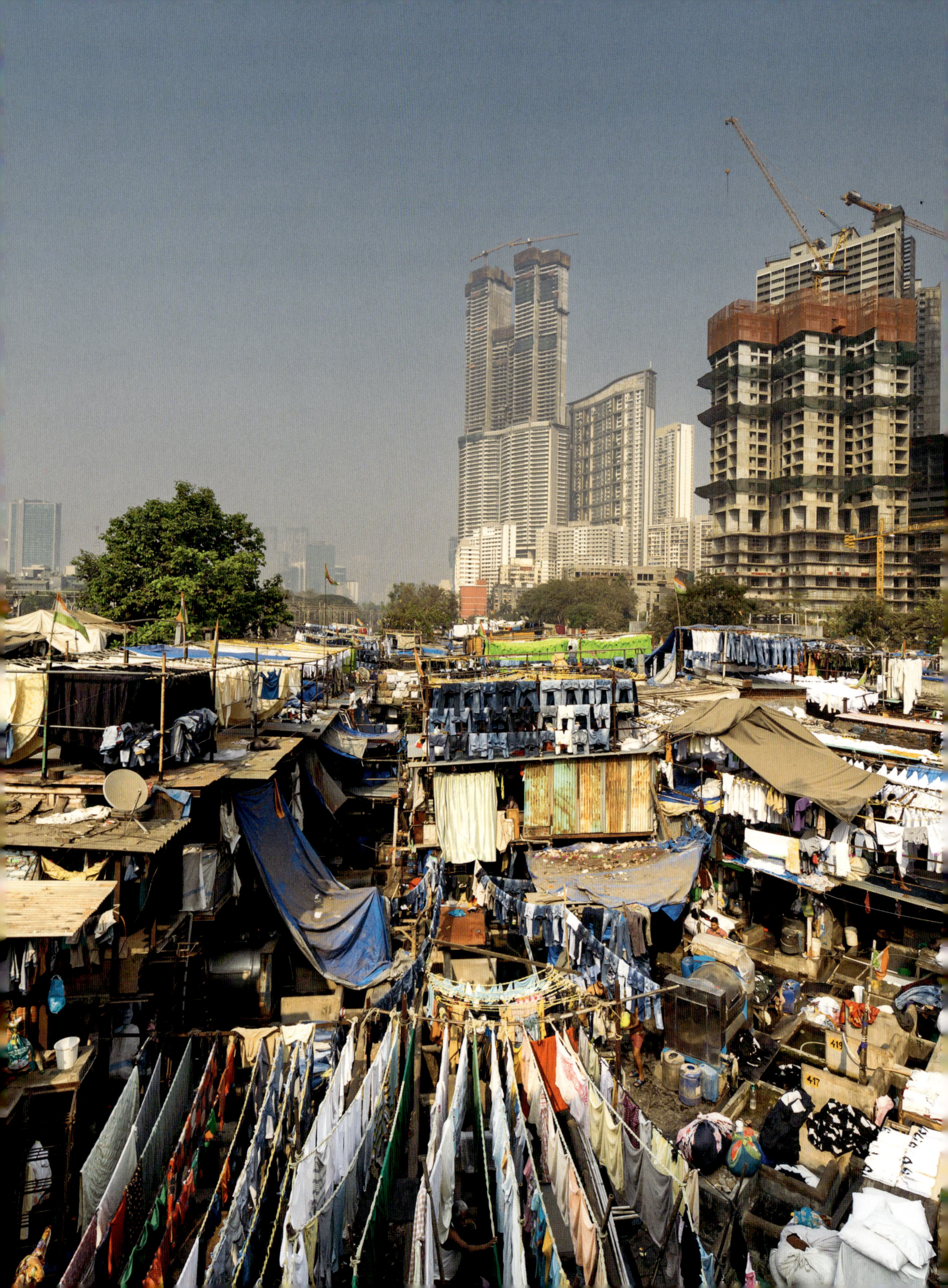

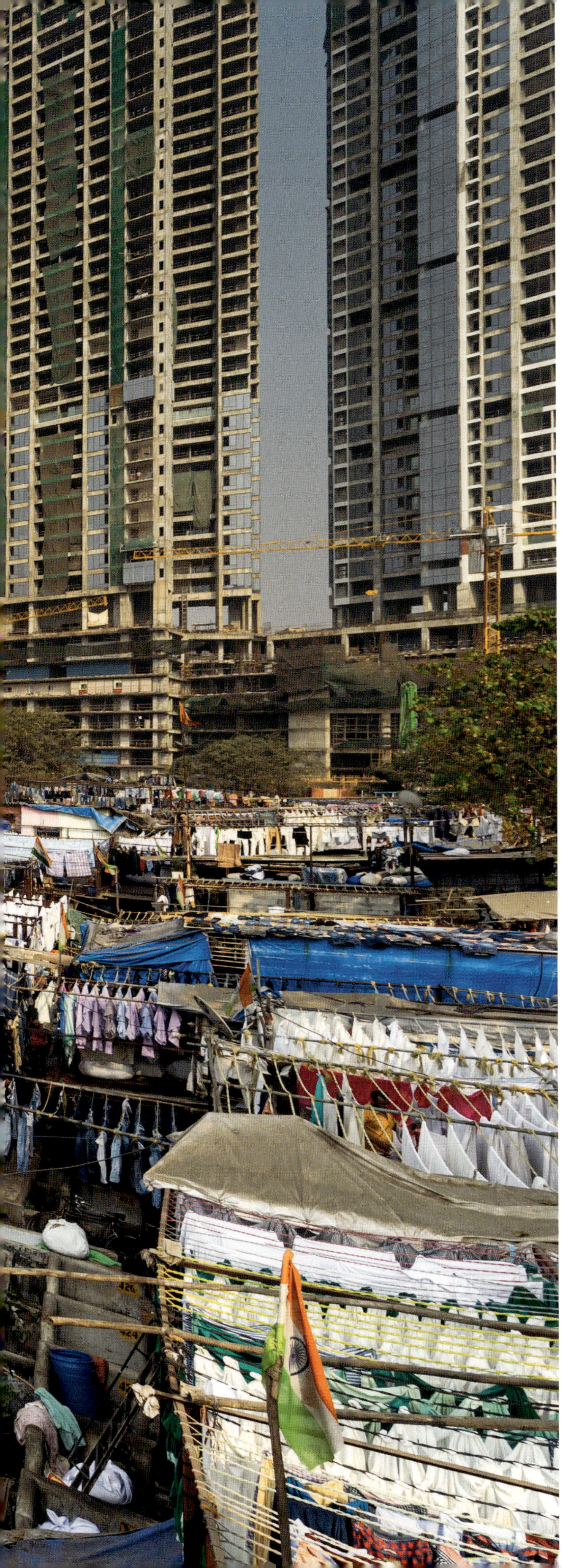

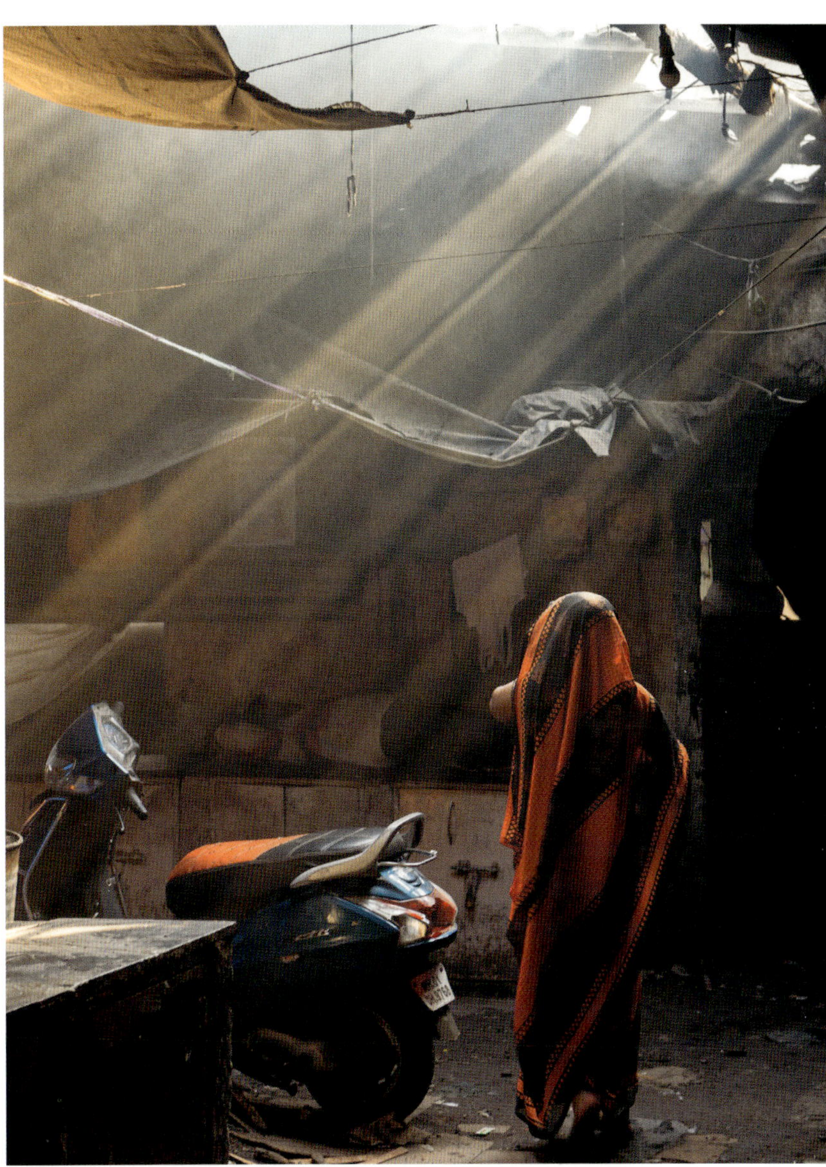

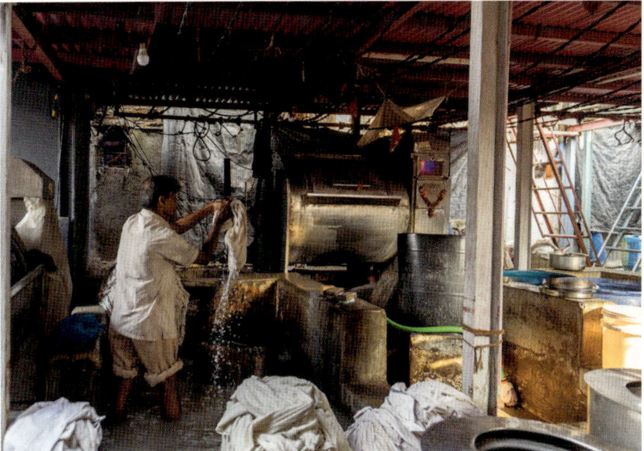

Nowhere else in the world do so many people wash such vast amounts of laundry by hand in one location as in Dobi Ghat, the "laundry room of Mumbai".

Nirgendwo sonst auf der Welt waschen so viele Menschen auf einem Areal per Hand solche Massen an Wäsche wie in Dobi Ghat, der „Waschküche Mumbais".

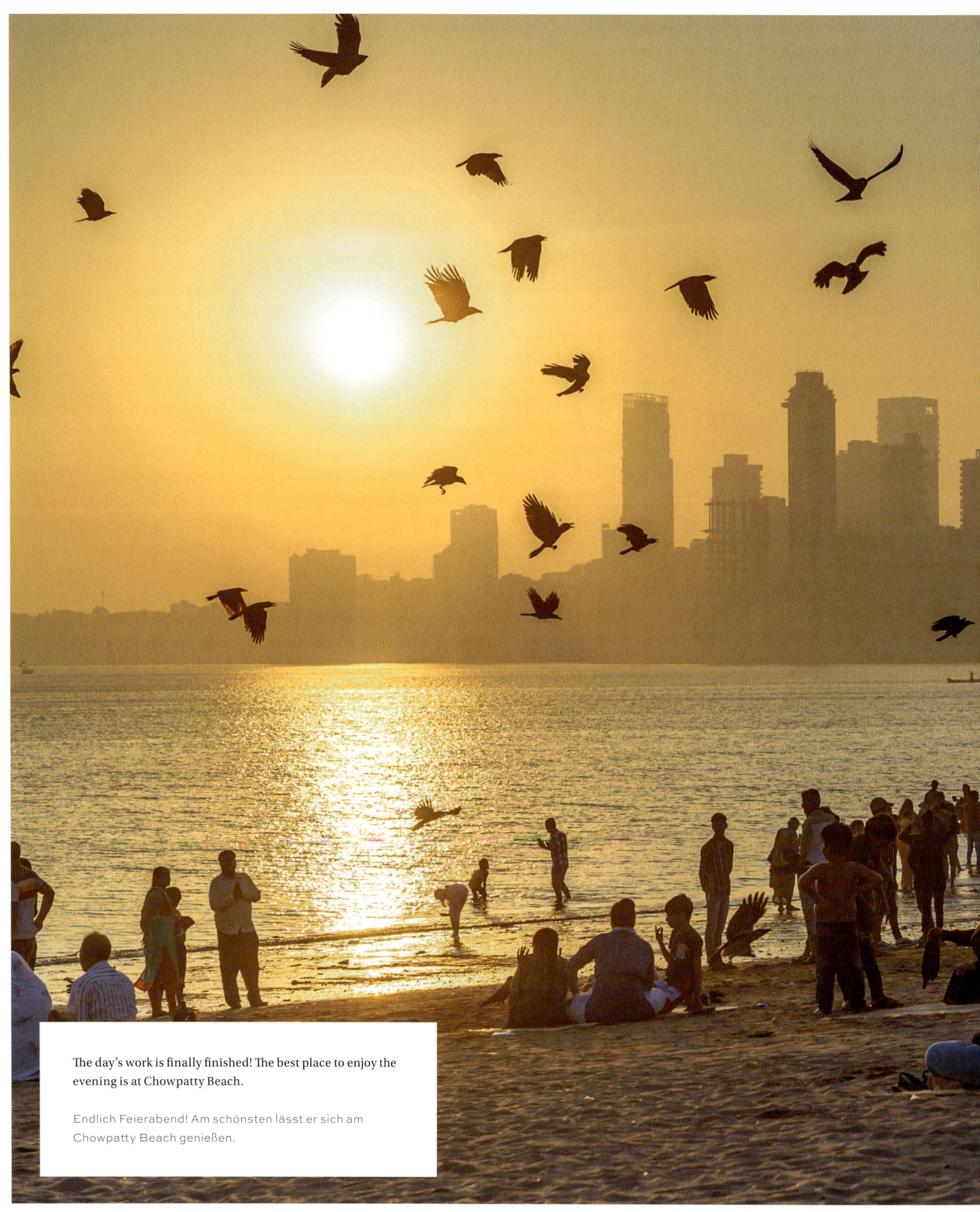

The day's work is finally finished! The best place to enjoy the evening is at Chowpatty Beach.

Endlich Feierabend! Am schönsten lässt er sich am Chowpatty Beach genießen.

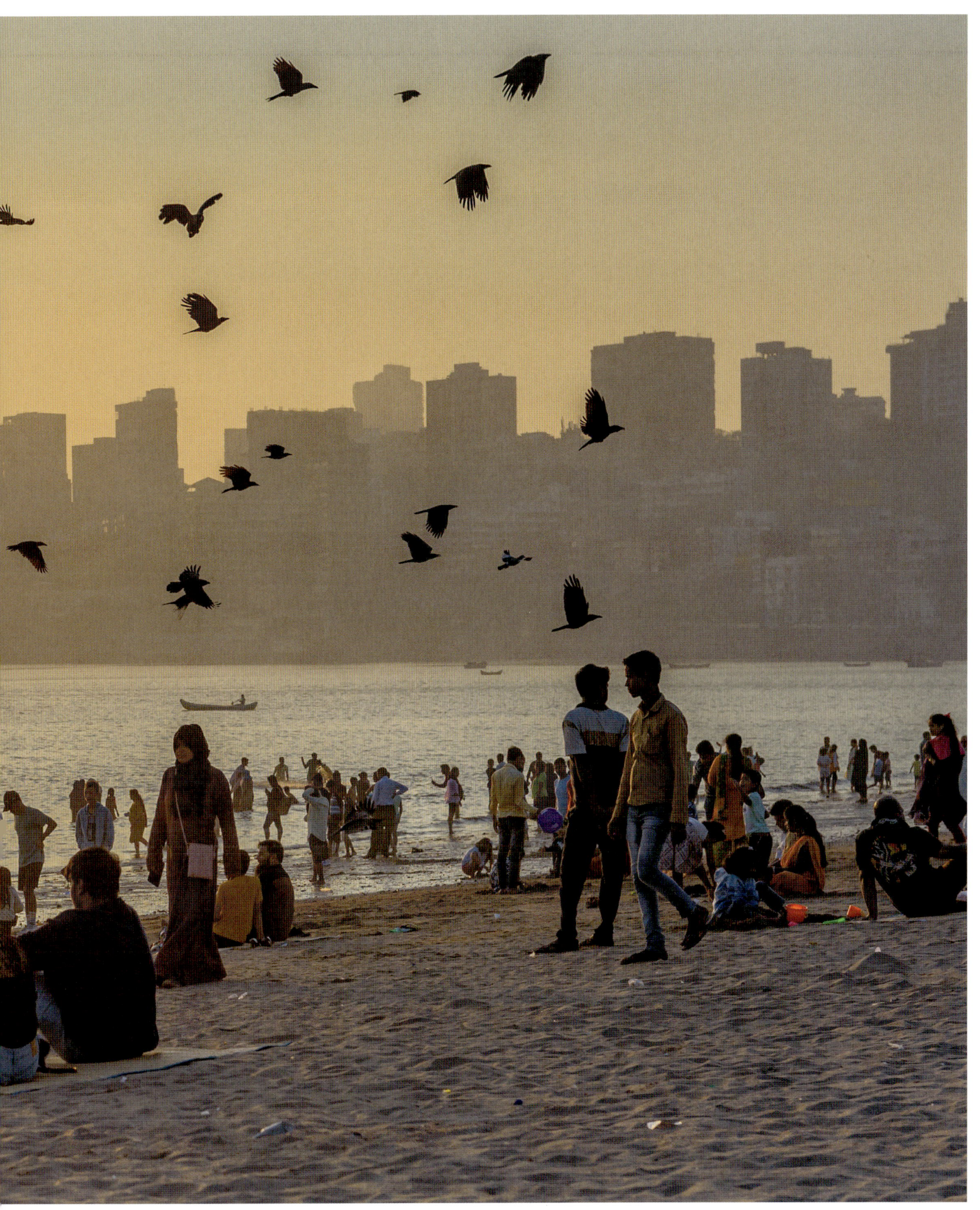

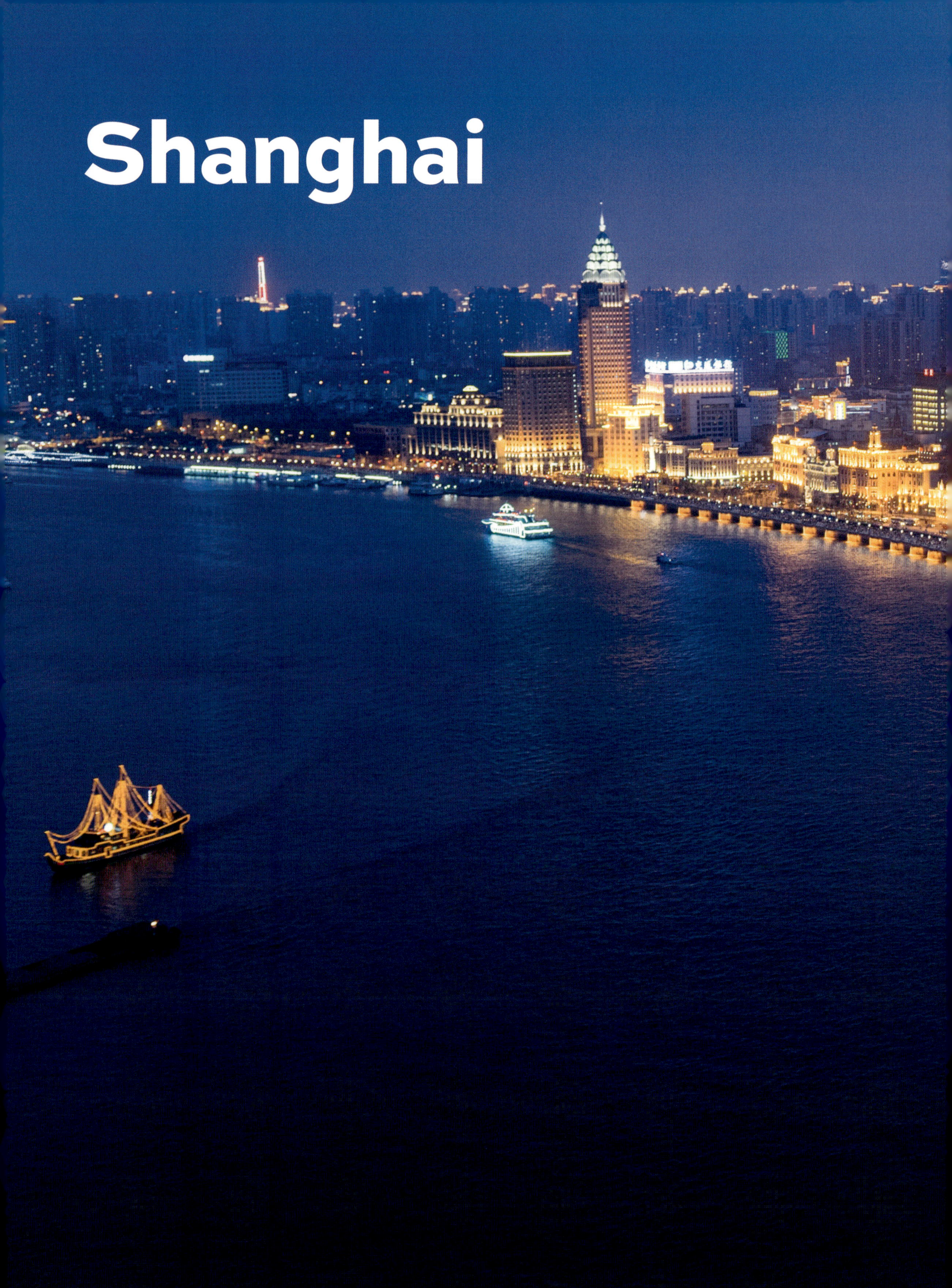
Shanghai

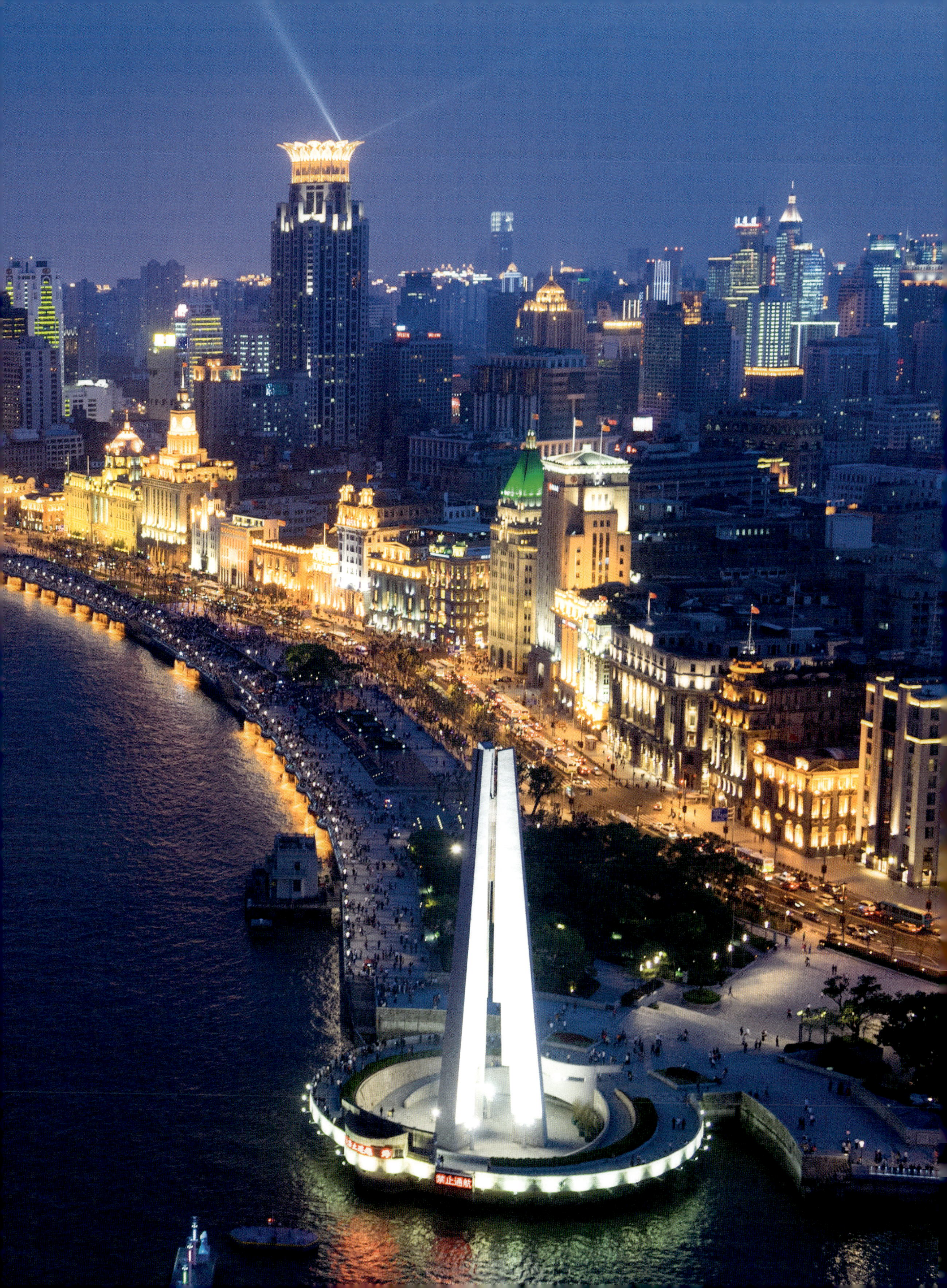

"Better City Better Life"

"Shanghai has a very positive image for Chinese people. If you think about the three megacities of Beijing, Guangzhou, and Shanghai, maybe more than half of the Chinese think Shanghai is the most beautiful and best to live in, not Beijing, not Guangzhou. Shanghai is magic for us, a magical city, the city of wonder." (Ming Yu)

Shanghai is a kind of optical illusion. No sooner do you think you've captured it when it has changed again. The city is cool, exciting, and exhausting. It doesn't necessarily captivate people with charm, but it is China's trendsetter when it comes to fashion and lifestyle. The metropolis draws its self-confidence from its eventful history, yet the city is building for the future. The "head of the dragon" has one mission above all: to equip the Middle Kingdom for the future. For over a hundred years, Shanghai has seemed to be a giant testing ground. How much change can people be expected to endure, how quickly can change be implemented, how much of the future is already feasible now? The outcome materializes in the merciless demolition of everything old, in the tallest buildings, the most exciting nightlife, the fastest means of transportation, the most important investors, and the most international population in China.

To this day, the Shanghainese people draw their extraordinary self-confidence from the fact that their city has always been and still is more modern, better, more fashionable, more advanced, and faster than any other city in China. Without batting an eye, they are unshakably convinced that their subways, skyscrapers, restaurants, shopping malls, and traffic infrastructure are the most modern and best in the world, and in all of China, of course. Powerful politics might well take place in distant and conservative Beijing. Here, it is only the power of money that counts, expressed in towering skyscrapers and glittering temples of consumption. Immigrants make this self-confidence their own, because those who have made it this far have the opportunity, with hard work and perseverance, to participate in the phenomenon that is Shanghai.

But is there such a thing as the real, typical Shanghainese person? Every resident of the city would likely respond indignantly to this question in the affirmative. But if you ask more precisely what it is that characterizes the true Shanghainese, it becomes more difficult. If one believes the people of the metropolis, then you can recognize them by their language, by their unique dialect, spoken within the city limits and almost

"Better City Better Life"

„Also Shanghai hat für Chinesen ein sehr positives Image. Wenn man an die drei Megacities Peking, Guangzhou, Shanghai denkt, dann findet vielleicht über die Hälfte der Chinesen Shanghai am schönsten und am besten zum Leben, nicht Peking, nicht Guangzhou. Shanghai ist für uns Magie, eine Magic City, die Stadt des Wunders." (Ming Yu)

Shanghai ist wie ein Vexierbild. Kaum meint man, es erfasst zu haben, hat es sich schon wieder verändert. Die Stadt ist cool, aufregend und anstrengend. Sie besticht nicht unbedingt durch ihren Charme, aber sie ist Chinas Trendsetterin in Sachen Mode und Lifestyle. Die Metropole bezieht ihr Selbstbewusstsein aus ihrer bewegten Geschichte, doch gebaut wird für die Zukunft. Der „Kopf des Drachen" hat vor allem eine Aufgabe: das Reich der Mitte zukunftsfähig zu machen. Seit über hundert Jahren erscheint Shanghai als ein gigantisches Experimentierfeld. Wie viel Veränderung kann man Menschen zumuten, wie schnell lässt sich Veränderung durchführen, was ist an Zukunft schon jetzt machbar? Das Ergebnis materialisiert sich im gnadenlosen Abriss alles Alten, in den höchsten Gebäuden, dem aufregendsten Nachtleben, den schnellsten Verkehrsmitteln, den wichtigsten Investoren und dem internationalsten Publikum Chinas.

Bis heute ziehen die Shanghaier ihr außerordentliches Selbstbewusstsein daraus, dass ihre Stadt immer moderner, besser, modischer, fortschrittlicher und schneller war und ist als alle anderen Städte Chinas. Ohne mit der Wimper zu zucken, sind sie unerschütterlich davon überzeugt, dass ihre U-Bahnen, Hochhäuser, Restaurants, Einkaufszentren oder Verkehrswege die modernsten und besten der Welt und Chinas sowieso sind. Mag sich die politische Macht ruhig im entfernten und biederen Beijing befinden. Hier zählt nur die Macht des Geldes, die sich ihren Ausdruck in himmelstürmenden Wolkenkratzern und glitzernden Konsumtempeln schafft. Die Zuwanderer machen sich dieses Selbstbewusstsein zu

The 632-meter Shanghai Tower symbolizes China's and especially Shanghai's dynamic future, according to its builders.

Der 632 Meter hohe Shanghai Tower steht laut seinen Erbauern symbolisch für Chinas und besonders für Shanghais dynamische Zukunft.

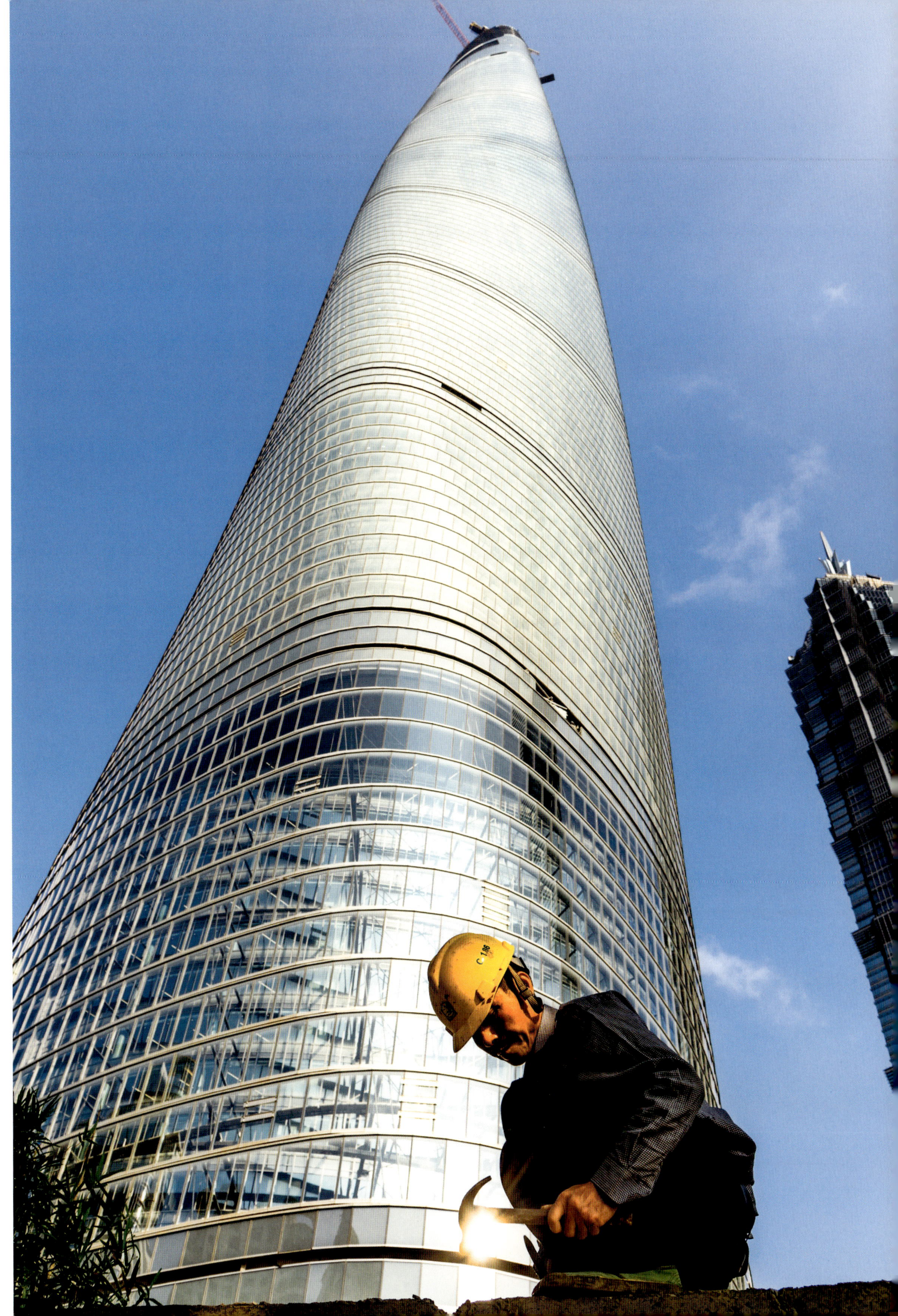

incomprehensible to Chinese people from other regions. The Mandarin "ni hao" for hello becomes "nong ho", and "zai jian" for goodbye becomes "ze wei". And even there, there are nuances, the even more original pronunciation, and thus the even more genuine, even more unmistakable Shanghainese.

"Are immigrant workers important to Shanghai? Of course they are. Without immigrant workers, the Shanghai of today would not exist. People here have this attitude: I have my dream there, I'm working with all my might to make it come true."

Shanghai has been a country of immigration since the mid-19th century; a magnet then and now for all those seeking the new and the exciting, riches and quick good fortune. Shanghai residents owe their self-confidence to the city's success, its dynamism and progress, even if they do not share in any of this materially.

"Better City, Better Life" was the motto of the World Expo in Shanghai in 2010, with the underlying vision of a livable city where cultural diversity, economic development, scientific and technical innovations, the redesigning of city districts, and the coexistence of urban and rural areas were to be made a reality. If the people were largely forgotten in all these visions until that point, a lot has happened for the residents since then as well. Public spaces, waterfront promenades, cultural centers, parks, and much more have been developed to improve the quality of life. In just a few years, the city has become one of China's most important artistic and cultural centers.

The Shanghainese people never fail to take advantage of opportunities. Here, you can experience first-hand the emergence of a huge industrial society that is also able to culturally compete with the West. It is possible to use this development to whip up fear, or perhaps to think about it the way Gottfried Leibniz did, when he wrote in 1705: "For I fear that, when the Chinese have learned our sciences, they will one day drive the Europeans out. So it seems to me that we should not lose the opportunities to be compensated, by making an exchange of their knowledge for ours."

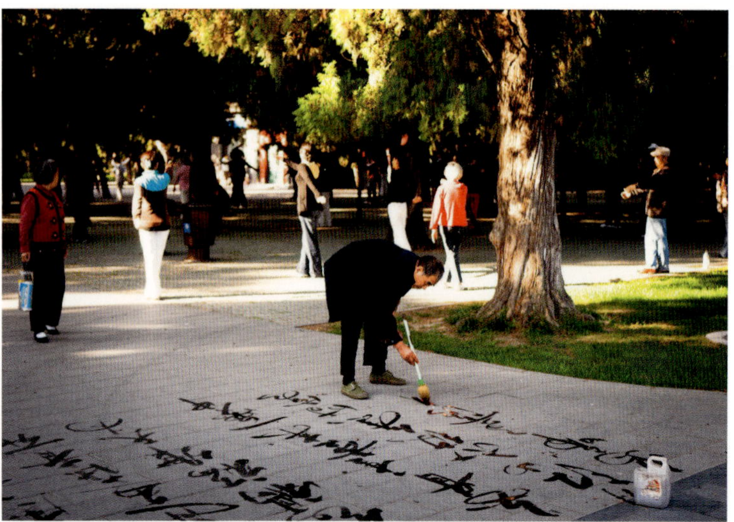

Eigen, denn wer es bis hierher geschafft hat, dem steht mit Fleiß und Ausdauer der Weg offen, an eben diesem Phänomen Shanghai teilzuhaben.

Aber gibt es den echten, den typischen Shanghaier? Wohl jeder Bewohner der Stadt wird diese Frage empört bejahen. Fragt man jedoch genauer danach, was denn den echten Shanghaier ausmacht, wird es schon schwieriger. Glaubt man den Bewohnern der Metropole, dann erkennt man ihn an der Sprache, am eigenwilligen Dialekt, der innerhalb des Stadtrings gesprochen wird und für Chinesen anderer Regionen nahezu unverständlich ist. So wird aus dem hochchinesischen *ni hao* für „Guten Tag" *nong ho* und aus *zai jian* für „Auf Wiedersehen" *ze wei*. Und selbst da gibt es Nuancen, die noch originalere Aussprache und damit den noch echteren, noch unverwechselbareren Shanghaier.

„Ob Wanderarbeiter für Shanghai wichtig sind? Natürlich sind sie es. Ohne die Wanderarbeiter gäbe es das Shanghai von heute nicht. Die Menschen hier sind so eingestellt: Ich habe da meinen Traum, ich arbeite mit allen Kräften an der Verwirklichung."

Dabei ist Shanghai seit Mitte des 19. Jh. ein „Einwanderungsland". Magnet für all jene, damals wie heute, die das Neue und Aufregende, den Reichtum und das schnelle Glück suchen. Sein Selbstbewusstsein verdankt der Bewohner Shanghais dem Erfolg der Stadt, der Dynamik und dem Fortschritt, selbst dann, wenn er an alldem nicht materiell teilhat.

„Better City, Better Life" hieß das Motto der Weltausstellung in Shanghai 2010. Dahinter verbarg sich die Vision für eine lebenswerte Stadt, in der kulturelle Vielfalt, Wirtschaftsentwicklung, wissenschaftliche und technische Innovationen, die Neugestaltung von Stadtvierteln sowie das Zusammenleben von städtischen und ländlichen Räumen verwirklicht werden sollen. Sind die Menschen bei all diesen Visionen bis dahin weitgehend vergessen worden, hat sich seitdem auch für die Einwohner viel getan. Öffentliche Räume, Uferpromenaden, Kulturzentren, Parks u.v.m. wurden geschaffen, um die Lebensqualität zu verbessern. In nur wenigen Jahren hat sich die Stadt zu einem der bedeutendsten Kunst- und Kulturzentren Chinas entwickelt.

Die Shanghaier haben nie geschlafen, wenn es um die Nutzung von Chancen ging. Hier erlebt man live, wie eine riesige Industriegesellschaft entsteht, die mit dem Westen auch kulturell konkurrieren kann. Man kann von dieser Entwicklung Ängste schüren oder es vielleicht mit Leibniz halten, der 1705 schrieb: „Wenn die Chinesen unsere Wissenschaft gelernt haben, jagen sie eines Tages die Europäer fort, sodass es mir scheint, dass keine Gelegenheit versäumt werden sollte, sich durch einen Austausch ihrer und unserer Kenntnisse zu entschädigen."

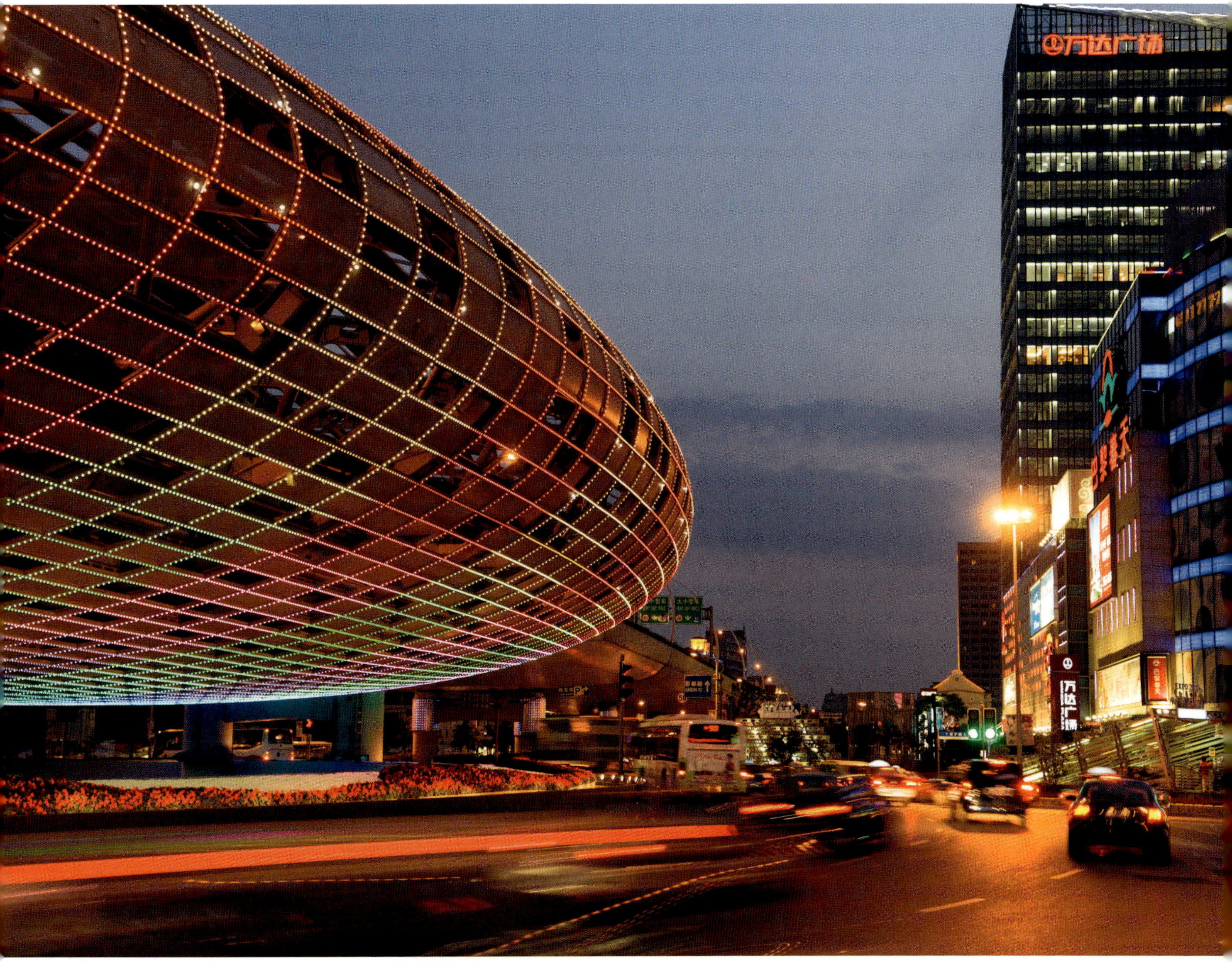

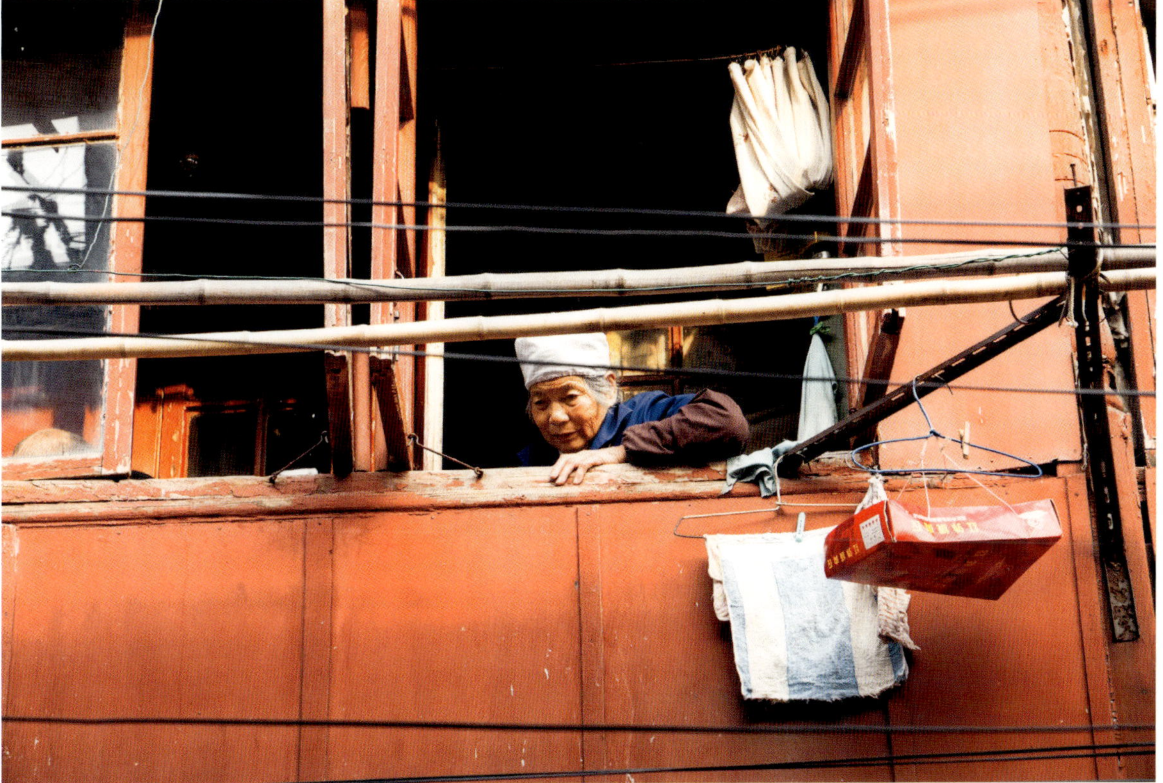

The things of the past are disappearing faster and faster. The Shanghai of the present is also a little like the characters of water calligraphy: a fleeting moment in time.

Das Alte verschwindet immer schneller. Auch das Shanghai der Gegenwart ist ein wenig wie die Schriftzeichen der Wasserkalligraphie: ein flüchtiger Moment.

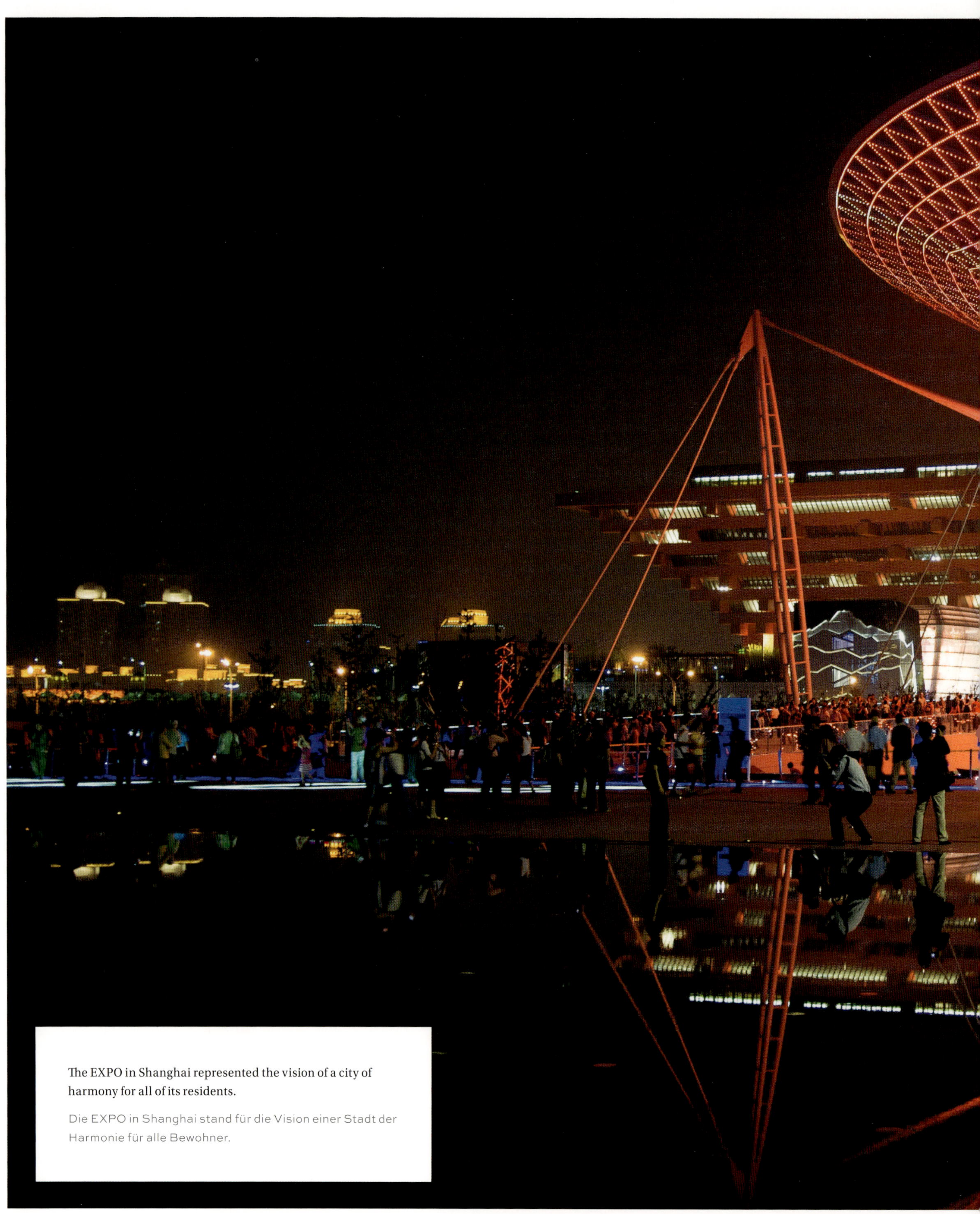

The EXPO in Shanghai represented the vision of a city of harmony for all of its residents.

Die EXPO in Shanghai stand für die Vision einer Stadt der Harmonie für alle Bewohner.

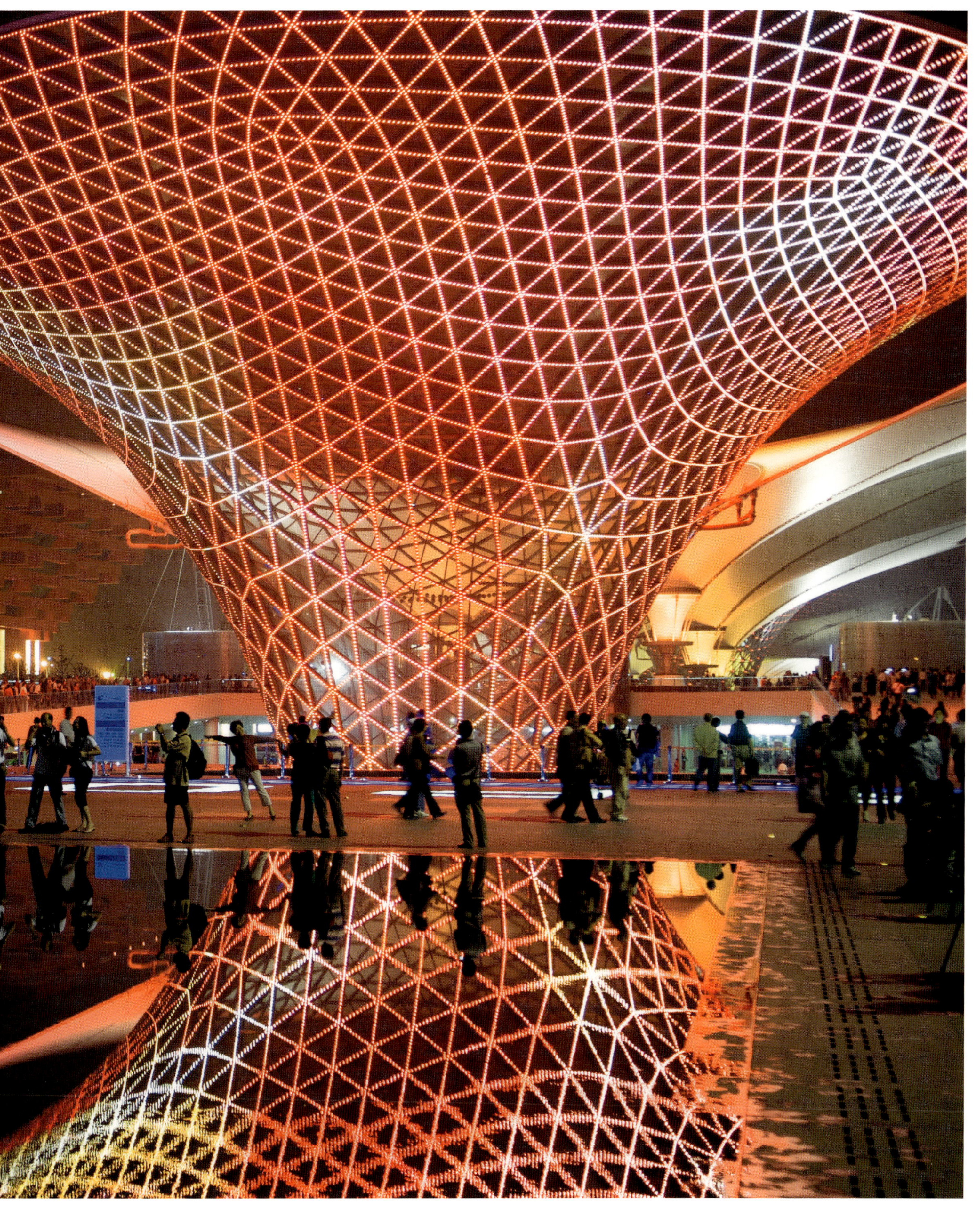

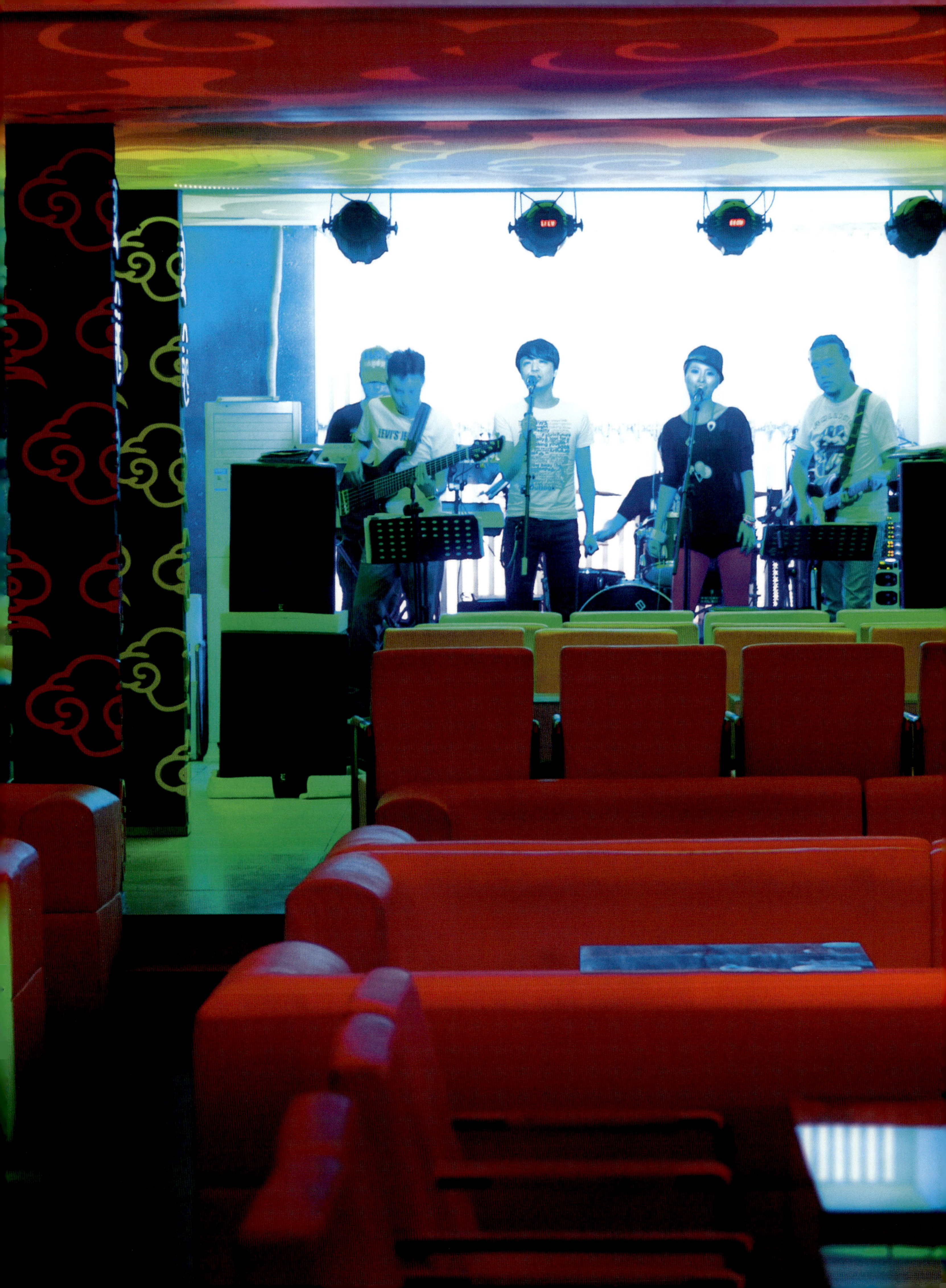

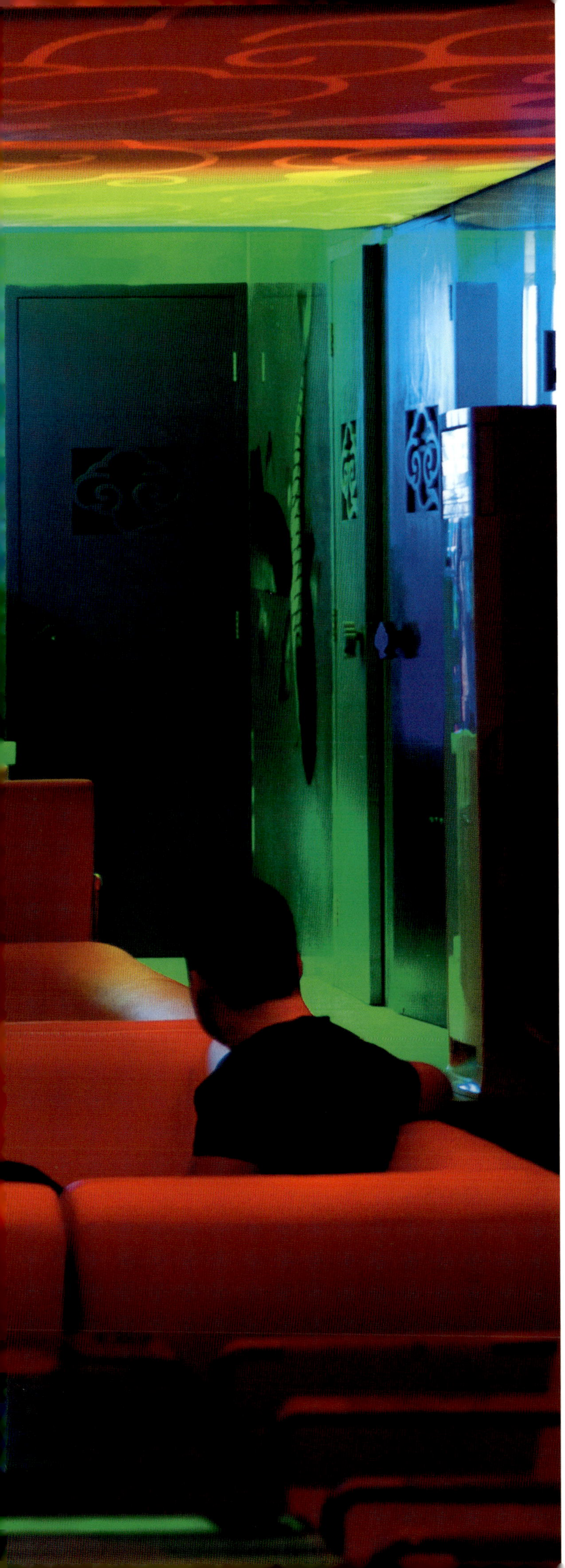

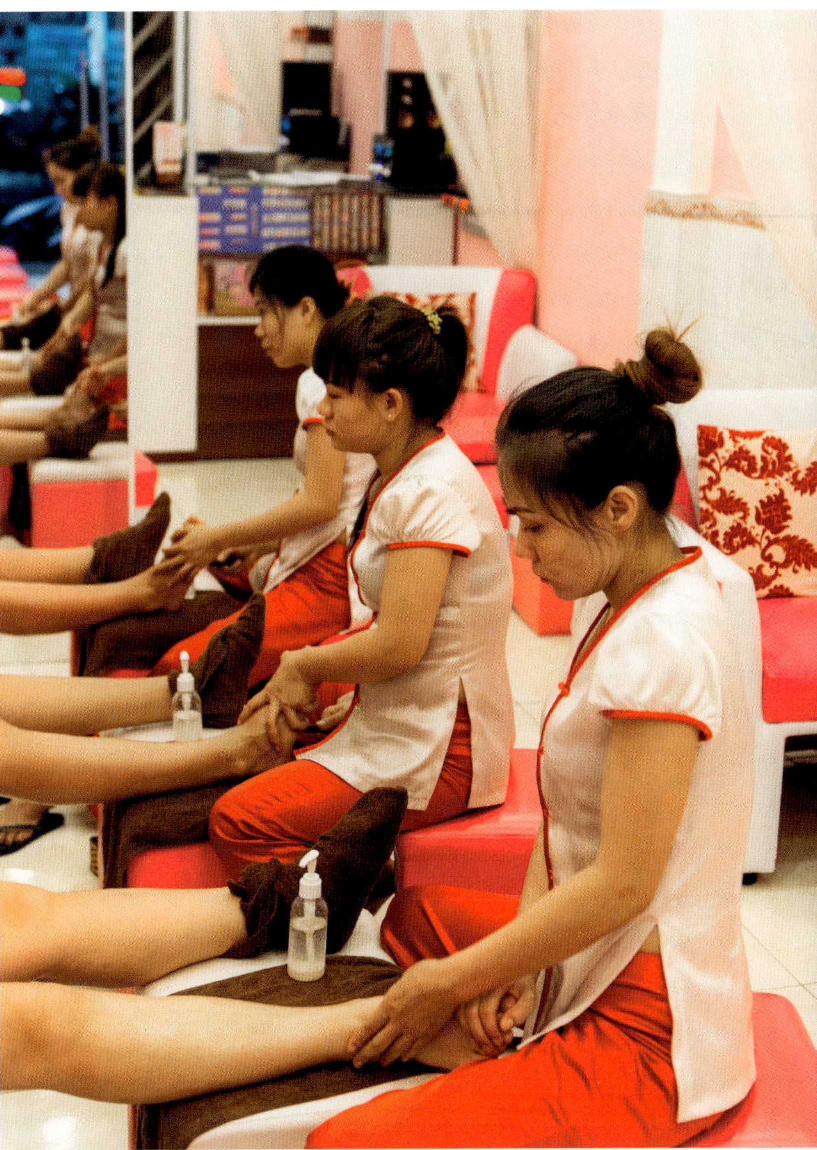

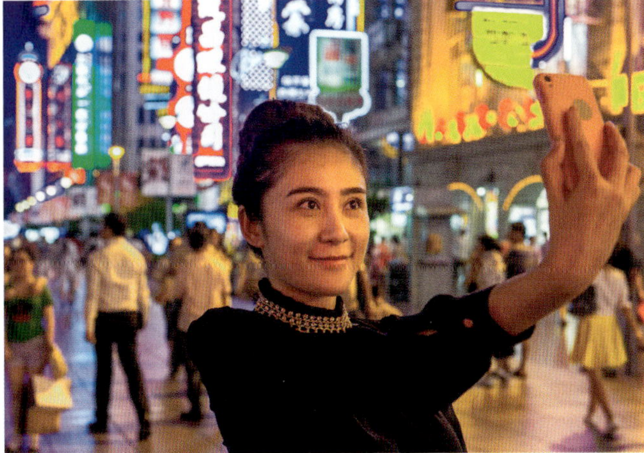

People in Shanghai work long and hard, but
they don't neglect the enjoyment of recreational
pleasures either.

In Shanghai wird viel und hart gearbeitet,
aber auch die Freizeitvergnügungen kommen
nicht zu kurz.

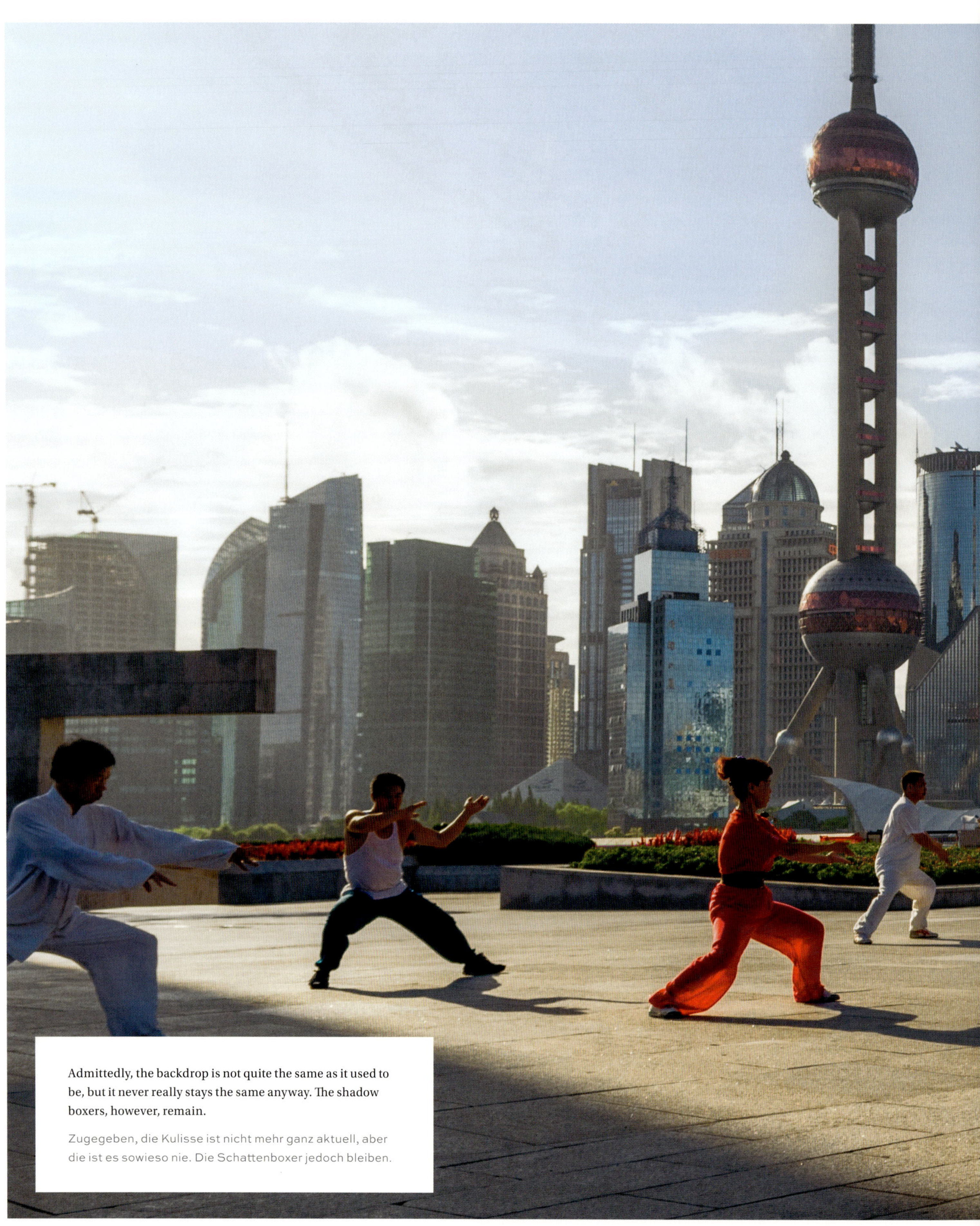

Admittedly, the backdrop is not quite the same as it used to be, but it never really stays the same anyway. The shadow boxers, however, remain.

Zugegeben, die Kulisse ist nicht mehr ganz aktuell, aber die ist es sowieso nie. Die Schattenboxer jedoch bleiben.

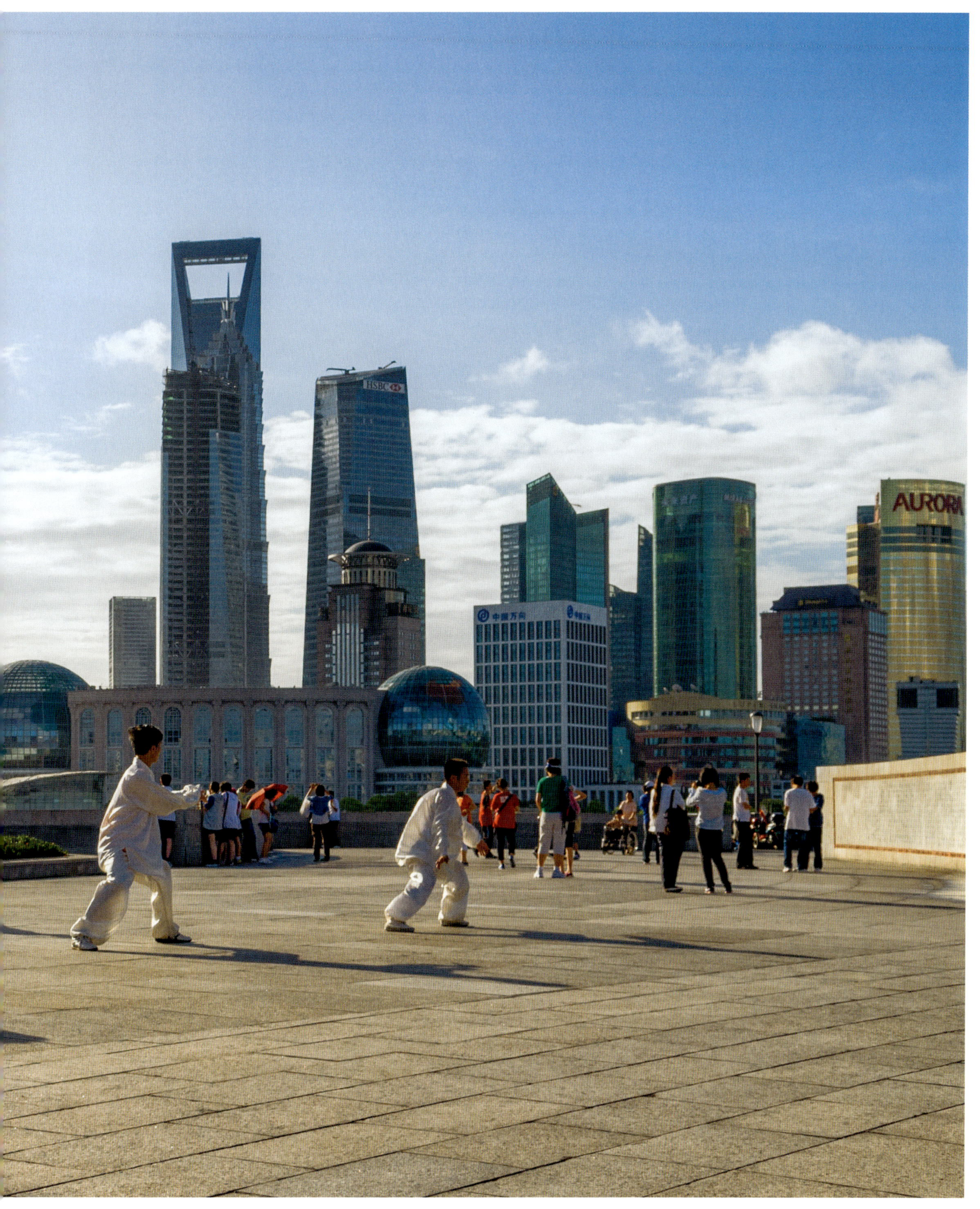

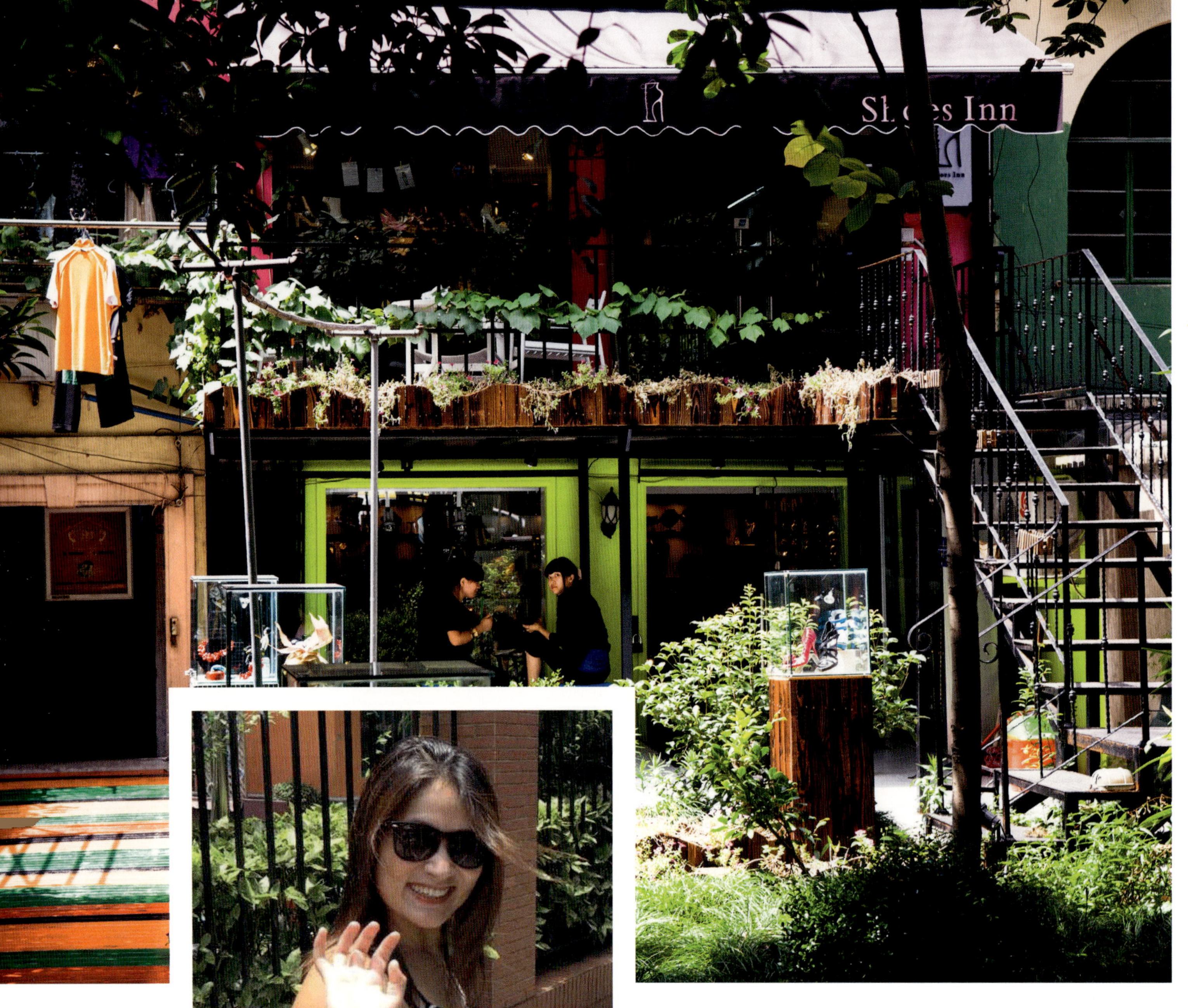

MING YU

"Well, my favorite place, where I also lived for years, is the former French Concession (...), a neighborhood full of flair." (Ming Yu)

„Also mein Lieblingsort, an dem ich jahrelang auch gelebt habe, ist die ehemalige Französische Konzession (...), ein Viertel voller Flair." (Ming Yu)

...ON THE APPEAL OF LIVING IN THIS MEGACITY

"City or countryside, this question doesn't necessarily come up in China. For the Chinese, cities are much more attractive than the countryside. There, the quality of life is significantly worse, job opportunities are not as good, and there are far fewer educational opportunities. The gap between the countryside and the city is simply far too great in China. That's why the Chinese tend to move to the city, everything for a better future. It's ultimately about resources: Everyone wants a piece of the pie, to share in the success."

... ON THE CHANGES

"I came to Shanghai in 2009 for my master's degree. I can still remember sitting in the subway from the main station to the university, when I wrote to one of my aunts, 'Oh, look, I'm here and there are so many skyscrapers.' Unfortunately, I didn't know then that I could have bought an apartment here. And ten years later, when I wanted to buy an apartment in Shanghai, I couldn't afford anything because the prices had skyrocketed. And the cityscape? In

2017, when I left Shanghai, there were maybe three, four times more high-rises than in 2009."

...ON THE LIMITS OF MEGACITIES

"But what I do know is that China once started thinking about merging Hong Kong, Shenzhen, and Guangzhou. And that would be about 40 million residents, 35 to 40 million. At least, Chinese city planners say that would be the current limit. More than 40 million is not possible, because the infrastructure for garbage, mail, traffic, and everything else has to be built. A city would not be able to cope with more at the present time. On the other hand, it is important to point out that large cities have existed for a long time. People have been living in big cities for thousands of years, especially in China. In Shanghai, 24 million people live together peacefully. So it works if the overall conditions are right."

...ON THE PROBLEM
OF TOO MANY HIGH-RISES

"Shanghai means 'city on the sea,' but the city is built on silt. That's not a problem initially, but in recent decades many thousands of skyscrapers have been built. And now Shanghai is too heavy, and it's sinking. Just a little every year, but the city is only a few meters above sea level. The Yangzi River continues to deposit a lot of mud and is rising, the sea level is rising... the authorities realized that reducing groundwater increases the sinking of the city. Now, water that has been extracted is being replaced using active and passive measures. This is already helping to prevent Shanghai from becoming a 'city beneath the sea'."

...ÜBER DEN REIZ IN DER
MEGACITY ZU LEBEN

„Stadt oder Land, diese Frage stellt sich in China nicht unbedingt. Für Chinesen sind Städte viel attraktiver als das Land. Dort ist die Lebensqualität bedeutend schlechter, die Jobchancen sind nicht so gut und die Bildungschancen sind viel geringer. Die Kluft zwischen Land und Stadt ist in China einfach viel zu groß. Deswegen ziehen die Chinesen eher in die Stadt – alles für eine bessere Zukunft. Es geht letztendlich um die Ressourcen: Jeder will was vom Kuchen abhaben, am Erfolg teilhaben."

...ÜBER DIE VERÄNDERUNGEN

„Also ich bin 2009 für mein Masterstudium nach Shanghai gekommen. Ich kann mich noch gut erinnern, als ich in der U-Bahn vom Hauptbahnhof zur Uni saß, da habe ich noch einer Tante geschrieben „Oh, schau ich bin hier und es gibt so viele Hochhäuser". Da wusste ich leider noch nicht, dass ich hier eine Wohnung hätte kaufen können. Und zehn Jahre später, als ich dann in Shanghai eine Wohnung kaufen wollte, konnte ich mir nichts mehr leisten, weil die Preise explodiert sind. Und das Stadtbild? 2017, als ich Shanghai verlassen habe, gab es vielleicht drei-, viermal mehr Hochhäuser als 2009."

...ÜBER DIE GRENZEN
VON MEGASTÄDTEN

„Was ich aber weiß ist, dass China mal Überlegungen gestartet hat, Hongkong, Shenzhen und Guangzhou zusammenzulegen. Und das wären dann etwa 35 bis 40 Millionen Einwohner. Zumindest sagen chinesische Städteplaner, das wäre die momentane Grenze. Also mehr als 40 Millionen geht nicht, weil eine Infrastruktur für Müll, Post, Verkehr, ja für alles Mögliche aufgebaut werden muss. Mehr würde eine Stadt nach momentanem Stand nicht verkraften. Auf der anderen Seite muss man auch ganz klar sagen, dass es Großstädte ja schon lange gibt. Menschen leben seit Jahrtausenden in Großstädten, auch und gerade in China. In Shanghai leben 24 Millionen Menschen friedlich zusammen. Es funktioniert also, wenn die Rahmenbedingungen stimmen."

...ÜBER DAS PROBLEM
ZU VIELER HOCHHÄUSER

„Shanghai bedeutet „Über dem Meer", doch die Stadt ist auf Schlick erbaut. Das ist ja erst mal kein Problem, aber in den letzten Dekaden wurden viele Tausend Wolkenkratzer gebaut. Und nun ist Shanghai zu schwer und sinkt. Jedes Jahr nur ein bisschen, aber die Stadt liegt nur wenige Meter über dem Meeresspiegel. Der Yangzi lagert immer viel Schlamm ab und steigt, der Meeresspiegel steigt... die Behörden haben erkannt, dass die Absenkung des Grundwassers das Absinken der Stadt fördert. Nun wird entnommenes Wasser daher durch aktive und passive Maßnahmen ersetzt. Das hilft schon mal, damit Shanghai nicht die Stadt „Unter dem Meer" wird."

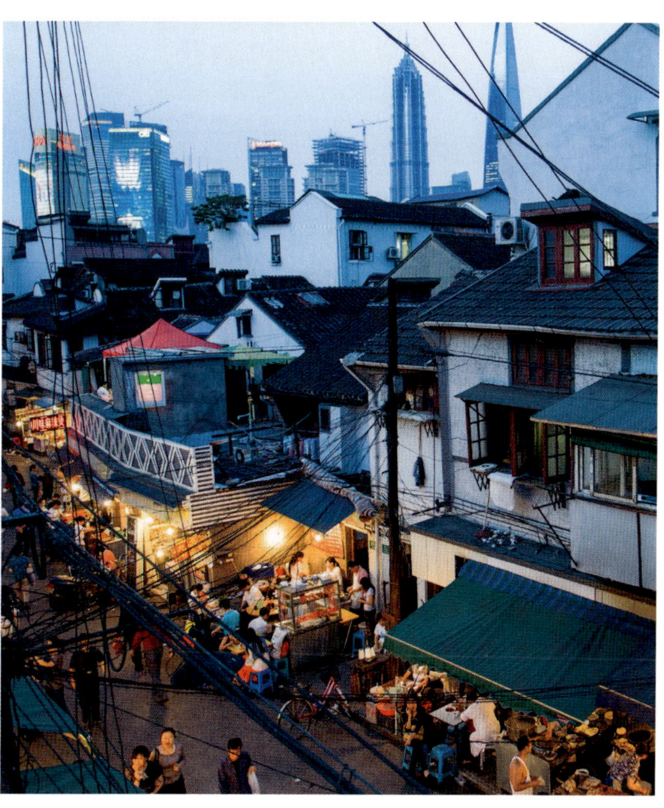

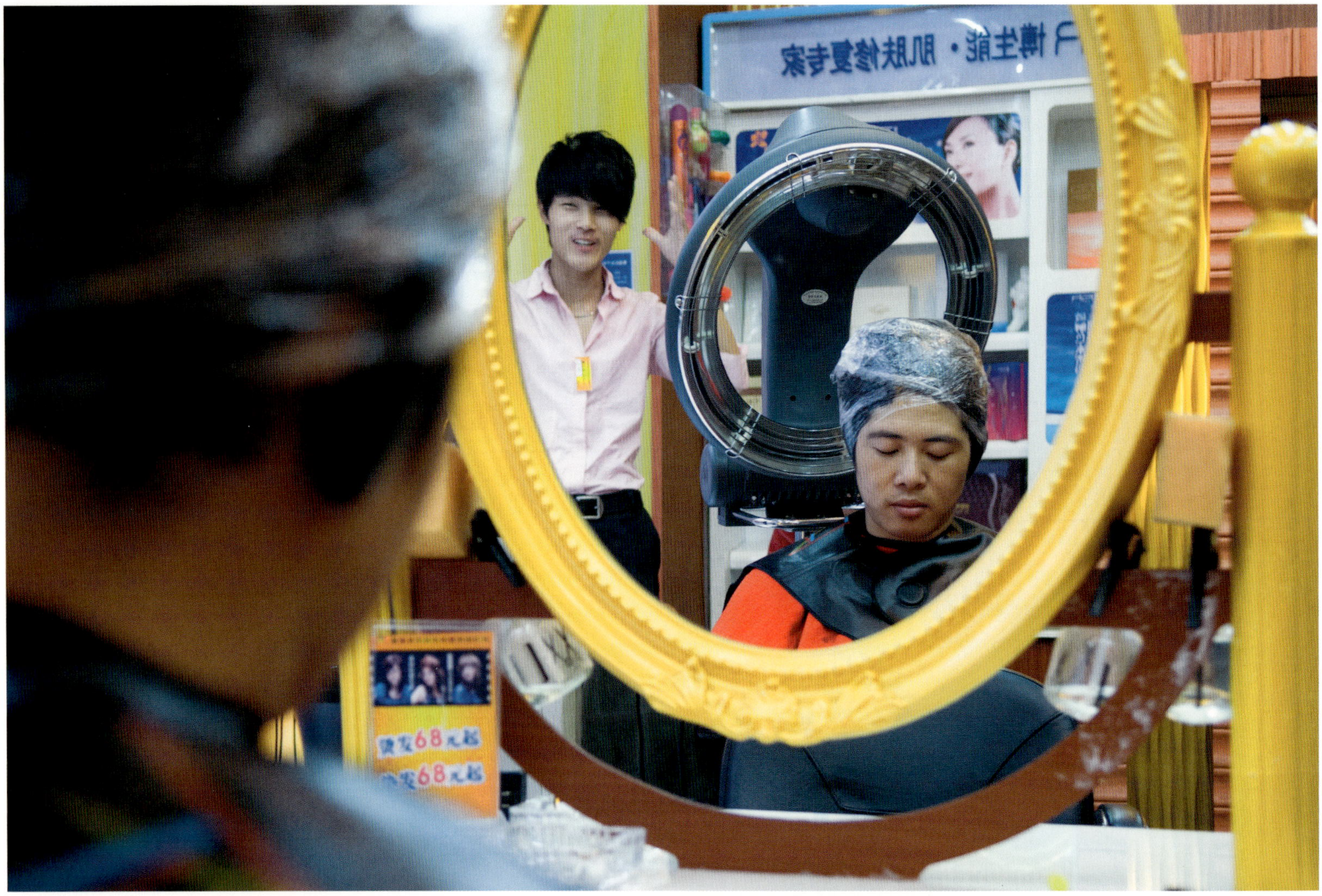

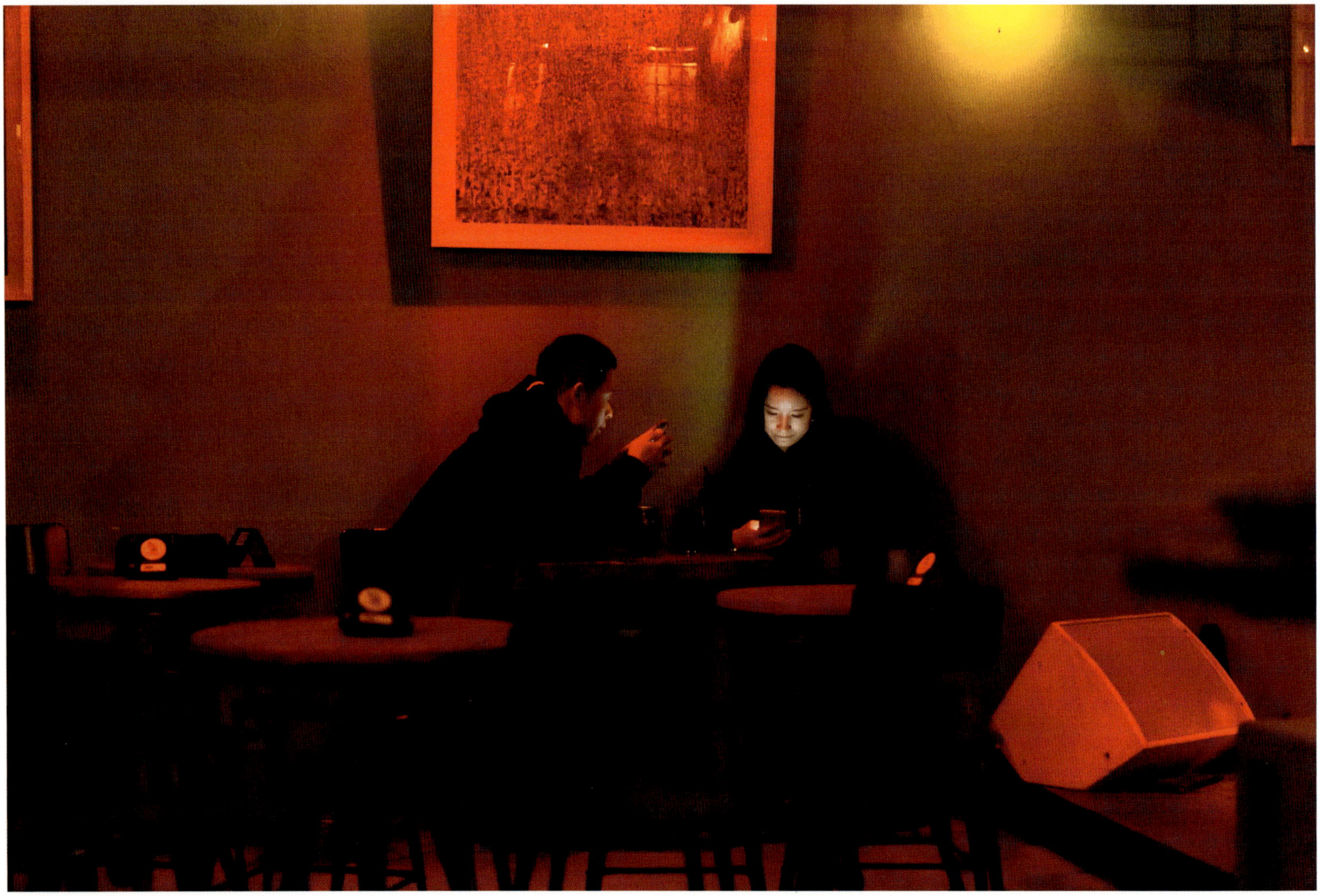

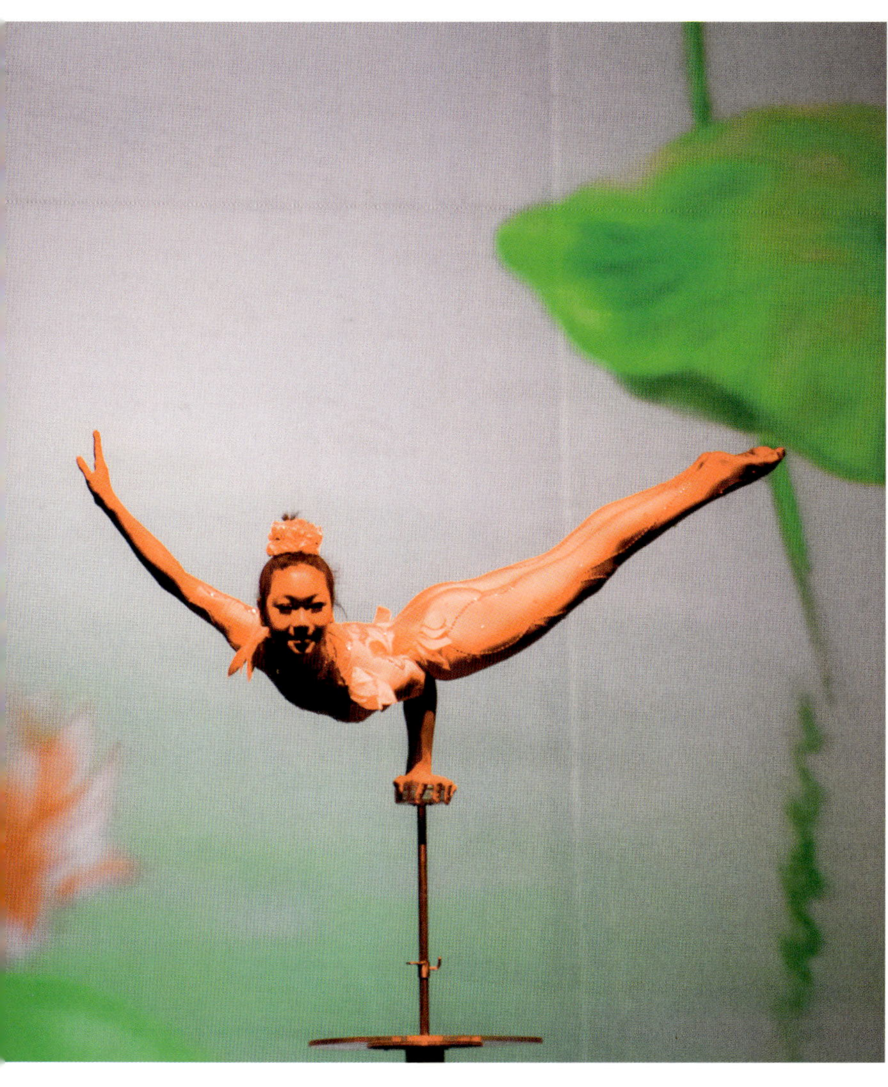

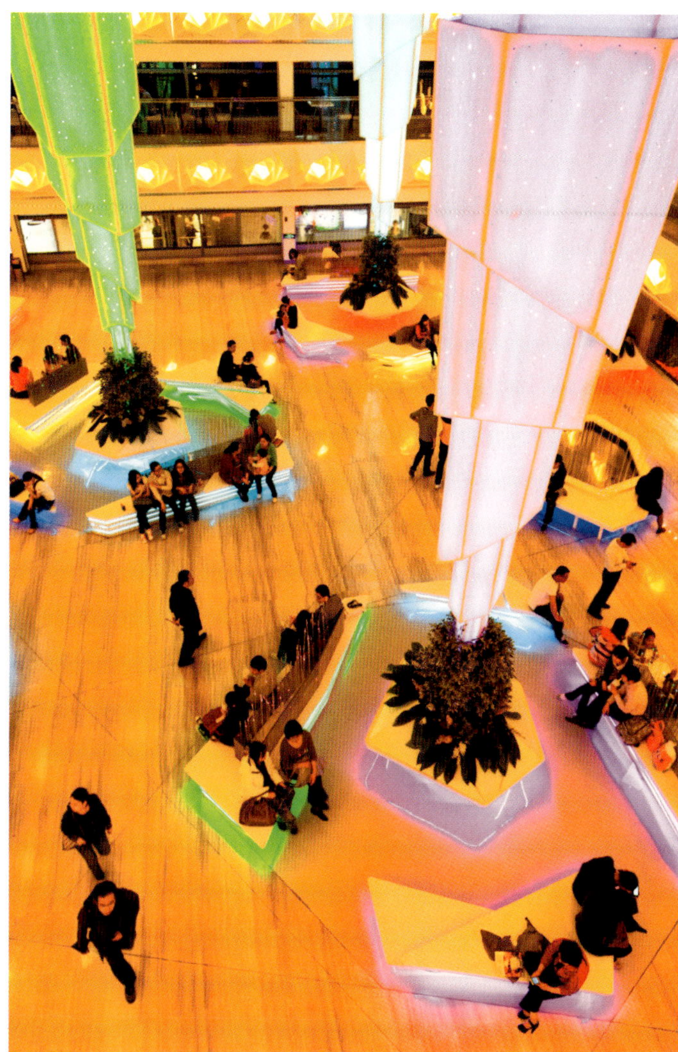

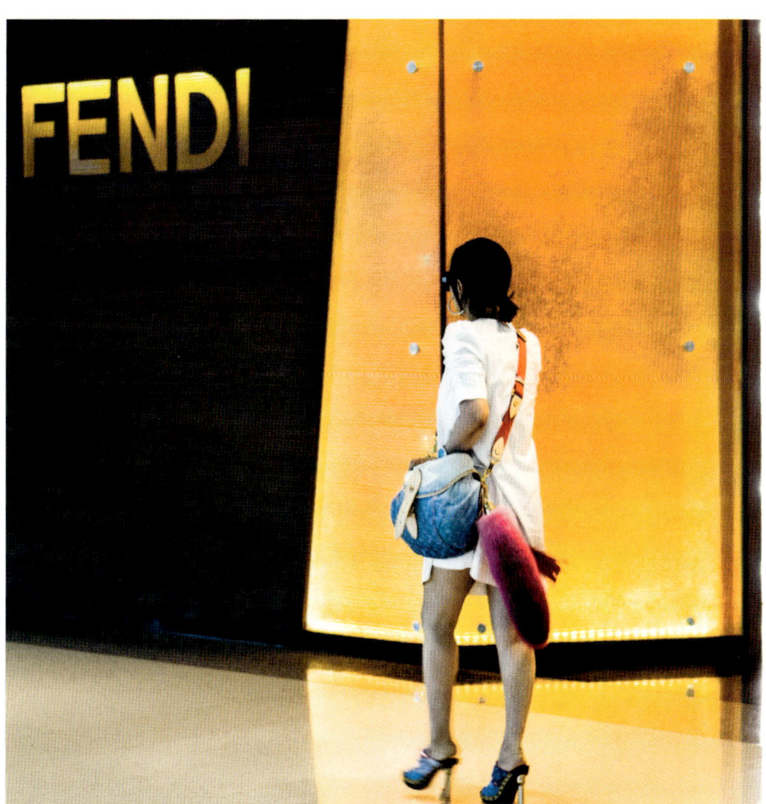

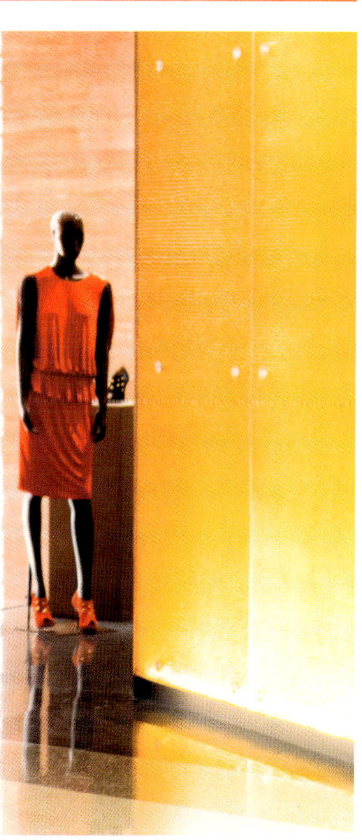

Cool, modern, nostalgic, and yes, traditional
too–everything is represented here.

Cool, modern, nostalgisch und ja,
auch traditionsbewusst –
alles ist vertreten.

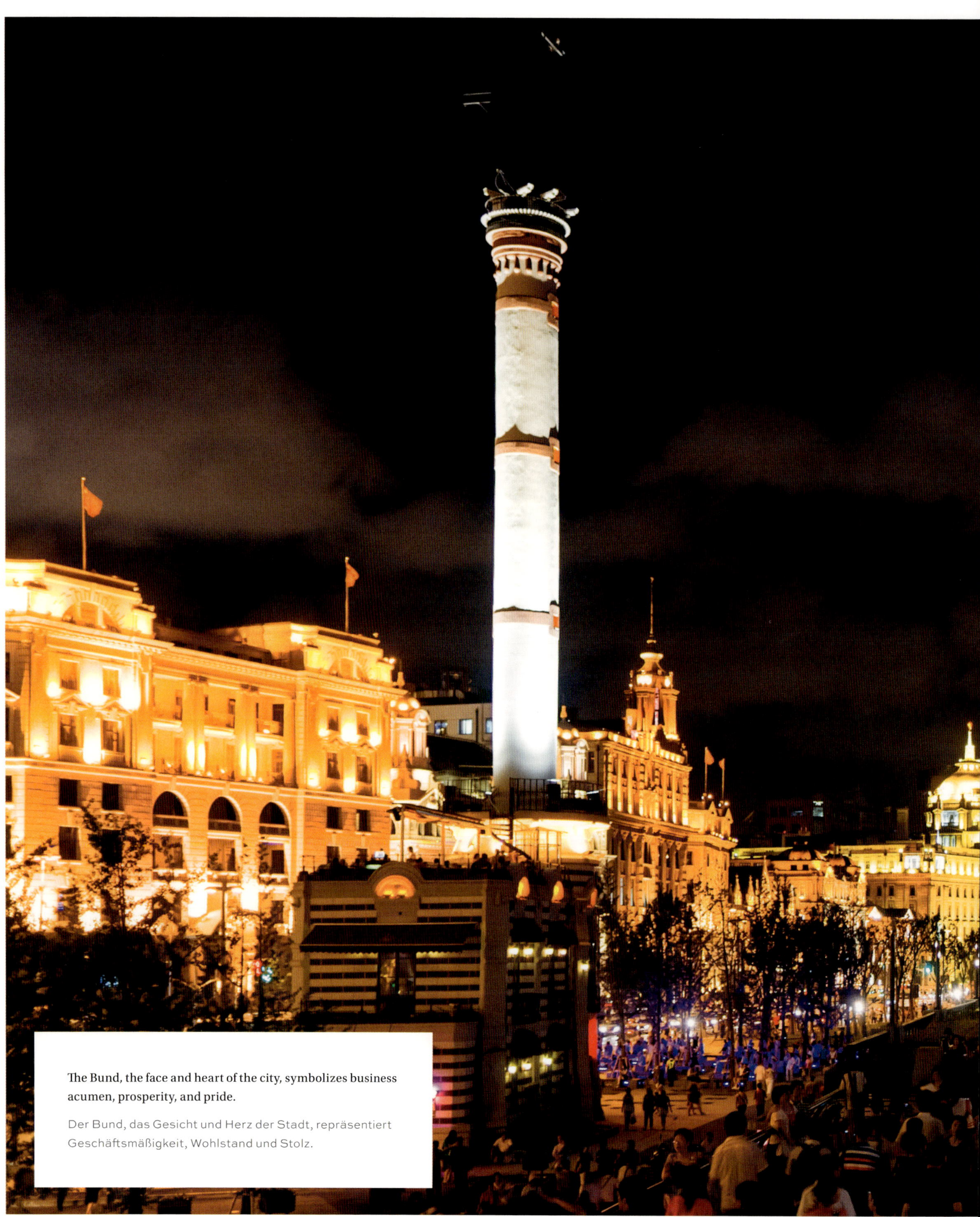

The Bund, the face and heart of the city, symbolizes business
acumen, prosperity, and pride.

Der Bund, das Gesicht und Herz der Stadt, repräsentiert
Geschäftsmäßigkeit, Wohlstand und Stolz.

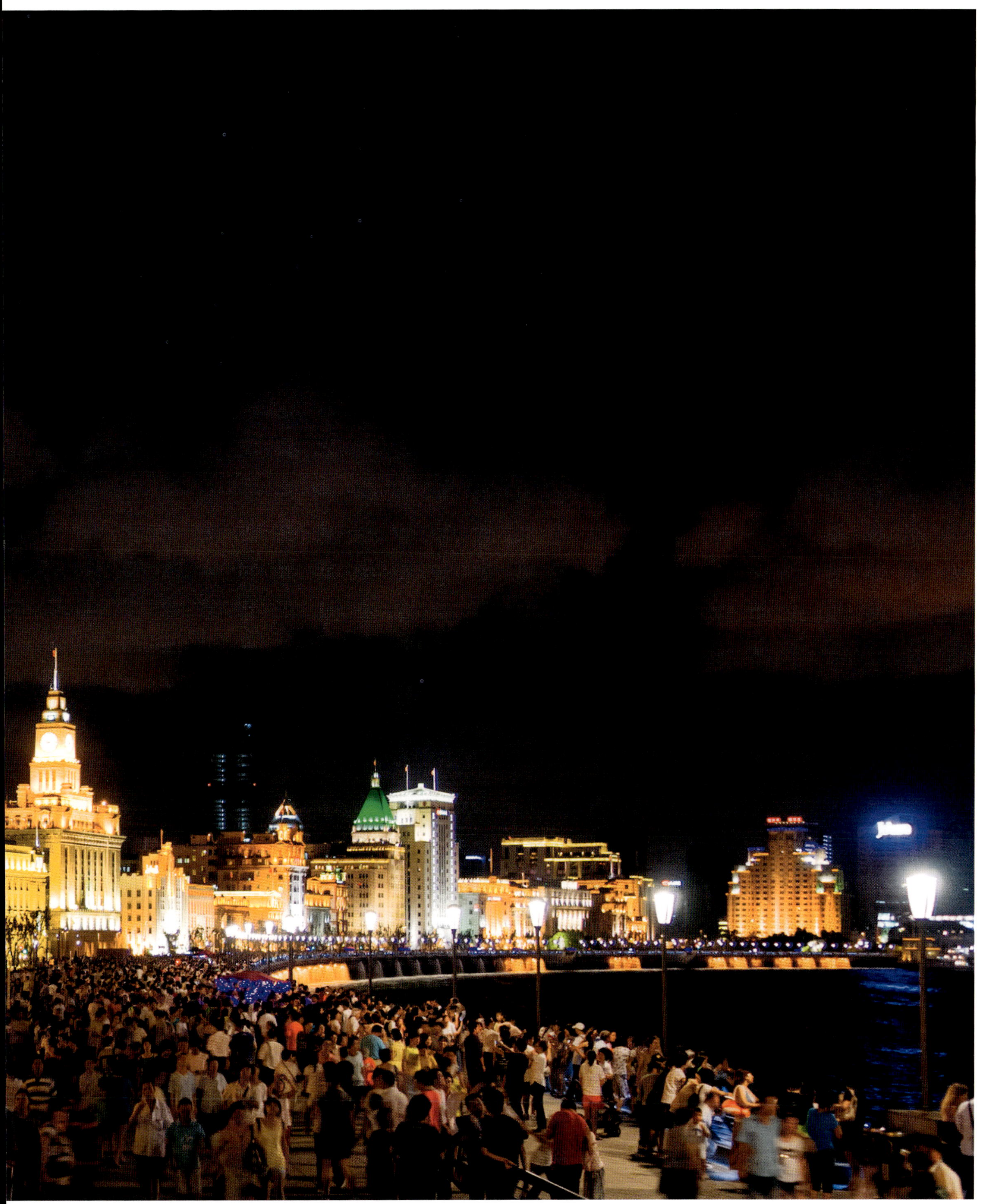

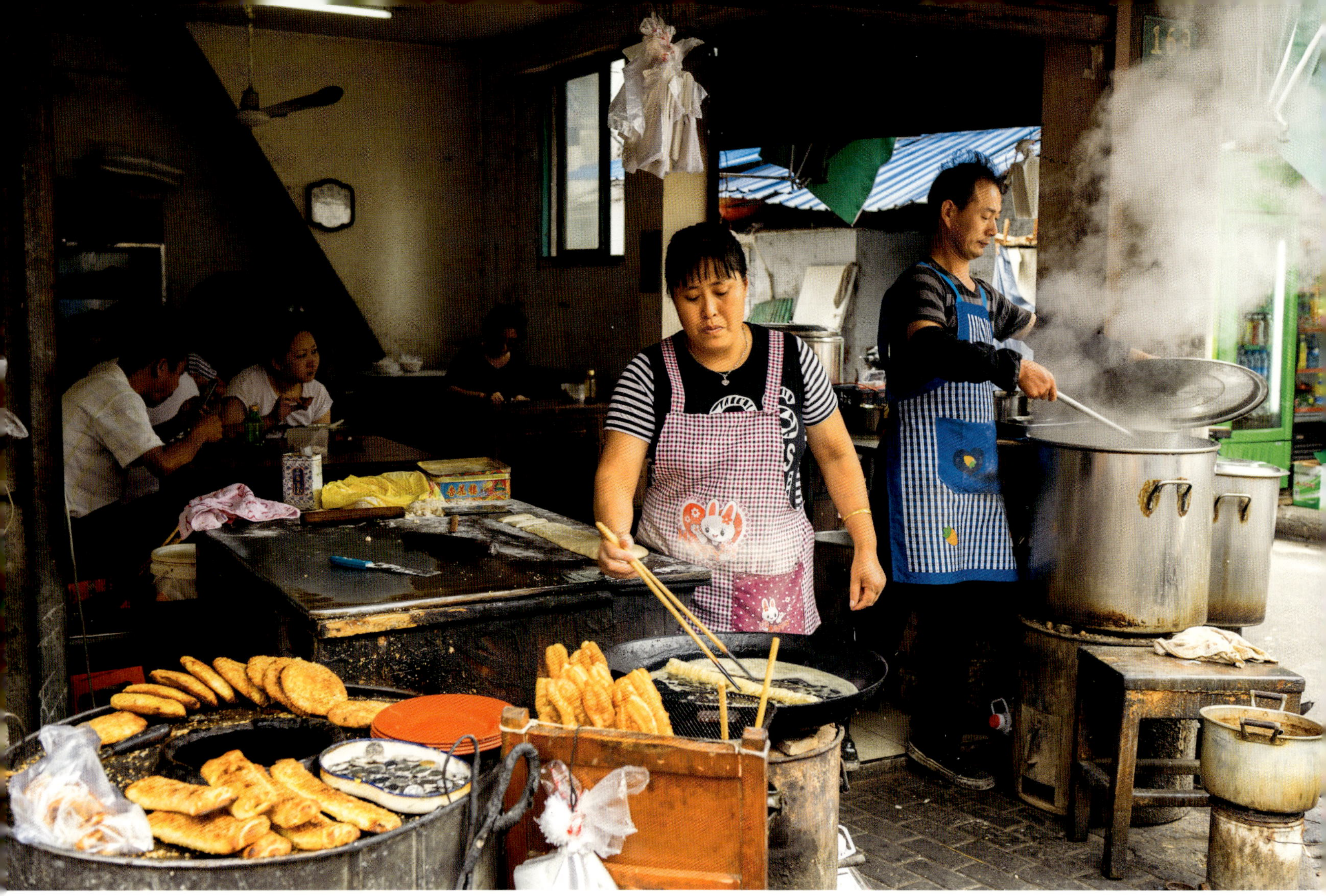

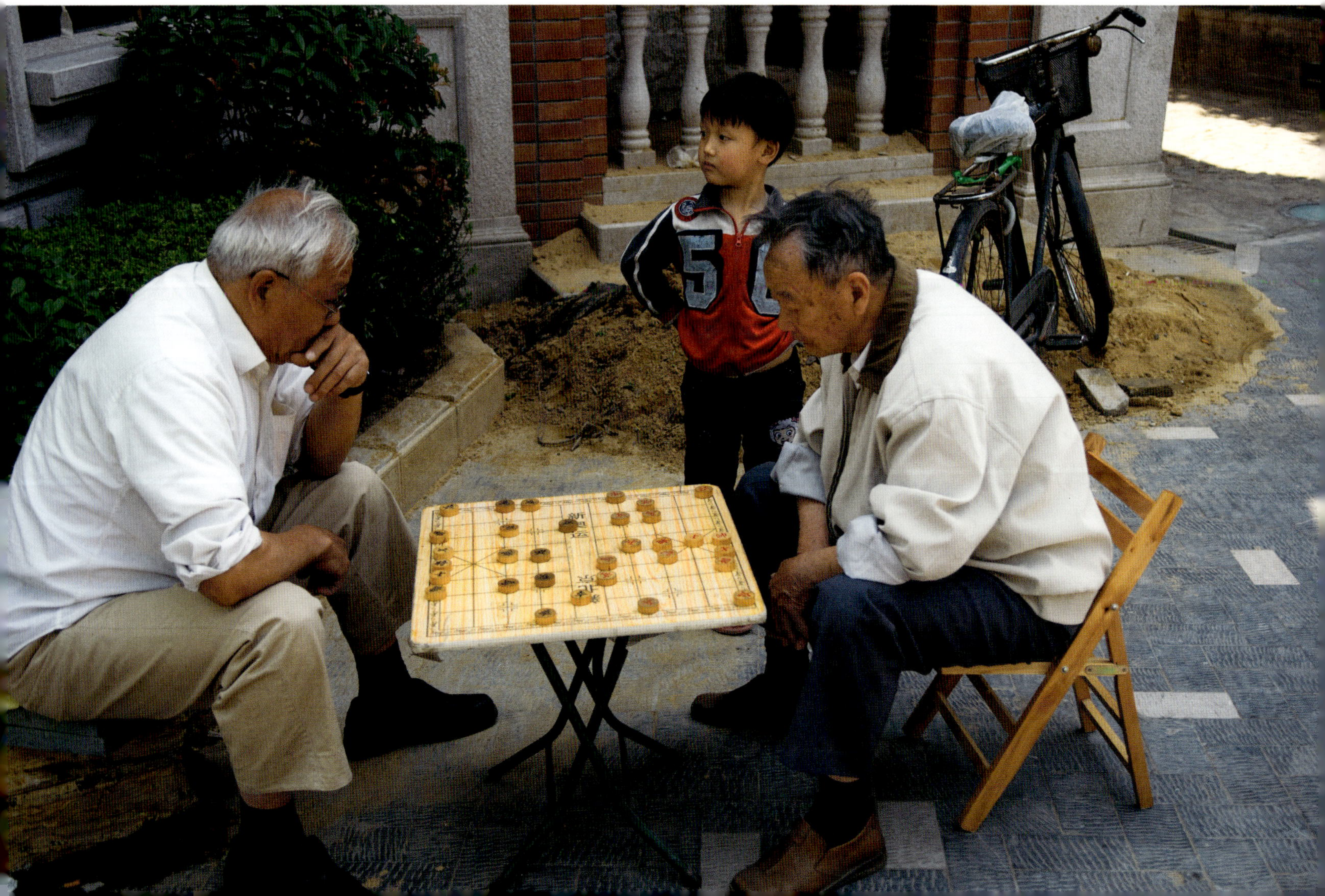

*"I don't know if I would like Shanghai to become
the number one city in the world, but at the very least,
I would like the city to continue to grow in a healthy and
sustainable way." (Ming Yu)*

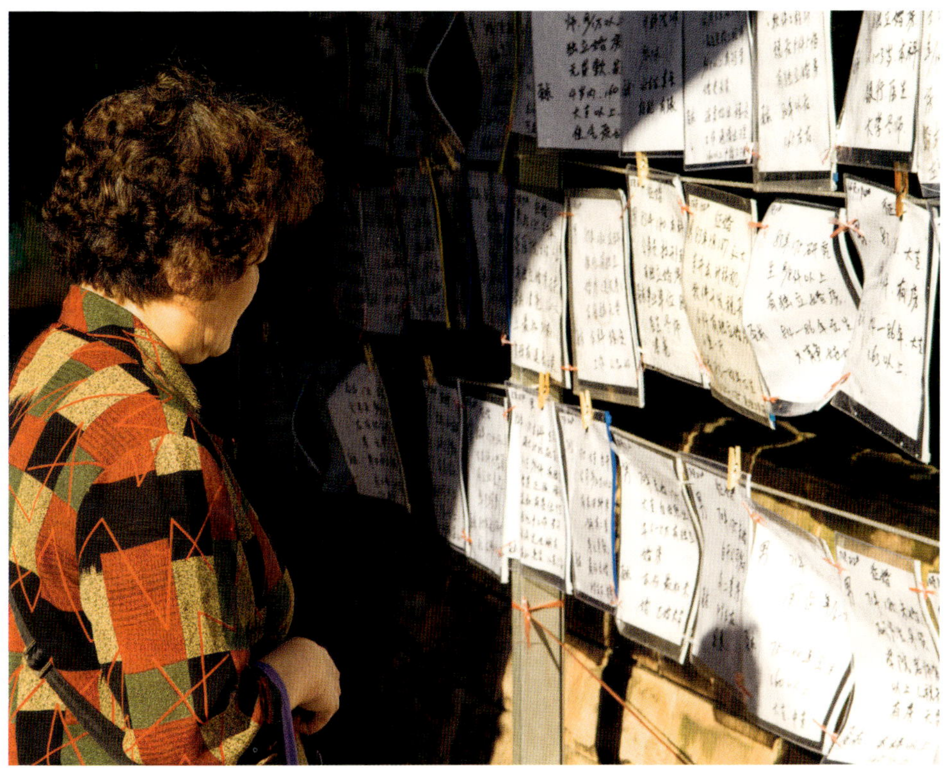

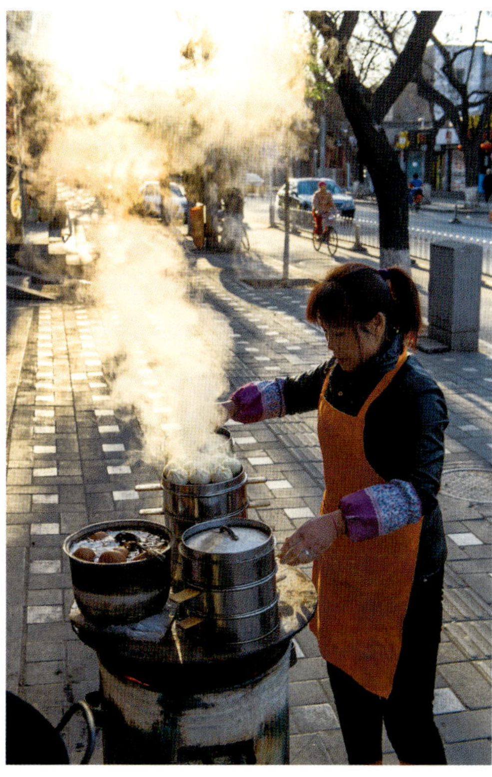

„Ich weiß nicht, ob ich mir
wünsche, dass Shanghai die
Nummer eins unter den Welt-
städten werden soll, aber
mindestens, dass die Stadt
gesund und nachhaltig weiter
wächst." (Ming Yu)

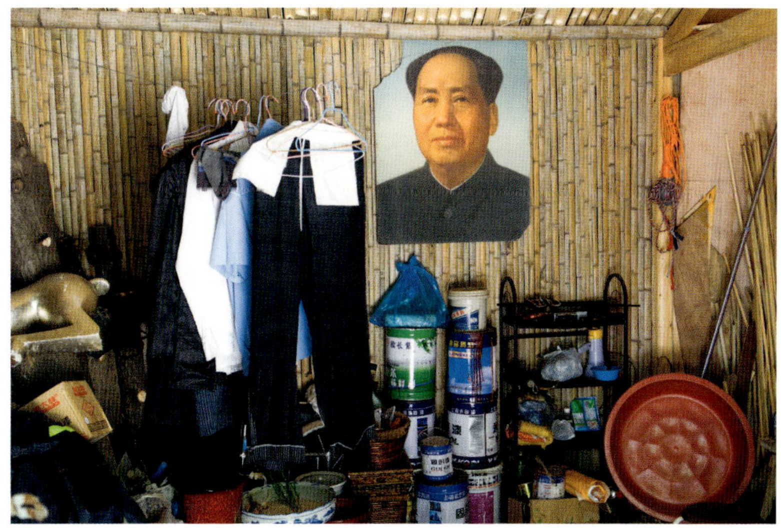

The old "Chinese Old Town" has been almost
completely demolished, but there are still a few
pockets left where life remains tranquil.

Die alte „chinesische Altstadt" wurde fast
vollständig abgerissen, aber noch gibt es ein
paar Winkel voller beschaulichem Leben.

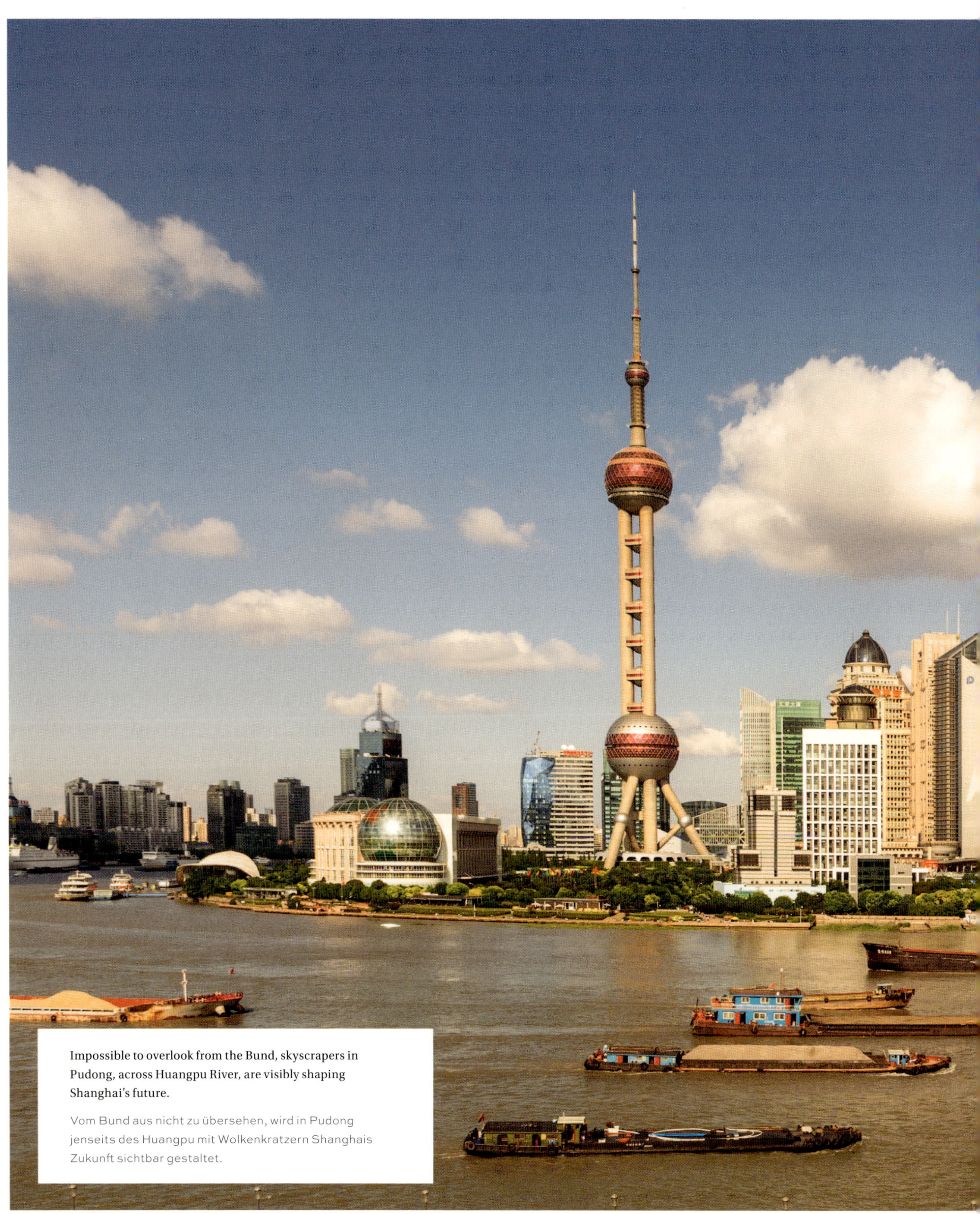

Impossible to overlook from the Bund, skyscrapers in Pudong, across Huangpu River, are visibly shaping Shanghai's future.

Vom Bund aus nicht zu übersehen, wird in Pudong jenseits des Huangpu mit Wolkenkratzern Shanghais Zukunft sichtbar gestaltet.

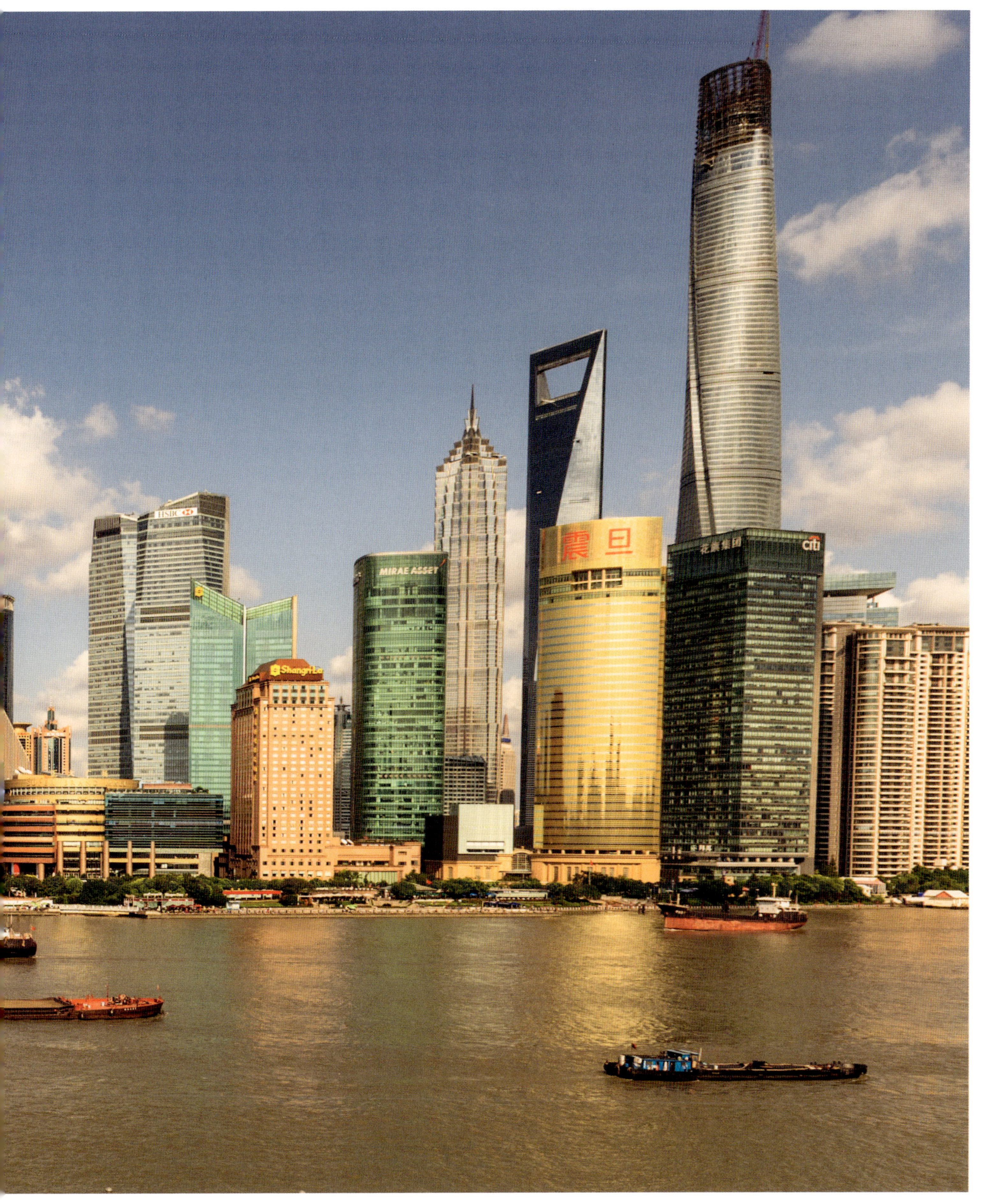

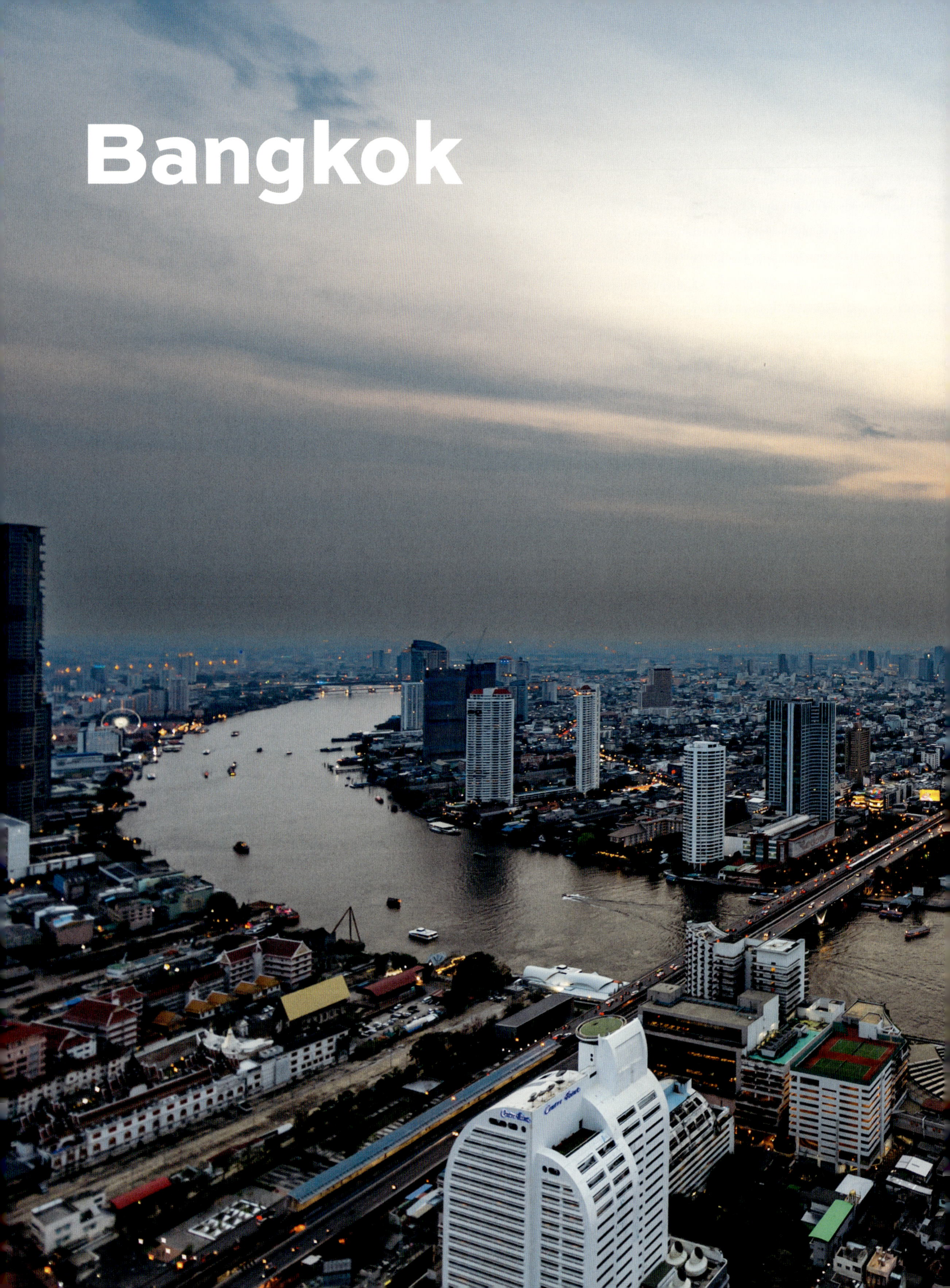

Bangkok

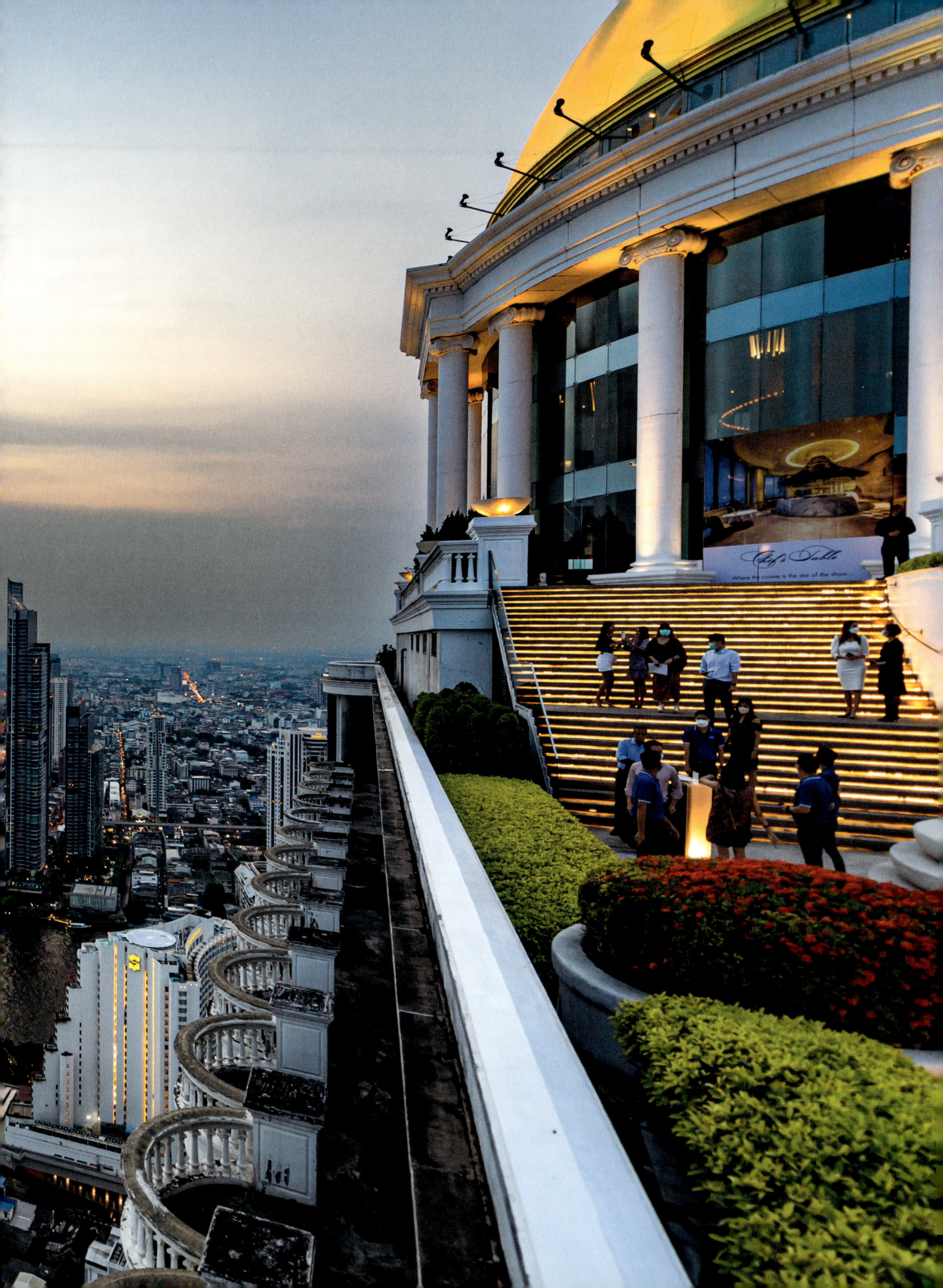

Living Vertically

Leben in der Vertikalen

"And as a city cannot go horizontal, they go vertical, that's very common. The point is going vertical is fine, but we're actually not accepting the landscape's layer, the layer of ecology on the ground. We actually put the concrete all over that layer as well. Humans can go vertical, but humans have to understand that the land is actually bigger than the city. It's not about the city overtaking the land." (Kotchakorn Voraakhom)

It all began in 1782, when King Rama I moved his court to Bangkok, a village on the Chao Phraya River delta. There were no roads, the only transportation routes were the *klongs*, canals winding throughout the entire delta. Life took place on the water, floating markets supplied the population's needs, boats connected the various sections of the city, which was growing at an ever-faster pace. People lived with the water, on the water, and in houses above the water. Regular floods were as much a part of everyday life as rain during the rainy season.

Two hundred years later, all that is beginning to change. Bangkok is growing increasingly faster and higher. Klongs are being filled in by the hundreds, converted into streets, with the remaining canals degenerating into stinking cesspools. Water has become an enemy to be bent to the city's will. The result of this development is a vibrant, modern, cool, colorful, exciting, and, in many areas, still exotic city. But it is now growing upward. The streets are packed with vehicles, and people are relegated to the second, third, fourth floors above the urban canyons. This keeps them dry when the 'ground floor' is flooded yet again.

"I think (…) the temples in the city area are the places that so many people come to, people who had a nightmare, for example, they came from the countryside to find a better job, to seek a better life. And then they were cheated. They're disappointed. They have no hope, no way out for their lives. The first place that they think about, that they think of, is the temple." (Ajahn PM Napan)

„Wenn eine Stadt sich nicht horizontal ausbreiten kann, geht sie in die Vertikale, (…). Vertikal zu gehen ist in Ordnung, aber wir müssen auch die Landschaftsschicht, die Schicht der Ökologie auf dem Boden akzeptieren. Wir bedecken auch diese Schicht mit Beton. Der Mensch kann in die Vertikale gehen, aber er muss verstehen, dass das Land größer ist als die Stadt. Es geht nicht darum, dass die Stadt das Land überwindet." (Kotchakorn Voraakhom)

Alles begann 1782, da verlegte König Rama I. seinen Hof nach Bangkok, ein Dorf im Delta des Menam Chao Phraya, Straßen gab es nicht, die einzigen Transportwege waren die *Klongs*, Kanäle die das gesamte Delta durchzogen. Das Leben spielte sich auf dem Wasser ab, Schwimmende Märkte dienten der Versorgung der Bevölkerung, Boote verbanden die einzelnen, nun immer schneller wachsenden Teile der Stadt. Die Menschen lebten mit dem Wasser, auf dem Wasser und in Häusern über dem Wasser. Regelmäßige Fluten gehörten zum Alltag wie der Regen in der Regenzeit.

Zweihundert Jahre später beginnt sich das alles zu ändern. Bangkok wächst immer schneller und höher. Klongs werden zu Hunderten zugeschüttet und zu Straßen, die verbliebenen Kanäle verkommen zu stinkenden Kloaken. Das Wasser ist zum Feind geworden, den es zu bändigen gilt. Das Ergebnis dieser Entwicklung ist eine lebensfrohe, moderne, coole, bunte, aufregende und in vielen Winkeln immer noch exotische Stadt. Doch nun wächst sie nach oben. Die Straßen sind voller Fahrzeuge, die Menschen werden in die zweite, dritte, vierte Etage über den Straßenschluchten verbannt. So bleiben sie trocken, wenn das „Erdgeschoss" mal wieder überflutet wird.

Not just an icon in name only: The ICONSIAM Mall is considered one of the largest luxury department stores in all of Asia. Its light show is fittingly magnificent.

Nicht nur dem Namen nach eine Ikone: Die ICONSIAM Mall gilt als eines der größten Luxuskaufhäuser ganz Asiens. Entsprechend prunkvoll fällt das Lichterfest aus.

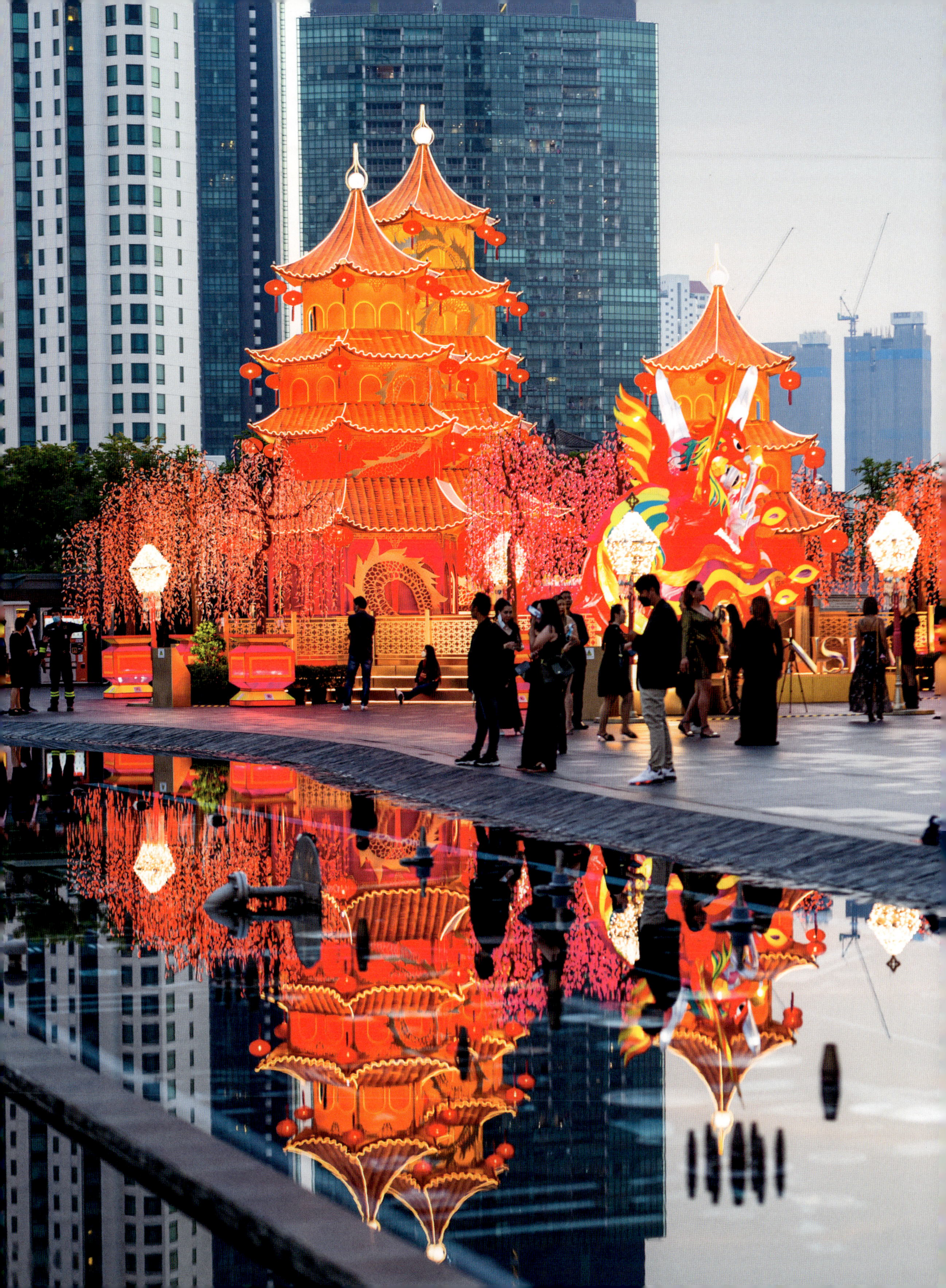

The people who bear the brunt of this development are those living in the slums scattered throughout the city, in the suburbs, along the klongs, and around the railroad tracks. They have no other option. When the floods come, they have to stay in the floodwaters to look after their belongings, their family members. Yet they are the ones who keep the city running, who work in the restaurants, who are literally building Bangkok. These people contribute to the vibrancy of the city with their very energy.

And when that energy needs to be recharged? Then they're off to one of the city's countless temples. These are spiritual "parks" for all those seeking respite in the hustle and bustle of the city. Because real parks have been forgotten. Green sanctuaries are a rarity. Yet green spaces not only serve as public spaces for relaxation and recreation, in Bangkok they also have an important function in regulating the water supply. Like so many cities in delta regions, Bangkok is in danger of sinking.

„Ich denke, (...) die Tempel im Stadtgebiet die Orte, zu denen viele Menschen kommen, die zum Beispiel einen Albtraum hatten, vom Land kamen, um eine bessere Arbeit zu finden, um ein besseres Leben zu suchen. Und dann wurden sie betrogen. Sie sind enttäuscht. Sie haben keine Hoffnung, keinen Ausweg für ihr Leben. Der erste Ort, an den sie denken, ist der Tempel." (Ajahn PM Napan)

Die Leidtragenden dieser Entwicklung sind die Menschen in den überall in der Stadt verteilten Slumvierteln, in den Vorstädten, an den Klongs, entlang der Schienenwege. Denn sie haben keine Wahl. Wenn die Fluten kommen, müssen sie in der Flut bleiben, weil sie sich um ihr Hab und Gut, ihre Familienangehörigen kümmern müssen. Dabei sind nicht zuletzt sie es, die die Stadt am Laufen halten, in den Restaurants arbeiten, die Bangkok buchstäblich erbauen. Diese Menschen tragen mit ihrer Energie zur Lebendigkeit der Stadt bei.

Und wenn die Energie mal aufgeladen werden muss? Dann geht es in einen der zahllosen Tempel der Stadt. Sie sind spirituelle „Parks" für alle, die in der Hektik der Stadt Ruhepunkte suchen. Denn echte Parks wurden einfach vergessen. Grüne Rückzugsorte haben eher Seltenheitswert. Dabei dienen Grünanlagen nicht nur als öffentliche Räume der Entspannung und Erholung, in Bangkok kommt ihnen auch eine wichtige Funktion zur Regulierung des Wasserhaushaltes zu. Wie so viele Städte in Deltaregionen ist nämlich auch Bangkok vom Versinken bedroht.

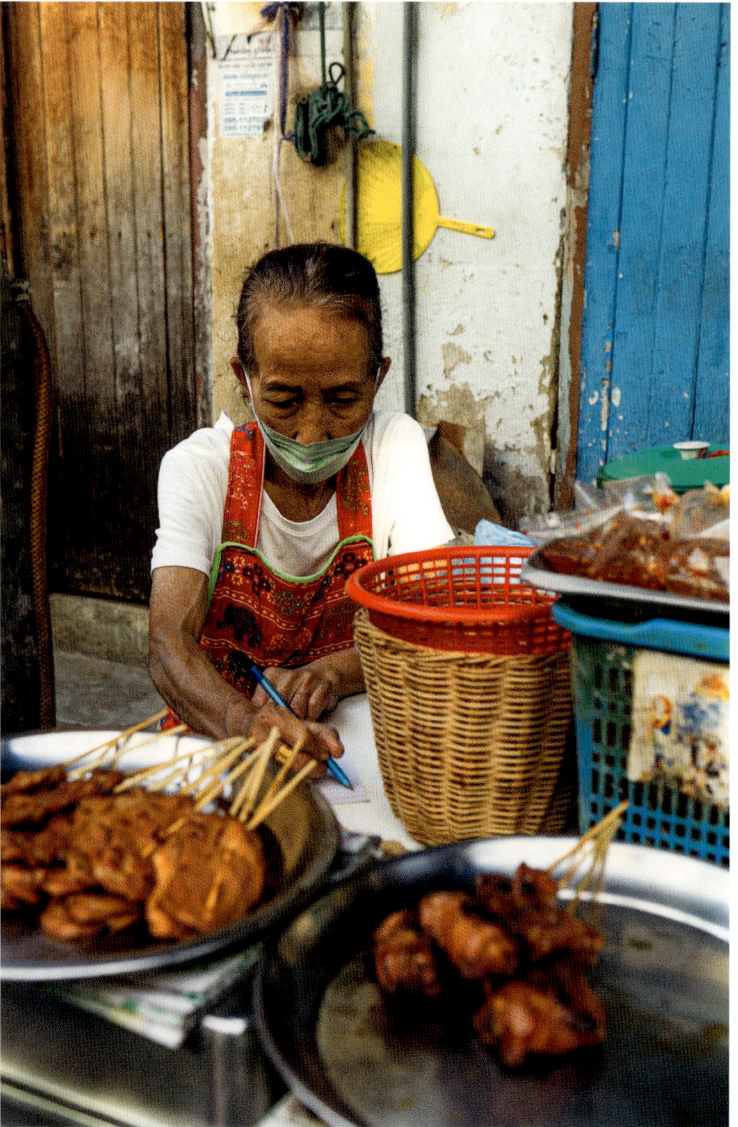

Eat until you can't eat anymore. It feels like you have the chance to sample little tidbits everywhere you go all day long.

Essen bis zum Abwinken. Gefühlt kann man überall den ganzen Tag Kleinigkeiten kosten.

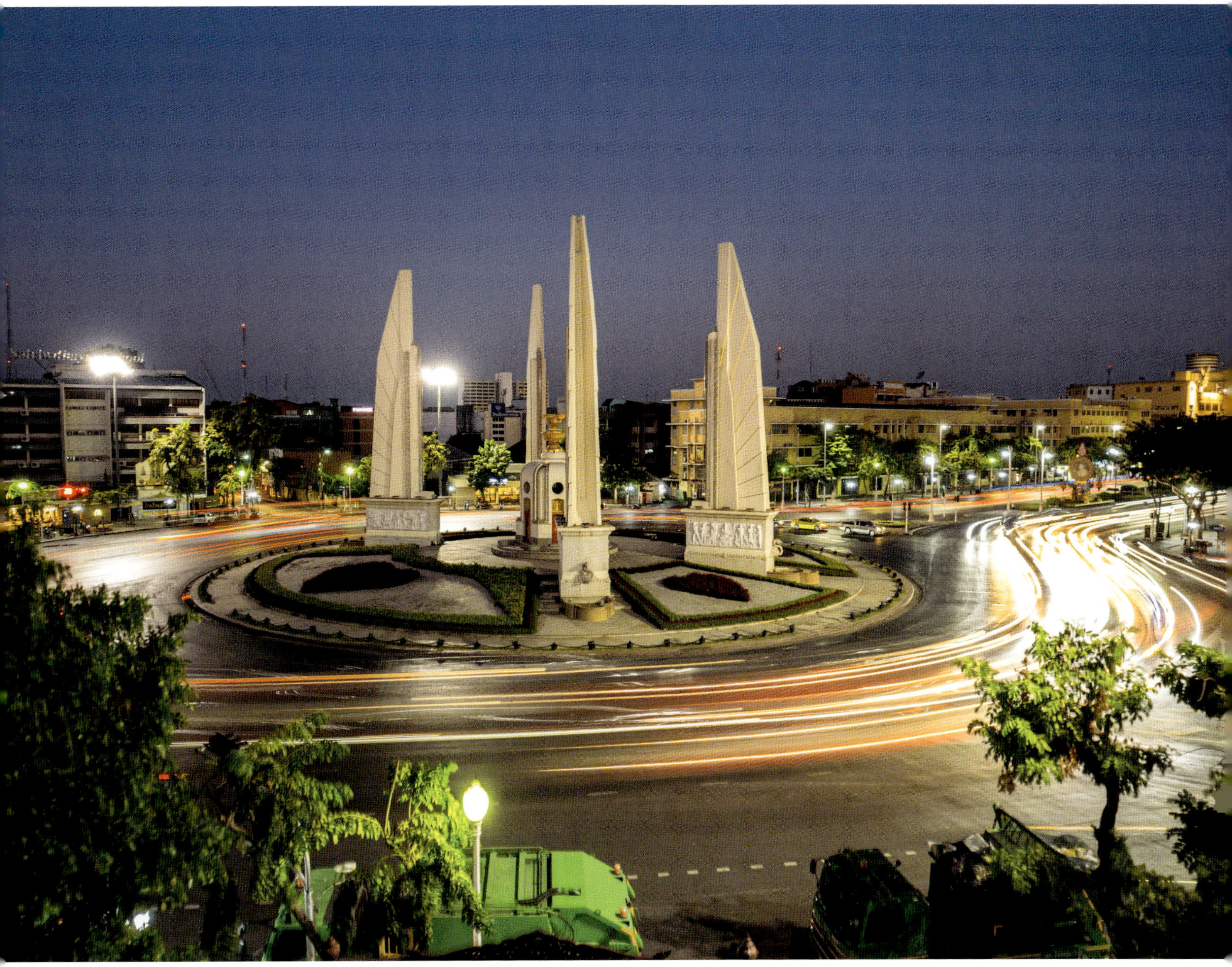

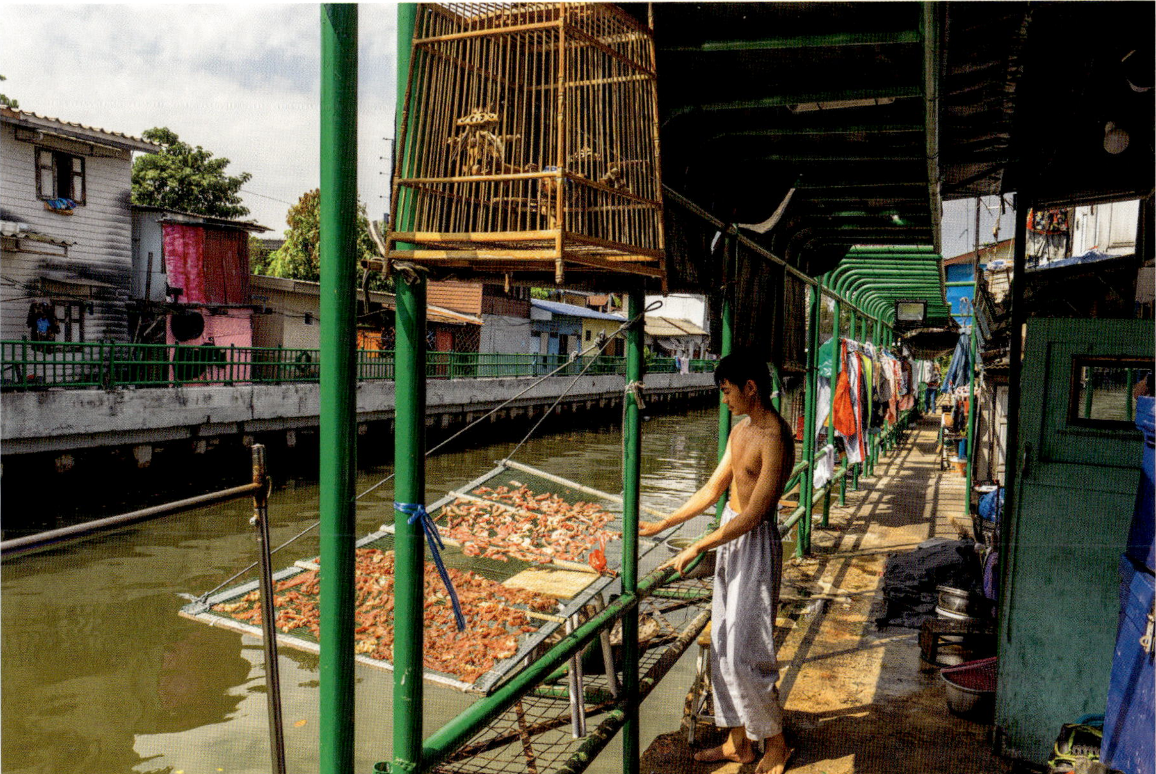

True democracy or just a facade?
The four wings of the Democracy
Monument symbolize the Thai military.
The shrimper likely has more
day-to-day issues to deal with.

Echte Demokratie oder Fassade? Die
vier Flügel des Democracy Monument
stehen für das thailändische Militär.
Für den Krabbenfischer stellen sich
wohl eher alltäglichere Fragen.

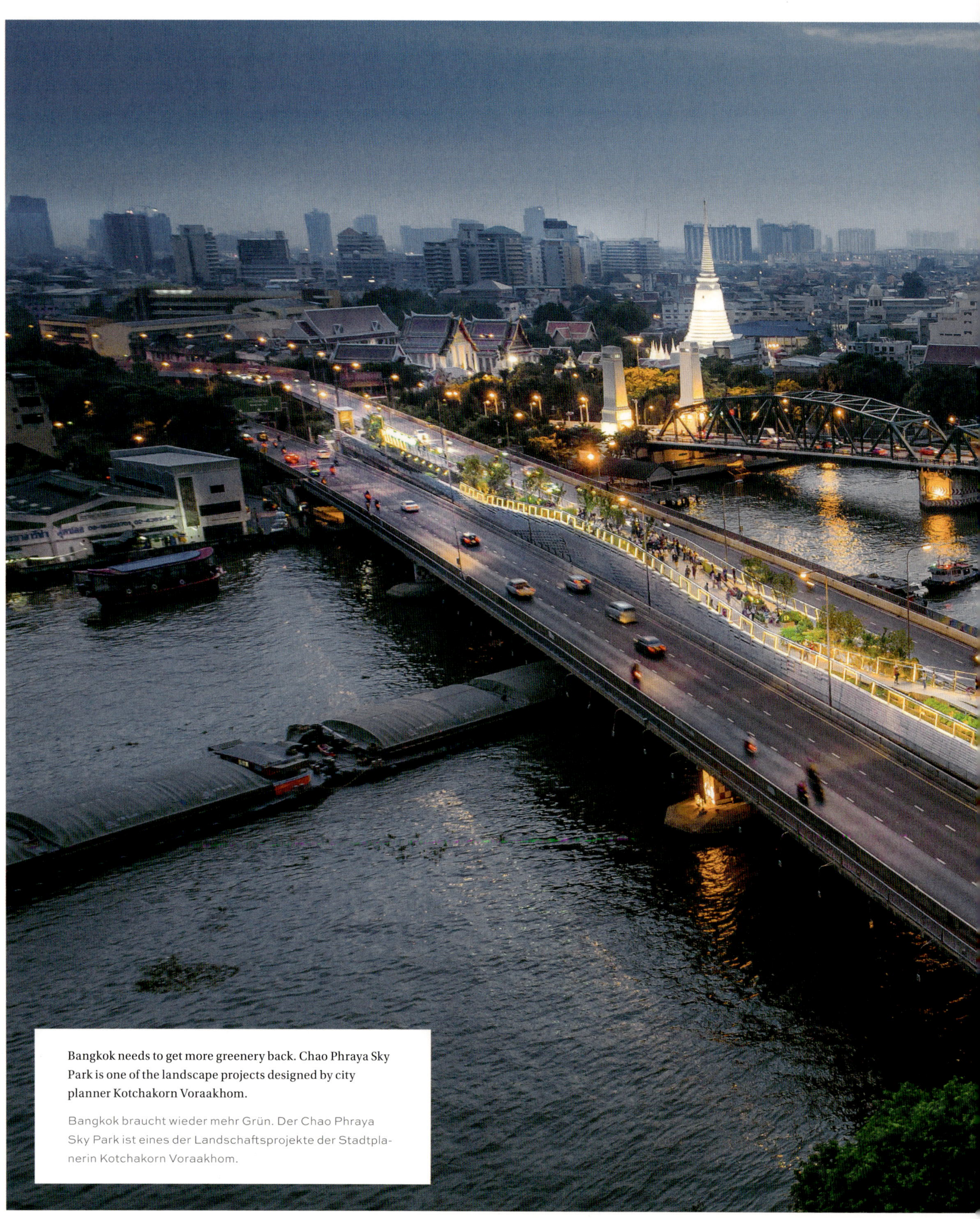

Bangkok needs to get more greenery back. Chao Phraya Sky
Park is one of the landscape projects designed by city
planner Kotchakorn Voraakhom.

Bangkok braucht wieder mehr Grün. Der Chao Phraya
Sky Park ist eines der Landschaftsprojekte der Stadtplanerin Kotchakorn Voraakhom.

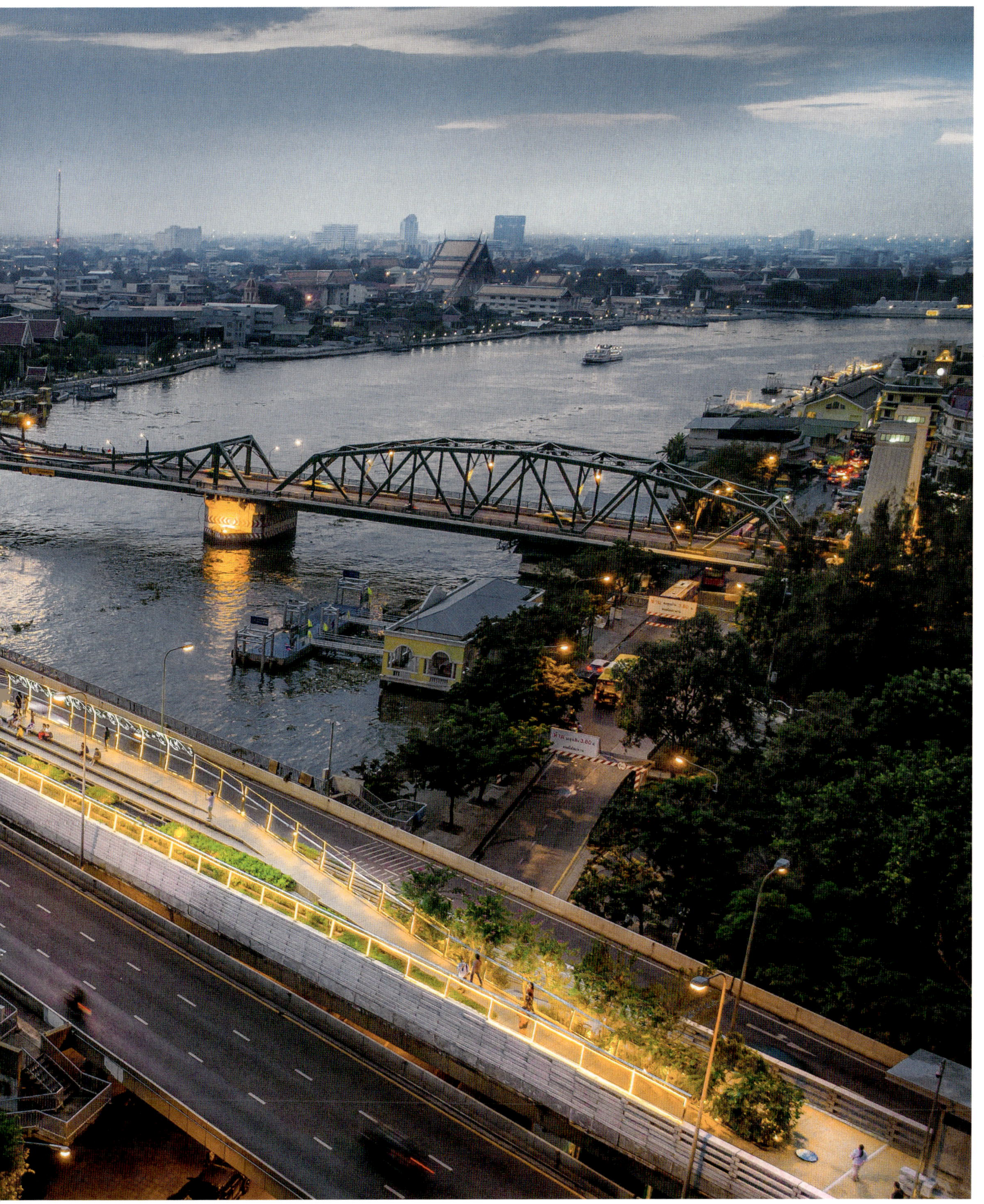

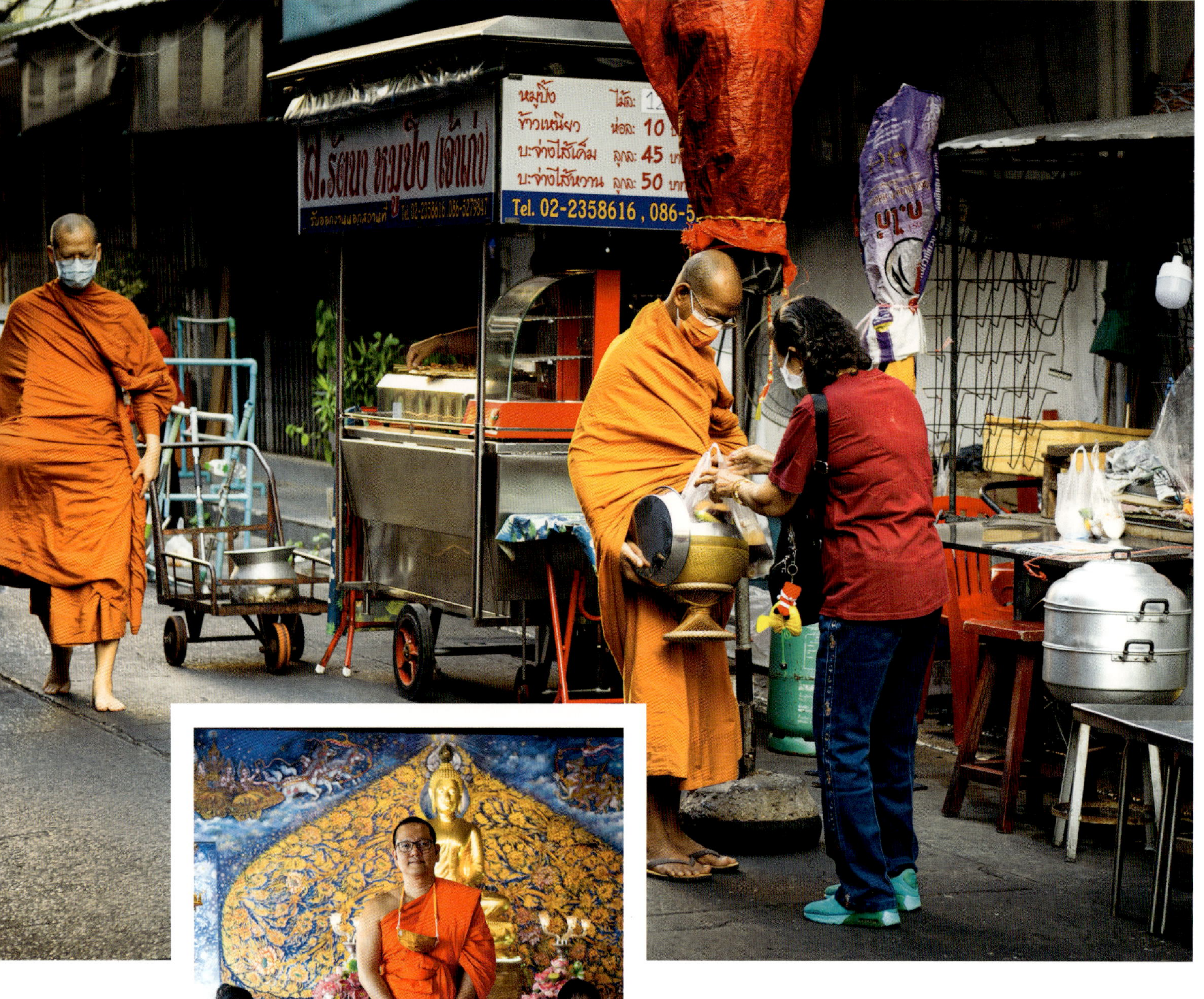

AJAHN PM NAPAN

DEPUTY ABBOT OF
WAT SAKET

STELLVERTRETENDER
ABT VON WAT SAKET

...ON THE IMPORTANCE OF TEMPLES

"I think in the past the temple was the center of the community. We have a specific time for men to become a monk for three months, kind of in the culture of tradition. Because of that, people from their families come to the temple to learn how to take care of the monk and the religion. And because of that, they learn to take care of themselves. But right now, because of the modern era or because of globalization, right now we have maybe just two weeks to become a monk and learn about everything, which is not enough to feel it inside (...) I think if we can improve this situation by maybe bring the temple to a virtual space through Facebook, to platforms on social media, and then make it a part of daily life for everyone, they can reach that inner peace and also create an outer peace for themselves. I think this way we can bring the physical and also virtual space together, to achieve a peaceful space inside our homes."

"I think the most important thing that temples can provide for people who are stressed in the modern age is how to pause, how to take a deep breath and stay focused on your breath. We call that mindfulness. And not just only mentally, also physically as well.

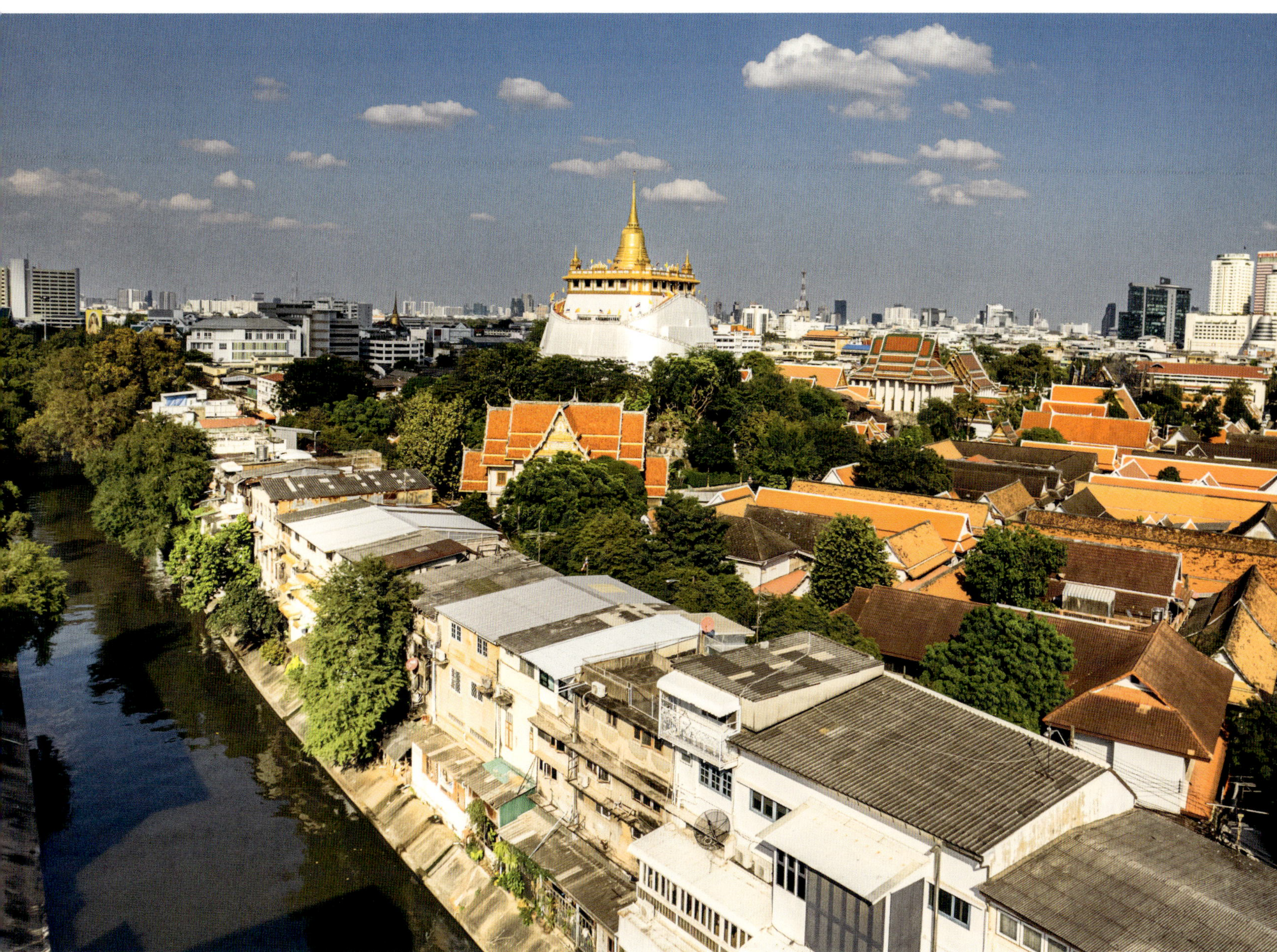

Because when you enter the area of the temple, you can feel the sense of calmness and mindfulness and peacefulness. And I think this is kind of a spiritual park for people who live in the city."

...ÜBER DIE BEDEUTUNG DER TEMPEL

„Ich glaube, in der Vergangenheit war der Tempel das Zentrum der Gemeinschaft. So haben wir für Männer die Tradition, für drei Monate ein Mönch zu werden. Aus diesem Grund kommen auch die Mitglieder ihrer Familien in den Tempel und lernen, wie sie sich um die Mönche und die Religion kümmern müssen. Und dadurch lernen sie, für sich selbst zu sorgen. Aber jetzt, aufgrund der modernen Ära oder der Globalisierung, haben wir nur vielleicht zwei Wochen Zeit, um Mönch zu werden und alles zu lernen. Das reicht nicht aus, um einen inneren Zugang zu bekommen (...). Ich denke also, wenn wir diese Situation verbessern können, indem wir den Tempel in den virtuellen Raum bringen, über Facebook, über Plattformen in den sozialen Medien, und ihn dann zum täglichen Leben eines jeden machen, können sie diesen inneren Frieden erreichen und auch einen äußeren Frieden für sich selbst schaffen. Ich denke also, dass wir auf diese Weise den physischen und den virtuellen Raum zusammenbringen können, um einen friedlichen Raum in unserem Haus zu schaffen."

„Ich denke, das Wichtigste, was die Tempel Menschen bieten können, die in der modernen Zeit gestresst sind, ist, innezuhalten, tief einzuatmen und sich auf den Atem zu konzentrieren. Wir nennen das Achtsamkeit. Und zwar nicht nur geistig, sondern auch körperlich. Denn wenn man den Bereich des Tempels betritt, spürt man das Gefühl von Ruhe, Achtsamkeit und Frieden. Und ich denke, das ist eine Art spiritueller Park für Menschen, die in der Stadt leben."

The daily practice of alms giving is an important part of the life of the monks, as well as for the givers and followers of Theravada Buddhism.

Der tägliche Almosengang ist ein wichtiger Bestandteil im Leben der Mönche, aber auch für die Spender und Anhänger des Theravada-Buddhismus.

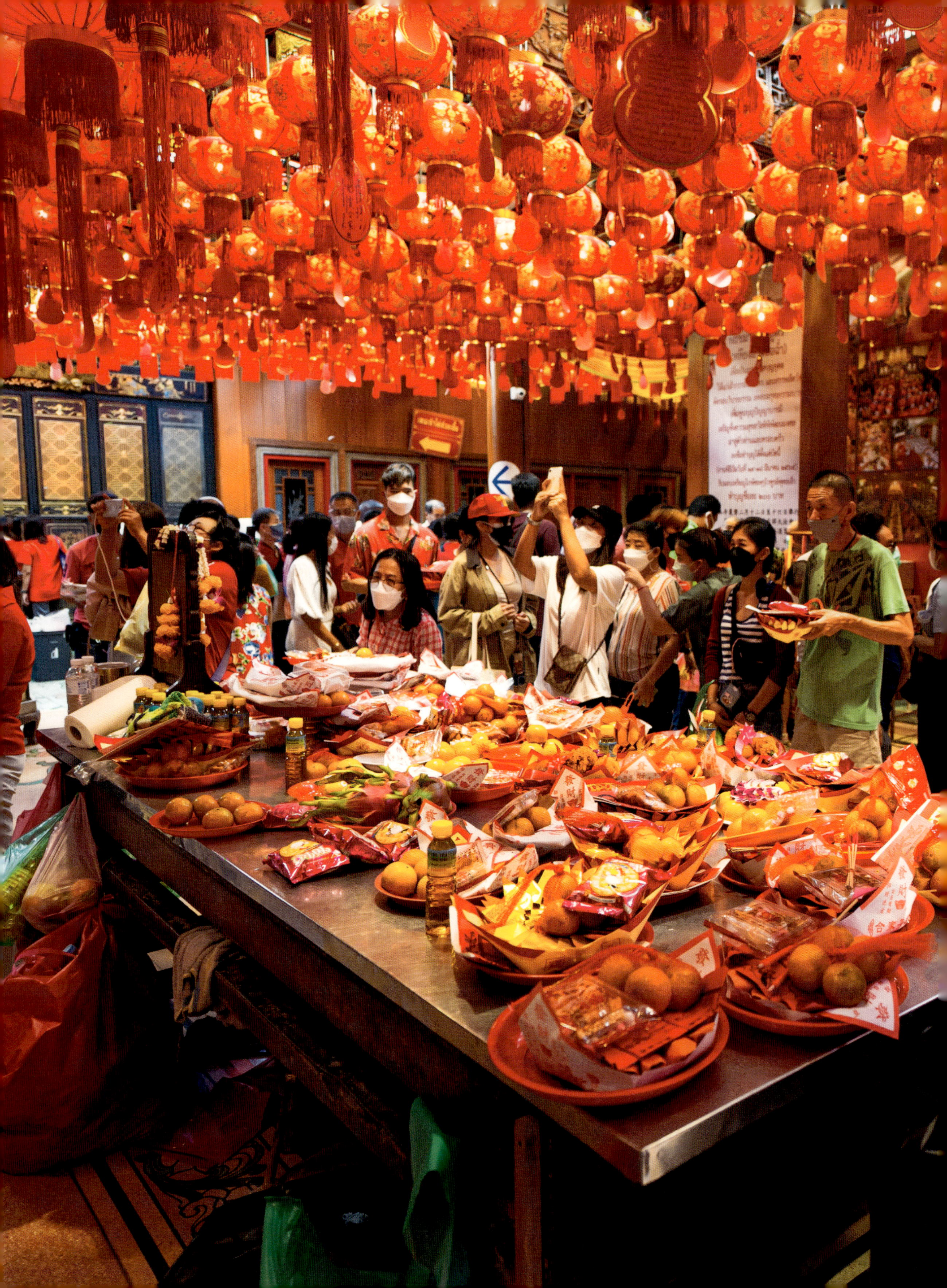

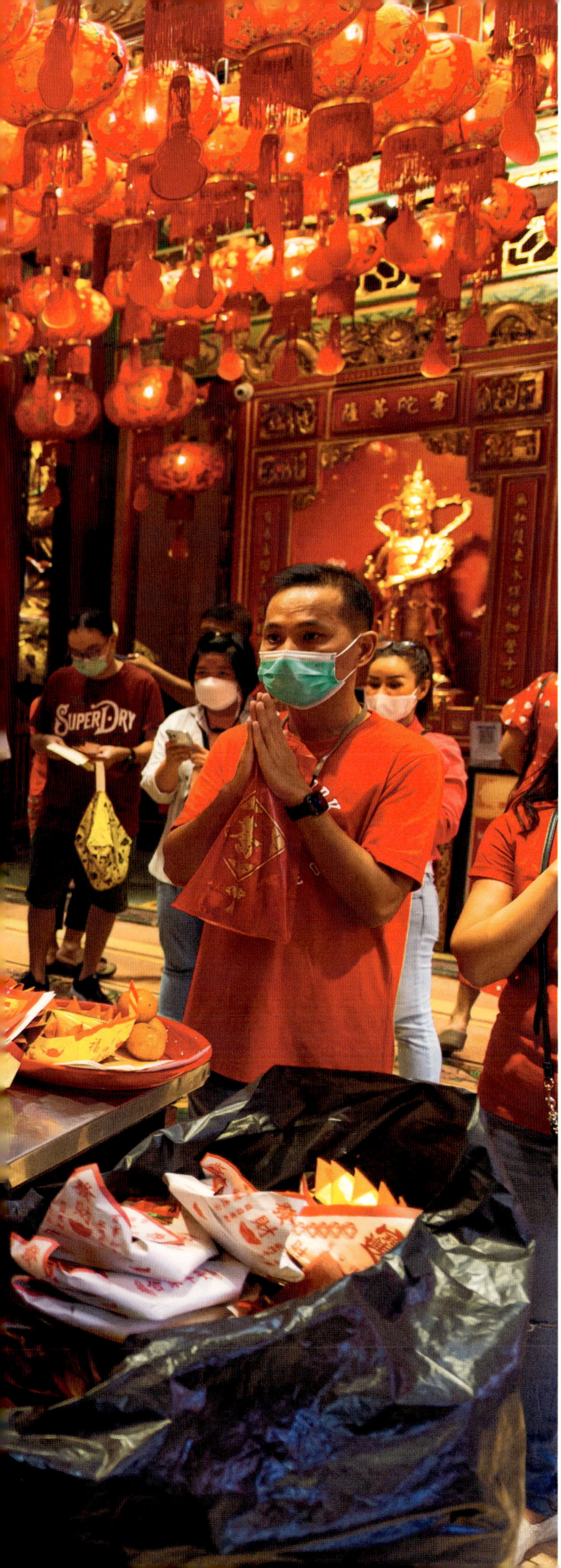

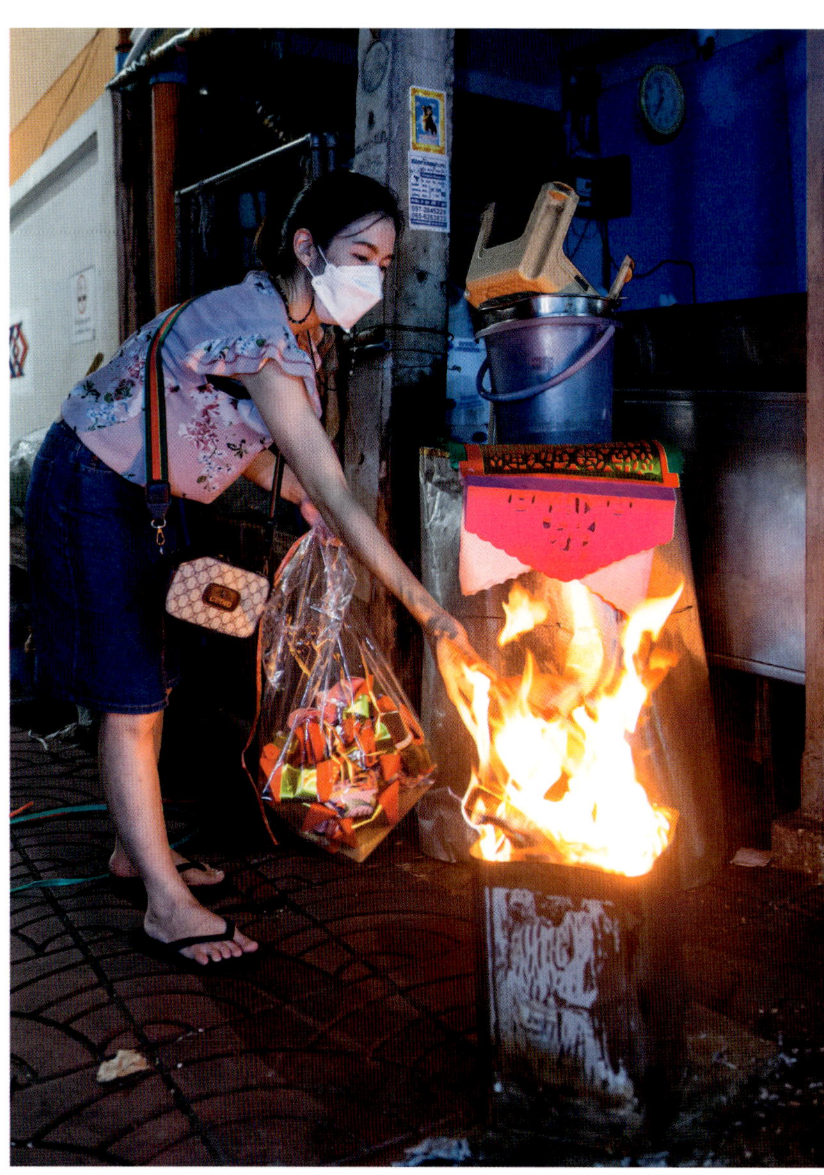

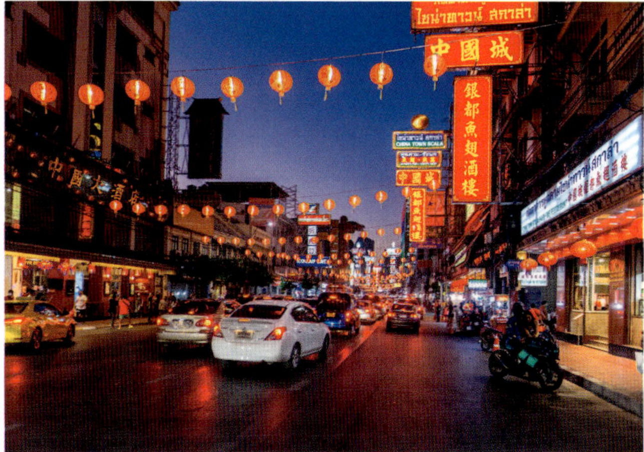

A feast for the deities, for the eyes, and for the believers. Sacrifices are made before the New Year's Eve meal of the Chinese New Year for good luck and wealth in the coming year.

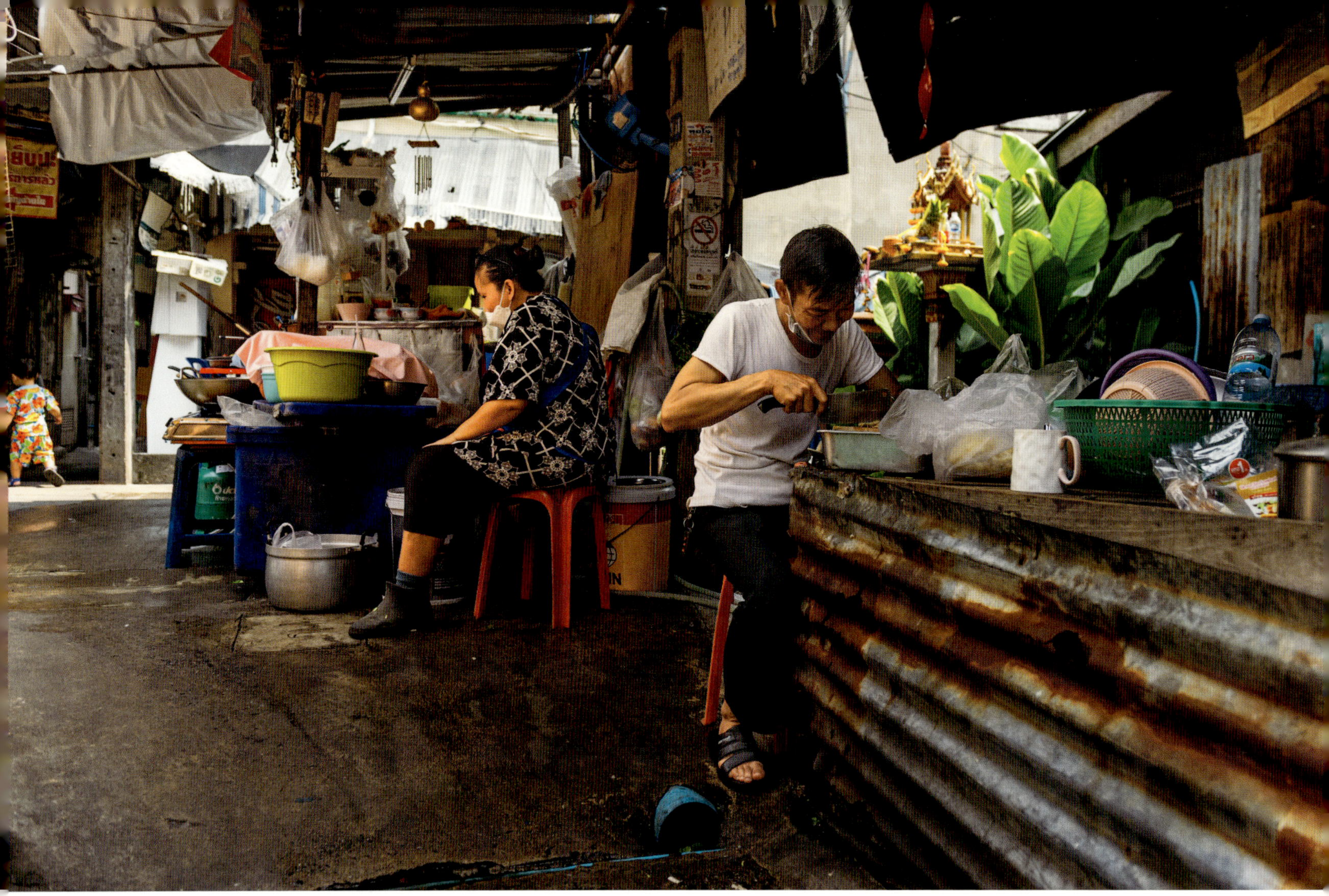

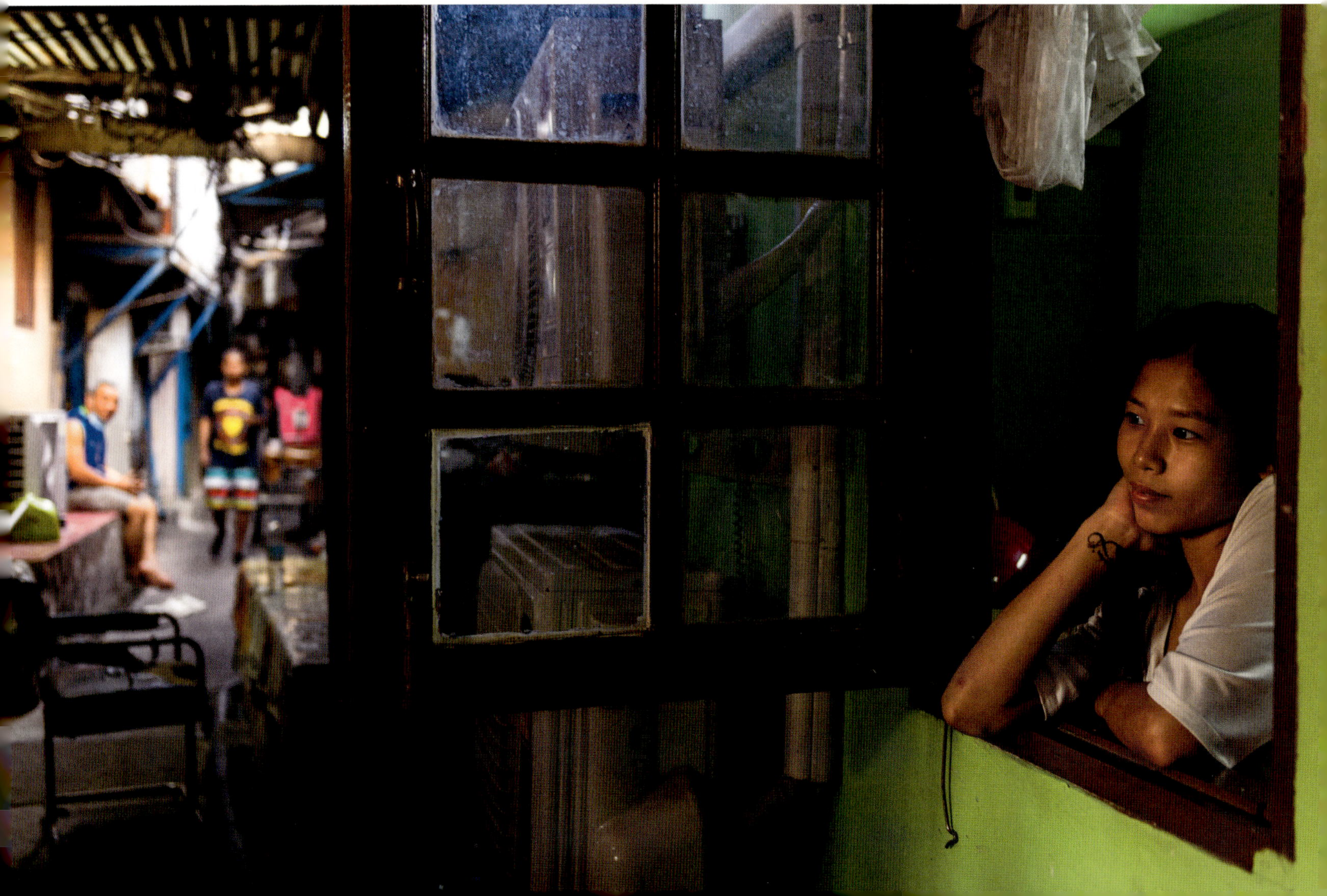

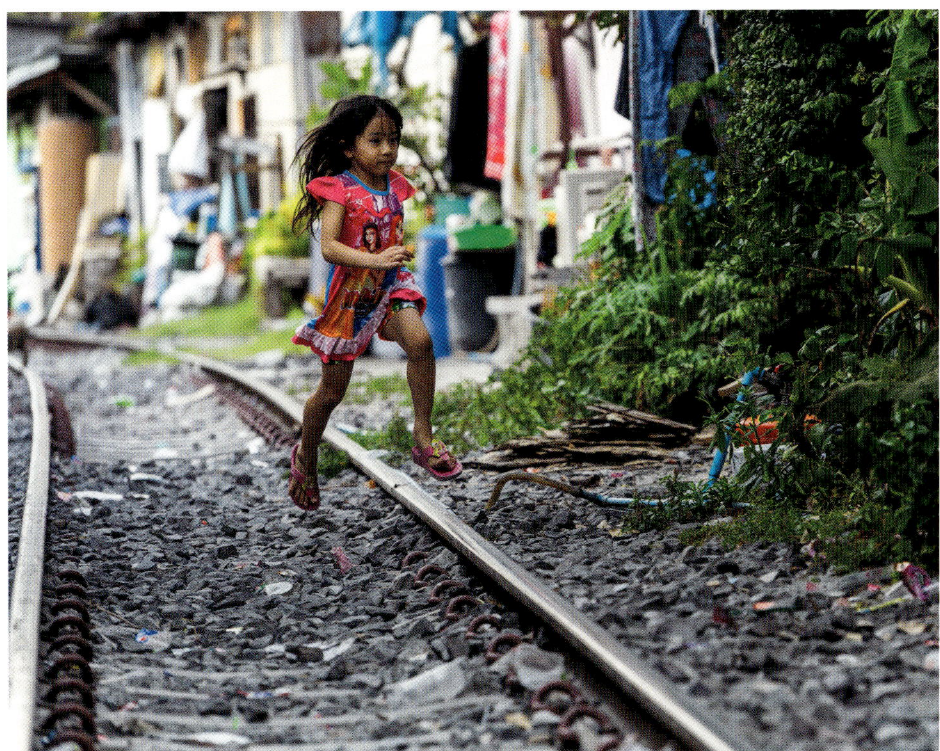

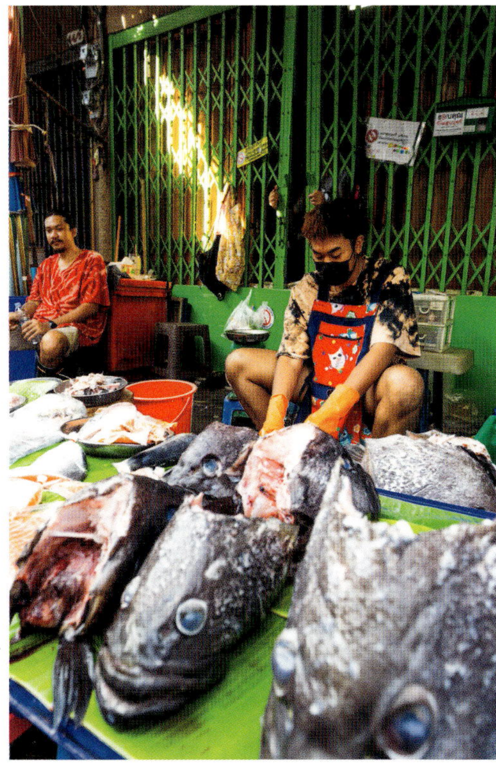

„Selbst wenn Sie etwas verlieren, atmen die Menschen noch. Sie haben ihr Leben noch nicht verloren. Also lassen Sie sich das von niemandem nehmen."
(Ajahn PM Napan)

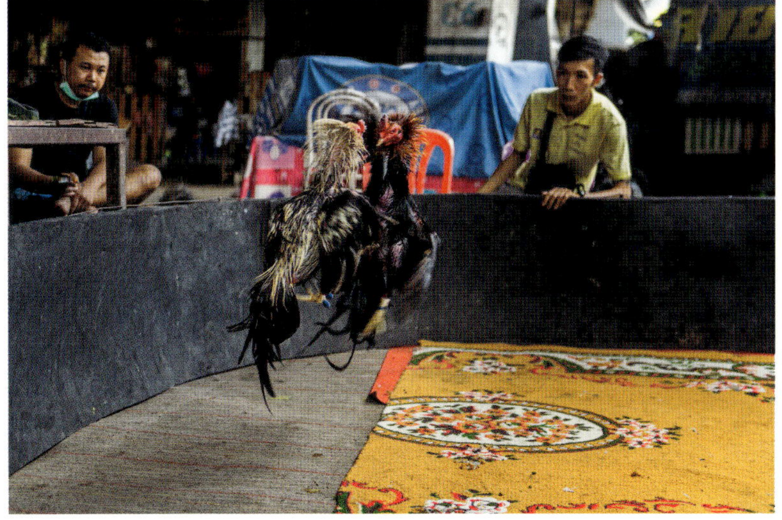

Life in the slums is a daily struggle, but the demand for cheap labor is creating more and more illegal and precarious makeshift dwellings.

Das Leben in den Slums ist ein täglicher Kampf, doch die Nachfrage nach billigen Arbeitskräften lässt immer mehr illegale prekäre Behausungen entstehen.

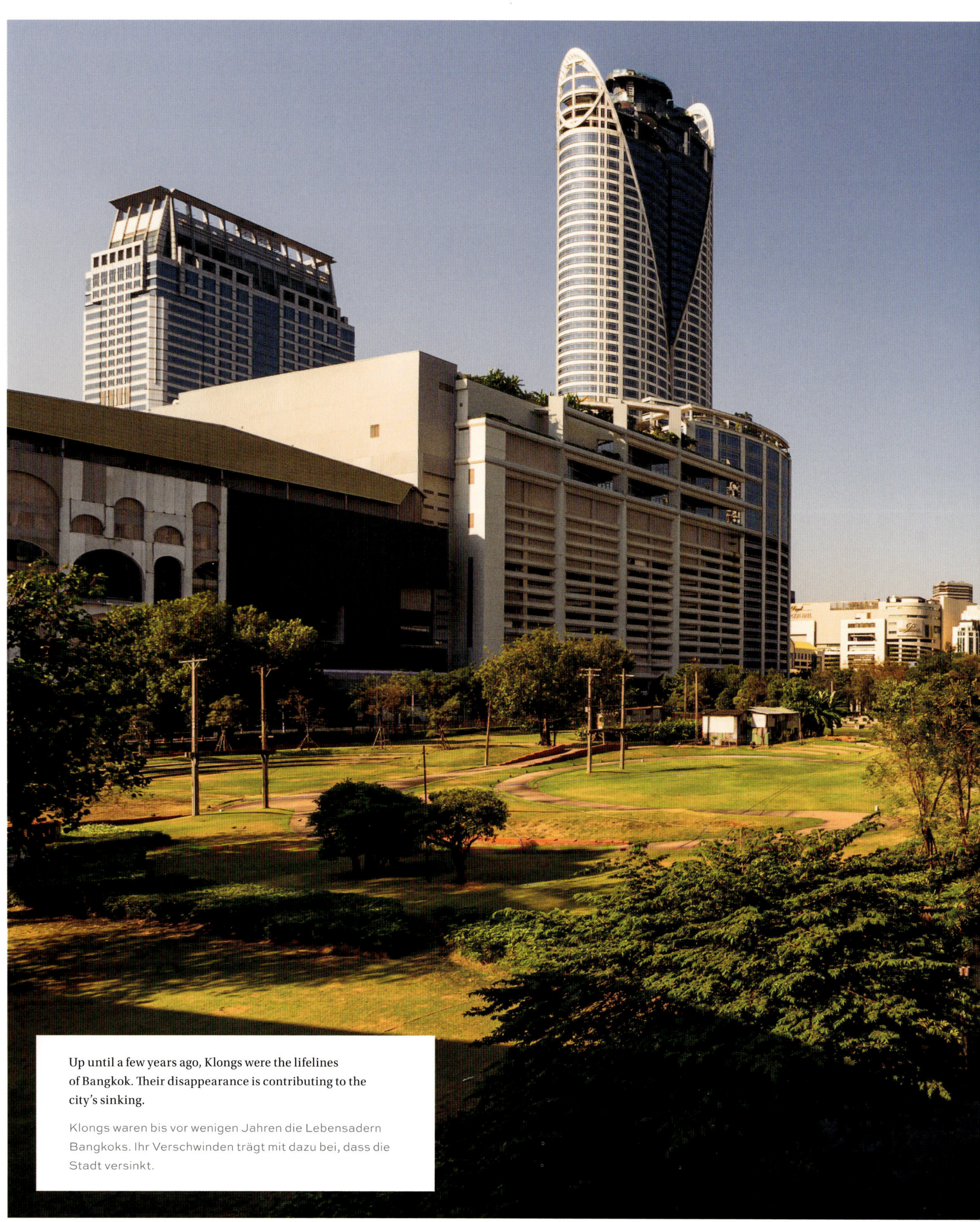

Up until a few years ago, Klongs were the lifelines of Bangkok. Their disappearance is contributing to the city's sinking.

Klongs waren bis vor wenigen Jahren die Lebensadern Bangkoks. Ihr Verschwinden trägt mit dazu bei, dass die Stadt versinkt.

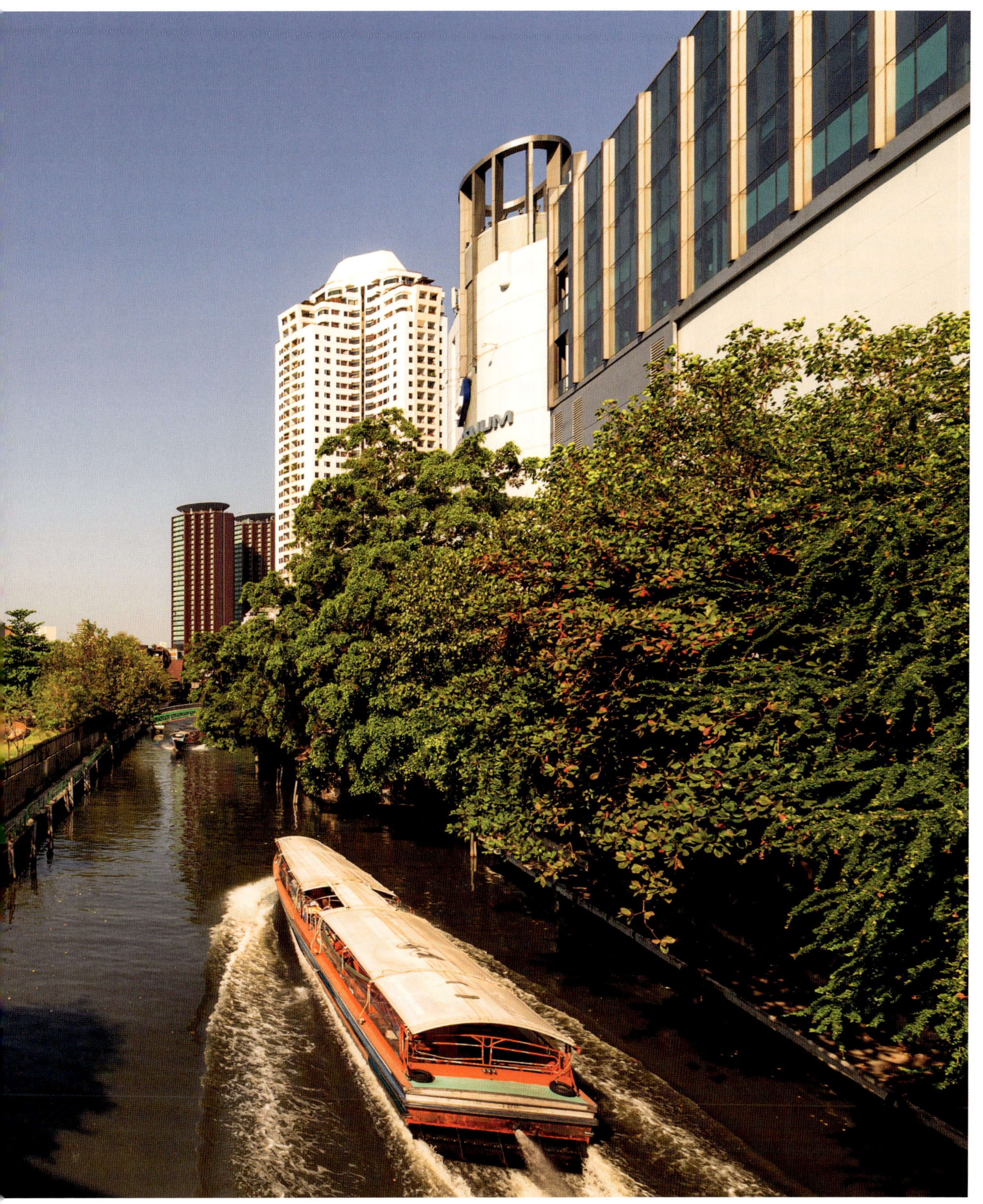

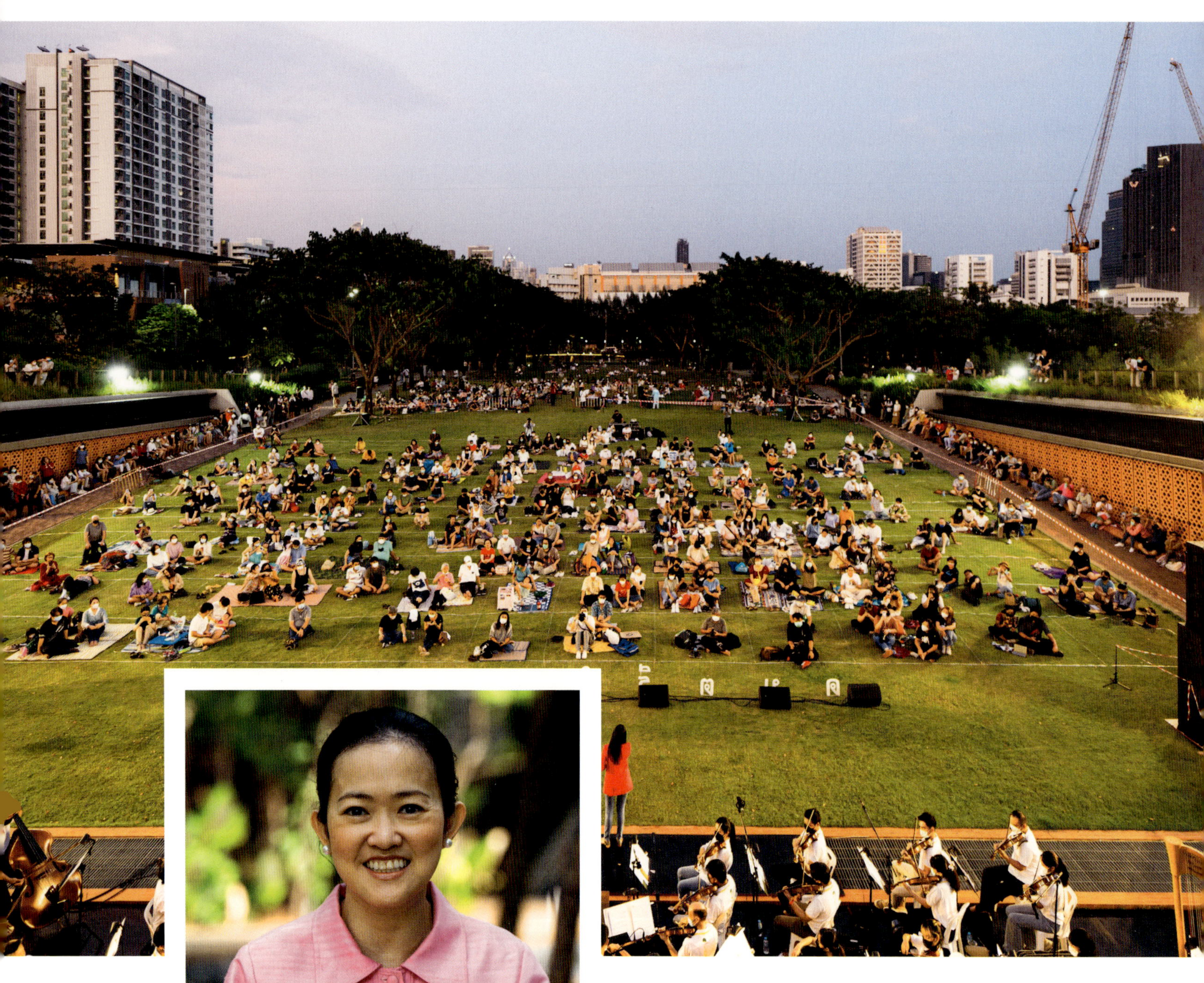

KOTCHAKORN VORAAKHOM
CITY PLANNER
STADTPLANERIN

A major success: Kotchakorn Voraakhom won the tender to redesign CU Centenary Park based on ecological criteria.

Ein großer Erfolg: Kotchakorn Voraakhom gewann die Ausschreibung für die Neugestaltung des CU Centenary Park nach ökologischen Kriterien.

...ON THE IMPORTANCE OF THE KLONGS

"Canals are life, canals are part of food, canals are part of transportation. But 100 years ago, city planning changed, and we are so focused on automobiles and buildings, we're actually turning our back on the canals. Nowadays when you want to see a canal, it doesn't feel like it's actually part of the city. And don't forget that we used to be called the Venice of the East. We used to have more than 2,000 canals. But nowadays there are only 1,300 left, and they are covered in concrete (...) And we have to understand the dynamic of the landscape, the flood season, the flow of the water, the green surfaces that we need to breathe. And all those infrastructures have been forgotten, have been destroyed for decades."

... ON THE JOY OF BEING A CITY PLANNER

"As a child I loved to see all the cracks in the concrete and all these little plants sneaking out from that pattern of cracks. And I thought, these are such lovely friends or lovely creatures that were actually part of my playground. I would imagine breaking up all these areas, and maybe expanding the selection of these plants. This was actually my wishful thinking when I was young. But now that I have become a landscape architect, I'm actually breaking up a bigger piece of the city's concrete. And I actually relate this to that experience of playing in my past. It's just so connected, unplanned or unexpected. And my being a landscape architect is actually turning the city back into my playground."

...ON WHAT CLIMATE CHANGE MEANS FOR BANGKOK

"The whole city is actually vulnerable, you know, Bangkok is on top of the list of cities at risk when it comes to flooding and water, and when it comes to climate change. So as a population we are all vulnerable. (...) Of course, there are areas that flood first or are impacted by climate change before other areas in this wetland. Big wetlands. Bangkok is a big wetland. The most vulnerable people are actually those who live in informal settlements or slums, because they live next to the canals or waterways, and it is actually the flood of the runoff from the city that goes into the river. And it doesn't mean that those who live in a high-rise and many other small places that seem safe are safe, because Bangkok is very flat. When it floods, when it rains, it actually creates flash floods, and the whole city actually shuts down in 20 or 30 minutes. We are all vulnerable."

...ÜBER DIE BEDEUTUNG DER KLONGS

„Der Kanal ist Leben, der Kanal ist Teil der Ernährung, der Kanal ist Teil des Verkehrs. Aber vor 100 Jahren hat sich die Stadtplanung geändert, und wir haben uns so sehr auf Autos und Gebäude konzentriert, dass wir dem Kanal den Rücken zugekehrt haben. Wenn man heutzutage einen Kanal sehen will, hat man nicht das Gefühl, dass er wirklich Teil der Stadt ist. Und vergessen Sie nicht, dass wir früher ‚Venedig des Ostens' genannt wurden. Früher hatten wir mehr als 2 000 Kanäle. Aber heute sind es nur noch 1 300, und die sind von einer Betondecke überdeckt. (...) Doch wir müssen die Dynamik der Landschaft verstehen, die Überschwemmungssaison, den Fluss des Wassers, die grüne Oberfläche, die wir zum Atmen brauchen. Und all diese Infrastrukturen wurden vergessen und jahrzehntelang zerstört."

...ÜBER DIE FREUDE, STADTPLANERIN ZU SEIN

„Als Kind liebte ich es, die Risse im Beton zu sehen und all die kleinen Pflanzen, die aus den Rissen herauskriechen. Und ich dachte, das sind so nette Freunde oder nette Kreaturen, und die sind tatsächlich Teil meines Spielplatzes. Ich stellte mir vor, all diese Flächen zu knacken und damit vielleicht die Auswahl dieser Pflanzen zu vergrößern. Das war eigentlich meine Fantasie, als ich jung war. Aber jetzt, wo ich Landschaftsarchitektin bin, breche ich tatsächlich größere Stücke Beton in der Stadt auf. Und ich beziehe mich tatsächlich auf diese Spieler-

fahrung in der Vergangenheit. Und es ist einfach so verbindend, ungeplant oder unerwartet. Und Landschaftsarchitektin zu sein bedeutet, dass ich die Stadt wieder zu meinem Spielplatz mache."

...ÜBER DEN KLIMAWANDEL FÜR BANGKOK

„Die ganze Stadt ist gefährdet, wenn man weiß, dass Bangkok auf der Liste der gefährdeten Städte ganz oben steht, wenn es um Überschwemmungen und Wasser geht und wenn es um den Klimawandel geht. Als Bevölkerung sind wir also alle gefährdet. (...) Aber natürlich gibt es Gebiete, die zuerst überflutet werden oder von den Auswirkungen des Klimawandels früher betroffen sind als andere Gebiete in diesem Feuchtgebiet. Große Feuchtgebiete. Bangkok ist ein großes Feuchtgebiet. Die am meisten gefährdeten Menschen sind also diejenigen, die in informellen Siedlungen oder Slums leben, weil sie neben den Kanälen oder Wasserstraßen leben, dem Abfluss aus der Stadt, der in den Fluss fließt. Und das bedeutet nicht, dass diejenigen, die in einem Hochhaus oder an einem anderen scheinbar sicheren Ort leben es auch sind, denn Bangkok ist sehr flach. Wenn es also zu einer Überschwemmung kommt, wenn es regnet, kommt es zu einer Sturzflut und die ganze Stadt wird innerhalb von 20 oder 30 Minuten geflutet. Wir sind also alle verwundbar."

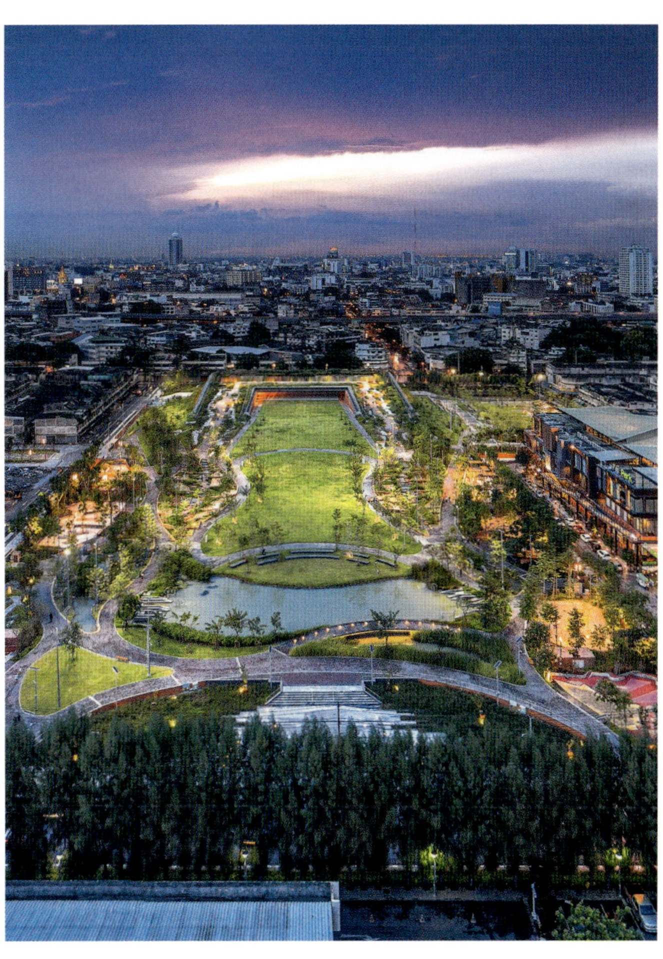

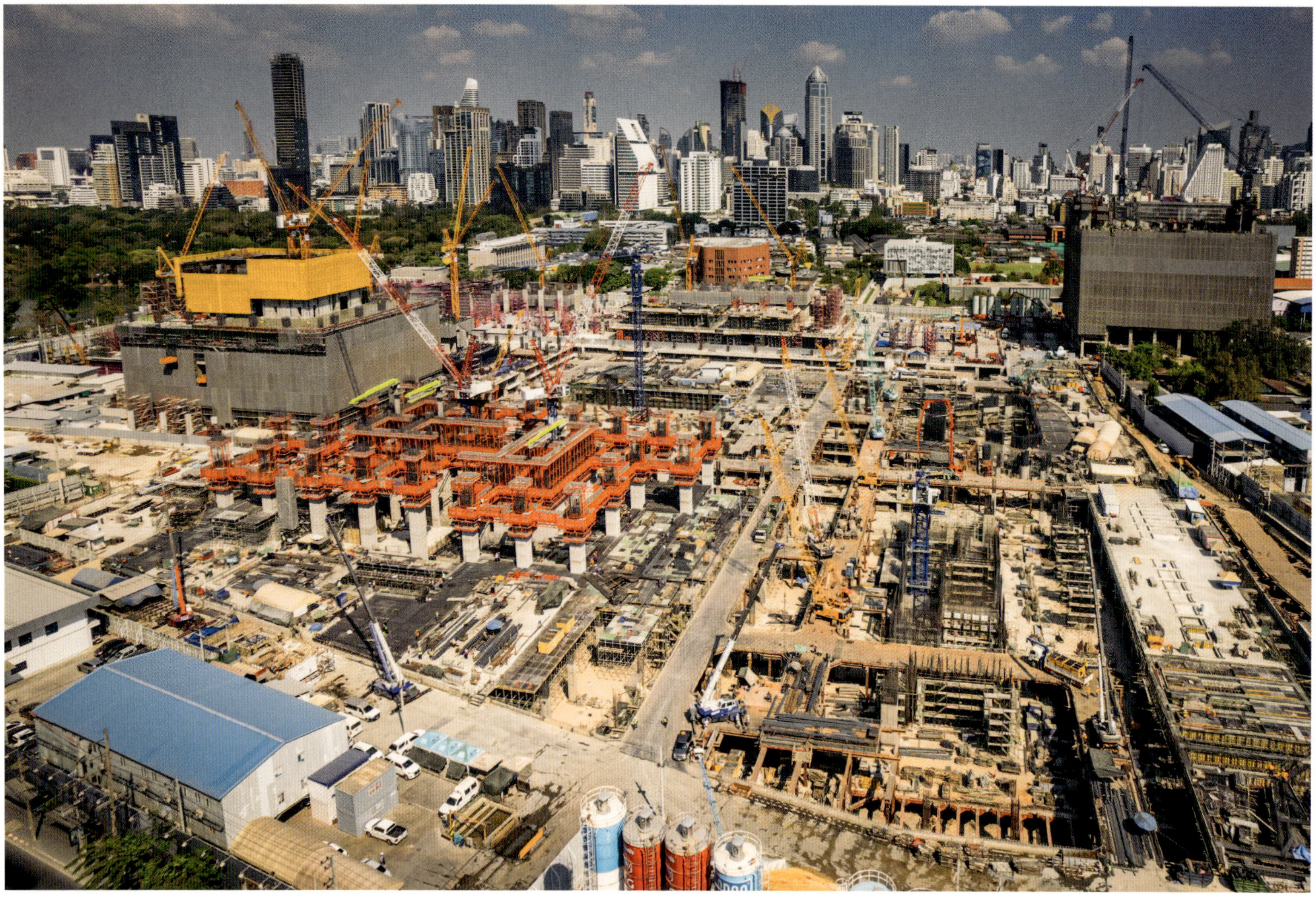

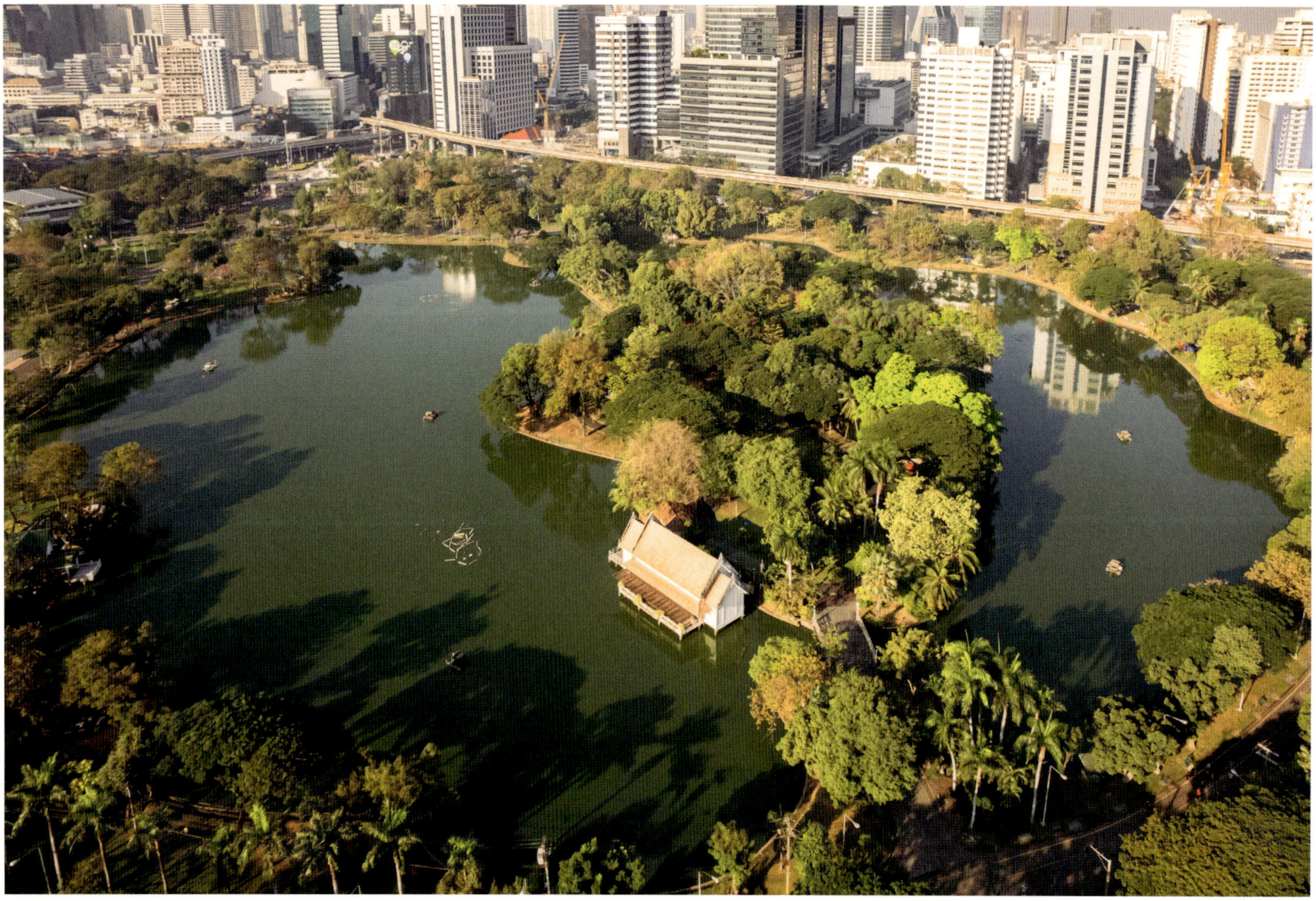

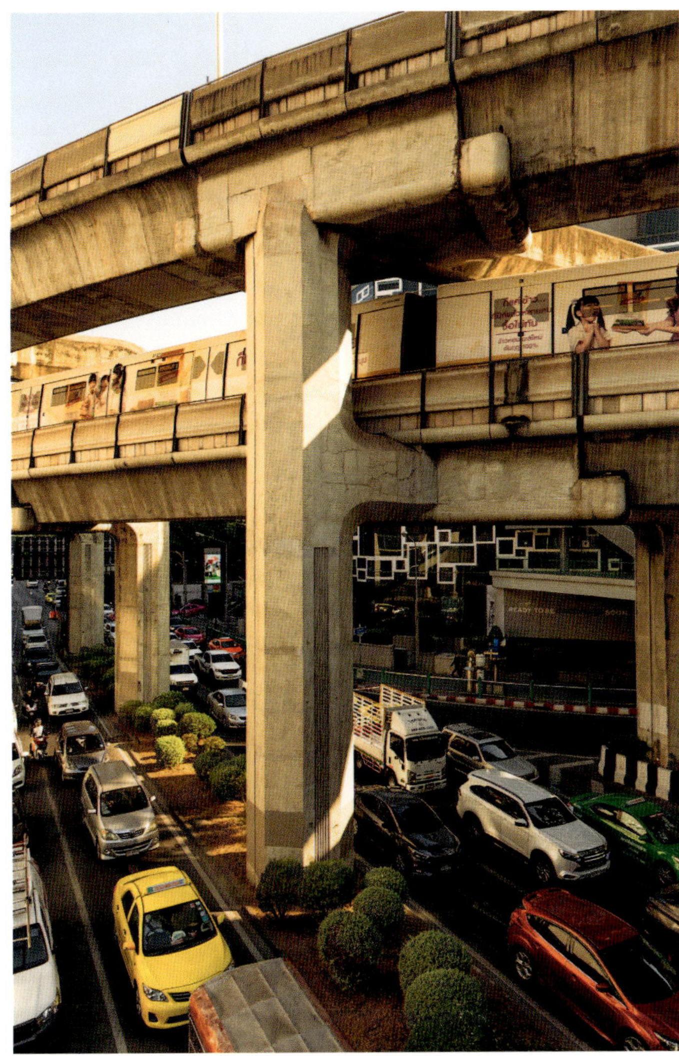

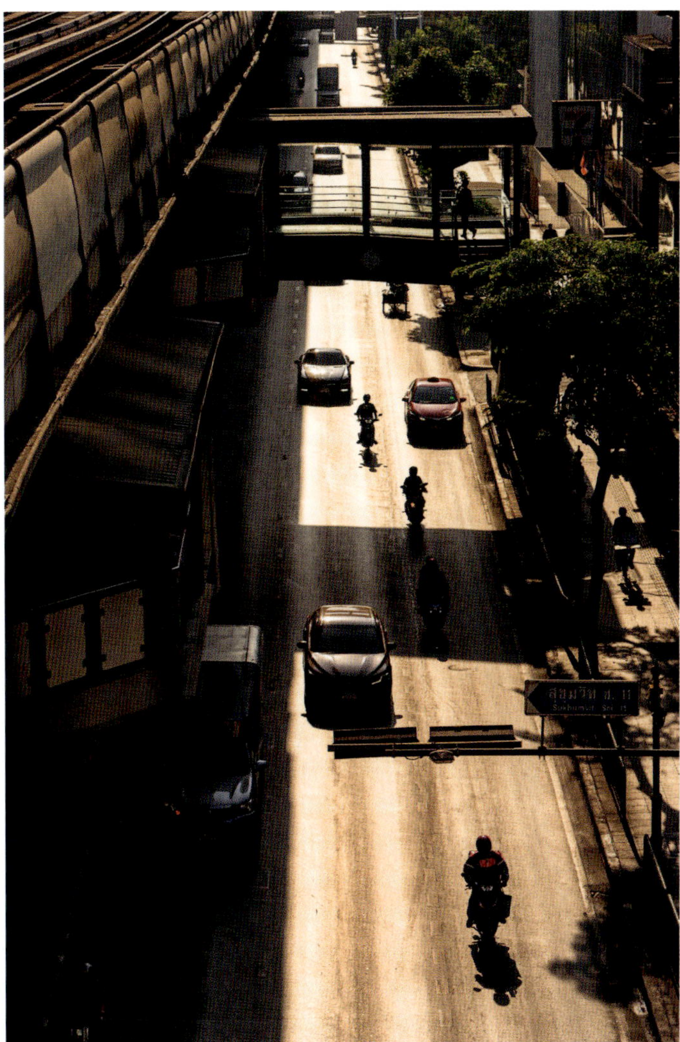

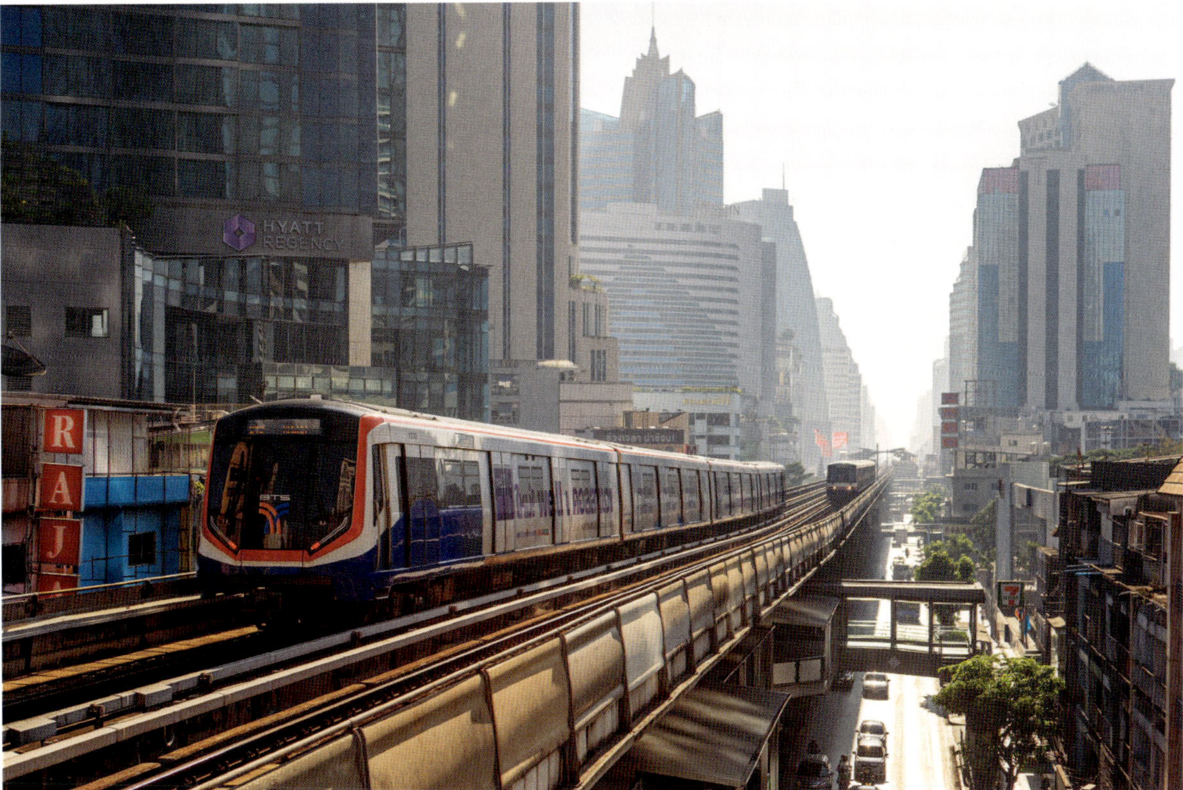

Living vertically: Bangkok is growing and expanding upward in every respect.

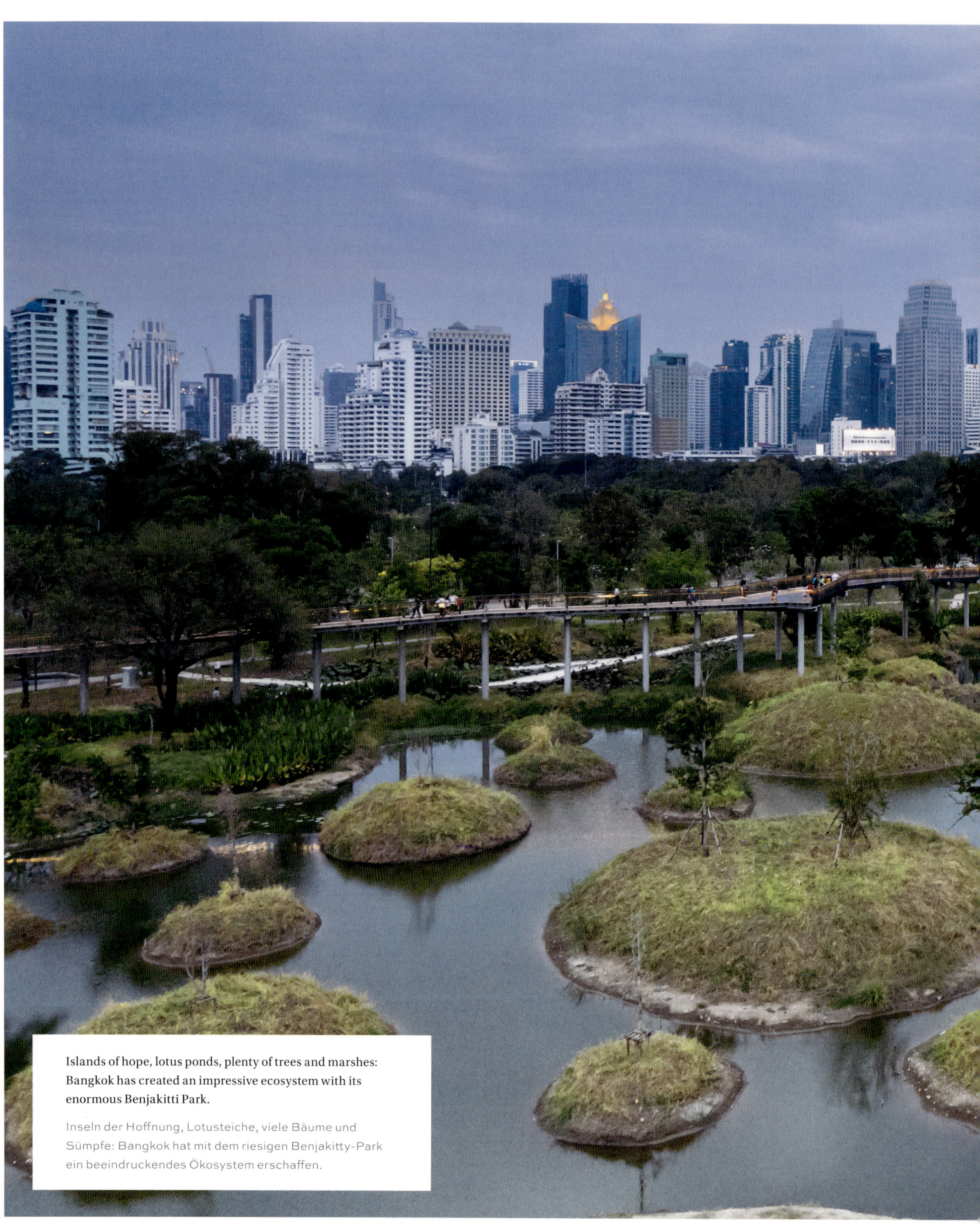

Islands of hope, lotus ponds, plenty of trees and marshes: Bangkok has created an impressive ecosystem with its enormous Benjakitti Park.

Inseln der Hoffnung, Lotusteiche, viele Bäume und Sümpfe: Bangkok hat mit dem riesigen Benjakitty-Park ein beeindruckendes Ökosystem erschaffen.

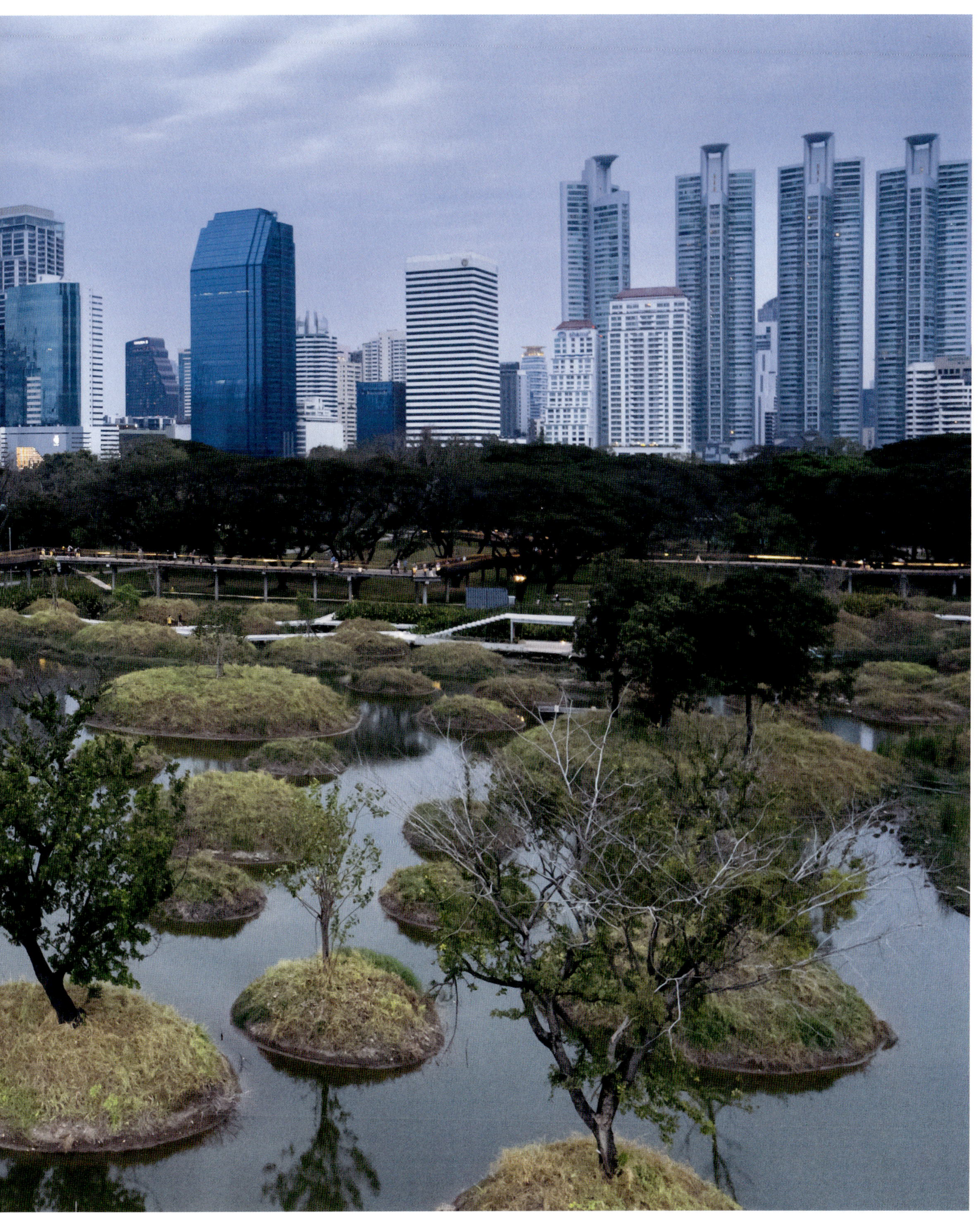

Christoph Mohr has lived and worked in Cologne since 1999. As a camera assistant, he worked on feature films as well as documentaries. After filming in Manila, Christoph was so enthusiastic about the photos he brought back that he decided to become a photographer. Through his artistic use of light and color, he succeeds in taking impressive snapshots of the regions he travels to. He is particularly interested in the developing countries of the southern hemisphere. In addition to rural and urban life, he focusses on the local social, cultural, and political conditions. People are at the center of his work. This results in a balanced mixture of portrait, landscape, urban, documentary, and reportage photography, with which he provides interesting, and comprehensive insights. His main clients include major publishers and NGOs. After the volume *Sacred Spaces – The Holy Sites of Buddhism*, his path took him in the social documentary direction again and he launched the cross-media project *Megacities.*

Christoph Mohr lebt und arbeitet seit 1999 in Köln. Als Kameraassistent wirkt er an Kino- und Dokumentarfilmen mit. Nach Dreharbeiten in Manila war er von den mitgebrachten Fotos so begeistert, dass er beschloss Fotograf zu werden. Durch seinen künstlerischen Umgang mit Licht und Farbe gelingen ihm eindrucksvolle Momentaufnahmen der bereisten Regionen. Sein besonderes Interesse gilt den Entwicklungsländern der südlichen Erdhalbkugel. Neben dem Leben auf dem Land und in der Stadt interessieren ihn die gesellschaftlichen, kulturellen und politischen Verhältnisse vor Ort. Der Mensch steht im Mittelpunkt seiner Arbeiten. So entsteht eine ausgewogene Mischung aus Porträt-, Landschafts-, Urbaner-, Dokumentar- und Reportage-Fotografie, mit der er interessante und umfassende Eindrücke liefert. Zu seinen Hauptkunden gehören die großen Verlage und NGOs. Nach dem Band *Heilige Stätten des Buddhismus* ging sein Weg wieder verstärkt in die sozial dokumentarische Richtung und er rief das medienübergreifende Projekt *Megacities* ins Leben.

www.christophmohr-fotografie.de

Bastian Barenbrock is a freelance documentary and landscape photographer, as well as a cameraman and drone photography specialist based in Cologne. Driven by his passion for travel and curiosity about different cultures and landscapes, the focus of his work is on high-quality documentaries for renowned, international production companies and TV stations for which he works worldwide. Years of experience in documentary filmmaking have enabled him to develop a cinematic visual language that uses aerial shots and unusual perspectives to create new angles and tell multi-faceted stories.

Bastian Barenbrock ist freiberuflicher Dokumentar- und Landschaftsfotograf, sowie Kameramann und Spezialist für Drohnenaufnahmen mit Sitz in Köln. Angetrieben von seiner Reiseleidenschaft und Neugierde für unterschiedliche Kulturen und Landschaften, liegt der Schwerpunkt seiner Arbeit auf hochwertigen Dokumentarfilmen für renommierte, internationale Produktionsfirmen und TV-Sendern, für die er weltweit tätig ist. Durch jahrelange Erfahrung im Dokumentarfilm konnte er eine filmische Bildsprache entwickeln, die unter Verwendung von Luftaufnahmen und ungewöhnlichen Perspektiven neue Blickwinkel ermöglicht und es ihm erlaubt facettenreiche Geschichten zu erzählen.

www.instagram.com/bastian_barenbrock

Oliver Fülling is a freelance author and editor for various publishing houses and is based in Oberallgäu. A passionate traveler, he published his first China travel guides while still studying sinology. His part-time work as a trekking guide in Central and East Asia has inspired him to also publish several books on Tibet, the Himalayas, and Buddhism. In total, Oliver Fülling has now published over 30 books on various topics. Three books were written in collaboration with Christoph Mohr, including *Sacred Spaces – The Holy Sites of Buddhism* published by teNeues. Always on the lookout for new forms of expression, the collaboration on the *Megacities* project has been a very special experience for him.

Oliver Fülling ist freier Autor und Lektor für verschiedene Verlage mit Sitz im Oberallgäu. Als Reisender aus Leidenschaft, hat er schon während seines Sinologiestudiums die ersten Chinareiseführer publiziert. Seine nebenberufliche Tätigkeit als Trekkingführer in Zentral- und Ostasien, hat ihn dazu inspiriert, auch mehrere Bücher über Tibet, den Himalaya und den Buddhismus zu veröffentlichen. Insgesamt hat Oliver Fülling mittlerweile über 30 Bände zu verschiedenen Themen veröffentlicht. Drei Bücher entstanden in Zusammenarbeit mit Christoph Mohr, u. a. *Heilige Stätten des Buddhismus* im teNeues-Verlag. Immer auf der Suche nach neuen Ausdrucksformen, war die Mitarbeit am *Megacities Projekt* eine ganz besondere Erfahrung.

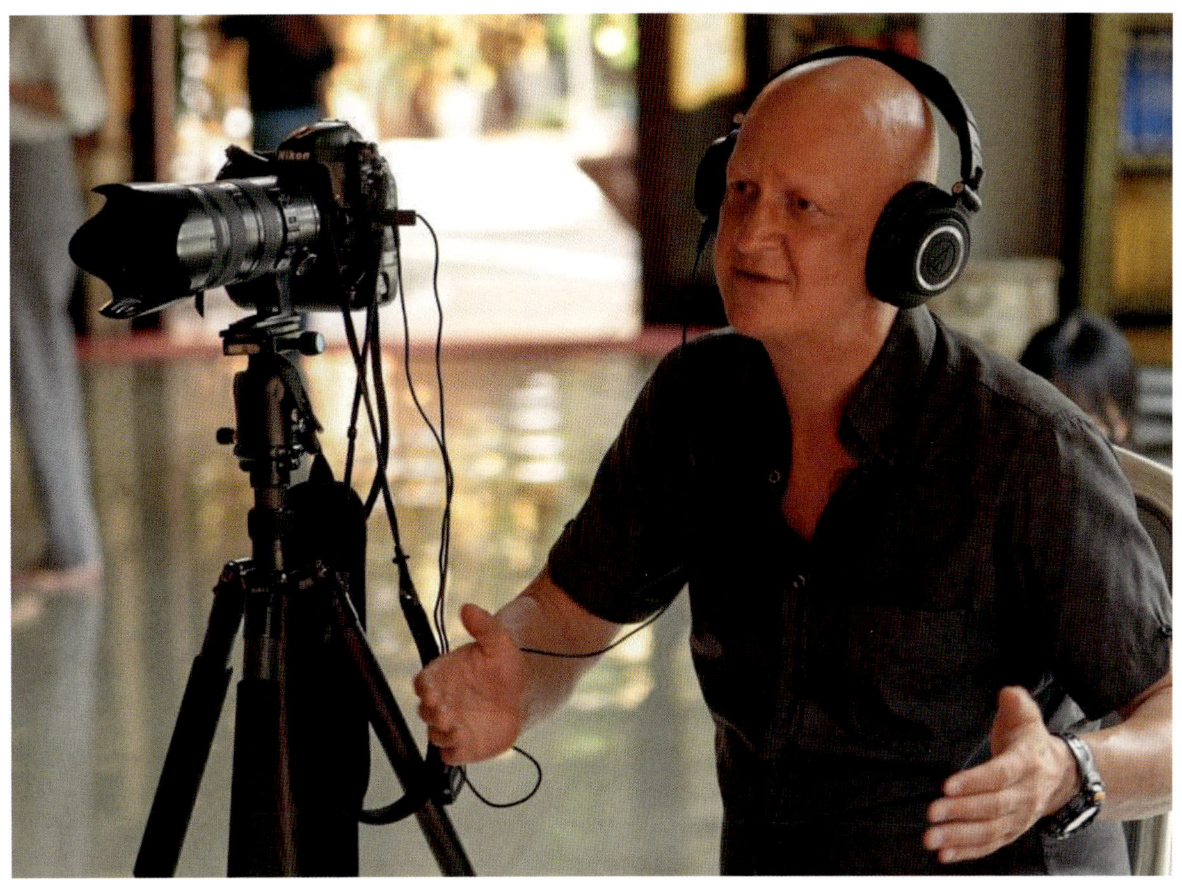

Christoph Mohr

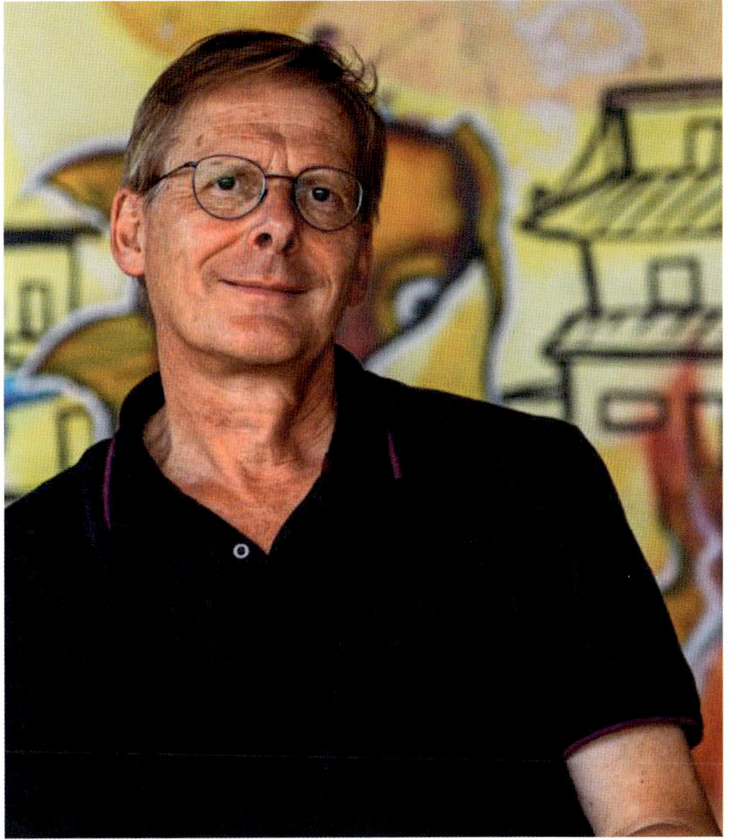

Oliver Fülling

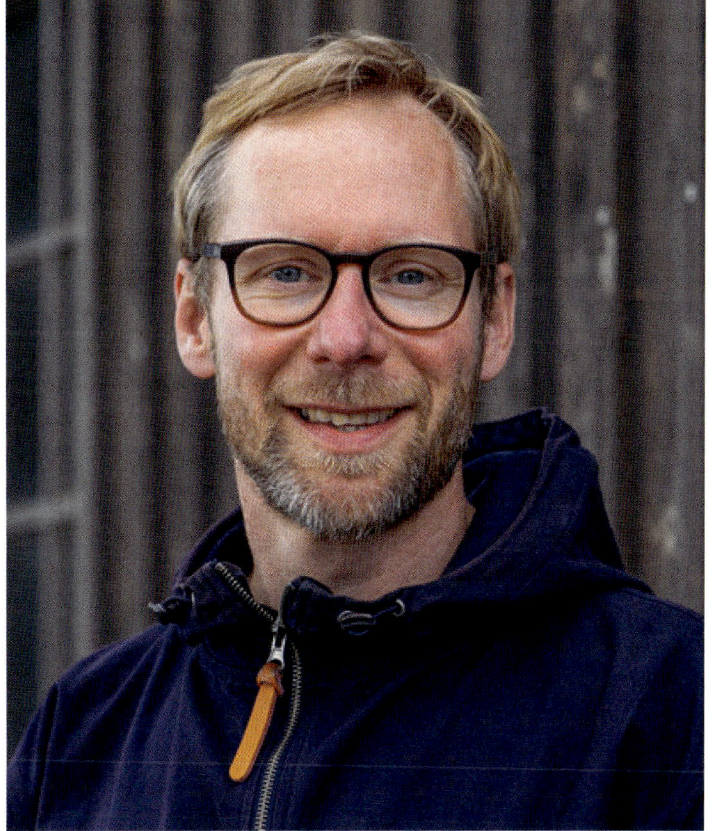

Bastian Barenbrock

Concept & Idea by Christoph Mohr
Texts & Captions by Oliver Fülling
Interviews by Christoph Mohr,
Oliver Fülling & Bastian Barenbrock

Editorial Coordination by Nadine Weinhold, teNeues Verlag
Production by Alwine Krebber, teNeues Verlag
Design (Cover) by Jens Grundei, teNeues Verlag
Design (Backcover) by Anika Lethen
Design (Content) by Eva Stadler
Layout by Anika Lethen
Color Separation by ORT Medienverbund GmbH

Translation (English) by Robin Limmeroth
Proofreading by Nadine Weinhold, teNeues Verlag

ISBN: 978-3-96171-499-5
Printed in Slovakia by Neografia a.s.
Library of Congress Control Number: 2023942516

Published by teNeues Publishing Group

teNeues Verlag GmbH
Ohmstraße 8a
86199 Augsburg, Germany

Düsseldorf Office
Waldenburger Straße 13
41564 Kaarst, Germany
e-mail: books@teneues.com

Augsburg/München Office
Ohmstraße 8a
86199 Augsburg, Germany
e-mail: books@teneues.com

Press Department
e-mail: presse@teneues.com

teNeues Publishing Company
350 Seventh Avenue, Suite 301
New York, NY 10001, USA

www.teneues.com

teNeues Publishing Group
Augsburg / München
Berlin
Düsseldorf
London
New York

teNeues

FSC
MIX
Paper | Supporting responsible forestry
www.fsc.org FSC® C020353